BASICS OF FINANCIAL MANAGEMENT

SECOND EDITION

Frank Bacon
Longwood College

Ramesh Garg
Eastern Michigan University

Tai S. Shin
Virginia Commonwealth University

Suk H. Kim
University of Detroit Mercy

Copley Publishing Group
Acton, Massachusetts 01720

Copyright © 2002 by Copley Publishing Group. All rights reserved
Printed in the United States of America

ISBN 1-58152-138-3

Contents

Preface vii

PART 1   INTRODUCTION   1

Chapter 1   **Goals and Functions of Finance**   3

Evolution of Finance • Objective of the Firm • Place of Finance in a Business Organization • Functions of Financial Management • Principles of Finance • Summary

Chapter 2   **Operating Environment of Financial Management**   15

Circular Flow of Income • Financial Institutions • Financial Markets • Inflation • Forms of Business Organization • Tax Treatment of Corporate Income • Summary • List of Key Terms

PART 2   FINANCIAL PLANNING AND CONTROL   33

Chapter 3   **Financial Statement Analysis**   35

Background Information • Financial Analysis • Comparative Ratio Analysis • Limitations of Ratio Analysis • Summary • List of Key Terms • Problems

Chapter 4   **Leverage and Risk Analysis**   61

Break-Even Analysis and Leverage • Operating Leverage • Financial Leverage • Combined Effect of Operating Leverage and Financial Leverage • Business Risk, Financial Risk, and Total Risk • Summary • List of Key Terms • Problems

Chapter 5   **Financial Planning and Forecasting**   77

Nature of Budgeting • Relationships among Various Budgets • Types of Pro Forma Financial Statements • Percent-of-Sales Method • Summary • List of Key Terms • Problems

PART 3   WORKING CAPITAL MANAGEMENT   91

Chapter 6   **An Overview of Working Capital Management**   93

Basic Concepts of Working Capital Management • Alternative Financing Plans • Short-Term versus Long-Term Debt • Summary • List of Key Terms • Problems

Chapter 7	**Current Asset Management**	109

Cash Management • Marketable Securities • Management of Accounts Receivable • Inventory Management • Summary • List of Key Terms • Problems

Chapter 8	**Sources of Short-Term Financing**	133

Trade Credit • Short-Term Bank Loans • Commercial Paper • Accounts Receivable Financing • Inventory Financing • Summary • List of Key Terms • Problems

PART 4	**CAPITAL EXPENDITURE ANALYSIS**	149

Chapter 9	**Time Value of Money**	151

Compound or Future Value versus Present Value • Financial Calculators • Compound Value of a Lump Sum • Compound Value of an Annuity • Present Value of a Future Lump Sum • Present Value of an Annuity • Other Common Applications of Future Value and Present Value • Perpetuities • Summary • List of Key Terms • Problems

Chapter 10	**Capital Budgeting under Certainty**	189

Capital Budgeting Process • Capital Budgeting Techniques under Certainty • Ranking and Selection • Summary • List of Key Terms • Problems

Chapter 11	**Other Issues in Capital Budgeting**	213

Factors Influencing Cash Flows • Special Topics • Summary • List of Key Terms • Problems

Chapter 12	**Capital Budgeting under Uncertainty**	225

The Basic Concept of Risk • Methods to Adjust for Risk • Portfolio Risk and Return • Summary • List of Key Terms • Problems

Chapter 13	**Valuation and Cost of Capital**	235

Valuation • Component Costs of Capital • Weighted Average Cost of Capital • Weighted Marginal Cost of Capital • Weighted Marginal Cost of Capital and Investment Decisions • Summary • List of Key Terms • Problems

PART 5	**LONG-TERM FINANCING**	257

Chapter 14	**Investment Bankers and Capital Markets**	259

The Primary Market • Secondary Markets • How to Read the Stock Quotations • Regulations of Security Markets • Summary • List of Key Terms • Problems

Chapter 15	**Fixed Income Securities: Bonds and Preferred Stock**	271

Differences between Bonds, Preferred Stocks, and Common Stocks • Characteristics of Bonds • Types of Bonds • Bond Ratings • Reasons for Using Bonds • Hybrid Nature of Preferred Stock • Characteristics of Preferred Stock • Reasons for Using Preferred Stock • Refunding Analysis • Summary • List of Key Terms • Problems

Chapter 16	**Common Stock**	285

Accounting Terms as Applied by Common Stock • Rights of Common Stockholders • Reasons for Using Common Stock • Convertible Securities • Warrants • Fully Diluted Earnings per Share • Summary • List of Key Terms • Problems

Chapter 17	**Dividend Policy and Retained Earnings**	299

Factors Affecting Dividend Policy • Alternative Dividend Policies • Theories of Dividend Policy • Stock Dividends and Stock Splits • Repurchase of Common Stock • Summary • List of Key Terms • Problems

Chapter 18	**Term Loans and Leases**	313

Bank Term Loans • Other Term Loans • Leases • Summary • List of Key Terms • Problems

PART 6	**SPECIAL TOPICS IN FINANCE**	**327**

Chapter 19	**Corporate Growth through Mergers**	329

Internal Growth versus External Growth • Types of Business Combination • Terms of Combination • Some Accounting Aspects of Business Combinations • Holding Companies • Summary • List of Key Terms

Chapter 20	**Corporate Growth through Multinational Operations**	339

Motives for World Trade • Motives for Foreign Investment • Political Risks • Foreign Exchange Market and Risks • Financing Foreign Trade • Financing Foreign Investment • Summary • List of Key Terms

PART 7	**CASE PROBLEMS IN FINANCE**	**361**

Case Study 1: Ratio Analysis—Wayne Airlines
Case Study 2: Cash Budgeting—Canton Toy Company
Case Study 3: Profitability Analysis—Midwest Business Instruments
Case Study 4: Inventory Management—Miller Toy Company

Case Study 5:	Secured Short-Term Financing—Lewis Clothing Company	
Case Study 6:	Cash Flow Analysis for Capital Budgeting—York Fiber Corporation	
Case Study 7:	Weighted Average Cost of Capital—Advanced Technology Company	
Case Study 8:	Valuation—Wayne Gifts Incorporated	
Case Study 9:	Debt Financing—Central Power Company	
Case Study 10:	Ethics in Financing—Advanced Technology's Ethical Dilemma	
Case Study 11:	International Finance—GM Operations in Mexico and The Peso Crisis	

Appendix A   Interest Tables — 397

Glossary of Financial Terms — 417

Answers to Selected End-of-Chapter Problems — 435

Index — 447

Preface

The objective of this text is to introduce students to those principles essential to an understanding of financial problems and the policies financial managers use to contend with these problems. To achieve this objective, the text stresses practical application in a user-friendly format. *Basics of Financial Management* is an introductory text for practitioner-oriented finance courses and provides a reference for case-oriented courses in finance. We have written the text in a clear, concise, and practical manner. Readers will be exposed to all the basic tools and techniques of financial management without a complex treatment of theoretical financial concepts.

The new edition expands the explanation of investment and financing decisions with emphasis on providing the student with a more practical, real-world understanding of the concepts. More attention is given to linking complex investment and financing decision models to every-day business application. In particular, greater emphasis is placed on valuation and cost of capital. Throughout the text, we have incorporated more examples to illustrate problem-solving, especially in present value analysis. Also, the new edition illustrates problem-solving for all concepts by financial calculator. Overall, the new edition is designed to be more "user-friendly" to the student while also enhancing the content of corporate finance fundamentals.

The text's structure was carefully designed to ensure a smooth transition from accounting to financial management. A number of the earlier chapters in *Basics of Financial Management* include a thorough review of accounting principles, finance terminology, and financial statements. A variety of financial problems are examined as they relate to the financial statements and their impact on return, risk, and stock price.

The last section of the text contains eleven short cases designed to illustrate major points in key chapters. This case study approach allows instructors to use a "hand-on" orientation. They can use these cases for student presentations, homework assignments, or classroom discussions. These cases should enable students to strengthen their practical understanding of financial concepts and techniques. Without the added expense of a separate casebook, students can apply what they have learned in practical settings.

We used many numerical examples throughout the text to clarify discussions of financial concepts and techniques. In addition, a generous number of end-of-chapter problems support text discussions by emphasizing the application of theory. Most chapters have numerical examples within the text and end-of-chapter problems. Answers to end-of-chapter problems are found at the end of the text. Students may refer to these answers to check computation results for accuracy. All end-of-chapter problems are tied or keyed to the numerical examples presented in each chapter. We have highlighted key terms in bold type. Students may test their comprehension and retention by using the list of key terms provided at the end of each chapter. Another friendly feature of the text is a quick reference glossary with 300 terms.

We encourage you to visit a website devoted to *Basics of Financial Management* at <http://www.mich.com/~kimsuk>. This website is an integral part of the 2nd edition. This site will direct visitors to the World Wide Web in three related areas: international business, investments, and student needs. To help visitors use our website more effectively, we have developed 40 Internet Exercises and posted them in our home page. Moreover, professors may use these Internet Exercises to achieve two objectives: (1) explain how the Internet can be used to access necessary information on a variety of topics and (2) teach students how to use this information. Internet Exercise 24, for example, may be used to achieve Objective One by asking how one obtains information about careers in finance. As another example, Internet Exercises 16 and 25 may be used to achieve Objective Two by asking how one performs a comparative financial analysis of two competing companies.

Lecture notes prepared by authors are available through our website. To print or view these lecture notes, visit <http://www.mich.com/~kimsuk>, then click Finance Notes. To print or view 40 Internet Exercises, visit <http://www.mich.com/~kimsuk>, then click Internet Exercises.

The text has seven parts. Part 1 (Chapters 1 and 2) discusses the primary goal of a firm and the operating environment of financial management. Part 2 (Chapters 3 through 5) explains key concepts and tools of financial planning and control. Part 3 (Chapters 6 through 8) covers management of working capital. Part 4 (Chapters 9 through 13) covers the time value of money and long-term investment decisions. Part 5 (Chapters 14 through 18) analyzes various sources of long-term financing. Part 6 (Chapters 19 and 20) examines topics of special interest, such as mergers and multinational finance. Part 7 contains eleven cases.

Part 1

INTRODUCTION

Nearly all individuals or organizations raise money and spend it. The field of finance provides the necessary decision framework for raising money (known as financing decisions) and spending money (known as investment decisions). Any decision must have an appropriate goal for the individual or the firm. Therefore, Chapter 1 develops the goal of the firm to be used in the financial decision-making process and examines the role of financial management necessary to achieve this goal. The process of financial management (financing and investment decisions) involves individuals, business firms, governments, and other institutions as they enter various markets to exchange money. Chapter 2 reviews this operating environment where these financing and investment decisions are made.

1

GOALS AND FUNCTIONS OF FINANCE

A college student, such as yourself, should study the subject of finance. "I am not a finance major!" you say. "Why should I have to take a course in finance?" That is a reasonable question. It is true that most of the readers of this book will not end up working in the finance department of a large company such as General Motors. However, you may take a job as a buyer for a large department store, become a general manager, or even start your own business. Although these are not finance jobs, they all require significant knowledge of finance to succeed. Since almost every transaction involves either an investment or financing decision, the knowledge of finance can empower the individual to succeed in all business activities whether personal or job-related. Should you pursue a career in finance, many opportunities exist including pension fund manager, credit analyst, financial analyst, cash manager, stock broker, or capital budgeting manager to name a few. Regardless of what path you take, a strong background in finance will definitely increase your chances of success.

In essence, business finance is concerned with the money that flows through a company. Because almost every managerial job in a company involves the proper management of money, most managerial jobs require some knowledge of the financial area. For example, the production manager needs to understand financial techniques in order to evaluate purchases of equipment, inventories, labor, and maintenance for that division. The marketing department must make estimates of sales, delivery costs, and advertising costs. The purchasing manager must be able to evaluate quantity discounts, cost of varying credit terms, and numerous other types of financial data.

The fact is, finance is an essential part of every company. It does not matter if the company is a Mom & Pop grocery store or a large multinational company. Someone in the company must make estimates of how much money is needed for the firm's operations, raise that amount of cash, and then see that the money is spent properly to achieve the company's goals. In essence, raising needed funds requires financial decisions and deciding what to buy with the funds are investment decisions. The process of financial analysis is described in Table 1-1:

Table 1-1
The Process of Financial Management

	BALANCE	SHEET	
INVESTMENT DECISIONS	Current Assets	Current Liabilities	FINANCING DECISIONS
	Long Term Assets	Long Term Debt and Equity	

3

On the left side of the balance sheet, investment decisions determine "what to buy" and the proper mix of short-term and long-term assets. On the righthand side, we decide "how to pay" for the asset we choose, either through current liabilities or long-term debt or equity funds. For the firm to be successful, investment and financing decisions must achieve the maximum return relative to risk to increase the firm's common stock price.

This book deals with these financial decisions which both large and small companies must make. Thus, the underlying financial principles are basically the same for both types of companies. This chapter consists of five sections: the evolution of finance; the primary goal of the firm; where finance fits in a business organization; the three important functions of the financial manager; the major principles of finance.

EVOLUTION OF FINANCE

Finance evolved from the field of institutional economics that attempted to explain the economic behavior of various organizations. The study of finance first emerged as a separate field of study in the early 1900s. Since then, the content and focus of finance have undergone significant changes over the years.

Around the turn of the century, giant industrial corporations such as U.S. Steel and Standard Oil were created by combining smaller firms in the industries. This started a trend of combinations which required large amounts of cash to buy out the smaller firms. Huge blocks of stocks and bonds were sold to raise the money for these ventures. Thus, the emphasis during this period was largely on legalistic matters such as mergers, combinations, the formation of new firms, and the issuance of securities.

During the great bull market of the 1920s, everyone thought that business conditions were soaring. Finance focused on raising funds necessary for expansion. However, with the October 1929 stock market crash the fortunes of many people crashed as well. The depression of the 1930s caused an unprecedented number of large-scale bankruptcies. This abrupt turn of events forced financial managers to focus on defensive aspects, such as bankruptcy, reorganization, liquidity, and government regulation of securities markets. Finance was still a legalistic subject, but the emphasis shifted from expansion to survival.

During the 1940s and 1950s, finance continued to take the traditional approach that had evolved during the previous two decades. The study of finance was largely descriptive rather than analytical. Emphasis focused on describing the firm's financial status rather than analyzing the effects of financial and investment decisions. However, after World War II, the U.S. embarked on an unprecedented economic expansion. This expansion led to a greater examination of opportunities on the part of financial managers. Analysis of investment opportunities and more efficient use of assets gained in importance. Financial managers gradually became more interested in analysis and less interested in description.

The evolutionary pace began to accelerate during the late 1950s. The increased utilization of computers in the 1960s and the development of mathematical models contributed to an increased emphasis on analysis and internal decision-making. The financial manager made extensive use of analytical and mathematical techniques for the systematic solution of financial problems.

Chapter 1: Goals and Functions of Finance

From the late 1960s through the current decade, financial management focused on risk-return tradeoffs, capital structure, and the maximization of stockholder wealth for a given level of risk. The importance of these concepts was apparent as three American finance professors, Hary Markowitz, William Sharpe, and Merton Miller, received their Nobel Prize in economics for their contributions to finance theories of risk-return, portfolio management, and capital structure. Financial risk as a financial variable drew particular attention in the 1980s because record numbers of companies declared bankruptcy. Companies that operated in only one industry—air transportation, energy production, and agriculture—were particularly hard hit, thereby forcing them to reduce risk through diversification. Asset diversification came about through mergers and acquisitions, internal production expansions, and increased emphasis on multinational operations. In recent years, capital budgeting under uncertainty gained popularity as a result of unprecedented changes in the U.S. economic system: supply-side economic policies, deregulation of major industries, strong international competition, rapid advances in technology, constant restructuring, and joint venture activities.

OBJECTIVE OF THE FIRM

Management is motivated to achieve a number of objectives, some of which are conflicting. Such conflicts arise because the firm has a number of constituents such as stockholders, employees, customers, creditors, and suppliers whose desires do not necessarily coincide with each other. Hence, the conflicting objectives confronting management raise the problem of setting priorities.

In this book, we assume that the primary goal of the firm is to maximize stockholder wealth, as reflected by stock price. At any given point in time, the dollar value of a stockholder's wealth in the firm is obtained by multiplying the current stock price per share by the number of common shares owned. In addition, this market price reflects stockholder wealth since stock price reflects the effects of management's financial and investment decisions.

Wealth Maximization versus Profit Maximization

Should the major goal of private business be profit maximization? Profits are indeed essential ingredients of business survival for any length of time. But the profit maximization goal falls short of the stockholder wealth maximization goal for at least four reasons.

Timing

Maximization of profits does not take into account the timing of the expected earnings, while wealth maximization does. Consider Projects A and B which have the same total earnings of $10 million over the next five years. Project A is expected to receive earnings of $2 million a year for five years. On the other hand, Project B would generate no earnings for the first four years but would receive earnings of $10 million in the fifth year. Business concerns and investors prefer to receive income as soon as possible rather than at some distant time in the future. Since money has time value, the sooner the firm receives the income, the quicker it can invest the funds to earn interest. Thus, investors place a higher value on the shares of the company's stock if it accepts Project A instead of Project B.

Risk

Maximization of profits does not recognize risk, whereas wealth maximization takes risk into account. Suppose that Project C is expected to produce profits of $10 million, while Project D is expected to generate profits of $12 million. Let us further assume that the probability of receiving Project C's income is almost 100%, while Project D is quite risky. Therefore, Project C will almost certainly produce profits of $10 million while the expected $12 million of Project D is most unlikely. If investors are adverse to risk, they would naturally prefer Project C. But the profit maximization goal completely ignores the significance of risk.

Dividend Payments

If the firm's primary objective is to increase profits, then dividends would never be paid to stockholders since all profit would be retained and reinvested to boost profit. If the firm never pays dividends, many stockholders would view this as a negative signal and sell the firm's stock, thus reducing stockholder wealth by depressing stock price. The payment of dividends helps the firm attract investors seeking dividends and thus increases the value of the stock in the market.

Qualitative Factors

Finally, maximization of profits does not allow for quality aspects of future activities, such as growth of sales, stability, and diversification. A large, stable, and diversified volume of sales gives the firm a cushion against business setbacks, such as recessions and changes in consumer preferences. The current market value of the stock reflects these quality aspects of future activities.

Stock Price Maximization

For all these reasons, stock price maximization is more important than profit maximization. The market price of the firm's stock represents the present value of the firm as viewed by its owners. More specifically, it reflects the market's evaluation of the firm's prospective earnings stream over time, the riskiness of this stream, the dividend policy of the firm, and quality aspects of the firm's future activities.

Because investors want to maximize their own wealth, they prefer that the firm adopt policies that maximize its stock price. Essentially, the market price of the stock is a performance index of the firm's progress. Thus, the greater the price of the stock, the more favorable the investors' view of management's performance. If stockholders are not satisfied with management's performance, they may sell all or part of their stock holdings and reinvest in other securities or assets. This action will place downward pressure on the market price of the firm's stock.

Management versus Stockholders

We may think of managers as agents of the owners. Stockholders delegate decision-making authority to managers and expect these agents to act in the stockholders' best interest. However, the objectives of managers may differ from those of the firm's stockholders. Because the stockholders of most large corporations today are well diversified, the control of these companies is separated from ownership. This situation allows managers to act in their own best interests rather than in the best interests of the stockholders. Thus, some managers are likely more concerned with their own welfare or their own survival. In other words, they may attempt to maximize their own total utility by amassing income, power, self-esteem, and prestige. The total utility of managers, therefore, could be increased by management decisions that in fact tend to lower stockholder wealth. For example, managers may acquire expensive jets or limousines, throw extravagant parties, or even join elite country clubs for personal benefit but at the company's expense. To protect job security, managers may be reluctant to make important financing decisions involving appropriate risks. For example, one sure way for the firm to avoid bankruptcy and protect the manager's job is for the firm to never borrow any money. While such action would benefit the manager personally, a company with no debt cannot compete with other firms in the same industry where the benefits of debt are commonly enjoyed. The manager's low-risk, no-debt position would cause the firm's stock price to fall and thus hurt the owners of the firm.

To ensure that managers act in the best interest of the stockholders, appropriate incentives should be given to them and they have to be monitored. Incentives include stock options, bonuses, and perquisites. Monitoring can be done by reviewing management perquisites, auditing financial statements, and limiting management decisions. In summary, it appears reasonable to believe that managers will undertake actions that are relatively consistent with stockholder wealth maximization. This is because over the long run, their own goals, including survival, will largely depend on the value of the firm and the wealth of the stockholders.

Place of Finance in a Business Organization

Modern organization theory above all looks upon an organization as a system consisting of many departments and divisions which are directly or indirectly interrelated. It is therefore important to recognize that the financial manager works as part of the total management team.

Organization structures vary from company to company, but Figure 1-1 shows a typical organization chart. The functional areas of business operations for manufacturing companies are production, marketing, and finance. Production and marketing are critical for the survival of the company, because they determine its very existence—its ability to produce products and sell them at a profit. But finance is an integral part of total management and cuts across functional boundaries, because it expresses inputs, outputs, plans, and results in monetary terms.

Thus, in order to evaluate resource allocation possibilities, the financial manager is concerned with production and marketing. The decision to buy a new machine, for example, cannot be made by the financial manager alone. Other functional areas must be consulted: marketing, production, engineering, and accounting. The marketing department may estimate the sales volume of the industry, the annual percentage growth of market demand for the product, the percentage market share of the company, and the selling price per unit. The production department may estimate the requirements of labor, materials, and facilities. The engineering department may estimate the variable cost per unit, fixed costs, the cost of a new project, and the life of the project. The accounting department may estimate the expected net cash flows of the project. The problem of the financial manager is to determine the expected value of the project and its risk.

Figure 1-1
Typical Organization Chart

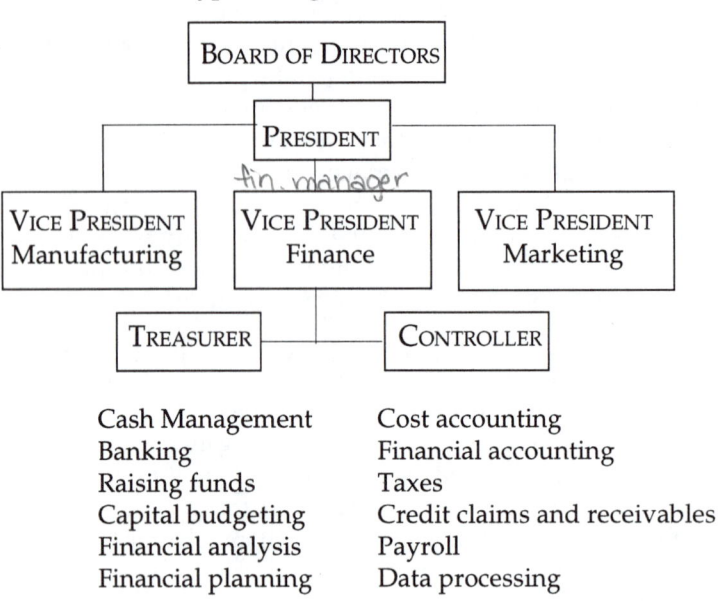

```
                    BOARD OF DIRECTORS
                            |
                        PRESIDENT
                       (fin. manager)
          _____|_____
         |              |              |
    VICE PRESIDENT  VICE PRESIDENT  VICE PRESIDENT
    Manufacturing     Finance        Marketing
                    ____|____
                   |         |
               TREASURER  CONTROLLER
```

Cash Management	Cost accounting
Banking	Financial accounting
Raising funds	Taxes
Capital budgeting	Credit claims and receivables
Financial analysis	Payroll
Financial planning	Data processing

In the typical organization chart (Figure 1-1), the vice-president for finance is the financial manager of the firm. The financial manager reports to the president of the firm and has direct authority over the treasurer and the controller. The treasurer is responsible for cash management, banking, raising funds, capital budgeting, and financial planning. The controller is responsible for accounting, taxes, credit claims, payroll, and data processing.

FUNCTIONS OF FINANCIAL MANAGEMENT

In order to achieve the firm's primary goal of maximizing stockholder wealth, the financial manager performs three major functions: (1) financial planning and control, (2) the efficient allocation of funds among various assets (investment decisions), and (3) the acquisition of funds on favorable terms (financing decisions). The balance sheet summarizes the assets owned and claims on assets as of a specific time. Because assets are investments and claims are financing, we can present the current position of investment and financing decisions in the form of a simplified balance sheet, as shown in Table 1-2.

Table 1-2
A Simplified Balance Sheet

	Investments (Assets)	Financing (Claims)
Short-term	Current Assets	Current Liabilities
Long-term	Fixed Assets	Long-term Debt and Equity

In the past, the role of financial management was largely limited to the acquisition of funds. Little weight was attached to the allocation of these funds within the firm. As business firms continued to become bigger, more complex, and more diversified, however, the role of financial management changed. Today, financial managers are involved in all aspects of acquiring and allocating funds. Hence, the importance of the financial manager within the company has increased. He or she assumes responsibility for an information system which measures the results of operations in order to evaluate performance and plan future strategies. This puts the financial manager in a key position in the company hierarchy. The position of the financial manager has become even more important as an increasing number of chief executive officers for major business concerns have been selected from the finance area.

Financial Planning and Control

Financial planning and control must be considered simultaneously. For purposes of control, the financial manager establishes standards, such as budgets for comparing actual performance with planned performance. The preparation of these budgets is a planning function, but their administration is a controlling function.

The basic purpose of planning for future years is to anticipate problems and opportunities, analyze them, and determine the actions that will guide the firm to its established goals. The primary policy decision is the selection of the industry in which to operate. Decisions must then be made concerning the firm's brand of products, its size, types of both human and capital resources it needs, and its liquidity position. Once the company's goals and long-range plans are established, its subgoals, organizational framework, and programs are developed. On the basis of these plans and estimates of sales for the near future, the financial manager must also project upcoming cash inflows and outflows. Financial planning and control are a prerequisite for making sound financial decisions.

Allocation of Funds

As the financial manager plans for the allocation of funds, the most urgent task is to invest funds wisely within the firm. Every dollar invested has alternative uses. Thus, funds should be allocated among assets in such a way that they will maximize the wealth of the firm's stockholders. In the past, the management of current assets was the main role of the financial manager for three reasons. First, current assets represented a larger proportion of the firm's total assets than fixed assets. Second, current-asset investment was more volatile than fixed-asset investment. Third, current-asset management represented the day-to-day internal operations of the firm.

In addition to current asset management, the financial manager must perform a major role in capital investment decisions and divestiture decisions. These decisions involve the allocation and commitment of funds to large investment projects whose returns are expected to extend beyond one year. Because the future returns are not known with an absolute degree of accuracy, investment projects necessarily involve risk. Consequently, they should be evaluated in the terms of their expected risk-return tradeoff.

Acquisition of Funds

The third role of the financial manager is to acquire funds on favorable terms. If projected cash outflow exceeds cash inflow, the financial manager must obtain additional funds from outside the firm. Funds are available from many sources at varying costs, with different maturities, and under various types of agreements. The critical role of the financial manager is to determine the combination of financing that most closely suits the planned needs of the firm. This requires obtaining the optimal level of funds that minimizes the cost of capital while also insuring the firm against the risk of not being able to pay bills as they become due.

Figure 1-2
Integrated Financial Decision Making Model

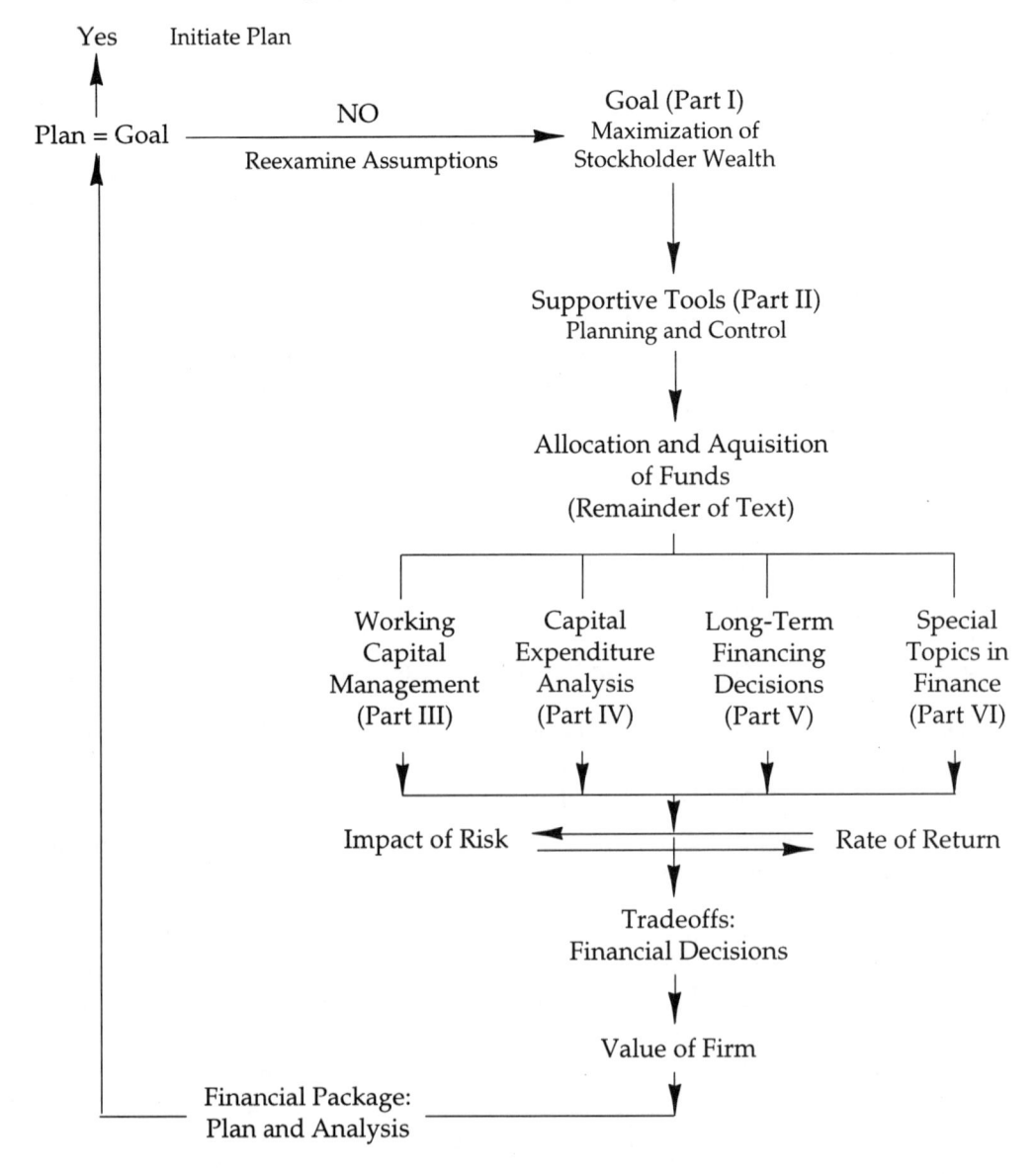

```
Yes       Initiate Plan
 ▲
 |              NO              Goal (Part I)
Plan = Goal  ─────────────▶    Maximization of
         Reexamine Assumptions  Stockholder Wealth
 ▲                                     |
 |                                     ▼
 |                              Supportive Tools (Part II)
 |                              Planning and Control
 |                                     |
 |                                     ▼
 |                              Allocation and Aquisition
 |                                    of Funds
 |                              (Remainder of Text)
 |                   ┌───────────┬─────┴─────┬───────────┐
 |               Working      Capital     Long-Term    Special
 |               Capital    Expenditure   Financing    Topics in
 |              Management    Analysis    Decisions    Finance
 |              (Part III)   (Part IV)   (Part V)    (Part VI)
 |                   ▼           ▼           ▼           ▼
 |            Impact of Risk ◀─────────────▶ Rate of Return
 |                                     ▼
 |                                 Tradeoffs:
 |                              Financial Decisions
 |                                     ▼
 |                                Value of Firm
 |                                     ▼
 └─────── Financial Package: ──────────┘
          Plan and Analysis
```

Principles of Finance

A primary objective of this book is to help the reader understand some of the basic principles of finance. Understanding of these basic principles is necessary to carry out the three major functions of finance: financial planning and control, the allocation of funds, and the acquisition of funds. The most important of these principles follows:

Risk-Return Tradeoff

The maximization of stockholder wealth depends on the tradeoff between risk and return. Generally, **the higher the risk of a project, the higher the expected return from the project.** For example, if you are offered a chance to invest in a project which offers an extremely high rate of return, you should immediately suspect that the project is very risky.

The financial manager must assess the optimal risk/return tradeoff that will maximize the wealth of the firm's stockholders. Figure 1-2 shows how the financial manager assesses the various risk-return tradeoffs available to support the wealth maximization goal. Practically all financial decisions involve such tradeoffs. Most of these decisions include financial planning and control, working capital management, capital budgeting decisions, long-term financing, and special decisions.

Time Value of Money

There is an old cliche regarding the time value of money which states: "a dollar in hand today is worth more than a dollar due some time in the future." The reason for this is that a dollar today can be invested so that, in the future, it will be worth more than a dollar received later. Another way of saying this is that the timing of the cash flows is important. Given the choice of when to receive a specified income, one would choose to receive it as soon as possible.

Financial managers are constantly confronted with decisions that involve exchanging "dollars today" for "dollars in the future." For example, the time value of money is the foundation on which commercial banks and other lending institutions were based. If money had no time value, no one would be willing to pay interest in order to use the money now. Also, firms purchase equipment now in exchange for expected dollar returns from the equipment in the future. In essence, the concept of time value is crucial to all investment and financing decisions.

Leverage

The principle of leverage refers to the level of fixed costs embedded in the firm's asset and financing mixes. A firm with a high level of fixed costs will find that a small change in sales will cause a large change in the earnings of the business. Higher fixed costs increase the firm's leverage and risk. Likewise, this allows the firm to magnify its rate of return when sales increase. As an example, consider a theme park like Disney World. Virtually all of the park's expenses are fixed in nature. Once the decision has been made to open the gates on a given day, the park's expenses are almost totally fixed. The staff has been hired, the equipment has been purchased, and the advertising has been conducted.

Now assume that enough tickets have been sold to cover that day's expenses, i.e., the park is at breakeven. If one more ticket is sold, how much do the park's expenses increase as a result of the additional customer? Virtually none. As an economist would say, the marginal cost is zero. Because none of the money is needed to pay expenses, all of the extra money goes into the profit of the park. A very small percentage increase in sales has led to a large percentage increase in earnings. (fixed costs)

Liquidity versus Profitability

Liquidity refers to the ability to pay your bills when they come due. Higher liquidity strengthens the firm's ability to pay its bills but likewise reduces its profitability resulting in a **tradeoff between the two goals.** For example, an increase in the cash position increases liquidity, but it also reduces profitability because cash is not an earning asset. Buying productive equipment reduces liquidity, but it raises profitability. The appropriate combination of liquidity and profitability requires balancing the risk of not being able to pay bills as they come due against obtaining the maximm profitability possible to increase stockholder wealth. Decisions involving this tradeoff occur so often that the principle has often been called "the financial manager's dilemma."

Matching Principle

The matching principle states that **short-term assets should be financed with short-term liabilities and long-term assets should be financed with long-term sources of funds.** If the matching principle is violated, the company may experience a number of problems. If excessive amounts of long-term funds are used to finance current assets, the firm's profitability may suffer. If fixed assets are financed with short-term sources, severe cash shortages may result.

Portfolio Effect (Diversification)

The portfolio effect states that **as more assets are added to a portfolio, the risk of the total portfolio decreases.** This principle explains much of the rationale for large conglomerates. For example, some companies have operations in industries as diversified as energy, financial services, consumer goods, and transportation. Since it is impossible to predict which industries will outperform others in the future, these diversified conglomerates are spreading their risk so as not to "put all of their eggs into one basket." The energy operations of a company, for example, may be hurt if world oil prices unexpectedly take a nosedive. However, this might be offset by one of the other industries performing better than expected. Overall, the company earns its desired rate of return even though the profitability of the individual divisions may be unpredictable.

Valuation

The valuation principle states that **the economic value of an asset is equal to the present value of its expected cash flows.** By determining the present value of expected cash flows, all such assets are valued in essentially the same way. First, the cash flow stream is estimated. Second, the required rate of return for each cash flow is established. Third, each cash flow is discounted by its required rate of return, and these present values are then summed to find the value of the asset.

We may buy an asset for any number of reasons. Some people buy art objects because they enjoy looking at them daily. Others buy a new car because it gives them basic, dependable transportation. However, most business purchases are made for economic reasons. The business owner expects the asset to generate cash inflows in excess of its purchase price. If we can estimate these cash inflows, we can calculate how much the asset is worth to us.

Summary

This chapter has given an overview of the environment of the financial manager. The financial manager has the same objective as every other manager in the firm: to maximize the wealth of the stockholders. If the firm's stock price goes up as a result of the managers' decisions, the decisions were good ones. The stockholders would recognize that the value of the company has been enhanced by the managers' efforts.

The financial manager has three primary duties: to plan and control the company's financial future, to raise the funds needed for the firm's operations, and to allocate those funds to the most profitable opportunities in the company.

In conducting his or her duties, the financial manager must be aware of certain financial principles and relationships. These principles are crucial to the successful operation of the firm. Some of the principles are simply common sense relationships expressed in the form of a simple statement. Some require a quantitative analysis to see if they are being applied correctly. All, however, are vital to the financial well-being of a business operation.

2

Operating Environment of Financial Management

Business firms operate in a complex environment of financial, legal, economic, and political forces that continually influence their actions. To maximize stockholder wealth, a number of external factors provide essential inputs in the decision-making process. These factors include financial system, forms of business organization, and corporation taxation. The financial system consists of financial institutions, financial markets, and financial instruments.

This chapter discusses the following topics: circular flow of income; financial institutions; financial markets where financial instruments are traded; the impact of inflation and interest on financial management; key aspects of the various forms of business organization; and the tax treatment of corporate income.

Circular Flow of Income

Figure 2-1 shows how households exchange their economic resources for money income, which can then be spent on goods and services. Business firms are the primary production agents in the economy, while households are the primary providers of resources in the economy. Firms produce products and then sell them to households. In order to produce goods and services, firms buy economic resources, such as capital, land, labor, and entrepreneurial ability. To acquire these resources, business firms make income payments such as interest, rent, wages, and profits which represent the economic cost of production.

Business firms must acquire funds to engage in production activities. Many of these funds come from cash flows that the firms themselves generate, but other funds are provided by investors through financial intermediation. **Financial intermediation** is the process of transferring funds from surplus economic units (those who earn more money income than they spend in a year) to deficit economic units (those who spend more than their money income in a year). Financial institutions and markets exist for the primary purpose of facilitating the intermediation process.

To obtain funds from investors, firms issue financial (or paper) assets. Financial or paper assets fall into three general classes: money-market instruments, capital-market instruments, and money. **Money-market instruments** are those whose maturities are less than one year. **Capital-market instruments** are those whose maturities are longer than one year. Money is used as a medium of exchange, a store of value, and a standard

Figure 2-1
Circular Flow of Income

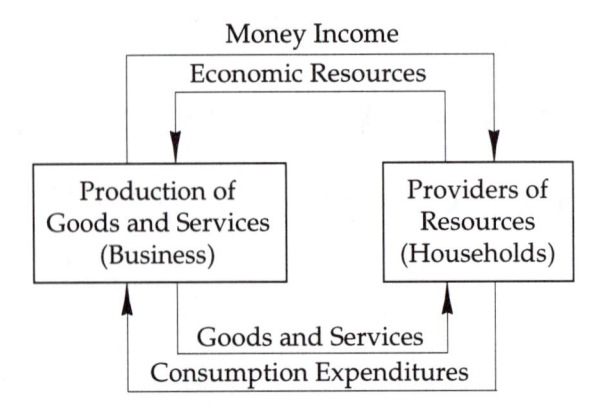

```
                        Money Income
                    Economic Resources
        ┌──────────────────┐      ┌──────────────────┐
        │   Production of  │      │    Providers of  │
        │ Goods and Services│     │     Resources    │
        │    (Business)    │      │   (Households)   │
        └──────────────────┘      └──────────────────┘
                    Goods and Services
                  Consumption Expenditures
```

of value. The following list shows various ways to measure the money supply, but all counts include coin, currency, demand deposits, and negotiable-order-of-withdrawal (NOW) accounts.

- M-1 Demand deposits at commercial banks, currency in circulation, balances in NOW accounts, plus other transaction accounts at financial institutions.
- M-2 M-1 plus savings and small-denomination time-deposit accounts, plus money market mutual fund shares.
- M-3 M-2 plus large-denomination time deposits.
- L   M-3 plus other liquid assets such as commercial paper, Treasury bills, etc.

FINANCIAL INSTITUTIONS

Financial institutions serve as intermediaries who channel funds from those who earn more than they spend in a year (or surplus savers who are primarily individuals) to those who spend more than they earn in a year (or deficit spenders who are mainly governments and businesses). There are two major types of financial institutions: private and governmental. This section concentrates on the private financial institutions of most interest to individuals and business firms which include: depository financial institutions, insurance companies, and others. The many government agencies that play an important role in various parts of the financial system are as follows:

1. U.S. Department of the Treasury

2. Regulatory agencies
   a. Federal Reserve System
   b. Federal Home Loan Bank System
   c. Federal Deposit Insurance Corporation
   d. Comptroller of the Currency
   e. Securities and Exchange Commission
   f. State regulatory agencies

Chapter 2: Operating Environment of Financial Management

3. Agencies that support housing and urban renewal
   a. Federal Housing Administration
   b. Veterans Administration
   c. Federal National Mortgage Association
   d. Government National Mortgage Association
   e. Federal Home Loan Mortgage Corporation
   f. Public Housing Administration

4. Financial agencies that support the agricultural industry
   a. Farm Credit Administration
      Federal Land Banks
      Federal Intermediate Credit Banks
      Banks for Cooperatives
   b. Commodity Credit Corporation
   c. Farmers Home Administration
   d. Rural Electrification Administration

5. Agencies that provide loans and insurance to business firms
   a. Small Business Administration
   b. Export-Import Banks
   c. Agency for International Development
   d. Overseas Private Investment Corporation

6. State and local government retirement funds

Depository Financial Institutions

Commercial banks, mutual savings banks, savings and loan associations, and credit unions are sometimes called **depository financial institutions** because they accept demand and/savings deposits.

Commercial Banks

Commercial banks are the largest type of financial institution in terms of the amount of financial assets they hold. Business firms depend heavily upon commercial banks, both as borrowers and as lenders. They borrow short-term funds from banks to run their daily operations. They also borrow intermediate-term funds from banks to finance their plant-and-equipment costs. As lenders, they deposit funds in checking accounts so they can write checks and invest some of their funds on a temporary basis. Commercial banks specialize in such loans as short-term and intermediate-term business loans, consumer loans, and mortgage loans.

Mutual Savings Banks

Mutual savings banks acquire their funds in the form of NOW accounts, savings accounts, and various time deposit accounts. These funds are used to finance home purchases and to purchase corporate bonds. While savings and loan associations hold primarily conventional (uninsured) mortgages, mutual savings banks invest primarily in those mortgages insured and guaranteed by the Federal Housing Administration and the Veterans Administration. In addition to their heavy investment in home mortgages, mutual savings banks buy large quantities of high-quality corporate bonds.

Practically all mutual savings banks presently operate under state charter, even though federal charter is available. Mutual savings banks operate in about 20 states, but their real strongholds are New York, Massachusetts, Connecticut, Pennsylvania, and New Jersey. Approximately 90 percent of their deposits are concentrated in those five states.

Savings and Loan Associations

Savings and loan associations presently serve purposes similar to those of mutual savings banks. They are chartered either by the federal government or by the state in which the association wishes to operate. Savings and loan associations may have a mutual or a stock form of ownership. The depositors and borrowers of a mutual savings and loan association elect a board of directors who oversee the association as any other corporate board of directors would do. With the stock form of ownership, stockholders own the association, elect the directors, and face risk and returns just as stockholders in other corporations do. Savings and loan associations specialize in mortgages even though they make some consumer loans. Unlike mutual savings banks, they are found in every state.

Credit Unions

Four major ingredients of a credit union are a group of people, a common interest, pooled savings, and loans to each other. It is a cooperative self-help thrift and loan society composed of individuals bound together by some tie such as a common employer, membership in a labor union, a church, or a fraternal order. Members purchase ownership "shares" similar to savings accounts, and each in turn may borrow from the credit union. Members own, control, and operate the credit union themselves under either a federal or a state charter. While credit unions are relatively small financial institutions, there are many of them throughout the country and their growth has been rapid. With minimal operating costs and limited collection problems, credit unions are able to offer competitive interest rates on deposits and still provide loans at rates below those available from other institutions.

Insurance Companies

Insurance companies can be divided into two broad categories: life and property-casualty. Life insurance companies dominate in terms of assets held. This is because the life insurance business involves receipt of premiums during a given year, but payments from these premiums occur over many years in the future. Many other types of insurance involve collection of premiums during a given year and payments from these premiums during the same year.

Life Insurance Companies

Life insurance companies set premiums at levels that enable them to cover benefit payments on the basis of prior mortality statistics. In the process of providing death benefits, they accumulate vast amounts of "policy reserves" by charging premiums that exceed the cost of benefit payments during the early years of a policy. These reserves (which are not needed until the benefits fall due) are invested, and the income is used mainly to reduce the net amount of premiums that a policyholder must pay. Such earnings on policy reserves are similar to interest on savings. Because life insurance companies invest large amounts of money in corporate securities, they are a major source of business financing. They also invest heavily in mortgages.

Property and Casualty Insurance Companies

Property-casualty insurance companies provide their policyholders with protection against financial losses from fire and other perils. Policyholders suffering no fire or casualty damage get their money's worth out of their premiums through the peace of mind that comes from the fact that they are protected against loss. Property-casualty insurance companies might well be called "department stores" of insurance. Some specialize in particular types of policies, but most sell many kinds of insurance. Among these are the following:

1. Property coverage such as fire, hail, and windstorms.
2. Casualty insurance such as workmen's compensation, automobile liability, miscellaneous liability, plate glass, and burglary and theft.
3. Fidelity and surety bonds.
4. Accident and health insurance.
5. Multiple peril insurance that provides protection against a number of different types of risks under a single policy.

All basic insurance policies sold provide property-casualty insurance companies with investable funds because premiums are paid in advance. However, these funds are relatively temporary. Thus, these insurance companies hold large amounts of state, municipal, and U.S. government bonds, although they also invest heavily in corporate securities.

Other Financial Institutions

Many other types of private financial institutions operate in the financial system. Pension funds, mutual funds, and finance companies are briefly discussed in this section.

Pension Funds

Pension funds fall into two broad categories: private pension funds and government-sponsored pension funds. Both types are established to provide income to retired or disabled persons in the economy. Most private pension funds established by business firms are operated by the trust departments of commercial banks and by life insurance companies. Government-sponsored pension funds are controlled by legislation of the sponsoring governmental unit. Private pension funds invest heavily in corporate stocks. Pension funds for the employees of state and local governments invest heavily in corporate bonds and stocks.

Mutual Funds

Mutual funds acquire small amounts of money from numerous individuals and then invest them in various securities for the benefit of these individuals. Mutual fund shares are financial assets whose values equal the value of the securities and cash owned by the fund. Shareholders have the right to sell their shares back to the mutual fund at their current asset value whenever they wish to do so. Mutual fund assets are actually managed by a management company which consists of professionals in the field of investments. Mutual funds invest heavily in corporate securities.

Finance Companies

Finance companies differ sharply from deposit-type financial institutions. They usually do not have access to deposit funds and must compete for higher cost funds in financial markets. Of course, they have far greater flexibility in the acquisition of assets and liabilities. They depend heavily on open market commercial paper and also borrow considerable money from banks. Finance companies use their funds to make loans to individuals and business firms. Some finance companies are formed by parent firms to finance the sales of the firm's goods. These finance companies are frequently called **"captive" finance companies.** A familiar example is General Motors Acceptance Corporation (GMAC), a subsidiary of General Motors.

Deregulation of Financial Institutions

Depository financial institutions—commercial banks, mutual savings banks, savings and loan associations, and credit unions—have been among the most heavily regulated areas of the economy. The present structure of regulatory restraints on depository financial institutions was imposed primarily in response to the collapse of the banking system in the 1930s. Price regulation, entry restrictions, and portfolio regulation were pervasive in the financial industry. Substantial and numerous innovations in the financial system in the last decade largely preceded and were later facilitated by recent deregulation.

Deregulation of depository financial institutions was carried out under provisions of the Depository Institutions Deregulation and Monetary Control Act of 1980 and the Garn-St. Germain Depository Institutions Act of 1982. These two acts marked the culmination of two decades of effort by members of the Congress, the regulatory agencies, and the financial industry to change some of the regulations under which U.S. financial institutions have operated for the last five decades. Many of these regulations have been made obsolete by changes in the economy, the structure of credit markets, technology, consumer demands for financial services, and the competitive environment.

The Depository Institutions Deregulation and Monetary Control Act of 1980 is summarized below:

1. Interest rate ceilings on savings and time deposits were phased out by the end of 1986.
2. All depository financial institutions are permitted to offer NOW accounts (interest-earning checking accounts) to individuals and nonprofit organizations.
3. State limits of interest rates (usury ceilings) on first residential mortgage loans were eliminated as of March 31, 1980.
4. Federal deposit insurance at depository financial institutions was increased from $40,000 to $100,000.
5. Any reserve requirement will be uniformly applied to all transaction accounts at all depository financial institutions. Transaction accounts include demand

deposits, NOW accounts, automatic transfer service accounts, telephone transfer service accounts, and share drafts.
6. Thrift institutions (mutual savings banks, savings and loan associations, and credit unions) may provide a broader range of services to their savings customers and manage their assets in a more flexible way.

The Act opens many opportunities for depository institutions to compete more effectively with other financial institutions such as money market funds. It also poses substantial challenges. With competition enhanced, less efficient institutions may find it difficult to provide quality service at competitive prices. In addition, the Act opened the door for the entry of new competitors into the financial industry.

Transitional problems are inevitable as depository financial institutions bring their operations into conformity with the new rules. The 1980s has been a period of adjustment. While it is difficult to predict, the U.S. financial system in the 1990s and beyond is likely to be considerably different than it is today. Depository institutions have to evaluate carefully the costs and benefits of doing business in the new environment. Thus, they will have to reexamine their pricing policies and service levels.

FINANCIAL MARKETS

Deficit spenders and surplus savers meet in financial markets to transact business (exchange money for paper assets such as checking deposits, CDs, loans, securities, etc.). Financial markets consist of money markets and capital markets. These two types of financial markets are similar in that they provide an investment outlet for those with excess funds and a source for those in need of funds. But they differ with regard to the type of funds involved. Money markets deal in short-term credit instruments, while capital markets deal in long-term debts and stocks. This section briefly describes financial markets and instruments.

Money Markets

Money markets are a group of markets where short-term credit instruments such as Treasury bills, commercial paper, bankers' acceptances, negotiable certificates of deposit, repurchase agreements, and federal funds are traded. In general, money market instruments are issued by obligors of the highest credit rating and are characterized by a high degree of safety of principal. Maturities may be as long as one year but usually are of 90 days or less. Some instruments span only a few days or even one day. The major issuers of money market instruments are financial institutions, major corporations, and governmental units.

Treasury Bills

Treasury bills are direct obligations of the U.S. government. They are perhaps the single most important type of money market instrument. Although one-year bills are auctioned on a monthly basis, Treasury bills with maturities of 91 days and 182 days are auctioned on a weekly basis. These bills are sold on a discount basis.

Commercial Paper

Commercial paper consists of short-term unsecured promissory notes sold directly or through dealers by finance companies and certain industrial concerns. Commercial paper is unsecured and bears the name of the issuer. Consequently, the market has generally been dominated by large corporations with the highest credit ratings. These notes have maturities of anywhere from three days to 270 days.

Bankers' Acceptances

Bankers' acceptances are short-term credit instruments that arise out of foreign transactions. They are time drafts (orders to pay) issued by a business firm (usually an importer) and "accepted" by a bank. They entail very little risk because the accepting bank bears the primary responsibility of providing payment at maturity. Bankers' acceptances carry an average maturity of 90 days.

Negotiable Certificates of Deposits

Commercial banks began to issue large-denomination certificates of deposits (negotiable CDs of $100,000 or more) in 1961 in order to attract idle corporate funds. **Negotiable CDs** are formal negotiable receipts for funds left with the bank for a specified period of time, usually from 30 days to one year.

Repurchase Agreements

Repurchase agreements are arrangements whereby a securities dealer sells its short-term securities with a simultaneous agreement to buy them back at a later date. In general, they are known as "repos" or "RPs." RPs involve little default risk because such transactions use U.S. Treasury bills or other high-quality debt securities as collateral.

Federal Funds

Federal funds are loans between banks on an overnight basis—funds lent out on one day and repaid the following morning. These funds arise from the requirement that commercial banks hold certain levels of liquid reserves in the form of deposit with their Federal Reserve Bank. A bank with excess reserves can lend them to another bank with insufficient reserves.

Capital Markets

Capital markets deal in long-term securities such as stocks, bonds, and mortgages. There are two types of capital markets: primary markets and secondary markets. When the firm sells its new securities, the transaction takes place in the **primary market**. Most new securities are sold through either a public offering or a private placement. In a public offering, new issues are sold through investment bankers such as Merrill Lynch, Solomon-Smith-Barney, and E. F. Hutton. The private placement involves the sale of an entire issue to a limited number of ultimate investors. The **secondary market** deals with those securities that have already been issued and sold. There are two major secondary markets: organized securities exchanges and the over-the-counter market. Organized securities exchanges are physical locations such as the New York Stock Exchange (NYSE) and the American Stock Exchange (AMEX) where buyers and sellers come together to trade large volumes of selected securities on an auction basis. For example, suppose Bill Jones desired to buy 100 shares of IBM Corporation at the current market price. Since Bill has an account with E*Trade, he could either log on to his E*Trade internet account and execute the order on-line or call his broker who would relay his order to E*Trade's clerk on the floor of the NYSE. The clerk would forward the order to one of E*Trade's seat holders who would carry the order to IBM's trading post and execute the order. Once placed, orders are usually executed in seconds with confirmation either via internet, phone, or by mail. The over-the-counter market is not a tangible location but rather a sophisticated circuit of many stockbrokers and dealers whose offices are linked by telephones, teletypes, and computers.

Bonds

A **bond** is a written promise to make payments of interest and principal on a specified future date to the holder of the bond. Most bonds are issued in units of $1,000 maturity or par value. They are usually called a fixed-income security because they have a fixed-interest payment made semiannually. The annual interest is expressed as a percentage of the maturity value and is called the coupon rate. Bonds fall into four general categories: U.S. Treasury issues, U.S. agency issues, municipal issues, and corporate bonds. For example, assume that Kenbridge Corporation, who needs long term funds to purchase a plant, decides to issue 10 percent coupon interest, 20-year, $1000 par value bonds that pay interest to the bondholder semiannually. An investor (surplus saver) who buys one of these bonds would hold the contractual right to receive $100 interest per year (10 percent of $1000) in two equal payments of $50 every six months ($100/2) for 20 years and the right to receive the $1000 par or principal from Kenbridge Corporation at the end of the 20th year.

The U.S. government offers two types of fixed-income securities with maturities greater than one year: Treasury notes and Treasury bonds. These Treasury issues are considered to be the safest long-term debt securities because they are guaranteed by the U.S. government. Treasury notes are issued with an original maturity of one to ten years. Treasury bonds are issued with an original maturity over ten years.

Various U.S. government agencies issue fixed-income securities to support their financial activities. Although U.S agency issues are not direct obligations of the U.S. government, many of them are supported by the Treasury Department. Some major issuers are the Federal National Mortgage Association, the Federal Home Loan Banks, the Federal Land Banks, and the Federal Intermediate Credit Banks.

Municipal issues represent bonds sold by states, counties, cities, and other political incorporations. They are normally called tax-exempt bonds because their interest income is totally exempt from federal income taxes. This tax-exempt feature enables state and local governments to issue bonds at lower interest costs. Municipal issues are of two basic types: general obligation bonds and revenue bonds. General obligation bonds are backed by the issuer and repaid from taxes received by the issuing body. Revenue bonds are sold to finance a particular public project and repaid from the income earned on the project.

Corporate bonds are marketable debt instruments of corporations with maturities between 5 and 30 years. When a firm issues bonds to the public, it designates a trustee who represents the interest of the bondholders. The bond **indenture** constitutes a contract between the borrower and the trustee. The indenture specifies the bond's repayment schedule, restrictions on dividend payments and liquidity, and types of collateral.

Stocks

Stocks consist of common stocks and preferred stocks. The common stockholders of a corporation represent the firm's ownership. They have a claim to any asset returns after all debt and preferred stock obligations are fully satisfied. Their ownership is represented by a stock certificate. This stock certificate shows the name of the company, the name of the owner of the shares, the number of shares owned, the name of the registrar, and the par value of the stock. When the stockholder decides to transfer the ownership of the shares, the form on the back of the stock certificate must be completed. Common stockholders have a number of rights:

1. The right to elect the board of directors
2. The right to receive dividends
3. The right to examine the books of the corporation
4. The right to vote on mergers
5. The right to preserve their percentage ownership in the company.

Preferred stock is actually a hybrid security with features of both common stock and debt. Preferred stock carries a stated dividend rate but its dividend is paid only if voted each period by the board of directors. Preferred stock issues do not have definite maturity dates but are retired through call features and other means. Preferred stockholders generally do not have a voice in management but are entitled to elect a specified number of directors if the company fails to pay dividends during a specified period of time.

INFLATION

Inflation is a measure of the percentage increase in the general price level. Inflation's intensity is usually measured through indexes that are designed to reflect changes in the general level of prices. Analysts and policy makers thus monitor movements of the major price indexes very carefully. As a result, the indexes are of considerable importance in determining both governmental and business strategies.

One of the oldest surviving economic doctrines is the quantity theory of money, a hypothesis about the main cause of inflation which states that changes in the general level of commodity prices are determined primarily by the quantity of money in circulation. This represents the popular axiom that attributes inflation to "too much money chasing too few goods." When we talk about business and finance, however, the two major causes most widely cited for inflation are demand-pull and cost-push.

Demand-pull inflation describes a situation where the price of a product increases because its demand exceeds its supply. Increases in money supply, federal income tax rebates, and expectations of further price increases can cause demand-pull inflation. **Cost-push inflation** represents a situation where price rises because of increases in labor costs. Organized unions demand and obtain wage increases. Large employers then "push" their increased wage costs on to consumers by raising the price of their products.

Interest Rates

The investor's required rate of return or the interest rate serves as the market price of money. The market interest rate is the pricing mechanism which balances the flow of funds between the surplus savers and the deficit spenders. Lower interest rates usually stimulate greater economic growth while higher borrowing costs generally stagnate the economy. The **nominal rate of interest** consists of the real interest rate and the expected rate of inflation or:

Nominal Market Interest Rate = Real Interest Rate + Rate of Inflation

This assumption is usually called the **Fisher effect**. The real interest rate is therefore the nominal market interest rate less the rate of inflation and is thought to be relatively stable over time. It is determined by the productivity of investment in the economy and a risk premium commensurate with risk of the borrower. Therefore the:

Nominal Market Interest Rate = Risk-Free Real Rate + Risk Premium + Inflation

A proxy for the nominal risk-free rate is typically the U.S. Treasury Bill or the investor's required return on a risk-free asset. Thus, the nominal rate of interest embodies in it an inflation premium sufficient to compensate lenders for the expected loss of purchasing power. Consequently, nominal interest rates are higher when people expect higher rates of inflation and are lower when people expect lower rates of inflation. Of course, inflation-induced increases in the nominal interest rate mean higher business-borrowing rates. The Board of Governors of the Federal Reserve closely monitors the condition of the economy and at its discretion initiates actions to raise and lower the nominal market rate of interest to keep inflation in check and maintain economic stability and growth.

Financial Difficulty

For the last few years, business firms have experienced difficulty obtaining long-term, fixed-rate loans. Bond prices fall as interest rates rise. In an effort to protect themselves against such capital losses, some lenders have put more funds into short-term rather than long-term debt and have insisted on floating-rate bonds whose interest rate varies with short-term interest rates.

Demand for Capital

Inflation increases the amount of funds required to conduct a given volume of business. When expected inflation is high, workers demand and obtain higher wages. Sold inventories should be replaced with more expensive goods. The cost of new equipment also increases. All these things require financial managers to raise additional capital.

Investment Planning

Companies are finding it more and more difficult to estimate expected future cash inflows and plan their investment accordingly. High and volatile inflation is the root of the uncertainty. Virtually all investment projects provide expected future cash inflows in nominal dollars rather than real dollars. The real value of each dollar received falls if there is inflation after the project is undertaken.

Forms of Business Organization

The three basic forms of business organization in the United States are the **sole proprietorship, the partnership, and the corporation**. The sole proprietorship is the dominant form of organization with respect to numbers, but the corporation is the dominant form of organization with respect to total sales and total profits.

Sole Proprietorship

A **sole proprietorship** is a business owned by an individual who is solely responsible for all aspects of the business. The owner is personally responsible for all debts of the firm, even in excess of the amount invested in the business. Its major advantages are:

1. Low start-up costs
2. Greatest freedom from regulation
3. Owner in direct control
4. Minimum working capital requirements
5. Tax advantage to small business owner
6. All profits to owner.

Its major disadvantages include unlimited liability, lack of continuity, and the difficulty involved in raising capital.

Partnership

A **partnership** is a legal entity that is jointly owned by two or more individuals. The articles of partnership are a written contract between the partners necessary to establish most partnerships. This contract specifies the capital contribution of each partner, the share of each partner both in the assets and in profits of the firm, provisions for salaries, and provisions for the withdrawal or death of a partner. As in the sole proprietorship, the owners of the partnership are personally responsible for all debts of the firm, even those debts in excess of the amount invested in the business. The major advantages of the partnership include:

1. Ease of formation
2. Low start-up cost
3. Additional sources of venture capital
4. Broader management base
5. Possible tax advantages
6. Limited outside regulation.

Its major disadvantages include unlimited liability, divided authority, lack of continuity, and difficulty in raising additional capital.

Corporation

In terms of revenue and profits produced, the corporation is the most important type of economic unit. Although only 17 percent of U.S. business firms are corporations, they account for over four-fifths of total business sales and earn almost two-thirds of total business profits. Accordingly, corporations play a major role in the U.S. economy.

A **corporation** is a separate legal entity empowered to own assets, incur liabilities, and engage in certain activities. This definition should not obscure the fact that the corporation is owned by real people called stockholders. The corporation is simply a legal device that allows its stockholders to act and to be treated as a single person in order to achieve a common purpose.

A corporation is incorporated in a particular state. To form a corporation, the corporate founders must file an application, commonly known as articles of incorporation, with the secretary of state or some other state official. The articles of incorporation include the location of the company, the purpose of the business, the names of the owners and directors, the names of the management, the number of shares of stock authorized, the paid-in capital, and the length of the corporation's life. Once the articles of incorporation are approved by the appropriate state official, a charter is issued to establish the corporation as a legal entity and spell out the conditions under which it can exist. Bylaws are then drawn up by the corporation's founders and approved by the board of directors. The bylaws include such operational matters as the rights of the stockholders, the election of the board of directors, the appointment of officers, the selection of standing committees of the board, and the issue and transfer of stock. Thus, the corporation is governed by the state's bylaws.

Advantages

The corporate form of organization has three major advantages over both the proprietorship and the partnership: limited liability, transferability of ownership, and ease of raising funds.

Both sole proprietors and partners are fully and personally liable for all the liabilities of their company. In contrast, because the corporation has a separate existence from its owners, the owners' liability is limited to their investment after they have fully paid for their shares in the corporation. That is, the stockholders' personal assets cannot be taken by creditors to settle the debts of the business.

Each stockholder owns a certain portion of the corporation, expressed in shares of stock. Corporate ownership is evidenced by stock certificates, which can easily be sold to new owners without the prior consent of other stockholders. The legal existence of the corporation is not jeopardized by the partial transfer of ownership or the death of any of its owners.

The corporate form of organization is also greatly advantageous for a large business because the corporation can easily raise large sums of capital. Because corporate shares are readily marketable and per-share price is relatively low, capital can be raised from any individuals who are willing to invest their money.

Disadvantages

Although the corporation has emerged as the most important form of organization, mainly because of its advantages, it also has certain disadvantages. Because the corporation is a separate entity created by law, it is subject to regulation by the state in which it was organized. The corporation must also fulfill the requirements set forth by federal regulatory agencies. Organizational expenses and red tape are another drawback. The length of time required to form a corporation, the cost of incorporation, and the issuance of shares may be serious problems, especially for small businesses.

An additional disadvantage is the fact that the portion of corporate earnings distributed to stockholders in the form of dividends is taxed twice. In contrast, the earnings of sole proprietors and partners are taxed only once as the personal income of the owners. In addition, corporate laws and tax laws vary from state to state. Some states levy special taxes and fees on the corporation and restrict its activities to that type of business for which it was chartered.

TAX TREATMENT OF CORPORATE INCOME

Because the net income shown on the firm's income statement measures corporate performance, it is important to understand the basic concepts used in calculating that income. The key items to be examined are depreciation, interest and dividends.

Depreciation

Depreciation charges are usually treated as tax-deductible expenses. The three depreciation methods generally used are straight-line, double declining-balance, and sum-of-years-digits. The straight-line depreciation method results in a uniform deduction from revenues each year. The double declining-balance and sum-of-years-digits methods allow the company to allocate a larger proportion of the asset's cost during its early life and a smaller proportion of its cost during its later years. Thus, these two depreciation methods are forms of accelerated depreciation.

The accelerated depreciation methods are based on the hypothesis that depreciation charged under these methods results in a more accurate matching of expense with revenue. Assets usually produce large revenues during their early years of use and smaller revenues during their later years of use. Hence, these two methods permit the company to match larger depreciation charges with larger revenues during the early years of use and to match smaller depreciation deductions with smaller revenues during the later years of use. Increasing maintenance expenses are offset by falling depreciation charges so that the company can achieve a better matching of expense and revenue.

Example 2-1. Assume that a machine is purchased for $15,600. It has an estimated useful life of five years and an estimated salvage value of $600 at the end of five years. Table 2-1 compares the three depreciation methods in terms of the annual depreciation charges over the five-year period.

Straight-Line

The straight-line depreciation method is a function of time. The cost of an asset less its estimated salvage value is allocated in an equal amount each year over its useful life. With this method, a uniform annual depreciation of $3,000 is computed as follows:

$$\text{Annual Charge} = \frac{\text{Cost} - \text{Salvage Value}}{\text{Asset Life}} = \frac{\$15{,}600 - \$600}{5 \text{ Years}} = \$3{,}000$$

Chapter 2: Operating Environment of Financial Management

Double Declining Balance

Under the declining-balance method of depreciation, the same depreciation rate is applied each year to the undepreciated value of the asset at the end of the previous year.

Table 2-1
Comparison of Three Depreciation Methods

Year	Straight-Line	Double Declining-Balance	Sum-of-Years-Digits
1st	$ 3,000	$ 6,000	$ 5,000
2nd	3,000	3,600	4,000
3rd	3,000	2,160	3,000
4th	3,000	1,296	2,000
5th	3,000	1,944	1,000
Total	$15,000	$15,000	$15,000

Under the double declining-balance method, the annual depreciation rate is twice the straight-line rate. Because the straight-line rate of the five-year machine is 20 percent, the double declining-balance rate would be 40 percent. This rate is applied to the asset's cost of $15,600 less its salvage value of $600. The first year's depreciation under the this method is $6,000 = $15,000 x 0.40; the second year's depreciation is $3,600 = ($15,000 – $6,000) x 0.40; and the process continues. It is important to understand that under the double declining-balance method the cost of the asset is not fully depreciated at the end of its useful life. Thus, the remaining undepreciated cost at the end of the second-to-last year is included in the last year's depreciation. The third column of Table 2-1 shows annual depreciation charges computed under the double declining-balance method.

Sum-of-Years Digits

Under the third depreciation method, a firm applies a varying fraction each year to the cost of the asset less its salvage value. The denominator of the fraction is the total of the years digits which represent the asset's useful life. The numerator of the fraction is the total of the years digits which represent the asset's useful life. The numerator of the fraction is the number of remaining years of the asset's useful life. The sum of the digits as the denominator may be computed as follows:

$$\text{Sum of Digits} = N\left(\frac{N+1}{2}\right) \qquad (2\text{-}1)$$

where N is the estimated useful life of the asset. For example, if an estimated useful life of the asset is five years, the sum is 15 = 5[(5+1)/2]. The numerator of the fraction is changed each year to represent the years of useful life remaining at the beginning of the year in which the depreciation computation is made. For example, if a machine has an estimated useful life of five years, the numerator for the first year would be 5, and the numerator for the second year would be 4. The first year's depreciation under this method is $5,000 = $15,000 x 5/15, the second year's depreciation is $4,000 = $15,000 x 4/15. The annual depreciation for other years can be computed in the same way. The last column of Table 2-1 shows annual depreciation charges computed under this method.

Accelerated Cost Recovery System

For financial reporting purposes, a variety of depreciation methods—straight line, double declining, and sum-of-the-years digits—can be used. However, for tax purposes, the depreciation of assets is regulated by the Internal Revenue Code, which experienced major changes under the Revenue Reform Act of 1986. The Accelerated Cost Recovery System (ACRS) is used to determine depreciation for tax purposes. Under the 1986 law, business assets are classified according to six recovery periods: 3, 5, 7, 10, 15, and 20. Table 2-2 shows the first four property classes—those routinely used by business. Using ACRS recovery periods, the first four property classes are depreciated by the doubledeclining balance method and switching to straight-line depreciation when advantageous. These rates are given in Table 2-3 and are developed with the use of the half-year convention, which treats all property as if it were placed in service in midyear. As shown in Table 2-3, the depreciation percentages for an N-year class asset are given for (n + 1) years. For example, a 3-year asset is depreciated over a 4-year recovery period.

Table 2-2
First Four Categories for Depreciation Write-Off

Class	Definition
3 year	Research and experiment equipment plus certain special tools.
5 year	Light duty trucks, autos, and technological equipment such as computers and copiers.
7 year	Office furniture, fixtures, and most types of manufacturing equipment.
10 year	Petroleum refining products, railroad track cars, and manufactured homes.

Table 2-3
Depreciation Percentages by Recovery Year

Recovery Year	3 year	5 year	7 year	10 year
1	.333	.200	.143	.100
2	.445	.320	.245	.180
3	.148	.192	.175	.144
4	.074	.115	.125	.115
5		.115	.089	.092
6		.058	.089	.074
7			.089	.066
8			.045	.066
9				.065
10				.033
11				
Totals	1.000	1.000	1.000	1.000

Interest and Dividends

Corporations pay interest on their bonds and dividends on their stocks. They also receive interest on credit made to their customers and dividends on their investment in the stocks of other corporations.

Interest and Dividend Payments

Interest payments made by a corporation are treated as a tax-deductible expense, but dividends paid on its stock are not. Hence, interest is paid with before-tax earnings, whereas dividends are paid with after-tax earnings. The use of debt by profitable companies results in a significant tax advantage relative to the use of preferred or common stock. Thus, this differential tax treatment of interest and dividends paid by a corporation has a significant impact on the manner in which the company raises capital.

Interest and Dividend Income

Interest earnings made by a corporation are treated as ordinary income and thus taxed at regular corporate tax rates. However, only 15 percent of dividends received by one corporation from other corporations is taxed at the ordinary tax rate, and 85 percent is exempt from taxation. The 85 percent-exclusion clause helps to reduce the effect of triple taxation. Consider the case where Company A received dividends from Company B:

1. Company B paid taxes on its income before the payment of dividends.
2. Company A would then add its dividends to taxable income and pay a tax on this dividend income.
3. The stockholders of Company A would receive dividends and pay a tax on this dividend income.

SUMMARY

This chapter covered a number of important topics which affect stockholder wealth maximization: financial system, forms of business organization, and corporate taxation. The financial system consists of financial institutions, financial markets, and financial assets. Financial institutions exist to acquire surplus funds from economic units and then make them available to other economic units. Financial markets consist of money markets and capital markets. Money markets deal in short-term securities and capital markets deal in long-term securities. Money market instruments and capital market instruments are usually called financial assets.

The emphasis in this book is on the corporation because it is the dominant form of business organization in terms of total sales and profits. In a modern economy, the corporation has certain advantages over other forms of business organization: limited liability, transferability of ownership, and ease of raising capital. This chapter also examined a number of important factors in measuring corporate income: depreciation, interest and dividends.

List of Key Terms

financial intermediation
capital market instruments
captive finance companies
Treasury bills
bankers' acceptances
repurchase agreements
capital markets
secondary market
stocks
cost-push inflation
sole proprietorship
corporation

money market instruments
depository financial institutions
money markets
commercial paper
negotiable CDs
federal funds
primary market
bond
demand-pull inflation
nominal rate of interest
partnership
depreciation charges

Part 2

Financial Planning and Control

Before we proceed to the management of assets and the acquisition of funds, certain foundation concepts and tools must be understood. These important areas include financial planning and control. As such Part Two presents financial analysis (Chapter 3), financial and operating leverage (Chapter 4), and various budgets (Chapter 5). These tools and concepts allow the financial manager to accurately assess the firm's financial and operating performance, to locate potential problem areas, to take corrective action, and to plan for the future. The ideas and terminology developed here will facilitate an understanding of the remainder of this text.

3

FINANCIAL STATEMENT ANALYSIS

The two fundamental corporate financial statements are the balance sheet and the income statement. The analysis of these two statements combined with the analysis of other financial data is called financial statement analysis. Ratio analysis is perhaps the most important part of financial statement analysis. The absolute dollar amounts in financial statements become more meaningful when they are converted to ratios. For example, suppose Corporation X produces an annual profit after taxes of $50,000 compared to competitor Corporation Y which earned only $20,000 for the same time period. Because X's absolute profit is greater than Y's, can you conclude that X outperformed Y and therefore the market price of X's stock will rise faster than Y's? Absolutely not, because what if X employed total assets of $500,000 while Y utilized only $100,000. In essence, Y earned $20,000 on an investment of $100,000 (or $20,000/$100,000 = 20%) compared to X's 10% (or $50,000/$500,000). Even though X's profit after taxes exceeds Y's, X's and Y's profits relative to total assets clearly identify Y as the stronger company in this one area.

Thus, ratios provide relative measures of the firm's performance. Ratio analysis is used to evaluate the past, current, and projected performance of the business firm. There are two broad groups of ratios: financial ratios and common-size statements. Financial ratios relate balance-sheet and income-statement items to one another. Common-size statements express balance-sheet and income-statement items as percentages.

This chapter has four major sections. The first section examines some background information about ratio analysis: financial statements, uses of ratio analysis, and inflation. The second section describes how to compute various ratios and discusses their implications. The third section discusses industry average ratios and trend analysis, which can be used as criteria to indicate the strengths and weaknesses of the ratios computed for a particular company at a given point in time. The fourth section describes some problems one encounters in ratio analysis.

BACKGROUND INFORMATION

A meaningful ratio analysis requires us to understand a number of financial factors: financial statements, uses of ratio analysis, and inflation. Ratios are computed on the basis of data taken from the balance sheet and the income statement. Many diverse groups of people are interested in various ratios, but different ratios mean different

PART 2: FINANCIAL PLANNING AND CONTROL

Table 3-1
Lewis Clothing Company Balance Sheet
December 31, 2000 (thousands of dollars)

Cash	$40	Accounts payable	$40
Marketable securities	30	Notes payable	30
Accounts receivable	60	Accrued taxes	10
Prepaid expenses	20	Other accruals	60
Inventories	150	Total current liabilities	$140
Total current assets	$300		
		Long-term debt	$110
Gross plant & equipment	$245	Common stock	100
Accumulated depreciation	−45	Paid-in capital	50
Net plant & equipment	$200	Retained earnings	100
Total assets	$500	Total debt & equity	$500

Current stock price $50/share
Dividend per share $3
Common shares outstanding 10,000

things to different groups of people. Inflation could distort the results of ratio analysis because some financial-statement items are expressed at the historical cost, while other items are expressed at market prices.

Financial Statements

Ratio analysis involves the use of the balance sheet and the income statement. The **balance sheet** summarizes a firm's assets, liabilities, and stockholders' equity on a given date. The **income statement** reveals a firm's revenues, expenses, taxes, and profits during a particular period of time. While the balance sheet represents a snapshot of the firm's financial position at a given point in time, the income statement represents a dynamic (flow) concept of the firm's operations over time. In essence the balance sheet indicates the firm's financial position at a point in time, while the income statement provides something like a "report card" of performance for a designated period of time.

Balance Sheet

Table 3-1 shows the balance sheet of the Lewis Clothing Company for the fiscal year ending December 31, 2000. The left-hand side shows the assets, while the right-hand side shows claims against these assets. Assets are listed in order of liquidity or how quickly they can be converted into cash. Liabilities are listed in order of liquidation or payment.

Current assets are cash and other assets that are expected to be converted into cash and to be available for the operation of the firm within one year. Cash is any item that is immediately available and acceptable as a means of payment. It includes coins, currency, checks, bank drafts, money orders, and demand deposits. Marketable securities are Treasury bills and other securities which companies hold to earn interest. Accounts receivable represents the amount due from customers for services rendered or for goods sold on credit. Prepaid expenses such as prepaid insurance are current assets which have been acquired but not used at the statement date. Inventories consist of raw mate-

Chapter 3: Financial Statement Analysis

Table 3-2
Lewis Clothing Company Income Statement
December 31, 2000 (thousands of dollars)

Net sales			$ 1,000
Cost of goods sold			− 700
Gross profit			$ 300
Less	Operating expenses		
	Selling expenses	$ 30	
	General and administrative expenses	35	
	Lease payments	10	− 75
	Gross operating income		$ 225
Less:	Depreciation		− 75
	Earnings before interest and taxes (EBIT)		$ 150
Less:	Interest		− 50
Net income before taxes			$ 100
Less:	Taxes		− 50
Net income after taxes			$ 50
EPS = 50/10 = $5			

rials, work in process, and finished goods available for sale. Plant and equipment represent fixed assets to be used over a long period of time in the operation of the firm.

Current liabilities represent those liabilities or claims which will require the use of cash to pay off or liquidate within one year. Accounts payable result from purchases on credit and represent the amounts owed to creditors. Notes payable are formal written promises to pay. A trade note payable arises from the credit purchase of goods and services used in the course of business. A note payable to a bank arises when a firm borrows money from a bank. Accrued taxes and other accruals are debts that are owed because of the passage of time but have not been paid because they are not yet due (i.e. income taxes payable). Long-term debts such as mortgages payable and bonds payable are debts payable beyond one year. Stockholders' **equity** or **net worth** consists of common stock, paid-in capital, and retained earnings. Common stock and paid-in capital arise from the sale of common stock by the company to raise capital. A par value is generally assigned to common stock. The excess of the stock's market price over its par value is assigned to paid-in capital. The profits of the corporation may be distributed to the stockholders in the form of dividends or they may be retained in the corporation. Retained earnings are the accumulated profits earned by the company that were not paid out as dividends.

Income Statement

Table 3-2 shows the 2000 income statement for the Lewis Clothing Company. Net sales are such assets as cash and accounts receivable received in exchange for services rendered, sales of goods, and gains from sales or exchanges of assets other than stock in trade. The cost of goods sold represents the actual production cost of goods and services sold. It consists of purchases of raw materials, labor costs associated with production, and other production-related expenses. Operating expenses are shown separately from the cost of goods sold so that we can analyze them directly. Depreciation appears as a separate entry in the income statement, although it may be included as a part of the company's cost of goods sold or as its administrative expenses. Net income after taxes may be paid out to stockholders as dividends or retained and reinvested in the business.

Uses of Ratio Analysis

The four major interest groups of the company are short-term creditors, long-term creditors, management, and stockholders. The viewpoint of each group differs because the nature of the financial relationship to the firm is different. Ratios mean different things to different people. Each group studies the financial statements carefully and interprets the information that relates to their particular interest in the company.

Short-term creditors are primarily interested in the ability of the company to meet its short-term obligations. Long-term creditors such as bondholders are usually more interested in the ability of the firm to service its debt over the long run. In other words, long-term creditors want to assure themselves that the company will be able to make its interest and principal payments when they come due. Management uses ratio analysis to measure the firm's performance from period to period in an effort to identify and correct problem areas. From a more selfish point of view, managers may place more emphasis on those ratios contributing to the survival of the firm so as to protect their jobs. Stockholders may be more concerned with those ratios closely related to the value maximization of their stock.

Security analysts, government agencies, and labor unions are also interested in the company's performance. In order to determine the desirability of the firm's stocks and bonds as an investment, security analysts frequently examine its ratios. Many industries such as utilities and financial institutions are regulated by the government agencies. Some government agencies use ratios to appraise the financial health of the regulated firm and to set the firm's rate of return or price as with electric utilities. Labor unions sometimes employ ratios to show that the firm's profits justify wage increases.

Inflation

Because inflation can distort some financial data, the financial manager should explore the impact of inflation on ratios. Inflation causes phantom sources of profit that may lead even the most alert analyst to derive a faulty assessment of the firm's financial condition. The major problem arises because certain financial statement items such as net sales are stated in current dollars, whereas other items such as fixed assets and inventory may be stated at the historical cost. For example, suppose a firm purchased a building 20 years ago for $100,000 and its current book value is $10,000 (historical cost less accumulated depreciation). Due to inflation, the current price (or replacement cost) of the building is $400,000. Had the firm converted the value of the building on the books from historical cost to market value, depreciation charges would have to rise and net income after taxes would have to fall to more accurately describe the economic consequences of inflation. But historical cost accounting required the firm to account for the building at cost less accumulated depreciation. Thus the accounting treatment resulted in understating depreciation expenses and overstating net income giving rise to so-called phantom profits or fake book profits which would not have surfaced if current economic values were applied. And since financial ratios are based on these phantom values, distorted performance ratios result since they may vary because assets were purchased at different times. This problem becomes even more pronounced since income taxes and dividends, which are current cash values, are calculated on the basis of these economically, nonexistent, phantom profits. In essence, the firm's taxes and dividends were overstated resulting in a real economic drain of capital over time.

Another problem of inflation centers around the accounting for inventory. The total cost of goods available for sale must be allocated between the cost of goods sold and the cost of goods on hand (inventory). The two major methods of allocation are the first in-first out (FIFO) and the last in-first out (LIFO). The **FIFO method** is based on the assumption that the units of a product are sold in the order in which they were acquired. In other words, the oldest units on hand are sold first, the units acquired later are the next to be sold, and so on. In periods of rapidly rising inflation, the use of the FIFO method overstates reported earnings and taxes because it charges off the least expensive inventory against sales. A remedy to this problem is to use the LIFO method.

The **LIFO method** of allocation is based on the assumption that the cost of goods sold should be based on prices paid for the most recently acquired units, and the inventories consist of the oldest units on hand. The major advantage claimed for this procedure is that during periods of rapidly rising prices, the higher prices of the most recent purchases are included in the cost of goods sold, thereby reducing reported earnings and income taxes. It is further claimed that the cost of goods sold is more realistic because the LIFO cost approximates the replacement cost. Even the LIFO may distort certain ratios such as the ratio of sales to inventory because sales are stated in current dollars while inventory may be stated at the historical cost. Inflation may distort the results of ratio analysis. The financial performance of a company may be attributable to external factors over which management has little control. For example, reported earnings may be a function of increasing prices rather than a function of satisfactory performance. Thus, in an inflationary environment, particular caution is necessary to differentiate between performance attributable to inflation and performance that is directly under management's control.

FINANCIAL ANALYSIS

Different types of ratios are important for two reasons. First, no single ratio provides us with sufficient information to determine the financial condition and performance of the company. Reasonable judgement about the firm's financial condition and performance requires examination of a group of ratios. Second, ratios mean different things to different people, and people differ in the ratios they find useful.

We divide financial ratios into five categories: liquidity or debt ratios, leverage ratios, activity ratios, profitability ratios, and common stock ratios.

1. Liquidity ratios measure the company's ability to pay its short-term bills.
2. Leverage ratios indicate the company's capacity to meet its long-term obligations and interest charges.
3. Activity ratios measure how effectively the company is using its resources.
4. Profitability ratios indicate the returns on sales and investments.
5. Common stock ratios measure market performance.

To illustrate the ratios discussed in this chapter, we use the financial statements of the Lewis Clothing Company shown in Tables 3-1 and 3-2. Table 3-3 summarizes the individual types of ratios.

Table 3-3
Ratio Definitions and and Values for Lewis Clothing Company

Ratio	Ratio Definition	Calculation	
Liquidity Ratios			
Current ratio (CR)	$\dfrac{\text{current assets}}{\text{current liabilities}}$	$\dfrac{\$300}{\$140}$	2.14 to 1.00
Quick or acid test ratio (QR)	$\dfrac{\text{current assets} - \text{inventories}}{\text{current liabilities}}$	$\dfrac{\$300-150}{\$140}$	1.07 to 1.00
Leverage Ratios			
Debt ratio (DR)	$\dfrac{\text{total debt}}{\text{total assets}}$	$\dfrac{\$250}{\$500}$	0.50 or 50%
Times interest earned ratio (TIER)	$\dfrac{\text{EBIT}}{\text{interest charges}}$	$\dfrac{\$150}{\$50}$	3.00 times
Activity Ratios			
Inventory turnover (IT)	$\dfrac{\text{cost of goods sold}}{\text{inventory}}$	$\dfrac{\$700}{\$150}$	4.70 times
Accounts receivable turnover (ART)	$\dfrac{\text{annual sales}}{\text{receivables}}$	$\dfrac{\$1{,}000}{\$60}$	16.70 times
Average collection period (ACP)	$\dfrac{365 \text{ days}}{\text{receivable turnover}}$	$\dfrac{365}{16.7}$	22.00 days
or ACP	$\dfrac{\text{accounts receivable}}{\text{credit sales}/365}$	$\dfrac{60}{1{,}000/365}$	22.00 days
Average payment period (APP)	$\dfrac{\text{accounts payable}}{*\text{credit purchases}/\text{day}}$	$\dfrac{40}{800/365}$	18.25 days
Asset turnover (AT)	$\dfrac{\text{sales}}{\text{total assets}}$	$\dfrac{\$1{,}000}{\$500}$	2.00 times
Profitability Ratios			
Gross margin on sales (GM)	$\dfrac{\text{sales} - \text{cost of goods sold}}{\text{sales}}$	$\dfrac{\$1{,}000 - \$700}{\$1{,}000}$	0.30 or 30%
Profit margin on sales (PM)	$\dfrac{\text{net income after taxes}}{\text{sales}}$	$\dfrac{\$50}{\$1{,}000}$	0.05 or 5%
Return on equity or net worth (ROE)	$\dfrac{\text{net income after taxes}}{\text{net worth}}$	$\dfrac{\$50}{\$250}$	0.20 or 20%
Return on assets or investment (ROA)	$\dfrac{\text{net income after taxes}}{\text{total assets}}$	$\dfrac{\$50}{\$500}$	0.10 or 10%

*Assumes credit purchases of $800,000 per year.

Common Stock Ratios (CSR)

Earnings per share (EPS)	$\dfrac{\text{net income after taxes}}{\text{\#common shares outstanding}}$	$\dfrac{\$50}{10}$	$5 per share
Payout ratio (PO)	$\dfrac{\text{dividend per share}}{\text{earnings per share}}$	$\dfrac{\$3}{\$5}$	0.60 or 60%
Dividend per share (DPS)	PO x EPS	0.60 x $5	$3 per share
Price to earnings (PE)	$\dfrac{\text{market price per share}}{\text{earnings per share}}$	$\dfrac{\$50}{\$5}$	10 to 1

Liquidity Analysis

Net working capital (NWC) provides a measure of the firm's liquidity. The net working capital for the Lewis Clothing Company is as follows:

Net working capital = current assets – current liabilities
= $300 – $140
= $160

Although not a ratio, NWC provides an important measure for the company and can be used to track liquidity over time. NWC represents those assets which will convert to cash within a year less those claims which will require liquidation with cash within a year. The higher the value, the greater is the firm's liquidity position. Thus NWC can be viewed as that short-term capital that is not committed to the payment of a debt within the next year and is free to be used for available investment or financing opportunities. In essence, Lewis has $160,000 available for this purpose. Stated differently, Lewis could spend $160,000 over the next year and still have enough liquidity to cover existing short-term debts.

Liquidity ratios examine the adequacy of funds, the solvency of the company, and the ability of the company to meet its short-term commitments. Two commonly-used liquidity ratios are the current ratio and the quick ratio.

Current Ratio (CR)

The current ratio is the ratio of current assets to curent liabilities. The current ratio of the Lewis Clothing Company is

Current ratio = $\dfrac{\text{current assets}}{\text{current liabilities}}$ = $\dfrac{\$300}{\$140}$ = 2.14 to 1.00

Thus, the Lewis Clothing Company has $2.14 of current assets for every $1 of current liabilities. This means that, even if the value of the firm's current assets were to decrease by as much as 53 percent [or 1–(1/2.14)], it could still pay its short-term obligations in full. Stated differently, Lewis could reduce current assets by $160,000 or to the point of zero NWC and still pay off short-term debts.

The current ratio is a rough indication of a firm's ability to service its current obligations. Generally, the higher the current ratio, the greater the "cushion" between current obligations and a firm's ability to pay them. Although the stronger ratio reflects the excess of current assets over current liabilities, the composition and quality of current assets is a critical factor in the analysis of an individual firm's liquidity.

An unusually high current ratio indicates that the financial manager has invested excessive funds in low-return short-term assets and suggests a shift of funds from low-return, short-term assets to high-return, long-term assets would be in the best economic interests of the firm's owners. An unusually low current ratio suggests that the firm may have some difficulty in paying its bills. The traditional rule of thumb states that the current ratio should be at least 2. However, the financial manager must also consider certain other factors, such as the line of business, the size of the firm, the season of the year, and the composition of current assets.

Table 3-4
The Composition of Current Assets and Current Ratio

	Firm A	Firm B
Cash and securities	$ 1,000	$ 4,000
Accounts receivable	2,000	25,000
Inventories	27,000	1,000
Total current assets (1)	$30,000	$30,000
Total current liabilities (2)	$15,000	$15,000
Current ratio = (1)/(2)	2 to 1	2 to 1

The composition of current assets is extremely important in evaluating a firm's liquidity. To illustrate, suppose Firms A and B have the characteristics indicated in Table 3-4. Each firm has a current ratio of 2. But it should be clear from this analysis that Firm B is in a much better position than Firm A to meet its currently maturing obligations. This is because Firm A has far more inventories, thus indicating that it may have some conversion problem with the sale of inventories. Firm A must first sell its $27,000 worth of inventories and then convert the resulting accounts receivable into cash. Because Firm B has only $1,000 in inventories, it would not have such a conversion problem. Hence, although Firm A's current ratio appears favorable, because of its high level of inventories, it may not be able to pay some of its bills on time.

Quick Ratio or Acid Test Ratio (QR)

A way to uncover the current ratio's inventory problem when comparing Firm A and B is to examine the quick ratio. Simply recalculate the current ratios, but this time exclude inventories from current assets. The result is the quick ratio (QR) which is an "acid test" of the firm's ability to meet its current obligations. The quick ratio of the Lewis Clothing Company is as follows:

$$\text{Quick ratio} = \frac{\text{current assets} - \text{inventories}}{\text{current assets}} = \frac{(\$300 - \$150)}{\$140} = 1.07 \text{ to } 1.00$$

Thus, the Lewis Clothing Company has $1.07 of quick assets for every $1 of current liabilities.

The quick ratio excludes inventories from current assets to determine quick assets. Normally, inventories are the least liquid current asset and thus have the highest risk in the event of liquidation. Hence, it is important for the financial manager to measure the ability of the firm to meet its short-term obligations without relying on inventories.

Debt Analysis

Firms with high financial leverage or debt have heavy debt in relation to total assets. These firms are more vulnerable to business downturns than those with lower debt-to-total assets ratios. Debt ratios help to measure this vulnerability. More specifically, they measure the extent to which borrowed funds are used to finance the firm and the extent to which earnings can decline before the firm is unable to meet its fixed charges. The higher the financial leverage, the higher the risk and likewise the higher is the expected earnings per share (EPS) and rate of return. Many financial analysts agree that leverage ratios are as important as liquidity ratios for indicating financial strength and sound management. No generally accepted percentage relationships exist as guides for leverage ratios, but the larger the stockholders' equity, the stronger the financial condition of the firm.

Total Debt to Total Assets (DR)

Generally known as the debt ratio, the ratio of total debt to total assets measures the percentage of total funds provided by creditors. Debt includes current liabilities and all bonds. The debt ratio of the Lewis Clothing Company is

$$\text{Debt ratio} = \frac{\text{total debt}}{\text{total assets}} = \frac{\text{(current debt + long-term debt)}}{\text{total assets}} = \frac{\$140 + \$110}{\$500} = .50 \text{ or } 50\%$$

Half of Lewis's assets were paid for with borrowed money and the other half were financed with the owner's money. Creditors and stockholders have an equal claim of 50 cents for each asset dollar.

The debt ratio expresses the degree of protection provided by the owners for the creditors. The higher the ratio, the greater the risk being assumed by the creditors. A lower ratio generally indicates greater long-term financial safety. A firm with a low debt ratio has greater flexibility to borrow in the future. A highly leveraged company has a more limited debt capacity.

Creditors prefer moderate debt ratios, because the lower debt ratios mean the greater safety of their claims. In contrast, the owners may seek high leverage to magnify earnings. The use of leverage magnifies the impact on the owners' rate of return on investment in both favorable and unfavorable ways. Favorable leverage occurs when the firm's rate of return on assets is greater than the cost of its debt, which magnifies the owners' rate of return. Table 3-5 illustrates this magnification effect. Unfavorable leverage occurs when the firm's rate of return on assets is smaller than the cost of its debt, which reduces the owners' rate of return. While many firms tend to use a higher leverage in order to magnify earnings for their stockholders, greater leverage also tends to increase the cost of debt. Thus, it is desirable to strike a proper balance between debt and equity.

Times Interest Earned (TIER)

This ratio is net operating income divided by interest charges. The net operating income consists of earnings before interest and taxes (EBIT). The reason for using income before taxes is simple. The ability of the firm to pay its interest is not affected by taxes, because interest payment is a tax-deductible expense. For the Lewis Clothing Company, the ratio is as follows:

$$\text{Times interest earned} = \frac{\text{earnings before interest and taxes}}{\text{interest}} = \frac{\$150}{\$50} = 3 \text{ times}$$

Thus, the company earns before taxes three times as much as its interest charges.

This ratio is a measure of a firm's ability to meet its interest payments. A high ratio indicates that the firm would have little difficulty in meeting the interest obligations of a loan. A low ratio would indicate that the firm may face some difficulty if it wants to borrow additional funds.

Activity Analysis

Activity ratios (or asset utilization ratios) are useful in judging how effectively the firm utilizes its assets. These ratios involve comparisons between the level of sales and the investment in various asset items. Hence, they are based on data from both the balance sheet and the income statement.

Inventory Turnover (IT)

The inventory turnover equals the cost of goods sold divided by inventory. For the Lewis Clothing Company,

$$\text{Inventory turnover} = \frac{\text{cost of goods sold}}{\text{inventory}} = \frac{\$700}{\$150} = 4.7 \text{ times}$$

An inventory turnover of 4.7 indicates that Lewis sold and replaced its inventory about 5 times over the past year or every 78 days (365 days in a year/4.7). On average, it took Lewis 78 days to convert inventory into sales. This 78 day period is often referred to as the **inventory conversion period**. The inventory turnover measures the number of times inventory is turned over during the year. High inventory turnover can indicate better liquidity or superior merchandising. Conversely, it can indicate a shortage of needed inventory for sales or frequent stock outs. Low inventory turnover can indicate poor liquidity, possible overstocking, or obsolescence; in contrast to these negative interpretations, it can indicate a planned inventory buildup in anticipation of material shortages. A problem with this ratio is that it compares one day's inventory to the cost of goods sold and does not take seasonal fluctuations into account.

Average Collection Period (ACP)

Because the accounts-receivable turnover and the average collection period are inverses of each other, either of these two ratios can be used to measure the activity of a firm's accounts receivable. Annual credit sales are divided by receivables to obtain the receivable turnover. Thus, average collection period can be calculated as 365 days divided by the receivable turnover. The receivable turnover of the Lewis Clothing Company is as follows:

$$\text{Receivable turnover} = \frac{\text{annual credit sales}}{\text{receivables}} = \frac{\$1{,}000}{\$60} = 16.7 \text{ times}$$

And the corresponding average collection period is:

$$\text{Average collection period} = \frac{365 \text{ days}}{\text{receivable turnover}} = \frac{365}{16.7} = 22 \text{ days to collect.}$$

Or, alternatively, average collection perod can be calculated as:

$$\text{Average collection period} = \frac{\text{receivables}}{\text{credit sales per day}} = \frac{\$60}{\$1000/365} = 22 \text{ days}$$

A receivable turnover of 16.7 means that the company's accounts receivable turned over almost 17 times for the year. An average collection period of 22 days means that, on the average, the firm has waited for 22 days to collect its accounts receivable. Stated differently, on average it takes Lewis 22 days to convert a receivable into cash. The turnover of a firm's accounts receivable is a measure of its liquidity or activity. The higher the turnover of receivables, the shorter the time between sale and cash collection. If the firm's receivables appear to be turning slower than the rest of the industry, further research is needed and the quality of the receivables should be examined closely. A problem with this ratio exists when only one observation or the year-end balance of accounts receivables is used to estimate accounts receivable turnover and the average collection period. Using only one observation would not allow the ratio to capture the effects of seasonal fluctuations in sales. To correct this problem, simply use a monthly average of accounts receivables in the calculation so as to control for the variability in sales and receivables. An additional problem in interpretation may arise when there is a large proportion of cash sales since such data might not be readily available since the financial statement does not segregate sales into cash and credit portions.

The average collection period expresses the average time in days that receivables are outstanding. Generally, the greater number of days outstanding, the greater the probability of delinquencies in accounts receivable. The terms (i.e. 2/10/n30) offered by a company to its customers may differ from terms within the industry and should be taken into consideration.

Average Payment Period (APP)

The reciprocal of the average collection period is the average payment period. An accounts receivable on Lewis Company's books exists as an accounts payable on the other party's books. Therefore, while the average collection period indicates how long it takes Lewis's customers to pay on account, the average payment period determines how long it takes Lewis to pay off its outstanding accounts. Accounts receivables result from credit sales while accounts payables result from credit purchases. If credit purchases were $800,000, the average payment period for Lewis Clothing Company is:

$$\text{Average payment period} = \frac{\text{accounts payable}}{\text{credit purchases/day}} = \frac{\$40}{\$800/365} = 18.25 \text{ days}$$

On average it takes Lewis 18.25 days to pay off creditors. Stated differently, 18.25 days lapse from time of purchase on credit until the account payable is paid off. This information is especially significant to lenders and suppliers since it provides a measure of the firm's timeliness in paying of its bills.

Asset Turnover (AT)

This ratio relates the firm's sales to its assets. Ideally, every dollar in assets ought to help generate sales. Thus, the asset turnover is sales divided by total assets. For the Lewis Clothing Company, the ratio is

$$\text{Asset turnover} = \frac{\text{sales}}{\text{total assets}} = \frac{\$1000}{\$500} = 2 \text{ times}$$

turnover on generated revenue.

An asset turnover of 2 times means that the firm sold $2 for every $1 of its total assets. The firm sold an amount equal to its total assets twice during the year. A high ratio is desirable since it implies that the firm employs as few assets as possible to create the highest sales possible. The asset turnover is a general measure of a firm's ability to generate sales in relation to total assets. It should be used only to compare firms within specific industry groups and in connection with other operating ratios to determine the effective employment of assets.

Profitability Analysis

Profitability ratios are designed to assist in the evaluation of management performance. There are various measures of profitability. Each of these ratios relates earnings to sales, assets, or equity. Creditors, owners and management pay close attention to various profitability ratios, because in order to stay in existence the firm must be profitable. Without profits, a firm could not attract outside capital. Creditors and owners would become concerned about the firm's future and attempt to withdraw their funds.

Gross Profit Margin on Sales (GM)

This ratio measures the firm's markup or the percentage amount by which price exceeds the cost of the product that was sold. The gross profit margin for Lewis Clothing Company is

$$\text{Gross profit margin} = \frac{(\text{sales} - \text{cost of goods sold})}{\text{sales}} = \frac{(\$1000 - \$700)}{\$1000} = .30 \text{ or } 30\%$$

Chapter 3: Financial Statement Analysis

For every dollar in sales, Lewis has 30 cents left after paying for the product that generated the sale. The higher the gross profit margin the better as it implies either the ability to sell at a higher price or buy merchandise at a lower cost.

Profit Margin on Sales (PM)

affected by expenses.

This ratio is net income after taxes divided by sales. The profit margin of the Lewis Clothing Company,

$$\text{Profit margin on sales} = \frac{\text{net income after taxes}}{\text{sales}} = \frac{\$50}{\$1000} = .05 \text{ or } 5\%$$

Lewis Company clears 5 cents after all costs, expenses, interest, and taxes for every dollar in sales. The profit margin on sales indicates management's ability to operate the business with sufficient success not only to recover both fixed and variable costs, but also to leave a margin of reasonable profit for the stockholders.

Return on Net Worth or Equity (ROE)

This ratio is net income after taxes divided by net worth or equity. For the Lewis Clothing Company,

$$\text{Return on equity} = \frac{\text{net income after taxes}}{\text{equity or net worth}} = \frac{\$50}{\$250} = .20 \text{ or } 20\%$$

every $1 invested by stockholders, earns 20%.
(regardless of where $ came from) ($1 provided by stockholders).

The return on equity measures the return available to stockholders. While it can serve as an indicator of management performance, the analyst is cautioned to use it in conjunction with other ratios. A high return, normally associated with effective management, could indicate an undercapitalized firm with a high debt ratio and a high level of risk. In contrast, a low return, usually an indicator of inefficient management performance, could reflect a highly capitalized, conservatively operated business with low financial leverage.

(ROE) stockholders should earn more than ROA. ROE > ROA.

Return on Assets (ROA)

Also known as return on investment (ROI), ROA is net income after taxes divided by total assets. The return on assets of the Lewis Clothing Company is as follows

$$\text{Return on assets} = \frac{\text{net income after taxes}}{\text{total assets}} = \frac{\$50}{\$500} = .10 \text{ or } 10\%$$

every $1 invested in business, earns 10% of income.

(regardless of where $1 came from.)

This ratio measures the overall effectiveness of management in employing the resources available to it. A heavily depreciated plant and a large amount of intangible assets or unusual income or expense items will cause distortions of this ratio.

Common Stock Ratios

Common stock ratios provide internal and external users with the ability to compare the firm to the industry on the basis of market performance by computing net income after taxes and dividends on a per share basis. These ratios provide important information in determining the value of the firm's stock and its growth potential.

Earnings Per Share

Earnings per share scales the earnings of the firm on a per share basis to allow investors to compare firms in the same industry. The earnings per share for Lewis Clothing Company is

$$\text{Earnings per share (EPS)} \quad \frac{\text{net income after taxes}}{\text{\#common shares outstanding}} \quad \frac{\$50,000}{10,000} = \$5$$

Thus, the Lewis Clothing Company earned net income after taxes of $5 for each of the 10,000 common shares outstanding.

Payout (PO) and Dividend Per Share (DPS)

The payout ratio indicates what percent of the earnings per share the firm paid to the stockholders in dividends. The Lewis Clothing Company earned $5 per share and paid 60 cents on the dollar in dividend. Stated differently, Lewis' dividend per share represents 60% of the firm's earnings per share of $5. The firm paid out 60% of the earnings available to common stockholders and retained 40%.

Using the PO ratio and the EPS, we can calculate the firm's dividend per share. For the Lewis Clothing Company, the PO of 60% times its EPS of $5 produces a dividend per share of $3 as shown below.

$$\text{Payout ratio (PO)} \quad \frac{\text{dividend per share}}{\text{earnings per share}} \quad \frac{\$3}{\$5} = .6 \text{ or } 60\%$$

$$\text{Dividend per share (DPS)} \quad \text{PO} \times \text{EPS} \quad .6 \times \$5 = \$3 \text{ per share}$$

Price to Earnings Ratio (PE)

The PE ratio published in the financial news compares the firm's current stock price to its most recent EPS. For the Lewis Clothing Company, the PE is 10 as shown below. The ratio indicates that the investor is paying $50 in market price for $5 in earnings, which reduces to $10 in market value for every $1 in EPS.

$$\text{Price to earnings (PE)} \quad \frac{\text{market price per share}}{\text{earnings per share}} \quad \frac{\$50}{\$5} = 10 \text{ to } 1$$

The PE is often used as a valuation tool. The PE is basically an earnings multiple. Stated differently, the Lewis Clothing Company's stock, currently at $50 per share, is selling in the open market at 10 times its most recent EPS of $5. So if we can project the firm's future earnings and assuming the average firm in the industry has a PE of around 5, then we can estimate what the firm's share value ought to be when compared to the industry. Suppose we project Lewis's EPS to be $6 next year, then applying the industry PE of 5 we find that Lewis's share value ought to be $30. Compared to the industry, the Lewis Clothing Company's stock ought to be worth only $30 per share (or 5 times its expected EPS of $6). *Standard and Poor's Industrial Ratios* publishes industry PE averages.

Likewise the PE can be used to identify potential earnings growth for a given firm. An unusually high PE for a firm sometimes suggests growth. For example, if the industry average PE is 5 while the Lewis Clothing Company's is 10, it appears that the market is paying more for a dollar of Lewis's past earnings than the industry in general. Remember, the PE ratio represents two perspectives; one, the most recent book EPS in the denominator which is a result of past performance and, two, in the numerator the firm's market price which is a present gauge of the firm's future performance. In essence, the market price is a prediction of future performance and cash flows while the EPS encompasses the results of past decisions and cash flows. A high PE when compared to the industry may suggest that the market view of the firm's future in the numerator relative to a dollar of past earnings far exceeds the industry average. Therefore, the unusually high PE compared to the industry may suggest that the market sees significant growth and a bright future for the Lewis Company.

DuPont System

The DuPont system is an important technique for examining the relationships among factors affecting the rate of return on equity. The system was developed by the DuPont Company in 1959. Since then, it has been widely recognized as an effective planning and control technique. The system is illustrated in Figure 3-1, using the Lewis Clothing Company as an example.

The important point of the figure is the return on investment (ROA):

$$ROA = \text{profit margin} \times \text{asset turnover}$$

$$= \frac{NIAT}{sales} \times \frac{sales}{total\ assets} = \frac{NIAT}{tot.\ assets}$$

$$= \frac{\$50}{\$1000} \times \frac{1000}{\$500} = 0.05 \times 2 = .10\ or\ 10\%$$

The ROA is a product of the profit margin and the asset turnover. The asset turnover and the profit margin for the Lewis Clothing Company are two times and 5 percent, respectively, thereby producing a 10 percent ROA.

Figure 3-1 illustrates the DuPont analysis which identifies the three sources of profitability that account for the return to the firm's owners or ROE. The upper branch focuses on profit margin as a key component in building profitability. The middle branch links to volume or turnover as a critical determinant of the firm's rate of return to its stockholders. The product of profit margin and asset turnover produces the return on assets. For example, a grocery retailer and an equipment sales firm may offer the same ROA but trace it back to extremely different margins and sales volumes because of competitive conditions in the industry and the nature of the product over the course of the business cycle. Generally, highly competitive, nondurable goods firms like the grocery retailer

Figure 3-1
DuPont Analysis

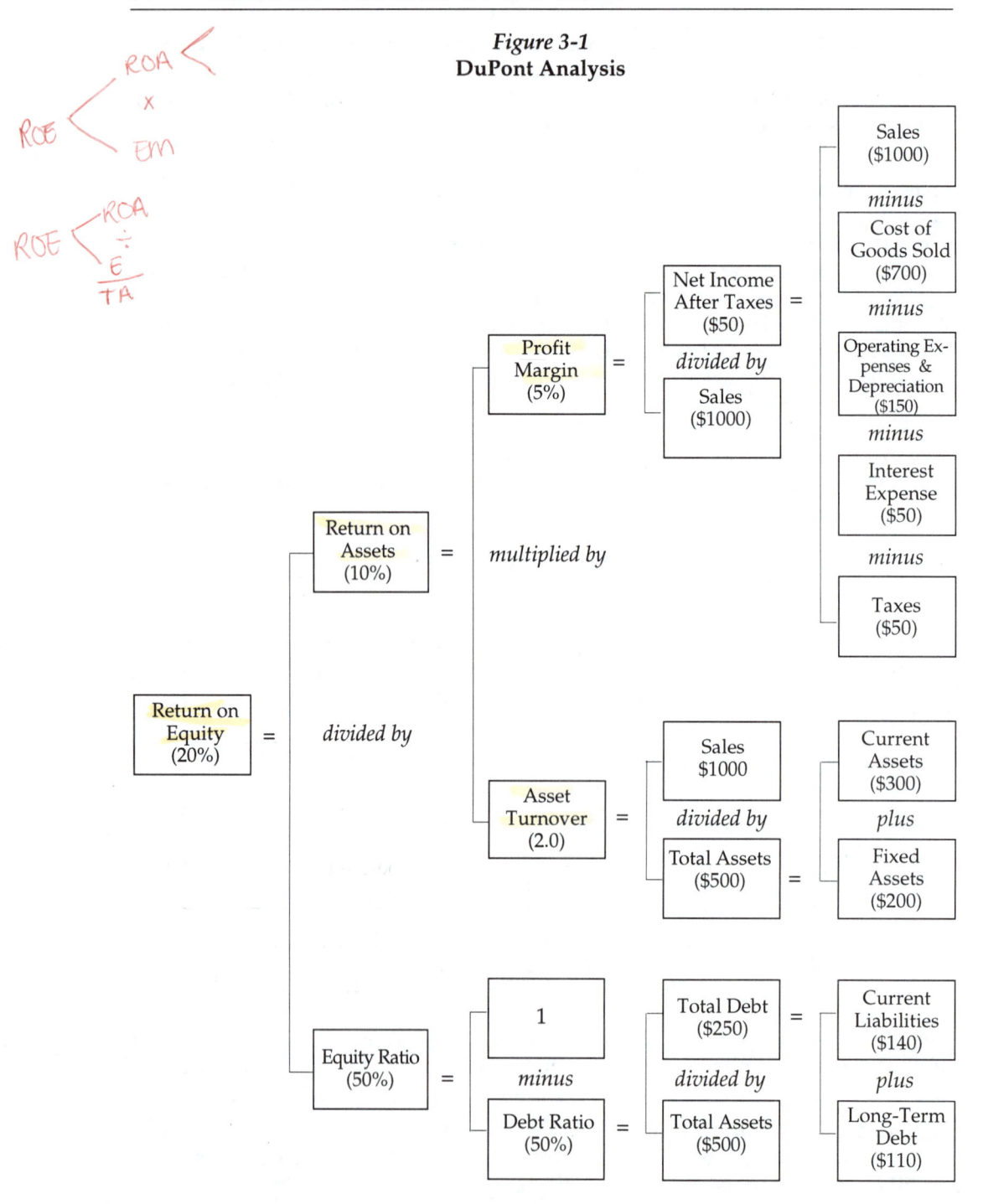

will produce ROA by selling in large volume (high asset turnover) but clear a very small profit per unit due to the extreme competition. On the other hand, the equipment sales firm faces much less price competition but experiences considerable fluctuation in sales and output over the course of the business cycle since such durable products are generally repaired and maintained during a recession and traded in for new ones on economic upturns. Therefore, the equipment firm builds its profitability by earning a relatively large margin on a very small turnover or volume. In essence, margin and turnover are pretty much dictated by the nature of the product, which explains the firm's level of business risk.

A third source of ROE is explained by the firm's financial leverage or level of debt relative to total assets. As shown in the bottom branch of Figure 3-1, under certain circumstances, a firm can increase ROE by increasing its level of debt to some threshold which lenders will tolerate without raising the firm's interest rate. Financial leverage, although influenced by the firm's level of business risk, is solely a function of management's discretion and generally moves inversely with the firm's level of business risk. Firms with high business risk usually control total risk (financial and business risks) by carrying less debt, and vice versa.

The DuPont system may be extended to measure the effect of financial leverage (the use of debt).

As shown in the bottom branch, return on equity is magnified by the use of debt. For example, assume that another company called Lewis #2 exists and is identical to Lewis Clothing Company in every way except that Lewis #2 has no debt. Imagine that both experienced identical operations over the past year and their balance sheets only differ due to the existence of debt for Lewis Clothing Company. Table 3-5 compares the two firms.

Table 3-5
Effects of Financial Leverage

Lewis Clothing Company (with 50% debt)		Lewis #2 (with no debt)	
Sales	$1000	Sales	$1000
Less: Operating costs	-850	Less: Operating costs	-850
EBIT	150	EBIT	150
Less: Interest on debt	-50	Less: Interest on debt	0
Net income before tax	$100	Net income before tax	$150
Less: Income tax (50%)	-50	Less: Income tax	-75
Net income after tax (NIAT)	$50	Net income after tax	$75
$\text{ROE} = \dfrac{\text{NIAT}}{\text{Equity}} = \dfrac{50}{250} = 20\%$		$\text{ROE} = \dfrac{75}{500} = 15\%$	
$\text{ROE} = \dfrac{37.50}{250} + \dfrac{37.50 - [50 \times (1-t)]}{250}$			
where t = tax rate			
$\text{ROE} = \dfrac{37.50}{250} + \dfrac{37.50 - 25}{250}$			
ROE = 15% + 5% = 20%			

In essence, the firm's owners earned $37.50 on their own capital ($250) and $12.50 (after tax) on the borrowed capital generating a return to the owners of 20%. The tax deductibility of the $50 of interest cut the owners' tax bill by $25.00 resulting in net cost of funds of

$25. This allowed the owners to lever the borrowed funds for a net advantage of $12.50 (or $37.50 − $25.00) for a clear 5% bonus, thus explaining the total return on capital of 20% (or 15% + 5%). In this case, the total advantage of financial leverage was due to tax savings since the 15% return on capital did not exceed the 20% before tax interest rate on debt. But the 15% return on capital does exceed the after tax interest rate on debt of 10% or [20%(1−tax rate)], thus explaining the advantage of debt financing. Had the interest rate been 10% (or 25/250), then the firm would have gained 25(1−.5)/250 or 5% from tax saving and 5% for pure leverage for a total of 25%. In essence you borrow at 10% and invest at 15% to clear the difference of 5%. In this case, the capital was invested at a return of 15% which is higher than the before-tax interest rate on debt of 10% so the benefit of financial leverage would have been expanded by two sources, leverage generating an additional 5% (15% return less 10% interest on debt) and tax savings generating another 5% (or the savings of 12.50/250).

Common-Size Statements

Another type of ratio analysis is the analysis of common-size statements. **Common-size statements** present individual statement figures as percentages of a base total. It is important for the financial manager to compare changes on the financial statements that take place from period to period with certain base totals within those periods. Hence, total assets, total sales, or some other established norm are each converted to a base of 100. Each item within each classification is then stated as a percent of the base. For example, the common-size balance sheet states each asset, liability, and owners' equity as a percent of total assets. By the same token, the common-size income statement expresses each entry as a percent of sales.

Tables 3-6 and 3-7 show the common-size statements of the Lewis Clothing Company. By providing a common basis for analysis, common-size statements allow comparisons within the company over time, with other companies in the same industry, or with other companies of similar asset size. To illustrate, let us compare operating expenses of the Lewis Clothing Company with those of other companies in the clothing industry. Operating expenses of the Lewis Clothing Company are 7.5 percent of sales. If similar companies in the clothing industry had operating expenses of 4.8 percent of sales, it would be clear that the Lewis Clothing Company is out of line with the industry and may have to take immediate steps to bring its operating expenses in line.

The common-size statements, supplemented by additional analytical financial data, can be a very powerful tool for financial analysis in evaluating a particular company's performance in comparison with the industry. If meaningful comparisons are to be made between companies in the same industry or between companies of similar asset size, the data in the comparison must be based on reasonably uniform and consistent account methods.

COMPARATIVE RATIO ANALYSIS

The ratios discussed in this chapter are those developed for a particular company at a given point in time. Thus, they may have little meaning unless they are compared with some standards. For instance, the current ratio of the Lewis Clothing Company is 2.14; it shows the relationship between current assets and current liabilities as of December 31, 2000. We cannot say for sure whether it is too high or too low unless the ratio is related to the industry average or some other criterion. There are two basic sources of criteria to be used: historical standards and industry standards.

Table 3-6
Lewis Clothing Company Common-Size Balance Sheet
December 31, 2000 (thousands of dollars)

Cash	$ 40	8%
Marketable securities	30	6
Accounts receivable	60	12
Prepaid expenses	20	4
Inventories	150	30
Total current assets	$300	60%
Gross plant & equipment	$245	49%
Accumulated depreciation	45	9
Net plant & equipment	$200	40%
Total assets *use as base*	$500	100%
Accounts payable	$ 40	8%
Notes payable	30	6
Accrued taxes	10	2
Other accruals	60	12
Total current liabilities	$140	28%
Long-term debt	$110	22%
Common stock	100	20
Paid-in capital	50	10
Retained earnings	100	20
Total debt & equity *use as base*	$500	100%

*compare w/ other co. in industry.
compare over years in co.*

Table 3-7
Lewis Clothing Company Common-Size Income Statement
December 31, 2000 (thousands of dollars)

Net sales			$1,000	100.0%
Less:	Cost of goods sold		- 700	- 70.0
Gross profit			$ 300	30.0%
Less:	operating expenses			
	selling expenses	$30		
	general and administrative expenses	35		
	lease payments	10	- 75	- 7.5
	Gross operating income		$ 225	22.5%
Less: depreciation			- 75	- 7.5
EBIT		$ 150	15.0%	
Less: interest			- 50	- 5.0
Net income before taxes			$ 100	10.0%
Less: taxes			50	5.0
Net income after taxes			$ 50	5.0%

Table 3-8
Lewis Clothing Company Compared to the Industry

Ratios	Definition	Calculation For Lewis Clothing Company	Industry Average*	
Liquidity				
Current ratio	Current Assets / Current Liabilities	$300 / $140 = 2.14	2.3	Worse
Quick or Acid Test	CA − Inventory / Current Liabilities	$300−150 / $140 = 1.07	1.0	Better
Leverage				
Debt ratio	Total debt / Total assets	$250 / $500 = .5	.49	Higher
Times Interest Earned	EBIT / Interest charges	$150 / $50 = 3	5.2	Worse
Activity				
Inventory Turnover	Cost of goods sold / Inventory	$700 / $150 = 4.7	3.5	Higher
Receivable Turnover	Annual credit sales / Receivables	$1000 / $60 = 16.7	7.6	Higher
Average Collection Period	Receivables / (Credit sales/365) or 365 days / Receivables turnover	$60 / (100/365) = 22	48	Lower
Asset Turnover	Sales / Total assets	$1000 / $500 = 2	.9	Higher
Profitability				
Profit Margin	Net income after taxes / Sales	$50 / $1000 = .05	.077	Lower
Return on Equity or Net Worth	Net income after taxes / Net worth	$50 / $250 = .2	.142	Higher
Return on Assets or Investment	Net income after taxes / Total assets	$50 / $500 = .1	.13	Lower

Source: *Almanac of Business and Industrial Financial Ratios*, 30th Annual Edition, 1999, Leo Troy, Ph.D., Prentice Hall.

Historical Standards

To analyze the financial condition and performance of the company, the financial manager should compare its recent ratios with its past ratios. A ratio may fluctuate considerably over time, so that sole reliance on a single ratio may at times give a misleading indication of financial condition. When ratios are calculated over a number of years and compared with one another, we may determine whether the firm's financial condition is improving or worsening.

Industry Standards

The second standard that the financial manager can use to examine the company's financial condition is industry average ratios. It is important to remember that companies in the same industry should be used for comparisons. The increasing diversification of company operations and the accelerated tempo of changes in specifications and technologies have made it extremely difficult to identify a particular company with a given industry. But proper classification by industry is a necessity for meaningful ratio analysis, because the characteristics of financial ratios vary from industry to industry. Industry averages can be obtained for many ratios and most industries from credit reporting firms such as Robert Morris Associates and Dun and Bradstreet.

Table 3-8 illustrates how Lewis Clothing Company compares with standard industry ratios. For example, Lewis's liquidity when compared to the average firm in the industry, reveals mixed results with a worse current ratio along with a higher quick ratio of 1.07. Similar comparisons for leverage, activity and profitability can also be made.

LIMITATIONS OF RATIO ANALYSIS

Because of certain limitations great care must be taken when ratios are interpreted. In this section, we discuss some of the limitations of ratio analysis.

Distortion of Comparative Data

Inflation distorts the firm's balance sheets. Moreover, profits are also affected by inflation because past inflation affects both depreciation charges and the cost of goods sold. Hence, ratio analysis for one company over time, a comparative analysis of companies of different ages, or a comparative analysis of companies using different accounting methods should be interpreted with great caution. This is why we discussed inflation's effects on ratio analysis in detail early in this chapter.

Varied Product Lines

Many large companies operate a number of different divisions in quite different industries. However, most credit reporting firms categorize companies by their primary product Standard Industrial Classification (SIC) number only. Furthermore, many U.S. companies have recently become more internationalized, more diversified, and adopted modern technologies. All these have made it very difficult to identify a particular firm with a given industry of about the same size.

Differences in Accounting Methods

Companies within the same industry may differ in their method of operations and accounting practices which in turn can directly influence their financial statements. Because credit reporting firms include them in their sample, these statements can significantly affect their composite calculations.

Window Dressing

Companies often use "window dressing" techniques to make their financial statements look better to financial analysts. In other words, financial statements can be greatly affected by accounting window dressing, which can conceal the true value of ratios.

Other Limitations

There are many other considerations that can result in variations among different companies engaged in the same general line of business. They include different labor markets, geographical location, quality of products handled, sources and methods of financing, terms of sale, notes to financial statements, and industry sizes.

SUMMARY

Ratio analysis relates balance sheet and income statement items to one another. It permits the financial manager to chart the firm's history and to evaluate its present position. It also allows the financial manager to anticipate reactions of creditors and stockholders.

Ratios are classified into four categories: liquidity, leverage, activity, and profitability. In addition to these four types of ratios, it is often useful to express balance sheet and income statement items as percentages. The evaluation of trends in common-size statements over time affords the financial analyst insight into the underlying movements of funds.

The DuPont system shows how the return on investment depends on the profit margin and the asset turnover. The profit margin multiplied by the asset turnover equals the rate of return on investment. The intelligent use of the system provides management with an opportunity to effect needed changes in the profit margin and the asset turnover, thereby improving the return on investment.

A ratio becomes a meaningful number when it is compared with some standards. The two basic types of comparative analysis are trend analysis and comparisons of a firm's ratios with the firm's industry average ratios. The financial manager can compare the firm's recent ratios with its past ratios to see if it is improving or deteriorating. The financial condition of a firm can be evaluated by comparing its ratios at a certain point in time with the ratios of companies in the same industry. The two types of comparative analysis are useful, but analysts should use them with caution and judgement because they have a variety of limitations.

List of Key Terms

- balance sheet
- current assets
- equity or net worth
- LIFO method
- leverage ratios
- profitability ratios
- DuPont chart system

- income statement
- current liabilities
- FIFO method
- liquidity ratios
- activity ratios
- common-size statements

Problems

3-1 Nancy Corporation's financial statements for 2000 are given below:

Cash	$60	Accounts payable	$20
Marketable securities	40	Notes payable	60
Accounts receivable	20	Accrued taxes	80
Inventories	80	Accrued wages	40
Total current assets	$200		
		Total current liabilities	$200
Gross plant & equipment	$345	Long-term debt	$100
Accumulated depreciation	45	Common stock	100
Net plant & equipment	$300	Retained earnings	100
Total assets	$500	Total claims on assets	$500

Net sales		$1,000
Less: Cost of goods sold		600
Gross profit		$400
Less: operating expenses		
selling expenses		$100
general and administrative expenses		50
lease payments		50
Gross operating income		$200
Less: depreciation		50
Net operating income		$150
Less: interest		50
Net income before taxes		$100
Less: taxes		50
Net income after taxes		$50

Compute the following ratios: current ratio, quick ratio, debt ratio, times interest earned, inventory turnover, receivable turnover, average collection period, asset turnover, profit margin on sales, return on equity, and return on assets.

PART 2: FINANCIAL PLANNING AND CONTROL

3-2 Boot Corporation has current assets of $20,000 and current liabilities of $10,000. If we assume that each transaction is independent, what is the effect of each of the following transactions on Boot Corporation's current ratio?

(a) $2,000 of accounts payable are paid off with cash.
(b) Inventories of $5,000 are purchased on credit.
(c) Additional common stock is sold for $4,000 cash.
(d) A long-term debt of $2,000 is obtained, and the proceeds are used to buy a new machine.
(e) Accounts receivable of $1,000 are collected in cash.

3-3 Given the following financial data, complete the balance sheet below:

Total debt to net worth			1.5 to 1	
Quick ratio			1 to 1	
Asset turnover			2 times	
Average collection period			18.25 days	
Sales/inventory			10 times	
Cash	_____	Notes payable	_____	
Receivables	_____	Long-term debt	$20,000	
Inventories	_____	Common stock	15,000	
Net plant	_____	Retained earnings	25,000	
Total assets	_____	Total debt & equity	_____	

3-4 The sales, total assets, and net income for five companies of about the same size in the same industry are given in the following table.

(a) Determine the asset turnover, profit margin on sales, and return on assets for each of these five companies.
(b) Examine the ratios of those companies that seem to be out of line in relation to the five company norms.

Item\Firm	A	B	C	D	E
Sales ($000)	600	610	700	850	600
Assets ($000)	200	400	300	500	280
Net income ($000)	60	74	55	67	80

3-5 Given the following financial data, construct the income statement of the Alco Toy Company:

Times interest earned	5 times
Tax rate	40%
Cost of goods sold to sales	80%
Sales	$100,000
Interest expense to sales	2%

3-6 Below are the balance sheets and income statements of the Sunshine Company for 2000 and 2001.

(a) Express each balance sheet item as a percent of total assets and each income statement item as a percent of net sales (common-size statements).

(b) Using the common-size statements produced in part a), evaluate the financial condition and the operating results of the company, indicating favorable and unfavorable trends.

SUNSHINE COMPANY
Balance Sheet
December 31

	2000	2001
Cash	$ 8,000	$ 16,000
Accounts receivable	13,000	17,000
Inventories	18,000	22,500
Total current assets	$ 39,000	$ 55,500
Net plant and equipment	75,500	73,000
Total assets	$114,500	$128,500
Accounts payable	$ 13,000	$ 17,000
Notes payable	10,000	9,500
Accrued payables	4,000	5,500
Total current liabilities	$ 27,000	$ 32,000
Long-term debt	30,000	27,500
Total liabilities	$ 57,000	$ 59,500
Common stock	50,000	54,500
Retained earnings	7,500	14,500
Total stockholders' equity	$ 57,500	$ 69,000
Total claims on assets	$114,500	$128,500

SUNSHINE COMPANY
Income Statement
December 31

	2000	2001
Net sales	$ 75,500	$ 98,500
Cost of goods sold	46,000	61,500
Gross profit	$ 29,500	$ 37,000
Operating expenses	14,000	13,900
Depreciation expense	2,500	2,500
Interest expense	1,500	1,375
Total expenses	$ 18,000	$ 17,775
Net income before taxes	$ 11,500	$ 19,225
Income taxes at 30%	3,450	5,768
Net income after taxes	$ 8,050	$ 13,457

3-7 Using the financial data in Problem 3-6, (a) calculate the following ratios of the Sunshine Company for 2001 and (b) compare Sunshine Company ratios with the industry averages. Indicate whether Sunshine compares favorably or unfavorably when compared to the industry.

Ratio	Sunshine	Industry	Comparison
Current ratio		2.0 times	
Quick ratio		1.0 times	
Debt to total assets		45.5%	
Times interest earned		17.0 times	
Inventory turnover		3.5 times	
Average collection period		63 days	
Asset turnover		1.5 times	
Profit margin on sales		18.0%	
Return on total assets		27.0%	

4

Leverage and Risk Analysis

The ratios described in the preceding chapter are tools that enable creditors and investors to evaluate the attractiveness of a company's stock as a potential investment or to determine whether the financial position of a firm is good enough to protect creditors or to borrow new funds. Two other tools available to help the financial manager in financial planning and control are leverage analysis and budgets. The term **leverage** means the use of special force and effects to produce more than normal results from a given course of action. For example, by himself a man can lift only so much weight but with an appropriately applied lever he can multiply his strength to move extremely heavy objects. In finance, this concept is applied with the emphasis on the use of "fixed cost" items in anticipation of magnifying returns at high levels of operations. But leverage is a two-edged sword—producing highly favorable returns when things go well and highly unfavorable results when things go wrong.

This chapter examines both operating leverage and financial leverage. **Operating leverage** is the ratio of fixed assets to total assets. **Financial leverage** is the ratio of total debt to total assets. Thus, in this chapter we consider the proper mix of current assets and fixed assets as well as the proper mix of debt and owners' equity. In the next chapter, budgets, which express the plans, goals, and programs of a business in monetary terms, are examined.

Break-Even Analysis and Leverage

Basically, **break-even analysis** is a mathematical device used to estimate how many units of a product should be produced to cover total operating costs. Total operating costs consist of variable costs and fixed costs. **Variable costs** are those that have a direct relationship with sales volume: they include direct labor, raw materials, and sales commissions. These costs vary directly with sales. For example, when a shoe manufacturer produces an additional pair of shoes, more leather is needed so the cost of the leather increases with each additional pair made. **Fixed costs**, on the other hand, remain constant as sales volume changes (i.e. depreciation, utilities, and supervisory salaries). Since the supervisor's salary is fixed in the short run, it doesn't matter whether his factory produces 1,000 pairs of shoes per month or 5,000 per month, the salary cost remains the same.

The formula for determining the break-even point of the product is

$$Q = \frac{F}{P - V} \qquad (4\text{-}1)$$

PART 2: FINANCIAL PLANNING AND CONTROL

where Q = break-even point in units, F = fixed costs, P = price per unit, and V = variable cost per unit.

Another way of explaining the concept of break-even analysis is to use a break-even chart, as illustrated in Figure 4-1. Revenues and costs are measured on the vertical axis and sales are measured on the horizontal axis. Fixed costs of $400 are represented by a horizontal line, because they are assumed to remain unchanged as sales change. As shown in Figure 4-1, the company's revenue increases by $5 per unit sold (or the selling price per unit), whereas its total cost increases by $3 per unit sold (the amount of the variable cost per unit). Hence, the slope of the revenue line in the chart is steeper than that of the total cost line, so that these two lines intersect at a point called the break-even point. Up to the break-even point of 200 units the company incurs losses, but it begins to realize profits after that point. In essence, the higher the fixed costs, the greater the risk, since the firm must count on selling more units just to break even. Look at fixed costs sort of as the barrier that the firm must overcome before reaching the profit zone. But after break-even, the firm with high fixed cost will enjoy greater magnification of operating profits, the reward for taking more risk.

Example 4-1. Company A sells its products for $5 per unit and has annual fixed costs of $400. This company's variable costs are $3 per unit regardless of the volume sold.

The break-even point is

$$Q = \frac{\$400}{\$5 - \$3} = 200 \text{ units}$$

Thus, the company must sell 200 units to make its total revenues equal its total costs. If sales are greater than 200 units, the company will make a profit. If sales are less than this amount, it will incur a loss.

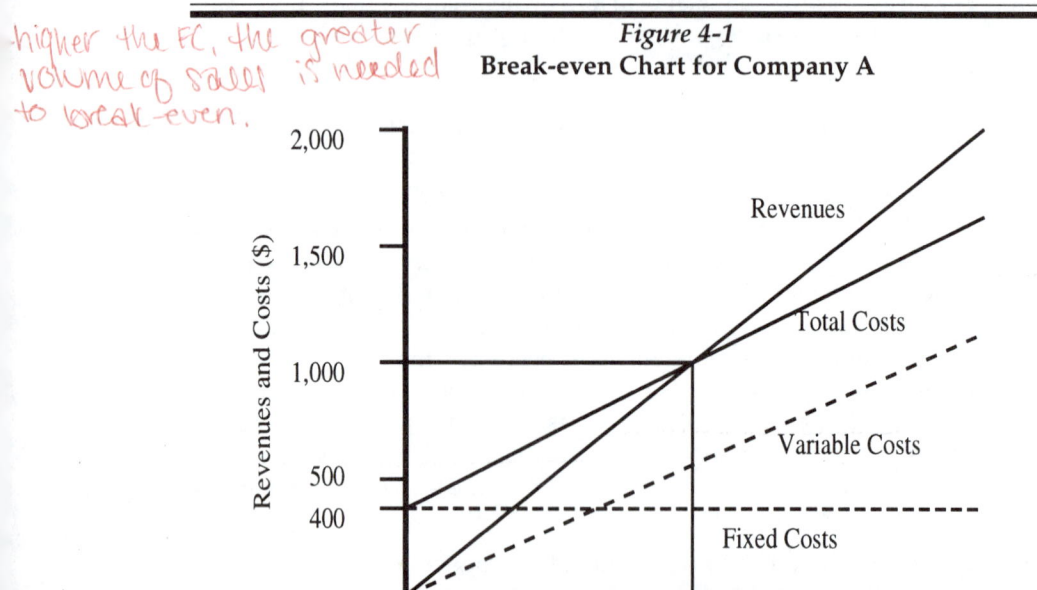

---

higher the FC, the greater volume of sales is needed to break-even.

Figure 4-1
Break-even Chart for Company A

Although break-even analysis is useful in describing the relationship between costs and revenues, it has a number of limitations. An obvious weakness is the rather convenient assumption that costs can be separated into two groups, fixed costs and variable costs. In practice, many costs are semivariable costs, because they are partly fixed and partly variable. Another weakness is that the break-even chart and the break-even point are valid only if the stated costs and prices remain constant. If any one or more of these change, the entire computation process must be repeated. The third limitation applies to companies that sell a wide variety of products. When the proportion of these products changes, a separate break-even chart is necessary for each product and expenses common to all products must be allocated to each product. Finally, break-even analysis is basically a short-term tool. Thus, it cannot be used as a major technique for an economic evaluation of long-term investment projects.

Leverage or risk surfaces in two forms, operating and financial. Operating leverage is traced to the relative asset mix, that is the degree of current relative to fixed assets. Given a certain level of total assets, the firm determines its level of operating risk or leverage by how it allocates total assets between the current and fixed categories. Firms confident that "good times" or high sales will occur in the future might assume a high degree of operating leverage by employing high levels of fixed assets and thereby low amounts of current assets. For example, suppose management is faced with the decision to either buy or lease a new building needed to operate the firm. The decision to buy would increase the proportion of fixed assets relative to total assets and elevate operating risk. Buying the building commits the firm to paying for the building out of expected future sales and cash flow. Obviously, the rational decision to buy transfers the risk of ownership to the firm and the transaction should result in acquiring necessary space at a cheaper cost per square foot than if the same area were leased. Thus, with the long-term commitment comes lower total operating costs allowing for greater magnification of operating profits or EBIT. The choice of higher fixed assets creates higher fixed costs (high operating risk) which cause lower total costs, and higher profits (high return). Likewise, if the firm's future sales turn negative, the effects of this decision path would reverse causing magnification of losses. The choice to lease by the month rather than buy the building follows the low risk route since risk of ownership now remains with the landlord. Clearly, since the landlord now faces the risk of ownership, he will charge a lease rate per square foot high enough to compensate him for the risk. Now, opposite of the buy-decision, the firm will face higher total operating costs and lower EBIT, but to acquire the lower risk the firm had to sacrifice some return. The firm is not committing the firm's future sales to paying for the building. In this case, if sales don't occur in the future, the firm can simply cancel the lease and eliminate its losses. In sum, compared to the buy-decision the decision to lease decreases the proportion of fixed assets to total assets, reduces operating leverage, increases total operating costs, and reduces operating profitability.

Using the same rationale, but switching now to the right-hand side of the balance sheet, the degree of financial leverage traces to the level of fixed cost financing (either debt or preferred stock) versus common equity chosen to buy the firm's assets. Remember, the left-hand side of the balance sheet reveals "what you bought" while the right-hand side tells "how you paid for it." The "how to pay for it" decision has to be one of two choices. Either you pay with your own money (or common equity financing) or you get fixed cost funds by borrowing or selling preferred stock. But with greater debt comes greater fixed cost of financing known as interest. So if the firm opts for a high degree of debt, like the rationale with fixed assets, it is committing the firm's expected future sales and cash flow to the required payment of interest which would not be the case with equity financing since there is no legal requirement to pay

64   PART 2: FINANCIAL PLANNING AND CONTROL

dividends to the firm's stockholders. The company which desires to sell common stock (equity financing) rather than borrow assumes less financial risk since it is not legally binding the firm to future interest costs but rather will only pay for the use of the stockholders' money in the form of dividends if sales and profits occur. But there is no "free lunch." By opting for higher common equity, the firm sacrifices the benefits of financial leverage (see Table 3-5 in chapter 3). In sum, higher debt equates higher financial leverage, greater financial risk, and greater potential return.

Table 4-1 identifies the sources of operating, financial, and total leverage.

Table 4-1
Sources of Operating, Financial and Combined Leverage

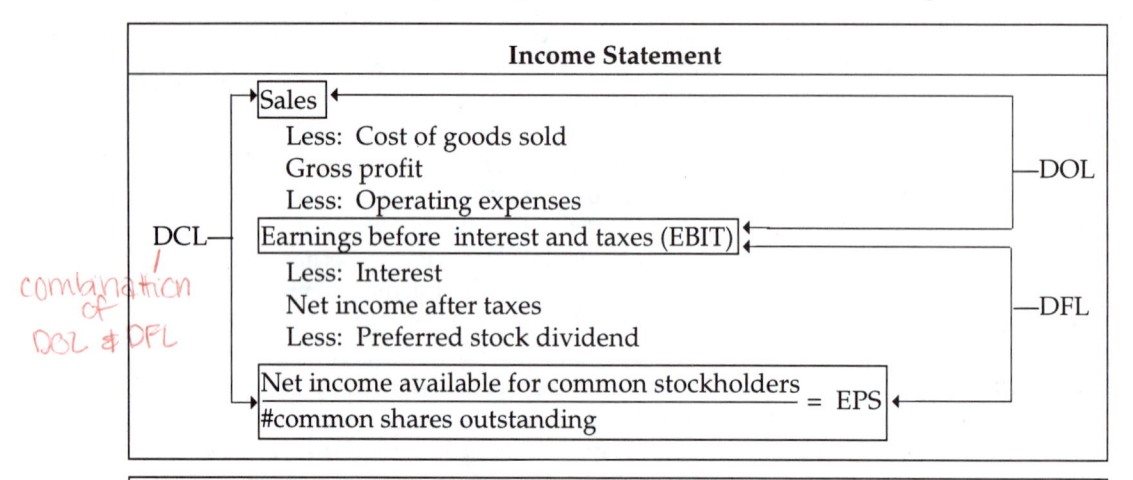

Income Statement

DCL —
- Sales
  - Less: Cost of goods sold
  - Gross profit
  - Less: Operating expenses — DOL
- Earnings before interest and taxes (EBIT)
  - Less: Interest
  - Net income after taxes
  - Less: Preferred stock dividend — DFL
- Net income available for common stockholders / #common shares outstanding = EPS

Balance Sheet

DOL	Asset Mix	Current Assets	Debt	Financing Mix	DFL
		Fixed Assets	Preferred		
			Common Equity		
	Total Assets		Total Debt + Preferred + Common		

OPERATING LEVERAGE

As shown earlier, operating leverage is a concept which enables the financial manager to use break-even data to determine the sensitivity of operating profits to changes in sales volume. **Operating leverage refers to the extent to which fixed assets are used in operations.** That is, a company with a high operating leverage uses more fixed assets than companies with a low operating leverage. A highly capital-intensive company tends to have a higher break-even point than less capital-intensive companies. But once it reaches its break-even point, its operating profits increase faster than do those of less capital-intensive companies. This is because the capital-intensive company uses very little labor per unit produced.

As shown in Table 4-1, operating leverage explains the sensitivity of EBIT to change in sales volume. The **degree of operating leverage** is therefore defined as the percentage change in earnings before interest and taxes (EBIT) that results from a given percent change in units sold, or:

$$DOL = \frac{\% \text{ CHANGE IN EBIT}}{\% \text{ CHANGE IN SALES (UNITS)}}$$

A simple formula for calculating the degree of operating leverage may be derived from this definition:

$$DOL = \frac{Q(P-V)}{Q(P-V)-F} \text{ or } \frac{\text{Sales} - \text{Variable Costs}}{\text{Sales} - \text{Variable Cost} - \text{Fixed Cost}} \quad (4\text{-}2)$$

where DOL is the degree of operating leverage at a sales volume Q. Using Equation (4-2), Company A's degree of operating leverage at 300 units of output is

$$DOL = \frac{300(\$5-\$3)}{300(\$5-\$3)-\$400} = 3$$

A degree of operating leverage of 3 indicates that a 1 percent increase in sales volume will result in a 3 percent increase in EBIT. Likewise, a 1 percent decline in sales volume will magnify into a 3 percent drop in EBIT.

To illustrate how different operating leverages affect EBIT, consider Company B, which produces the same product as Company A. The company sells its product for $5 per unit, has annual fixed costs of $750, and has variable costs of $2 a unit. Company B's break-even point is

$$Q = \frac{\$750}{\$5-\$2} = 250 \text{ units}$$

and its DOL at 300 units of output is

$$DOL = \frac{300(\$5-\$2)}{300(\$5-\$2)-\$750} = 6$$

Although Companies A and B produce the same product and sell it at the same price, both the break-even point and the DOL are greater for Company B. This means that the higher the operating leverage, the greater are the break-even point and the effect on EBIT from a given change in sales volume. Company B uses more expensive machinery requiring less labor per unit produced. With the higher fixed costs and operating leverage, Company B would experience a 6 percent change in EBIT for every 1 percent change in volume, whereas Company A would have only a 3 percent change in EBIT for every

1 percent change in volume. Therefore, operating leverage tends to magnify operating profits or losses, depending on whether sales increase or decrease.

The most interesting aspect of break-even analysis is that, the further the volume is from the break-even point, the less the DOL. That is, a series of 1 percent increases in output above the break-even point would produce smaller jumps in EBIT growth. To see this, compute the DOL for Company B when it sells 350 units of its output:

$$DOL = \frac{350(\$5 - \$2)}{350(\$5 - \$2) - \$750} = 3.5$$

For Company B, the 3.5 DOL at 350 units of output is much smaller than the 6 DOL at 300 units of output.

FINANCIAL LEVERAGE

Financial leverage is defined as the extent to which funds with a fixed cost are used in company operations. The use of funds obtained at a fixed cost is intended to increase the return to common stockholders. However, financial leverage works in both favorable and unfavorable ways. Favorable leverage occurs when the firm earns more on these funds than the associated fixed cost. Unfavorable leverage occurs when the firm earns less on these invested funds than the related fixed cost.

Whereas operating leverage determines the mix of current assets and fixed assets, financial leverage influences how these assets are financed. Hence, the source of operating leverage relates to the asset mix found on the left-hand side of the balance sheet, while financial leverage stems from the financing mix on the right-hand side.

Impact of Financial Leverage on Earnings Per Share

Perhaps the best way to understand the proper use of financial leverage is to analyze its effect on earnings per share (EPS):

Example 4-2. Suppose that a firm has $100-par value common stock outstanding in the amount of $10,000 and needs an additional $5,000 to buy a new plant. The firm is considering three alternatives to raise the money: (1) issue 50 new shares of common stock at $100 par value to raise $5000, (2) issue 50 new shares of preferred stock at $100 par with a fixed 6 percent preferred stock dividend, or (3) issue bonds (debt) at a 5 percent interest rate. We assume an EBIT of $2,000 and a federal income tax rate of 50 percent for the firm for each alternative. Table 4-2 shows EPS under these three financing plans.

Table 4-2 and Figure 4-2 show that at an EBIT above $750, as in the case with EBIT at $2,000, EPS under the debt alternative is superior to either the preferred stock alternative or the common stock alternative. But if EBIT declines below $750, the indifference point, the common stock alternative is more attractive than the debt alternative. If the choice is between the debt and the preferred stock alternatives, then the debt

Chapter 4: Leverage and Risk Analysis   67

decision is the clear winner at any EBIT level above $250. Thus, to choose the best alternative for the stockholders, it is important to determine the level of EBIT at which we will be indifferent between the two alternative sources of funds.

Table 4-2
Impact of Leverage on Earnings Per Share

	Common Stock	Preferred Stock	Debt
Common stock	$10,000	$10,000	$10,000
Additional funds	5,000	5,000	5,000
Total funds	$15,000	$15,000	$15,000
EBIT	$ 2,000	$ 2,000	$ 2,000
Less: interest	0	0	250
Earnings before taxes	$ 2,000	$ 2,000	$1,750
Less: taxes at 50%	1,000	1,000	875
Earnings after taxes	$ 1,000	$ 1,000	$ 875
Less: preferred dividends	0	300	0
Earnings available to stockholders	$ 1,000	$ 700	$ 875
Number of Common shares	150	100	100
EPS	$ 6.67	$ 7.00	$ 8.75

Graphic Analysis of EPS Fluctuation

In Figure 4-2, the vertical axis represents EPS, and the horizontal axis represents EBIT. We need two sets of calculations to draw the linear functions of EPS and EBIT for the various situations. Recall that for $2,000 EBIT, we had EPS of $6.67, $7, and $8.75 for the common stock, preferred stock, and debt financing alternatives. For the second set of points, it is common to use the intersection of each line with the horizontal axis (where EPS is zero). The horizontal-axis intercept for the common stock alternative is at $0 EBIT, because there are no fixed interest costs. The intercept for the preferred stock alternative is $600, because this amount is necessary to cover the $300 preferred stock dividends after taxes. Specifically, with $600 before taxes and taxes of $300 (or 50% of $600), the firm will have exactly $300 left to pay the preferred stock dividend of $300 (or 6% of $5000). The intercept for the debt alternative is at $250 EBIT. If EBIT is $250, then the interest cost of $250 (or 5% of $5000) will be deducted from the $250 EBIT to leave zero income before tax and therefore no tax. Remember that interest cost is deducted "before tax" while any dividends must come from "after tax" dollars. Using the two points (at EPS for EBIT of $2000 and EBIT at EPS of zero) for each alternative, we find the three straight lines for the debt, preferred stock, and common stock alternatives. Wherever the lines intersect, we say that firm would be indifferent between the two alternatives; that is, at that precise cross-over point for the EBIT, either alternative would produce the same EPS.

Figure 4-2 can be used to approximate the indifference point between two alternatives, but the following equations enable us to accurately calculate the indifference point:

$$\text{EPS} = \frac{(\text{EBIT} - I)(1 - t) - D_p}{n} \qquad (4\text{-}3)$$

where I = annual interest expenses, D_p = annual preferred stock dividends, and n = number of shares of common stock outstanding.

Suppose that we are comparing debt and common stock alternatives. The debt alternative has an associated interest expense of $250, with 100 shares of common stock outstanding. The stock alternative has no interest charges but would require the firm to issue an additional 50 shares raising total outstanding common shares to 150. To find the indifference point between these two alternatives, we set the two expressions equal to each other and then solve for EBIT:

Debt Alternative   Common Stock Alternative

$$\frac{(\text{EBIT} - \$250)(1 - 0.5) - \$0}{100} = \frac{(\text{EBIT} - \$0)(1 - 0.5) - \$0}{150}$$

$$25 \, \text{EBIT} = \$18{,}750$$

$$\text{EBIT} = \$750$$

In effect, we are seeking the precise EBIT where the two alternatives yield the exact same EPS. Similarly, the EBIT indifference point between the preferred stock and common stock alternatives is

Preferred Stock Alternative   Common Stock Alternative

$$\frac{(\text{EBIT} - \$0)(1 - 0.5) - \$300}{100} = \frac{(\text{EBIT} - \$0)(1 - 0.5) - \$0}{150}$$

$$\text{EBIT} = \$1{,}800$$

Thus, the EPS indifference point is $750 in EBIT for the debt and common stock alternatives. At an EBIT of $750, the common stock and debt alternatives yield the same EPS. Below the $750 level of EBIT, the common stock alternative will yield higher EPS, and above that point the debt alternative will yield higher EPS. The EPS indifference point is $1,800 in EBIT for the preferred stock and common stock alternatives. Below that point the common stock alternative will yield higher EPS, and above that point the preferred stock alternative will yield higher EPS.

Chapter 4: Leverage and Risk Analysis 69

Figure 4-2
Indifference Chart for Three Alternative Sources of Funds

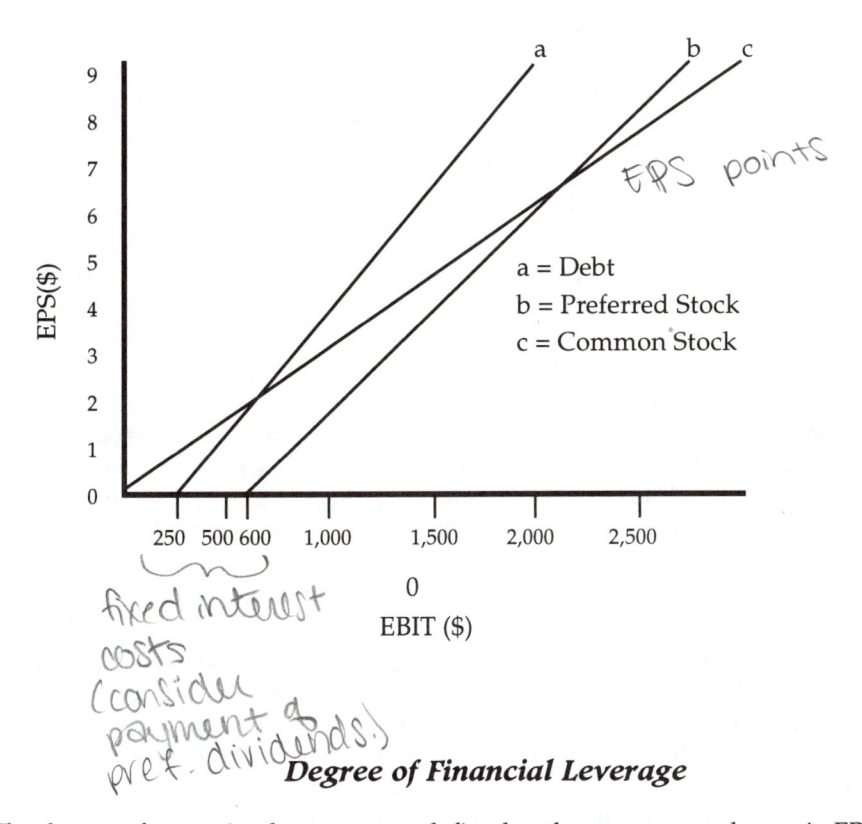

[Graph showing EPS($) on y-axis (0-9) vs EBIT($) on x-axis (250, 500, 600, 1,000, 1,500, 2,000, 2,500) with three lines labeled a, b, c]

a = Debt
b = Preferred Stock
c = Common Stock

[Handwritten annotations: "EPS points", "fixed interest costs (consider payment of pref. dividends)"]

Degree of Financial Leverage

The degree of operating leverage was defined as the percentage change in EBIT in relation to a given percent change in sales volume. The **degree of financial leverage** can also be defined as the percentage change in EPS associated with a given percent change in EBIT, or:

$$DFL = \frac{\% \text{ CHANGE IN EPS}}{\% \text{ CHANGE IN EBIT}}$$

A simple formula for calculating the degree of financial leverage may be derived from its definition:

$$DFL = \frac{EBIT}{EBIT - I - (Dp/1 - t)} \qquad (4\text{-}4)$$

where DFL = degree of financial leverage at a particular level of EBIT and I = annual interest expenses, Dp = annual preferred stock dividends, t = tax rate. Dp/1 – t computes preferred stock dividends on a before-tax basis. This is what the firm must earn before taxes to generate enough funds after tax to pay preferred stockholders their fixed dividend.

For the debt alternative at an EBIT of $2,000,

$$DFL = \frac{\$2,000}{\$2,000 - \$250} = 1.14$$

With preferred stock financing,

$$DFL = \frac{\$2,000}{\$2,000 - \$600} = 1.43$$

Where: $\$600 = \dfrac{\text{preferred stock dividends}}{1-t} = \dfrac{\$300}{1-.5} = \$600$

Thus, with the debt alternative, a 1 percent increase in EBIT would cause EPS to increase by 1.14 percent. With the preferred stock financing, a 1 percent increase in EBIT would lead to a 1.43 percent increase in EPS. A greater degree of financial leverage exists for the preferred stock alternative because it has a higher financial cost on a before-tax basis. It is important to understand that even though the preferred stock alternative provides greater financial leverage, this alternative produces the smaller EPS at all viable levels of EBIT than the debt alternative. With a DFL of 1.14 , for every 1% increase in EBIT the debt alternative will yield a 1.14% increase in an already higher EPS compared to preferred stock financing which would produce a 1.43% in a smaller EPS. Preferred stock's higher financial leverage number is simply due to the higher fixed cost of financing when compared to debt financing. This is because preferred stock financing receives no tax benefit in that its dividend payments to preferred stockholders are not deductible before taxes. Thus, with a 50% tax rate, for every $1.00 needed for preferred dividends, the firm needs $2.00 (or 1/1 – .5) , so if $300 is needed after tax, then $600 is necessary before tax. On the other hand, debt financing receives a tax benefit since interest payments to bondholders is tax deductible. Thus, at the 50% tax rate, every dollar in interest expense saves the firm 50 cents in taxes, so for any EBIT of $250 or above, the fixed cost of debt financing is only $125 or $250 x (1 – t). Therefore, the likely after-tax cost of debt is 2.5% or (5% x .5).

Combined Effect of Operating Leverage and Financial Leverage

The use of operating leverage magnifies fluctuations in EBIT. When sales volume rises, EBIT increase at a faster rate; when sales volume falls, EBIT decline more rapidly. The use of financial leverage causes any change in EBIT to have a magnified effect on EPS. Therefore, the combined effect of these two types of leverage allows changes in sales volume to produce even further fluctuations in EPS. This combined effect can be obtained by multiplying the DOL by the DFL. Because EBIT = Q(P – V) –F, Equation (4-4) can be restated as:

$$DFL = \frac{EBIT}{EBIT - I} = \frac{Q(P-V) - F}{Q(P-V) - F - I}$$

(4-5)

Combining Equation (4-2) with Equation (4-5), we obtain

$$DCL = (DOL)(DFL)$$

$$= \frac{Q(P-V)}{Q(P-V)-F} \times \frac{Q(P-V)-F}{Q(P-V)-F-I}$$

$$= \frac{Q(P-V)}{Q(P-V)-F-I} \qquad (4\text{-}6)$$

where DCL is the degree of combined leverage. Likewise:

$$DCL = (DOL) \times (DFL)$$

Or

$$DCL = \frac{\%\ \text{CHANGE IN EBIT}}{\%\ \text{CHANGE IN UNIT SALES}} \times \frac{\%\ \text{CHANGE IN EPS}}{\%\ \text{CHANGE IN EBIT}}$$

And

$$DCL = \frac{\%\ \text{CHANGE IN EPS}}{\%\ \text{CHANGE IN UNIT SALES}}$$

Suppose we illustrate the DCL calculation for our hypothetical Firm A which has $1,000 in debt at 8 percent interest. Recall that the firm's selling price is $5 a unit, fixed costs are $400, and variable costs are $3 a unit. The degree of combined leverage at an output of 300 units is

$$DCL = \frac{300(\$5-\$3)}{300(\$5-\$3)-\$400-\$80} = \frac{\$600}{\$120} = 5$$

Thus, a 1 percent increase in sales volume will lead to a 5 percent increase in EPS. This combined leverage effect of 5, of course, is much greater than the degree of operating leverage alone, which was 3 at 300 units. Hence, if this particular company employs a substantial amount of both operating and financial leverage, even small changes in the amount of sales will produce wide fluctuations in EPS.

To confirm that a 1 percent increase in sales volume will increase EPS by 5 percent, we compute earnings per share at the two levels of sales of 300 units and 303 units (or 300 plus 1% of 300). This is given in Table 4-3. As expected, when sales increased by 1 percent = (303 – 300)/300, EPS increased by 5 percent = ($6.30 – $6.00)/$6.00. So 1% or 3 unit increase in sales volume magnified EPS by 5% or 30 cents from $6.00 to $6.30.

Table 4-3
Earnings per Share at the Two Levels of Sales for Firm A

Items	300 units	303 units
Sales (price per unit = $5)	$1,500	$1,515
Less: variable costs (cost per unit = $3)	900	909
Sales less variable costs	$ 600	$ 606
Less: fixed costs	400	400
EBIT	$ 200	$ 206
Less: interest	80	80
Profit before taxes	$ 120	$126
Less: taxes at 50%	60	63
Earnings after taxes	$ 60	$ 63
Common shares outstanding	10	10
Earnings per share	$ 6.00	$ 6.30

Business Risk, Financial Risk, and Total Risk

Both operating leverage and financial leverage have a direct relationship to certain risks found in the firm. Operating risk (business risk) is related to operating leverage. Financial risk is related to financial leverage. Total risk is associated with the combined effect of operating leverage and financial leverage.

Business risk refers to the variability of operating profits or the possibility that the firm will not be able to cover its fixed operating costs. Business risk may be caused by such factors as business cycles, competition, labor strikes, and the nature of the industry to which the firm belongs. Business risk also depends on operating leverage. The higher the operating leverage, the greater are the break-even point and the effect on operating profits from a given change in sales volume. Thus, (1) as the firm increases the use of fixed assets, its sales volume necessary to cover its fixed costs increases; and (2) when fixed costs are high, even a small decrease in sales volume can lead to a large decrease in operating profits. Simply stated, by increasing the use of operating leverage, the firm can increase the variability of earnings, thus increasing the probability of not being able to meet its fixed costs.

Financial leverage affects not only expected EPS but also financial risk. **Financial risk** refers to the possibility that the firm will not be able to meet its fixed charges (loan repayments and interest). The higher the financial leverage, the greater are the fixed charges and the effect on EPS from a given change in operating profits. Hence, (1) as the firm increases the use of fixed-income securities (debt and preferred stock), its operating profits necessary to cover its fixed charges increase; and (2) when fixed charges are high, even a smaller decrease in operating profits can lead to a large decrease in earnings available to common stockholders. Simply stated, the use of more fixed-income securities increase the probability that the firm will not be able to meet its fixed charges.

Business risk from the use of fixed assets and financial risk from the use of fixed-income securities constitute corporate total risk. Recall that the combined-leverage effect causes changes in sales to result in even greater fluctuations in EPS than the mere sum of two individual effects. This is because the combined-leverage effect is multiplicative rather than additive. Thus, total risk is a product of business risk and financial risk.

The total risk is a key factor used by investors and lenders when deciding to entrust funds with the firm. Thus the firm must closely monitor and manage its total risk so as to remain competitive when entering the financial markets in search of new funds. For example, compare the risk profile of the electric utility with the auto firm. Both industries are capital intensive since they require heavy investment in expensive fixed assets (i.e. state-of-the-art generating plants and auto production facilities). At first glance, one would expect both firms to face high business or operating risk. But further investigation reveals a significant difference in the cyclical nature of each firm's product and competitive position. Even though the generation and transmission side of the electric utility industry is gradually making the transition to competition, still for the most part the industry remains largely a regulated monopoly. Likewise, the electric utility is selling an on-line, upon-request commodity which consumers depend on continuously, without interruption. Also, if consumers don't pay their bills, the utility firm can disconnect service. Thus, the nature of the product and the industry insures stable, dependable sales and cash flows over the course of the business cycle, even during economic recession. This grants the electric utility the comfort of low business risk when compared to the auto firm. The durability and cyclical nature of the auto firm's product raises its business risk. When recession hits, consumers don't trade for new cars, rather they repair and run the old cars longer for fear of losing their jobs and income stream. Thus unlike the electric utility, the auto firm faces extreme fluctuations in sales over the course of the business cycle. In order to compete against the electric utility for needed funds in the financial markets, the auto firm must lower its financial risk so that its total risk is not out of line with other firms like utilities. In fact, this is the case since existing evidence shows that electric utilities engage significantly higher levels of debt than auto firms. Because of lower business risk, the electric utility can afford higher financial risk and still compete against the auto firm for funds in the financial markets.

Financial Risk and Business Failure

The cost of business failure is extremely high, because not only those persons directly involved but also the entire community or even the entire nation are adversely affected by corporate collapse. Thus, an investigation of how to identify the causes and symptoms of failures could be extremely valuable for those concerned with the sustained well-being of business firms.

The major causes most frequently cited for business failures are poor planning, inadequate capital, poor working capital management, and so on. These elements are often excuses for poor performance rather than its causes. The underlying cause of most business failures is incompetent management. However, the two most important factors for our purposes are business risk and financial risk. Because business risk depends largely on such external factors as business cycles and the industry to which the firm belongs, even competent management has very little or no control over it. Financial risk, in contrast, is under the direct control of management.

Financial leverage usually raises expected earnings available to common stockholders, but it also increases the riskiness of the firm's securities. Therefore, financial leverage produces two conflicting results: (1) higher earnings available to common stockholders, which lead to a higher stock price, but (2) increased riskiness, which leads to a lower stock price. However, some writers argue that there is an optimum capital structure. **Optimum capital structure** refers to a financing mix that maximizes the price of the firm's stock.

It is not easy to determine a firm's optimum capital structure, but the ratios described in Chapter 3 can be used to measure the firm's financial risk. These ratios are the total debt/total assets ratio and times interest earned. The degree of financial leverage is also an important tool to determine whether the use of fixed-income securities is justified.

Summary

The principles of financial projection covered in this chapter revolved around the use of both operating leverage and financial leverage. A firm has many alternative sources of funds available to it when it seeks financing. The major determinant of which sources should be chosen is the principle of leverage and its relationship with the capital structure of the firm.

Operating leverage refers to the extent that fixed assets are used in company operations. The use of operating leverage tends to magnify profits during periods of high sales, as each additional unit of output contributes to a considerable margin of profit, based on variable costs only. Unfortunately, a similar condition holds for declining sales. Acceleration of losses is out of proportion to the rate of sales reduction, because fixed costs must be paid even though sales are short of the expected level.

Financial leverage refers to the extent of fixed-income securities used in company operations. Whenever the return on assets exceeds the cost of the funds raised by the debt or the preferred stock, leverage is favorable and increases earnings per share. If the return on assets is less than the cost of these funds, leverage is unfavorable and reduces earnings per share.

List of Key Terms

leverage	operating leverage
financial leverage	break-even analysis
variable costs	fixed costs
degree of operating leverage	degree of financial leverage
operating or business risk	financial risk
optimum capital structure	

Problems

4-1 Find the break-even point if the selling price is $8 per unit, variable costs are $3 per unit, and fixed costs are $3,000.

4-2 Determine the degree of operating leverage at 800 units of output if the selling price is $8 per unit, variable costs are $3 per unit, and fixed costs are $3,000.

4-3 A company has 200 common shares outstanding. The company needs an additional $10,000 to buy a new machine. It is considering two alternatives to raise the money: (1) issue 100 new shares of common stock at $100 par value, and (2) issue bonds at a 6 percent interest rate. With either the common stock or the debt alternative, it is expected that the firm's EBIT will be $2,400 and its tax rate is 50 percent. See Example 4-2 and Table 4-2 for help.

(a) Determine the earnings per share for each financing option.
(b) Determine the EBIT indifference point between the two methods of financing.
(c) Determine the earnings per share at the EBIT indifference point (see p. 68 for help).

4-4 Colby's Shirts, Inc. has started a new line of shirts with the symbol of a duck over the pocket. This new line will sell for $50 per shirt. The shirts are made in a new plant facility in Ann Arbor, Michigan. Fixed costs are $60,000, variable costs are $30 per shirt, sales volume is 4,000 shirts, and interest expenses are $10,000.

(a) What is the degree of operating leverage?
(b) What is the degree of financial leverage?
(c) What is the degree of combined leverage?

4-5 The ABC Company sells its product for $20 per unit. Its fixed costs are $10,000 and the variable cost per unit is $10.

(a) Determine the break-even point in units and dollars.
(b) Determine the earnings before interest and taxes at sales of 1,500 units.
(c) What is the new break-even point if the price per unit increases from $20 to $30?
(d) Determine the degree of operating leverage at sales of 2,000 and 4,000 units, respectively.

4-6 The College Company has 10,000 shares of common stock outstanding with a par value of $40, and its tax rate is 48 percent. The company is weighing the choice among three financing alternatives for a major expansion program which would require $100,000 and increase its operating profit from $90,000 to $125,000. The financing alternatives are as follows:

(a) 2,000 common shares at $50 net to the company.
(b) $100,000 of 7 percent preferred stock.
(c) $100,000 of 6 percent bonds.

Assuming an EBIT of $125,000 for each alternative, determine the earnings per share for each financing plan (see Example 4-2 and Table 4-2). Compute the EPS indifference points (see p. 68 for help) for the common stock vs. preferred stock plan and common stock vs. bond debt plan. Discuss the computation results.

4-7 The Western Glass Company sells its glass by the square foot. The price per square foot is $5 and variable costs are $3 per square foot. Fixed costs are $60,000, and the company has $100,000 worth of debt with an interest rate of 10 percent. The company is operating at 50,000 square feet.

(a) What is the degree of operating leverage?
(b) What is the degree of financial leverage?
(c) What is the degree of combined leverage?

4-8 A company sells two products, A and B. The price per unit is $12 for A and $8 for B. The variable cost per unit is $6 for A and $4 for B. Total fixed costs on both products are $80,000.

(a) Calculate the break-even point if these two products are sold in the same proportions.
(b) Calculate the break-even point if they are sold in the ratio of 3 to 2 in favor of A.

5

FINANCIAL PLANNING AND FORECASTING

A budget is a management tool for getting the most profitable use out of the company's resources by improving the firm's internal coordination. Management must plan its economic activities in advance, carry out its plans, and make sure that deviations are properly evaluated and handled. Thus, budgeting relates to the fundamentals of the management process: planning, execution, and control.

This chapter has three primary objectives. The first is to provide an overview of the firm's total budgetary system. The overall budgetary system of a company consolidates all departmental budgets and covers all phases of its operations. The second objective is to discuss financial planning budgets; these budgets consist of the cash budget, the pro forma income statement, the pro forma balance sheet, and the pro forma funds-flow statement. The third objective is to describe the percent-of-sales method as an alternative to financial planning budgets.

NATURE OF BUDGETING

A **management information system** is a comprehensive system to provide all levels of management in a firm with information so that production, marketing, and financial functions can be effectively performed to achieve the objectives of the firm. It should be emphasized that budgeting is only a part of the overall management information system. The budgetary system integrates the operational plans to express the financial results and economic performance of the firm. But this financial information is central in any management information system, because the final measure of economic performance depends on the total financial consequences from the sum of all operations.

Budgets are preestablished standards to which operations are evaluated, compared, and adjusted by the exercise of control. For example, actual sales and profit contribution are compared with previous plans. Actual production costs are compared with previous plans over materials, labor, and manufacturing overhead costs. Like any other control methods, budgetary standards measure the progress of actual performance and provide information which permits management to anticipate change and adapt to it.

It is important for a firm to allow a certain degree of flexibility and adaptability in its budgetary program. This flexibility is essential to cope with rapidly changing conditions in the modern business world. Although most companies choose the period of one year as their budget period, some firms break down the planned annual budget by quarters, months, or even weeks. Alternative budgets are another method for obtaining flexibility in a budgetary program. This method establishes separate budgetary programs for different operation conditions. For example, a firm may prepare three different types of budgets: one geared for a high level of sales, another for a normal level, and a third for a low level.

Relationships among Various Budgets

To simplify our discussion of an overall budgetary program, budgets are grouped by function or area—sales budget, production budget, sales expense budget, administrative budget, and financial planning budget. Figure 5-1 shows the relationships among these budgets.

Budgeting is part of the total planning activity of the firm. This total planning activity usually begins with long-range objectives over four, five, or even more years. This establishes the stage for the first year's detailed planning, of which budgeting is a part. Long-range objectives of the firm may provide for plant expansion, machinery and equipment acquisitions, and other resources which require capital expenditures. Most capital decisions depend mainly upon expected demand for the product. Thus, the sales budget provides the basis for establishing the capital budget. Capital expenditures are covered by specific financing programs; the portion of the capital expenditure budget which will materialize during the current year is reflected in the other budgets. These two factors suggest that the long-range capital budget should be treated as a special budget.

In most cases, the sales budget is the first step in the entire budgeting process. Sales for the coming year are estimated to reach a certain minimum number of units or a certain dollar volume on the basis of past experience, general economic conditions, and other planning considerations. The sales budget is the basis for the firm's activities not only in the finance department but also in the production and marketing departments. As shown in Figure 5-1, the sales budget flows in five directions.

1. The **sales budget** gives a basis for a **production budget** which reflects the use of materials, labor, and facilities. Although the sales budget does not necessarily reflect the production schedule, it is a prerequisite for establishing the production budget which, in turn, determines sales requirements and desired inventory levels.
2. After sales are estimated and the product is produced to meet sales requirements, the next step in the budgeting process calls for a sales expense budget. Both the sales budget and production budget flow directly to the **sales expense budget** which consists of various budgets such as advertising, selling, and other sales expenses.
3. Anticipated sales figures determine the general office and executive requirements which are reflected in the general administrative budget.
4. The source side of the cash budget depends upon anticipated sales revenues. The cash budget arises due to the gap in time between the expenditure and receipt of funds. A large amount of money must be spent for materials, labor, and selling expenses several months before sales are made and accounts receivable are collected.

5. The sales budget is also used to estimate the revenues which are reflected in the income budget.

Figure 5-1
Relationships Among Various Budgets

```
                    ┌─────────────┐
                    │  Objectives │
                    └──┬───────┬──┘
                       │       │
                       ▼       ▼
              ┌──────────────┐  ┌────────────────┐
              │ Sales Budget │─▶│ Capital Budget │
              └──────────────┘  └────────────────┘
```

Production Budget	Sales Expense Budget	Administration Budget
Cash Budget		Income Budget
Sources		Revenues
Uses		Expenses
Cash Budget		Income Budget

Balance Sheet Budget

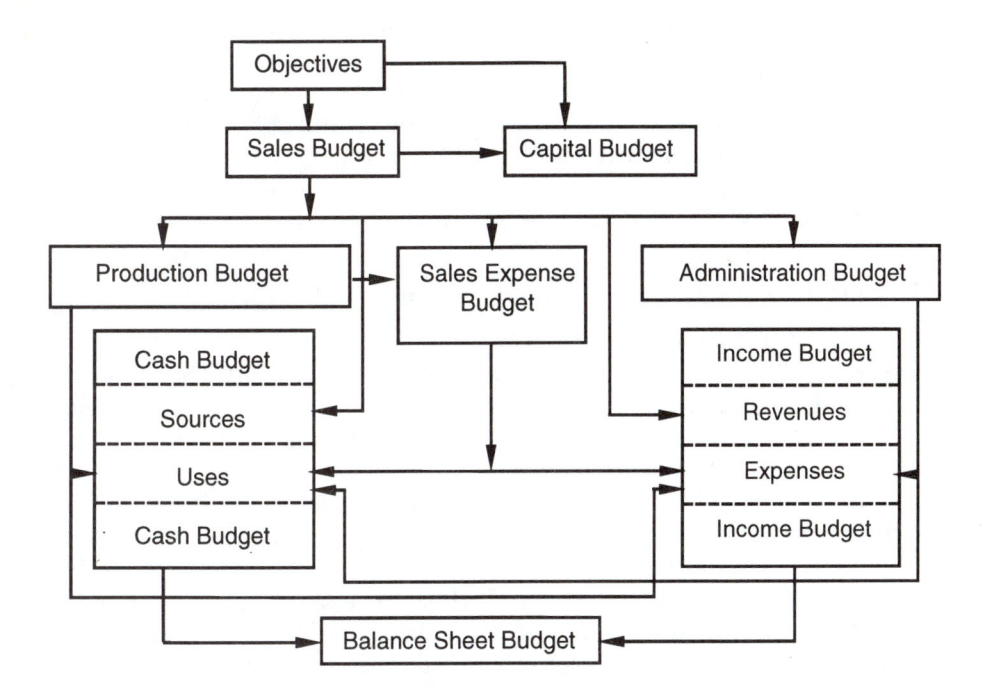

Figure 5-1 also shows that the budgets of the production, marketing and general administrative expenses flow into both the cash and income budgets to project the costs of company operations. The results of estimating all these elements of cost and revenue are reflected in the cash and income budgets, which summarize all budgets. A comprehensive budgetary program usually includes a balance sheet budget. The balance sheet budget summarizes the effect of the firm's budgeting system on its assets, liabilities, and net worth. The balance sheet budget is in fact the all-inclusive expression of the conditions and assumptions for the period ahead.

Types of Pro Forma Financial Statements

It should be obvious by now that the various budgets presented here are closely related. Figure 5-1 has shown us that there is a significant interrelationship between the cash budget, pro forma income statement, and pro forma balance sheet. Normally, all three types of analyses are based on the same set of assumptions about operating rates, receipts and collections, payments, inventory levels, and so forth. The remaining portion of this chapter is designed to illustrate a numerical example of the cash budget, the

Cash Budget

A **cash budget** summarizes projected cash receipts and cash disbursements of the firm over various intervals of time. The regular cash requirements of the firm should be forecasted to make certain that (a) adequate cash funds are available for the timely payment of credit purchases, payrolls, and other costs; (b) funds will be available for additional capital assets; and (c) excess funds, if any, are wisely invested. Cash budgets enable management to synchronize cash outflows with cash inflows. Although cash budgets may be prepared for any period of time, monthly cash budgets are most widely used because they consider seasonal fluctuations in cash flows. However, when sales are erratic and the cash balance is low, cash budgets at more frequent intervals such as weekly periods may be more desirable.

The cash budget of the ABC Company for the first six months of 2001 is prepared from the following estimates:

a. Sales are $20,000 a month from December 2000 to June 2001. These sales are 90 percent for credit and 10 percent for cash.
b. Monthly purchases of merchandise are $8,000. The purchase breakdown is 80 percent credit and 20 percent cash.
c. Accounts receivable are collected in the month following the sales. Payments for raw materials are also made in the month following the month in which these costs were incurred.
d. Wages and salaries used in the production process are $4,000 each month and are paid in the month they are incurred; factory overhead is $1,500 per month; selling expenses are $1,100 each month; and monthly administrative expenses are $800.
e. The company's capital budget calls for the purchase of a new machine costing $20,000 whose payment is expected to be made in May; income tax payments of $10,000 are planned in March; dividend payments of $8,700 are planned in March; and a semiannual interest payment of $1,200 on $20,000 of 12 percent bonds is due in June.
f. The company has a cash balance of $10,000 on December 31, 2000. This amount is the minimum cash balance which should be maintained throughout the budget period.

The cash requirements are estimated in the cash budget shown in Table 5-1. The top half of the table illustrates the worksheets for calculating total cash receipts and total cash expenses. Schedule A shows that the total sales are estimated to be $20,000 a month, of which 10 percent or $2,000 are cash sales and $18,000 are credit sales; the credit sales are collected in the following month. As shown in Schedule B, total purchases of raw materials are forecasted at $8,000 a month, of which 20 percent or $1,600 are cash purchases and $6,400 are credit purchases; there is a one-month lag between purchases on credit and payments. All monthly expenses are added to total cash payments for raw materials to complete the worksheet for total cash expenses.

Total cash receipts are given on the top line of the cash budget. Next comes an estimate of cash disbursements. In addition to the total cash expenses shown in Schedule B of Table 5-1, we must include occasional cash outflows such as capital expenditures, income taxes,

Chapter 5: Financial Planning and Forecasting   81

Table 5-1
ABC Company Cash Budget for Six Months Ending June 30, 2001

Schedule of Cash Receipts (A)

	Dec.	Jan.	Feb.	Mar.	April	May	June
Credit Sales	$18,000	$18,000	$18,000	$18,000	$18,000	$18,000	$18,000
Collections		18,000	18,000	18,000	18,000	18,000	18,000
Cash Sales		2,000	2,000	2,000	2,000	2,000	2,000
Total Cash Receipts		$20,000	$20,000	$20,000	$20,000	$20,000	$20,000

Schedule of Cash Expenses (B)

	Dec.	Jan.	Feb.	Mar.	April	May	June
Credit Purchases	$6,400	$6,400	$6,400	$6,400	$6,400	$6,400	$6,400
Payments		6,400	6,400	6,400	6,400	6,400	6,400
Cash Purchases		1,600	1,600	1,600	1,600	1,600	1,600
Wages and Salaries		4,000	4,000	4,000	4,000	4,000	4,000
Factory Overhead		1,500	1,500	1,500	1,500	1,500	1,500
Selling Expenses		1,100	1,100	1,100	1,100	1,100	1,100
Administrative Expenses		800	800	800	800	800	800
Total Cash Expenses		$15,400	$15,400	$15,400	$15,400	$15,400	$15,400

Cash Budget

	Jan.	Feb.	Mar.	April	May	June
Total Cash Receipts (A)	$20,000	$20,000	$20,000	$20,000	$20,000	$20,000
Cash Expenses (B)	15,400	15,400	15,400	15,400	15,400	15,400
Capital Expenditures			10,000		20,000	
Income Taxes			8,700			
Dividend payments						1,200
Interest Expenses						
Total Disbursements	$15,400	$15,400	$34,100	$15,400	$35,400	$16,600
Net Cash Gain (loss) During Month	4,600	4,600	(14,100)	4,600	(15,400)	3,400
Beginning Cash Balances	10,000	14,600	19,200	5,100	9,700	(5,700)
Cumulative Cash	$14,600	$19,200	$5,100	$9,700	($5,700)	($2,300)
Minimum Cash Balance	(10,000)	(10,000)	(10,000)	(10,000)	(10,000)	(10,000)
Cash Surplus	$4,600	$9,200		300		
Cash Shortage			$4,900		$15,700	$12,300

dividend payments, and interest. Once all foreseeable cash inflows and outflows have been taken into account, we subtract the anticipated cash disbursements for any month from the estimated cash receipts for that month to get the net gain or loss during that month; for January, there is a net gain of $4,600. To compute the cash balance at the end of the month, the beginning cash balance is added to the net cash gain or loss for that month. Note that the cumulative or ending cash balance of any month is the beginning balance of the next month. Finally, the minimum cash balance of $10,000 is subtracted from the cumulative cash balance to get the cash surplus or deficit.

The next to last line of Table 5-1 shows that the firm is expected to have a cash surplus for the first two months of the budget period, whereas the last line of the table indicates that the firm is expected to have a cash deficit for the last four months of the cash budget period. Now, the financial manager can use this cash forecast to determine not only what to do with the anticipated cash surplus during some months, but also whether to borrow or to defer some of the cash outflows to meet the estimated cash deficit during the last four months of the budget period.

Pro Forma Income Statement

Once the detailed cash budget has been prepared, we can proceed to develop a set of pro forma statements. Since the changes in retained earnings will have to be reflected in the pro forma balance sheet, we start with the **pro forma income statement**. To prepare a pro forma income statement of the ABC Company for the first half of 2001, we need a number of additional assumptions.

g. The firm had an inventory of $2,000 at the close of 2000 and wishes to increase its inventory level to $13,000 by the end of June, 2001.
h. Depreciation charges are $500 a month.
i. The firm's tax rate is 50 percent.

Table 5-2
ABC Company Six-Month Pro Forma Income Statement, June 30, 2001

			Explanation
Sales		$120,000	6 mo. @ $20,000
Cost of goods sold			
Beginning inventory	$ 2,000		Given
Raw materials used	48,000		6 mo. @ $8,000
Direct labor	24,000		6 mo. @ $4,000
Factory overhead	9,000		6 mo. @ $1,500
Depreciation	3,000		6 mo. @ $500
Total	$86,000		
Ending inventory	13,000	73,000	
Gross profit		$47,000	
Selling expenses	$ 6,600		6 mo. @ $1,100
Administrative expenses	4,800	11,400	6 mo. @ $800
Operating profit (EBIT)		$ 35,600	
Interest expense		1,200	
Earnings before taxes		$ 34,400	
Taxes at 50%		17,200	
Earnings after taxes		$ 17,200	

Chapter 5: Financial Planning and Forecasting

Table 5-2 shows the pro forma income statement of the firm for June 30, 2001. It begins with a sales forecast. The cash budget shows that sales would be $20,000 a month during the budget period. Therefore, sales for the first six months of 2001 should be $120,000. Given this sales forecast, production schedules can be formulated and estimates of production costs can be made for the products. Table 5-2 shows that the cost of goods sold is affected by both beginning and ending inventories, raw materials, production wages, factory overhead, and depreciation. The values of these items are derived from the cash budget and the additional assumptions made to develop the pro forma income statement.

The six-month total expenditures for selling and administration shown in the pro forma income statement represent the sums of the monthly figures appearing in the cash budget. Next, interest expenses are deducted to obtain earnings before taxes; the interest expense figure is given in Table 5-1. Income taxes are then estimated on the basis of a 50 percent tax rate and deducted to determine earnings after taxes; the firm is expected to have a net income after taxes of $17,200. Basically, the pro forma income statement serves as an estimate of profits for the six months. But, with a detailed breakdown of expenses, it may serve as a device to control expenses.

Pro Forma Balance Sheet

To illustrate the preparation of a **pro forma balance sheet**, suppose that Table 5-3 presents the balance sheet for the ABC Company as of December 31, 2000. From this table, along with the cash budget and the pro forma income statement, we can begin to construct the pro forma balance sheet for June 30, 2001 shown in Table 5-4.

Because the firm has the policy of maintaining a minimum cash balance of $10,000, the cash balance on June 30 will be $10,000. The accounts receivable represent the credit sales for June. The inventory level is obtained from the ending inventory figure in the pro forma income statement. Gross fixed assets have increased by $20,000 for the period, but the pro forma income statement shows that the estimated deprecation for the six-month period is $3,000; this charge raises the net fixed assets by only $17,000.

Table 5-3
ABC Company Balance Sheet as of December 31, 2000

Cash	$10,000	Accounts payable	$ 6,400
Accounts receivable credit sales	18,000	Accrued income taxes	13,600
Inventory	2,000		
Total current assets	$30,000	Total current debts	$20,000
Gross fixed assets	$87,000	Bonds, 12%	$20,000
Accumulated depreciation	27,000	Common stock	15,000
Net fixed assets	$60,000	Retained earnings	35,000
Total assets	$90,000	Total debt & equity	$90,000

Let us turn to the other side of the pro forma balance sheet. The cash budget indicated that to assure a minimum cash balance of $10,000, the firm is expected to have a cash deficit of $12,300 as of June 30; it is assumed that this plug amount will be financed by a short-term bank loan. Accrued income taxes are determined by adding the projected income taxes for the six-month period to the December 31 tax balance and by subtracting the actual tax payments during the budget period from the sum. Assume that long-term debt and common stock are constant. Retained earnings would be the retained earnings at December 31 plus earnings after taxes minus the amount of cash dividends paid.

Table 5-4
ABC Company Six-Month Pro Forma Balance Sheet for June 30, 2001

Cash	$10,000	Accounts payable	$ 6,400
Accounts receivable *credit sales*	18,000	Notes payable (plug)	12,300
Inventory	13,000	Accrued income taxes	20,800
Total current assets	$41,000	Total current debts	$39,500
Gross fixed assets	$107,000	Bonds, 12%	$20,000
Accumulated depreciation	30,000	Common stock	15,000
Net fixed assets	$77,000	Retained earnings	43,500
Total assets	$118,000	Total claims	$118,000

All the estimated balance sheet items must be combined to prepare a pro forma balance sheet. The six-month pro forma balance sheet of the ABC Company for June 30, 2001 is given in Table 5-4.

Pro Forma Sources and Uses of Funds Statement

In analyzing the financial operations of a firm, there must be an offsetting source for every use of funds. The asset items represent the financing sources of the assets. A funds-flow statement based on historical data indicates where funds came from and how they were used between the past two points in time. A future flow-of-funds statement based on forecasts shows how a firm plans to obtain and use funds during a future time period. The funds-flow statement is an important planning tool to estimate the firm's financial requirements and to determine the best way to meet these requirements. It can also serve as a control device to check if the funds were used according to the plan.

To develop a funds-flow statement, we have to tabulate the changes in the balance sheet items from one period to the next and classify these changes as follows: sources of funds include increases in liability and equity items, decreases in asset items, and deprecation; uses of funds include increases in asset items and decreases in liability and equity items. Table 5-5 shows a pro forma sources-and-uses-of-funds statement of the ABC Company for the first six months ending June 30, 2001. It is important to note that to reflect earnings after taxes and dividends, some adjustments were made in the pro forma funds-flow statement. The firm is expected to earn $17,200 after taxes, and it is planned to pay dividends of $8,700 in March. The $17,200 is treated as a source of funds and the $8,700 is treated as a use of funds. An $8,500 increase in retained earnings for the first half of 2001 is not included in the table to avoid double counting.

The **pro forma funds-flow statement** constructed on the basis of the projected balance sheet and the supplementary projected data on earnings, dividends, and depreciation summarizes the firm's projected operations over the budget period. An examination of Table 5-5 shows that the principal uses of funds will be an addition to fixed assets and

Chapter 5: Financial Planning and Forecasting   85

a sizable increase in inventory. The firm will need funds to meet these working and fixed asset demands. These funds are expected to come from operations, an increase in notes payable, and an increase in accrued income taxes.

Table 5-5
ABC Company Pro Forma Sources-and-Uses-of-Funds Statement
For Six Months Ending June 30, 2001

Sources		
Earnings after taxes	$17,200	43.3%
Depreciation	3,000	7.6
Increase in notes payable	12,300	31.0
Increase in accrued taxes	7,200	18.1
Total sources of funds	$39,700	100.0%
Uses		
Inventory investment	$11,000	27.7%
Gross fixed asset expansion	20,000	50.4
Dividends paid	8,700	21.9
Total uses of funds	$39,700	100.0%

PERCENT-OF-SALES METHOD

The **percent-of-sales** method is an alternative to the financial planning budgets discussed. This method assumes that certain accounts on the balance sheet change in some fixed proportion to changes in sales. In other words, it estimates the level of each asset, liability or owners' equity account for a future period as a percent of the sales forecast. This percentage can come from the most recent balance sheet item as a percentage of current sales.

Many balance sheet items vary directly with sales. A higher level of sales necessitates more cash, more accounts receivable, and higher inventory levels. If the current sales of the company are its capacity limit, increases in sales also necessitate additional plant capacity. On the liability side, both accounts payable and accruals are expected to increase with increases in sales. Increases in accounts payable and accruals are frequently called spontaneously generated liabilities, which would automatically finance a part of sales increases. Although retained earnings are not expected to increase proportionally with increases in sales, they will rise as long as the company is profitable and does not pay out 100 percent of earnings. Neither common stock nor bonds will increase spontaneously with increases in sales.

Example 5-1. Assume that the balance sheet relationships of Table 5-3 are constant. The current sales of the ABC Company are $200,000 a year, which is its capacity limit. The company's profit margin after taxes on sales is 10 percent, half of which is paid as dividends. Both common stock and bonds are expected to stay the same and all the other balance sheet items are expected to vary directly with sales. If sales expand to $300,000 during 2001, what additional funds will be needed?

Table 5-6
ABC Company Balance Sheet Items as a Percent of Sales as of December 31, 2000

Cash	5.0	Accounts payable	3.2
Accounts receivable	9.0	Accrued income taxes	6.8
Inventory	1.0	Total current debts	10.0
Total current assets	15.0	Bonds, 12%	na
Net fixed assets	30.0	Common stock	na
		Retained earnings	na
Total assets	45.0	Total debt & equity	10.0
Assets as percent of sales			45.0
Less: spontaneous liabilities			10.0
Additional financing as percent of incremental sales			35.0

naNot applicable.

Table 5-6 shows that cash of $10,000 represents 5 percent of sales; accounts receivable of $18,000 are 9 percent of sales; and so on. No percentages are computed for bonds, common stock, and retained earnings, because they are not assumed to vary with sales. Assets must increase by 45 cents for every $1 increase in sales. Out of this 45 percent, 10 percent will be automatically financed through accounts payable and accrued income taxes. The remaining 35 percent should be financed by profit or additional outside sources of funds.

Recall that sales are scheduled to increase by $100,000 from $200,000 to $300,000. The $100,000 increase in sales necessitates $35,000 or (35% of sales) in additional financing. Because the ABC Company will retain 5 percent of its earnings (half of 10 percent profit margin on sales), its retained earnings will increase by $15,000 or (5% of $300,000 sales). If we subtract these retained earnings of $15,000 from $35,000 that must be financed, we find that the ABC Company will need an additional amount of $20,000 from new sources.

SUMMARY

In this chapter, we continued our examination of financial planning and control. An essential part of the financial manager's role is short-term budgeting. Short-term financial planning budgets include the cash budget, the pro forma income statement, the pro forma balance sheet, and the pro forma sources-and-uses-of-funds statement. These budgets are utilized for both planning and control purposes. Budgets establish standards of performance; these standards are compared with actual results; and corrective action is taken if actual results are below standards.

The cash budget shows various cash receipts and disbursements expected by a firm during the coming year, usually on a monthly basis. This budget is particularly useful to determine when additional financing will be required and when a surplus will occur. The pro forma income statement provides the financial manager with insight into the prospective future performance of the firm. The pro forma balance sheet indicates the financial condition of the firm at the end of the budget period. The sales budget is the key input to all of these three budgets. The pro forma sources-and-uses-of-funds statement shows where funds will come from and how these funds will be used. The percent-of-sales method estimates financial requirements on the basis of the sales forecast. Because the method assumes that the relationships between the balance sheet and sales will remain constant, it is only useful for relatively short-run forecasting.

LIST OF KEY TERMS

management information system
sales budget
production budget
proforma income statement
proforma funds flow statement

budgets
cash budget
proforma balance sheet
percent-of-sales method
sale expense budget

PROBLEMS

5-1 Prepare the cash budget of the Lee Company for the first six months of 2001 on the basis of the following estimates (see ABC Company example on p. 80 for help):

(1) Credit sales are $20,000 a month from December 2000 to June 2001.
(2) Monthly credit purchases of raw materials are $10,000 from December 2000 to June 2001.
(3) Accounts receivable are collected in the month following the sales. Payments for raw materials are also made in the month following the month in which these costs were incurred.
(4) Wages and salaries used in the production process are $3,000 each month, paid in the month they are incurred; factory overhead is $1,000 per month; selling expenses are $1,500 each month; and monthly administrative expenses are $500.
(5) The company's capital budget calls for the purchase of a new machine costing $10,000 whose payment is expected to be made in May; income tax payments of $5,000 are due in March; dividend payments of $10,000 are planned in March; and a semiannual interest of $1,000 on $20,000 of 10 percent bonds is due in June.
(6) The company has a cash balance of $10,000 on December 31, 2000. This amount is the minimum cash balance which should be maintained throughout the budget period.

5-2 Using the cash budget worked out in Problem 5-1 and the following additional information, prepare an income statement for the Lee Company for the six months ending June 30, 2001.

(7) The company's tax rate is 50 percent.
(8) Depreciation charges are $500 a month.
(9) The company had an inventory of $1,000 at the close of 2000 and wishes to increase its inventory level to $8,000 by the end of June 2001.

PART 2: FINANCIAL PLANNING AND CONTROL

5-3 Use the information given in Problems 5-1 and 5-2 and the following information to construct a balance sheet for the Lee Company for June 2001. The amount of the firm's short-term bank loan (notes payable) is expected to be $2,000 at the end of June 2001.

Balance Sheet (December 31, 2000)

Cash	$10,000	Accounts payable	$ 10,000
Accounts receivable	20,000	Accrued income taxes	15,000
Inventory	1,000	Total current debts	$25,000
Total current assets	$31,000		
Gross fixed assets	$77,000	Bonds, 10%	$20,000
Accumulated depreciation	27,000	Common stock	10,000
Net fixed assets	$50,000	Retained earnings	26,000
Total assets	$81,000	Total claims	$81,000

5-4 Using the actual December 31, 2000 balance sheet (above), the pro forma June 30, 2001 balance sheet, the pro forma income statement for the first six months of 2001, and the cash budget for the first six months of 2001, construct a sources-and-uses-of-funds statement for the Lee Company for the first six months of 2001.

5-5 The current sales of the XYZ Company are $200,000 a year. The sales for the forthcoming year (2001) are expected to expand to $240,000. The company's profit after taxes on sales is 8 percent, 70 percent of which is paid as dividends. Assuming that the XYZ Company is operating below its capacity, determine the amount of new funds required to finance this growth.

Balance Sheet (December 31, 2000)

Cash	$10,000	Accounts payable	$ 60,000
Accounts receivable	60,000	Notes payable	15,000
Inventory	40,000	Accrued expenses	5,000
Current assets	$110,000	Current liabilities	$ 80,000
Fixed assets	$40,000	Common stock	55,000
		Retained earnings	15,000
Total assets	$150,000	Total claims	$150,000

5-6 Lakewood Corporation projects the following sales:

April = $75,000; May = $95,000; and June $110,000. Ninety percent of Lakewood's sales are on credit; 60 percent of accounts receivable are collected in the month after the sale and the rest of accounts receivable are collected in the second month after the sale. February sales were $60,000 and March sales were $70,000. There are no bad debt losses.

(a) Prepare a monthly schedule of cash receipts for April–June.
(b) Determine the balance of accounts receivable at the end of June.

Chapter 5: Financial Planning and Forecasting

5-7 Sales for next year are expected to be $3 million. Given the following data, develop a pro forma balance sheet.

Minimum cash balance = $90,000
Accounts receivable = 15% of annual sales
Inventory = 10% of annual sales
Fixed assets = $1,275,000 (no change)
Accounts payable = 4% of annual sales
Long-term debt = $360,000
Common stock = $300,000 (no change)
Retained earnings = $720,000 plus any additional earnings during the year
Net income = 6% of annual sales and no dividends planned.

Cash	_____	Financing required	_____
Accounts receivable	_____	Accounts payable	_____
Inventory	_____	Long-term debt	_____
Fixed assets	_____	Common stock	_____
		Retained earnings	_____
Total assets	_____	Total debt & equity	_____

5-8 Given the following balance sheet changes, what change, if any, should appear in retained earnings?
marketable securities = +$3,000; inventories = +$10,000; depreciation = +$3,000; accounts payable = +$11,000; and notes payable = -$6,000

5-9 The balance sheet of the Sayer Company on December 31, 2000 is given below. The company's sales for 2000 were $100,000.

Cash	$ 2,000	Accounts payable	$ 10,000
Accounts receivable	17,000	Accruals	5,000
Inventories	20,000	Mortgage bonds	14,000
Fixed assets (net)	$30,000	Common stock	20,000
		Retained earnings	20,000
Total assets	$69,000	Total debt & equity	$69,000

The company's profit margin after taxes on sales is 4 percent, half of which is paid as dividends. Both mortgage bonds and common stock are expected to stay the same and all the other balance sheet items are expected to vary directly with sales. Sales are expected to be $160,000 for 2001.

(a) Prepare Sayer Company's balance items as a percent of sales for 2000. See Table 5-6 and Example 5-1 for help.
(b) What additional funds will be needed in 2001?

Part 3

WORKING CAPITAL MANAGEMENT

Part Three deals with the techniques for managing working capital, which refers to the firm's current assets and liabilities. Chapter 6 covers the theory of working capital management; Chapter 7 discusses current assets; and Chapter 8 discusses current liabilities. Current assets include cash, marketable securities, accounts receivable, and inventories. Current liabilities consist of trade credit, commercial paper, short-term bank loans, accounts receivable loans, and inventory loans.

6

AN OVERVIEW OF WORKING CAPITAL MANAGEMENT

In Part Three, we developed tools of analysis for long-term investment and financing decisions. This part places the emphasis of analysis on short-term accounts: current assets and current liabilities. Working capital, sometimes called gross working capital, simply refers to current assets. Net working capital is defined as current assets minus current liabilities. The management of current assets and current liabilities constitutes working capital management.

BASIC CONCEPTS OF WORKING CAPITAL MANAGEMENT

Current assets are defined as assets that are reasonably expected to be converted into cash and to be available for the operation of the business within one year. They are listed on the balance sheet in the order of their expected conversion into cash. Current liabilities are all liabilities to be paid within one year and listed on the balance sheet in the order of their probable liquidation.

Working capital management is important not only because it involves the largest proportion of the financial manager's time, but also because current assets represent more than half the total assets of a business firm. In addition, there is a close relationship between sales growth and the level of current assets. For example, increases in credit sales require more accounts receivable and inventories. Finally, working capital management is particularly important for small companies. It is possible for them to minimize their investments in fixed assets through leases, but it is practically impossible to avoid an investment in current assets.

The two important aspects of working capital management are (1) how to determine the optimal amount of investment in current assets, and (2) how to determine the appropriate mix of short-term and long-term capital. The optimal amount of investment in current assets is the level of current-asset holdings that maximizes the overall profitability of the firm. The appropriate mix of short-term and long-term capital is a particular combination of current liabilities and long-term debt that minimizes the company's overall cost of capital. Before we discuss these two aspects of working capital management in detail, we examine reasons for investing in current assets.

Operating Cycle

All business firms go through a period of organization during which the owners make an investment, acquire plant and equipment, purchase raw materials, and hire workers. If companies expect to increase their sales and profits, their assets should be expanded. Success requires that new investments be made not only in fixed assets but also in current assets. Additional current liabilities, long-term debt, and equity funds are needed to finance these needs. Current asset management and current liability management go hand in hand because increases in short-term assets should usually be financed by short-term capital. The operating cycle explains the interrelationship between current assets and current liabilities. Figure 6-1 below outlines the elements of the Operating Cycle (OC).

Figure 6-1
Operating Cycle

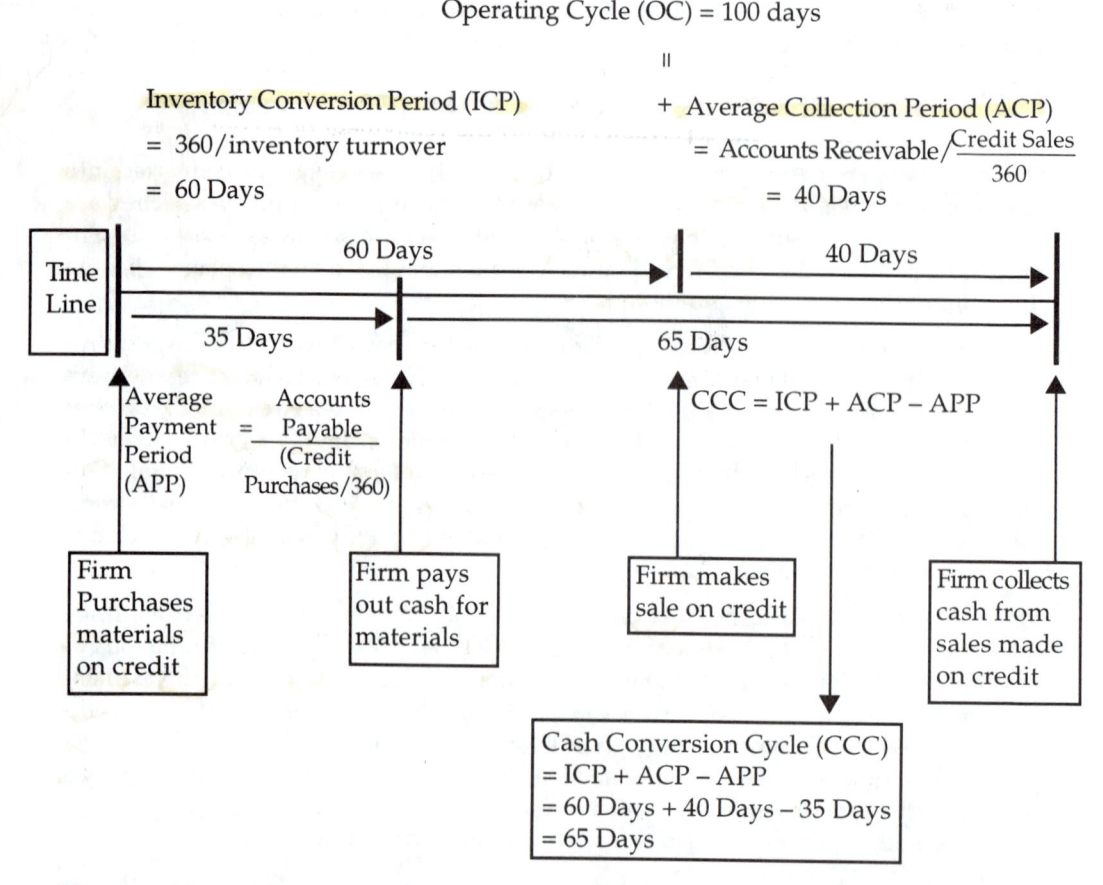

Operating Cycle (OC) = 100 days
||

Inventory Conversion Period (ICP) + Average Collection Period (ACP)
= 360/inventory turnover = Accounts Receivable/$\frac{\text{Credit Sales}}{360}$
= 60 Days = 40 Days

Time Line:
- 60 Days | 40 Days
- 35 Days | 65 Days

Average Payment Period (APP) = $\frac{\text{Accounts Payable}}{\text{(Credit Purchases/360)}}$

CCC = ICP + ACP − APP

- Firm Purchases materials on credit
- Firm pays out cash for materials
- Firm makes sale on credit
- Firm collects cash from sales made on credit

Cash Conversion Cycle (CCC)
= ICP + ACP − APP
= 60 Days + 40 Days − 35 Days
= 65 Days

The **operating cycle** is the length of time that elapses from the point when the firm purchases raw materials and other inputs into the production process until the point when it collects cash from the sale of its finished product. As shown above, the cycle consists of the inventory conversion period and the average collection period. For example, suppose Jason Corporation (see Figure 6-1), a shoe manufacturer, sells all its

Chapter 6: An Overview of Working Capital Management

merchandise on credit and on average its customers pay off their accounts in 40 days. If it takes Jason Corporation an average of 60 days from the time it buys raw materials and other inputs until it sells the finished product, then the operating cycle is 100 days. Also, If Jason buys all its materials on credit and pays the accounts after about 35 days, then 65 days elapse from the time cash leaves the firm until cash flows back in. This information is important to management since this cash conversion period is the time period during which money is tied up and sufficient funds or financing must be available on the right-hand side of the balance sheet to cover the investment on the asset side. During this time period, Jason must count on either unsecured or secured short-term bank loans. Ideally, the firm would perfer to buy its production inputs on credit, then make, sell, and collect on its customers' accounts before its bill for the original inputs comes due. If this were the case, the cash conversion period would be negative since the average payment period would exceed the operating cycle. In the Jason Corporation example, if the operating cycle equaled 30 days then the cash conversion period would be a negative 5 days or (CCC = OC of 30 days minus APP of 35 days). Unfortunately, this is generally not the case for most manufacturing firms.

Ordinarily, the operating cycle starts with short-term bank loans or trade credit and ends with the repayment of these loans. In other words, the operating cycle represents the amount of time that the firm's cash is tied up in its operation. Normally, the operating cycle consists of several steps: (1) the purchase of raw materials on credit; (2) the conversion of raw materials into finished goods; (3) the sale of finished goods on credit; (4) the collection of accounts receivable; and (5) the repayment of accounts payable. This operating cycle indicates what gives rise to differences in the amount and timing of cash flows. Table 6-1 shows such an operating cycle.

The company purchases raw materials on credit in the first period. Thus, both accounts payable and inventory increase simultaneously. If the company's current assets exceed its current liabilities, this transaction would decrease both the current ratio and the quick ratio. In the second period, raw materials are transformed into finished goods. If we ignore production costs such as labor, this event would change only the form of inventories from raw materials to finished goods. Because the company must spend some money on labor to transform raw materials into finished goods, its accrued wages should increase or its cash holdings should decline. It is also possible that this event

Table 6-1
Operating Cycle: Changes in Balance Sheet Items

Accounts	Period 1 Purchase	Period 2 Transfer	Period 3 Sell	Period 4 Collect	Period 5 Repay
Accounts payable	+				-
Inventory: raw materials	+	-			
Inventory: finished goods		+	-		
Accounts receivable			+	-	
Cash				+	-

96   PART 3: WORKING CAPITAL MANAGEMENT

causes accrued wages to rise and cash holdings to fall simultaneously. But it is important to recognize that finished goods can be used as collateral for short-term loans.

The sale of finished goods on credit in the third period reduces inventories and increases accounts receivable. Inventories are sold on credit with the markup reflected as retained earnings. Hence, this transaction causes the debt ratio to decline and the current ratio to rise. However, the third period represents the peak in financing requirements. The collection of accounts receivable in the fourth period increases cash holdings and reduces accounts receivables. This cash is used to pay off the accounts payable and other loans in the fifth period and thus the company is in a highly liquid position.

Retailers and wholesalers avoid the manufacturing portion of the operating cycle. Normally, service companies do not have the inventory problem. It is also important to note that management can, within limits, alter the time required to complete the operating cycle. The use of overtime can reduce the time required to complete the production process. Aggressive selling techniques and more lenient credit terms may immediately lower the time required to convert inventories into accounts receivable. Greater cash discounts and tighter collection policies may considerably reduce the time required to convert accounts receivable into cash. All such policy changes require additional costs. Thus, companies should reduce the operating cycle until the marginal revenue generated thereby equals the marginal cost; at this point they maximize their profits.

Risk-Return Tradeoffs: Current Assets and Liabilities

A tradeoff exists between risk and profitability. The degree of risk and the level of profitability depend upon the amount of investment in current assets and the amount of current liabilities used in the operation of the business. Thus, the profitability associated with various levels of current assets and current liabilities should be evaluated relative to the risk associated with those levels. Profitability is measured by profits after taxes, while risk is measured by the probability that a company will be unable to pay its obligations as they come due. Risk-return tradeoffs and alternative working capital policies with respect to the levels of current assets and current liabilities are illustrated in Table 6-2.

Table 6-2
Profitability and Risk of Alternative Working Capital Policies

Classification	Amount	Resulting Profitability	Resulting Risk	Alternative Policies
Current Assets	High	Low	Low	Conservative
Current Liabilities	Low	Low	Low	Conservative
Current Assets	Moderate	Moderate	Moderate	Moderate
Current Liabilities	Moderate	Moderate	Moderate	Moderate
Current Assets	Low	High	High	Aggressive
Current Liabilities	High	High	High	Aggressive

Chapter 6: An Overview of Working Capital Management

The underlying foundation concept that explains this risk-return tradeoff is simple. Long-term investments or the commitment of funds for longer periods of time face greater risk because the future is uncertain and this uncertainty grows the further into the future we look. So a higher return on long-term investment is necessary to compensate long-term investors for higher risk. Therefore, on the left-hand side of the balance sheet, investment in fixed or long-term assets are riskier and generally earn a higher return; thereby using the same logic, investments in short-term assets would be safer and earn a lower return. Likewise, if the firm has a high proportion of total assets in the short-term category, risk is lower since its liquidity is higher making it more certain about its ability to pay bills as they come due. If this logic is rational when analyzing the asset side of the balance sheet, then it should also hold true for the right-hand side. But on the right-hand side, we must take the viewpoint of outside investors looking in. For example, when a stockholder buys stock in a company, it appears on the stockholder's books as an asset. Or if a creditor like a bank makes a loan to the firm, this liability (or notes payable) on the firm's balance sheet would appear as an asset (or notes receivable) on the bank's books. Transferring this logic to the right-hand side of the firm's balance sheet, the firm's long-term debt (or long term assets to the lenders) or equity (long-term assets on the stockholders' books) must carry a higher rate of return to compensate the providers of capital for the greater risk. Similarly, the less risky short-term debt (or short-term assets to the lenders) ought to carry a lower return. And since the return earned by the lenders and stockholders is equal to the cost of financing to the firm, generally short-term liabilities carry lower interest cost while the cost of long-term funds is more expensive.

To illustrate a risk-return tradeoff, let us assume that the amount of the firm's total assets is constant and that the amount of its current assets or current liabilities varies. As shown in Table 6-2, a higher level of current assets coupled with a lower level of current liabilities portrays a conservative working capital management policy. The greater the proportion of current assets to total assets, the lower the profitability and the lower the degree of risk. As the ratio of current assets to total assets rises, the firm's profitability falls because current assets are less profitable than fixed assets. The risk of not being able to pay bills as they come due decreases because the increase in current assets improves the firm's liquidity position. As the ratio of current liabilities to total assets decreases, the firm's profitability and its risk both fall. A reduction in current liabilities may compel the firm to borrow heavily on a long-term basis. Long-term debt and equity are more expensive than short-term debt and consequently reduce the firm's profitability. If the firm's current assets remain unchanged, its net working capital increases as its current liabilities decrease. A rise in net working capital means a decrease in overall risk.

A low level of current assets alongside a high level of current liabilities provides an aggressive working capital management approach. The smaller the proportion of current assets to total assets, the higher the rate of return and the higher the degree of risk. As the ratio of current assets to total assets decreases, the firm's profitability increases because fixed assets produce greater returns than current assets. The risk of technical insolvency also increases because the firm's net working capital decreases with the decrease in current assets. When the ratio of current assets to total assets is low, the greater profitability is essential to compensate for possible lost sales, lost customer goodwill, and bad credit ratings caused by poor liquidity ratios. As the ratio of current liabilities to total assets increases, both the firm's profitability and its risk increase. Its profitability increases because short-term debt is typically less costly than long-term debt. Its risk increases with the increase in current liabilities for two reasons: (1) short-term interest rates fluctuate more widely than long-term

98   PART 3: WORKING CAPITAL MANAGEMENT

interest rates; (2) if short-term loans come due or come up for renewal when earnings are low, the firm may find it impossible to repay them or difficult to refinance them.

Moderate levels of current assets and current liabilities would result in intermediate levels of profitability and risk between the conservative and aggressive policies.

Combined Effects

We can determine the combined effects of changes in current assets and changes in current liabilities on profitability and risk by considering them simultaneously.

Example 6-1. The Temple Company has $5,000 of fixed assets and this amount is expected to remain the same for the period under review. The company intends to choose one of the following working capital policies for the coming year: (1) a conservative policy that calls for $6,000 of current assets and no short-term debt; (2) an intermediate policy that calls for $5,000 of current assets and $2,500 of short-term debt; or (3) an aggressive policy that calls for $4,000 of current assets and $4,500 of short-term debt. The company requires its total debt to be 50 percent of its total assets. It expects sales of $20,000 and its rate of return before interest and taxes on the sales is expected to be 10 percent.

Table 6-3 illustrates the three working capital policies and shows the alternative effects on profitability as measured by the rate of return on equity and the alternative effects on

Table 6-3
**Combined Effects of Changes in Current Assets
and Liabilities on Profitability and Risk for Alternative Policies**

	Conservative	Intermediate	Aggressive
Current assets	$ 6,000	$ 5,000	$ 4,000
Fixed assets	5,000	5,000	5,000
Total assets	$11,000	$10,000	$ 9,000
Current liabilities (5%)	$ 0	$ 2,500	$ 4,500
Long-term debt (10%)	5,500	2,500	0
Total debt	$ 5,500	$ 5,000	$ 4,500
Equity	5,500	5,000	4,500
Total liabilities and net worth	$11,000	$10,000	$ 9,000
Sales in dollars	$20,000	$20,000	$20,000
EBIT	2,000	2,000	2,000
Less: interest	550	375	225
Taxable income	$ 1,450	$ 1,625	$ 1,775
Less: tax (50%)	725	812.5	887.5
Earnings on equity	$ 725	$ 812.5	$ 887.5
Rate of return on equity	13.2%	16.3%	19.7%
Current ratio	Infinite	2.00:1	0.89:1

Chapter 6: An Overview of Working Capital Management

risk as measured by the current ratio. The conservative policy provides the company with the lowest rate of return on equity but gives it the highest current ratio. It is important to note that under this working policy, the current ratio is infinitely high. Although we recognize that the company would have some spontaneous credit such as accounts payable, the current ratio would still be very high. In contrast, the aggressive policy provides the company with the highest rate of return on equity but gives it the lowest current ratio.

In theory, it is possible to determine precisely the optimum working capital policy, but in practice, it is very difficult. The **optimum working capital policy** refers to the amount of investment in current assets and the level of current liabilities to be employed that will maximize the market value of the company's common stock. A determination of the optimum policy would require unobtainable information on a complex set of variables. However, management can establish guidelines to determine an appropriate amount for each type of current asset. It also can examine the various types of short-term debt and their effects on the cost of capital.

ALTERNATIVE FINANCING PLANS

Although the operating cycle does not tell us the level of current assets to be maintained, it provides us with the rationale for investing in current assets. Current assets consist of permanent current assets and temporary current assets.

Ordinarily, cash, accounts receivable, and inventories rarely drop to zero. Hence, a part of the current asset category becomes a permanent investment in the firm. **Permanent current assets** are a minimum level of current assets that the firm must always maintain. Minimum cash balances and safety stocks of inventories are a part of permanent current assets. As the company grows in size, sales, and output over the long-run, its permanent current assets must also increase.

Temporary current assets are current assets that fluctuate with sales. These assets fluctuate with seasonal patterns whose durations are less than a year. Some industries such as the canning industry, the clothing industry, and the farm industry depend heavily upon sales at a certain time of the year. As the company gears production to meet the seasonal peak, it needs large sums of money to finance inventories and to meet related financial requirements. When the season ends, the financial need also declines on a decreasing scale until all of the accounts receivable are collected.

Earlier, it was noted that the way to finance current assets involves a tradeoff between risk and profitability. However, it is important to remember that spontaneous sources of short-term credit such as accounts payable and accruals are not active decision variables. Accounts payable and accruals tend to increase spontaneously with sales and to finance a part of the buildup in current assets. Thus, the financial manager is usually concerned with how current assets not supported by these spontaneous sources of credit are financed.

One financing plan utilizes a **matching principle** where the firm matches the maturity structure of its assets with the maturity structure of liabilities and equity. In other words, the firm should finance its short-term financial needs with short-term funds and its long-term financial needs with long-term funds. Under this approach, temporary current assets or current assets with seasonable variations would be financed with short-term sources of funds such as short-term bank loans. On the other hand, permanent current assets and fixed assets would be financed with long-term sources of funds such as long-term debt or equity funds.

It is desirable to finance a five-year machine with a five-year bank loan, to finance accounts receivable with an average collection period of 20 days with a 20-day bank loan, and so on. To illustrate, assume that a firm finances its temporary current assets with a 20-year bank loan. If the expected net cash flows occur, the firm may have to pay interest on this debt when the funds are not needed. On the other hand, suppose that the firm finances its five-year machine with a three-month bank note. The expected net cash flows from the machine would not be sufficient to pay off the loan at the end of three months. Therefore, the loan must be renewed. The financial manager must consider a number of worst possible occurrences with respect to the renewal of this loan. The bank may refuse to renew the loan, demand an extremely high interest, or impose highly restrictive provisions in exchange for the renewal of the loan. If the machine is financed by long-term debt, the company would have no renewal problem and its cash flows would be sufficient to retire the loan.

Figure 6-2 illustrates the synchronization of the asset maturity with the liability maturity. If total financing requirements behave in the manner shown, only the short-term fluctuations at the top of the figure would be financed with short-term sources of funds.

Some companies may elect a more conservative approach (see Figure 6-3) by financing all of their permanent assets plus a portion of their temporary current assets with long-

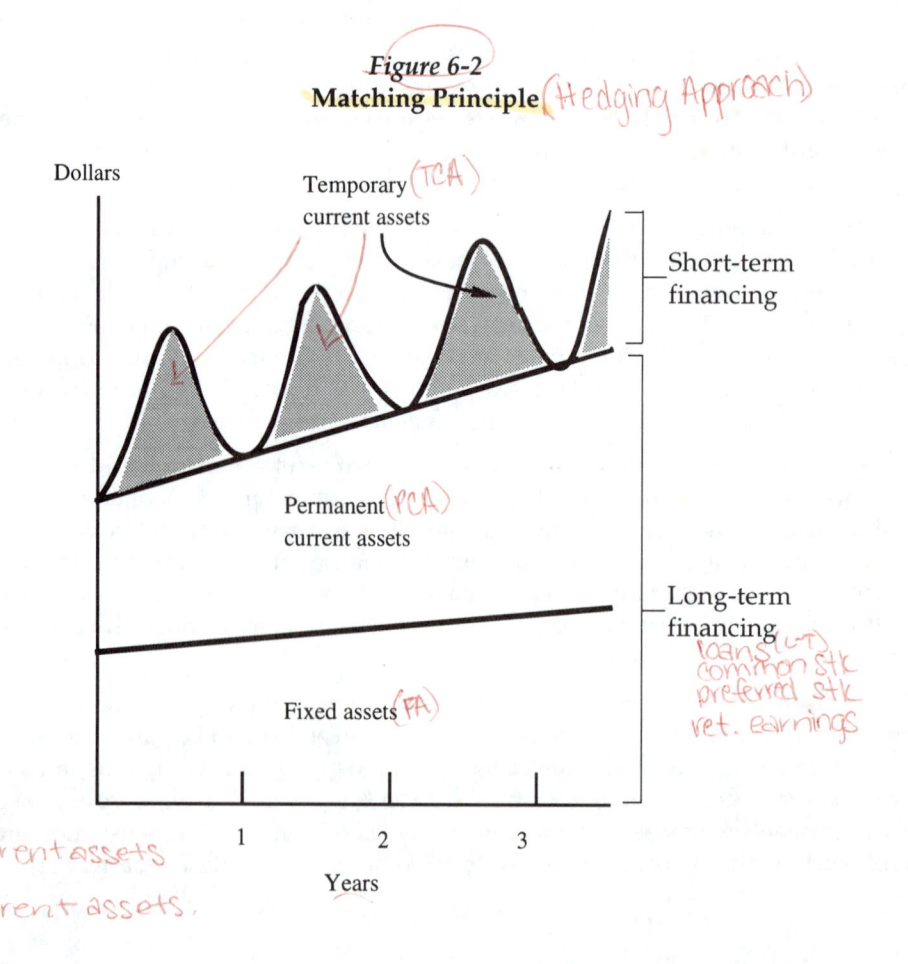

Figure 6-2
Matching Principle

term funds. Such a margin of safety may be desirable to offset expected adverse fluctuations in cash flows under conditions of uncertainty. Adverse fluctuations in the business cycle may make short-term loans very difficult or even practically impossible to obtain. A drawback of this approach occurs when adverse fluctuations in net cash flows do not occur and the firm ends up paying interest on this debt when the funds are not needed. For example, at time 1 in Figure 6-3, the firm is paying interest on long-term funds (represented by distance ab) that are not needed. This added expense reduces profitability and risk.

On the other hand, some other companies may take the more aggressive financing route (see Figure 6-4) and finance all of their temporary current assets plus a portion of their permanent current assets with short-term credit. At time 1, the distance ab now represents that portion of permanent funding needs that is dependent on obtaining short-term credit. This option results in lower interest expense, higher profitability, and higher risk. Suppose that the firm finances its five-year machine with a three-month bank note. The expected net cash flows from the machine would not be sufficient to pay off the loan at the end of three months. Therefore, the loan must be renewed. The financial manager must consider a number of worst possible occurrences with respect to the renewal of this loan. The bank may refuse to renew the loan, demand an extremely high interest, or

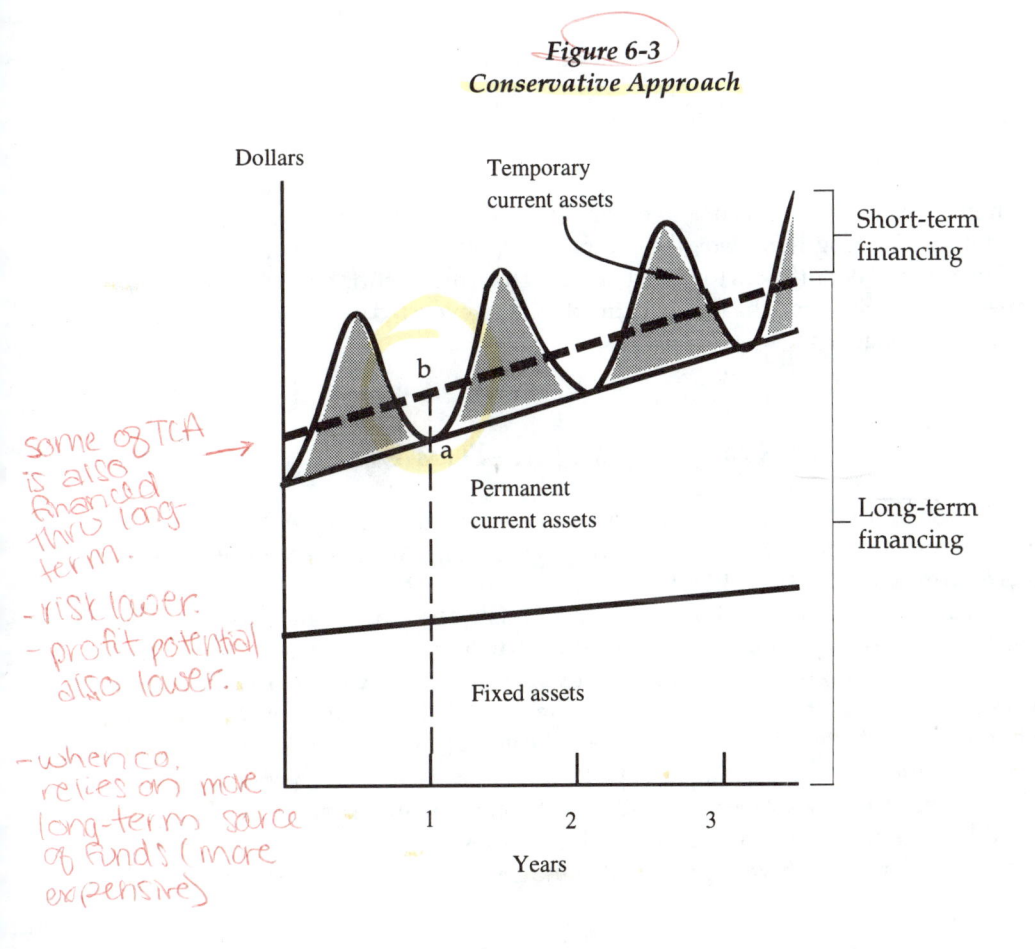

Figure 6-3
Conservative Approach

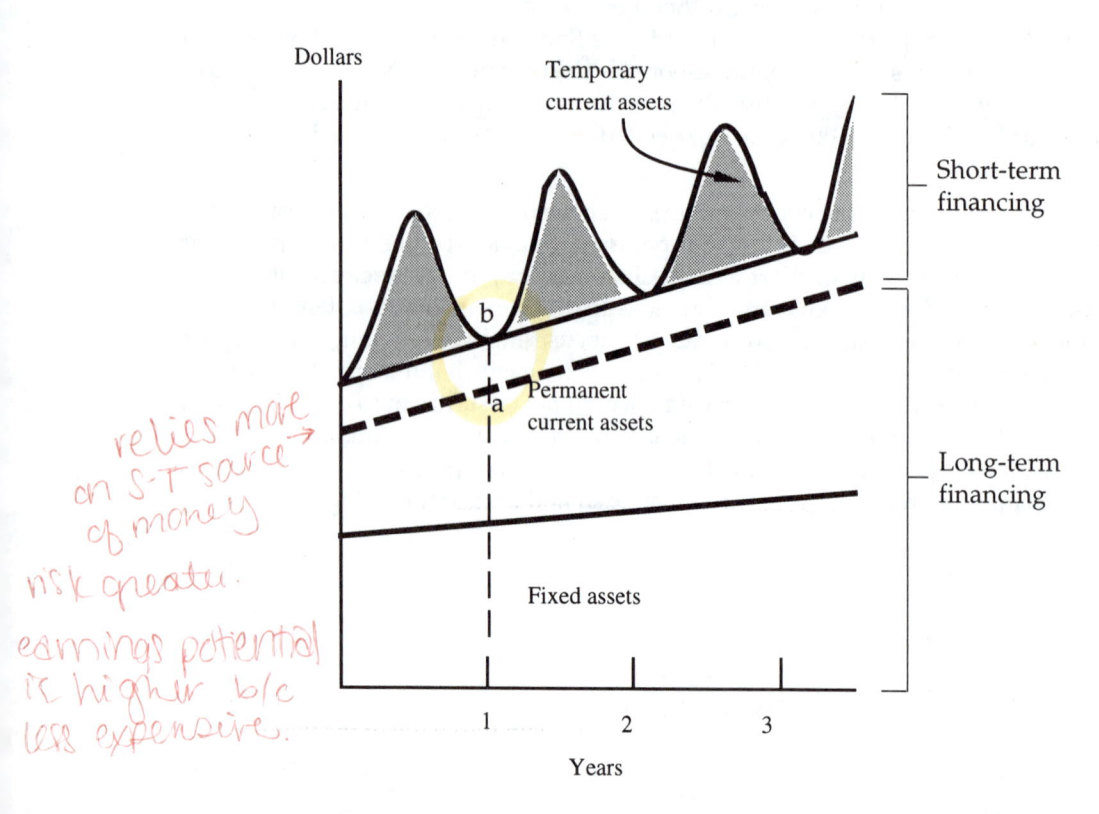

Figure 6-4
Aggressive Approach

(Figure shows temporary current assets as peaks financed by short-term financing, with permanent current assets and fixed assets financed by long-term financing, over years 1, 2, 3.)

Handwritten margin note: relies more on S-T source of money → risk greater. earnings potential is higher b/c less expensive.

impose highly restrictive provisions in exchange for the renewal of the loan. If the machine is financed by long-term debt, the company would have no renewal problem and its cash flows would be sufficient to retire the loan. Thus, the maturity-matching policy of a firm depends heavily upon the risk associated with its expected cash flows and the risk preference of management.

SHORT-TERM VERSUS LONG-TERM DEBT

While there are times when interest rates on short-term loans are higher than those on long-term loans, short-term rates are usually less than long-term rates. This is because short-term loans are less risky. Thus, the financial manager should balance this interest differential against the firm's willingness to accept risk. The mix of long-term debt and short-term debt is greatly influenced by the term structure of interest rates, which represents the relationship between the maturity of debt and its yield (cost). The **term structure of interest rates** at any given time is characterized by a yield curve. The yield curve identifies the linear relationship between the yield-to-maturity (YTM) on the vertical axis and time on the horizontal. The yield curve shows this relationship at a point in time and generally uses treasury bonds for the comparison. A treasury bond is a piece of debt that has a time to maturity and an interest rate. For example, if the U.S. treasury (borrower) sells a 5-year bond, with annual interest payments, $1000 par, with

Chapter 6: An Overview of Working Capital Management

a 10% coupon or contract rate, the borrower contracts to pay the buyer (or lender) end-of-year interest payments of $100 (or 10% of par) a year for 5 consecutive years and pay the bondholder the $1000 principal at the end of the 5 years.

The goal of the yield curve analysis is to isolate the effect of time to maturity on the interest rate or YTM. So the interest here is to seal off all other possible effects on YTM except for time. As an example, assume that a researcher is interested in examining the effects of smoking on the likelihood of getting cancer. In designing the experiment, the researcher would statistically compare the incidence rate of cancer on a sample of non-smokers with a sample of smokers, expecting to find a higher rate of cancer among the smoking group. Would the researcher select people from all different ages and occupations to place in the samples? Obviously not, since age and occupation could have an effect on the probability of one getting cancer, the researcher's results would be contaminated by these other effects making it impossible to isolate just the sole effect of smoking. To correct the problem, the researcher would choose samples that were identical in every way possible except for one smoked and the other did not. Transferring this logic to the yield curve analysis, we are interested in examining "only" the effect of time on YTM. Would we use corporate bonds to do the analysis? Absolutely not, since corporate bonds bear varying levels of default risk; that is, the possibility that the firm might not be able to pay the contracted interest and principal to the lender when it comes due. Since treasury bonds have no default risk (because the federal government has the power to print money if necessary to pay lenders), yield curve analysis of these treasury securities can accurately isolate the relationship of YTM and time. To produce the yield curve, we compute the YTM on the 1-year T-bond, 2-year T-bond, 3-year T-bond, and so on. Then we plot the corresponding YTM-year points on a graph as shown in Figure 6-5. There are three main theories used to explain the shape of the yield curve: expectation theory, liquidity preference theory, and market segmentation theory.

The **expectation theory** states that yield curves reflect investors' expectations of future short-term interest rates. In other words, expectations about future short-term rates are used to predict the shape of the yield curve.

Figure 6-5
Expectation Theory and Yield Curves

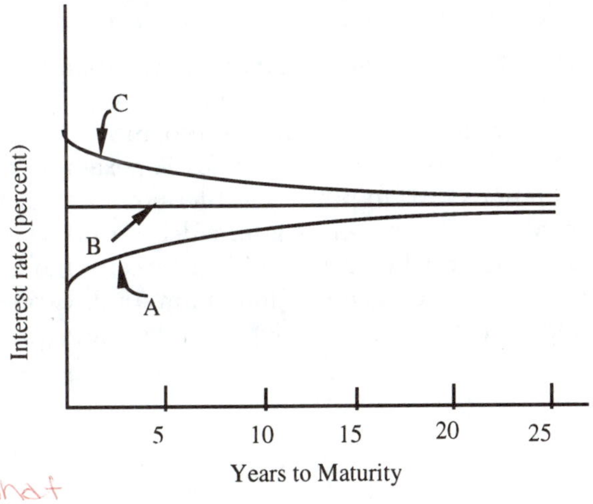

Figure 6-5 shows three possible shapes of the yield curve. **Curve A**, the upward sloping curve, depicts the normal yield curve. In this case lenders and borrowers expect future short-term rates to rise. This expectation motivates them to carry out certain actions which make their expectation come true. For example, expecting interest rates to rise, borrowers try to borrow long-term by selling long-term bonds. The excess supply pushes long-term bond prices down and yields up, thus fulfilling their expectations. Similarly, lenders worried about their long-term bond prices falling when interest rates rise quickly try to sell long- and buy short-term bonds. This activity pushes the prices on long bonds down and yields up and forces the price of short bonds up and yields down, thereby explaining the upward sloping curve.

Curve C, the downward sloping curve, depicts the inverted yield curve. In this case lenders and borrowers expect future short-term rates to fall. For example, waiting for interest rates to fall, borrowers seeking short-term loans sell short-term bonds. The excess supply of short-term bonds pushes short-term bond prices down and yields up, thus fulfilling their expectations. On the other hand, lenders hoping to gain on their long-term bond when interest rates fall, quickly try to buy long- and sell short-term bonds. This activity pushes the prices on long bonds up and yields down and forces the price of short bonds down and yields up, thereby explaining the downward sloping curve.

Flat yield curves such as B in Figure 6-5 exist when future short-term interest rates are expected to stay the same. In this case, lenders and borrowers expect future short-term interest rates to remain the same.

The **liquidity preference theory** asserts that long-term loans command higher rates of return because they involve more risk than short-term loans. This theory explains the traditional upward-sloping or normal yield curve. In essence, lenders require a liquidity premium in the way of extra yield to compensate them for having to wait longer periods of time before liquidation of their bond at maturity. Likewise, this liquidity premium compensates the lender for two types of risk that increase with time to maturity: default risk and interest rate risk. The **default risk** is the possibility that interest and principal payments will not be made on schedule. The longer the maturity of a loan, the higher the possibility of being unable to pay off the loan and interest. The **interest rate risk** is the possibility that interest rates will continue to increase after loans have been made. If interest rates continue to increase, the long-term lender suffers the financial sacrifice of foregoing more profitable uses for his or her money.

The **market segmentation theory** implies that there are separate markets for each maturity, and that interest rate differentials are determined by supply and demand conditions in the various maturity markets. This theory recognizes that different investors prefer to invest in debt securities of different maturities. For example, commercial banks and nonfinancial corporations tend to prefer short-term debt securities, while insurance companies and pension funds prefer long-term debt securities. For example, low rates in the short-term segment (when demand for short-term funds is less than supply) along with high rates (when demand for long-term funds exceeds supply) in the long-term segment help explain the upward sloping or normal yield curve.

Summary

Working capital management covers all areas of the administration of both current assets and current liabilities. The operating cycle indicates that cash inflows are not matched in both timing and amount by cash outflows, thereby giving the rationale for investment in working capital. Management must decide the level of current assets to be held and the way these assets are financed. These two types of decisions involve tradeoffs between risk and profitability.

The greater the ratio of current assets to total assets, the less the risk of technical insolvency and the less the profitability. In contrast, the lower the ratio of current assets to total assets, the higher the risk of cash insolvency and the higher the rate of return. Although the amount and composition of current assets to be maintained vary with sales, they depend considerably upon the risk preference of management. Conservative companies are likely to hold relatively large stocks of current assets, while aggressive companies are likely to hold relatively small stocks of current assets. The same is true of types of current assets. Conservative companies are more likely than aggressive companies to maintain more liquid current assets such as cash and marketable securities.

The greater the ratio of current liabilities to total assets, the higher the rate of return and the higher the risk. The lower the ratio of current liabilities to total assets, the lower the rate of return and the lower the risk. The composition and amount of current liabilities are also policy matters. If the firm elects to operate aggressively, it borrows heavily on a short-term basis. This aggressive policy would increase the expected rate of return because short-term debt is less costly. However, short-term loans are subject to the risk of fluctuating interest rates and refunding or renewal problems.

One working capital policy calls for matching asset and liability maturities. In other words, short-term needs are financed with short-term funds, while long-term needs are financed with long-term funds. Although it is possible to synchronize the maturity structure of current assets with current liabilities precisely under conditions of certainty, it usually is not possible under conditions of uncertainty. Under conditions of uncertainty, some companies may wish to finance a portion of their temporary current assets with long-term funds to allow for adverse fluctuations in cash flows. Management's risk preferences are also an important factor that affects the way assets are financed. Conservative managers are likely to rely more heavily on long-term funds than aggressive managers.

List of Key Terms

current assets
permanent current assets
matching principle
expectation theory
default risk
market segmentation theory

operating or cash cycle
temporary current assets
term structure of interest rates
liquidity preference theory
interest rate risk

PROBLEMS

6-1 A company has $500,000 of sales and earns 10 percent or $50,000 before taxes on these sales. Its total assets are $200,000, of which $50,000 are current assets and $150,000 are fixed assets. The firm's tax rate is 40 percent and its short-term borrowing rate is 5 percent.

(a) What are earnings after taxes?
(b) What is the after-tax rate of return on total assets?
(c) If the company increases its current assets by $50,000 through short-term loans making total assets $250,000, what would be the new after-tax rate of return on total assets? (Assume that everything else remains constant).

6-2 A company's ratio of current assets to sales has been 80 percent for the past ten years. The financial manager has decided to formulate some alternative policies based on current assets at 30, 50, and 70 percent of sales for next year. Sales are expected to be $200,000 and earnings after taxes are forecast to be 10 percent of sales. Fixed assets totaling $50,000 remain the same for each alternative. Determine the rate of return on total assets under each of these three alternatives.

6-3 A firm has $200,000 of total assets and earns 20 percent before interest and taxes on these assets. The ratio of total debts to total assets has been set at 50 percent. The cost of short-term debt is 7 percent, while the cost of long-term debt is 10 percent. A conservative policy calls for only long-term debt; an intermediate policy calls for 50 percent short-term debt and 50 percent long-term debt; and an aggressive policy calls for 100% short-term debt. The firm's tax rate is 50 percent. See Example 6-1 and Table 6-3 for help.

(a) What is the rate of return on equity under each of these three policies?
(b) If current assets are 50 percent of total assets, what is the current ratio under each of these three policies?

6-4 A company has $1 million of fixed assets and requires its total debt to be 50 percent of its total assets. Two alternative working capital policies are as follows: alternative A calls for $1 million of current assets and $100,000 of short-term debt, while alternative B calls for $400,000 of current assets and $500,000 of short-term debt. The cost of short-term debt is 5 percent, whereas the cost of long-term debt is 10 percent. The firm's tax rate is 50 percent. Earnings before interest and taxes are expected to be $200,000. Calculate the current ratio and the rate of return on equity. See Example 6-1 and Table 6-3 for help.

6-5 Canton Toy Company has the following balance sheet.

Cash	$2,000	Accounts payable	$ 10,000
Marketable securities	1,000	Notes payable	4,000
Accounts receivable	10,000	Accrued wages	2,000
Inventories	7,000	Current liabilities	16,000
		Long-term debt	$10,000
Current assets	$20,000	Common stock	8,000
Fixed assets	$20,000	Retained earnings	6,000
Total	$40,000	Total	$40,000

(a) Determine Canton's net working capital.
(b) If Canton increases sales by $40,000, it would require another $12,000 of working capital. Trade credit would finance 25 percent of this increase. How should the rest of the working capital be financed to maintain the current financial structure between short-term and long-term financing?
(c) How could Canton adopt a more aggressive working capital strategy?

6-6 A company has sales of $100,000 on which it earns 20 percent before interest and taxes. The firm has $20,000 in fixed assets and $30,000 in current assets.

(a) Compute the asset turnover and the pretax rate of return on assets.
(b) If the company reduces its current assets to $10,000, what would be its pretax return on assets?
(c) If the company increases its current assets to $50,000, what would be its pretax return on assets?

6-7 A company requires $1 in current assets for each $5 of sales. If the company has a net profit margin of 10 percent and the level of fixed assets does not change, what will be the amount of external financing required? Assume that sales increase from $100,000 to $200,000 and that all earnings are retained.

6-8 A company expects next year's sales to be $100,000 if the economy is strong, $70,000 if the economy is steady, and $50,000 if the economy is weak. Assume there is a 40 percent probability that the economy will be strong, a 10 percent probability of a steady economy, and a 50 percent probability of a weak economy. What is the expected level of sales for next year?

7

CURRENT ASSET MANAGEMENT

In Chapter 6 we discussed the overall problems involved in working capital management. In this chapter we focus our attention on the company's investment in specific current assets: cash, marketable securities, accounts receivable, and inventories. Because cash and marketable securities are the company's most liquid assets, the financial manager must place the primary emphasis on safety and liquidity in the management of these assets. Here we present techniques for improving the efficiency of cash management and study the investment of excess funds in marketable securities. As we move to accounts receivable and inventories, profitability becomes more important. The management of accounts receivable involves credit standards, credit terms, and collection policies. Each of these areas will be discussed, with primary emphasis on how they can be varied to obtain the optimum investment. Because inventories represent a large proportion of the total assets for most companies, major attention is given to the development of a basic model for inventory control.

CASH MANAGEMENT

Cash provides the firm with the ability to pay bills as they come due, but it is not an earning asset. Thus, it is very important for the company to determine an optimal level of investment in cash. The major sources of cash flow into the firm are cash sales, collections on accounts receivable, sales of new securities, loans from banks or non-bank financial institutions, and advance cash payments on contracts. In contrast, cash outflows are necessary for interest and dividend payments, retirement of debt and other securities, income tax payments, payments on accounts payable, wages and salaries, and purchases of fixed assets.

The overall efficiency of cash management depends on various collection and disbursement policies. To maximize available cash, the firm must speed up its collection process and delay its payments. Hence, it must consider these two policies simultaneously to improve its overall cash management efficiency.

Motives for Holding Cash

John M. Keynes suggested that there are three main reasons why households and businesses prefer to hold cash rather than other forms of assets: the transaction motive, the precautionary motive, and the speculative motive.

The **transaction motive** relates to the need for cash in order to carry on routine activities. Businesses need certain average levels of cash and deposits to make ordinary day-to-day transactions. If cash inflows and cash outflows were always synchronized perfectly with respect to time, such idle cash balances would not be necessary. Because this synchronization does not usually occur, companies must have some cash on hand. The **precautionary motive** relates to the need for cash to meet any rainy-day contingencies that might arise. Particularly relevant are such risks as strikes and the business failures of important customers. Precautionary balances can be held in marketable securities such as Treasury bills and commercial paper. The **speculative motive** relates to the holding of cash in order to take advantage of profit-making opportunities. Suppose that the rate of interest is low and bond prices are high. Individuals and businesses are likely to withhold a part of their savings that would otherwise flow into the money market or the stock market, because they expect that the interest rate will rise in the future and bond prices will fall. However, most companies do not hold cash to take advantage of expected changes in interest rates and security prices. Many individual investors do hold cash for such speculative purposes.

These three motives for money obviously depend on the level of money income and the rate of interest. The greater the money income, the greater the ability of the firm to hold cash. The higher the rate of interest, the higher the cost to hold cash relative to other assets.

Float

Float refers to the status of funds in the process of collection. Float can be viewed as the period of time that elapses from the point that a payer writes and sends out a check to make a payment to a payee until the funds are actually withdrawn from the payer's checking account. Nearly all aspects of cash management are associated with the concept of float. Thus, a thorough understanding of float is essential to effectively evaluate the collection and disbursement procedures of any cash management system. For purposes of measurement and analysis, we can break down float into five categories:

1. **Invoicing float** refers to funds tied up in the process of preparing invoices. Because this float is largely under the direct control of the company, it can be reduced through more efficient clerical procedures.
2. **Mail float** includes funds tied up from the time customers mail their remittance checks until the company receives them.
3. **Processing float** consists of funds tied up in the process of sorting and recording remittance checks until they can be deposited in the bank. Like invoicing float, this float is under the company's internal control and thus can be reduced through more efficient clerical procedures.
4. **Transit float** involves funds tied up from the time remittance checks are deposited until these funds become usable to the company. This float occurs because it takes several days for deposited checks to clear through the commercial banking system.
5. **Disbursing float** refers to funds available in the company's bank account until its payment check clears.

The Acceleration of Collection

There are three useful techniques which the financial manager can use to speed cash flows into the firm: lock box system, concentration banking, and pre-authorized checks. Although the firm cannot persuade its customers to pay their bills more promptly, it can often reduce the size of the float—the difference between the amount of deposit and the amount of available funds in a bank. To illustrate this, assume that the Mink Company in New York sells a mink coat to a customer in Los Angeles by mail. It takes about three days for the check to arrive in New York after the customer drops it into a Los Angeles mailbox. The company needs a day to process the check, and should wait two more days to have the funds available for disbursement, because it usually takes two days for the check to clear through the commercial banking system. Thus, the company would be able to use the funds about six days after the check was mailed.

Lock-Box System

One way to speed up this process in many cities is to rent post-office lock boxes. The company instructs its customers to send their payments to the lock box in their city. The company authorizes a bank of its choice in each of these cities to pick up the checks daily and credit them to its account. The bank microfilms the checks for record purposes and begins the clearing process. If checks are drawn on and deposited in the same bank, they are cleared by transferring funds from one account to another. If only two banks are involved in the same city, they exchange their checks directly with each other. Once the checks are cleared in the local area, the bank remits balances over a certain amount by wire to the firm's main bank or its bank of deposit. This procedure enables the firm to reduce the period that elapses between the time customers pay their bills and the moment it has the use of the funds.

Concentration Banking

Another way to speed up the collection process is to use geographically dispersed collection centers. Customers are instructed to remit their payments to a center in their city. When payments are received, they are deposited in a local bank close to the collection center. These local banks then transfer surplus funds to the company's concentration bank or banks. The company maintains a major account with its concentration bank, usually a disbursement account. Thus, it uses the concentration bank not only for the collection of payments but also for disbursements. The funds are usually unavailable to the company until its concentration bank collects the checks. The use of concentration banking allows the company to save time in both mailing and clearing customer payments.

Pre-Authorized Checks

Pre-authorized checks (PACs) are a commercial demand deposit instrument, which is used to transfer funds from an individual to a company. PACs are similar to ordinary checks, but do not require the signature of the individual on whose account they are being drawn. They are created only with the depositor's legal authorization.

Customers authorize firms to draw checks on their respective demand deposit accounts. This authorization usually involves a fixed amount at specific intervals. The customers also sign indemnification agreements, which authorize their bank to honor PACs when presented for payment. The firm typically provides the bank with magnetic tapes that contain all necessary information to print PACs. The company retains a hard copy that lists all tape data for control and balance purposes. Upon receipt of the tapes the bank will produce PACs, deposit them to the company's account, clear them through the banking system, and return a control report to the firm.

A PAC system provides companies with a number of advantages. The cash flows from this system are highly predictable. Billing and postage costs are eliminated. Mail and processing costs are drastically reduced as compared with alternative systems, so that the company can enjoy more cash. Moreover, many customers prefer this system over their own payment system, because it does not bother them with a regular billing.

The Delay of Disbursement

In addition to the acceleration of collections, the efficient control of disbursements can produce a faster turnover of cash. Delaying disbursements enables the firm to keep cash on hand for longer periods. For example, if the firm buys materials on terms of 2/10, net 30, it should pay suppliers on the tenth day in order to take the 2 percent cash discount. If the firm pays the account on the tenth day rather than the third day, it will be able to use the funds for an additional seven days. By the same token, if the firm fails to take the 2 percent cash discount for some reason, it should pay the account on the 30th day, as late as possible. In other words, it must delay its payments until the last day in order to have the additional funds for the extra time.

A firm can also delay actual disbursements of funds through the use of drafts. A check is payable on demand, but a **draft** is payable only when the bank presents it to the issuer for payment. The issuing firm then deposits funds to cover the draft. In other words, the firm must have the funds in the bank when it draws the check, but it should provide cash to meet a draft only when its bank presents the draft to it for collection. Thus, the use of drafts allows the firm to maintain smaller deposits in its banks.

More frequent requisitions of funds by divisional offices from the firm's central office in conjunction with the centralization of disbursements make it possible for the firm to use large sums of money on a temporary basis. For example, if the firm switches its requisition policy from monthly requisitions to weekly requisitions, it can keep cash on hand as much as three weeks longer. The centralization of disbursements enables the firm to pool cash at its headquarters which would otherwise stay idle at the division level. This idle cash may be invested in marketable securities on a temporary basis.

The use of a float is yet another method used to maximize cash availability. At any given time, there are checks written by a firm that have yet to be cleared through the banking system because that process takes a number of days. Thus, it is possible for the firm to have a negative balance on its checkbook but a positive balance in its bank book. If the amount of the float can be estimated accurately, this technique can be used to maintain smaller bank balances.

Cost of Cash Management

A company may use various collection and disbursement procedures to improve its cash management efficiency. Because these two types of procedures constitute two sides of the same coin, they have a joint effect on the overall efficiency of cash management. Banks provide client companies with a variety of services. Most cash collections and disbursements for corporations are made through commercial banks. They also prepare activity reports, monthly statements, and reconciliation for their client companies, information which the companies can use for purposes of internal control. These bank services help companies develop a cash management system that best meets company objectives. The operation of a simplified cash management system is illustrated in Figure 7-1.

Both the acceleration of collections and the delay of disbursements involve additional costs. Hence, it is important for the company to determine how far it should go to make its cash operations more efficient. In theory, the company should adopt various collection and disbursement methods as long as their marginal returns exceed their marginal expenses.

The value of careful cash management depends on the opportunity cost of funds invested in cash. The **opportunity cost** of these funds in turn depends on the company's required rate of return on short-term investments. For example, assume that the adoption of a lock-box system under consideration is expected to reduce the investment in cash by $100,000. If the company earns 11 percent on short-term investments, the opportunity cost of the current system is $11,000. Thus, if the cost of the lock-box system is less than $11,000, it should be adopted to improve earnings performance.

Determining an Optimum Cash Balance

To establish its optimum cash balance, the firm must consider the transaction demand for cash, the efficiency of cash management, and the compensating-balance requirements of its banks. As a general rule, the **optimum cash balance** is the greater of (1) the firm's transactions balances plus its precautionary balances, or (2) its required compensating balances. **Compensating balances** are those that borrowers are required by their bank to keep in their account. Banks typically require their customers to maintain balances equal to 15 percent of outstanding loans.

Figure 7-1
Cash Management System

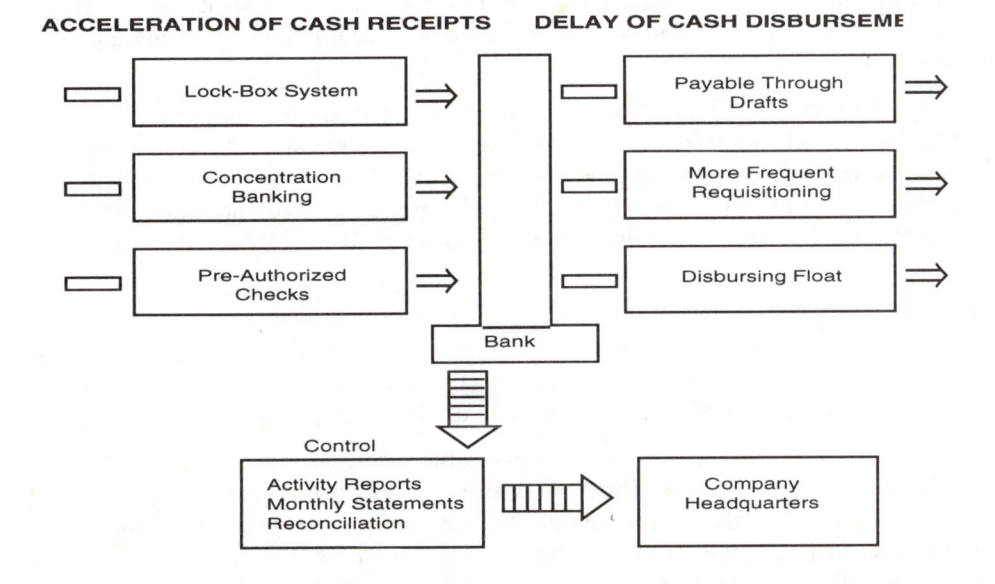

Required compensating balances are used to cover the cost of accounts and to increase the effective cost of borrowing. We have seen that banks clear checks, operate lock-box plans, and provide credit information for their customers. They obviously incur some expenses to provide their customers with such services. If a bank can lend a depositor's funds at a return of $1,000, the account is worth $1,000 to the bank. Hence, it would be beneficial for the bank to attract and hold the account if it spends less than $1,000 to serve the account. Compensating-balance requirements also raise the effective cost to the borrower. For example, if a firm must maintain 20 percent of its outstanding loan with an interest rate of 10 percent in its checking account, its effective cost increases to 12.5 percent (0.10 ÷ 0.80). However, unless these required compensating balances exceed those balances that borrowers would maintain ordinarily, such requirements do not raise the effective cost of borrowing. Finally, compensating balances not only keep money in the bank that can be loaned to others but also increase the liquidity position of the borrower that can be used to pay off the loan in case of default.

MARKETABLE SECURITIES

Some companies do not permit temporarily idle funds to remain in their demand deposit accounts. They invest those funds in marketable securities. The securities are held for two reasons: (1) to give a buffer against cash shortages, and (2) to earn interest on a temporary basis. If companies have some marketable securities, they can liquidate part of their holdings to increase their cash balances when cash outflows exceed cash inflows. Some companies frequently have large sums of surplus cash flows during part of the year. They may invest these idle funds in marketable securities to earn interest on a strictly temporary basis. However, most companies hold the securities for future needs of liquidity.

Factors Affecting Selection

Most surplus cash flows are temporary. Thus, if funds are invested in marketable securities such as Treasury bills, these securities should be virtually riskless, highly marketable, and of short maturity.

Normally, the securities chosen should be limited to those with a minimum risk of default. The **default risk** refers to the possibility that loans will not be repaid or that investments will deteriorate in quality. The credit standing of the issuers directly affects both income and risk. Generally speaking, the higher the credit standing, the lower the yield. At the same time, the risk of market loss is smaller on high-quality securities such as Treasury bills.

Marketability is another important factor that affects the selection of securities. For companies that hold marketable securities for near-future needs of liquidity, marketability considerations are of major importance. These firms must be able to sell most of their holdings for cash on short notice and with a minimum of loss.

The third factor affecting the selection of marketable securities is maturity. The longer the maturity, the higher the risk. The risk consists of two factors: a credit factor and an interest factor. There is always the possibility that the financial position of the issuer will vary over time. The longer the time, the greater the possibility of change. There is also the possibility that interest rates will vary over time. The longer the maturity, the greater the possibility that income or bond prices will be affected by changes in the level of rates.

Types of Short-Term Marketable Securities

To ensure convertibility without delay and appreciable loss, the marketable securities chosen for temporary investment of idle funds must meet the three requirements of high quality, marketability, and short-term maturity. In other words, they must be free of risk and salable in the market on short notice.

Treasury Securities

Treasury securities are the most popular securities for the temporary investment of idle funds, because they meet the tests of high quality and marketability. There are three basic types of marketable U.S. government securities: bonds, notes, and bills.

Although one-year bills are auctioned on a monthly basis, **Treasury bills** with maturities of 91 days and 182 days are auctioned on a weekly basis. Treasury bills are currently sold in minimums of $10,000 and multiples of $5,000 above the minimum. These readily marketable securities are sold on a discount basis. The return to the investor is the difference between the purchase price of the bill and its face value or par value. The quoted (published) interest rate is obtained by dividing the discount by par and expressing this percentage at an annual rate, using a 360-day year.

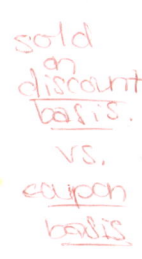

Example 7-1. A bid of $96.295 per $100 of face amount is accepted on 91-day Treasury bills. What annual interest rate would be published? What is the true yield of the Treasury bill that would make it comparable to rates quoted on many other instruments such as bonds?

The quoted (published) interest rate on a bank discount basis would be

$$\frac{\$100 - \$96.295}{\$100} \times \frac{360}{91} = 14.657\%$$

To calculate the true yield of a Treasury bill for comparison with other yields such as the bond's yield to maturity, the discount must be divided by the price and a 365-day year is used. The true yield of the above example is

$$\frac{\$100 - \$96.295}{\$96.295} \times \frac{365}{91} = 15.432\%$$

As this example demonstrates, the quoted yield can seriously understate the true yield of a Treasury bill. The difference between these two yields is greater the longer the maturity of the bill and the higher the level of interest rates.

Treasury notes are issued with an original maturity of one to ten years. **Treasury bonds** are issued with an original maturity of over ten years. Notes and bonds may be offered to the public for cash subscription or in exchange for outstanding or maturing securities. Offerings are generally announced one to three weeks in advance of the issue date. They are sold on a coupon basis.

Commercial Paper

Commercial paper consists of short-term promissory notes sold directly or through dealers by finance companies and certain industrial concerns. Commercial paper has maturities of anywhere from three days to 270 days, and its interest rates are usually somewhat higher than rates on Treasury bills of the same maturity. This paper is generally sold on a discount basis and is payable at its face value. Major financial services such as Standard & Poor's and Moody's provide investors with credit reports and ratings on commercial paper.

Banker's Acceptance   *arise from international trade.*

Banker's acceptances are generally used to finance foreign trade. The exporter prepares a draft with a definite maturity such as 90 days after shipment has been made. To assure payment for the shipment, the exporter may ask the importer to have the draft accepted by a commercial bank. When the bank agrees to make the payment by writing "Accepted" on the draft along with the signature of an authorized bank official, it becomes a banker's acceptance. By this process the bank guarantees the payment of the draft at maturity, and the exporter can sell it in the marketplace. Banker's acceptances are sold on a discount basis, and their rates are modestly above rates on Treasury bills.

Repurchase Agreement

The **repurchase agreement** is an arrangement by which a bank or a security dealer sells its short-term securities with an agreement to buy them back on a specified future date at an agreed price. The agreed price includes interest to the maturity. Rates on repurchase agreements are related to rates on Treasury bills. Repurchase agreements can be made for maturities of one day to several months, but most of the transactions are of a short maturity, usually a few days. They involve little default risk, because such transactions use U.S. government securities as collateral.

Negotiable "Jumbo" Certificates of Deposit

Commercial banks began to issue **negotiable certificates of deposit** (CDs) in 1961 in order to attract idle corporate funds. Negotiable CDs are formal negotiable receipts for funds left with the bank for a specified period of time, usually from 30 days to one year. They are offered in various denominations, but most negotiable CDs are issued in exchange for the deposit of funds of $100,000 or more. They trade in active secondary markets. Rates on negotiable CDs are ordinarily somewhat higher than those on Treasury bills. The bank pays interest on these CDs if the funds are left with it until maturity.

Money Market Funds

A new and increasingly popular instrument is the money market fund, a product of the tight monetary policy during the 1970s. The money market fund is a financial intermediary. It sells its shares to a large number of small investors and then reinvests the proceeds in money market instruments such as high-yielding $100,000 CDs and $25,000-to-$100,000 commercial paper. A major advantage of the fund is to permit an investor with as little as $100 to directly participate in high-yielding securities. Investments are usually made with open maturities and frequently require one day's notice for withdrawal.

Others

U.S. agency securities and state and local government securities are also used for temporary investment of idle funds. Such government agencies as the Government National Mortgage Association and the Federal Home Loan Bank are authorized to issue securities. Agency securities are highly marketable, and they have higher yields than Treasury securities with similar maturities. The securities issued by state and local governments usually have higher after-tax yields than Treasury and agency securities, because their interest earnings are exempt from federal income taxes.

Portfolio Management

Portfolio management depends on the amount of investment in marketable securities and type of securities. If future cash flows can be estimated accurately, idle funds can be invested in such a way that securities will mature on the dates when the funds will be needed. If future cash flows cannot be estimated accurately, the company's investment policy involves a tradeoff between risk and profitability. Conservative financial managers usually restrict their investments to Treasury bills, whose quality and marketability are the highest among competing securities for excess funds. In contrast, aggressive financial managers allocate a greater portion of their portfolios to high-return securities such as agency securities, commercial paper, and tax-free municipal bonds.

Most surplus funds are temporary. If companies invest funds in marketable securities such as Treasury bills, they should follow sound portfolio guidelines. First, instruments in the short-term investment portfolio should be diversified to maximize the yield for a given amount of risk or to minimize the risk for a given amount of return. Second, for companies that hold marketable securities for near-future needs of liquidity, marketability considerations are of major importance. Third, the maturity of the investment should be tailored to the company's projected cash needs. Fourth, the securities chosen should be limited to those with a minimum risk of default. Fifth, the portfolio should be reviewed daily to decide what new investments will be made and which securities will be liquidated.

Short-Term Investment Pools

Over the last decade numerous types of **short-term investment pooling arrangements** (STIPs) have emerged in the nation's financial system. The most well-known and widely publicized form of STIP is the money market fund. However, the money market funds are only one of many types of STIP. Some other STIPs include short-term tax-exempt funds, short-term investment funds, local government investment pools, credit union pools, and short-term investment trusts.

While the various types of STIPs differ in some respects, such as the kind of asset held or the type of investor, they are all alike in their basic function, which is to purchase large pools of short-term financial instruments and sell shares in these pools to investors. In almost all instances discussed here, the pool allows participants to invest a much smaller amount of money than would be necessary to directly purchase the individual securities held by the pool.

While all STIPs basically function as intermediaries for short-term securities, they can differ in several ways. First, some STIPs are open to a wide variety of investors while others cater only to a narrow group. Second, some STIPs hold many different money market instruments while other confine their investment to one type of security. Third, some STIPs are "open-ended" arrangements that allow investors to purchase and redeem shares of an ever-changing pool of underlying securities. In other STIPs, investors buy shares of a specific pool of underlying securities. Other features that vary among STIPs include minimum investment size, expense ratios, and methods of investing and withdrawing funds.

MANAGEMENT OF ACCOUNTS RECEIVABLE

The level of accounts receivable depends on the volume of credit sales and the average collection period. These two variables, in turn, depend on two types of factors: uncontrollable and controllable ones. Controllable factors include credit standards, credit terms, and collection policy.

Credit Standards

Credit standards are the minimum criteria that customers must meet to purchase merchandise on credit. Financial managers can use such information as credit ratings, past payment records, credit references, and certain ratios to establish the credit standards for their customers. How do they determine what grade of risk to accept? As management moves from customers who are more likely to pay their bills to those who are less likely to pay, sales tend to increase. However, a lenient credit policy is also likely to increase bad-debt losses, clerical expenses, and investments in accounts receivable. In theory, the firm should liberalize its credit standards to the point at which the marginal profit on its increased sales equals the marginal cost of credit.

Example 7-2. A company's current annual credit sales are $12,000; the selling price per unit is $10; and the variable cost per unit is $8. If the company adopts new credit standards that are under consideration, its sales are expected to increase by 15 percent, and its average collection period is also expected to increase from the current level of 30 days to 45 days. The company's required rate of return is 10 percent on investments in accounts receivable. Clerical expenses and bad-debt losses are expected to stay the same. Because the company is operating at less than full capacity, an increase in sales can be achieved without any increase in fixed assets.

To determine whether the company should relax its current credit standards, it must calculate the marginal profit on sales and the cost of marginal investment in accounts receivable. The additional unit sales multiplied by the profit per unit represent the company's marginal profit on sales. The profit per unit is the difference between the selling price per unit and the variable cost per unit. Thus, the marginal profit per unit is $2 or ($10 – $8). With a 15 percent increase in sales, $1,800 of new sales or ($12,000 x 0.15) would be generated. The $1,800 increase in sales represents 180 additional units or ($1,800 ÷ $10). Hence, the marginal or extra profit on the extra 180 units sold is equal to $360 or (180 units x $2 profit per unit).

To determine the cost of the marginal investment in accounts receivable, we have to compute the current level of accounts receivable before implementing the new credit policy and the level of accounts receivable after the new credit policy is in place. We can compute the level of accounts receivable (AR) with either the accounts receivable turnover (ART) or the average collection period (ACP) formula (see chapter 3). ART = credit sales/AR and ACP = AR/(Credit sales/360) and likewise ART = 360/ACP. Therefore, credit sales/AR = 360/ACP and solving AR, AR = credit sales/(360/ACP) and is calculated as follows:

Accounts receivable before and after new policy implementation:

AR (before) = credit sales/(360/ACP) = $12,000/(360/30) = $1,000
AR (after) = credit sales/(360/ACP) = $12,000+$1,800)/(360/45) = $1,725
Additional accounts receivable   = $1,725 – $1,000   = $ 725

The company requires all investments to earn a 10 percent return or the investment is not considered. With the company's 10 percent required rate of return, the cost of the marginal or extra investment in accounts receivable is $72.5 or ($725 x 0.10).

Because the marginal profit on sales of $360 exceeds the cost of the marginal investment in accounts receivable of $72.50, the company would be well advised to relax its credit standards. An optimum credit policy involves the liberalization of credit standards until the marginal profit on sales equals the cost of the marginal investment in accounts receivable. It is important to recognize that additional sales could mean additional bad-debt losses, more clerical expenses, and additional investments in fixed assets. These occurrences would necessitate additional analysis.

Credit Terms

Credit terms involve the length of the period for which the company will grant credit and the amount of any cash discount that it will allow for early payment. The terms 2/15, net 40 means that a 2 percent discount is granted if payment is made within 15 days from the invoice date; otherwise the full invoice price is due in 40 days.

Credit Period

Although the length of the credit period frequently depends on the customers of the industry, the credit manager can use it to increase profitability. An extension of the credit period should increase sales, but it should cause both the average collection period and the bad-debt losses to rise as well. Suppose, for the purpose of illustration, that Example 7-2 involved the extension of the credit period instead of the relaxation of credit standards. Assume also that this extension would cause the average collection period to increase from 30 days to 45 days and sales to increase by 15 percent. All other assumptions stay the same. Because the figures in this example are identical with those in Example 7-2, the results should be the same. Such a policy should be adopted because the marginal profit on sales exceeds the cost of the marginal investment in accounts receivable.

Cash Discount

Many companies frequently alter the cash discount to speed up the payment of accounts receivable. A cash discount of 2/10/net 30 indicates that if the customer pays off the account by the tenth day, 2% will be deducted from the bill. If the customer doesn't pay by the tenth day, he is expected to pay the full balance off by the 30th day. An increase in the cash discount (i.e. from 2/10/net 30 to 3/10/net 30) tends (1) to stimulate sales, (2) to shorten the average collection period, and (3) to reduce bad-debt losses. These advantages are offset by a reduced profit margin per unit sold, because more customers take the discount and pay the reduced price.

Example 7-3. Assume the Johnson Company is considering a plan to increase the cash discount for the purpose of speeding up collections or shortening the average collection period (ACP). Johnson assumes that this action will not affect annual sales which will remain constant. Currently, annual credit sales are $240,000, the ACP is 45 days, and the variable costs are 80% of sales. The company intends to increase its cash discount from 0/net 45 to 2/10/net 45. The discount increase is expected to reduce the ACP from 45 days to 30 days for a net reduction in the ACP of 15 days. Half of the customers are expected to take advantage of the 2 percent cash discount. Thus half of credit sales (or $120,000) will be reduced by the discount of 2%, since customers get this benefit by paying on or before the 10th day. Johnson assumes that bad-debt losses will not be affected by the change in the cash discount and will remain constant.

To begin the analysis, we must first (as in Example 7-2) determine the level of investment in accounts receivable (AR) before and after the change in the cash discount.

AR (before) = credit sales/(360/ACP) = $240,000/(360/45) = $30,000
AR (after) = credit sales/(360/ACP) = $240,000/(360/30) = $20,000
                                         Reduction in AR = $10,000

Thus, because Johnson's customers are paying off their accounts 15 days quicker, the company's investment in AR will drop by $10,000 which will free up these funds to be used elsewhere in the business. And since Johnson's opportunity cost of funds (what the firm can earn elsewhere on these funds) is 20%, the company can save $2,000 or ($10,000 x 20%). Thus, the cash discount is expected to speed up collections, reduce AR by $10,000, allowing this $10,000 to be invested elsewhere at 20% to save the company $2,000.

But an increase in the cash discount will cause the firm to sacrifice some of its sales, since half of the customer are expected to take the discount. Therefore, half of credit sales (or .5 x $240,000) would be affected by a reduction of 2% and since credit sales will remain constant at $240,000 after the change in the cash discount, the firm will lose $2,400 (or 2% of $120,000). Thus, we compare the marginal gain from the change in the discount policy to marginal loss:

Marginal Gain = Extra return on funds freed up by drop in AR = $2,000
Marginal Loss = Loss in sales revenue from discount takes   = $2,400
                                        Net Marginal Loss   = $ 400

Based on the analysis, if Johnson Company changes its cash discount, the marginal loss would exceed the marginal gain by $400, so the firm's stockholders would be worse off by offering the 2% cash discount. The firm should reject the new cash discount policy.

Stated differently, the opportunity cost to the company from increasing the discount is the total amount of the cash discounts taken by the customers, or $2,400 or (0.02 x 0.50 x $240,000). Because the opportunity cost of $2,400 exceeds the dollar saving of $2,000, the company should not adopt its proposed cash discount policy.

So far, our examples assumed no bad-debt losses. But different credit policies affect both the average collection period and bad-debt losses. Now we consider a change in both.

Example 7-4. In this example, assume that Johnson Company is considering a plan to loosen its credit standards by selling to marginal customers or those customers with worse credit records. By selling to less credit-worthy customers, Johnson must compare the gains from the additional sales (or marginal profit on sales to these marginal customers) to marginal losses (additional bad debt losses and extra investment in AR due to slower collections) resulting from selling to the same. In total the new policy to reduce credit standards is expected to

- Increase credit sales by 360 units
- Increase bad debts from 1% of credit sales to 2%
- Increase the ACP by 15 days or from 30 days to 45 days

Current annual credit sales are 2,400 units, the selling price is $10 per unit, and the variable cost is $8 per unit. The firm's required rate of return on short-term investment is 20%.

MARGINAL GAIN FROM NEW POLICY:

Additional sales of 360 units x selling price of $10   = $3,600
Variable cost of selling 360 units x variable cost of $8 = $2,880

Marginal Profit = $ 720

MARGINAL LOSS FROM NEW POLICY:

Cost of extra investment in AR:

AR (before) = credit sales/(360/ACP) = $24,000/(360/30)   = $2,000
AR (after) = credit sales/(360/ACP) = (24000 + $3,600)/(360/45) = $3,450

Increased Investment in AR = $1,450

Marginal cost of tying up additional $1,450 in AR = $1,450 x 20% = ($290)

Extra bad debts (BD) losses:

BD (before) = credit sales of $24,000 x 1% BD loss = $240
BD (after) = credit sales of ($24,000 + $3,600) x 2% BD loss = $552

Extra bad debts losses = ($312)

SUMMARY OF ANALYSIS:

Marginal profit on new sales	$720
Marginal Cost of new Sales:	
Cost of extra investments in AR ($290)	
Extra bad debt losses ($312)	($602)
Marginal Gain of New Policy	$118

The analysis indicates that Johnson Cmpany should adopt the change in the credit policy since it should result in a marginal gain of $118 to the firm's owners.

Collection Policy

Collection policy refers to the procedure a firm undertakes to collect its past-due accounts. The costs of a tight collection policy are additional collection expenditures and lost sales. These advantages are offset by decreases in both bad-debt losses and the average collection period. Two major variables involved in the determination of an optimum collection policy are collection expenditures and bad-debt loses. Although these two variables are inversely related to each other, their relationship is not linear. Initial collection expenditures usually have a small impact on the reduction of bad-debt losses. Additional collection expenditures begin to produce a substantial reduction in bad-debt losses. Beyond a certain point, however, additional collection expenditures do not reduce bad-debt losses enough to justify the further outlay of funds. In theory, the company should increase its collection expenditures to the point at which the revenues of its additional collection effort equal additional costs of this effort.

To establish clear-cut collection procedures for past-due accounts, the firm must decide how overdue it should allow an account to become before collection procedures are started. If collection procedures are begun too early, they may be too expensive in terms of both out-of-pocket expenditures, and lost goodwill in relation to the additional revenues that may be gained. As an account becomes older, however, it becomes more expensive and more difficult to collect.

A polite letter is usually sent to an account that is overdue for a certain number of days. If payment is not received within a certain period of time, letters with a more forceful tone are mailed. If letters fail, a telephone call from the credit manager, followed by additional calls from such persons as the firm's attorney, can be used. Personal visits can be employed to collect the account if letters and telephone calls prove unsuccessful. If all else fails, the firm can turn the account over to a collection agency or take direct legal action against the account. Both alternatives are extremely costly.

Example 7-5. The expected bad-debt losses for the Service Company are computed as shown in Table 7-1. This means that $5,000 of the firm's outstanding accounts receivable may be uncollectable. The credit manager estimates that $1,000 in additional collection expenditures can generate the following collection probabilities: a 40 percent chance to collect 10 percent of the expected bad-debt losses; a 50 percent chance to collect 20 percent of the estimated bad-debt losses; and a 10 percent chance to collect 40 percent of the expected bad-debt losses.

Table 7-1
Expected Bad Debt Losses

	Amount Outstanding	Estimated Bad Debt Losses (%)	Expected Bad debt Losses
Not yet due	$50,000	2	$1,000
1-30 days past due	20,000	6	1,200
31-60 days past due	10,000	11	1,100
Over 61 days past due	8,500	20	1,700
Totals	$88,500		$5,000

Table 7-2
Total Expected Value from Collection of Bad Debt Losses

Probability		Amount Collected	Expected Value
0.4	x	$500 or (0.1 of $5,000)	$200
0.5	x	1,000 or (0.2 of $5,000)	500
0.1	x	2,000 or (0.4 of $5,000)	200
Total expected value			$900

To determine the additional revenues that can be gained from the $1,000 in additional collection expenditures, multiply the probability of collection by the amount to be collected and sum these products. Table 7-2 shows this computation process. Because the anticipated collection expenses of $1,000 exceed the expected additional revenues of $900, this collection policy should not be accepted.

Analysis of Individual Accounts

Once the firm has established general guidelines to an optimum credit policy, it must develop procedures to evaluate individual credit applicants. The purpose of credit analysis is to determine the ability and willingness of these applicants to repay their credit in accordance with the credit terms. The credit evaluation process consists of three steps: (1) obtain credit information on a specific account, (2) analyze this information, and (3) make the credit decision.

Sources of Credit Information

The important sources of credit information include financial statements, reports of credit-reporting agencies, bank checking, and credit interchange bureaus.

Credit applicants may be requested to submit detailed financial reports, such as balance sheets, income statements, sources-and-uses-of-funds statements, and pro forma financial statements. These financial reports can be used to determine the applicant's liquidity, profitability, and debt capacity.

Dun and Bradstreet, the best known credit-reporting agency, collects financial information on over three million U.S. and Canadian firms and makes it available to subscribers. It publishes credit reports and credit ratings on each of these companies in its national and regional reference books.

A credit check through the applicant's bank is another important source of credit information. Many banks have large credit departments that maintain central files of all their depositors and borrowers and that undertake credit checks for their customers. These files show the payment record on previous loans, the average cash balance carried, and sometimes financial information.

The Credit Interchange Service of the National Association of Credit Management is a national network of local credit bureaus that exchange credit information on a reciprocal basis. Participating companies provide their local credit bureaus with information on their customers such as the amount of credit, the payment record on past credit, and the length of service.

Credit Analysis

Credit information collected through these sources and the company's own experience can be used to determine the applicant's ability and willingness to pay its obligation. The essential factors in credit analysis are the five C's of credit: character, capacity, capital, collateral, and condition.

Character refers to the willingness of applicants to honor their obligations. Because character is largely a function of such qualitative factors as honesty and integrity, it is difficult to evaluate. **Capacity** consists of two elements: (1) the borrowers' ability to repay their obligations, and (2) their legal capacity to enter into a loan contract. The amount of credit requested should be within the applicant's ability to repay. It is also important for the company to check whether the applicant has authority to borrow money. Minors and limited partners usually do not have such authority. **Capital** has to do with the general financial position of the applicant. Various ratios and financial statements are very important sources of information to determine the financial strength of the customer. **Collateral** refers to assets that can be used as a pledge for security of the credit. **Conditions** are economic factors that affect the ability of borrowers to repay their obligations. But these conditions are beyond the control of individual credit applicants.

Credit Decision

The first two steps of the credit evaluation process should enable the firm to judge the applicant's credit-worthiness. This worthiness is then compared with the firm's credit standard to make the full decision on the credit application. If the firm decides to grant the credit to the applicant, it usually sets a maximum amount of credit to extend.

INVENTORY MANAGEMENT

Managing inventory efficiently is extremely important for two reasons. First, inventories represent a significant segment of total assets for most business firms, especially those in the retail trade. Second, they are the least liquid of current assets; thus, errors in inventory management are not quickly remedied. Hence, it is not surprising that the greatest improvement in current asset management in the last few decades has been made in the area of inventory control and investment. With the application of computers and mathematical models, the size of inventories in relation to sales has been greatly reduced.

In manufacturing firms, inventories consist of raw materials, work in process and finished goods. The amount of raw materials depends on anticipated production, seasonal factors in production and product demand, reliability of suppliers, and efficiency of production operations. Work-in-process inventories are strongly influenced by the length of the production period, the level of current output, and the efficiency of production engineers and planners. The level of finished goods is determined by the level of current market demand and the seasonality of sales.

Optimum Investment in Inventory

The level of sales, the length of the production cycle, and the durability of the product are the major determinants of investment in inventory. To determine the optimum investment that minimizes the total cost of inventory, management must evaluate both carrying costs and ordering costs.

Carrying costs include interest on funds tied up in inventory, insurance premiums, storage costs, and taxes. Carrying costs rise as the size of inventory increases. Ordering costs are the costs of placing an order, of shipping and handling, and of lost quantity discounts. Ordering costs fall as the average inventory increases. Management must also consider some implicit costs associated with the size of inventory. The cost of lost sales, lost customer goodwill, and potential disruption in production schedules rise with smaller inventories. Adverse changes in price, obsolescence, and pilferage rise with larger inventories.

The total cost of inventory consists of carrying costs and ordering costs. Figure 7-2 illustrates these three costs curves. Carrying costs are upward sloping. This is because, as the order size increases, the average inventory on hand also increases. Ordering costs are downward sloping. This is because, as the order size increases, the company can reduce the number of orders. The total-cost curve falls at first as the order size increases, because the rate of decrease in ordering costs is greater than the rate of increase in carrying costs. The total cost curve begins to rise after point EOQ, however, because the increase in carrying costs exceeds the decrease in ordering costs. Hence, point EOQ represents the minimum total cost; this particular point is usually called the **economic order quantity**. In other words, the economic order quantity refers to the size of the order that minimizes the total cost of inventory.

126   PART 3: WORKING CAPITAL MANAGEMENT

Figure 7-2
Relationship Between Order Size and Total Inventory Cost

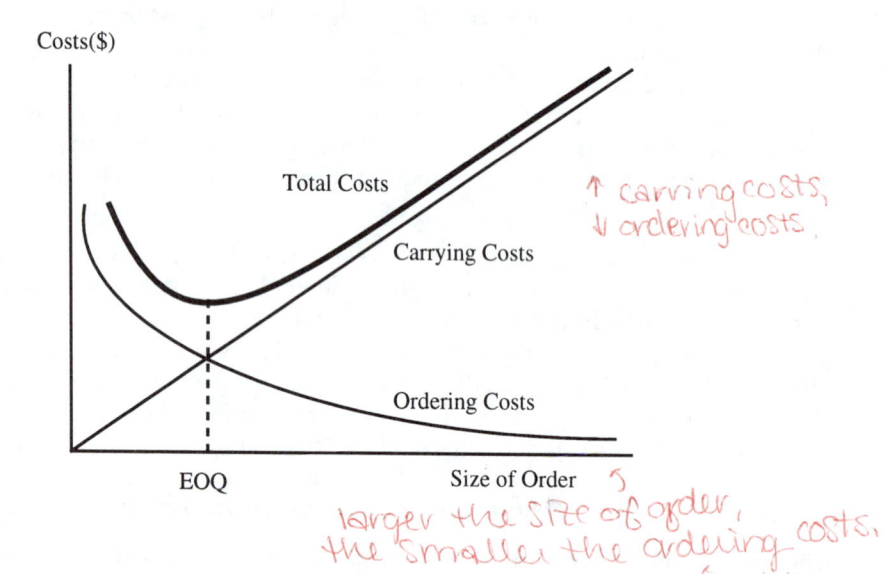

[Figure: Graph showing Costs($) on vertical axis and Size of Order on horizontal axis. Total Costs curve is U-shaped with minimum at EOQ. Carrying Costs line rises linearly. Ordering Costs curve declines.]

Economic Order Quantity

Under certain fairly reasonable assumptions we can develop a formula to determine the economic order quantity. Assume: (1) the usage of a particular inventory item can be estimated accurately; (2) the usage rate of the item is constant over a period of time; (3) there are no additional inventories carried to guard against changes in sales or delivery; (4) there are no quantity discounts; (5) inventory orders are received immediately; (6) the ordering cost per unit is the same regardless of the order size; and (7) carrying cost per unit is constant. Some of these assumptions will be removed a little later.

The following symbols are used to present the analysis in a simple manner:

C = carrying cost per unit per period
Q = quantity ordered in units
S = total usage in units over time period
O = ordering cost per order.

The total carrying costs for a period of time are the carrying cost per unit (C) times the average inventory (Q/2), or C(Q/2). The total ordering costs for the same period of time are the ordering cost per order (O) times the number of orders (S/Q), or SO/Q. Because total inventory costs are the total carrying costs plus the total ordering costs, we obtain

$$\text{Total inventory cost} = \frac{CQ}{2} + \frac{SO}{Q} \qquad (7\text{-}1)$$

Chapter 7: Current Asset Management

The economic order quantity (EOQ) can be obtained from Equation (7-1):

$$EOQ = \sqrt{\frac{2SO}{C}} \qquad (7\text{-}2)$$

Example 7-6. A firm sells 640 units of a product over each 64-day period of business. Carrying costs are $10 a unit for each 64 days and ordering costs are $50 an order. The economic order quantity is

$$EOQ = \sqrt{\frac{2(640)(\$50)}{\$10}} = 80 \text{ units}$$

Thus, the firm must order 80 units at a time to minimize its total inventory cost. The number of orders during the period under consideration is the total usage of 640 units divided by the EOQ of 80 units, or eight orders.

Given the EOQ of 80 units, the firm can also determine its total inventory costs as follows.

$$\text{Total inventory cost} = \frac{\$10 \times 80}{2} + \frac{640 \times \$50}{80} = \$800$$

This amount is the lowest possible total cost of inventory. The optimum average inventory is the EOQ divided by two, or 40 units.

If the total inventory costs are not particularly sensitive to the order size, it may be useful to compute an EOQ range rather than a point. To illustrate, assume that the firm wants to determine the percentage change in total costs for a 10 percent increase in the order size (8 units). Because the new order size is 88 units, we can calculate the total inventory costs as follows:

$$\text{Total inventory cost} = \frac{\$10 \times 88}{2} + \frac{640 \times \$50}{88} = \$804$$

Thus, the percentage change in total costs for a 10 percent increase in the order size is 0.5 percent or ($4 ÷ $800). It is fair to conclude that the sensitivity is not great; consequently, the firm has greater flexibility in ordering merchandise.

The EOQ is strongly influenced by quantity discounts, because they affect the price per unit. It should be noted that the relaxation of our earlier assumption on quantity discounts does not greatly change our basis calculations. To illustrate, suppose that a quantity discount of $0.10 per unit in price is available to the firm if it increases its order size from 80 units to 100 units. Total inventory costs are

$$\text{Total inventory cost} = \frac{\$10 \times 100}{2} + \frac{640 \times \$50}{100} = \$820$$

Because the total cost for the order size of 80 units was $800, the increase in the order size would cause the total cost to increase by $20 or ($820 – $800). On the other hand, the saving available to the firm in the form of lower purchase price is the discount per unit times the total usage, or $64 or ($0.10 x 640). The saving is greater than the increase in total costs; thus, the firm should use an order quantity of 100 units instead of 80 units.

Safety Stocks

A level of **safety stocks** in all three inventory categories (raw materials, work in process, and finished goods) is maintained to absorb random fluctuations in purchases, production, or sales. Some safety stocks in the form of raw materials are necessary in case the supplier is slow in delivery. Safety stocks of work in process assure a continual flow of materials even when there are occasional delays in the production cycle. Safety stocks of finished goods are maintained so that customers will not have to wait for delivery.

Although we assumed that inventory orders are received immediately, in practice a lead time must be established to cover the span between the time an order is placed and the time it is delivered. When usage is known with certainty, the reorder point is the lead time in days times the daily usage. Assume that inventories are used at an even rate of 40 units a day and that there is a lead time of five days. The reorder point would be 200 units or (40 units X 5 days).

With a safety stock of 100 units to protect the firm against a further delay in delivery beyond the lead time of five days, the reorder point must be set at 300 units of inventory as opposed to the previous 200 units. The 300 units consist of the safety stock of 100 units plus the 200 units expected to be used during the lead time. When the firm allows for uncertainty in demand for inventory, the size of safety stocks becomes even greater.

Safety stocks allow the firm to protect itself from conditions of uncertainty, but they also increase total inventory costs. Thus, it is extremely important for management to determine the proper amount of safety stocks. This amount depends on many factors, such as the degree of uncertainty in demand for inventory, the lead time, the cost of stockouts, and so on.

SUMMARY

In this chapter we discussed four types of current assets: cash, marketable securities, accounts receivable, and inventories. In managing cash, a firm's management must attempt to accelerate collections and to delay disbursements so that it will have a maximum availability of cash. Lock-box systems, concentration banking, and pre-authorized checks can be used to speed up the collection process. Drafts, more frequent requisitions, and floats can be used to delay disbursements. If the firm has some idle funds, they should be invested in marketable securities such as Treasury securities, commercial paper, banker's acceptances, and negotiable certificates of deposit.

The management of accounts receivable involves a firm's credit standards, credit terms, and collection policy. In each case, the credit decision involves a tradeoff between additional cost and the profitability that may be gained from a change in the firm's credit policy.

The efficient management of inventories is very important for two reasons. First, inventories represent a large segment of total assets for most business firms. Second, they are the least liquid of current assets. Thus, changes in levels of inventory have important economic effects on the overall profitability of the firm. Like the management of any current asset, the efficient management of inventory requires the firm to balance the costs of increases in the levels of inventory against the profits that can be gained from these increases. The economic order quantity is an important inventory control tool, which determines the optimal size of order to place. Some safety stocks must be maintained to protect the firm from conditions of uncertainty.

LIST OF KEY TERMS

transaction motive
speculative motive
pre-authorized checks
optimum cash balance
default risk
Treasury notes
commercial paper
repurchase agreement
credit standards
collection policy
capacity
collateral
ordering cost
safety stocks

precautionary motive
float
draft
compensating balance
Treasury bills
Treasury bonds
bankers' acceptances
negotiable certificates of deposit
credit terms
character
capital
carrying cost
economic order quantity

PROBLEMS

7-1 The Simple Company has an average collection period of 60 days; its inventory conversion period is 80 days; and its average payment period is about 50 days. The company spends a total of $2 million per year at a constant rate. The firm's required rate of return on investment is 20 percent.
(a) What is the company's cash conversion cycle? (See Figure 6-1 for help.)
(b) What is the company's cash turnover or (360/cash-cycle)?
(c) Calculate the minimum amount of cash that the company must maintain to meet its payments as they come due. (Hint: Total Spending ÷ Cash Turnover.)
(d) How much can the company save if it stretches its accounts payable to 68 days?

7-2 An average of six days elapses between the time customers pay their bills and the moment the company deposits these checks. The adoption of a lock-box system under consideration is expected to reduce the mailing time from four and one-half days to two days and the processing time from one and one-half days to one daily. The company collects $1 million daily. The annual cost of the lock-box system is estimated to be $50,000 and the company's required rate of return on short-term investments is 5 percent.
(a) What is the amount of reduction in cash balances that would be realized through the adoption of a lock-box system?
(b) What is the opportunity cost of the current system?

(c) Should the company adopt its proposed lock-box system?

7-3 The Complex Company has sales of $12.5 million a year and credit sales account for 80 percent of this amount. The vice president of marketing believes that sales could be increased very sharply if the company relaxes its credit policy. The company's average collection period is currently 36 days, its selling price per unit is $1,000, and its variable cost per unit is $800. The adoption of a new credit policy under consideration is expected to increase sales by 20 percent, the average collection period will increase to 72 days, and bad-debt losses will rise from 1 percent to 2 percent. The company's required rate of return on short-term investment is 10 percent. Should the Complex Company change its current credit policy? (See Example 7-2 and 7-4)

7-4 The ABC Company has recently lost a substantial portion of its market to its competitors. The major cause for this decline and a subsequent decrease in its profit was found to be its tight credit policy. As a result, management intends to change its current credit policy. The following information is available.

	Policy A	Policy B	Policy C	Policy D	Policy E
Marginal profits on sales	$ 5,000	$ 4,000	$ 3,000	$ 2,000	$ 1,000
Additional receivables	18,000	15,000	15,000	16,000	14,000

Determine which policy the ABC Company should adopt if its required rate of return on short-term investments is 20 percent. (See Example 7-2)

7-5 The Truth Company purchases 40,000 boxes of ice cream cones over each 200-day period of business. Carrying costs are $2 per box and ordering costs are $100 per order. The company desires to maintain a safety stock of 500 boxes (on hand initially) and two days are required for delivery.

(a) What is the economic order quantity?
(b) What is the minimum number of orders to be placed?
(c) What is the total inventory cost associated with the economic order quantity?
(d) What is the reorder point?
(e) The company can obtain a quantity discount of $0.02 per box if it increases its order size to 3,000 boxes. Should the company increase its order size to take the cash discount offered?

7-6 A watch store sells 1,600 watches a year. The store estimates that it costs $2 per year to carry a watch in inventory and $100 to place an order for watches. Thus, its economic order quantity is 400 watches. Determine the total inventory costs associated with an order size of (a) 800, (b) 533, (c) 400, (d) 320, and (e) 267 watches. Verify that an order size of 400 units is the economic order quantity.

7-7 A bid of $98 per 100 of face amount is accepted on 91-day Treasury bills. A bond has an annual coupon rate of 7.5 percent and is sold for 90 percent of face value. (See Example 7-1 for help.)

   (a) What would be the published annual interest rate of the Treasury bill?
   (b) What is the true yield of the Treasury bill?
   (c) Which instrument has a higher yield: the Treasury bill or the bond?

7-8 Kono Electronics has decided to extend trade credit to some customers previously considered poor risks. Sales would increase by $200,000 if credit is extended to these new customers. However, 10 percent of these new accounts will be unccollectable. The cost of producing and selling the product will be 80 percent of the sales. The firm is in the 40 percent tax bracket.

   (a) What is the incremental income after tax?
   (b) What is the firm's incremental return on sales if these new credit customers are accepted?

7-9 West Electronics is experiencing some inventory control problems. The company currently orders 5,000 radios four times a year to handle annual demand of 20,000 radios. Each order costs $15 and each costs $1.50 to carry. The company maintains a safety stock of 200 radios.

   (a) What is West Electronics' current total annual inventory cost?
   (b) Compute the economic order quantity.
   (c) Compute total annual inventory cost under the economic order quantity.

7-10 A company has improved its production process and is able to reduce inventory by $500,000. This change will cost $60,000 per year. The company has an opportunity cost on inventory of 15 percent. What is the profit (loss) of the improved production process?

8

Sources of Short-Term Financing

Once the firm has decided on the nature of its needs for funds, the next step is to secure the funds. There are a variety of short-term credits available. Short-term credit refers to debt that is reasonably expected to be repaid within one year. This chapter covers such short-term sources of funds as trade credit, short-term bank loans, commercial paper, accounts receivable financing, and inventory financing. The first three sources of funds are often called **unsecured loans** because they do not require collateral. The last two sources of funds are frequently called **secured loans** because they require collateral.

Most business firms prefer to borrow on an unsecured basis because secured loans frequently have high bookkeeping costs and also contain a number of highly restrictive provisions. However, some companies cannot obtain loans on an unsecured basis because they are either financially weak or have not established a satisfactory performance record. Companies may be anxious to pledge security if they can obtain a reduction in interest rate, but this rarely occurs.

Trade Credit

Profitable business operations give rise not only to needs for funds but also to certain sources of continuing credit. Trade credit and accruals are the two major spontaneous sources of credit, and they constitute a substantial offset to the gross need for funds in the business. These two types of funds result from normal patterns of successful operations without special effort or negotiation on the part of the financial manager.

Trade credit or accounts payable occur when a firm purchases its supplies and raw materials on credit from other firms. Trade credit represents the largest source of short-term funds. It is a particularly important source of funds for small companies, because they may not qualify for loans from banks or other institutional lenders.

Open account, notes payable, and trade acceptances are the three major forms of trade credit. **Open account** does not require the buyer to sign a formal note that evidences liability to the seller; credit is extended on the basis of the seller's credit investigation of the buyer. This is the most common type of trade credit. **Promissory notes** are employed when jewelry and other expensive items are involved or when customers are well overdue on their accounts. In this case, the buyer is asked to sign a note that officially recognizes an obligation to the seller. **Trade acceptances** are drafts accepted by

134   PART 3: WORKING CAPITAL MANAGEMENT

the buyer. When shipment is made, the seller draws a draft on the buyer. When the buyer or his bank accepts the draft, it becomes a trade acceptance.

Terms of Trade Credit

Our discussion of credit terms is restricted to open trade credit because it is most commonly used in practice. To use open account trade credit effectively, one must understand four possible aspects of credit terms: the credit period, the size of the cash discount, the cash discount period, and the date the credit period begins. The terms "2/10, net 25 EOM" contain these four aspects. These terms state that a 2 percent discount (the size of the cash discount) is granted if payment is made within 10 days (the cash discount period) from the end of the month (the date the credit period begins); otherwise, the full invoice price is due in 25 days (the credit period) from the end of the month or by the 25th day of the following month.

COD and CBD

COD (cash on delivery) involves risk that the buyer may refuse the shipment. CBD (cash before delivery) involves no credit at all because the buyer must pay for the goods in advance. Some sellers use CBD terms to avoid all risks.

Ordinary Terms

Most credit terms include a net period which refers to the period of time allowed for payment. The terms "net 30" mean that the invoice price must be paid within 30 days. The terms "2/10, net 30" indicate that a 2 percent discount is offered if payment is made within 10 days; otherwise, the full amount of the bill must be paid within 30 days. The true price of any product or service is the discounted price. Therefore, if on a $100 purchase, a borrowing firm (or firm considering financing the transaction with trade credit) is offered terms 2/10/n30, then the true price is $98, or $100 less 2% of $100. Therefore, the seller/lender is saying "if you don't pay on or before the 10th day, I will charge you $2 interest on the net amount of $98 for the remaining 20 days by adding $2 to the price." In effect the buyer, by not paying the net due of $98 on the 10th day, automatically assumes a $98 loan at a cost of $2 for the remaining 20 days. And with roughly eighteen 20-day periods in a year the annualized rate comes to over 36% (or 2% x 18). This can be viewed as the effective interest rate the borrowing trade creditor faces by failing to take the cash discount of 2% on the 10th day. The effective annual interest rate of failing to take the cash discount may be computed on a non-compounded basis as follows:

$$i^* = \frac{\text{Discount}}{(100 - \text{Discount})} \times \frac{360}{(\text{Final due date} - \text{Discount period})} \quad (8\text{-}1)$$

Thus, the effective annual interest rate (or i*) of foregoing the terms "2/10, net 30" is

$$\frac{2}{100-2} \times \frac{360}{20} = 36.73\%$$

Here we used 360 rather than 365 as the number of days in the year for ease of calculation. If 365 days are used, the cost of the cash discount foregone increases to 37.24 percent. Thus the annual interest rate that the borrower faces for 20 days is around 37%. Let's say this firm can borrow money at its local bank at an effective annual interest rate of 12%. Then the firm should take out a 12% loan for $98 and pay off the trade credit on the 10th day and thus pay about a third of the interest or 12% compared to 37%.

Datings

Datings are frequently used by such seasonal businesses as clothing and sporting goods to level out their production and shipping activities. For example, sporting goods manufacturers may encourage their customers to send in their orders for the fall during the spring or summer months, with the understanding that shipments on these orders will be made at the discretion of the manufacturer. If sporting goods are sold with the terms of net 30 October 15 dating, the buyers do not have to pay their bills until November 15, even if they may have received the goods during January or February.

Stretching Accounts Payable

In practice, many companies stretch or postpone their payments beyond the end of the credit period without severe consequences.

Suppliers are in business to sell goods; thus, they may permit accounts to become overdue for some time. However, companies should not stretch their payables too often and too excessively, because the cash discount foregone and the possible deterioration in credit rating may outweigh the benefit.

Evaluation of Trade Credit

The major advantages of trade credit are its availability and flexibility. The accounts payable of most firms require few formalities and represent a continuous form of credit. Once the initial credit application passes a credit check by the supplier, the company can buy goods and services from the supplier without further negotiation of credit terms. Changes in the amount of accounts payable are usually in line with changes in the amount of funds needed. As the firm reaches the selling season, it increases its investment in inventories. A part of the additional investment in inventories is financed by an automatic increase in trade credit. As the firm enters the selling season, it can gradually reduce its accounts payable from collections on its accounts receivable.

The two major disadvantages of trade credit are the cost of the cash discount foregone and the opportunity cost associated with the firm's practice of stretching its payables. Excessive use of trade credit may cause the firm to have a liquidity crisis, because it may base its expansion on trade credit rather than on the owners' equity. Thus, the effective use of trade credit requires companies to weigh its advantages against its disadvantages.

SHORT-TERM BANK LOANS

Trade credit appears on the balance sheet as accounts payable, whereas bank loans appear as notes payable. Most short-term bank loans are made on an unsecured basis for business firms to cover their seasonal increases in inventories or accounts receivable. Short-term bank loans to business firms make up about two-thirds of the dollar amount of all commercial and industrial loans. The important users of such loans are retail firms, food processors, and manufacturing firms with seasonal operations. Unsecured short-term business loans by commercial banks play a critical role in the growth of firms, because they are non-spontaneous funds.

Types of Unsecured Bank Loans

Banks lend short-term funds in three basic ways: notes, lines of credit, and revolving credit agreements.

Notes

When companies need short-term funds for only one purpose, they can obtain the funds from their banks by signing promissory notes. These notes contain the amount of payment, the time of payment, and the interest rate charged. Such one-shot loans typically have maturities from 30 to 90 days.

Lines of Credit   clean-up period

A **line of credit** is an agreement between a business firm and a bank specifying the maximum amount of unsecured credit that its customer will be permitted to owe during a specified period of time, usually one year. These loans are usually extended in the form of authorized overdrafts; customers are allowed to overdraw their deposit balance at the bank up to an agreed amount.

Ordinarily, a line of credit is in the form of a letter to the customer and is not legally binding. While it is not a guaranteed loan, the bank informally allows the borrower to owe up to some maximum amount provided the funds are available. Customers usually do not pay a commitment fee on the unused portion of the line. The credit-worthiness of the customers and their credit needs are used to determine the amount of the line. The line of credit is especially helpful to both the customer and the bank in cutting down the time-consuming "red-tape" of a loan application and approval every time the borrower needs a quick loan.

There are two protective devices in most credit lines: an annual cleanup period and a compensating balance. Banks require customers to clean up their entire credit for a certain number of days during the year. The cleanup feature encourages borrowers to switch their loans from one bank to another. It also gives banks an opportunity to review the accounts before taking them on again. Compensating balances are sometimes required by banks to increase the effective cost of interest and to protect their loans against financial difficulties of the borrower. When default occurs, the bank may be able to apply the borrower's deposits to the balance of the loan.

Revolving Credit Agreements

A **revolving credit agreement** is a legal commitment on the part of a bank with respect to the maximum amount of credit that its customer can borrow during a specified period of time. Unlike the line of credit, with this agreement the bank guarantees the borrower that a specified amount of funds will be available for loan regardless of the availability or scarcity of money. The terms of the agreement are prepared in writing for two reasons: (1) it is legally binding, and (2) it normally runs from one to three years. Because the bank guarantees the availability of funds to the borrower, a commitment fee is usually charged on a revolving credit agreement. The commitment fee applies to the unused portion of the borrower's credit line.

Interest Rates

Interest rates on most business loans are determined through direct negotiation between the borrower and the bank. The prevailing prime rate and the credit worthiness of the borrower are the two major determinants of the interest rate charged. The prime rate is the rate of interest charged by the country's largest banks on short-term business loans to the most credit-worthy customers. The effective interest rate on a loan varies according to the type of loan. Interest may be paid on a collect or regular basis (see Example 8-1).

Example 8-1. Assume that a firm borrows $10,000 at 10 percent for a year. Compute the effective rate of interest for the loan on a collect basis as well as on a discount basis.

The effective rate of interest on a collect basis is

$$i^* = \frac{\$1000}{\$10000} = 10\%$$

The effective rate of interest on a discount basis is

$$i^* = \frac{\$1000}{\$10000 - \$1000} = 11.11\%$$

If the loan and its interest are paid in equal monthly installments, the effective rate of interest becomes even higher. The effective rate of interest on an installment loan is computed as follows:

$$i^* = \frac{24c}{P(n+1)} \qquad (8\text{-}2)$$

where r = effective rate of interest, c = true dollar cost of the credit, or the sum of all payments less the amount borrowed, P = amount borrowed, and n = life of the credit.

If the loan of Example 8-1 and its interest are paid in 12 monthly installments, its effective rate of interest is

$$i^* = \frac{24 \times \$1000}{\$10000(12+1)} = 18.46\%$$

Under a collect or regular type of loan, the borrower gets the full use of the principal until maturity when he pays off the principal and the interest. With the discounted loan, the borrower pays the interest (called the discount) at the beginning of the loan period and returns to pay the principal at maturity. Usually the borrower pays the interest by having the bank deduct the interest from the principal in the beginning. By deducting the interest "up front," the bank is said to discount the note. In essence, the firm has to borrow the principal and the interest, thereby driving up the effective interest rate when compared to the same loan made on a collect or regular basis. By paying the interest in the beginning, the borrower loses use of the interest which in effect causes him to pay interest on interest.

Another type of loan is the compensating balance loan. The compensating balance is an amount of funds that the bank requires the customer to keep in the borrowing firm's checking account. This amount is usually 10 to 20 percent of the loan. By requiring a compensating balance, the bank can insure that the borrower will be a good, regular customer and not

138 PART 3: WORKING CAPITAL MANAGEMENT

borrow at this bank and deposit funds in another. For example, assume a business firm borrowed $100,000 for one year at an interest rate of 10% from its bank which required a 20% compensating balance and the borrower currently had no money in a checking account. In effect, under a collect basis loan the borrower would leave the bank with only $80,000 of net proceeds since $20,000 would have to stay in the firm's checking account. So the firm is borrowing and paying interest on $100,000 but getting the use of only $80,000. At maturity the borrower comes in and pays the principal plus $10,000 (or 10% of $100,000) for use of $80,000. This is like renting a 10 room house and after execution of the lease, the landlord tells you that two of the rooms are his so you can't use that space, thus driving up the effective rent per square foot of the remaining 8 rooms.

Suppose Jones Company needs to borrow $100,000 for 30 days to pay one of its suppliers. Four different banks provide offers. Table 8-1 provides formulas and illustrates the analysis of the four types of loans:

- Bank A: $100,000 for 30 days at an interest cost of $1,000 for a regular bank loan
- Bank B: $100,000 loan for 30 days at an interest cost of $800 on a discounted basis
- Bank C: $100,000 regular loan at an interest cost of $700 with a 10% compensating balance requirement
- Bank D: $100,000 discounted loan at an interest cost of $700 with a 10% compensating balance requirement

Table 8-1
Effective Interest Rates on Short-Term Loans

Bank	Loan Type	i^* = effective interest rate; Compensating Balance (CB) = CB% × P I = interest in dollars; P = principal; I = principal × rate × time		
A	Collect or Regular	$i^* = \dfrac{I}{P} \times \dfrac{360}{\text{\#days of note}}$	$i^* = \dfrac{1{,}000}{100{,}000} \times \dfrac{360}{30}$	$= 12\%$
B	Discounted	$i^* = \dfrac{I}{P-I} \times \dfrac{360}{\text{\#days of note}}$	$i^* = \dfrac{800}{(100{,}000-800)} \times \dfrac{360}{30}$	$= 9.68\%$
C	Regular with 10% comp. bal.	$i^* = \dfrac{I}{(P-CB)} \times \dfrac{360}{\text{\#days of note}}$	$i^* = \dfrac{700}{(100{,}000-10{,}000)} \times \dfrac{360}{30}$	$= 9.33\%$
D	Discounted and 10% comp. balance	$i^* = \dfrac{I}{(P-CB-I)} \times \dfrac{360}{\text{\#days of note}}$	$i^* = \dfrac{700}{(100{,}000-10{,}000-700)} \times \dfrac{360}{30}$	$= 9.41\%$

The analysis in Table 8-1 essentially scales the four different offers to a common effective annual interest rate that is comparable. By calculating the effective annual interest rate on a loan the manager can zero in on the "true" cost of the money regardless of the variety of terms that may accompany the agreement. A business confronted with the four loans above would select Bank C with the lowect cost of the money at an effective annual interest rate of

9.33%. But if the firm needs to walk away from the bank with the full $100,000 to use in its business, then it must borrow an amount such that after deducting the 10% compensating balance, $100,000 in proceeds would remain. To compute the amount of the loan necessary to produce the amount of funds needed simply:

$$\text{Amount of Loan} = \frac{\text{Amount needed}}{(1 - CB\%)} \quad \text{Where: CB\% = Compensating Balance as a percent.}$$

For above Bank Loan C: Amount of loan = $\frac{\$100,000}{(1-.1)}$ = $111,111.11

So the business firm would have to borrow $111,111.11 in order to leave the bank with the $100,000 it needs.

Selection of the Bank

Many business firms rely heavily on money markets (i.e. commercial paper) for loans. However, it is important to recognize that such sources are typically more volatile and less dependable in availability during times of financial strain than are banks as a source of funds. Moreover, most banks are willing to discuss the business problems of borrowers and to provide them with informal management counseling services. However, there are important differences among banks with respect to their views of risk and their role in the community.

Banks vary widely in their basic policies toward risk. Some banks prefer to remain conservative, others are more liberal, and still others are quite aggressive. Some banks may ask the firm to renew its loans in bad times.

Although the firm may get more personal attention from smaller banks, it may want to maintain close relations with larger banks because they are able to accommodate its growing loan demands. Banks also vary widely in their lending policies. Lending policies are, in effect, screening devices by which bank managers seek to restrict loans to the type and character that they feel appropriate. For example, banks in a rapidly growing residential community would have a higher proportion of mortgage loans than those in a stable industrial area.

Thus, there are important differences in the lending practices between banks. The bank's attitude toward risk, its loyalty to the customer, its size, and the type of loan that it specializes in are important factors that affect the selection of the bank from which to borrow money. Because short-term bank loans are critical to assure the continuous growth of a business, the selection of the bank requires a careful analysis of these factors.

COMMERCIAL PAPER

Commercial paper consists of unsecured short-term promissory notes sold by finance companies and certain industrial concerns. These notes are issued only by the most credit-worthy companies because they are not secured. Business firms with temporary surplus cash, commercial banks, and non-bank financial institutions purchase commercial paper.

Commercial paper is sold either directly to investors or through dealers. Since the 1920s, some large finance companies such as the General Motors Acceptance Corporation have sold their commercial paper directly to their ultimate investors. These companies

Figure 8-1
Commercial Paper

```
Date  Jan 15, 2001                          Payable on   April 15, 2001


Pay to the Order of _____Bearer_____         $ 100,000


One Hundred Thousand and no/100 _____ Dollars

Drawn on:
K&G NATIONAL BANK
ANYWHERE, USA
```

issue their paper in such a way that the maturity and the amount fit the needs of investors. Industrial firms, utility companies, and relatively small finance companies sell their notes through dealers, five or six of whom dominate the dealer market for commercial paper. They purchase the paper from the issuers and sell it to investors.

Cost of Commercial Paper

Business firms are able to raise funds through the sale of commercial paper more cheaply than through bank loans. The business firm can either sell the commercial paper directly to investors (known as a direct placement) or through commercial paper dealers. In essence, commercial paper is the corporate equivalent of U.S. Treasury bills or T-bills. In general, only large, well-established, credit-worthy firms (i.e. General Motors Corporation) have access to this sector of the money market. The rate on prime commercial paper, in general, is 0.25 to 1 percent below the prime rate for bank loans to the most credit-worthy customers. This rate differential tends to rise in periods of easy money and to fall in periods of tight money.

Commercial paper has maturities from only a few days to 270 days with an average of five months, and it is sold on a discount basis. The borrower is generally required to maintain a back-up line of credit. If the paper is sold through dealers, the effective rate of interest depends on the amount of interest, the amount of discount, and the dealer commission. Typically, the dealer commission is 0.125 percent.

Evaluation of Commercial Paper

As a source of short-term funds, commercial paper has a number of advantages. It is less costly than bank credit. It allows the issuer to avoid the inconvenience and expense of financial arrangements with a number of banks; most short-term bank loans require a compensating balance. It is free of bank regulations that restrict the maximum loan by a national bank to a single borrower. The maximum amount of credit to a single borrower is limited to 10 percent of the bank's capital and surplus.

Example 8-2. A company wants to sell $100,000 of commercial paper every five months at an annual rate of 8 percent and a dealer commission of 0.125 percent.

The dollar amount of interest is $8,000 or ($100,000 × 0.08); the market price of the paper is $92,000 or ($100,000 − $8,000); and the dealer commission is $125 or ($100,000 × 0.125%). The effective annual cost is

$$i^* = \frac{\$8000}{\$92,000 - \$125} = 8.71\%$$

The principal disadvantage of commercial paper is that it is highly impersonal. Thus, although the firm can raise all of its short-term funds through the sale of commercial paper, it must be careful not to impair relations with its bank. Bank relations are much more personal; consequently, banks are more likely to help their loyal customers in periods of tight money. Another disadvantage of commercial paper is the size of funds available. Because yield rates on commercial paper are lower than those on most other market instruments, the size of the funds available to the commercial paper market depends on the excess liquidity that corporations may have at any particular time.

Accounts Receivable Financing

Accounts receivable is a highly liquid asset on the business firm's balance sheet. As such, this asset offers strong collateral for a short-term source of funds. There are two types of accounts receivable financing: **pledging (assigning)** and **factoring**. The pledging of accounts receivable creates a short-term secured loan while factoring involves the actual sale of accounts receivable to another party at a discount. The pledging of accounts receivable can be on a non-notification or notification basis. When a receivable loan is made on a non-notification basis, the borrower's customers are not notified that their accounts have been pledged to the lender. Under this arrangement, the lender trusts the borrowing firm to forward the payments on to the lender as received from the customer. If made on a notification basis, the customers liable for the accounts are notified to send their payments to the lender (usually a bank). Basically, the bank is willing to loan money to the firm with the expectation that as the customers pay on their bills, the borrowing firm will pay off the debt. Accounts receivable is pledged with recourse. **Recourse** means that the borrower absorbs the loss if customers do not pay their accounts. When the firm pledges its receivables, it retains title to the receivables.

However, when the firm "factors" its receivables, it actually sells the receivables to a financial institution called a factor. The sale of accounts receivable is typically made with notification and without recourse.

Pledging Accounts Receivable

An accounts receivable loan is initiated by a legally binding agreement between the borrower and the lender. The agreement specifies the procedures to be followed and the obligations of both parties. Once the working relation has been established, the borrower periodically takes a stack of invoices to the lender. These invoices represent the bills that customers owe the business firm. The lending institution then screens these invoices and rejects those that do not meet its credit standards.

The amount of advance or loan against the accounts receivables depends on the credit worthiness of the borrower and the quality of the receivables themselves. Ordinarily, the maximum amount of advance ranges from 50 to 90 percent of the face value of accounts receivable assigned. This means that a safety margin for the lending institution runs from 50 to 10 percent depending on the quality of the pledged receivables and the credit-worthiness of the firm. The lower the receivable quality and/or borrower's credit-worthiness, the higher the safety margin. If the borrower's customers do not pay their invoices, the lender still has recourse against the borrower.

The cost of an accounts receivable loan tends to be higher than the cost of an unsecured loan for two major reasons. First, companies that borrow against accounts receivable are financially weaker than those that can borrow without the collateral. Second, the accounts receivable loan requires a considerable amount of paperwork for the lending institution and careful supervision.

Factoring Accounts Receivable

The factor purchases the accounts of a client (borrowing firm) on a non-recourse basis and performs a number of additional services such as credit checking, bookkeeping, the collection of accounts, and risk bearing. The factor reviews the credit of the borrower's customers and establishes credit limits in advance. The maximum amount of advance against uncollected accounts receivable ranges from 80 to 90 percent of the invoice value. When the sales are made, the borrower's customers are instructed to make payment directly to the factoring company. For example, suppose John Doe bought $1000 of merchandise from X Corporation on account with terms net, 30 days. Historical analysis indictes that John usually waits 45 days to pay his account. In need of cash on or before the end of the 30 days, X sells John's $1000 account to Factor Company Y for $800 (at a 20% discount based on results of Y's credit analysis) and notifies John of the sale and instructs him to make payment directly to Y. The $200 discount includes compensation for risk and commission (see Example 8-3). Any interest charges would depend on when Y makes the deposit to X's account. Usually Y doesn't have to deposit the $800 into X's account until either John pays or the end of the credit period (30 days in this case), whichever comes first. Let's say John waits his usual 45 days to pay his account. In this case, Y must deposit the $800 in X's account by the end of the 30th day. If Y made the deposit on the 10th day, X would have to pay interest to Y at a predetermined rate for the 20-day interim. And if John never pays his bill, then Y loses the $800, the result of a bad credit analysis decision.

The factor receives the interest charge on the daily balance of advances plus a commission of 1 to 2 percent of the factored receivables for credit analysis, bookkeeping, the collection of accounts, and risk taking. The commission usually depends on the typical size of individual accounts, the volume of receivables factored, and the level of risk. If the borrower does not draw on this account until the receivables are collected, there is no interest charge.

Example 8-3. A company has recently sold its accounts receivable of $10,000. The factor advances 80 percent of the receivables, charges 1 percent interest per month, and charges a 2 percent factoring commission. Both the interest and the commission are paid on a discount basis. Discount basis means that the costs are deducted from the principal at the beginning of the loan period.

The firm's net proceeds are computed as follows:

Face value	$10,000
Less: Reserve due from factor (0.20 x $10,000)	$ 2,000
Factoring fee (0.02 x $10,000)	200
Funds available for advance	$ 7,800
Less: Interest on advance (0.01 x $7,800)	78
Net proceeds from advance	$ 7,722

Thus, the firm receives a cash advance of $7,722 now and expects to recover the $2,000 reserve later. Its total factoring cost of $278 consists of a factoring commission of $200 and an interest charge of $78.

Evaluation of Accounts Receivable Financing

The principal advantage of accounts receivable financing is flexibility. The amount of credit available to the firm increases as the need for credit rises. The firm needs more funds when its sales expand. The amount of credit available to the borrower increases as the firm's sales expand, because the dollar amount of invoices varies directly with sales. The second advantage is that accounts receivable allow the firm to obtain a loan that it might otherwise be unable to obtain. The third advantage is that the factor makes credit checks on the firm's customers; thus, the firm does not need to maintain its own credit department.

Accounts receivable financing also has a number of disadvantages. The cost of borrowing on the security of accounts receivable is usually higher than the cost of an unsecured loan. If invoices are numerous and relatively small in dollar amount, the cost of this credit may be even higher. Another disadvantage is that loans against such liquid assets as receivables may be viewed as a sign of financial weakness. If the firm's suppliers learn about it, they may refuse to sell their goods to the firm on credit.

INVENTORY FINANCING

In addition to accounts receivable, short-term loans may also be secured by a pledge of inventories. Finished goods offer greater collateral value than goods-in-process. Since certain types of raw materials (i.e. lumber, grain) have readily available markets for immediate sale, they offer strong collateral value to lenders. Take furniture for instance. First there is the lumber, then the table partially built, and then the final product, a completed table ready for sale. In terms of collateral value, the raw lumber ranks first, then the finished table, and finally the table-in-process. The desirability of inventories as security of a loan depends on marketability, price stability, durability, and the degree of physical control. For example, such products as grains, sugar, coffee, and major appliances are highly marketable and non-perishable. Hence, the advance against these products may be as high as 80 or 90 percent of their market value. On the other hand, such commodities as highly specialized machinery and fresh foods are not very attractive as collateral for obvious reasons.

From the simple to the more complex, the three approaches to using inventories as security for a short-term loan include: floating (blanket) inventory liens, trust receipts, and warehouse receipts. The complexity of the lending arrangements focuses on the issue of who has physical control over the inventory. The more security the lender demands, the greater will be the lender's physical control over the inventory and the more complex the agreement. Under the simple method, it is relatively cheap to administer the pledged inventories but difficult to police them on the part of the lender. The more complex method requires considerable administrative costs but provides the lender with control over the collateral.

Floating Inventory Liens

The borrowing firm may pledge its entire inventory as security for a loan. This arrangement is generally most convenient when the inventory consists of a lot of different relatively inexpensive items (i.e. small tools, tires, etc.). Due to the nature of the inventory it is virtually impossible for the lender to maintain physical control over the many different, unidentifiable objects. Thus, because the lender cannot exercise tight control over the collateral, enabling the borrower to sell these inventories at will, this type of arrangement is generally used only to provide additional protection and safety to the lender and does not play a major role in the determination of whether the loan will be made. If a loan is made solely on the basis of this type of inventory as collateral, the lender usually advances less than 50% against its book value.

Trust Receipts

A **trust receipt** acknowledges that a borrower is holding goods in trust for the lender. This form of inventory financing is quite favorable when the inventory consists of large, easily identifiable (i.e. by a serial number) products. Automobile dealers frequently use this arrangement. Under a trust-receipt financing arrangement, a finance company may actually buy cars from an automobile manufacturer and then deliver them to an automobile dealer, who executes a trust receipt in favor of the lender. As the dealer sells the cars, the proceeds of the sale are given to the finance company in payment of the loan. The lender periodically checks the cars on the premises of the dealer against the outstanding trust receipts. When the cars that are held in trust are identified by serial number, the serial numbers on the cars are compared with those shown on the security agreement. The audit verifies that the credit system is functioning properly.

In other cases where the borrower purchases the inventory, the lender may advance 80 to 100% of the book value and take a formal lien against the ones used as collateral. As the items are sold, the lender trusts the borrower to promptly pay back any principal and interest applicable to the correspondng collateral. The risk to the lender is a function of the amount of trust placed in the borrower to forward payments honestly. Periodic on-site checks are made to keep the borrower honest.

If the inventory consists of many items whose values are relatively small, the process of verification becomes burdensome and expensive. The lender must place a greater reliance on the borrower's honesty because the goods are on the premises of the borrower and frequently difficult to identify.

Warehouse Receipts

A **warehouse receipt** specifies that inventory is in a warehouse. Two types of warehouses are employed: public warehouses and field warehouses. A public warehouse represents an independent third party that rents space to the storer of goods. Under this arrangement, goods are transported to a public warehouse at the borrower's expense. The warehouse then issues a receipt that evidences title to the goods, and it will release the goods only on the presentation of this receipt. The use of a public warehouse provides the lender with the best protection over the collateral.

A public warehousing arrangement is extremely costly or inconvenient for the borrower because of the space required or the need to move inventory in and out of the borrower's premises at frequent intervals. To overcome these problems, field warehouses are frequently used. In field warehousing, the goods are stored on the premises of the borrower, but they are under the control of a field warehousing company. The company issues a warehouse receipt in the same manner as in public warehousing. The borrower obtains funds from the lender on the basis of the collateral value of the inventory.

The total costs of the warehousing arrangement consist of interest and service charges. Interest charges are imposed by the lender and depend on the size of the loan and the credit worthiness of the borrower. Service charges are costs incurred to check inventory and to assure compliance with the security agreement. They are charged by the warehouse company and depend on the handling charges and the period the goods are in storage. Typically, the costs are higher when the inventories are relatively small or when the number of deposits and withdrawals from the inventory is large.

It is important to recognize that warehouse receipts are as good as the borrower and the warehouse company. The lender wants to be sure that the inventories will actually be there to satisfy the loan if the borrower defaults in making payments. This concern becomes particularly high when the services of a field warehousing company are used.

Summary

In this chapter, both unsecured short-term loans and secured short-term loans have been discussed. Trade credit, bank credit, and commercial paper are the most widely used forms of unsecured short-term loans. The two basic forms of secured short-term loans are accounts receivable financing and inventory financing.

Trade credit represents the largest source of short-term funds for most companies. This credit is particularly important for small companies, because they usually do not have easy access to other sources of funds. There is no explicit cost associated with trade credit, but there is an implicit cost—the cost of the cash discount foregone. Short-term bank loans consist of notes, lines of credit, and revolving credit agreements. Both the line of credit and the revolving credit agreement usually require compensating balances. It is important to recognize that banks provide business firms with non-spontaneous funds. Commercial paper is used only by highly credit-worthy companies. Large finance companies sell their paper directly to investors, whereas medium-size finance companies and utility companies sell their paper through dealers. The major advantage of commercial paper is that it is cheaper than bank credit.

Many firms are unable to obtain unsecured credit, because they are either financially weak or have not established a record of satisfactory earnings. The two principal assets used to secure short-term loans are accounts receivable and inventories. Accounts receivable can be pledged to secure short-term business loans or sold to a factor. Advantages of accounts receivable financing are flexibility, strong collateral, and the elimination of credit investigation fees. Inventory loans may involve a floating inventory lien, a trust receipt, a public warehouse receipt, or a field warehouse receipt. There is always a definite risk that pledged inventories will be liquidated before the loan is repaid, regardless of whether they are left in control of the borrower or a third party.

List of Key Terms

unsecured loans
open account
trade acceptances
line of credit
commercial paper
factoring accounts receivable
trust receipt

secured loans
promissory notes
datings
revolving credit agreement
pledging accounts receivable
recourse
warehouse receipt

Problems

8-1 For each of the following purchases, (a) calculate the effective interest rate of failing to take the discount, and (b) determine the date and amount paid if the discount is taken. Assume that the invoice date is March 10 and that there are 30 days in a month.

(1) $500, 2/10, net 30
(2) $3,500, 4/20, net 60
(3) $1,500, 3/30, net 40
(4) $4,400, 2/10, net 70

8-2 There are three alternatives to increase a net working capital by $10,000:

(1) Forego cash discounts with the terms of 2/10, net 40.
(2) Borrow the money at 7 percent from the bank on a regular basis. This bank loan requires a minimum compensating balance of 20 percent.
(3) Sell commercial paper at 8 percent. The underwriting fees of the issue are 2 percent of the face value.

Calculate the effective annual interest rate of each alternative.

8-3 The Symplex Company has recently factored its accounts receivable at a rate of $10,000 a month. The factor advances 80 percent of the receivables, charges 1 percent interest per month on advances, and charges a 3 percent factoring fee. The interest and fee are paid on a discount basis.

(a) Determine the net proceeds to the company.
(b) Determine the effective annual cost of this financing arrangement.

8-4 A $10,000 bank loan has a stated interest rate of 10 percent.

(a) Calculate the effective interest cost if the loan is on a discount basis.
(b) Calculate the effective interest cost if the loan requires a minimum compensating balance of 20 percent and it is on a discount basis.
(c) Calculate the effective interest cost if the loan requires a 25 percent compensating balance but it is on a collect or regular basis.

8-5 For each of the following installment transactions, calculate the effective interest cost:

Creditor	Cash Price	Down Payment	Monthly Payment	Term of Sale
(a)	$12,500	$500	$300	60 months
(b)	3,250	250	120	36
(c)	1,500	300	102	12
(d)	600	100	51	10
(e)	350	50	80	4

8-6 The ABC Company sells its accounts receivable at a rate of $300,000 per month. The factor advances 80 percent of the receivables for an annual interest of 9 percent. A 2 percent factoring commission is charged on all receivables purchased. Both the interest and the factoring commission are paid on a collect basis. The factor's services are expected to save the company a credit department expense and bad-debt expense of $3,000 a month. What is the effective interest cost of this service?

8-7 A company has a $50,000 revolving credit with its bank. The interest rate of the credit is 10 percent. In addition, there is a 1 percent commitment fee on the unused portion of the revolving credit.

(a) If the company expects to use on average 70 percent of the total commitment, what is the expected annual dollar cost of this credit arrangement?
(b) What is the percentage cost when both the interest rate and the commitment fee paid are considered?
(c) What happens to the percentage cost if on average only 40 percent of the total commitment is used?

8-8 A company needs to borrow $45,000 in order to finance its accounts receivable. Two banks in town offered different terms: Wayne National Bank offered the company a 10 percent loan with a 10 percent compensating balance to be paid back in quarterly payments. Detroit State Bank offered the company an 11 percent loan to be paid back semiannually. Which loan term should the company take?

8-9 You can borrow $50,000 at 10 percent interest from a local bank. What is the effective rate of interest under the following conditions?

(a) The principal and interest are to be repaid at the end of one year, but there is a 20 percent compensating balance requirement.
(b) The loan is discounted and the principal is repaid at the end of one year.
(c) The loan is to be repaid in 12 monthly installments.

8-10 A company finds that it will need another $50,000 in August to build up inventory. The First National Bank has offered to make a loan at 10 percent annually, provided the company maintains a 20 percent compensating balance. The Second National Bank, a competing bank, indicated that it will lend the company $50,000 for 13 percent with no compensating balance. Which bank is making the better offer?

Part 4

Capital Expenditure Analysis

Part Four moves into an analysis of capital investment decisions. Capital expenditure analysis is defined as the entire process of allocating limited capital resources among various investment projects whose benefits are expected beyond one year. Chapter 9 discusses the time value of money which is basic to investment decisions. This concept permits us to make benefits and costs in different time periods comparable. Chapters 10 and 11 evaluate investment projects under certainty. Chapter 11 analyzes investment projects under uncertainty. Chapter 12 describes the cost of capital. We first discuss such component costs as the cost of debt and the cost of owners' equity. Then we obtain the weighted average cost of capital by bringing together the individual component costs.

9

TIME VALUE OF MONEY

Capital budgeting decisions involve the allocation and commitment of funds to investment projects whose returns are expected to extend beyond one year. Such investments usually require very large sums of money and are made in expectation of benefits to be realized over an extended period of time. Thus, the rational use of capital resources is critical for the future well-being of the company. Moreover, once capital investment decisions are made, they are not easily reversible. Used plants and most used equipment have a limited market. In certain areas, production methods are rapidly outmoded by increasingly higher levels of technology.

The five chapters in Part Four describe capital expenditure analysis. In this chapter we deal with the time value of money, which is basic to investment decisions. In Chapters 10 and 11, we discuss capital budgeting under certainty, which relies heavily on the time value of money. Uncertainty is explicitly and formally discussed in Chapter 12. The cost of capital and its application to capital budgeting problems are considered in Chapter 13.

Since money has time value, present dollars do not equate future dollars. And since almost all investment and financing decisions involve a trade of present dollars for future dollars, concepts of present and future value lay the foundation of the finance discipline. The concept of compound value or present value refers to the conversion of cash flow over a period of time to a common point in time. The concepts of compound value and present value are used in this conversion process. The value of any investment project is the present value of the future benefits that will flow to its owner. In order to convert future benefits into present value, the future benefits must be discounted to reflect the time value. The **discount rate** consists of the rate of return on a riskless investment plus a premium based on the perceived risk that expected benefits will not materialize. The concept of present value is important to an understanding of such topics as capital budgeting under certainty (Chapters 10 and 11), the cost of capital (Chapter 13), lease versus purchase decision (Chapter 18), and mergers (Chapter 19).

COMPOUND OR FUTURE VALUE VERSUS PRESENT VALUE

Assuming a zero rate of inflation, would you prefer to receive $100 today or $100 three years from now? Clearly, you would rather receive the $100 today since you could invest it at the current market rate of interest and your investment would grow to

PART 4: CAPITAL EXPENDITURE ANALYSIS

something greater than $100 at the end of three years. Similarly, would you pay out $100 today for the right to receive $100 three years hence? Absolutely not, if you did, you would earn no return. So you would discount (or back out interest at the compounded market interest rate) the future dollars back to the present. Assuming a market interest rate of 10%, Figure 9-1 outlines the process with a time line.

Figure 9-1
Present Value and Future Value Time Line

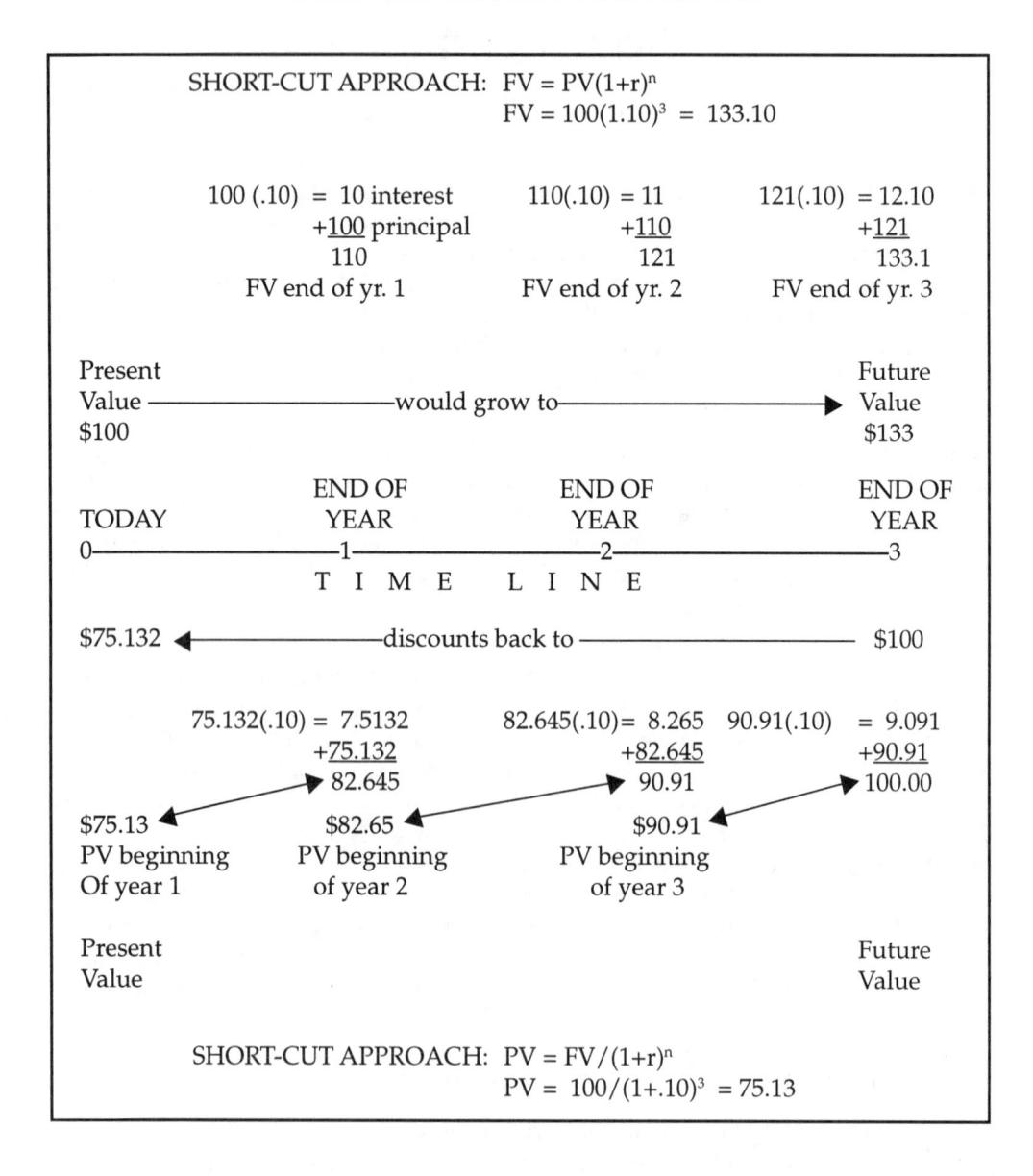

SHORT-CUT APPROACH: $FV = PV(1+r)^n$
$FV = 100(1.10)^3 = 133.10$

100(.10) = 10 interest	110(.10) = 11	121(.10) = 12.10
+100 principal	+110	+121
110	121	133.1
FV end of yr. 1	FV end of yr. 2	FV end of yr. 3

Present Value $100 ———would grow to———▶ Future Value $133

TODAY 0 ——— END OF YEAR 1 ——— END OF YEAR 2 ——— END OF YEAR 3

TIME LINE

$75.132 ◀——— discounts back to ——— $100

75.132(.10) = 7.5132	82.645(.10) = 8.265	90.91(.10) = 9.091
+75.132	+82.645	+90.91
82.645	90.91	100.00

$75.13 — PV beginning Of year 1
$82.65 — PV beginning of year 2
$90.91 — PV beginning of year 3

Present Value ——— Future Value

SHORT-CUT APPROACH: $PV = FV/(1+r)^n$
$PV = 100/(1+.10)^3 = 75.13$

Compound or future value represents what present dollars in hand will grow to in the future if compounded for some number of periods at some given rate of interest. Figure 9-1 illustrates this process of $100 growing, at an annually compounded rate of 10%, to $110 at the end of year 1, to $121 at the end of year 2, and finally to $133.10 at the end of year 3. As Figure 9-1 shows, compounding is simply computing interest at certain intervals and adding it back to the principal so that in the periods that follow, interest is earned on the principal plus the accumulated interest. For example, suppose someone offers you a value equivalent to $125 three years from today in exchange for $100 today. If you demand at least a 10% (as in Figure 9-1) return on your money, would you pay $100 for this offer today? Absolutely not, since doing so would force you to lose roughly $8 or ($133 – $125) or stated differently, you would not earn the 10% return you could have gotten elsewhere. On the other hand, if the future value of the offer was $140, you should quickly accept the offer since you would realize a $7.00 gain or ($140 – $133) resulting in a return greater than 10%.

Present value represents future values discounted back (reverse compounding) to the present at some rate of interest for some number of periods. Figure 9-1 demonstrates how a future value of $100 discounts to $90.91 at the beginning of year 3, to $82.645 at the beginning of year 2, and finally it reverse compounds to a present value of $75.13 at the beginning of year 1. In this case, what if the ask price for an offer to receive $100 three years from now is currently $80? Assuming your opportunity cost of money is 10%, if you make this trade at the $80 asking price, you will lose roughly $5.00 or ($80.00 – $75.00) today and your rate of return is less than 10%. Alternatively, at any asking price below $75.13, you would reap an immediate gain and earn a rate of return greater than the 10% you can get elsewhere. Since almost every business decision involves a trade of present dollars (the current price) for some future dollar offer, the understanding and application of these concepts is critical to financial decisions.

FINANCIAL CALCULATORS

Powerful financial calculators, priced under $30, currently exist that can assist in completing most financial problems. These calculators are pre-programmed to carry out numerous finance routines with a few key strokes. The financial calculator can not teach you the fundamental concepts but can only serve as a useful tool in working problems in the fastest and most efficient manner. Simply understanding how to use the calculator is no substitute for knowledge of the underlying concepts of finance. The calculator can aid in the application of the concepts through problem-solving. It is of little value to know how to produce the "right numeric answer" and not know what it means. While, the emphasis of this text is on the basic understanding and application of fundamental finance concepts, problem-solving via the Texas Instruments (TI) *BA II PLUS* financial calculator will be illustrated to students with their work. In addition to our illustrations, the calculator comes with the *BA II PLUS BUSINESS CALCULATOR MANUAL*. Students should note because of the greater precision of the calculator, small differences will result between solving problems with the calculator and the financial tables.

154 PART 4: CAPITAL EXPENDITURE ANALYSIS

Figure 9-2 below describes the major keys used in solving finance problems.

Figure 9-2
Major Keys for TI BA II Plus Calculator

Rows					
1	Quit Func. Above Key	Set Func. Above Key	Del. Func. Above Key	Ins. Func. Above Key	
2	CPT Key	Enter Key	Scroll Up ↑ Key	Scroll Down ↓ Key	On/Off Key
3	2nd Key	CF Key	NPV Key	IRR Key	Right Arrow Key
4	XP/Y Func. above Key	P/Y Func. above Key	Amort. Func. above Key	BGN Func. above Key	CLR TVM Func. above Key
5	N Key	I/Y Key	PV Key	PMT Key	FV Key

As shown, the first and fourth rows represent the functions labeled above the keys. By pressing 2nd and the actual key, you access the function above the key. For example, to clear the TVM registry exhibited by all values in the TVM row or row five above, simply press 2nd and KEY FV which activates the CLR TVM function. This action will clear the values in the terminal value row five above. To clear the calculator of all previous operations so that you can begin new TVM calculations, always press 2nd QUIT and 2nd FV key. These instructions provide only a brief overview for getting started. Detailed instructions and steps to use the calculator in solving problems are in the *BA II PLUS BUSINESS CALCULATOR MANUAL* that is acquired with purchase of the calculator.

Rows four and five (described below) and the CPT key are of particular interest here since they involve present value/future value calculations. Other keys will be explained as they become relevant to later chapter material.

Keys:

CPT	=	Computes a desired value after entering appropriate input values
N	=	Number of periods
I/Y	=	Interest rate per year
PV	=	Present value
PMT	=	Amount of payment when working with annuities
FV	=	Future value

Functions Above Keys (Activated by pressing 2nd and the desired key):

xP/Y	=	Multiplies a value in the display by the number of payments per year
P/Y	=	Sets the number of payments per year and the number of compounding periods per year

Chapter 9: Time Value of Money

Amort	=	Performs amortization calculations for annuities
BGN	=	Set for end of period (ordinary annuity) or beginning of period payments (annuity due)
CLR TVM	=	Clears the terminal value worksheet

COMPOUND OR FUTURE VALUE OF A CURRENT LUMP SUM

Interest is said to **compound** when the interest for each period is added to the principal and the interest for the next period is computed on the total. The time of computation could be the end of a quarter, a year, etc. To treat the matter systematically, let us define the following notations.

FV_n = value at the end of n periods (compound value)
PV = initial sum of money (present value)
i = interest rate or discount rate
n = number of periods.

If a company invests PV on a project that earns i percent per period, the company would have at the end of one period:

$$FV_1 = PV(1 + i) \qquad (9\text{-}1)$$

If the initial investment and the accumulated interest continue to earn at the i percent per period, the company would have at the end of two periods:

$$FV_2 = PV(1 + i)^2 \qquad (9\text{-}2)$$

Under the same assumption, the company would have at the end of n periods:

$$FV_n = PV(1 + i)^n$$
$$= PV \times IF_{FV_{n,i}} \qquad (9\text{-}3)$$

where $IF_{n,i}$ = compound-value interest factor or simply interest factor.

Example 9-1. A person deposits $100 in a savings account that pays 8 percent interest compounded annually. How much money would the person have at the end of three years?

At the end of three years, the person would have

$$FV_3 = \$100(1 + 0.08)^3 = \$125.97$$

When the value of n is relatively small, it is fairly simple to compute the compound value using Equation $FV_n = PV(1 + i)^n$. But when the value of n becomes large, it takes a considerable amount of time to determine the compound value this way. To simplify the computation procedure, it is essential to tabulate the value of the compound interest factor $IF_{FV_{n,i}}$. Table A in Appendix A shows the values of $IF_{FV_{n,i}}$ covering a wide range of n and i.

The interest factor in Example 9-1 is 1.260, which is found in the intersection of the three-year row and the 8 percent column in Table A. This interest factor would be used rather than raising (1 + i) to the third power:

$$FV_3 = \$100 \times IF_{FV_{3,8\%}} = \$100 \times 1.260 = \$126$$

The small difference between $125.97 from the previous computation and $126 from this computation results from rounding the decimals.

By financial calculator:

Table 9-1
Financial Calculator Solution of Example 9-1

Problem	CLEAR TVM Registry	SET Compounding periods per year	ENTER N, I/Y, and PV	SET as ordinary	COMPUTE ANSWER
Calculating future value	Press 2nd QUIT and 2nd CLR TVM	Press 2nd P/Y; Press 1 and hit ENTER; then 2nd QUIT	Press 3 and hit N; Press 8 and hit IY; Press 100 and +/− and hit PV	Press 2nd BGN; Press 2nd SET until END appears; Press 2nd QUIT	Press CPT FV; Result is $125.97 Future Value at end of 3 Years

Now, suppose that interest is calculated and added back to the principal more frequently than one time a year. This process of compounding more frequently is quite common among financial institutions. We continue with Example 9-1 to illustrate semiannual, quarterly, monthly, weekly, daily, and even continuous compounding. According to Formula 9-3

$$FV_n = PV(1+i)^n \quad \text{for annual compounding.}$$

To compound at shorter intervals, we amend formula 9-3 to

$$FV_n = PV(1+\frac{i}{m})^{mn} \quad (9\text{-}3a)$$

where m = number of times per year interest is compounded. Table 9-2 solves Example 9-1 for semiannual, quarterly, monthly, weekly, daily, and continuous compounding by formula and by financial calculator.

Table 9-2
**Financial Calculator Solution of Example 9-1
with Compounding More than Once a Year**

COMPOUNDING INTERVAL	BY FORMULA	BY FINANCIAL CALCULATOR
SEMIANNUAL	$FV_n = 100(1+\frac{.08}{2})^{2\times3}$ Where: i= 8%, n=3 years, and m= 2 compounding periods per year	2nd P/Y; enter 2; 2nd QUIT; now enter 2x3 or 6 for N, 8 for I/Y, 100 for PV, and hit CPT, then FV; answer = $126.53
QUARTERLY	$FV_n = 100(1+\frac{.08}{4})^{4\times3}$ Where: i= 8%, n=3 years, and m= 4 compounding periods per year	2nd P/Y; enter 4; 2nd QUIT; now enter 4X3 or 12 for N, 8 for I/Y, 100 for PV, and hit CPT, then FV; answer = $126.82
MONTHLY	$FV_n = 100(1+\frac{.08}{12})^{12\times3}$ Where: i= 8%, n= 3 years, and m= 12 compounding periods per year	2nd P/Y; enter 12; 2nd QUIT; now enter 12x3 or 36 for N, 8 for I/Y, 100 for PV, and hit CPT, then FV; answer = $127.0237
WEEKLY	$FV_n = 100(1+\frac{.08}{52})^{52\times3}$ Where: i= 8%, n=3 years, and m= 52 compounding periods per year	2nd P/Y; enter 52; 2nd QUIT; now enter 52x3 or 156 for N, 8 for I/Y, 100 for PV, and hit CPT, then FV; answer = $127.1015
DAILY	$FV_n = 100(1+\frac{.08}{365})^{365\times3}$ Where: i= 8%, n=3 years, and m= 365 compounding periods per year	2nd P/Y; enter 365; 2nd QUIT; now enter 365x3 or 1095 for N, 8 for I/Y, 100 for PV, and hit CPT, then FV; answer = $127.1216
HOURLY	$FV_n = 100(1+\frac{.08}{8,760})^{8,760\times3}$ Where: i= 8%, n=3 years, and m= 8,760 compounding periods per year	2nd P/Y; enter 8,760; 2nd QUIT; now enter 8,760x3 or 26,280 for N, 8 for I/Y, 100 for PV, and hit CPT, then FV; answer = $127.1248
PER SECOND or CONTINUOULSY	$FV = 100(1+\frac{.08}{525,600})^{525,600\times3}$ Where: i= 8%, n=3 years, and m= 525,600 compounding periods per year	2nd P/Y; enter 525,600; 2nd QUIT; now enter 525,600x3 or 1,576,800 for N, 8 for I/Y, 100 for PV, and hit CPT, then FV; answer = $127.1249

Extending the number of compounding periods to a "per second" basis is equivalent to continuous compounding. But if we continue to increase the number of compounding periods, we find that FV_n approaches:

$$FV_n = PV \times (e^{rxn}) \qquad (9\text{-}3b)$$

where e is the exponential function having a value of 2.71828, r= the annual interest rate, and n = number of years so for Example 9-1:

$$FV_n = 100 \times (2.71828)^{.08 \times 3} = 127.1249$$

As shown in Table 9-2, compounding the $100 present value every second at 8% for 3 years results in a future value of $127.1249 that is likewise equivalent to multiplying the $100 present value by e^{rn} where e is the limit of the expression $(1+1/m)^m$ as m approaches infinity. In essence, as the number of compounding periods or m approaches infinity, one dollar compounded continuously for 3 years at 8% approaches $(2.17828)^{.08 \times 3}$ or e^{rn} which comes to $1.271249. And for $100 such dollars the future value is simply 100(1.271249) or roughly $127.12.

Additional Problems

Example 9-2. Calculating future value with multiple compounding periods.

Suppose you invest $10,000 in a CD at 6% for the next 11 years. How much money will you accumulate by the end of the 11-year period if compounded annually, semiannually, quarterly, monthly, weekly, daily, or continuously? Table 9-3 provides results by financial calculator as demonstrated in previous Table 9-2.

Table 9-3
Solving for FV when Compounding More than Once Per Year

Compounding Intervals Per Year	Future Value at end of 11 years
Annually	$18982.98
Semiannually	$19161.03
Quarterly	$19253.33
Monthly	$19316.13
Daily	$19346.87
Hourly	$19347.8796
Continuously or per second	$19347.9226

Chapter 9: Time Value of Money   159

Example 9-3. Finding the number of periods.

Suppose you currently have a $10,000 CD in the bank that is earning 6% compounded annually and this interest rate is expected to remain constant in the future. How many years will it take for the value of your investment to double or increase to $20,000? (See Table 9-4 for solution by financial calculator.)

Table 9-4
Finding Number of Periods

Problem	CLEAR TVM Registry	SET Compounding periods per year	ENTER I/Y, PV, and FV	SET as ordinary	COMPUTE ANSWER
Calculating the number of periods	Press 2nd QUIT and 2nd CLR TVM	Press 2nd P/Y; Press 1 and hit ENTER; then 2nd QUIT	Press 6 and hit I/Y; Press 10000 +/- and hit PV; Press 20000 and hit FV	Press 2nd BGN; Press 2nd SET until END appears; Press 2nd QUIT	Press CPT N; Result is 11.90 years for the value to double to 20000

Example 9-4. Finding the rate or I/Y

Suppose you observe that the price of a loaf of bread increased from $.95 per loaf to $1.30 per loaf over 8 years. What is the annual rate of inflation on the bread over this time period? (See Table 9-5 for the financial calculator solution.)

Table 9-5
Finding the Rate

Problem	CLEAR TVM Registry	SET Compounding periods per year	ENTER N, PV, and FV	SET as ordinary	COMPUTE ANSWER
Calculating the annual rate of inflation	Press 2nd QUIT and 2nd CLR TVM	Press 2nd P/Y; Press 1 and hit ENTER; then 2nd QUIT	Press 8 and hit N; Press .95 +/- and hit PV; Press 1.30 and hit FV	Press 2nd BGN; Press 2nd SET until END appears; Press 2nd QUIT	Press CPT I/Y; Result is 3.99% annual rate of inflation on the bread

160 PART 4: CAPITAL EXPENDITURE ANALYSIS

COMPOUND VALUE OF AN ANNUITY

An ordinary **annuity** is a series of equal cash flows that occur at the end of each period over a specified number of periods. The term annuity usually refers to a series of fixed annual deposits or payments, but it may also apply to a deposit or payment schedule with various intervals. An annuity may be made annually, quarterly, or even daily. An annuity due is a series of equal cash flows that occur at the beginning of each period for a specified number of periods.

Example 9-5 Ordinary Annuity. You deposit $100 at the end of each year in a savings account that pays 8 percent interest compounded annually. How much money would you receive at the end of three years?

Figure 9-3
Compound Value of a $100 Three-Year Ordinary Annuity

End of Period

0	1	2	3		
Deposits ($CF)	-100	-100	-100	= +100	CF
			$100(1 + 0.08)^1$	= +108	$CF(1+i)^1$
			$100(1 + 0.08)^2$	= +117	$CF(1+i)^2$
				+325 = FVA	

Where CF = equal cash flows of annuity.

Because deposits are made at the end of each year, the last deposit earns no interest; the second deposit earns interest for one year; and the first deposit earns interest for two years. Figure 9-3 depicts this process. The compound value of the $100 three-year annuity is $325 or (117 + 108 + 100). Expressed algebraically, the future or compound value of the annuity is

$$FVA = CF(1 + i)^2 + CF(1 + i)^1 + CF$$
$$= \$100(1 + 0.08)^2 + \$100(1 + 0.08)^1 + \$100$$
$$= \$325$$

where FVA = future value of an ordinary annuity and CF = periodic deposit or payment.

Thus, the future value of an ordinary annuity at the end of any year n is

$$FVA = CF(1 + i)^{n-1} + CF(1 + i)^{n-2} + ... + CF$$
$$= CF[(1 + i)^{n-1} + (1 + i)^{n-2} + ... + 1]$$
$$= CF \times IF_{FVA_{n,i}} \quad (9\text{-}4)$$

where $IF_{FVA_{n,i}}$ = annuity interest factor.

Table B in Appendix A shows the values of $IF_{FVA_{n,i}}$ covering a wide range of n and i. The annuity interest factor of three years and 8 percent is found to be $IF_{FVA_{3,8\%}} = 3.246$ in Table B. Hence, the compound value of the $100 three-year annuity with an interest rate of 8 percent is

$$FVA = \$100 \times IF_{FVA_{3,8\%}} = \$100 \times 3.246 = \$324.6$$

By financial calculator:

Setting:

Function	entry	
2nd P/Y	1	(for one compounding period per period)
2nd PMT	Display should show END, if not hit 2nd ENTER to activate the SET function to convert to end-of-period payments for ordinary annuity. Then, press 2nd CPT to activate the QUIT function.	

Input	KEY
3	N
8	I/Y
$100	+/- to convert to negative, then press PMT

Computation:

Press CPT   FV = $324.64

Example 9-6. Annuity Due. You deposit $100 at the beginning of each year in a savings account that pays 8 percent interest compounded annually. How much money would you receive at the end of three years?

Figure 9-4
Compound Value of a $100 Three-Year Annuity Due

```
-$100              -$100              -$100         FV= +$350.60
0_____1_____2_____3
           T    I    M    E    L    I    N    E
```

Because deposits are made at the beginning of each year, each deposit earns an additional year's interest. Figure 9-4 depicts this process. The compound value of the $100 three-year annuity is $351 or (126 + 117 + 108). Expressed algebraically, the compound value of the annuity is

$$\begin{aligned} FVA &= CF(1+i)^3 + CF(1+i)^2 + CF(1+i) \\ &= \$100(1+0.08)^3 + \$100(1+0.08)^2 + \$100(1+.08) \\ &= \$351 \end{aligned}$$

where FVA = future value of an annuity due and CF = periodic deposit or payment.

Thus, the compound value of an annuity due at the end of any year n is

$$FVA = CF(1+i)^n + CF(1+i)^{n-1} + \ldots + CF(1+i)$$
$$= CF[(1+i)^n + (1+i)^{n-1} + \ldots + (1+i)]$$
$$= CF \times (IF_{FVA_{n+1,i}} - 1) \qquad (9\text{-}4a)$$

Table B in Appendix A shows the values of $IF_{FVA_{n,i}}$ covering a wide range of n and i. The annuity interest factor in Table B for four years and 8 percent is found to be 4.506 and subtracting 1 gives us 3.506. Hence, the compound value of the $100 three-year annuity due with an interest rate of 8 percent is

$$FVA = \$100 \times [IF_{FVA_{4,8\%}} - 1] = \$100 \times 3.506 = \$350.60$$

By financial calculator:

Setting:

Function	entry	
2nd P/Y	1	(for one compounding period per year)

2nd PMT — If display shows END, hit 2nd ENTER to activate the SET function to convert to beginning-of-period payments to display BGN for annuity due. Then, press 2nd CPT to activate the QUIT function.

Input	KEY	
3	N	
8	I/Y	
$100	+/– to convert to negative, then press PMT	

Computation:

Press CPT   FV = $350.61

Additional Problems

Example 9-7. Solving for the annual and quarterly payment of an ordinary annuity and an annuity due.

Suppose you desire to accumulate $20000 at the end of the next 8 years. If you can earn a 10% return on your investment, what necessary payment would you have to deposit into your savings plan if: (calculator solution in table 9-6 below)

A) Annual and at the end of the period for an ordinary annuity?

B) Annual and at the beginning of the period for an annuity due?

C) Quarterly and at the end of the period?

D) Quarterly and at the beginning of the period?

Table 9-6
Solving for Payment under Ordinary Annuity and Annuity Due

Problem	CLEAR TVM Registry	SET Compounding periods per year	ENTER N, FV, and I/Y	SET as ordinary or annuity due	COMPUTE ANSWER
A) Ordinary and annual	Press 2nd QUIT and 2nd CLR TVM	Press 2nd P/Y; Press 1 and hit ENTER; then 2nd QUIT	Press 8 and hit N; Press 20000 and hit FV; Press 10 and hit I/Y	Press 2nd BGN; Press 2nd SET until END appears; Press 2nd QUIT	Press CPT PMT; Result is -$1748.88 per year at end of year
B) Annuity Due and annual	Press 2nd QUIT and 2nd CLR TVM	Press 2nd P/Y; Press 1 and hit ENTER; then 2nd QUIT	Press 8 and hit N; Press 20000 and hit FV; Press 10 and hit I/Y	Press 2nd BGN; Press 2nd SET until BGN appears; Press 2nd QUIT	Press CPT PMT; Result is -$1589.89 per year at beginning of year
C) Ordinary and quarterly	Press 2nd QUIT and 2nd CLR TVM	Press 2nd P/Y; Press 4 and hit ENTER; then 2nd QUIT	Press 32 and hit N; Press 20000 and hit FV; Press 10 and hit I/Y	Press 2nd BGN; Press 2nd SET until END appears; Press 2nd QUIT	Press CPT PMT; Result is -$415.37 per qtr. at end of each quarter
D) Annuity Due and quarterly	Press 2nd QUIT and 2nd CLR TVM	Press 2nd P/Y; Press 4 and hit ENTER; then 2nd QUIT	Press 32 and hit N; Press 20000 and hit FV; Press 10 and hit I/Y	Press 2nd BGN; Press 2nd SET until BGN appears; Press 2nd QUIT	Press CPT PMT; Result is -$405.24 per qtr. at beginning of each quarter

Example 9-8. Solving for the future value of an ordinary annuity and an annuity due.

Your child has just been born and you want to plan for his education. If you can save $100 per month and can earn a 12% return, how much money will you have at the end of 18 years when your son is ready for college if: (calculator solution in Table 9-7)

A) Ordinary Annuity?

B) Annuity Due?

Table 9-7
Solving for the Future Value of an Ordinary Annuity and Annuity Due

Problem	CLEAR TVM Registry	SET Compounding periods per year	ENTER N, PMT, and I/Y	SET as ordinary annuity due	COMPUTE ANSWER
A) Ordinary	Press 2nd QUIT and 2nd CLR TVM	Press 2nd P/Y; Press 12 and hit ENTER; then 2nd QUIT	Press 216 and hit N; Press 100 and hit -/+ and hit PMT; Press 12 and hit I/Y	Press 2nd BGN; Press 2nd SET until END appears; Press 2nd QUIT	Press CPT FV; Result is $75,786.06 accumulated at end of 18 years
B) Annuity Due	Press 2nd QUIT and 2nd CLR TVM	Press 2nd P/Y; Press 12 and hit ENTER; then 2nd QUIT	Press 216 and hit N; Press 100 and hit -/+ and hit PMT; Press 12 and hit I/Y	Press 2nd BGN; Press 2nd SET until BGN appears; Press 2nd QUIT	Press CPT FV; Result is $76,543.92 accumulated at end of 18 years

Example 9-9. Solving for the interest rate on an ordinary annuity and an annuity due.

You plan to build a home in 10 years. If the house will cost $350,000 ten years from today, what rate of return would you have to earn on your set-aside savings to achieve your goal if you can: (Calculator solution in Table 9-8)

A) Save $10,000 per year at the end of each year?

B) Save $10,000 per year at the beginning of each year?

C) Save $1,000 per month at the end of each month?

D) Save $1,000 per month at the beginning of each month?

Table 9-8
Solving for Rate of Return or Interest Rate on an Ordinary Annuity and on Annuity Due

Problem	CLEAR TVM Registry	SET Compounding periods per year	ENTER N, FV, and PMT	SET as ordinary annuity due	COMPUTE ANSWER
A) Ordinary and annual	Press 2nd QUIT and 2nd CLR TVM	Press 2nd P/Y; Press 1 and hit ENTER; then 2nd QUIT	Press 10 and hit N; Press 350000 and hit FV; Press 10000, +/-, and hit PMT	Press 2nd BGN; Press 2nd SET until END appears; Press 2nd QUIT	Press CPT I/Y; Result is 26.03% required return to achieve goal
B) Annuity Due and annual	Press 2nd QUIT and 2nd CLR TVM	Press 2nd P/Y; Press 1 and hit ENTER; then 2nd QUIT	Press 10 and hit N; Press 350000 and hit FV; Press 10000, +/-, and hit PMT	Press 2nd BGN; Press 2nd SET until BGN appears; Press 2nd QUIT	Press CPT I/Y; Result is 22.02% required return to achieve goal
C) Ordinary and monthly	Press 2nd QUIT and 2nd CLR TVM	Press 2nd P/Y; Press 12 and hit ENTER; then 2nd QUIT	Press 120 and hit N; Press 350000 and hit FV; Press 1000, +/-, and hit PMT	Press 2nd BGN; Press 2nd SET until END appears; Press 2nd QUIT	Press CPT I/Y; Result is 18.87% required return to achieve goal
D) Annuity Due and monthly	Press 2nd QUIT and 2nd CLR TVM	Press 2nd P/Y; Press 12 and hit ENTER; then 2nd QUIT	Press 120 and hit N; Press 350000 and hit FV; Press 1000, +/-, and hit PMT	Press 2nd BGN; Press 2nd SET until BGN appears; Press 2nd QUIT	Press CPT I/Y; Result is 18.62% required return to achieve goal

PRESENT VALUE OF A FUTURE LUMP SUM

Investment projects involve the exchange of present dollars for some offer of future dollars. And since present dollars differ from future dollars because of time value, PV and FV are not comparable. The concept of present value can be used to simplify this problem. As explained earlier in the chapter, the future dollar offer must be discounted

$$PV = FV \times IF_{PV,n,i}$$

to its present value at the interest rate the firm requires on all its investments, usually referred to as the opportunity cost of capital. This process is simply reverse compounding or the process of backing interest out to account for the time value lost by not having those dollars today. By converting FV to its PV equivalent, we now have values that are economically comparable for decision purposes. Essentially this concept evaluates the future cash flows in terms of their worth today. When this is done for all projects, one has a common basis from which to make the selection decision.

The **present value** of a lump sum represents the current value of a future payment. Because discounting (finding present value) is simply the reverse of compounding, one can readily transform Equation (9-3) into a present value formula as follows:

$$PV = \frac{FV_n}{(1+i)^n} = FV_n \times \frac{1}{(1+i)^n}$$

$$= FV_n \times IF_{PV_{n,i}} \quad (9\text{-}5)$$

where $IF_{PV_{n,i}}$ = discount factor. Table C in Appendix A shows the values of $IF_{PV_{n,i}}$ covering a wide range of n and i. Table 9-9 represents selected portions of Table C.

Example 9-10. Suppose a firm is offered $1,000 at the end of three years. How much is it willing to pay for this offer today if the firm's opportunity cost of funds is 6 percent?

PV=?   FV offer = $1000

0_____1_____2_____3

T I M E   L I N E

A) Solved by tables:

To find a discount factor of $IF_{PV_{3,6\%}}$, look down the 6 percent column in Table 9-9 to the three-year row. We find it to be 0.840, which is underlined. Thus, the present value of $1,000 due in three years and discounted at 6 percent is

$$PV = \$1{,}000 \times IF_{PV_{3,6\%}} = \$1{,}000 \times 0.840 = \$840$$

Table 9-9
Present Value of $1

Period	1%	2%	3%	4%	5%	6%	7%	8%
1	.990	.980	.971	.962	.952	.943	.935	.926
2	.980	.961	.943	.925	.907	.890.	873	.857
3	.971	.942	.915	.889	.864	.840	.816	.794
4	.961	.924	.888	.855	.823	.792	.763	.735
5	.951	.906	.863	.822	.784	.747	.713	.681
6	.942	.888	.837	.790	.746	.705	.666	.630
7	.933	.871	.813	.760	.711	.665	.623	.583
8	.923	.853	.789	.731	.677	.627	.582	.540

B) Solved by financial calculator:

Table 9-10
Solving for Present Value

Problem	CLEAR TVM Registry	SET Compounding periods per year	ENTER N, FV, and I/Y	SET as ordinary	COMPUTE ANSWER
Find present value of future sum of $1,000	Press 2nd QUIT and 2nd CLR TVM	Press 2nd P/Y; Press 1 and hit ENTER; then 2nd QUIT	Press 3 and hit N; Press 1000 and hit FV; Press 6 and hit I/Y	Press 2nd BGN; Press 2nd SET until END appears; Press 2nd QUIT	Press CPT PV; Result is $839.62 present value

Additional Problems

Up to now, it has been assumed that the unknown variable was the present value of a future lump sum. But there are numerous occasions in business when it becomes necessary to determine the interest rate or the number of periods. To find the interest rate or the number of periods, we can change Equation 9-5 as follows:

$$PV = FV_n \times IF_{PV_{n,i}}, \text{ or } IF_{PV_{n,i}} = \frac{PV}{FV_n} \tag{9-6}$$

Example 9-11 Find the rate of interest. You can borrow $5,400 from a bank if you contract to pay the bank $10,000 at the end of eight years. What is the rate of interest you will have to pay on this loan?

168 PART 4: CAPITAL EXPENDITURE ANALYSIS

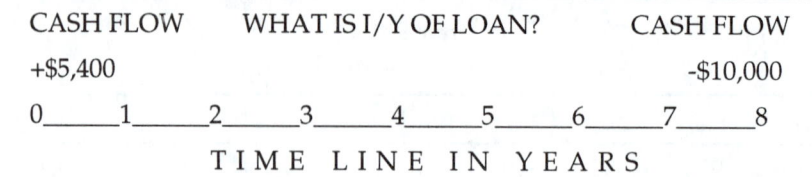

```
CASH FLOW       WHAT IS I/Y OF LOAN?        CASH FLOW
+$5,400                                      -$10,000

0_____1_____2_____3_____4_____5_____6_____7_____8
              TIME LINE IN YEARS
```

If you solve Equation (9-6) for the discount factor of eight years and i percent interest, you obtain

$$IF_{PV_{8,i}} = \frac{\$5,400}{\$10,000} = 0.540$$

Look across the eight-year row of Table 9-9 to find that the discount factor for 0.540 is under the 8 percent column; 8 percent is the implicit interest rate of the loan.

By financial calculator:

Table 9-11
Solving for the Interest Rate on a Loan

Problem	CLEAR TVM Registry	SET Compounding periods per year	ENTER N, PV, and FV	SET as ordinary	COMPUTE ANSWER
Finding the annual rate of interest on the loan	Press 2nd QUIT and 2nd CLR TVM	Press 2nd P/Y; Press 1 and hit ENTER; then 2nd QUIT	Press 8 and hit N; Press 5400 and hit PV; Press 10000 and hit +/- and hit FV	Press 2nd BGN; Press 2nd SET until END appears; Press 2nd QUIT	Press CPT IY; Result is 8.01% annual rate of interest on loan

---

Example 9-12 Computing the number of periods. At an annual growth rate of 4 percent, how long does it take $1,462 to accumulate to the amount of $2,000?

```
OUTFLOW        IF I/Y IS 4%, WHAT IS N?        INFLOW
-$1,464                                         +$2,000
0_____2_____3_____4_____N?
                    TIME    LINE
```

The discount factor of n years and 4 percent is

$$IF_{PV_{n,4\%}} = \frac{\$1,462}{\$2,000} = 0.731$$

In the 4 percent column of Table 9-9, the discount factor 0.731 is in the eight-year row; it will take eight years to accumulate $1,462 to the amount of $2,000 at 4 percent compounded annually. By financial calculator:

Table 9-12
Solving for the Number of Periods

Problem	CLEAR TVM Registry	SET Compounding periods per year	ENTER I/Y, PV, and FV	SET as ordinary	COMPUTE ANSWER
Finding the number of periods	Press 2nd QUIT and 2nd CLR TVM	Press 2nd P/Y; Press 1 and hit ENTER; then 2nd QUIT	Press 4 and hit I/Y; Press 1462 and hit +/- and hit PV; Press 2000 and hit FV*	Press 2nd BGN; Press 2nd SET until END appears; Press 2nd QUIT	Press CPT N; Result is 7.99 years for $1462 to grow to $2000 at a 4% rate

*Inputs
$1462
+2000

Key
+/- to convert to negative since this is a cash outflow at beginning of year 1, then press PV
FV

Example 9-13 Compounding More than One Time per Year. Find the present value of $1,000 due at the end of two years if money is worth (a) 8 percent compounded annually, (b) 8 percent compounded semi-annually, and (c) 8 percent compounded quarterly.

A) Solved using tables:

We can use Equation (9-5) to solve Problem (a):

$$PV = FV_n \times IF_{PV_{2,8\%}} = \$1,000 \times 0.857 = \$857$$

To solve Questions (b) and (c), two adjustments to Equation (9-5) should be made: (1) divide the nominal annual rate by the number of compounding periods during the year, and (2) multiply the number of years by the number of compounding periods during the year. Thus, for Question (b), we obtain

$$i = 8\% \div 2 = 4\%; n = 2 \times 2 = 4$$

$$PV = \$1,000 \times IF_{PV_{4,4\%}} = \$1,000 \times 0.855 = \$855$$

and for Question (c), we obtain

$$PV = \$1,000 \times IF_{PV_{8,2\%}} = \$1,000 \times 0.853 = \$853$$

or in general form:

$$PV = \frac{FV}{(1 + \frac{i}{m})^{mn}} \qquad (9\text{-}6a)$$

where m = number of compounding periods per year.

We can use the same procedure to cover all cases—discounting, compounding, single payments, and annuities.

Solved by formula and financial calculator (see Table 9-13 below):

Table 9-13
Solving for Present Value when Compounding More than One Time Per Year

COMPOUNDING INTERVAL	BY FORMULA	BY FINANCIAL CALCULATOR
SEMIANNUAL	$PV = \frac{1000}{(1 + \frac{.08}{2})^{2 \times 3}} = \$790.31$ Where: i= 8%, n=3 years, and m= 2 compounding periods per year	2nd P/Y; enter 2; 2nd QUIT; now enter 2x3 or 6 for N, 8 for I/Y, 1000 for FV, and hit CPT, then PV; answer = $790.31
QUARTERLY	$PV = \frac{1000}{(1 + \frac{.08}{4})^{4 \times 3}} = \$788.49$ Where: i= 8%, n=3 years, and m= 4 compounding periods per year	2nd P/Y; enter 4; 2nd QUIT; now enter 4x3 or 12 for N, 8 for I/Y, 1000 for FV, and hit CPT, then PV; answer = $788.49
MONTHLY	$PV = \frac{1000}{(1 + \frac{.08}{12})^{12 \times 3}} = \$787.25$ Where: i= 8%, n=3 years, and m= 12 compounding periods per year	2nd P/Y; enter 12; 2nd QUIT; now enter 12x3 or 36 for N, 8 for I/Y, 1000 for FV, and hit CPT, then PV; answer = $787.25

Chapter 9: Time Value of Money 171

WEEKLY	$PV = \dfrac{1000}{(1 + \frac{.08}{52})^{52 \times 3}} = \$786.77$ Where: i= 8%, n=3 years, and m= 52 compounding periods per year	2nd P/Y; enter 52; 2nd QUIT; now enter 52x3 or 156 for N, 8 for I/Y, 1000 for FV, and hit CPT, then PV; answer = \$786.77
DAILY	$PV = \dfrac{1000}{(1 + \frac{.08}{365})^{365 \times 3}} = \$786.65$ Where: i= 8%, n=3 years, and m= 365 compounding periods per year	2nd P/Y; enter 365; 2nd QUIT; now enter 365x3 or 1095 for N, 8 for I/Y, 1000 for FV, and hit CPT, then PV; answer = \$786.6485
HOURLY	$PV = \dfrac{1000}{(1 + \frac{.08}{8760})^{8,760 \times 3}} = \$786.63$ Where: i= 8%, n=3 years, and m= 8760 compounding periods per year	2nd P/Y; enter 8,760; 2nd QUIT; now enter 8760x3 or 26280 for N, 8 for I/Y, 1000 for FV, and hit CPT, then PV; answer = \$786.6287
PER SECOND or CONTINUOULSY	$PV = \dfrac{1000}{(1 + \frac{.08}{525,600})^{525600 \times 3}} = \$786.63$ Where: i= 8%, n=3 years, and m= 525600 compounding periods per year	2nd P/Y; enter 525600; 2nd QUIT; now enter 525600x3 or 1576800 for N, 8 for I/Y, 1000 for FV, and hit CPT, then PV; answer = \$786.627875

Example 9-14 Return on Investment. Suppose you bought Lawson Company stock 10 years ago at \$25 per share and the same stock is currently selling for a market price of \$130 per share. What is your compounded annual rate of return on this investment? (See Table 9-14 for the solution by financial calculator)

PART 4: CAPITAL EXPENDITURE ANALYSIS

Table 9-14
Solving for Return on Investment

Problem	CLEAR TVM Registry	SET Compounding periods per year	ENTER N, PV, and FV	SET as ordinary	COMPUTE ANSWER
Compound annual rate of return on stock investment	Press 2nd QUIT and 2nd CLR TVM	Press 2nd P/Y; Press 1 and hit ENTER; then 2nd QUIT	Press 10 and hit N; Press 25 and +/- and hit PV; Press 130 and hit FV	Press 2nd BGN; Press 2nd SET until END appears; Press 2nd QUIT	Press CPT I/Y; Result is 17.92% annual rate of return

Example 9-15 Finding the rate of return on house investment. If you bought your house 12 years ago for $50,000 and just sold it for $180,000, what is your annual rate of return on your investment? (See Table 9-15 for the solution)

Table 9-15
Solving for Rate of Return

Problem	CLEAR TVM Registry	SET Compounding periods per year	ENTER N, PV, and FV	SET as ordinary	COMPUTE ANSWER
Compound annual rate of return on house investment	Press 2nd QUIT and 2nd CLR TVM	Press 2nd P/Y; Press 1 and hit ENTER; then 2nd QUIT	Press 12 and hit N; Press 50,000 and +/- and hit PV; Press 180,000 and hit FV	Press 2nd BGN; Press 2nd SET until END appears; Press 2nd QUIT	Press CPT I/Y; Result is 11.26% annual rate of return

PRESENT VALUE OF AN ANNUITY

As with the future value of an annuity, present-value analysis can be extended to cover the case of a series of periodic payments or withdrawals. The present value of an annuity refers to the value at the beginning of the term of the annuity (time 0) that is equivalent to the future cash flows discounted (reverse compounded) at some rate of interest. For ex-

$PVA = CF \times IF_{PVA_{n,i}}$

ample, Table 9-16 shows that equal cash flows of $1 to be received at the end of each of the next three years is equivalent to $2.58 today if the opportunity cost of funds is 8%. We simply back the interest out of the consecutive cash flows at a discount rate of 8%.

Example 9-16. Suppose someone offered you $100 a year for the next three years and the price of this offer today is $285. If you are able to earn 8% interest on your money, would you accept this offer?

The first $100 is paid at the end of the first year, which is one year after the beginning of the term of the annuity. Hence, the present value of the first payment is found by discounting the payment for one year. The present value of the second payment is obtained by discounting the payment for two years, and so on. Figure 9-5 explains the computation procedure. The present value of the annuity is $257.7 or (92.6 + 85.7 + 79.4).

Figure 9-5
Present Value of a $100 Three-Year Annuity

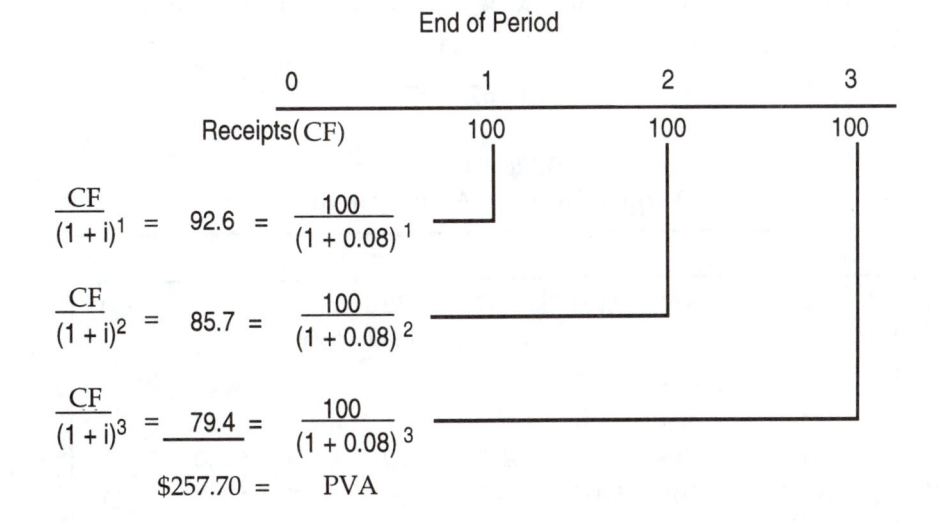

End of Period

	0	1	2	3
Receipts(CF)		100	100	100

$$\frac{CF}{(1+i)^1} = 92.6 = \frac{100}{(1+0.08)^1}$$

$$\frac{CF}{(1+i)^2} = 85.7 = \frac{100}{(1+0.08)^2}$$

$$\frac{CF}{(1+i)^3} = 79.4 = \frac{100}{(1+0.08)^3}$$

$$\$257.70 = PVA$$

Because the cost of the offer or ($285) is greater than its present value by $27.3 or ($285 − $257.70), you would definitely refuse the deal. If you demand a return of 8%, then all you can afford to pay for this offer today is $257.70. Paying anything more would yield you a return under 8%.

Algebraically, the present value of the annuity is

$$PVA = \frac{CF}{(1+i)^1} + \frac{CF}{(1+i)^2} + \frac{CF}{(1+i)^3}$$

$$= CF \left(\frac{1}{(1+i)^1} + \frac{1}{(1+i)^2} + \frac{1}{(1+i)^3} \right)$$

$$= \$100 \left(\frac{1}{(1.08)^1} + \frac{1}{(1.08)^2} + \frac{1}{(1.08)^3} \right) = \$257.7$$

where PVA = present value of an annuity and CF = periodic payment or deposit. In general, the present value of an annuity at the end of any year n is

$$PVA = CF \left(\frac{1}{(1+i)^1} + \frac{1}{(1+i)^2} + \cdots + \frac{1}{(1+i)^n} \right)$$

$$= CF \times IF_{PVA_{n,i}} \qquad (9\text{-}7)$$

where $IF_{PVA_{n,i}}$ = annuity discount factor.

Table D in Appendix A shows the values of $IF_{PVA_{n,i}}$ covering a wide range of n and i. Table 9-16 illustrates selected portions of Table D.

With Table 9-16, you can easily solve your annuity problem. The annuity discount factor of three years and 8 percent is found to be 2.577, which is underlined. The present value of your annuity is

$$PVA = CF \times IF_{PVA_{3,8\%}} = \$100 \times 2.577 = \$257.7$$

Table 9-16
Present Value of an Annuity of $1

Period	1%	2%	3%	4%	5%	6%	7%	8%
1	0.990	0.980	0.971	0.962	0.952	0.943	0.935	0.926
2	1.970	1.942	1.913	1.886	1.859	1.833	1.808	1.783
3	2.941	2.884	2.829	2.775	2.723	2.673	2.624	<u>2.577</u>
4	3.902	3.808	3.717	3.603	3.546	3.465	3.387	3.312
5	4.853	4.713	4.580	4.452	4.329	4.212	4.100	3.993
6	5.795	5.601	5.417	5.242	5.076	4.917	4.767	4.623
7	6.728	6.472	6.230	6.002	5.786	5.582	5.389	5.206
8	7.652	7.325	7.020	6.733	6.463	6.210	5.971	5.747

Additional Problems

Up to now we have assumed that the only unknown variable was the present value of an annuity and that all the other variables were known. However, there are cases in which the size of each periodic payment, the interest rate, or the number of periods must be determined when the present value of an annuity is known. If the present value of an annuity is given, one can algebraically manipulate Equation (9-7) to determine the value of a variable other than the present value.

If the value of an annuity is not known, the present value of the annuity, the interest rate, and the number of periods are usually given.

Example 9-17.

Solved using financial tables:

Suppose you need to borrow $13,548 today to buy a car. If the bank agrees to loan you the $13,548 today at 7% interest for four years, what would your four equal year-end payments be? Clearly this example fits the present value of an annuity where the present value is the principal borrowed and the annuity is the loan payment.

Because the discount factor $IF_{PVA_{4,7\%}}$ is found to be 3.387 from Table 9-16, the size of annual withdrawal is

$$PVA = CF \times IF_{PVA_{n,i}}, \text{ or } CF = \frac{PVA}{IF_{PVA_{n,i}}} \qquad (9\text{-}8)$$

$$CF = \frac{\$13,548}{IF_{PVA_{4,7\%}}} = \frac{\$13,548}{3.387} = \$4,000$$

In essence, it will take four equal annual payments of $4,000 each to pay off a loan of $13,548 at an interest rate of 7%. The sum of the four payments is $16,000 (or 4 x $4,000). Thus, you pay total interest in the amount of $2,452 (or $16,000 − $13,548) for the rent or interest cost on the money borrowed.

Now let us extend the loan problem in Example 9-17 to include semi-annual, quarterly, and monthly payments and solve by financial calculator: (See financial calculator solution in Table 9-17)

Table 9-17
Solve for Payment in Loan Problem

Problem	CLEAR TVM Registry	SET Compounding periods per year	ENTER N, PV, and I/Y	SET as ordinary	COMPUTE ANSWER
Annual loan payment	Press 2nd QUIT and 2nd CLR TVM	Press 2nd P/Y; Press 1 and hit ENTER; then 2nd QUIT	Press 4 and hit N; Press 13548 and hit PV; Press 7 and hit I/Y	Press 2nd BGN; Press 2nd SET until END appears; Press 2nd QUIT	Press CPT PMT; Result is -$3,999.75 annual loan payment

176 PART 4: CAPITAL EXPENDITURE ANALYSIS

Semi-annual loan payment	Press 2nd QUIT and 2nd CLR TVM	Press 2nd P/Y; Press 2 and hit ENTER; then 2nd QUIT	Press 8 and hit N; Press 13548 and hit PV; Press 7 and hit I/Y	Press 2nd BGN; Press 2nd SET until END appears; Press 2nd QUIT	Press CPT PMT; Result is -$1,970.91 semi-annual loan payment
Quarterly loan payment	Press 2nd QUIT and 2nd CLR TVM	Press 2nd P/Y; Press 4 and hit ENTER; then 2nd QUIT	Press 16 and hit N; Press 13548 and hit PV; Press 7 and hit I/Y	Press 2nd BGN; Press 2nd SET until END appears; Press 2nd QUIT	Press CPT PMT; Result is -$978.16 quarterly loan payment
Monthly loan payment	Press 2nd QUIT and 2nd CLR TVM	Press 2nd P/Y; Press 12 and hit ENTER; then 2nd QUIT	Press 48 and hit N; Press 13548 and hit PV; Press 7 and hit I/Y	Press 2nd BGN; Press 2nd SET until END appears; Press 2nd QUIT	Press CPT PMT; Result is -$324.42 monthly loan payment

Example 9-18 *Solving for the interest rate.* Charles borrowed $10,000 from his sister Susan and agreed to repay in ten equal semiannual payments of $1,295. The repayment starts six months from today. Charles wants to determine the implicit annual rate of interest.

Solved by financial tables:

The implicit annual rate of interest is

$$PVA = CF \times IF_{PVA_{n,i}}, \text{ or } IF_{PVA_{n,i}} = \frac{PVA}{CF} \quad (9-9)$$

$$IF_{PVA_{10,i}} = \frac{\$10,000}{\$1,295} = 7.722$$

Look across the ten-period row of Table D and locate the discount factor 7.722. It is under the 5 percent column. Because 5 percent is the six-month interest rate, the implicit annual interest rate of the loan is 10 percent. See Table 9-18 for the solution by financial calculator:

Table 9-18
Solving for the Interest Rate on a Loan

Problem	CLEAR TVM Registry	SET Compounding periods per year	ENTER N, PV, and PMT	SET as ordinary, or annuity due	COMPUTE ANSWER
Determine the implicit interest rate on a loan	Press 2nd QUIT and 2nd CLR TVM	Press 2nd P/Y; Press 2 and hit ENTER; then 2nd QUIT	Press 10 and hit N; Press 10000 and hit PV; Press 1295, +/-, and hit PMT	Press 2nd BGN; Press 2nd SET until END appears; Press 2nd QUIT	Press CPT I/Y; Result is 9.998% effective annual interest rate on the loan

To determine N or the term of an annuity, the size of each periodic payment, the present value of the annuity, and the interest rate must be known.

Example 9-19 Solving for N, the number of periods. The price of a small building is $60,000. The buyer made a down payment of $10,000 and agreed to pay $6,279 at the end of each year. The annual installment of $6,279 includes principal and 11 percent compound interest. How long does it take the buyer to pay the principal and the interest?

By financial tables:

The amount borrowed, or the present value of a $6,279 annuity at 11 percent is $50,000 (price of $60,000 - down payment of $10,000). The discount factor $IF_{PVA_{n,11\%}}$ is

$$IF_{PVA_{n,11\%}} = \frac{\$50,000}{\$6,279} = 7.963$$

In the 11 percent column of Table D, the discount factor 7.963 is found to be in the 20-period row; the term of the annuity is 20 years.

Now let us extend this problem and determine the number of payments if annual or monthly by financial calculator: (See Table 9-19 below)

178   PART 4: CAPITAL EXPENDITURE ANALYSIS

Table 9-19
Solving for the Number of Payments on a Loan

Problem	CLEAR TVM Registry	SET Compounding periods per year	ENTER PV, PMT, and I/Y	SET as ordinary or annuity due	COMPUTE ANSWER
Determine the number of annual payments of $6,297 each needed to pay off the loan	Press 2nd QUIT and 2nd CLR TVM	Press 2nd P/Y; Press 1 and hit ENTER; then 2nd QUIT	Press 50000 and hit PV; Press 6297 and +/- and hit PMT; Press 11 and hit I/Y	Press 2nd BGN; Press 2nd SET until END appears; Press 2nd QUIT	Press CPT N; Result is 19.81 annual payments to pay off loan
Determine the number of monthly payments of $500 each needed to pay off the loan	Press 2nd QUIT and 2nd CLR TVM	Press 2nd P/Y; Press 12 and hit ENTER; then 2nd QUIT	Press 50000 and hit PV; Press 500 and +/- and hit PMT; Press 11 and hit I/Y	Press 2nd BGN; Press 2nd SET until END appears; Press 2nd QUIT	Press CPT N; Result is 272.32 monthly payments to pay off loan

Example 9-20 Retirement annuity problem. Suppose you plan to accumulate $150,000 at retirement. If you are expected to live another 20 years after retirement and you can purchase an annuity with the $150,000 that yields a return of 10%, what would your end of period annual benefits be? What would your end of period monthly benefits be? (See Table 9-20 for financial calculator solution)

Table 9-20
Solving for Annual and Monthly Benefits for a Retirement Annuity

Problem	CLEAR TVM Registry	SET Compounding periods per year	ENTER N, PV, and I/Y	SET as ordinary or annuity due	COMPUTE ANSWER
Determine annual benefit payment	Press 2nd QUIT and 2nd CLR TVM	Press 2nd P/Y; Press 1 and hit ENTER; then 2nd QUIT	Press 20 and hit N; Press 150000 and +/- and hit PV; Press 10 and hit I/Y	Press 2nd BGN; Press 2nd SET until END appears; Press 2nd QUIT	Press CPT PMT; Result is an annual payment of $17,619 received at end of year

| Determine the monthly benefit payment | Press 2nd QUIT and 2nd CLR TVM | Press 2nd P/Y; Press 12 and hit ENTER; then 2nd QUIT | Press 240 and hit N; Press 150000 and +/- and hit PV; Press 10 and hit I/Y | Press 2nd BGN; Press 2nd SET until END appears; Press 2nd QUIT | Press CPT PMT; Result is a monthly payment of $1,447.53 received at end of month |

Example 9-21 Loan and Amortization Schedule.

Assume that a firm borrowed $2,400 at 16 percent interest on the unpaid balance for two years and agreed to amortize it by making equal payments at the end of every six months. Determine the size of the semiannual loan payment and prepare the amortization schedule.

To find the size of the semiannual loan payment, we can use the formula for the present value of an annuity:

PVA = $2,400; i = 16% ÷ 2 = 8% (per six months); n = 2 x 2 = 4 (semiannual periods); and $IF_{PVA_{4,8\%}}$ = 3.312

$$PVA = CF \times IF_{PVA_{n,i}}, \text{ or } CF = \frac{PVA}{IF_{PVA_{n,i}}}$$

$$CF = \frac{\$2,400}{3.312} = \$724.60$$

A semiannual payment of $724.60 for two years will pay off a loan of $2,400 and give the lending institution a return of 8 percent every six months or 16 percent a year. To see this, we can construct the **amortization schedule**, as shown in Table 9-21.

Table 9-21
Amortization Schedule

(1) Period	(2) Beginning Balance (2)* − (5)*	(3) Interest (2) x 8%	(4) Semiannual Payment	(5) Principal Payment (4) − (3)
1	$2,400.0	$192.0	$724.6	$532.6
2	1,867.4	149.4	724.6	575.2
3	1,292.2	103.4	724.6	621.2
4	671.0	53.6	724.6	671.0

*Of the previous period. For example, $1,292.2 = $1,867.4 − $575.2.

180   Part 4: Capital Expenditure Analysis

Example 9-22 Loan and amortization schedule solved by financial calculator. Suppose you borrow $150,000 for 15 years to buy a house. If the interest rate on the loan is 10%, find the annual payment, monthly payment, and corresponding amortization schedules. (See Table 9-22 for financial calculator solutions)

Table 9-22
Solving for the Annual and Monthly Payments on a Loan

Problem	CLEAR TVM Registry	SET Compounding periods per year	ENTER N, PV, and I/Y	SET as ordinary or annuity due	COMPUTE ANSWER
Determine annual payment	Press 2nd QUIT and 2nd CLR TVM	Press 2nd P/Y; Press 1 and hit ENTER; then 2nd QUIT	Press 15 and hit PV; Press 150000 and hit PV; Press 10 and hit I/Y	Press 2nd BGN; Press 2nd SET until END appears; Press 2nd QUIT	Press CPT PMT; Result is an annual payment of -$19,721
Determine monthly payment	Press 2nd QUIT and 2nd CLR TVM	Press 2nd P/Y; Press 12 and hit ENTER; then 2nd QUIT	Press 180 and hit N; Press 150000 and hit PV; Press 10 and hit I/Y	Press 2nd BGN; Press 2nd SET until END appears; Press 2nd QUIT	Press CPT PMT; Result is an monthly payment of -$1,611.91

After computing the loan payment, proceed as shown in the following table to produce the corresponding loan amortizations.

Table 9-23
First Three Periods of Corresponding Loan Amortization Schedules

	End of →	PERIOD 1	PERIOD 2	PERIOD 3
Problem	SET P1 and P2 which identify the beginning and end of each period being reviewed	Hit 2nd AMORT; ENTER 1 for P1 and P2 and scroll down to observe period one data	Hit 2nd AMORT; ENTER 2 for P1 and P2 and scroll down to observe period two data	Hit 2nd AMORT; ENTER 3 for P1 and P2 and scroll down to observe period three data

Determine annual payment loan amortization schedule	End of period balance, principal portion, and interest portion	BAL = 145270.93 PRN = -4721.07 INT = -15000	BAL = 140085.76 PRN = -5193.17 INT = -14527.89	BAL = 134373.27 PRN = -5712.49 INT = -14008.56
Determine monthly payment loan amortization schedule	End of period balance, principal portion, and interest portion	BAL = 149638.09 PRN = -361.91 INT = -1250.00	BAL = 149273.17 PRN = -364.92 INT = -1246.96	BAL = 148905.20 PRN = -367.96 INT = -1243.94

OTHER COMMON APPLICATIONS OF FUTURE VALUE AND PRESENT VALUE

Sinking Fund Example

The principal of many long-term debts is repaid at maturity, but the interest is paid when it is due. Many corporate bond issues require the firm to make periodic deposits into a **sinking fund** established to retire the principal on the maturity date. The idea here is to assure the bondholders or lenders that the firm will be able to pay off the principal when it comes due. If periodic deposits are made in equal amounts at equal intervals, the deposits form an ordinary annuity problem. The size of the periodic deposit can be obtained from Equation (9-4).

Example 9-23. A $1,000 bond with a 4 year maturity is issued with a 3 percent interest payable at the end of each year. In essence, the firm agrees to pay 3% of the $1,000 principal (or 3% x $1,000 = $30) per year at the end of each year and must pay off the principal of $1,000 at the end of the 4 years. To make sure the firm who sold the bond has the $1,000 at maturity, the bond seller or debtor is required to establish a sinking fund schedule which earns 3% compounded annually. Under this process, the firm will make four equal periodic deposits at the end of each year into a savings account which in this case can earn an assumed interest rate of 3% compounded annually. If the firm earns 0% interest, it would have to make payments of $250 (or $1,000/4 years). But since it earns 3% on the funds while in the account during the four year period, some interest will accumulate to help make the required payment smaller than $250. This is simply a future value of an annuity problem where we are given N, I/Y, and FV and we desire to CPT the PMT.

With financial tables, the size of each annual deposit is determined as follows:

$$FVA = CF \times IF_{FVA_{4,3\%}}; \text{ the value of } IF_{FVA_{4,3\%}} \text{ is } 4.184.$$

$$CF = \frac{\$1,000}{4.184} = \$239.00$$

The sinking fund schedule is given in Table 9-24.

Table 9-24
Sinking Fund Schedule

(1) Period	(2) Interest on Sinking Fund 3% x (5)*	(3) Periodic Deposit in Sinking Fund	(4) Increase in Fund (2) + (3)	(5) Accumulated Sinking Fund (4) + (5)*
1	$ 0.00	$239	$239.00	$239.00
2	7.17	239	246.17	485.17
3	14.55	239	253.55	738.72
4	22.16	239	261.16	999.88

*Of the previous period. For example, $14.55 = $485.17 X 3%

Table 9.25
Solving for the Sinking Fund Payment by Financial Calculator

Problem	CLEAR TVM Registry	SET Compounding periods per year	ENTER N, FV, and I/Y	SET as ordinary or annuity due	COMPUTE ANSWER
Ordinary and annual	Press 2nd QUIT and 2nd CLR TVM	Press 2nd P/Y; Press 1 and hit ENTER; then 2nd QUIT	Press 4 and hit N; Press 1000 and hit FV; Press 3 and hit I/Y	Press 2nd BGN; Press 2nd SET until END appears; Press 2nd QUIT	Press CPT PMT; Result is -$239.03 per year at end of year into sinking fund

The concept of present value discussed thus far can be used to solve a number of frequently encountered financial problems. Some of these problems are the determination of (a) the present value of an unequal cash flow stream, (b) bond values, and (c) an amortization schedule.

Present Value of an Unequal Cash-Flow Stream

Many financial decisions are concerned with unequal cash flows. Common stock investments and most capital investment projects involve uneven cash flows.

Example 9-24. A project is expected to produce $500 at the end of one year, $700 at the end of two years, and $1,000 at the end of three years. Compute the present value of these cash flows at a 10% discount rate.

To obtain the aggregate present value of $1,783.7, multiply each periodic receipt by the appropriate discount factor $IF_{PV, n, 10\%}$ and then sum these products. Individual discount factors are obtained from Table C. This computation is given in Table 9-26.

Table 9-26
Present Value Computation

Year	Cash Flows	x	Interest Factor	=	Present Value
1	$ 500		0.909		$ 454.5
2	700		0.826		578.2
3	1,000		0.751		751.0
	Aggregate Present Value				$1,783.7

Present Value and Bond Valuation

A bond is a piece of debt usually bearing: a $1000 principal or par value, a coupon or contract rate of interest, periodic interest payments, and a time to maturity. The seller of the bond is the borrower and the buyer is the lender or investor. Consider a $1000 par, 10% coupon bond maturing in 5 years with annual interest payments. Under this agreement, the lender would receive 5 equal annual end-of-year interest payments of $100 each or (10% x $1000) and one principal payment of $1,000 at the end of the five year period. These two cash flow streams (equal interest payments and a one-time principal payment) fit present value analysis quite well with the interest payments representing an annuity and the principal payment resembling a fixed sum, all to be received in the future. Therefore, the investor can determine the appropriate value of the bond by summing up the present value of the interest payment annuity and the present value of the fixed principal payment. Suppose the investor demands a yield (or return on investment) of 12%, which is higher than the coupon rate offered on the bonds by the seller/borrower. If the investor were to pay the $1000 par for the bond, the maximum return on the investment would be only 10%, which is under the investor's desired yield of 12%. To earn the desired yield, the investor must discount the bond or pay some amount less than $1000 such that the difference (or capital gain) would raise the effective yield to 12%. The higher the desired yield, the lower the price of the bond and vice versa. If the coupon exceeded the desired yield, then investors, anxious to get this good deal, would bid the bond's price up resulting in a capital loss large enough to push the effective yield down to the market return. Thus yield and bond price move in inverse directions (see Table 9-27 below).

Table 9-27
Bond Yield and Price

If	Then Bond Sells at
Yield > Coupon	Discount
Yield = Coupon	Par
Yield < Coupon	Premium

Thus, the current value or the purchase price of a bond should be the discounted value of all future payments: that is, (1) the present value of the periodic interest payments, and (2) the present value of the maturity value. To find this value, one must solve Equation (9-10), which combines Equation 9-7 and Equation 9-5:

$$\text{Bond Value} = \underbrace{CF \times IF_{PVA_{n,i}}}_{(Eq.\ 9\text{-}7)} + \underbrace{FV_n \times IF_{PV_{n,i}}}_{(Eq.\ 9\text{-}5)} \quad (9\text{-}10)$$

Remember, Equation 9-7 is used to determine the present value of an annuity (or periodic interest payments on the bond), and Equation 9-5 is used to determine the present value of a future lump sum (or the maturity value of the bond).

Example 9-25. A particular bond pays coupon interest in the amount of $30 every six months (or an annual coupon rate of 6%). The bond, with a face value of $1,000, will mature in ten years. The desired discount rate (or yield) is 4 percent. What should be the current market value of the bond?

The buyer will receive an annuity of $30 each six months and a sum of $1,000 at the end of ten years. The number of discount periods is 20 or (10 years × 2 periods per year) and the six-month yield is 2 percent or (0.04 ÷ 2). Thus, its value of $1,163.50 is obtained as follows:

$$\begin{aligned}
\text{Bond Value} &= \$30 \times IF_{PVA_{20,2\%}} + \$1{,}000 \times IF_{PV_{20,2\%}} \\
&= \$30 \times 16.351 + \$1{,}000 \times 0.673 \\
&= \$490.50 + \$673 \\
&= \$1{,}163.50
\end{aligned}$$

Table 9-28
Solve for Price of Bond by Financial Calculator

Problem	CLEAR	SET Com-	ENTER N,	SET as	COMPUTE
Find price of bond	TVM Registry	pounding periods per year	PMT, FV, and I/Y	ordinary or annuity due	ANSWER

Solve example 9-25 by financial calculator	Press 2nd QUIT and 2nd CLR TVM	Press 2nd P/Y; Press 2 and hit ENTER; then 2nd QUIT	Press 20 and hit N; Press 30 and hit PMT; Press 1000 and hit FV; Press 4 and hit I/Y	Press 2nd BGN; Press 2nd SET until END appears; Press 2nd QUIT	Press CPT PV; Result is current price or PV of the bond -$1,163.51

PERPETUITIES

A **perpetuity** is a special form of an annuity whose term begins on a definite date but never matures. Perpetuities often stem from the establishment of an endowment. Bonds lacking any maturity, perpetual preferred stocks, and zero growth stocks also are examples of perpetuities. If a project with a net investment of PAV at time 0 is expected to earn CF at the end of each year forever, its yield is the discount rate i, which equates the present value of all future net cash flows with the present value of the net investment:

$$PVA = \frac{CF}{(1+i)^1} + \frac{CF}{(1+i)^2} + \ldots + \frac{CF}{(1+i)^n} \qquad (9\text{-}11)$$

When we multiply both sides of Equation (9-11) by (1 + i), we obtain:

$$PVA(1+i) = CF + \frac{CF}{(1+i)^1} + \frac{CF}{(1+i)^2} + \ldots + \frac{CF}{(1+i)^{n-1}} \qquad (9\text{-}12)$$

Subtracting Equation (9-11) from Equation (9-12):

$$PVA(1+i) - PVA = CF - \frac{CF}{(1+i)^n} \qquad (9\text{-}13)$$

As n approaches infinity, $CF/(1+i)^n$ approaches 0. Therefore:

$$PVA_i = CF \qquad (9\text{-}14)$$

and

$$PVA = \frac{CF}{i} \qquad (9\text{-}15)$$

Example 9-26. A bond promises to pay interest of $250 a year indefinitely. If the yield (the internal rate of return) of the bond is 10 percent, its value would be:

$$PVA = \frac{\$250}{0.10} = \$2,500$$

Thus, an investor requiring a 10 percent return would be willing to pay $2,500 for a perpetual bond that pays an annual interest of $250 forever.

Summary

The basic purpose of this chapter was to introduce the key mathematical concepts of finance. They are compounded values and present values, which play a significant role in such financial decisions as capital budgeting, valuation, leasing, and capital structure. But most problems involving compound interest and compound discount can be solved relatively easily with the basic equations described in this chapter and Tables A, B, C, and D at the end of this book.

List of Key Terms

discount rate
annuity
present value
perpetuity

compound value
sinking fund
amortization schedule

Problems

9-1 Determine the compound or future values of the following lump sum problems.

(a) $2,000 for ten years at 8 percent compounded annually.
(b) $2,000 for ten years at 8 percent compounded quarterly (2 percent a quarter).
(c) $2,000 for ten years at 12 percent compounded quarterly (3 percent a quarter).

9-2 Determine the compound or future values of the following annuity problems.

Each Periodic Payment	Payment Interval	Term	Compound Interest Rate per Period
(a) $3,000	1 year	10 years	8%
(b) $1,500	6 months	10 years	4%
(c) $ 100	1 month	3 $1/3$ years	1%

9-3 Determine the present values of the following lump sum problems.

(a) $1,000 due at the end of ten years if money is worth 6 percent compounded annually.
(b) $2,000 payable at the end of five years if money is worth 6 percent compounded semiannually (3 percent every six months).
(c) $2,000 payable at the end of five years if money is worth 10 percent compounded semiannually (5 percent every six months).

9-4 Determine the present values of the following annuity problems.

Each Periodic Payment	Payment Interval	Term	Compound Interest Rate per Period
(a) $2,000	6 months	10 years	5%
(b) $2,000	1 year	10 years	10%
(c) $3,000	4 months	4 years	3%

9-5 How long does it take $1 to triple if money grows at 6 percent compounded annually?

9-6 The present value of a five-year annuity is $20,000. What is each quarterly payment if the interest rate is 8 percent compounded quarterly (2 percent a quarter)?

9-7 A four-year note has a payment of $3,000 at the end of each year for four years. What is the implicit <u>interest rate</u> if the present principal of the note is $10,161?

9-8 The cash price of a small house is $19,000. The owner of the house agrees to sell you the house in return for your promise to pay $4,000 down and $383 at the end of each month. If money is worth 12 percent compounded monthly (1 percent a month), how long will it take you to pay off the balance and interest?

9-9 A 20-year bond promises to pay <u>$60 interest</u> at the end of every six months. The bond has a maturity value of $1,000 and its appropriate <u>yield</u> rate is 10 percent. What is the value of the bond?

9-10 A project is expected to earn $200, $300, and $400 for the next three years. What is the present value of these cash flows at a 10 percent discount rate?

9-11 Exactly 15 years from now Mr. Smith will start receiving a pension of $20,000 per year. The pension payments will continue for 10 years. How much is the pension worth now if money is worth 10 percent per year?

9-12 If you decide to buy a house, you have to pay $10,000 per year for nine years. What is the price of the house if paid in a lump sum today? Assume that the interest rate is 10 percent.

9-13 Assume that you are given the choice between $20,000 in cash and $2,000 per year for perpetuity. If money is worth 10 percent, which would you prefer?

9-14 Mary King is the winner of a $1 million state lottery. She is given the choice between $100,000 a year for ten years and $700,000 in cash. The annuity payment starts today. If the interest rate is 12 percent, which would Mary King prefer?

9-15 Thomas Lee is 51 years old and he decides to set aside a fixed amount of money every year in a pension plan. He wants to start the plan now and continue until he is 65 years of age. The money accumulated must allow him to receive $10,000 per year, starting at age 66 and continuing for 20 years to age 85. If the money is invested at 10 percent, how much does Mr. Lee need to set aside each year to meet his goal?

9-16 A corporate bond with a face value of $1,000 has a 10 percent coupon rate and will mature in 10 years. If the current market rate is 8 percent, what is the current value of the bond (assume annual interest payments)?

9-17 Lisa Kim purchased 100 acres of land for $51,600 in 1970. If she sells the land for $100,000 in 1990, what rate of return will she have earned on her investment?

9-18   Ms. Mary Estate purchases a share of stock for $20. She expects the stock to pay dividends of $1.05, $1.1025, and $1.1576 in years 1, 2, and 3, respectively. She also expects to sell the stock for $25 at the end of three years.

   (a) Calculate the dividend growth rate.
   (b) What is the current dividend yield?
   (c) If the computed growth rate is expected to continue, what is the expected total rate of return?

9-19   What is the maximum a person should pay for an annuity issued by an insurance company that would provide $200 a year for perpetuity? The person has other investment opportunities in a similar risk class that promises a 16 percent rate of return.

9-20   Linda Park borrows $52,000 at 10 percent to buy a home. Her mortgage is for 25 years.

   (a) How much will her annual payment be? Assume that mortgage payments will be made annually.
   (b) How much interest will she pay over the life of the loan?
   (c) How much should she pay to get out of a 10 percent mortgage into an 8 percent mortgage with 15 years remaining on the mortgage?

10

Capital Budgeting under Certainty

Capital assets such as machines, tools, factories, and transportation facilities are used by companies in the process of producing goods and services. U.S. businesses spend more than $1,000 billion a year on such capital assets. For the last three decades, they have increased their capital expenditures for new plant and equipment approximately 10 percent a year. Such large investments in capital assets and rapid growth in capital expenditures have significantly contributed to the improved U.S. standard of living through higher levels of Gross National Products (GNP) and increased disposable personal income. Efficient management of capital expenditures has become even more essential with the increasing recognition that the ultimate success of company operations depends on sound capital budgeting decisions.

This chapter consists of two major sections. The first section describes the entire capital budgeting process. The second section discusses a number of capital budgeting techniques under certainty designed to evaluate specific investment proposals.

Capital Budgeting Process

A long-term investment decision process may be viewed as a system with a number of interrelated parts. There are many steps and elements in the entire process of planning capital expenditures. Each step or element is a subsystem of the total capital budgeting system which is closely connected by a variety of other subsystems. Thus, the entire capital budgeting process may be viewed as an integral unit of many parts which are directly or indirectly interrelated. The capital budgeting process includes eight phases: goal establishment, new project ideas, cash flow analysis, evaluation, selection, implementation, control, and auditing.

Company Goals

The establishment of long-range goals is the first step in the capital budgeting process. These goals set the stage for the development, evaluation, and selection of proposals for plant expansion, equipment replacements, new product development, and the like. It is important to remember that the primary goal of the firm is to maximize stockholder wealth (see Chapter 1).

190 Part 4: Capital Expenditure Analysis

New Project Ideas

A system should be established to stimulate ideas for capital expenditures and to identify good investment opportunities. This is because the availability of good investment opportunities provides the foundation for a successful investment program. Moreover, good investment opportunities do not just appear. A continuous stream of attractive investment opportunities come from hard thinking, careful planning, and frequently large outlays for research and development.

Aside from the actual generation of ideas, the second step in the capital budgeting process is to classify projects according to certain common characteristics. Such classifications are established (1) to provide categories useful in summarizing the financial totals for a group of projects and (2) help identify the types of projects and necessary decisions. Although project classification practices vary from company to company, capital investment projects are frequently grouped according to the following categories: replacements, expansion (new products), expansion (existing products), and others such as pollution control equipment.

The replacement of obsolete or worn-out assets is intended to reduce operating expenses or to preserve production efficiency. If the replacement of an existing machine with a new machine enables the firm to produce the same product at a lower cost, the firm must analyze the incremental costs and benefits associated with this change.

A growing firm often finds it necessary to acquire fixed assets that will be used to produce a new product. This type of expenditure is expected to result in incremental sales revenue. To support the expected increase in sales, the firm must increase its costs for labor and material, maintenance, and advertising.

Expenditures to increase the output of existing products are often alternatives to replacements. Such expenditures may be suitable solutions to problems of both capacity and cost. Suppose that an existing machine is inadequate to meet the increasing demand for an existing product and that it is also very expensive to operate. If the existing machine is replaced with one that has greater productive capacity, the firm may be able to solve the cost and capacity problems simultaneously.

If a company has identified many investment opportunities of different types, it must screen and review all of them so that a limited number of projects are chosen for more complex and quantitative analyses. For the manager, such a screening process is a matter of judgement exercised without complete data and particularly without cash flow estimates.

Cash Flow Analysis

All investment opportunities surviving this screening test require cash flow estimates. The after-tax cash outflows and inflows associated with each project must be estimated to evaluate investment alternatives. There are two important concepts to note in cash flow analysis: (1) cash flows are different from profits or income and (2) cash flows must be estimated on an incremental basis.

Cash flows are not necessarily identical with accounting profits because generally accepted accounting principles treat certain non cash expenditures, such as depreciation charges, as operating expenses rather than as benefits. The concept of cash flow has certain advantages over the concept of profits. First, only cash flow affects the firm's ability to pay bills or buy assets. Second, the cash basis of accounting makes it easier and more objective to measure the benefit of an investment project.

It is important to recognize that only incremental future cash outflows and inflows are relevant in capital expenditure analysis. For example, general office expenses or sunk costs are treated as irrelevant costs because they are not changed by the acceptance of the project.

To determine the attractiveness of a project, we must have three elements: the net cash investment, the net cash flow, and the economic life of the project.

The cash investment refers to the net cash outlay associated with a specific project: the amount of the initial investment required by the project less any cash inflows that occur in the process of placing the asset into service. The initial investment usually consists of the purchase price of the new asset, the transportation costs, the installation costs, and any other costs incurred to put the asset into service. The cash inflows include the proceeds from the trade or sale of existing assets, and the tax saving from the sale of the assets.

The **net cash flows** are net economic benefits caused by an investment project. The benefits expected from the project must be measured on an incremental after-tax basis. The net cash flows are used here to mean the differences between incremental after-tax cash inflows and outflows. Incremental cash inflows include operating savings, increased sales revenues, and salvage value. Incremental cash outflows include labor and material costs, maintenance costs, and other costs directly related to the project. These cash inflows and outflows are normally transformed into an after-tax basis.

The **economic life** of the project is the time period during which we can expect to obtain the benefits from the project. It is very important to distinguish the economic life of a project from its physical life. For example, a machine with a physical life of ten years may have to be replaced after only two or three years because of the change in the nature of the business or advances in technology.

Economic Evaluation

Once cash flow estimates have been made, the company begins the formal process of evaluating investment projects. The method of analysis must take into account the tradeoff between net cash investment and net cash flows. This evaluation process proceeds in two stages: capital budgeting analysis under certainty and risk analysis. Both analyses are made to rank and select the available investment opportunities.

Many techniques have been developed for project evaluation under conditions of certainty. They range from simple rules of thumb to sophisticated mathematical programming methods. The five most commonly used methods for an economic evaluation of individual projects are payback, average rate of return, net present value, profitability index, and internal rate of return. Each of these methods measures the rate of return on a uniform basis for all projects under consideration. A project or a set of projects will be chosen at this stage if the following three assumptions hold: first, the company has a definite cutoff point which all projects must meet; second, all cash outflows and inflows from each project are known with absolute certainty; and third, the company's investment programs are not constrained by any lack of funds.

Estimated project inflows and outflows must somehow be adjusted for risk for at least two reasons. First, only a few of the financial variables are normally known in advance with a fair degree of accuracy. Second, investors and businessmen are basically risk averters. If we do not know in advance exactly what future events will occur, we will have to determine the risk-return tradeoff in order to choose more attractive projects. A number of techniques may be used to evaluate individual projects under conditions of uncertainty: probability theory, utility theory, computer simulation, sensitivity analysis, risk-adjusted discount rate, and certainty equivalent approach. Portfolio risk analysis and the capital asset pricing model may be used to analyze the riskiness of multiple projects.

Selection

The final selection of a project depends on the types of capital budgeting decisions being made: the accept-reject decisions, the mutually exclusive choice decision, and the capital rationing decision. Investment proposals are said to be mutually exclusive if the acceptance of one project means the rejection of all the other projects. Capital rationing is necessary when there is a ceiling on total capital expenditures during a given period of time.

The selected project must successfully pass the **accept-reject decision**. If projects under consideration are mutually independent and not subject to capital rationing constraints, the company must accept all projects whose expected rate of return exceeds its hurdle rate in order to maximize stockholder wealth. The **hurdle rate** may be based on the cost of capital, the opportunity cost, or some other arbitrary standard. However, it is important to recognize the possibility that (1) certain projects may compete with each other and (2) available projects may exceed available funds. Mutual exclusiveness and capital rationing constraints are two cases where otherwise profitable projects are rejected.

Implementation

Authorization to expend funds for the accepted projects may be obtained by submission of individual capital expenditure requests in accordance with formal procedures set forth by the budget director. These procedures typically cover the use of standard forms, the channels for submission and review, and the authority requirements and limits for approval. For instance, they may require the approval of the Chairman of the Board for requests of $1 million or more, of the President for requests of $100,000-$1 million, and of the appropriate division manager for requests of less than $100,000. Once funds have been authorized to implement the projects, the firm must acquire the funds, purchase assets, and begin operating the projects. This phase usually requires relatively little attention from the financial manager if all prior phases in the capital budgeting process have been correctly performed. However, if the necessary funds or assets are not available at the specific cost, the company may be forced to reevaluate all projects.

Expenditure Control

There is a specific phase of the capital budgeting process during which the practical cost control of a project becomes important. This is the time between the approval of the project and its completion. The expenditure control of a project in process is designed to increase the probability that it is completed within the established guidelines. The control also allows management to pinpoint the problem areas of a project so that it can take corrective action. In the case of cost overruns, there are three possible courses of action: complete the project with added cost, reanalyze its economic worth, or abandon it.

Post-Audits

Because capital expenditure decisions are made on the basis of assumptions, estimates and actual results may differ. Thus, when a project is completed, the firm should perform a post-audit on the entire project to determine its success or failure. Post-audits provide important feedback information: to evaluate the effectiveness of project analysis; to explore further investment opportunities; to determine if some corrective action is necessary to bring a project up to its full potential; and to assign responsibility for mistakes and mismanagement in project implementation.

The results of post-audits enable the firm to compare the actual performance of a project with established standards. If the capital budgeting process used by a firm has been successful, the system is likely to be reinforced. If the system has been unsatisfactory, it is likely to be revised or replaced.

Examples of Cash Flow Analysis

Capital expenditure decisions require knowledge of the cash outflows needed to acquire assets and the cash inflows expected from their use. These cash flows may be determined on the basis of sales and cost estimates combined with the relevant tax implications of the transactions under consideration. Business firms must consider the different impact of depreciation on tax payments when they use straight-line depreciation or accelerated depreciation.

Example 10-1: Replacement. A corporation is planning to replace an old machine with a new one. The firm purchased the old machine five years ago at a cost of $20,000, and it has been depreciated on a straight-line basis. The machine had an expected useful life of ten years at the time of purchase and no estimated salvage value at the end of ten years. The firm has found a person willing to buy the old machine for $5,000 and remove it at his own expense. The firm can buy the new machine for $12,000. The new machine has a useful life of five years and no salvage value at the end of five years. An additional $3,000 will be required to transport and install it. The new machine is not expected to change the firm's revenue but is expected to reduce its operating costs from $10,000 to $5,000 a year. It is to be depreciated on a straight-line basis for five years, and the firm's marginal tax rate is 50 percent.

The net cash investment consists of the purchase price of the new machine, freight and installation costs, tax effects, and the proceeds from the sale of the old machine. If the firm purchases the new machine and sells the old one, it incurs an operating loss of $5,000 (or the book value of $10,000 minus the market value of $5,000). The tax savings on the loss is $2,500 or ($5,000 x 0.50). Thus, the net cash investment for the project is

Purchase price of new machine		$12,000
Freight and installation costs		3,000
Total		$15,000
Less: tax savings	$2,500	
proceeds from sale of old machine	5,000	7,500
Net cash investment		$ 7,500

194 PART 4: CAPITAL EXPENDITURE ANALYSIS

The net cash flow is the difference between the cash flow of the firm with and without the new machine. The difference must be estimated on an incremental after-tax basis, and it is the net benefit for the project. The annual depreciation charge is $2,000 or ($20,000 x 0.10) on the old machine and $3,000 on the new machine or ($15,000 x 0.20). Hence, the incremental depreciation charges associated with the project are $1,000 a year. Because the new machine is expected to reduce the firm's operating expenses from $10,000 to $5,000 a year, it will result in an annual cash savings of $5,000 a year. The expected net cash flow from the acceptance of the project is

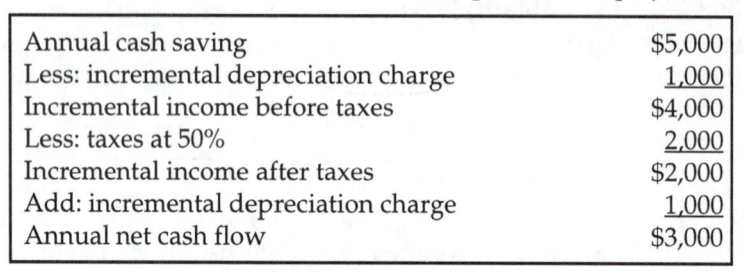

Annual cash saving	$5,000
Less: incremental depreciation charge	1,000
Incremental income before taxes	$4,000
Less: taxes at 50%	2,000
Incremental income after taxes	$2,000
Add: incremental depreciation charge	1,000
Annual net cash flow	$3,000

Thus, for a net cash investment of $7,500, the firm is expected to produce a net cash flow of $3,000 a year for the next five years.

Example 10-2: Expansion for New Products. A corporation is considering the introduction of a new product. To produce it, the firm will need to buy a new piece of equipment for $10,000. The equipment has no salvage value on retirement and an expected useful life of four years. The marketing department expects incremental sales revenue to be $11,000 a year, and the production department projects incremental operating expense to be $6,000 a year. It has been decided to use the double declining-balance method of depreciation. The firm's marginal tax rate is 40 percent. Determine the profit and net cash flow of the equipment.

The taxable income and income tax of each year are first computed, and then net cash flow for each year is determined. The expected net cash flow from the project is computed as follows:

	Year 1	Year 2	Year 3	Year 4
Revenues	$11,000	$11,000	$11,000	$11,000
Less: operating expenses	6,000	6,000	6,000	6,000
Depreciation charge	5,000	2,500	1,250	1,250
Taxable income	$ 0	$ 2,500	$ 3,750	$ 3,750
Less: taxes at 40%	0	1,000	1,500	1,500
Earnings after taxes	$ 0	$ 1,500	$ 2,250	$ 2,250
Add: depreciation charge	5,000	2,500	1,250	1,250
Annual net cash flow	$ 5,000	$ 4,000	$ 3,500	$ 3,500

The firm expects a net cash investment of $10,000 to result in net cash flows of $5,000, $4,000, $3,500, and $3,500 for the next four years.

Example 10-3: *Expansion for Existing Products.* A corporation is considering the purchase of a new press to replace an old one. The old press with a useful life of eight years was purchased four years ago at a cost of $8,000. It has been depreciated on a straight-line basis. The market value of the old press is negligible due to advances in technology. The new press requires a net cash investment of $10,000 and an expected useful life of four years. It is to be depreciated on the basis of the sum-of-years'-digits method. The new press is expected to expand sales from $15,000 to $17,500 a year. It is also expected to cut labor and maintenance costs from $7,500 to $6,000 a year. The firm's marginal tax rate is 40 percent. Determine the profit and net cash flow of the project.

The new press will produce an annual sales increase of $2,500 or ($17,500 − $15,000) and an annual cash saving of $1,500 or ($7,500 − $6,000). Given a depreciable value of $10,000 and useful life of four years, the annual depreciation charges of the new press for the sum-of-years-digits method are $4,000, $3,000, $2,000, and $1,000 over the next four years. Because the old press is depreciated on a straight-line basis at $1,000 a year, the additional depreciation charges will be $3,000, $2,000, $1,000, and $0 for the next four years. The net cash flows of the project are computed as follows:

	Year 1	Year 2	Year 3	Year 4
Additional sales	$2,500	$2,500	$2,500	$2,500
Add: cash savings	1,500	1,500	1,500	1,500
Incremental revenues	$4,000	$4,000	$4,000	$4,000
Less: additional deprec.	3,000	2,000	1,000	0
Taxable income	$1,000	$2,000	$3,000	$4,000
Less: taxes at 40%	400	800	1,200	1,600
Earnings after taxes	$600	$1,200	$1,800	$2,400
Add: additional deprec.	3,000	2,000	1,000	0
Net cash flows	$3,600	$3,200	$2,800	$2,400

Example 10-4: *ACRS.* A new machine costs $10,000 and is expected to have no salvage value on retirement. This machine falls in the three-year ACRS category. The ACRS is an acronym for the accelerated cost recovery system discussed in Chapter 2. The machine is expected to generate an annual revenue of $11,000 for the next four years and to require an annual operating cost of $6,000 (excluding the depreciation of the machine). The tax rate is 40 percent. Determine the deprecation and net cash flow of the machine.

This machine will be depreciated in four years because we get an extra year due to the mid-year convention. The deprecation schedule is shown in the following table:

PART 4: CAPITAL EXPENDITURE ANALYSIS

Year	Depreciation Base	Depreciation (%) (from Table 2-3)	Annual Depreciation
1	$10,000	0.333	$3,330
2	10,000	0.445	4,450
3	10,000	0.148	1,480
4	10,000	0.074	740
Total		1.000	$10,000

The expected net cash flows of the machine are computed as follows:

	Year 1	Year 2	Year 3	Year 4
Revenues	$11,000	$11,000	$11,000	$11,000
Less: operating expenses	6,000	6,000	6,000	6,000
deprecation charge	3,330	4,450	1,480	740
Taxable income	$ 1,670	$ 550	$ 3,520	$ 4,260
Less: tax at 40%	668	220	1,408	1,704
Earnings after taxes	$ 1,002	$ 330	$ 2,112	$ 2,556
Add: depreciation charge	3,330	4,450	1,480	740
Annual net cash flow	$ 4,332	$ 4,780	$ 3,592	$3,296

CAPITAL BUDGETING TECHNIQUES UNDER CERTAINTY

Chapter 9 and the first part of this chapter provided the necessary background for an economic evaluation of investment projects. This section begins the formal process of evaluating investment projects under conditions of certainty. The project evaluation process has two basic steps. The first is to rank available investment opportunities. The second is to determine a hurdle rate or a cutoff point that all projects must meet.

Many methods have been developed to guide management in the acceptance or rejection of proposed investment projects. The five most commonly used methods are payback, average rate of return, net present value, profitability index, and internal rate of return. Because the first two methods do not consider the time value of money, they are frequently called unsophisticated techniques. The last three methods are termed discounted cash-flow (DCF) approaches, which consider the time value of money. Each of these five methods is defined as follows:

1. **Payback.** The payback period is the number of years required to recover the original cost of a project by its net cash flows.
2. **Average rate of return.** This rate is the ratio of the average annual profits after taxes to the average net investment.
3. **Net present value.** This value is the present value of the net cash flows minus the present value of the net investment.
4. **Profitability index.** This index is the present value of the net cash flows divided by the present value of the net investment.
5. **Internal rate of return.** This rate is the discount rate that equates the present value of the net cash flows to the present value of the net investment.

The second major step in the project evaluation process is to establish the required rate of return (the hurdle rate or the cutoff point). We postpone an extensive discussion of this concept until Chapter 13, but a brief comment on the concept of the hurdle rate is included now because it has a direct influence on the investment decision. The choice of a minimum profitability standard is essential to maximize the value of the firm and thus the price of the common stock. The choice may be based on the cost of capital. If the cost of capital is used as a minimum acceptable level of return, the accepted project must earn at least as much as the cost of the funds invested in the project. If not, investors can find better yields elsewhere on equally risky investment opportunities. Under these circumstances, the investors will sell their shares, which in turn will depress the market price of the stock and increase the cost of capital. The cost of capital should include the cost of debt and the cost of equity, because almost no firms are financed solely from debt or equity. The quantity and the cost of the different forms of capital are not identical.

The selection of a required rate of return may also be based on the opportunity cost. The opportunity cost is defined as the rate of return the funds could earn if they were invested in the best available alternative project. Those projects that yield less than the opportunity cost will depress the market price of the common stock. On the other hand, those projects that yield more than the opportunity cost will increase the market price of the stock.

Before we turn to specific capital-budgeting techniques, we will describe four investment projects. These four projects are designed to make it possible to decide, within selected pairs, which project is clearly better than the other. Table 10-1 shows the net investment and net cash flows for each of the four projects.

To simplify the analysis, we make the following assumptions.

1. All costs and benefits for each project are certain to occur.
2. The firm has unlimited funds for investment, and the four projects are mutually independent. These two assumptions enable the firm to accept all profitable projects.
3. The net investment is made at the beginning of the first year, and the net cash flows are obtained at the end of each year.
4. All four projects have the same net investment, and the net cash flows are the earnings after taxes plus the annual depreciation charges. These assumptions will be removed in later chapters.

Table 10-1
Net Investment and Net Cash Flows for Four Projects

Project	Net Investment	Net Cash Flows Year 1	Net Cash Flows Year 2
W	$5,000	$5,000	$ 550
X	5,000	2,881	2,881
Y	5,000	5,000	0
Z	5,000	1,881	3,881

RANKING AND SELECTION

We can rank and select among some projects on the basis of intuition. First, if two projects have equal net cash flows each year through the last year of the shorter-lived

198 PART 4: CAPITAL EXPENDITURE ANALYSIS

project, we would definitely prefer the project that continues to produce earnings in subsequent years. Thus, Project W is more attractive than Project Y. Second, if the net investment, the total amount of net cash flows, and the project life are the same for any two projects, we would definitely prefer the project that has high net cash flows during its early years. Hence, Project X is more attractive than Project Z.

There are two basic unsophisticated techniques that can be used to rank and select investment projects: the payback method and the average rate of return method. They are easy to compute and popular in practice. However, these two methods are not theoretically complete because they do not consider the time value of money.

Payback

The payback period of a project is the number of years required to accumulate net cash flows sufficient to recover its net investment. If the annual net cash flows are equal, the net investment is divided by the annual net cash flows to obtain the payback period. If the annual net cash flows are not equal, we must add the net cash flows in successive years until we find a total of net cash flows equal to the net investment. Thus, the payback period of Project Y is one year or ($5,000 ÷ $5,000). For Project Z, $1,881 will be recovered in the first year, and the remaining balance of $3,119 or ($5,000 − $1,881) will be recovered in the second year. The payback period of Project Z is one year plus eight-tenths of one year or ($3,119 ÷ $3,881)) or 1.8 years.

The firm usually sets some maximum payback period and accepts all projects whose payback period of the four projects described in Table 10-1 and their rankings are shown in Table 10-2.

Table 10-2
The Payback Periods of Four Projects and Their Rankings

Project	Payback Period	Rankings
W	1.0 Years	1
X	1.7 Years	3
Y	1.0 Years	1
Z	1.8 Years	4

The payback method has a number of advantages. It is easy to compute and to understand. It also reflects investment liquidity. In other words, the payback period allows us to judge the length of time the funds will be tied up and to isolate projects with shorter payback periods. Although the payback period is easy to determine and popular in practice, its usefulness is limited because of its lack of theoretical validity. It ignores the amount and pattern of net cash flows beyond the payback period. For example, consider Projects W and Y, with an equal cost of $5,000 and an equal payback period of one year. Project W is the better investment because it is expected to produce $550 after the payback period. But this difference is completely ignored by the payback method, which rates these two projects equally. Another limitation is that it does not take into account the time value of money. Suppose that Project A yields $10 in the first year and $100 in the second year, whereas Project B earns $100 in the first year and $10 in the second year. If these two projects have an equal investment of $110, the payback method would rate them equally. Yet it is clear that most investors would prefer Project B, because it recovers the invest-

Average Rate of Return

There are many possible definitions of the average rate of return, depending on how benefits and costs are measured. The most common definition of the average rate of return, however, is the ratio of the average annual profits after taxes to the average net investment. When this method is used, the average profits are computed after depreciation. Assuming straight-line depreciation, the annual depreciation charge for Project Z is $2,500 or ($5,000 ÷ 2). Because the average annual net cash flows of the project are $2,881 or [($1,881 + $3,881) ÷ 2], its average annual profits are $381 after backing out our depreciation expense (or $2,881 − $2,500). The average net investment is half the original cost of the project. Project Z has a cost of $5,000. Thus, its average net investment is $2,500. Given the average annual profits and the average net investment, the average rate of return for Project Z is

$$\text{Average Rate of Return} = \frac{\$381}{\$2,500} = 15\%$$

Ordinarily, management preestablishes some minimum average rate of return as a cut-off point and accepts all projects whose average rates of return are greater than this minimum. For ranking projects, the greater the average rate of return, the better the project. The four projects listed in Table 10-1 are ranked by the average rate of return, as shown in Table 10-3.

Table 10-3
The Average Rates of Return for Four Projects and Their Rankings

Project	Average Profits	Average Net Investment	Average Rate Of Return	Ranking
W	$275	$2,500	11%	3
X	381	2,500	15	1
Y	0	2,500	0	4
Z	381	2,500	15	1

The average rate of return is easy to determine, but it has a number of serious shortcomings. It ignores the time value of money. Under the average rate-of-return method, profits in the last year are given the same weight as profits in the first year. For example, Projects X and Z have the same average rate of return. But most firms would definitely prefer Project X, because it has a large portion of total profits in the first year. Other deficiencies are (1) it uses accounting income rather than net cash flows, (2) it relies on a uniform income stream, and (3) it fails to take advantage of accelerated depreciation.

Because both the payback and average rate-of-return methods have the various limitations just described, discounted cash-flow approaches provide a more sophisticated basis for ranking and selecting investment projects. The net-present-value, profitability-index, and internal-rate-of-return methods clearly recognize that money has a time value. These three techniques also use the cash flows of a project over its entire life span. The use of cash flows avoids difficult problems underlying the measurement of accounting income.

Net Present Value

The measurement of a project by the net-present-value method (NPV) requires a determination of the following: (1) an appropriate rate of discount, (2) the present value of the net cash flows expected from the project, and (3) the net cash investment required by the project. The net present value of the project is the present value of the net cash flows minus the net cash investment:

$$NPV = \frac{CF_1}{(1+k)^1} + \frac{CF_2}{(1+k)^2} + \ldots + \frac{CF_n}{(1+k)^n} - C_o$$

$$= \sum_{t=1}^{n} \frac{CF_t}{(1+k)^t} - C_o$$

(10-1)

where Σ = capital Greek sigma, which denotes the sum of discounted net cash flows for the entire life of the project; CF_t = net cash flows in year t; k = cost of capital used as a discount rate; C_o = present cost of the investment; and n = number of years in life of the project.

With a rate of return to recover the cost of the invested funds, the net present value of Project Z is

$$NPV = \frac{\$1,881}{(1+0.05)^1} + \frac{\$3,881}{(1+0.05)^2} - \$5,000$$

$$= \$5,311 - \$5,000$$

$$= \$311$$

An easier way to solve the problem is:

1. Find the appropriate interest factor from Table C at the end of this book.
2. Multiply the annual net cash flow by that interest factor.
3. Add the present values of all net cash flow items.
4. Subtract the cost of the investment from the present value of the net cash flows. The results are shown in Table 10-4.

Table 10-4
Net Present Value Computation

Year	Net Cash Flow	Interest Factor at 5%	Present Value of Net Cash Flows
1	$1,881	0.952	$1,791
2	3,881	0.907	3,520
		Present value of net cash flows	$5,311
		Less: net investment	5,000
		Net present value (NPV)	$ 311

Solved by financial calculator:

1. Hit CF, and 2nd CLR Work.
2. Key in -5,000 for CF_0 and hit enter.
3. Scroll down to CO1 and key in +1881, scroll and enter 1 of F01 (frequency of one).
4. Scroll down, enter +3881 and 1 for C02 and F02, respectively.
5. Hit 2nd QUIT and then hit NPV.
6. Key in 5 for I and hit enter (this is the discount rate or cost of capital).
7. Scroll down to NPV and hit CPT to compute the NPV.
8. Result = $311.61 for the Net Present Value of the Investment.

For Investment X where net cash flows are equal:

1. Duplicate steps #1, 2, 5, 6, and 7.
2. For steps #3 and 4, key in +2881 for C01 and enter the frequency of 2 for F01.
3. Result = 356.96 for the Net Present Value of Investment X.

The present value of $5,311 for Project Z is the maximum amount that a firm could pay for the project and still earn the reqired cost of capital. To put the matter another way, the present value of the net cash flows expected from Project Z could pay off an investment of $5,000, its cost of 5 percent, and still leave $311 for the firm.

The net-present-value method tells us to accept all projects whose net present values are greater than zero and to reject all projects whose net present values are negative. Because the accept-reject decision is based on the zero net present value, the higher the positive net present value, the better the project. Table 10-5 ranks the four projects of Table 10-1 on the basis of the net-present-value method. As shown in Table 10-5, Projects W, X, and Z have positive net present values and consequently would be accepted by the firm. But Project Y has a negative net present value and therefore would be rejected. It is also important to note that Project X has the highest net present value among the four projects and thus should be ranked as the best project.

Table 10-5
Net Present Values at 5% and Their Rankings

Project	Present Value of Net Cash Flows	Net Investment	Net Present Value	Ranking
W	$5,259	$5,000	$259	3
X	5,356	5,000	356	1
Y	4,760	5,000	-240	4
Z	5,311	5,000	311	2

Profitability Index

An attempt to make the net-present-value method more meaningful can be made by introducing the profitability index (PI). The index is obtained by dividing the present value of the net cash flows by the net investment:

$$PI = \frac{PV}{COST} - 1$$

PART 4: CAPITAL EXPENDITURE ANALYSIS

$$\text{Profitability Index (PI)} = \frac{\sum_{t=1}^{n} \frac{CF_t}{(1+k)^t}}{C_o} \qquad (10\text{-}2)$$

Thus, the index uses the same information as the net-present-value method and measures the present value return per dollar of net investment. With a 5 percent discount rate, the profitability index for Project W is 1.05 or ($5,259 ÷ $5,000). Because the index criterion tells us to accept all projects whose indexes are greater than 1, Project W should be accepted. The greater the index, the better the project.

Table 10-6 shows the calculated profitability indexes of the four projects listed in Table 10-1 and their rankings. Because all the projects with positive net present values tend to have profitability indexes greater than 1, the net-present-value and profitability-index methods yield the same accept-reject decisions. Although these two methods rank the four projects in the same order, they can lead to different rankings under certain circumstances. This is because the net-present-value method measures a project's profitability on an absolute scale while the profitability index measures a project's profitability on a relative scale.

Table 10-6
Profitability Indexes of Four Projects and Their Rankings

Project	Present Value of Net Cash Flows	Net Investment	Profitability Index	Ranking
W	$5,259	$5,000	1.052	3
X	5,356	5,000	1.071	1
Y	4,760	5,000	0.952	4
Z	5,311	5,000	1.062	2

Internal Rate of Return

The internal rate of return is the discount rate that equates the present value of the net cash flows to the present value of the net cash investment, or the rate that provides a zero net present value:

$$\frac{CF_1}{(1+r)^1} + \frac{CF_2}{(1+r)^2} + \ldots + \frac{CF_n}{(1+r)^3} = C_o$$

$$\sum_{t=1}^{n} \frac{CF_t}{(1+r)^t} = C_o \qquad (10\text{-}3)$$

Here we know the value of net investment (C_o), net cash flows ($CF_1, CF_2, \ldots$), and project's life (n), but we do not know the value of the internal rate of return (r).

If the net cash-flow stream represents an even series or an annuity, we can closely approximate the internal rate of return by a relatively simple procedure. We solve for

Chapter 10: Capital Budgeting under Certainty

the implied discount factor, and we use it to search for the approximate internal return. The annuity discount factor for any project with an even series such as Project X can be found by applying Equation (9-7):

$$PVA = CF \times IF_{PVA_{n,i}} \quad \text{or} \quad IF_{PVA_{n,i}} = \frac{PVA}{CF}$$

$$IF_{PVA_{n,i}} = \frac{\$5,000}{\$2,881} = 1.736$$

Look across the two-year row of Table D in Appendix A to find that the annuity discount factor 1.736 is under the 10 percent column. This 10 percent is the internal rate of return for Project X.

When net cash flows are not the same in every year, it is necessary to use a trial-and-error procedure. The trial-and-error method requires the following steps:

1. Choose an arbitrary discount rate. The cost of capital is a good starting point, because the firm must earn at least as much as the cost of capital. Alternatively, a first estimate of the answer may be obtained by reconstructing the problem using an average net cash flow each year rather than the exact amounts given.
2. Compute the present value of net cash flows using an arbitrarily selected rate of the first estimate of the answer.
3. Compare the present value with the net investment. If the present value is higher than the net investment, try a higher rate and repeat the process. If the present value is lower than the net investment, try a lower rate and repeat the process.
4. Continue this process until you find the rate that equates the present value of net cash flows to the net investment. Or approximate the internal rate of return using linear interpolation.

To illustrate, consider Project Z, which has a net investment of $5,000 and is expected to yield $1,881 at the end of one year and $3,881 at the end of two years. Because the average annual net cash flow of Project Z is $2,881 or [($1,881 + $3,881) ÷ 2], the first estimate of the answer for Project Z is 10 percent. With the discount rate of 10 percent, the present value of the net cash flows for Project Z is $4,915.54. Because the present value of $4,915.54 is lower than the net investment of $5,000, we must try a rate lower than 10 percent. With a discount rate of 8 percent, the present value of the net cash flows for Project Z is $5,067.82. Because the present value of $5,067.82 is higher than the net investment of $5,000, we see that the internal rate of return is higher than 8 percent but lower than 10 percent. We can continue the trial-and-error procedure until we find the internal rate of return; or we can interpolate between 8 and 10 percent to approximate the internal rate of return. If we choose the latter method, it is convenient to diagram the data as follows:

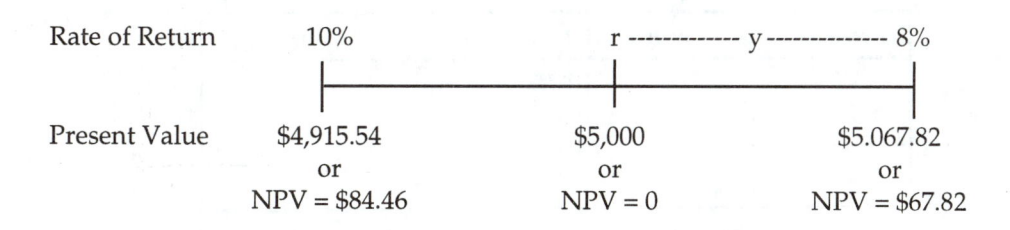

Rate of Return	10%	r ------------ y ------------ 8%
Present Value	$4,915.54	$5,000	$5,067.82
	or	or	or
	NPV = $84.46	NPV = 0	NPV = $67.82

$$\frac{\$5{,}067.82 - \$5{,}000.00}{\$5{,}067.82 - \$4{,}915.54} = \frac{y}{10\% - 8\%}$$

$$y = \frac{\$67.82}{\$152.28} \times 2\% = 0.9\%$$

$$r = 8\% + y = 8\% + 0.9\% = 8.9\%$$

Thus, the internal rate of return for Project Z is approximately 8.9 percent. It is important to note that interpolation fails to give an exact rate. Although we assumed that the rate difference ratio of y/2% is equal to the present value difference ratio of $67.82/$152.28, the true relationship between discount rates and present values is not linear.

The 8.9 percent represents the highest cost of financing that the firm could pay for all the funds to finance Project Z. To put the matter another way, the internal rate of return is the growth rate of a project. In other words, a net investment of $5,000 with an 8.9 percent growth rate will return $1,881 at the end of one year and $3,881 at the end of two years. This is verified as follows:

Year	Beginning Balance	Interest at 8.9%	Ending Balance	Annual Return
1	$5,000	$445	$5,445	$1,881
2	3,564	317	3,881	3,881

Solved by financial calculator:

1. Duplicate steps #1 through #4 exactly as illustrated earlier for calculating the NPV for Project Z. This simply enters the net cash flows.
2. Hit IRR and then CPT to compute the IRR.
3. Result = 8.89% as the Internal Rate of Return for Project Z.

The decision rule for the internal rate of return method is shown in Table 10-9 below. In essence, the decision rule compares the internal rate of return with a cutoff point, known as a minimum required rate of return. If the internal rate of return exceeds the cutoff point, the project should be accepted; if not, it should be rejected. The higher the internal rate of return, the better the project. Table 10-7 presents the internal rate of return for the four projects described in Table 10-1 and their relative rankings. If the minimum required rate of return is 5 percent and the projects are independent, Projects W, X, Z should be accepted, and Project Y should be rejected. It should be noted that this is precisely the same conclusion reached by the use of the net-present-value method with a discount rate of 5 percent.

Table 10-7
Internal Rates of Return for Four Projects and Their Rankings

Project	Internal Rate of Return	Ranking
W	10.0%	1
X	10.0	1
Y	0.0	4
Z	8.9	3

Table 10-8 summarizes a set of rankings by the five different techniques for the four projects listed in Table 10-1. We see that the techniques produce different rankings for the same set of investment projects. This strongly suggests that the correct choice of methods for the firm to use can be critical for its future well-being.

Table 10-8
Summary of Rankings

Project	Payback	Average Rate of Return	NPV at 5%	Profitability Index at 5%	IRR
W	1	3	3	3	1
X	3	1	1	1	1
Y	1	4	4	4	4
Z	4	1	2	2	3

Table 10-9
Internal Rates of Return and Net Present Value Decision Rules

if IRR = cost of capital, then NPV = 0

If	Then
IRR Greater than firm's cost of capital, NPV > 0 NPV greater than zero PI greater than 1	Accept Project
IRR less than the firm's cost of capital, NPV < 0 NPV less than zero PI less than 1	Reject Project

if PI =

Internal Rate of Return Versus Net Present Value

The current literature in the field of capital budgeting favors the use of the net-present-value and the internal-rate-of-return methods because they consider the time value of money. Their **accept-reject rules** are: (1) accept projects whose net present values are greater than 0, and (2) accept projects whose internal rates of return are greater than the firm's cost of capital. These two basic rules lead to the same decision if the following conditions hold:

1. Investment proposals under consideration are independent and free of capital rationing constraints.
2. All projects are equally risky so that the acceptance or rejection of any project does not affect the cost of capital.
3. A meaningful cost of capital exists to the extent that the company has access to capital at this cost.
4. A unique internal rate of return exists; every project has just one internal rate of return.

In the absence of these assumptions, the capital investment decision becomes more complex and these two discounted cash-flow approaches may lead to different decisions.

PART 4: CAPITAL EXPENDITURE ANALYSIS

For example, if we assume that the investment projects under consideration are mutually exclusive or that the firm has limited funds for investment, then the net present value and internal rate of return methods may give different answers. In the case of mutual exclusion, the firm must select only one project from two or more alternatives which accomplishes a single objective. Two projects might be to either build a new headquarters building or renovate the old. Obviously, the firm cannot do both since the acceptance of one would automatically eliminate the possibility of carrying out the other. Clearly, if the firm decides to renovate the old headquarters building, this action would mutually exclude the need for a new office building.

To illustrate, we will retabulate the results of the computation for Projects X, W, Y, Z of Table 10-1 with respect to the two discounted cash-flow approaches. It is clear from Table 10-10 that the two techniques do not rank the four projects in the same order of preference.

Table 10-10
Selection of Projects Under Net Present Value and Internal Rate of Return

Rank	Net Investment	Cumulative Net Investment	NPV Rank at 5%	% IRR Rank
1	$5,000	$5,000	X = $356	W = 10.0
2	$5,000	$10,000	Z = 311	X = 10.0
3	$5,000	$15,000	W = 259	Z = 8.90
4	$5,000	$20,000	Y = -240	Y = 0.0

Suppose Projects Z and W are **mutually exclusive** (that is acceptance of one precludes acceptance of the other), Project Z should be accepted when making a decision on the basis of net present value. On the other hand, Project W should be accepted over Project Z when making a choice on the basis of internal rate of return.

When **independent** projects are evaluated under a **capital-rationing constraint**, they are listed in the order of preference according to the net present value or the internal rate of return. Then projects are selected in descending order from the top of the list until the available funds have been consumed. If the firm has a capital budget of $10,000, net present value tells us to accept Projects X and Z, but internal rate of return tells us to accept Projects W and X.

Under ordinary circumstances, the two capital budgeting techniques yield identical decisions. Under certain circumstances, however, they produce different rankings, which make it impossible for us to avoid the necessity of choosing between the two methods of evaluating investment alternatives.

Net present value is better than internal rate of return for a number of reasons. First, net present value is easier to compute than the internal rate of return. Second, if the primary goal of a firm is to maximize its value, net present value leads to correct decisions, while internal rate of return may lead to incorrect decisions. Third, a single project has only one net present value at a particular rate of discount, though the same project may have more than one internal rate of return. Fourth, once computed, the internal rate of return remains constant over the entire life of the project. But uneven discount rates present no problems when net present value is used.

Finally, the reinvestment rate assumption under the NPV method is more sound than that of the IRR. In essence, the NPV assumes that all future cash flows from an investment will be reinvested at the firm's opportunity cost of capital while the IRR assumes all future cash flows will be reinvested at the projects initial IRR. The IRR assumption becomes unrealistic for projects with extremely high IRRs. For example, assume the firm randomly discovers and accepts a project yeilding a 70% IRR. For this 70% IRR to materialize or come true, the firm must reinvest all future cash flows from this project at the 70% rate of return. Obviously, it is unrealistic for the firm to assume that it will "run up on" such high return projects on a "regular" basis in coming years. The NPV makes the more conservative assumption that these same cash flows can be the reinvested at the firm's present opportunity cost of capital.

Internal rate of return has certain advantages, although net present value is superior theoretically. First, internal rate of return is easier to visualize and interpret because it is identical with the yield to the maturity of bonds or other securities. Second, we do not need to specify a required rate of return in the computations. In other words, internal rate of return does not require prior computation of the cost of capital.

Summary

Although the first part of this chapter broke down the capital budgeting process into components and relationships for a detailed inspection, these stages should not be used mechanically. Some steps may be combined, some may be subdivided, and others may be skipped altogether without jeopardizing the quality of the capital budgeting system. It is likely, however, that several of these steps will be in progress simultaneously for any project under consideration. For instance, if expenditure controls and post-audits are not planned until the economic evaluation of a project is completed, the capital budgeting process will hardly be realistic. Decisions for expenditure controls and post-audits affect plans, just as planning decisions affect controlling decisions. Thus, the capital budgeting process consists of several related activities that overlap continuously rather than following an ideally prescribed order. Because all steps in the investment decision-making process are interwoven, their relationships should not permanently place any one stage first or last in a sequence.

This chapter also examined various capital budgeting techniques with heavy emphasis on the net-present-value and internal-rate-of-return methods. In most situations, the two discounted cash-flow methods lead to the same decision. However, there are also situations in which these two techniques may lead to different decisions. Thus, the correct choice of capital budgeting techniques for the firm to use can be critical for its future well-being.

List of Key Terms

net cash flows
hurdle rate
average rate of return
profitability index
accept-reject decision rules
capital-rationing constraint

accept-reject decision
payback
net present value
internal rate of return
mutually exclusive choice

Figure 10-1
Sample Capital Budgeting Request Form

```
┌─────────────────────────────────────────────────────────────────┐
│                    CAPITAL BUDGETING REQUEST                    │
└─────────────────────────────────────────────────────────────────┘

┌─────────────────────────────────────────────────────────────────┐
│  Description of the Project:                                    │
│                                                                 │
│                                                                 │
│                                                                 │
│                                                                 │
└─────────────────────────────────────────────────────────────────┘
```

Authorization:		Post-Audit:			
<$ 1K	1st Supervisor ____	Yr.	Estimated	Actual	Error %
> 1K	2nd Supervisor ____	1	$_____	$_____	$_____ ___
> 10K	Dept. Manager ____	2	_____	_____	_____ ___
> 10K	Finance Staff ____	3	_____	_____	_____ ___
> 10K	Legal Dept. ____	4	_____	_____	_____ ___
> 10K	Purchasing ____	5	_____	_____	_____ ___
> 25K	V-P of Finance ____	6	_____	_____	_____ ___
>100K	President ____	7	_____	_____	_____ ___
>100K	Board Committee____	8	_____	_____	_____ ___

```
┌─────────────────────────────────────────────────────────────────┐
│                      Capital Requirements                       │
├─────────────────────────────────────────────────────────────────┤
│   Equipment . . . . . . . . . . . . . . . . . . . . . . . $____│
│   Transportation/Freight . . . . . . . . . . . . . . . .  ____│
│   Installation . . . . . . . . . . . . . . . . . . . . .  ____│
│   Buildings  . . . . . . . . . . . . . . . . . . . . . .  ____│
│   Feasibility Studies  . . . . . . . . . . . . . . . . .  ____│
│   Site Preparation . . . . . . . . . . . . . . . . . . .  ____│
│   Sale of Old Equipment (reduction of cost) . . . . . . (____)│
│   Tax on Sale of Old Equipment . . . . . . . . . . . . .  ____│
│   Working Capital  . . . . . . . . . . . . . . . . . . .  ____│
│                                                                 │
│ Total Capital Requirements . . . . . . . . . . . . . . . $____│
└─────────────────────────────────────────────────────────────────┘
```

```
┌─────────────────────────────────────────────────────────────────┐
│              Savings Before Depreciation and Taxes              │
├─────────────────────────────────────────────────────────────────┤
│ Yr.    Labor    +  Materials  +  Energy  +  Overhead  = Total Savings │
│  1  $_____  +  _____  +  _____  +  _____  =  $_____       │
│  2    _____  +  _____  +  _____  +  _____  =   _____       │
│  3    _____  +  _____  +  _____  +  _____  =   _____       │
│  4    _____  +  _____  +  _____  +  _____  =   _____       │
│  5    _____  +  _____  +  _____  +  _____  =   _____       │
│  6    _____  +  _____  +  _____  +  _____  =   _____       │
│  7    _____  +  _____  +  _____  +  _____  =   _____       │
│  8    _____  +  _____  +  _____  +  _____  =   _____       │
└─────────────────────────────────────────────────────────────────┘
```

Determination of Cash Flow

```
┌─────────────────────────────────────────────────────────────────────┐
│                    Determination of Cash Flows                      │
├─────────────────────────────────────────────────────────────────────┤
│ 1. Annual Cash Flows (excluding terminal cash flows)                │
│                                                                     │
│              Chg. in                              Chg. in           │
│ Yr.  Savings - Deprec.= Tax Inc. - Taxes = Net Inc. + Deprec.= Cash Flow │
│  1   $_____ - _____= _____ - _____ = _____ + _____=$_____│
│  2   _____ - _____= _____ - _____ = _____ + _____= _____│
│  3   _____ - _____= _____ - _____ = _____ + _____= _____│
│  4   _____ - _____= _____ - _____ = _____ + _____= _____│
│  5   _____ - _____= _____ - _____ = _____ + _____= _____│
│  6   _____ - _____= _____ - _____ = _____ + _____= _____│
│  7   _____ - _____= _____ - _____ = _____ + _____= _____│
│  8   _____ - _____= _____ - _____ = _____ + _____= _____│
├─────────────────────────────────────────────────────────────────────┤
│ 2. Terminal Cash Flows                                              │
│                                                                     │
│    Cash Flow in Terminal Year . . . . . . . . . . . .  $_____     │
│    Salvage Value . . . . . . . . . . . . . . . . . .   _____      │
│    Tax on Salvage Value . . . . . . . . . . . . . .    _____      │
│    Working Capital . . . . . . . . . . . . . . . . .   _____      │
│                                                                     │
│       Total Cash Flow in Terminal Year . . . . . . .   $_____     │
└─────────────────────────────────────────────────────────────────────┘

┌─────────────────────────────────────────────────────────────────────┐
│                    Present Value Analysis                           │
│                    Hurdle Rate = _____ %                            │
│                                                                     │
│          Total              Present Value         Present Value     │
│ Year   Cash Inflows    x      Factor        =    of Cash Inflows    │
│                                                                     │
│  1     $_____     x    _____        =    $_____         │
│  2      _____     x    _____        =     _____         │
│  3      _____     x    _____        =     _____         │
│  4      _____     x    _____        =     _____         │
│  5      _____     x    _____        =     _____         │
│  6      _____     x    _____        =     _____         │
│  7      _____     x    _____        =     _____         │
│  8      _____     x    _____        =     _____         │
│                                                                     │
│          Present Value of the Cash Inflows  =    $_____         │
└─────────────────────────────────────────────────────────────────────┘

┌─────────────────────────────────────────────────────────────────────┐
│                       Summary of Analysis                           │
├─────────────────────────────────────────────────────────────────────┤
│        Net Present Value   = $_____                             │
│   Internal Rate of Return  =  _____ %                           │
│         Payback Period     =  _____ years                       │
└─────────────────────────────────────────────────────────────────────┘

┌─────────────────────────────────────────────────────────────────────┐
│                        RECOMMENDATION:                              │
│                                                                     │
│              Purchase _____     Do Not Purchase _____           │
│                                                                     │
│ Reasons:                                                            │
│                                                                     │
│                                                                     │
└─────────────────────────────────────────────────────────────────────┘
```

PROBLEMS

10-1 The Hampton Machine Tool Company purchased a piece of equipment for $10,000 five years ago, and its current market value is $2,000. At the time of purchase, the equipment had an expected life of ten years and no expected salvage value on retirement. It has been depreciated on a straight-line basis. The firm wishes to buy new equipment at a cost of $20,000 with no expected salvage value. The new equipment has an estimated economic life of five years. It is expected to reduce operating costs by $2,000 a year and to increase sales by $4,000 a year. It has a depreciation life of five years and is expected to be depreciated on a straight-line basis. The tax rate is 50%.

(a) Determine the net cash investment of the project.
(b) Determine the project's incremental net cash flows.

10-2 A new machine costs $9,000 and is expected to have no salvage value on retirement. The machine will be depreciated for tax purposes in three years by the sum-of-the-years'-digits method. It is expected to generate an annual revenue of $20,000 for the next three years and to require an annual operating cost of $4,500 (excluding the depreciation of the machine). The tax rate is 40 percent.

(a) Compute the net cash flows of each year.
(b) How would the net cash flow of each year be changed if the firm used the double declining-balance method?

10-3 The West Company is contemplating the purchase of a new machine to replace an existing machine with a depreciable life of five years. The old machine has a book value of $5,000 and a market value of $4,000. The new machine costs $8,000. It has an expected economic life of six years, but can be depreciated for tax purposes in five years. The freight and installation costs will be $2,000. The new machine is expected to have no salvage value on retirement. The two machines have the following revenues and operating costs:

	Year 1	Year 2	Year 3	Year 4	Year 5	Year 6
OLD MACHINE						
Revenues	$ 2,000	$2,000	$2,000	$2,000	$2,000	$2,000
Costs	500	500	500	500	500	500
NEW MACHINE						
Revenues	$10,000	$9,000	$8,000	$7,000	$6,000	$5,500
Costs	3,500	3,500	3,500	3,500	3,500	3,500

Additional assumptions are: (1) the firm's tax rate is 40 percent and (2) the firm uses the straight-line depreciation method.

(a) Determine the net cash investment of the project.
(b) Determine the project's incremental net cash flow.

10-4 The Brown Company wishes to replace a current operation with a more efficient and reliable automatic process. This plan requires the purchase of a machine with a net cost of $35,000 and an estimated useful life of seven years. It will be depreciated over a seven-year period on a straight-line basis for tax purposes. The machine is expected to have no salvage value at the end of seven years and to reduce operating costs by $8,000 per year. The firm's marginal tax rate is 46 percent and its cost of capital is 5 percent. Determine (a) the payback period, (b) the average rate of return, (c) the net present value, (d) the profitability index, and (e) the internal rate of return.

10-5 Projects A and B have an identical cash investment of $1,000. Project A is expected to produce a net cash flow of $400 a year for the next five years. Project B will result in net cash flows of $500, $400, $500, and $400. Determine the payback period for Projects A and B.

10-6 Projects C and D have an identical cash investment of $2,000. Project C will yield $500 a year after taxes for the next five years. Project D is expected to earn $600 at the end of one year, $400 at the end of two years, and $200 at the end of three years. Determine the average rate of return for Projects C and D.

10-7 Projects E and F have an identical cash investment of $10,000. Project E will have a net cash flow of $4,000 a year for the next four years. Project F will have net cash flows of $5,000, $5,000, and $2,000 for the next three years. The cost of capital is 10 percent.

(a) Determine the net present value for Projects E and F.
(b) Determine the profitability index for Projects E and F.

10-8 Projects G and H have the same net investment of $10,000. Project G has a net cash flow of $2,637.83 a year for the next five years. Project H has net cash flows of $5,000, $5,000, and $2,000 for the next three years. Calculate the internal rate of return for Projects G and H.

10-9 Two mutually exclusive projects have the following cash flows:

Project	Year 0	Year 1	Year 2	Year 3	Year 4	Year 5
I	-$3,200	$1,600	$1,600	$800	$400	
J	-$3,200	$ 400	$ 800	$800	$800	$2,455

Rank the projects by the following methods: (a) the payback period, (b) the average rate of return (assume zero depreciation), (c) the net present value at 10 discount rate, and (d) the internal rate of return.

11

OTHER ISSUES IN CAPITAL BUDGETING

In Chapter 10 we ignored a number of important issues in investment analysis in order to simplify the analysis. This chapter addresses two major groups of additional issues in capital budgeting: factors influencing cash flows and special topics in capital budgeting.

FACTORS INFLUENCING CASH FLOWS

In the first part of Chapter 10, we discussed several factors which may influence cash flows. These factors included depreciation methods, proceeds from sales of used assets, and tax effects. In addition to these, the factors of sunk costs, interest charges, salvage value, and net working-capital requirement could affect the magnitude and timing of cash flows.

Sunk Costs

Sunk costs are those that stem from past decisions. They must be ignored because only incremental benefits and incremental costs are relevant in capital investment analysis. Sunk costs are irrelevant and should not enter into the decision process because they do not change with the acceptance of the project. Let us go back to Example 10-1. If the firm purchases the new machine and sells the old machine, it incurs an operating loss of $5,000 or (the book value of $10,000 minus the market value of $5,000). The tax saving on the loss is $2,500 or ($5,000 x 0.50), which leaves $2,500 yet to be recovered from the old machine. This $2,500 loss comes from the past decision and is a sunk cost. The recovery of past costs is irrelevant in capital investment analysis.

Example 11-1. The Detroit Fiber Corporation is reviewing a capital investment proposal for the production of polyester fiber. The company is currently a leading manufacturer of rayon and nylon fibers for tire cord in the United States. This market is shrinking, however, because of competitive inroads made by polyester fiber manufacturers. Top management of Detroit Fiber feels that an entry into polyester fiber could allow the company to preserve its leading market position in tire cord and to move into the production of polyester fiber for other end uses. The analysis of the polyester fiber project involves two troublesome areas. First, the company spent $1 million for market testing on this project two years ago. Second, the company has used only 60 percent of the nylon-rayon production capacity for the last five years and this 40 percent excess capacity can be used to produce polyester fiber. If an outside firm tried to rent it from Detroit Fiber, it would be charged somewhere in the neighborhood of $2 million.

Market test costs ($1 million) had already been incurred at the time the investment decision on the polyester fiber project was to be made. Thus, they are considered as sunk costs in investment analysis and should not enter into the decision process. Because the company uses its current excess capacity in the production of polyester fiber, no incremental cash flows are incurred and thus nothing should be charged against the project. However, if the excess capacity has an alternative use, the opportunity cost must be included in the project's evaluation. Let us assume that the 40 percent excess production capacity can be sold or rented for $2 million. This $2 million should be treated as a cash outlay at the outset of the project. It is important to recognize that such costs do not necessarily involve a dollar outlay.

Interest Expenses

Unlike depreciation charges, interest expenses involve actual cash outflows. However, interest expenses are normally excluded from the cash flow of the project in order to avoid a double-counting of the cost of funds. The basic purpose of the discounting process is to ensure that the net cash flow of accepted projects is sufficient to cover the cost of funds. Hence, the double counting of interest may lead to an incorrect decision to reject otherwise profitable projects. In other words, interest expenses are included in the opportunity cost or the cost of capital.

Salvage Value

When an asset's economic life is terminated, there is frequently still some value left in the asset. The sales proceeds of the used asset represents a cash inflow before tax from the disposal of the asset. Up to this point, we have assumed that there is no salvage value at the end of the project life. If the project is expected to have a **salvage value**, it may influence the net cash flows in the last year of the project life.

Assume that the estimated salvage of a new machine is $1,000 at the end of its life and the corporate tax rate is 40 percent. The salvage value of $1,000 to be realized is subject to taxation at the ordinary income tax rate because the machine will be fully depreciated at that time. The company would realize cash proceeds of $600 = $1,000(1 − 0.40) at the end of the last year. Hence, the total net cash flow in the last year would be $600 plus the net cash flow determined without salvage value. If the machine is sold before it is fully depreciated, the tax treatment is different.

Net Working Capital

In addition to the investment in a fixed asset, a revenue-expanding project may require additional current assets such as accounts receivable and inventories. Some portion of this investment in additional current assets would be offset by increases in current liabilities such as accounts payable and accruals. The remaining portion of the required increase in current assets—the excess of additional current assets over increased current liabilities—represents the **net working capital** requirement.

The net working capital requirement must be financed from long-term or permanent financing sources. When long-term capital sources are used to finance net working capital requirements, funds are tied up in the same way as investments in fixed assets tie up funds. Consequently, the additional net working capital should be included in the initial cash outlay of the project and this amount should be treated as a cash inflow if and when the project is terminated. Suppose that a new project would require $50,000 in additional net working capital to support the anticipated sales. This $50,000 should be treated as an initial cash outflow and a cash inflow at the end of the project life. Although the investment and subsequent recovery of funds balance each other out, they are not equal because of the time value of money.

SPECIAL TOPICS

This section considers three special topics in capital budgeting: projects with different life spans, abandonment (retirement) decision, and inflation.

Projects with Different Life Spans

When we compare mutually exclusive projects with different life spans, it is often useful to transform the net present value (present value) into an **annualized net present value** (annualized cost) over the project's life. Although this approach may be used to compare all types of alternative projects, it should not be used to analyze those projects whose cash flows are extremely irregular.

When mutually exclusive projects with unequal lives are under consideration, the financial manager has three basic choices of assumptions.

1. At the end of each project's life, the firm will reinvest in projects that earn its cost of capital.
2. The firm will make specific assumptions about the reinvestment opportunities that may be available to it in the future.
3. The firm will reinvest in projects of precisely the same characteristics as its current project under consideration.

The second assumption is the most realistic alternative of the three, but it is the most difficult to implement in practice. The third alternative requires the firm to compute the present value of the first round of the project with no further forecasts about the future. The following examples are based on the third assumption.

Example 11-2. The company's cost of capital is 10 percent. Two mutually exclusive projects have the following characteristics:

Project	Initial Cost	Year 1	Year 2	Year 3	Year 4
			Net Cash Flows		
A	$10,000	$9,000	$7,000		
B	12,000	6,000	4,000	$5,500	$7,400

The net present values of Projects A and B are computed as follows:

$$NPV_A = \frac{\$9{,}000}{(1.10)^1} + \frac{\$7{,}000}{(1.10)^2} - \$10{,}000$$

$$= \$3{,}963$$

$$NPV_B = \frac{\$6{,}000}{(1.10)^1} + \frac{\$4{,}000}{(1.10)^2} + \frac{\$5{,}500}{(1.10)^3} + \frac{\$7{,}400}{(1.10)^4} - \$12{,}000$$

$$= \$5{,}943$$

If one ignores the difference in project life, Project B is better than Project A. Equation (9-7) can be used to compute the annualized net present value:

$$PVA = CF \times IF_{PVA_{n,i}}, \text{ or } CF = \frac{PVA}{IF_{PVA_{n,i}}}$$

Project A: $\quad CF = \dfrac{\$3{,}963}{IF_{PVA_{2,10\%}}} = \dfrac{\$3{,}963}{1.736} = \$2{,}283$

Project B: $\quad CF = \dfrac{\$5{,}943}{IF_{PVA_{4,10\%}}} = \dfrac{\$5{,}943}{3.170} = \$1{,}875$

Project A is now better than Project B. The superiority of one project over the other, however, really depends on the expected returns from the reinvestment of Project A's cash benefits after year 2 and the potential earning rate of Project B's additional investment of $2,000.

Example 11-3. Two mutually exclusive projects are under consideration. Project C has a cost of $20,000, an annual operating expense of $4,000, and an economic life of three years. Project D has a cost of $60,000, an annual operating expense of $3,000, and an economic life of eight years. The time value of money is 10 percent.

The annual equivalent of a $20,000 investment every three years is

$$CF = \frac{\$20{,}000}{IF_{PVA_{3,10\%}}} = \frac{\$20{,}000}{2.487} = \$8{,}042$$

The annual equivalent of a $60,000 investment every eight years is

$$CF = \frac{\$60{,}000}{IF_{PVA_{8,10\%}}} = \frac{\$60{,}000}{5.335} = \$11{,}246$$

The annualized cost is the annual equivalent of each project's initial cost plus its annual operating cost. Thus, the annualized cost is $12,042 or ($8,042 + $4,000) for Project C and $14,246 or ($11,246 + $3,000) for Project D. Because the annualized cost of Project C is less than that of Project D, Project C should be accepted.

There are times when an alternative project may consist of several components of unequal lives. In this case, the company will have to take all of them or none of them. For instance, a building with a life of 20 years may cost $1 million. Assume that this building requires a furnace with a life of 15 years costing $200,000 and a lighting system with a life of 11 years costing $100,000. With a discount rate of 10 percent, the total annualized cost is computed as follows:

$$\text{Annual Cost of Building} = \frac{\$1,000,000}{IF_{PVA\,20,10\%}} = \frac{\$1,000,000}{8.514} = \$117,454$$

$$\text{Annual Cost of Furnace} = \frac{\$200,000}{IF_{PVA\,15,10\%}} = \frac{\$200,000}{7.606} = \$26,295$$

$$\text{Annual Cost of Lighting} = \frac{\$100,000}{IF_{PVA\,11,10\%}} = \frac{\$100,000}{6.495} = \underline{\$15,396}$$

Total Cost $\underline{\$159,145}$

If one or more mutually exclusive projects are made up of several components with different lives, the total annualized cost should be computed for each project so that the decision maker can compare these projects on the basis of a common denominator called an annualized cost. Although we assumed that these three components can be replaced for their original cost in later years, we can make specific assumptions about the replacement cost. Of course, these additional assumptions would make the computation process more difficult.

Retirement Decision

The literature on capital investment analysis pays insufficient attention to the possibility of future retirement. Ordinarily, a project is evaluated as though the company were committed to it over its entire economic life. However, it may become more profitable to retire a project before the end of its estimated economic life rather than continue its operation.

Retirement decisions are terminal decisions to the extent that an asset withdrawn from its original service will not be replaced by another asset which will perform the same service. When investment proposals are originally considered, key financial variables are identified and assumptions are made in order to arrive at a choice. As time passes, some unforeseen problems can occur and they could affect these key variables. Initial assumptions may turn out to be incorrect, or perhaps some additional investment opportunities may arise. If projects are no longer desirable, they should be retired. By the

218   PART 4: CAPITAL EXPENDITURE ANALYSIS

same token, if funds released from existing projects could be used for substantially better investment opportunities, these projects must be retired.

If the duration of the investment and production processes are well defined in the appraisal of an investment proposals, it is not difficult to determine the optimal length of the project. The economic rationale behind the investment decision rule can be applied directly to the retirement decision. If a firm uses the net-present-value method in its capital expenditure analysis, the firm should retire its project at that point in time when the retirement value of the project exceeds the present value of the project's subsequent net cash flows discounted at the firm's cost of capital. If the firm uses the internal-rate-of-return method, it should retire the project when the rate of return on its retirement value is less than the company's cost of capital. We employ the net-present-value method to determine the optimal length of a project.

Let us assume that the company has the option to retire an asset at various points throughout its economic life. If the asset has an economic life of n years, there are n opportunities for retirement; i.e., one at the end of each year. We may estimate the cash-flow series associated with each asset on the assumption that it will be retired at the end of each year, we then have n net present values to compare. Thus, this methodology basically finds the maximum net present value of the project's net cash flows by considering all possible periods when the project can be retired.

The net present value of a project can be expressed as a function of its retirement period:

$$NPV(n) = \sum_{t=1}^{n} \frac{CF_t}{(1+k)^t} + \frac{S_n}{(1+k)^n} - C_o$$

(11-1)

where NPV(n) = the net present value of the project if it is retired at the end of year n; CF_t = the net cash flow in year t; S_n = the salvage value of the project in year n; k = the firm's cost of capital used as a discount rate; and C_0 = the cost of the project.

Example 11-4. The Quick Transport Company provides scenic bus tours, cruises on the Great Lakes, and limousine shuttle service between the Renaissance Center in downtown Detroit and the Detroit Metropolitan Airport. Quick Transport has one limousine which has a cost of $2,500 and an economic life of five years. The limousine has a depreciation period of five years and is to be depreciated on a straight-line basis. The company has a contract with a group of Renaissance area companies to shuttle business executives between the Renaissance Center and the airport for the next five years. However, it may terminate the service at any time on a one-year notice. The contract assures stable revenues of $4,000 per year, but operating costs are expected to increase by $265 per year. Thus, the net cash flows from operation are expected to fall rather rapidly. The first-year operating costs for the limousine are $2,296. Quick Transport's marginal tax rate is 46 percent and its cost of capital is 12 percent. The after-tax salvage values of the limousine at the end of each year are estimated to be $2,500, $2,000, $1,500, $1,000, and $500 over the next five years.

First, we must compute the net present value of the project. To do so, the expected net cash flows from the limousine service must be computed, as shown in Table 11-1.

Table 11-1
Expected Net Cash Flows for Limousine

	Year 1	Year 2	Year 3	Year 4	Year 5
Revenues	$4,000	$4,000	$4,000	$4,000	$4,000
Less: operating expenses	2,296	2,561	2,826	3,091	3,356
depreciation	500	500	500	500	500
Taxable income	$1,204	$ 939	$ 674	$ 409	$ 144
Less: taxes at 46%	554	432	310	188	66
Earnings after taxes	$ 650	$ 507	$ 364	$ 221	$ 78
Add: depreciation	500	500	500	500	500
salvage value	—	—	—	—	500
Net cash flow	$1,150	$1,007	$ 864	$ 721	$1,078

Thus, for an investment of $2,500, Quick Transport expects annual net cash flows of $1,150, $1,007, $864, $721 and $1,078 over the next five years. The net present value of the project is

$$\text{NPV} = \frac{\$1,150}{(1.12)^1} + \frac{\$1,007}{(1.12)^2} + \frac{\$864}{(1.12)^3} + \frac{\$721}{(1.12)^4} + \frac{\$1,078}{(1.12)^5} - \$2,500$$

$$= \$1,015$$

The limousine project would be profitable because the net present value of the project is positive or ($1,015). When should Quick Transport retire the limousine to maximize its net present value?

We begin by calculating the cash-flow series associated with retirement at the end of each year. If the company retires the limousine at the end of one year, it would receive $1,150 from operation and $2,500 from salvage; at the end of two years, the company would receive $1,007 from operation and $2,000 from salvage, in addition to $1,150 from the first-year operation; and so on. We then compute the net present value of each cash-flow series by discounting the individual cash flows at the firm's cost of capital, 12 percent. For example, the net present value of the series associated with retirement at the end of two years is computed as follows:

$$\text{NPV} = \frac{\$1,150}{(1.12)^1} + \frac{\$1,007}{(1.12)^2} + \frac{\$2,000}{(1.12)^2} - \$2,500 = \$924$$

PART 4: CAPITAL EXPENDITURE ANALYSIS

The net present values of the project at the end of each year are given in Table 11-2. The table shows that the company can maximize net present value by retiring the limousine at the end of four years.

Table 11-2
Net Present Values of the Project at the End of Each Year

Holding Period	Present Value at 12%	Cash Outlay	NPV
1	$3,259	$2,500	$759
2	3,424	2,500	924
3	3,513	2,500	1,013
4	3,539	2,500	1,039
5	3,515	2,500	1,015

Inflation

Inflation has been one of the dominant economic problems in the United States since 1965. What effects does it have on the results of capital expenditure analysis? The presence of inflation in the economy distorts capital budgeting decisions. Hence, the financial manager should know how to incorporate inflation into capital investment analysis. We will begin with the standard capital budgeting case in which inflation is absent.

Example 11-5. A company wishes to buy a new machine with a net cash investment (depreciable value) of $5,000 and an estimated economic life of five years. This new machine would be depreciated on a straight-line basis over five years. It is not expected to change the firm's revenue but is expected to save the firm's operating expenses by $2,000 a year. The firm's marginal tax rate is 50 percent and its cost of capital is 10 percent. No inflation is expected.

The expected net cash flow of the project is computed as follows:

Annual cash saving	$2,000
Less: depreciation	1,000
Taxable income	$1,000
Less: taxes at 50%	500
Earnings after taxes	$500
Add: depreciation	1,000
Annual net cash flow	$1,500

Consequently, for a net cash investment of $5,000, the firm is expected to generate a net cash flow of $1,500 a year for the next five years. The net present value of the project is computed as follows:

$$NPV = \frac{\$1,500}{(1.10)^1} + \frac{\$1,500}{(1.10)^2} + \frac{\$1,500}{(1.10)^3} + \frac{\$1,500}{(1.10)^4} + \frac{\$1,500}{(1.10)^5} - \$5,000$$

$$= \$687$$

Chapter 11: Other Issues in Capital Budgeting 221

We would accept the project because it has an expected net present value of $687.

Consider a situation in which inflation at an annual rate of 10 percent is expected to take place during the five years of the project. The inflation-adjusted discount rate may have to be used as an appropriate cost of capital in order to reflect the anticipated inflation. It is customary practice to determine the **inflation adjusted discount rate** by making a simple addition of the firm's cost of capital (10%) and the inflation rate (10)%. In formal terms, we have:

$$k_I = [(1 + k)(1 + I)] - 1 \qquad (11\text{-}2)$$

where k_I = the inflation adjusted discount rate, k = the firm's cost of capital, and I = inflation rate. For our example, the inflation adjusted discount rate is 21 percent or [(1 + 0.10)(1 + 0.10) - 1]. The inflation adjusted net present value of the project (NPV_I) is

$$NPV = \frac{\$1{,}500}{(1.21)^1} + \frac{\$1{,}500}{(1.21)^2} + \frac{\$1{,}500}{(1.21)^3} + \frac{\$1{,}500}{(1.21)^4} + \frac{\$1{,}500}{(1.21)^5} - \$5{,}000$$

$$= -\$611$$

The project would be rejected because it has an expected net present value of -$611.

However, a sound analysis should also incorporate the anticipated inflation into the cash flow estimates as well. If cash savings are expected to grow at this overall rate of inflation or (10%), the annual cash savings are $2,200 = $2,000 x 1.10, $2,420 = $2,000 x $(1.10)^2$, $2,662 = $2,000 x $(1.10)^3$, $2,928 = $2,000 x $(1.10)^4$, and $3,222 = $2,000 x $(1.10)^5$. The expected net cash flows of the project are shown in Table 11-3.

Table 11-3
Impact of Inflation Net Cash Flow

	Year 1	Year 2	Year 3	Year 4	Year 5
Annual cash saving	$2,200	$2,420	$2,662	$2,928	$3,222
Less: depreciation	1,000	1,000	1,000	1,000	1,000
Taxable income	$1,200	$1,420	$1,662	$1,928	$2,222
Less: taxes at 50%	600	710	831	964	1,111
Earnings after taxes	$600	$710	$831	$964	$1,111
Add: depreciation	1,000	1,000	1,000	1,000	1,000
Annual net cash flow	$1,600	$1,710	$1,831	$1,964	$2,111

If we take the anticipated inflation of 10 percent into account in the cash flow estimates, the inflation-adjusted net present value of the project is:

$$NPV = \frac{\$1{,}600}{(1.21)^1} + \frac{\$1{,}710}{(1.21)^2} + \frac{\$1{,}831}{(1.21)^3} + \frac{\$1{,}964}{(1.21)^4} + \frac{\$2{,}111}{(1.21)^5} - \$5{,}000$$

$$= \$255$$

It is easy to assume mistakenly that this inflation-adjusted net present value of $255 should be identical with the net present value of $687 in the absence of inflation. Because the same inflation factor of 10% is now in both the numerator and the denominator of the equation for the net-present-value method, they cancel each other out. The principal reason for the distortion is that depreciation charges are based on original rather than replacement costs. Certainly, income grows with inflation, but the increased portion of the income is taxed and thus real net cash flows do not keep up with inflation.

Too often, capital investment analysts believe that inflation tends to be built into both the cost of capital and the cash flow estimates. In an inflationary environment, the cost of capital and the expected net cash flows reflect such price increases, so that no adjustment is necessary for inflation in the analysis of the firm's investment opportunities. But our example illustrates the necessity of incorporating inflation into investment analysis.

Summary

This chapter discussed a number of factors which could affect cash flows: sunk costs, interest charges, salvage value, and net working-capital requirement. Sunk costs should be ignored because they stem from past decisions. Interest expenses involve actual cash outflows, but they are usually excluded from the cash flows of the project in order to avoid a double counting of the cost of funds. If an asset has a salvage value at the end of the project life, its salvage value may affect the net cash flow in the last year of the project life. The net working-capital requirement should be treated as an initial cash outflow and a cash inflow at the end of the project life because it has an opportunity cost.

Special topics in capital budgeting include projects with different life spans, retirement decision, and the impact of inflation on capital budgeting decisions. When we compare mutually exclusive projects with different life spans, it is often useful to transform the net present value (present value) into an annualized net present value (annualized cost) over the project's life. This approach can be used to compare all types of alternative projects on the basis of a common denominator. Because the entire capital budgeting system is a dynamic process, capital investments cannot be viewed as an ultimate commitment. If the retirement value of a project is greater than the present value of its subsequent net cash flows, the project should be retired. The financial manager should incorporate inflation into investment analysis because its presence may distort the results of capital expenditure analysis.

List of Key Terms

sunk costs
net working capital
retirement decisions

salvage value
annualized NPV
inflation adjusted discount rate

PROBLEMS

11-1 A company bought a machine for $20,000 five years ago. Its current market price is $6,000. At the time of purchase, the machine had an expected useful life of ten years and no expected salvage value on retirement. It has been depreciated on a straight-line basis. Assume that the firm has decided to replace the old machine with the new one. The tax rate is 40 percent.

(a) Determine the book value of the old machine.
(b) Determine the sunk cost of the old machine.

11-2 A firm purchased a machine for $14,000. The machine is expected to have a salvage value of $2,000 at the end of its life. The regular tax rate is 46 percent.

(a) How much cash proceeds would the firm realize at the end of the machine's life as a result of its expected salvage value?
(b) Assume that the machine were sold at the end of the second year for $13,000 and that $4,000 in depreciation were claimed during the first two years. Determine the amount of taxes and the net cash proceeds.
(c) Assume that the machine were sold at the end of the second year for $15,000 and that $4,000 in depreciation were claimed during the first two years. Compute the amount of taxes and the net cash proceeds.

11-3 Two mutually exclusive projects have the following characteristics:

Project	Year 0	Year 1	Year 2	Year 3	Year 4
G	-$30,000	$15,000	$10,000	$20,000	$5,000
H	- 20,000	18,000	10,000		

The cost of capital is 10 percent. Choose the more desirable project on the basis of the annualized net present value.

11-4 Two mutually exclusive machines are under consideration. Machine A has a cost of $400,000, an annual operating expense of $10,000, and an economic life of four years. Machine B has a cost of $700,000, an annual operating expense of $6,000, and an economic life of seven years. The time value of money is 10 percent. Assume that the firm will invest in projects of precisely the same characteristics as its current project under consideration. Choose the more desirable project on the basis of the annualized cost (equivalent of a project's initial cost plus its annual operating cost).

11-5 A company wishes to build a warehouse with a life of 30 years costing $2 million. The warehouse requires a furnace with a life of 20 years costing $500,000 and a lighting system with a life of 15 years costing $200,000. With a discount rate of 10 percent, compute the total annualized cost of the three projects.

11-6 The net cash investment of Project A is $7,500. Project A is expected to produce a net cash flow of $2,000 a year for the next five years. The salvage values of the project at the end of each year are estimated to be $6,200, $5,200, $4,000, $2,200, and $0 over the next five years. The firm's cost of capital is 10 percent.

(a) What is the net present value of Project A if the project is held until the end of its life?
(b) What is the optimal time to retire the project using NPV(n) shown in Equation (11-1)?

11-7 Lee Corporation can invest in a project which costs $24,000 and has a useful life of four years. The project is expected to reduce the firm's operating expenses by $10,000 a year. Depreciation is straight line over four years, the tax rate is 50 percent, and the cost of capital is 10 percent in the absence of inflation.

(a) Compute the net present value of the project without the consideration of inflation.
(b) If inflation of 7 percent is expected over the life of the project and cash savings are adjusted upward, what is the project's net present value? Assume an inflation-adjusted discount rate of 17 percent.

11-8 A project with a cost of $10,000 is expected to produce a net cash flow of $4,000 a year for the next four years. The cost of capital is 10 percent.

(a) What is the net present value of the project?
(b) If an additional net working capital of $2,000 were required over the life of the project, what would be its effect on the net present value?

12

Capital Budgeting under Uncertainty

To develop the key concepts and techniques of capital budgeting in a systematic manner, we did not treat the riskiness of projects explicitly in the preceding chapters. Very few financial variables are known with certainty. Investors and financial managers are basically risk averters. This chapter considers the basic concept of risk and a number of approaches to risk analysis for individual projects.

The Basic Concept of Risk

In the preceding chapters, we assumed that cash flows are known with certainty. If we could always describe a project as a unique set of cash flows, it would be possible to make relatively simple and straightforward capital budgeting decisions. The shortcomings of such an assumption are obvious. It is extremely difficult to specify unique cash flows because we have an imperfect ability to predict future events that will affect the cash flows. If we do not know in advance exactly which of these events will occur, we have to estimate a number of possible cash flows for each period in the future.

The most appropriate classification of decisions may be based on the amount of information at the decision maker's disposal. Decision problems can be classified into certainty, risk, and uncertainty, depending on the amount of information available. Decisions are made under certainty when the decision maker knows all the available alternatives and their consequences. Decisions are made under risk when the decision maker knows all the available alternatives and can assign probabilities to the set of possible consequences for each alternative. Decisions are made under uncertainty when the decision maker knows all the available alternatives but does not have enough information to assign probabilities to the set of possible consequences for each alternative. Although a distinction can thus be made between risk and uncertainty, the two terms are used interchangeably in the remainder of this chapter.

Standard **probability theory** can be used to evaluate investment risk. This approach is based on the assumption that the investor identifies a large number of possible payoffs for a project and that he assigns a probability to each of these possibilities. A probability represents the likelihood that an event will occur; it can take on any value between 0 and 1. A probability of 1 means that an event is certain to occur. A probability of 0 means that an event will not occur. The sum of the probabilities for a set of mutually exclusive and completely exhaustive events must be equal to 1.

PART 4: CAPITAL EXPENDITURE ANALYSIS

Under conditions of **uncertainty**, we must analyze two factors for capital budgeting decisions, the expected value for a project and its risk. The expected value is a weighted average of cash flows times their probabilities, which is defined as follows:

$$\bar{R} = \Sigma RP \qquad (12\text{-}1)$$

where $\bar{R}$ = expected value of net cash flows, R = net cash flows, and P = probability.

The risk may be described by the dispersion of alternative returns around the expected value. The conventional measure of dispersion is the **standard deviation**, which is defined as follows:

$$\sigma = \left(\Sigma (R - \bar{R})^2 P \right)^{1/2} \qquad (12\text{-}2)$$

where σ = standard deviation.

Example 12-1. Assume that Project A has the following probability distributions of net cash flows:

Possible Event	Probability of Each Event	Net Cash Flow for Each Event
Boom	0.10	$1,100
Normal	0.80	1,000
Recession	0.10	900

The expected value of Project A and its standard deviation are computed as follows:

$$\bar{R} = (\$1{,}100)(0.10) + (\$1{,}000)(0.80) + (\$900)(0.10)$$

$$= \$1{,}000$$

$$\sigma = [(\$1{,}100 - \$1{,}000)^2 (0.10) + (\$1{,}000 - \$1{,}000)^2 (0.80) + (\$900 - \$1{,}000)^2 (0.10)]^{1/2}$$

$$= \$44.72$$

The standard deviation of $44.72 gives us a rough average measure of how far the three net cash flows fall away from the expected value of $1,000. Normally, the larger the standard deviation, the greater the risk. Although the standard deviation tells us the amount of risk for the project, it does not enable us to make accept/reject decisions. However, the standard deviation can be used to rank certain projects. In essence, for a normal probability distribution, there is a 68% chance that the project's net cash flow will fall within one standard deviation of the mean of 1,000, or between 955.28 or (1,000 − 44.72) and 1,000 + 44.72 or 1,044.72. Likewise, there is roughly a 95% chance that the project's net cash flow will fall within 2 standard deviations or (2 × 44.72 = 89.44) of the mean of 1,000 (between 910.56 and 1,089.44). And similarly, there is a 99% chance that the net cash flow will fall within 3 standard deviations, or between 865.84 and 1,134.16.

Solved by TI BA Plus financial calculator:

1. Hit 2nd Data. Hit 2nd CLR Work to clear the Data registry.
2. Key in 1100 for X01 and hit ENTER.
3. Scroll down, with down arrow, to X02, key 1000, hit ENTER and duplicate this step 7 more times for a total of 8 entries since the 1000 net cash flow outcome occurs 8 out of 10 times.
4. Key in 900 for X10 and hit ENTER. There is a 1 out of 10 chance for recession and the likely net cash flow is 900.
5. Now hit 2nd Stat. If LIN (for linear regression for two variables) appears, keep hitting 2nd SET and browse through the statistical programs until 1-V, for one variable (as in Example 12-1), appears.
6. Scroll down with the down arrow and observe n=10, mean of X=1000, Sx (or sample standard deviation) = 47.14, and the sigma x (for population standard deviation) = 44.72.

Example 12-2. Three pairs of mutually exclusive projects are described in Table 12-1.

For Pair 1, Projects B and C have an equal expected value of $1,000, but Project B has the smaller standard deviation. This leads us to conclude that Project B is better than Project C. For Pair 2, Projects D and E have an equal standard deviation of $400, but Project D has the higher expected value. Thus, Project D is better than Project E. For Pair 3, both the expected value and the standard deviation are greater for Project F than for Project G. Under these circumstances, we are not sure which project is better. To eliminate this problem, we must adjust the standard deviation for differences in project size. The coefficient of variation does this job. The **coefficient of variation** (CV) is computed by dividing the standard deviation by the expected value. Thus, the coefficient of variation is 0.60 or ($300 ÷ $500) for Project F and 0.70 or ($210 ÷ $300) for Project G. Because Project F promises the greater expected value for a lower degree of risk, Project F is better than Project G.

Table 12-1
Expected Value and Standard Deviation

Pair	Project	Expected Value	Standard Deviation	CV
1	B	$1,000	$400	.40
	C	1,000	700	.70
2	D	900	400	.44
	E	600	400	.67
3	F	500	300	.60
	G	300	210	.70

A more difficult problem arises when both the expected value and the coefficient of variation for a project exceed those for another project. Suppose that the expected value of Project J is $1,500 and its coefficient of variation is 0.60. The expected value of Project K is $2,000 and its coefficient of variation is 0.85. The expected value and the coefficient of variation are greater for Project K than for Project J. Hence, we are not sure which project is better. To overcome this and other problems, we need those methods which would adjust project estimates for risk.

METHODS TO ADJUST FOR RISK

The risk-adjusted discount rate, the certainty equivalent approach, and the capital asset pricing model are three formal approaches which are commonly used to incorporate risk into capital budgeting decisions. The first two methods are discussed in the remainder of this chapter, and the third is considered in Chapter 13.

Risk-Adjusted Discount Rate

The **risk-adjusted discount rate** adjusts for risk by varying the discount rate—increasing it for more risky projects and reducing it for less risky projects. Projects with average riskiness should be discounted at the firm's cost of capital because it reflects the normal risk faced by the firm. Those projects with greater-than-normal risk should be discounted at a rate in excess of the cost of capital. In contrast, those with less-than-normal risk should be discounted at a rate between the risk-free rate and the cost of capital. The risk-adjusted discount rate is computed as follows:

$$k' = R_f + R_p + R_a \qquad (12\text{-}3)$$

where k' = risk-adjusted discount rate, R_f = risk-free rate, R_p = premium for the firm's normal risk, and R_a = adjustment for above or below the firm's normal risk.

The sum of R_f and R_p is the firm's cost of capital or that rate of return the firm must earn on its investments to compensate bond holders and stockholders for the risk associated with entrusting capital with the firm. Therefore, if the firm uses its cost of capital as a hurdle rate in accepting investment projects, then the risk profile of the projects under consideration must exactly match the risk profile of the firm as embodied in the firm's cost of capital. If the projects bear risks different from the firm's risk profile, then the discount rate (or appropriate hurdle rate) must be tailored specifically for the risk characteristics of the particular project by adjusting it upward for projects with risk higher than the firm's and lower for projects less risky than the firm's risk profile.

The risk-adjusted NPV is computed by the following formula:

$$NPV_r = \sum_{t=1}^{n} \frac{\overline{X_t}}{(1+k')^t} - C_o \qquad (12\text{-}4)$$

where NPV_r = risk-adjusted NPV, X_t = expected value of possible net cash flows in period t, and C_o = expected value of possible costs.

Chapter 12: Capital Budgeting under Uncertainty

Example 12-3. Assume that the risk-adjusted discount rate for a project under consideration is 30 percent and the project has the cash flows listed in Table 12-2.

To determine the net present value of this project, we must first compute the expected value for each cash flow. The expected cost is $9,000; the expected value of cash flows for the first year is $7,700; and the expected value of cash flows for the second year is $9,100. Thus, the risk adjusted NPV of the project is computed as follows:

$$NPV_r = \frac{\$7,700}{(1.30)^1} + \frac{\$9,100}{(1.30)^2} - \$9,000 = \$2,308$$

← Table A, 30%, 1 yr.

Solved by financial calculator:

1. Hit CF, and 2nd CLR Work.
2. Key in -9,000 for CF_0 and hit enter.
3. Scroll down to C01 and key in +7,700 and hit ENTER; scroll and enter 1 for F01 (frequency of one).
4. Scroll down and enter +9,100 and 1 for C02 and F02, respectively.
5. Key 2nd QUIT and then hit NPV.
6. Key in 30 for I and hit ENTER (this is the discount rate).
7. Scroll down to NPV and hit CPT to compute the NPV.
8. Result = $2,307.69 for the Net Present Value of the Investment.

The decision rule is to accept the project if the risk-adjusted NPV is positive and to reject the project if the risk-adjusted NPV is negative. Because the project in this example has a positive risk-adjusted NPV, it represents a candidate for acceptance.

Table 12-2
Cash Flow and Probability Distribution

Original Cost		Cash Flow in Year 1		Cash Flow in Year 2	
Probability	Amount	Probability	Amount	Probability	Amount
0.3	$ 7,000	0.2	$7,000	0.2	$ 8,000
0.4	9,000	0.4	7,500	0.6	9,000
0.3	11,000	0.3	8,000	0.1	10,000
		0.1	9,000	0.1	11,000

While the simplicity of the concept of the risk-adjusted discount rate is appealing, it has a number of practical problems. First, it is extremely difficult to determine the appropriate discount rate of each project or each project class. Second, it does not adjust for the variability of the cash flow which is subject to risk throughout the project's useful life.

Certainty Equivalent Approach

The **certainty equivalent approach** incorporates the manager's preference for risk versus return directly into the capital budgeting decision. While the risk-adjusted discount

230   PART 4: CAPITAL EXPENDITURE ANALYSIS

rate adjusts for risk in the denominator of the NPV formula, the certainty equivalent approach adjusts for risk in the numerator of the same equation.

When the certainty equivalent approach is used, each cash flow is multiplied by a certainty equivalent coefficient, which is a certain cash flow divided by an uncertain cash flow. If management is indifferent between a certain $140 and an uncertain $200, its certainty equivalent coefficient is 0.70 or ($140 ÷ $200). The certainty equivalent coefficient has a value between 0 and 1. It varies inversely with risk. If the firm perceived greater risk, it would use a lower certainty coefficient, which would deflate the dollar return value. Once all the risky cash flows are adjusted downward to reflect uncertainty through the use of the certainty equivalent coefficient (CE), these certain cash flows are then discounted at the risk-free rate to determine the certain NPV:

$$NPV_c = \sum_{t=1}^{n} \frac{CE_t \overline{X}_t}{(1+X_f)^t} - C_o \qquad (12\text{-}5)$$

where NPV_c = certain net present value and CE_t = certainty equivalent coefficient in period t.

Example 12-4. A project with a cost of $10,000 is expected to produce net cash flows of $5,000, $6,000, and $8,000 for the next three years. Certainty equivalent coefficients for these three cash flows are 0.8, 0.7, and 0.6, respectively.

With a 5 percent risk-free discount rate, the certain NPV of the project is

$$NPV_c = \frac{\$5{,}000(0.8)}{(1.05)^1} + \frac{\$6{,}000(0.7)}{(1.05)^2} + \frac{\$8{,}000(0.6)}{(1.05)^3} - \$10{,}000$$

$$= \$1{,}764$$

The decision rule is to accept the project if the certain NPV is positive and reject it if the certain NPV is negative. Because the certain NPV is positive, we would accept this project.

Solved by financial calculator:

1. Hit CF, and 2nd CLR Work.
2. Key in -10,000 for CF_o and hit Enter.
3. Scroll down to C01 and key in +4,000; scroll and enter 1 for F01 (frequency of one).
4. Scroll down and enter +4,200 and 1 for C02 and F02, respectively.
5. Scroll down and enter +4,800 and 1 for C03 and F03, respectively.
6. Hit 2nd QUIT and then hit NPV.
7. Key in 5 for I and hit ENTER (this is the discount rate).
8. Scroll down to NPV and hit CPT to compute the NPV.
9. Result = $1,765.47 for the Net Present Value of the Investment.

The certainty equivalent approach may be able to adjust for risk more accurately than the risk-adjusted discount rate. First, the certainty equivalent approach adjusts for risk

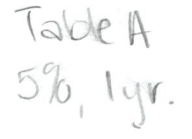

Chapter 12: Capital Budgeting under Uncertainty

in the expected cash flows which are subject to risk. Second, the certainty equivalent coefficient reflects the degree of confidence that the decision maker has in obtaining a particular cash flow. Third, the certainty equivalent approach allows us to use a different certainty equivalent coefficient for each year.

PORTFOLIO RISK AND RETURN

Up to this point we have focused on risk analysis of individual projects. In the real world, however, practically no company or individual invests everything in a single project. Rather, the firm invests in a combination of different projects, each with varying risk and return. In essence the firm could be viewed as one large "portfolio" of different, independent investments, each designed to increase the value of the entire firm or portfolio. The answer to the following question becomes important. Could an investment project be rejected when analyzed by itself but be accepted if analyzed in conjunction with others in the form of a portfolio? Or could several investment opportunites be acceptable when analyzed as a combination and rejected as individual projects? Clearly, the answer is yes since the risk and return profile of the combination may be different from the sum of the risk and return profiles of the individual projects. Thus, it is useful to analyze projects in conjunction with each other or in portfolio context. A **portfolio** is a collection of investment projects. Portfolio theory deals with the selection of investment projects that would minimize risk for a given return or that would maximize return for a given risk. Such a portfolio is an efficient portfolio.

The simultaneous risk-return analysis of multiple projects treats the combination of projects as a single investment. The expected value for a portfolio of investments is simply the sum of the individual present values for the projects that make up the portfolio. The risk for the portfolio of multiple investment projects is simply the standard deviation of the combined cash flows from the projects. By combining projects, the co-movement of different project cash flows tends to cancel out each other's variance and thus lower the total standard deviation or risk of the portfolio as a whole. "By not putting all its eggs into one basket," the firm balances the cash flow risk across a diversity of investment projects that co-move in such a way as to reduce the total cash flow risk.

The **Portfolio Effect** is defined as the extent to which the variations or risks of individual projects tend to offset each other. The portfolio effect depends on the degree of co-movement or correlation that exists between two or more projects. The **correlation coefficient** measures the degree of correlation between two projects and varies from zero (no correlation or independence) to ±1.0 (perfect correlation). A correlation coefficient of -1.0 means that the two sets of cash flows from two projects tend to move in exactly opposite directions. As shown in Example 12-5, if a boom occurs, Project X is expected to return $2,000, while Project Y is expected to return nothing. In contrast, if a recession occurs, Project X would earn nothing, whereas Project Y would earn $2,000. These two projects are perfectly negatively correlated. In this extreme case the two projects are perfectly negatively correlated allowing diversification to totally eliminate risk while assuring a positive NPV.

> **Example 12-5.** Project X has a cost of $800, while Project Y has a cost of $1,000. The firm's cost of capital is 5 percent. These two projects are

independent and their possible net cash flows at the end of one year are given below:

		Net Cash Flows	
Economic Condition	Probability	Project X	Project Y
Boom	0.50	$2,000	$ 0
Recession	0.50	0	2,000

Present value of Project X = (.5 x $2,000) + (.5 x $0)/1.05 = $952.

NPVx = project present value of $952 less project cost of $800 = +$152.

Similarly, the present value and NPV for Project Y are $952 and -$48, respectively. Their standard deviations are equal at $1,000. If analyzed individually, even with its positive NPV, Project X would clearly be undesirable due to its high risk and Project Y has no chance because of its negative NPV. But if we apply the portfolio effect, we can completely eliminate risk by combining these two projects and increase the value of the firm:

Present value of Project XY Combination = PVx of $952 + PVy of $952 = $1,904

NPVxy = PVxy of $1,904 less COSTxy of $1,800 = $104

Whether a boom occurs or a recession occurs, the expected net cash flow of this combination is $2,000 and the combined net present value is $104 (or $152 – $48). The standard deviation of this two-project portfolio is zero because the portfolio always produces a net present value of $104. When we consider Project X and Y separately, both projects are clearly undesirable. However, when we treat them as a portfolio, we find the portfolio quite attractive.

The positive portfolio effect is explained by the underlying correlation between the projects' cash flows.

A correlation coefficient of +1.0 means that the two sets of returns from two projects tend to move in exactly the same direction. Suppose that, if a boom occurs, Projects T and U would yield equal amounts of $2,000. On the other hand, if a recession occurs, each project would earn nothing. Then we can say that these two projects are perfectly positively correlated. In this case, diversification would not reduce risk at all. A correlation coefficient of 0 means that the two sets of returns from two projects are uncorrelated or independent of each other. If two projects are uncorrelated, diversification would reduce risk considerably.

Because the degree of correlation among projects depends on economic factors, most pairs of projects have correlation coefficients between 0 and +1.0. The argument is that most projects are likely to earn more during a boom and less during a recession. If so, diversification can reduce the overall risk somewhat. But different product lines and different geographic markets tend to have relatively low degrees of correlation with each other, thereby making it possible to reduce the overall risk considerably by diversification.

Chapter 12: Capital Budgeting under Uncertainty

SUMMARY

Some degree of risk exists in almost all investment decisions, and investors are basically risk averters. Given these two facts, it is necessary to consider risk in investment analysis. A general procedure for risk analysis involves these steps:

1. Identify a set of alternative projects available to the firm.
2. Define the possible events that are relevant to the alternatives.
3. Estimate the outcome of each alternative-event combination.
4. Assign an appropriate probability to each of the possible events.
5. Compute the expected value of each alternative project.
6. Calculate the standard deviation or the coefficient of variation for each alternative project.
7. Select the alternative project with the largest expected value for a given degree of risk.

Both the standard deviation and the coefficient of variation provide valuable information for effective capital budgeting decisions. However, they do not indicate whether a particular project should be accepted or rejected. We can use the certainty equivalent approach and the risk-adjusted discount rate method to adjust project estimates for risk.

LIST OF KEY TERMS

probability theory
risk-adjusted discount rate
portfolio effect

standard deviation
portfolio
coefficient of variation

PROBLEMS

12-1 A company has two investment projects under the different states of the economy: above normal, normal, and below normal. The probabilities of these states of the economy and their corresponding net cash flows are as follows:

		Net Cash Flows	
State of Economy	Probability	Project A	Project B
Above normal	0.50	$900	$700
Normal	0.30	500	700
Below normal	0.20	350	550

(a) Determine the following: expected value, standard deviation, and coefficient of variation.
(b) Interpret the measures.

12-2 A project has an initial cost of $2,800 and the firm's cost of capital is 10 percent. The project has the following probability distribution of expected net cash flows in each of the next three years:

Possible Market Reaction	Probability	Net Cash Flow
Low response	0.20	$1,000
Moderate response	0.10	2,000
High response	0.30	3,000
Very high response	0.40	4,000

(a) Determine the project's expected value of net cash flows in each of the next three years.
(b) Determine the net present value of the project.
(c) Determine the standard deviation of net cash flows in each of the next three years.

12-3 Five investment projects have the following expected net present values and standard deviations of returns:

Project	Expected Net Present Value	Standard Deviation
A	$7,000	$1,400
B	70,000	6,300
C	21,000	2,800
D	35,000	4,900
E	21,000	2,100

(a) Determine the coefficient of variation for these five projects and rank them from lowest risk to highest risk.
(b) If you were to choose between Projects C and E only, would you need to use the coefficient of variation?

12-4 A project with an initial cost of $15,000 is expected to produce net cash flows of $8,000, $9,000, $10,000, and $11,000 for each of the next four years. The firm's cost of capital is 12 percent, but the financial manager perceives the risk of this particular project to be much higher than 12 percent. The financial manager feels that a 20 percent discount rate would be appropriate for the project.

(a) Compute the net present value of the project at the firm's cost of capital.
(b) Compute the risk-adjusted net present value of the project.

12-5 A project has a cost of $1,400. Its net cash flows are expected to be $900, $1,000, and $1,400 for each of the next three years. The respective certainty-equivalent coefficients are estimated to be 0.75, 0.55, and 0.35. With a 6 percent risk-free discount rate, determine the certain net present value of the project.

12-6 Project F has a cost of $3,000 and Project G has a cost of $4,000. These two projects are mutually independent and their possible net cash flows are given below. Assume that the cost of capital is 10 percent.

		Net Cash Flows	
Economic Condition	Probability	Project F	Project G
Boom	0.50	$8,000	$0
Recession	0.50	0	8,000

(a) Determine the net present value of Projects F and G.
(b) Determine the standard deviation of Projects F and G.
(c) Determine the portfolio net present value and standard deviation.

13

VALUATION AND COST OF CAPITAL

Chapter 10 presented three discounted cash-flow approaches: the net-present-value method, the profitability index, and the internal-rate-of-return. These methods evaluate net cash flows of a project using the required rate of return to determine acceptability. The required rate of return for projects with normal risk is the firm's opportunity cost of capital.

This chapter addresses five major topics:

- Valuation concepts for debt, preferred stock, and common stock
- The required return of bondholders, preferred stockholders, and common stockholders and the respective component costs of capital for long-term debt, preferred stock, and common equity
- Combining the respective component cost to determine the weighted average cost of capital
- The marginal cost of capital for additional funds the firm decides to raise
- The relationship between marginal cost of capital and analysis of capital investments

VALUATION

The three major segments of the capital market are bonds, preferred stock, and common stock. This section reviews methods of determining the appropriate market value for these three segments. Once we know how investors determine the appropriate value of bonds, preferred stock, and common stock, we can then figure out or derive the rates of return these various investors expect on their respective investments. And the return that the firm's investors expect on the company's bonds, preferred stock, and common stock logically represents what it would cost the firm (i.e. market interest or yield on bond debt) should it decide to raise funds from either of these sources of capital. Stated differently, the return that the various providers of capital require has to equate the cost of the funds to the firm.

Bond Valuation

Chapter 9 illustrated the process of determining the market price of a bond having a semiannual interest payment and a lump-sum principal payment (see Example 9-25). The market price of a bond is the present value of the stream of interest payments and the $1,000 principal payment at maturity discounted at the current market yield as shown in the following formula 13-1 and illustrated in Example 9-25 in Chapter 9.

236   PART 4: CAPITAL EXPENDITURE ANALYSIS

$$P_b = \sum_{t=1}^{n} \frac{I_t}{(1+Y)^t} + \frac{P_n}{(1+Y)^n} \qquad (13\text{-}1)$$

where P_b = the market price of the bond, n = number of periods in the bond's life, I = the annual dollar amount of interest in time period t, Y = the bondholder's required yield to maturity on the investment or equivalently the firm's before-tax cost of the bond, and P_n = the face value of the bond or par value.

Example 13-1. St. Louis Company has bonds outstanding. Each bond has a face value of $1,000, an annual coupon rate of 9 percent or ($90 per year), 20 years to maturity, and the market yeild on similar bonds is 10%. What is the current price of this bond?

Equation (13-1) is used to compute the cost of the bond for St. Louis Company:

$$P_b = \sum_{t=1}^{20} \frac{\$90}{(1.10)^t} + \frac{\$1{,}000}{(1.10)^{20}}$$

$$= \$90 \times 8.514 + \$1{,}000 \times 0.149$$

$$P_b = \$915.26$$

Solved by financial calculator:

1. Hit 2nd QUIT and 2nd CLR TVM.
2. Hit 2nd P/Y, key in 1, hit ENTER, 2nd QUIT.
3. Key in 20, hit N.
4. Key in 10, hit I/Y.
5. Key in 90, hit PMT.
6. Key in 1000, hit FV.
7. Hit CPT and PV.
8. Result, PV = -$914.86 ~ 915.26

If we want to express all cost-of-capital rates on an after-tax basis, we must adjust this before-tax cost of the bond (or yield) for taxes, because interest charges are tax deductible. If we denote the after-tax cost of the bond by K_D, it can be approximated by

$$K_D = Y\,(1 - \text{tax rate}) \qquad (13\text{-}2)$$

If St. Louis Company has a marginal tax rate of 46 percent, the after-tax cost of its bond is

$$K_D = 10\%\,(1 - 0.46) = 5.4\%$$

Preferred Stock Valuation

As is the case for all securities, the value of a share of preferred stock equals the present value of all cash flows that will come from the stock. Because the preferred stock is scheduled to make payments indefinitely, it may be treated as a perpetuity for valuation purposes (see Chapter 9 and Example 9-26).

To determine the appropriate market value of preferred stock, divide the stock's annual dividend (D_p which is usually some fixed percentage of the preferred stock's par value) by the preferred stockholder's required reate of return on the investment (K_p). Given the annual dividend and the required rate of return on the preferred stock Equation (13-3) and Example 13-10 illustrate the solution as follows:

$$P_p = \frac{D_p}{K_p} \qquad (13\text{-}3)$$

Example 13-2. White Oak Inc. has preferred stock outstanding and it pays a dividend of $7 per year. If the required rate of return on the preferred stock is 10 percent, its value is $70, found by solving Equation (13-3) as follows:

$$P_p = \frac{\$7.00}{0.10} = \$70.00$$

Thus, an investor should not pay more than $70.00 per share in order to earn a desired 10% return on preferred stock which is paying $7 dividend per share forever. Stated differently, a $7 annuity forever equates a 10% return on an investment of $70.00.

Common Stock Valuation

The price of a share of common stock may be interpreted by the stockholder as the present value of the expected future dividends. Although in the short run stockholders may be affected by a change in earnings or other variables, the ultimate value of any common stock depends on the distribution of earnings in the form of cash dividends. The stockholder may benefit from the retention and reinvestment of earnings (referred to as retained earnings by accountants) by the company, but at some point earnings must be converted into cash flow for the stockholder. Therefore, to estimate the present value of future dividends some assumption about the company's expected dividend growth rate is necessary. Here we examine two cases: no-growth and constant growth in future dividends.

In the no-growth case, the firm's dividend is assumed to remain the same for indefinite periods in the future as illustrated by formula 13-4:

$$P_o = \frac{D_c}{K_e} \qquad (13\text{-}4)$$

where P_o = current market value at time 0 of common stock per share for no growth company
D_c = constant dividend on common stock per share expected to infinity
K_e = common stockholder's required return of the investment

As shown, this expression is equivalent to the present value of a perpetuity (as in the case of preferred stock and also see Chapter 9 and Example 9-26) and reduces to formula 13-4:

In the constant growth case, we assume the firm's dividend per share will grow at a constant rate indefinitely as shown by formula 13-5:

$$P_0 = \frac{D_0(1+g)^1}{(1+K_e)^1} + \frac{D_0(1+g)^2}{(1+K_e)^2} + \ldots + \frac{D_0(1+g)^\infty}{(1+K_e)^\infty} \qquad (13\text{-}5)$$

With algebraic manipulation, this expression reduces to formula 13-7:

$$P_0 = \frac{D_1}{K_e - g} \qquad (13\text{-}6)$$

where P_0 = current market value of common stock per share with constant dividend growth, D_1 = dividend per share expected at the end of year one, g = expected constant growth rate in dividend per share, D_0 = dividend per share at end of last year, and K_e = investor's required return on this company's common stock.

Example 13-3 illustrates a solution as follows:

Example 13-3. Assume that Richmond Motorola Inc. just paid a dividend of $1.00 (that is D_0 = $1.00) and that its required rate of return on its common stock is 15 percent. If investors expect that dividend will grow at an annual rate of 10 percent, then the estimated dividend one year later would be D_1 = $1.00 x 1.10 = $1.10. Inserting these values into Equation (13-6), we find the value of the common stock to be $22:

$$P_0 = \frac{\$1.10}{0.15 - 0.10} = \$22.00$$

COMPONENT COSTS OF CAPITAL

The weighted average cost of capital (WACC) generally represents a firm's opportunity cost of capital. The WACC depends on the capital structure. The primary components of the capital structure are long-term debt of various types, preferred stock, and common equity. They are principal sources of funds that are used to acquire fixed assets. Most companies use some combination of these sources in an effort to achieve the minimum cost of capital. To determine the WACC, we must compute the individual component costs of the firm's capital structure: the cost of debt, the cost of preferred stock, and the cost of common equity.

Component Cost of Debt

Only the cost of bonds is discussed here because the cost of other types of debt is usually determined by contracting lenders. Most corporate bonds carry a face value of $1,000. The borrower agrees to pay this full face value to the bondholders at maturity. Bond

Chapter 13: Valuation and Cost of Capital   239

issuers pay the fixed contract rate on the $1,000 face value of their bonds. This rate is called the **coupon rate**. For example, a $1,000 par value 8 percent bond indicates that the borrower will pay $80 in interest a year for every $1,000-face-value bond. The actual yield on the bond debt (cost to the firm for the borrowed funds) is defined as the discount rate that equates the market price of the bond with the present value of interest plus principal payments. This discount rate is also called the before-tax cost of the bond or the bond's yield to maturity. The before-tax cost of the bond is solved with formula (13-1).

The trial-and-error method described in Chapter 9 is used to determine the before-tax cost of the bond (Y). Essentially, the yeild on the bond is that precise rate of return that discounts all future cash flows from the bond to a value exactly equal to the bond's present value which is its current market price.

Example 13-4. St. Louis Company has bonds outstanding. Each bond has a face value of $1,000, an annual coupon rate of 9 percent ($90 per year), a market price of $915.26, and a maturity of 20 years. What is the before-tax cost of the bond (or yield)?

Equation (13-1) is used to compute the cost of the bond for St. Louis Company:

$$\$915.26 = \frac{\$90}{(1+Y)^t} + \frac{\$1,000}{(1+Y)^{20}}$$

$$\$915.26 = \sum_{t=1}^{20} \frac{\$90}{(1.10)^t} + \frac{\$1,000}{(1.10)^{20}}$$

D, 10%, 20 yr.

$$= \$90 \times 8.514 + \$1,000 \times 0.149$$

$915.26 = $915.26 at a Y value of .10

Y = 10%

Solved by financial calculator:
1. Hit 2nd QUIT and 2nd CLR TVM.
2. Hit 2nd P/Y, key in 1, hit ENTER, 2nd QUIT.
3. Key in 20, hit N.
4. Key in 915.26, hit +/- (to convert to -915.26), hit PV.
5. Key in 90, hit PMT.
6. Key in 1000, hit FV.
7. Hit CPT and I/Y.
8. Result, I/Y = 9.995% ~ 10%

Since we want to express all cost-of-capital rates on an after-tax basis, we must adjust this before-tax cost of the bond for taxes, because interest charges are tax deductible. If we denote the after-tax cost of the bond by K_D, it can be approximated by

$$K_D = Y(1 - \text{tax rate}) \qquad (13\text{-}7)$$

If St. Louis Company has a marginal tax rate of 46 percent, the after-tax cost of its bond is

$$K_D = 10\% (1 - 0.46) = 5.4\%$$

Component Cost of Preferred Stock

Preferred stock is viewed as a hybrid security bearing characteristics of both debt and common equity in a firm's capital structure. Like common stockholders, preferred stockholders are only entitled to dividends if the firm has profits and decides to pay them. Similar to debt securities, preferred stock generally carries no voting privilege and thus control remains with the common stockholders. Also, as debtholders receive a fixed payment called interest, preferred stockholders receive fixed payments in the form of preferred dividends which must be paid before common stockholders are eligible to receive dividends. Failure to pay interest on debt can result in bankruptcy, but inability to pay preferred dividends generally does not. In liquidation, the claims of the various creditors take precedence over those of the preferred stockholders. The claims of the preferred stockholders take precedence over those of the common stockholders. Thus, from the issuing firm's point of view, preferred stock is less costly than debt, but it is more costly than common equity.

The cost of preferred stock is a function of its stated dividend and flotation costs. For the firm to raise new capital through this source of capital, new preferred stock must be sold usually requiring the services of an investment banker. Flotation costs represent the fees paid for those investment banking services. Because most preferred stocks are perpetual in nature, their explicit cost is viewed in the same terms as that of a perpetuity. If preferred stock has no maturity date, its cost is

$$K_p = \frac{D_p}{P_p - F} \qquad (13\text{-}8)$$

where k_p = the cost of preferred stock, D_p = the stated annual dollar dividend per share, and P_p = the market price of preferred stock, F = flotation or selling costs charged by an investment banker.

Example 13-5. St. Louis Company has preferred stock outstanding. Each share of the preferred stock pays $3.60 dividends per year and has a market price of $31. Flotation costs are $1 per share. What is the cost of the preferred stock?

The cost of preferred stock for St. Louis Company is

$$K_p = \frac{\$3.60}{\$31 - 1} = 12\%$$

Component Cost of Common Equity

The dividend valuation model is one method of estimating the component cost of common equity. Referring to the constant growth model (formula 13-5 presented earlier in this chapter) the component cost of common equity can be determined by solving for K_e. If dividends per share are expected to grow at constant growth rate g indefinitely, the following equation can be used to compute the cost of common stock:

$$K_e = \frac{D_1}{P_o} + g \qquad (13\text{-}9)$$

where K_e = the cost of common stock, D_1 = dividends to be paid at the end of one year, P_o = the price of common stock, and g = dividend growth rate per year. In this case, the firm plans to use internally-generated earnings to finance its investments. Often, we refer to this as the investor's required return on retained earnings. It follows that if the firm retains and reinvests the stockholders' earnings, then the firm must earn a return at least equal to what investors could get elsewhere (or opportunity cost) under the same level of risk. By using internal funds, the firm avoids the flotation costs of selling new common stock to raise money.

Example 13-6. St. Louis Company's stock is currently selling for $40 a share. Dividends are expected to be $4 per share in the coming year and are expected to grow at a rate of 5 percent per year. What is the cost of common equity?

The cost of common equity for St. Louis company is computed as follows:

$$K_e = \frac{\$4}{\$40} + .05 = 15\%$$

If the St. Louis Company plans to sell new common stock to raise new capital then, similar to the preferred stock case, the firm must incur flotation costs. Suppose, in this example, St. Louis's investment banker indicates that the flotation cost will be $2 per share. Then:

$$K_n = \frac{D_1}{P_o - F} + g$$

$$K_n = \frac{4}{40 - 2} + .05$$

$$K_n = 15.5\%$$

Capital Asset Pricing Model

The Capital Asset Pricing Model (CAPM) can also be used to compute the cost of common equity. CAPM depends on a number of important concepts.

Efficient Capital Markets

Efficient capital markets exist when security prices reflect all available information and market prices adjust quickly to new information. Because capital markets are highly competitive, stock prices react to information so fast that market participants buy and sell securities in a way that eliminates all excess profits.

Capital markets are highly efficient for several reasons. Securities are traded by many companies and individuals who have broad market contacts, sophisticated analytical capabilities, and modern communications. Because new information is widely, quickly, and cheaply disseminated to investors, market prices quickly adjust to reflect significant developments. Various government agencies such as the Securities and Exchange Commission and various laws such as the Securities Act of 1933 are sometimes credited with enhancing efficiency.

Systematic and Unsystematic Risk

The CAPM implies that the total risk of a common stock consists of systematic (undiversifiable) risk and unsystematic (diversifiable) risk. **Systematic risk** is a reflection of the overall market risk—risk that is common to all stocks. Some common causes of systematic risk include changes in the overall economy, tax reform by the Congress, and a change in the world energy situation. Because it is common to all stocks, systematic risk cannot be eliminated by diversification. **Unsystematic risk** or diversifiable risk refers to "not putting all your eggs in one basket." This type of risk is unique to a particular company. Some causes of unsystematic risk include a wild strike affecting only the company, a new competitor producing essentially the same product, and a technological breakthrough making an existing product obsolete. As shown in Figure 13-1, unsystematic risk can be eliminated by diversification. By creating a portfolio of diversified stocks from different companies, the investor can virtually average away or eliminate this firm-specific risk. Notice that systematic risk, as measured by beta in the CAPM, cannot be eliminated.

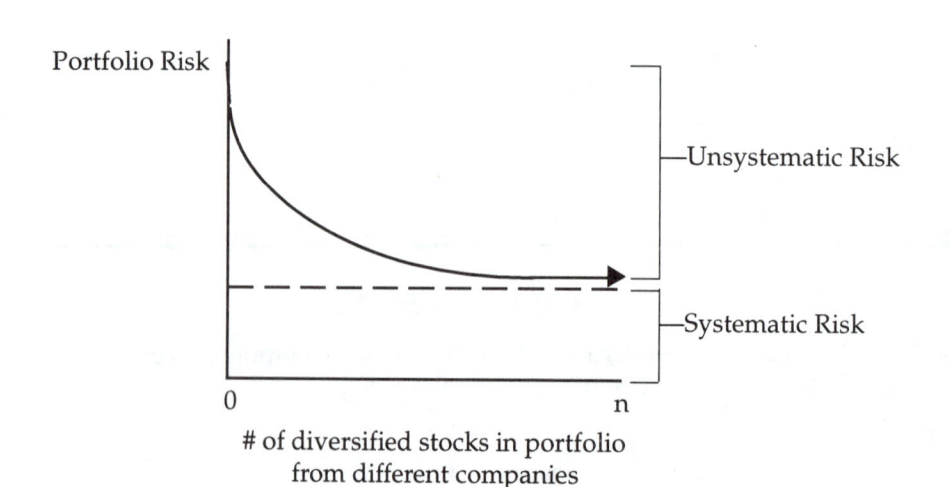

Figure 13-1
Effect of Diversification on Unsystematic Risk

Security Market Line

Therefore, if capital markets are efficient and investors are well diversified, unsystematic risk is almost nonexistent. Thus the only risk associated with a common stock is its systematic risk. If we assume that unsystematic risk is diversified away, the cost of common equity (K_i) is

$$K_i = R_f + (R_m - R_f)\beta_i \qquad (13\text{-}10)$$

where R_f = riskless rate of interest, R_m = expected rate of return on a market portfolio, which is a group of risky stocks such as Standard & Poor's 500 Stocks, and β_i = beta coefficient (systematic risk) for firm i's common stock, and K_i is the investor's risk adjusted reqiured rate of return on company i's common stock. Equation (13-10) is known as the **security market line**, which consists of the riskless rate of interest (R_f) and a risk premium $[(R_m - R_f)\beta_i]$—where β_i is an index of volatility in the excess return of one stock relative to that of a market portfolio.

Example 13-7. The expected rate of return on the market portfolio is 20 percent. The riskless rate of interest (the expected rate of interest on Treasury bills) is 10 percent. The beta for St. Louis Company's stock is 0.5. What is the cost of St. Louis Company's common equity using CAPM?

The cost of St. Louis Company's common equity is

$$K_i = 0.10 + (0.20 - 0.10)\,0.5 = .15 = 15\%$$

Figure 13-2
Security Market Line (SML) and St. Louis Company

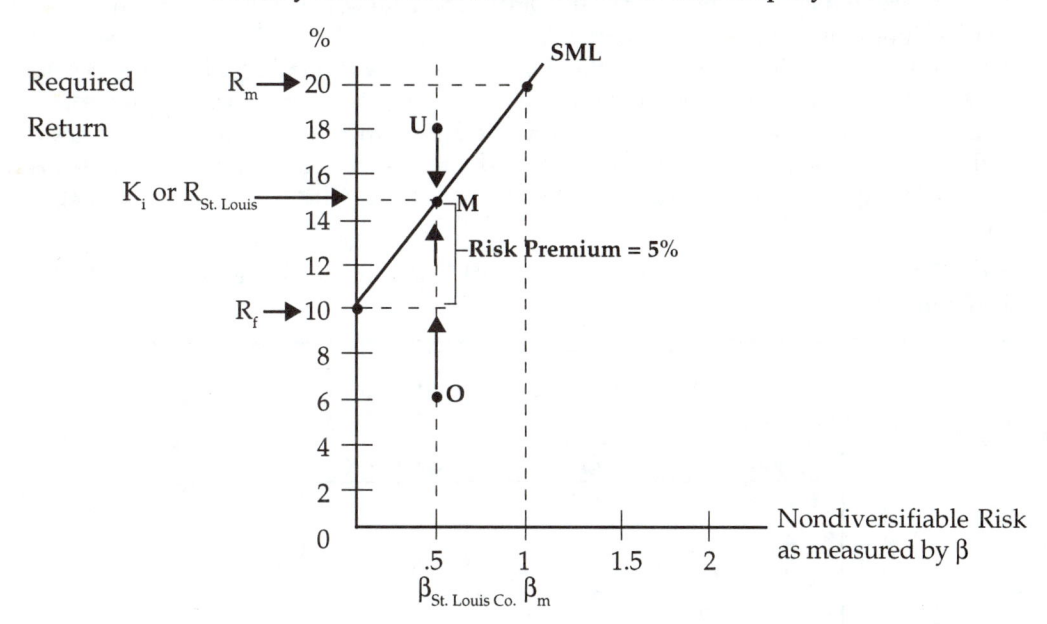

Where: $R_m = 20\%$, $R_f = 10\%$, $\beta_{\text{St. Louis Co.}} = .5$, and $\beta_m = 1$

244 PART 4: CAPITAL EXPENDITURE ANALYSIS

The betas for R_f and R_m investments are 0 and 1, respectively. By plotting these two points for the risk-free and market portfolio investments, we graph the SML. For St. Louis Company, with a beta of .5 and required return of 15% (see Example 13-7), investors require a risk premium (above the R_f rate) of 5%. If St. Louis's return fluctuates to point O, or 6%, investors would quickly sell its stock since they could earn a higher return, or 15%, with the market portfolio at the same level of risk, or .5 beta. Thus selling pressure would force St. Louis's stock price down and required return up to 15%, or market equilibrium.

At point U, St. Louis is underpriced relative to the market return and associated level of risk, or .5 beta. In this case buying pressure would push the firm's stock price up and required return down to the appropriate market return of 15% at point M.

Calculating Beta in Practice

Betas are estimated on the basis of weekly, monthly, or quarterly data for several months or several years in the past. The beta of a firm is calculated by regressing the firm's periodic stock returns on a corresponding periodic returns of a broad market index like the S&P 500. Current estimates of beta for actively traded stocks are available on a commercial basis. The better known services include those of Merrill Lynch, Wells Fargo Bank, and Value Line Investment Survey.

Because beta reflects the systematic risk of a stock relative to that of the market as a whole, the market index is assigned a beta of 1. Beta may be used to classify stocks into two broad categories: aggressive stocks and defensive stocks. **Aggressive stocks** are those stocks which have betas greater than 1. Their returns rise (fall) more than the market index rises (falls). For example, if a firm has a beta of 1.5, this suggests that when the market index rises by 1% this company's stock will increase by 1.5%. Defensive stocks are those stocks which have betas less than 1. Their returns fluctuate less than the market index. If a defensive firm's beta is .5, then an increase in the market index of 1% would lead to an increase in this company's stock of only .5%. Those stocks with betas equal to 1 are frequently called neutral stocks. The returns on these stocks move in step with the market index.

Example 13-8 illustrates the calculation of a stock's beta along with associated statistics by financial calculator.

Example 13-8. Stocks Y and market X produced the following % returns over the last five periods

Periods	Stock Y	Market X
1	14	8
2	3	5
3	-10	0
4	-12	-4
5	11	3

With these data, calculate the expected return, standard deviation, and coefficient of variation for X and Y. Also, find the correlation of X and Y and the beta of stock Y.

Solved by financial calculator:

1. Hit 2nd DATA. Hit 2nd CLR Work to clear the Data registry.
2. Key in 8 for X01 and 14 for Y01, hit ENTER. Scroll down and enter 5 for X02 and 3 for Y02 and so on until all five pairs of market X and stock Y returns are entered.
3. Now hit 2nd Stat. If LIN (for linear regression for two variable) does not appear, keep hitting 2nd SET and browse through the statistical programs until LIN appears.
4. Scroll down with the down arrow and observe n, the means, population and sample standard deviations, alpha, beta, correlation coefficient and so on.

Results	X	Y
a) Standard Deviation (population)	4.13	10.6
b) Expected Return	2.4	1.2
c) Coefficient of Variation	4.13/2.4 = 1.72	10.6/1.2 = 8.83
d) Alpha (Y intercept)		-4.25
e) Beta of Stock Y		2.27
f) Correlation of X and Y		.88

WEIGHTED AVERAGE COST OF CAPITAL

To compute the **weighted average cost of capital**: (1) calculate the cost of each component; (2) determine the weight of each component; (3) multiply each weight by its corresponding cost; and (4) sum these products. As shown in Table 13-1, the weighted average cost of capital for the St. Louis Company is 11.52%. Accordingly the company must earn at least 11.52 cents after taxes on every dollar it invests in assets in order to satisfy bondholders, preferred stockholders, and common stockholders with their respective required returns. For example, it takes 1.62 cents on every dollar of investment to cover an after-tax cost of debt of 5.4% and a before-tax yield to bondholders of 10% on the booked $60,000 of debt capital. To satisfy preferred stockholders, 2.40 cents out of the 11.52 is necessary. And finally, to provide common stockholders with return commensurate with risk, it takes 7.50 cents on every investment dollar. Suppose the firm made an investment that earned a return of only 9% or 9.00 cents on every dollar after taxes. Of this 9.00 cents, 1.62 would cover the cost of debt, 2.40 cents would cover the cost of preferred stock, leaving only 4.98 (or 9.00 − 4.02) cents available to common stockholders. This 4.98 cents would produce only about a 10% return to common stockholders who expected at least 15%. Logically, these dissatisfied common stockholders would sell this stock and buy another company's stock with the same level of risk but offering the desired 15% return. Similarly, if St. Louis Company made an investment yielding 18%, then the firm's common stockholders, happy with the 6.48 cents bonus (or 18 – 11.52) on every dollar after taxes and above expectations, would sell stock in other companies with similar levels of risk and buy St. Louis stock since its return exceeds what they can get elsewhere. Such would cause St. Louis's stock price to go up. Two alternative ways to specify the weights of the capital structure are used in practice: book value weights and market value weights.

Book Value Weights

Book value weights are derived from the stated values of individual components of the capital structure on the firm's current balance sheet. The amounts of long-term debt and preferred stock outstanding are used directly as stated. Common equity consists of common stock, paid-in-capital, and retained earnings.

Example 13-9. According to its latest balance sheet, St. Louis Company has outstanding common equity with a book value of $100,000, preferred stock with a book value of $40,000, and debt with a book value of $60,000. Recall that the component costs of the capital structure for St. Louis Company have been computed in the previous section: the cost of bonds = 5.4%; the cost of preferred stock = 12%; and the cost of common equity = 15%. The weighted average cost of capital (WACC) for St. Louis Company based on book value weights is given in Table 13-1, which indicates that the firm's WACC is 11.52 percent.

Table 13-1
WACC for St. Louis Company Based on Book Value

Capital	Component Book Value	Weight		Component Cost		Weighted Cost
Bonds	$ 60,000	0.30	x	5.4 %	=	1.62%
Preferred stock	40,000	0.20	x	12.0%	=	2.40%
Common equity	100,000	0.50	x	15.0%	=	7.50%
Total	$200,000	1.00		WACC		11.52%

There are two major advantages of book value weights. First, the proportions of the capital structure are stable over time because book value weights do not depend on market prices. Second, book value weights are easy to determine because they are derived from the stated values on the firm's balance sheet. However, the book value weights may misstate the WACC because the market values of bonds and stocks change over time.

Market Value Weights

Market value weights are based on the current market prices of stocks and bonds. The market value of stock is the number of shares outstanding times the current market price per share. The market value of debt is its stated value times its current market price. Bond prices are always quoted as a percent of their face value. If the stated (book) value of bonds is $1,000 and their quoted price is 90 percent, the market value of the bonds is $900.

> **Example 13-10.** St. Louis Company has outstanding common equity with a market value of $110,000, preferred stock with a market value of $36,000, and bonds with a market value of $54,000. The estimated WACC of St. Louis Company based on market value weights is shown in Table 13-2. As indicated, the firm's WACC is 11.868 percent.
>
> **Table 13-2**
> **WACC for St. Louis Company Based on Market Value Weights**
>
> | Capital | Market Value | Weight | Component Cost | Weighted Cost |
> |---|---|---|---|---|
> | Bonds | $ 54,000 | 0.27 | 5.4% | 1.458% |
> | Preferred stock | 36,000 | 0.18 | 12.0 | 2.160% |
> | Common equity | 110,000 | 0.55 | 15.0 | 8.250% |
> | Total | $200,000 | 1.00 | | 11.868% |

Because the primary goal of the firm is to maximize its market value, market value weights are consistent with the firm's objective. The market values of the firm's existing securities depend on the expected earnings of the company and the risk of the securities as perceived by investors. In other words, market values reflect the assessments by current buyers and sellers of future earnings and risk. Thus, the WACC computed with market value weights should be the valid average rate of return required by investors in the firm's securities. In essence, market value weights are superior since they are a reflection of the effect of current decisions on the firm's future, while book value weights reflect the results of past decisions.

WEIGHTED MARGINAL COST OF CAPITAL

Because the investment analyst is concerned with the cost of obtaining new funds, this section concentrates on incremental funds and their associated costs. The weighted marginal cost of capital (WMCC) refers to the cost incurred by the firm in acquiring an additional amount of capital for investment purposes. Underpricing and flotation costs involved in the sale of new securities affect the cost of capital. In many cases, the new issue must be sold below the market price of existing securities. In addition, there are out-of-pocket flotation costs such as underwriting fees, legal fees, and other costs associated with the new issue. Thus, in order for the firm to raise new funds by selling new bonds, preferred stock, or common stock, it generally contracts with an investment banking firm (i.e. Salomon-Smith-Barney) to sell or "float" the stock to the public. Thus F is the flotation cost or cost of selling the securities.

> **Example 13-11.** St. Louis Company intends to sell its new securities in the near future. Each new bond has a yield rate of 10 percent to maturity. The company's marginal tax rate is 46 percent. Each share of new

preferred stock pays $3.60 dividends per year, has a market value of $30, and has net proceeds of $25. Each share of new common stock has a market price of $40 and net proceeds of $35. Dividends are $4 per share in the coming year and are expected to grow at a rate of 5 percent per year.

Equation (13-2) can be adjusted to compute the after-tax cost of new bonds or K_{D_n}:

$$K_{D_n} = \frac{Y}{(1-F)} \times (1 - \text{tax rate})$$

For St. Louis if the flotation cost for selling the new bonds is 2% (or .02 of the bond's selling price)

$$K_{D_n} = \frac{10}{(1-.02)} \times (1-.46)$$

$$K_{D_n} = 10.2\% \times .54$$

$$K_{D_n} = 5.5\%$$

where: K_{D_n} = yield of new debt, F = flotation cost as percent of bond price (i.e. 2% of each bond's sales price).

For preferred stock as shown in Equation 13-8 as follows:

$$K_p = \frac{D_p}{P_p - F}$$

where: F = Flotation costs in dollars per share.

For St. Louis, whose preferred stock can be sold at $30 per share to net the company $25 per share, the flotation cost is $5 per share and the cost of new preferred stock is:

$$K_p = \frac{3.60}{(30-5)}$$

$$K_p = .144 \text{ or } 14.4\%$$

For the cost of new common stock (K_n), Equation 13-9 is similarly adjusted:

$$K_n = \frac{D_1}{P_o - F} + g$$

Now if the St. Louis Company decides to sell new common stock to raise needed capital, it must pay flotation costs and the dividend valuation model must be adjusted to reveal the net proceeds from the sale of the stock.

Therefore, with flotation costs of $5.00 per share, the cost of selling new common stock drives the cost of equity up to:

$$K_n = \frac{4}{40-5} + .05$$
$$K_n = .1643 \text{ or } 16.43\%$$

where: F = Flotation cost per share.

In essence, the firm sells the new common stock through an investment banker to the investor at a market price of $40 per share but after flotation cost, the company nets only $35 per share. For St. Louis, whose new common stock sold for $40 per share, but after deducting flotation costs of $5 per share, the company took in net proceeds of $35 per share.

Thus, the component costs of new securities are higher than those of the existing securities. This is mainly due to the flotation costs of issuing new securities, as well as underpricing.

Target Weights

Target weights are the proportions of additional funds which the company wants to raise. They reflect the **optimum capital structure**, which is defined as the combination of debt, preferred stock, and common equity that yields the lowest cost of capital. Evidence indicates that companies seek the optimum capital structure. For example, financial ratios published by Dun & Bradstreet, Robert Morris Associates, and other organizations show considerable similarities in the capital structure among companies in the same industry. Therefore, it appears that if firms in the same industry employ similar capital structures, then they probably perceive this capital structure as being optimal or one that produces the lowest possible WACC.

Actual measurement of the value of each capital component assumes that the company is concerned with the cost of new funds. To maximize its market value, the company should always expand its capital budget by raising funds in the same proportions as the optimum capital structure. Book value weights or market value weights are not necessarily identical with target value weights.

Example 13-12. The optimum capital structure of St. Louis Company consists of 20 percent debt, 15 percent preferred stock, 40 percent common stock, and 25 percent retained earnings. The company has decided to maintain this optimum capital structure in raising future long-term capital. Recall that the component costs of new securities have been computed in Example 13-11: the after-tax cost of new bonds = 5.5%; the cost of new preferred stock = 14.40%; and the cost of new common stock = 16.43%. Retained earnings do not involve flotation costs. Given the financial data in Example 13-11, the cost of retained earnings is 15 percent or ($4/$40 + .05). The WMCC of St. Louis Company (13.582%) is computed in Table 13-3.

Table 13-3
WMCC for St. Louis Company

Capital	Weight		Component Cost		Weighted Cost
Bonds	0.20	×	5.50 %	=	1.100 %
Preferred stock	0.15		14.40 %		2.160 %
Common stock	0.40		16.43 %		6.572 %
Retained earnings	0.25		15.00 %		3.750 %
Total	1.00		WMCC		13.582 %

Rationale for the Use of the WMCC

The weighted marginal cost of capital (WMCC) may have to be used as the firm's cost of capital for a number of good reasons. First, if a single component cost is used as the acceptance criterion, it is possible to accept projects with a low rate of return while rejecting projects with a high rate of return. Some low-return projects may be accepted because they can be financed with a cheaper source of funds such as debt. Some high-return projects would be rejected because they have to be financed with an expensive source of capital such as equity capital. If the firm uses up some of its potential for obtaining new low-cost debt, subsequent expansions will require it to use additional equity financing or the debt ratio will become too large.

To illustrate, assume that the firm has a 10 percent cost of debt and a 16 percent cost of common equity. In the first year it may use up its debt capacity to finance projects yielding 11 percent since the yield of 11 percent exceeds the cost of debt at 10 percent. In the second year the firm may discover projects that yield 15 percent, well above the return on the first-year projects. However, it cannot accept them because they would have to be financed with 16 percent equity money. To avoid this problem, the firm should use the WMCC.

Second, if the firm accepts those projects that yield more than its WMCC, the market value of its common stock will increase because the return on the project exceeds what the common stockholders expect on the common equity portion of the capital. This reward to the existing common stockholders signals success to the market and attracts new buyers who competitively bid up the company's stock price. Thus, accepting projects with this format supports the objective of the firm—to increase stockholder wealth.

WEIGHTED MARGINAL COST OF CAPITAL AND INVESTMENT DECISIONS

Using WMCC, the optimum capital structure and the optimum capital budget can be determined. To estimate the optimum capital structure, we hold the total amount of capital constant and change only the combination of financing sources to find the optimum (target) capital structure that yields the lowest cost of capital. The optimum capital budget exists where the market value of the firm is maximized which is that level of capital budget at which the marginal returns from investment are equal to the marginal cost of capital.

Optimum Capital Structure

The traditional approach to valuation and leverage assumes that an optimum capital structure exists. This model implies that the varying effects on the market capitalization rates for debt and equity allow the firm to lower its cost of capital by the intelligent use of leverage (debt). Debt has two types of cost: explicit cost and implicit (bankruptcy) cost. The **explicit cost** is the interest rate, whereas the **implicit cost** results from the increased cost of both equity and debt caused by the firm's higher level of debt and increased risk of bankruptcy.

Beginning with an all-equity capital structure, the addition of cheaper debt capital to the capital structure pulls the WMCC down and in turn increases the firm's market value. Figure 13-3 shows that at first both the cost of debt and the cost of common equity either remain constant or increase slowly with the increase of the debt ratio. But the WMCC falls with leverage, because the increase in the cost of equity does not offset completely the use of low-cost debt.

The traditional approach implies that beyond some point both the cost of equity and the cost of debt increase at an increasing rate due to the increased risk of bankruptcy. With the heavy use of leverage (or debt), the increase in the cost of equity more than offsets the use of low-cost debt. Thus, at a critical point, such as Point T in Figure 13-3, the subsequent introduction of additional debt causes the overall cost of capital to rise and the firm's market value to fall. The optimum capital structure is the point at which the WMCC bottoms out which is the point where the market value of the firm is maximized.

Figure 13-3
Debt Ratio and Cost of Capital

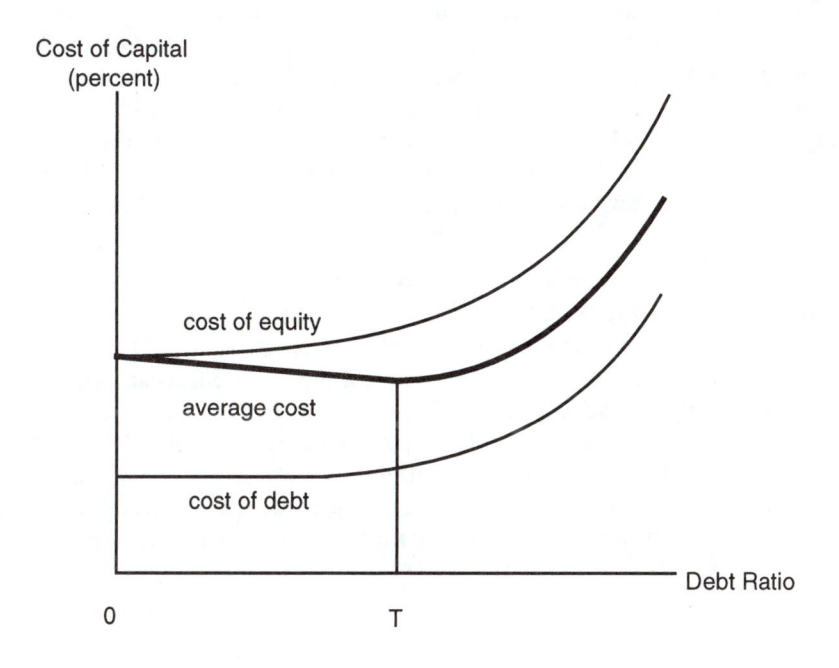

Optimum Capital Budget

Recall from Example 13-12 and Table 13-3 that the WMCC of St. Louis Company was 13.58 percent. Could St. Louis Company raise an unlimited amount of new capital at the 13.58 percent? The answer is no for two major reasons. First, once St. Louis Company exhausts its retained earnings and is forced to sell new common stock, its WMCC would rise. This is because the cost of new common stock is greater than the cost of retained earnings. Second, a company can only tap the capital market for some limited amount in the short-run before their WMCC goes up, even if the same optimum capital structure is maintained. As the company raises larger and larger sums of money during a given period of time, both the cost of debt and the cost of equity begin to rise, thereby pushing the WMCC up.

Example 13-13. St. Louis Company has only $25,000 of retained earnings available. Because retained earnings represent only 25 percent of the capital structure, the company has adequate retained earnings to support a capital budget up to $100,000 or ($25,000 ÷ 0.25). The company can raise another $60,000 at the same component costs: the cost of bonds = 5.5%; the cost of preferred stock = 14.40%; and the cost of common equity = 16.43%. Remember that the firm's optimum capital structure consists of 20 percent debt, 15 percent preferred stock, and 65 percent common equity. The new WMCC of St. Louis Company is about 13.93 percent or (0.20 x 5.5% + 0.15 x 14.40% + 0.65 x 16.43).

Because St. Louis Company wants to raise another $60,000 on top of the first $100,000, more new common stock must be sold to maintain the necessary common equity in the optimum capital structure. While the component costs of new securities do not initially change in this example, the WMCC increases from 13.58 percent to 13.93 percent with the loss of retained earnings because no more low-cost retained earnings are available for investment. To carry the example a bit further, we might find that if St. Louis Company tries to raise another $60,000 (a total of $220,000), its WMCC would rise to 14.50 percent. This increase might occur because no more low-cost debt is available for investment.

Table 13-4 shows six projects under consideration by St. Louis Company. Figure 13-4 graphs St. Louis Company's six projects and its WMCC schedule. The company should accept Projects A though D because their internal rates of return (IRR) exceed the cost of the capital that would be used to finance them. Projects E and F would be rejected because their internal rates are less than their costs of capital. The optimum capital budget of $160,000 is determined at the intersection of the IRR and WMCC schedules. Thus, the **optimum capital budget** can be defined as the amount of investment that would maximize the value of the firm.

Chapter 13: Valuation and Cost of Capital 253

Table 13-4
Optimum Capital Budget

Project	Investment	Cumulative Investment	Internal Rate of Return
A	$40,000	$ 40,000	18%
B	40,000	80,000	17
C	40,000	120,000	16
D	40,000	160,000	15
E	40,000	200,000	13
F	40,000	240,000	12

Figure 13-4
Optimum Capital Budget for St. Louis Company

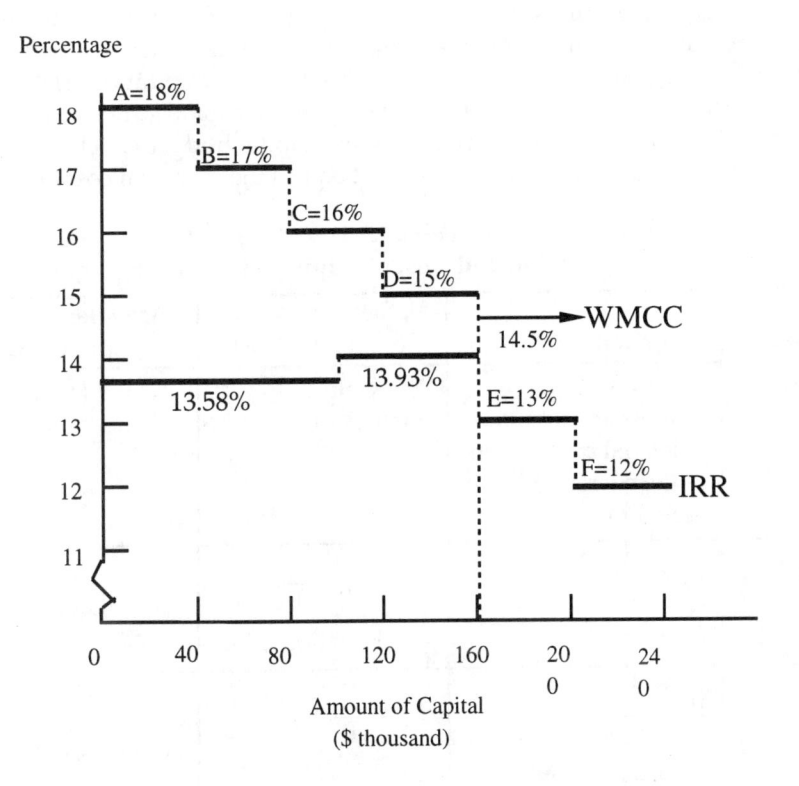

SUMMARY

The weighted average cost of capital or the weighted marginal cost of capital is used to represent the firm's opportunity cost of capital. The cost of capital is often employed to evaluate investment projects. To determine the weighted average cost of capital, first compute the individual component costs of the capital structure. The after-tax cost of debt is the bond's yield to maturity adjusted for the tax deductibility of interest. The cost of preferred stock is the stated dollar divided per share divided by the market price of the stock less flotation cost. The cost of common equity is the discount rate that equates the present value of all expected future dividends per share with the current market price of the stock. Another method (known as the Capital Asset Pricing Model) uses the beta of the stock, the riskless rate of interest, and the market risk premium to determine the cost of the common equity. There are three ways to specify the proportions of the capital structure: book value weights, market value weights, and target weights. Book value weights are derived from the stated values on the firm's balance sheet. Market value weights are based on the current market prices of bonds and stocks. Target weights are the proportions of additional funds which the company wants to raise. These three types of weights are used to determine the weighted average cost of capital. Valuation, component cost of capital, and WACC models are summarized in Tables 13-5 and 13-6 below.

The market value of the firm is maximized when the size of the total capital budget is determined by the level of investment at which the marginal returns from investment are equal to the marginal cost of capital. While holding the amount of capital constant and changing the mix of financing sources, the optimum capital structure exists where cost of capital is at its lowest point. The optimum capital budget is determined at the point where the marginal return on investment equals the marginal cost of capital.

Table 13-5
Valuation and Cost of Capital Models

Sources of Capital	Valuation	Before Tax Component Cost	After Tax Component Cost
Debt/Bonds	P_b = present value of interest annuity plus principal discounted at the current market yield (Y)	Y = yield-to-maturity on bond	$K_D = Y(1-t)$
Preferred Stock	$P_p = \dfrac{D_p}{K_p}$ (perpetuity)	$K_p = \dfrac{D_p}{P_p - F}$ F = Flotation Cost	K_p (no change)
Common Equity	$P_o = \dfrac{D_1}{K_e - g}$ (constant growth)	$K_e = \dfrac{D_1}{P_o} + g$	K_e (no change)
New Common Stock	Constant growth	$K_n = \dfrac{D_1}{P_o - F} + g$ F = Flotation Cost	K_n (no change)
Common Stock	CAPM	$K_i = R_f + (R_m - R_f)\beta_i$	K_i (no change)

Table 13-6
Component Cost of Capital and WACC

Source of Capital	Component Cost of Capital	Weight	Weighted Component Cost
Debt	K_D	W_D	$K_D \times W_D$ = Weighted Cost of Debt
Preferred Stock	K_p	W_p	$K_p \times W_p$ = Weighted Cost of Pf. Stock
Common Equity	K_e	W_e	$K_e \times W_e$ = Weighted Cost of Cm. Equity
WACC	K_i	(Proxy for K_e)	WACC = Sum

LIST OF KEY TERMS

coupon rate
systematic risk
security market line
defensive stocks
book value weight
marginal cost of capital
optimum capital structure
implicit cost

dividend valuation model
unsystematic risk
aggressive stocks
weighted average cost of capital
market value weight
target weight
explicit cost

PROBLEMS

13-1 Walter Corporation has bonds outstanding. The bond's yield to maturity (before-tax cost of the bond) is 12.4 percent and the firm's tax rate is 40 percent. What is the after-tax cost of the bond?

13-2 Walter Corporation has preferred stock outstanding. Each share of the preferred stock pays $4.20 and has a market price of $40 per share. What is the cost of the preferred stock?

13-3 The common stock of Walter Corporation is selling at $54 per share. It expects to pay a dividend of $4 per share and the dividend will grow at a rate of 9 percent per year. What is the cost of the common stock?

13-4 The component costs of the capital structure for Walter Corporation have been computed in Problems 13-1, 13-2, and 13-3: K_D = 7.4%, K_p = 10.5%, and K_e = 16.4%. According to its latest balance sheet, Walter Corporation has debt with a book value of $100,000, preferred stock with a book value of $50,000, and common equity with a book value of $50,000. What is the weighted average cost of capital for Walter Corporation?

13-5 Walter Corporation has debt with a market value of $90,000, preferred stock with a market value of $60,000, and common equity with a market value of $150,000. What is the weighted average cost of capital for Walter Corporation?

PART 4: CAPITAL EXPENDITURE ANALYSIS

13-6 A company is planning to launch a major expansion program which will require $1 million. The firm wants to maintain its current capital structure: debt = 30%, preferred stock = 20%, and common equity = 50%. New bonds will have an after-tax cost of 4.74 percent. New preferred stock will have a 9 percent dividend rate and will be sold at par. Common stock with a current market price of $50 can be sold to net the firm $40 per share. The firm currently pays a $2 dividend and plans to increase its dividend at the rate of 5 percent per year. The retained earnings available to the expansion program are estimated to be $200,000.

(a) To maintain the current capital structure, how much of the capital budget should be financed by external equity?
(b) Determine the cost of each individual component?
(c) Compute the weighted marginal cost of capital.

13-7 A company has the historical pattern of dividend payment as follows:

1991	$1.50
1992	1.48
1993	1.64
1994	1.87
1995	2.00
1996	2.00

The firm expects to pay a $2.10 dividend per share at the end of 1997. Dividends are expected to grow at the five-year average (1991-1996) per year. Common stock currently selling for $25 per share can be sold to net the firm $20.

(a) Compute the growth rate of dividends.
(b) Compute the cost of existing common equity.
(c) Compute the cost of new common stock.

13-8 The current capital structure of a firm is considered to be optimal. It has $5,000 in debt at 8 percent interest. The firm is expected to earn $1,500 before taxes of 50 percent per year, all of which will be paid in dividends. The cost of equity capital is 10 percent.

(a) Determine the total market value of the firm.
(b) Determine the overall cost of capital.

13-9 At present, the riskless rate of return is 10 percent and the expected rate of return on the market portfolio is 15 percent. The expected returns for five stocks are listed below, together with their expected betas:

Stock	Expected Return	Expected Beta
A	0.22	1.5
B	0.30	1.3
C	0.12	0.8
D	0.15	0.7
E	0.14	1.1

On the basis of these expectations, which stocks are overvalued? Which stocks are undervalued?

Part 5

LONG-TERM FINANCING

Part Five analyzes the various sources of long-term financing available to the firm. Chapter 14 considers the two types of capital markets: the primary market (e.g, investment bankers) and the secondary market (e.g., the organized security exchanges). Thus, the important role played by investment bankers in the operation of the capital markets and the function of the organized security exchanges (e.g, the New York Stock Exchange) are discussed. Then we take up the major sources of long-term capital: bonds and preferred stocks (Chapter 15), common stocks (Chapter 16), retained earnings (Chapter 17), and term loans (Chapter 18).

14

Investment Bankers and Capital Markets

This chapter presents an overview of the capital markets. The major focus is on two types of security markets: primary and secondary. Other topics covered include interpretation of the securities listings in financial news and the regulation of security markets.

The Primary Market

When the firm sells its new securities, the transaction takes place in the **primary market**. Most new securities are sold through either a public offering or a private placement. In a **public offering**, new issues are sold to the public through an investment banker. The **private placement** involves the sale of an entire issue to a single or a limited number of ultimate investors. An investment banker may arrange for the private sale of the issue.

Three Major Functions of the Investment Banker

The **investment banker** is a financial specialist who acts primarily as an intermediary between buyers and sellers of new securities. The investment banker provides the issuer with three services: advice and counsel, underwriting, and selling.

Advice and Counsel

The investment banker has the expertise to handle the distribution and sale of securities. As an advisor, the investment banker reviews the financial plans of the firm and offers detailed suggestions about the timing of the issue, its pricing, and other features designed to assure a successful sale.

Underwriting

Underwriting transfers the risk involved in the new issue from the issuing firm to the investment banker. When an investment banker underwrites the sale of a new issue, it actually buys the issue. Thus, the investment banker bears all the risk of adverse market price fluctuations during the period of distribution.

The compensation for this risk is the difference between the price the investment banker pays for the securities and the sale price of the securities. This price differential is known as the **spread,** underwriting fees, or underwriting profit. Underwriting fees average about 3 percent for large issues and probably as much as 10 for small issues.

259

Because common stocks are purchased by millions of individual investors, their underwriting fees are greater than those for preferred stocks and bonds. Normally, bonds are bought in large blocks by a limited number of institutional investors; consequently, their underwriting fees are smaller than those for common and preferred stocks.

Selling

The sale of the securities to the ultimate investors constitutes the last step in the investment banking process. For smaller issues, the investment banking firm usually sells the entire issue by itself. For large issues, it invites other investment bankers to form a syndicate. Syndicates are employed in the distribution of securities (1) to spread the risk, (2) to overcome the financial inability of a single investment banker to handle a large issue alone, and (3) to obtain a better market distribution.

When the issuer uses the services of the investment banker as a selling agent, it assumes the full risk of unsold securities on a best-efforts basis and returns all unsold securities to the issuer.

Investment Banking Operation

Perhaps the best way to clearly understand the investment banking operation is to trace the steps necessary to issue new securities.

Preselling Conferences

Before an underwriting takes place, the issuing firm and the investment banker hold a series of conferences which involve extensive discussions on the timing of the issue, the amount of capital to be raised, the type of securities to be issued, and the terms of the agreement. Once the conferees agree that a flotation sale will occur, the investment banker begins an investigation of the quality of the securities to be offered. In general, outside accounting, financial, legal, and engineering experts are hired by the investment banker to investigate the issuing firm. Once the investigation has been completed, a tentative underwriting agreement is drawn up.

Registration

After the firm and the investment banker have reached an agreement on all underwriting terms except the actual price of the security, they must file a registration statement with the Securities and Exchange Commission (SEC). The registration statement includes such information as the history of the firm, its financial statements, its management personnel, and the like. Before the SEC approves the sale of the security, it examines the registration statement to ensure the full disclosure of information with respect to the security. It usually takes 20 days for the SEC to complete its analysis of the registration statement.

Pricing the Issue

The purchase price the investment banker pays for a new issue can be determined either on a competitive basis or on a negotiated basis. When a new security is sold on a competitive basis, the investment banking firm must submit its bid on the price of the security. When the security is sold on a negotiated basis, the issuer and the investment banker discuss and negotiate its price. Because competitive bidding invites competition between investment bankers, it usually results in a higher price than a negotiated offering. For this reason, the law requires public utility and state bond issues to be sold on a competitive basis.

With a negotiated offering, the issuer and the investment banker jointly determine the resale price of the security to investors. Basically, the investment banker wants to set the price of the security relatively low to assure a successful sale, but the issuer wants as high a price as possible. Hence, the price should be low enough to assure a successful sale but high enough to satisfy the issuing firm.

The price of a new bond issue is generally determined in relation to the price of other new issues of the same risk class. If a firm's stock is already held by the public, the market price of the existing stock governs the price of its new stock issue. If the firm's stock is not held by the public, it has no current market price to use as a benchmark. If new securities do not have such a benchmark price, they are likely to be underpriced. To establish an appropriate price, the underwriter and the issuer must carefully analyze the tone of the market with respect to future interest rates, expected economic conditions, expected changes in monetary and fiscal policies, and the like.

Selling Activities

If the proposed issue is relatively small, an investment banker usually underwrites the entire issue by itself. If the issue is quite large or potentially risky, the originating underwriter invites other investment bankers to participate in the transaction on the basis of their ability to distribute securities. This particular group is called a syndicate. The members of the syndicate are called the underwriters. Each underwriter may sell a part of its participation directly to investors and the balance to a selling group. The selling group consists of dealers and other investment bankers that handle small quantities of the issue. In essence, the underwriters act as wholesalers and the members of the selling group as retailers.

After the selling group has been formed, the actual sales take place. Most public offerings are subject to market stabilization during the period of distribution. The manager of the underwriting group has the major responsibility for the stabilization of the market price at a level no lower than the offering price for the issue. The originating investment banker is frequently called the managing underwriter. The managing underwriter has two options to prevent a cumulative downward movement in the price:

1. It can peg the price for a limited number of days, usually 30 days. Once the price has been pegged, no member of the syndicate or the selling group may sell the issue below the stated price. This practice can be criticized on the ground that it involves a price-fixing arrangement.
2. It can enter the market as a buyer to support the price.

The Decision to Go Public

New public offerings by privately held firms are defined as **"going public."** Firms can go public with or without raising additional funds. If companies continue to grow, they may decide at some point to go public. We will evaluate the advantages and the disadvantages of public financing in the following section.

Advantages of Being Public

Going public makes it easier to raise new capital since the greatest pool of funds is channeled toward publicly held companies. Moreover, the prestige of a public company may be helpful in bank negotiations, executive recruitment, and the marketing of products. Other advantages include increased liquidity, stockholder diversification, and the establishment of a value for the firm.

Disadvantages of Being Public

Publicly held companies must have all information available to the public through the Securities and Exchange Commission and State filings. Not only are such disclosures tedious, time consuming, and expensive, but important corporate information on profit margins and product lines is exposed. Furthermore, publicly owned companies are under the heavy pressure for short-term performance placed on them by security analysts and large institutional investors. Other disadvantages include the dilution of control and earnings, and the high cost of reporting.

Alternative Methods of Distribution

Instead of selling a security issue to the general public through the underwriting procedure just described, many companies distribute their securities through two alternative methods: private placement and privileged subscription.

Private placement is the direct sale of an entire issue to a limited number of institutional investors. Most companies make heavy use of the underwriting method to market their new equity securities but employ private placement predominantly to sell their new debt issues.

When the firm sells its new issues through private placement, it can usually anticipate a number of benefits:

1. The private sale does not require the registration and disclosure procedures of the SEC, thereby saving the firm time, trouble and some costs.
2. Because private placement avoids the underwriting spread, the issuing costs are substantially lower.
3. Private placement makes it possible for the firm to modify the terms of the loan before its maturity, because of the small number of security holders.
4. Under private placement, the terms of the loan such as repayment schedules and maturity dates can be tailored to the precise needs of the borrowing firm.

When a market already exists for the firm's securities, it is logical to offer a new issue first to select potential investors on a **privileged-subscription basis.** These investors are usually of three types: employees, customers, and stockholders.

Most customers are not particularly responsive investors. Employees, too, are relatively small-scale buyers, but they deserve a brief mention. Many firms make stock available to key employees through a stock option plan. Under this arrangement, employees are given an opportunity to buy a certain number of shares at a specified price over a given period of time. The motive of the issuer is to increase employee loyalty.

Most privileged subscriptions are directed to existing stockholders, who often have a preemptive right under the corporate charter or state law. The **preemptive right** is a provision that gives the existing stockholders the ability to maintain their proportion-

Chapter 14: Investment Bankers and Capital Markets

ate ownership in the corporation. When the corporation issues additional common stock, the existing stockholders must be given the right to subscribe to the new stock so that they preserve their percentage ownership in the company.

When a privileged subscription is used to sell securities, each stockholder receives one right for each share of stock held. Usually, such stock-purchase rights must be exercised within 30 days. The stockholders who receive such a right have three choices: (1) they can exercise the right, (2) they can sell it in the market, or (3) they can let it expire.

The market value of a right depends on three factors: the market price of the stock, the subscription price, and the number of rights necessary to buy an additional share of stock. Stock-purchase rights may be valued either before or after the date of record. When the firm issues the rights, it specifies a **date of record** on which holders of record in the company's stock ledger are designated as the recipients of the rights. The company makes up a list of the stockholders as of that date, and those stockholders are called holders of record. Because it takes time for the company to be notified of the transfer of stock and to list the buyer as the holder of record, the stock usually goes **ex-rights** after the fourth business day before the date of record. That is, the new owner of this stock is not entitled to receive the rights.

The theoretical value of one right before the stock sells ex-rights is

$$R_o = \frac{M_o - S}{N + 1} \qquad (14\text{-}1)$$

Where R_o = market value of one right when stock is selling rights-on, M_o = market value of one share of stock when stock is selling rights-on, S = subscription price per share, and N = number of rights required to buy one new share of stock.

Example 14-1. The XYZ Company, with one million shares of stock outstanding, decides to issue 200,000 new shares. The market price of its stock is $50 a share, and the subscription price of its new stock is $38 per share.

Because it takes five rights to buy an additional share of stock (1,000,000/200,000), the theoretical value of one right is

$$R_o = \frac{\$50 - \$38}{5 + 1} = \$2$$

When the stock goes ex-rights, the new owner no longer receives the rights to subscribe to additional shares. Therefore, the market price of the outstanding stock declines by the value of one right. The theoretical value of one right when the stock goes ex-rights is

$$R_x = \frac{M_x - S}{N} \qquad (14\text{-}2)$$

Where R_x = market value of one right when the stock sells ex-rights, and M_x = ex-right market value of the stock.

In our example, the market price of the stock is $48 or ($50 – $2) when it goes ex-rights, and thus we obtain

$$R_x = \frac{\$48 - \$38}{5} = \$2$$

The theoretical value of one right when the stock goes ex-rights is the same as before.

SECONDARY MARKETS

The **secondary market** deals with those securities that have already been issued and sold. There are two major secondary markets: organized security exchanges and over-the-counter markets. On **organized security exchanges** such as the New York Stock Exchange, large volumes of selected securities are traded on an auction basis. The **over-the-counter markets** are informal markets where small volumes of many securities are traded on a bid-and-ask basis.

The organized exchanges essentially provide central marketplaces where individual and firm members can get together to trade securities. The over-the-counter markets are loose-knit networks of telephones and computers that connect numerous dealers.

Organized Exchanges

The New York Stock Exchange, the so-called Big Board, dominates all other organized stock exchanges. It accounts for more than 80 percent of the total dollar volume traded on all exchanges. The organized exchanges consist of the Big Board, the American Stock Exchange, and a number of regional stock exchanges such as those in Boston and Cincinnati.

Individuals or firms can become members of an exchange by buying seats. These seats represent the right to use the services of the exchange in the transactions of securities for their customers. Security transactions are conducted on a two-way-auction basis. Members with sales orders compete with one another to sell the securities at the highest possible price. In contrast, members with purchase orders compete to buy the securities at the lowest possible price. A successful transaction takes place when the highest bidder and the lowest offerer meet with each other.

Listed securities are those traded on the organized exchanges. **Unlisted securities** are those traded in the over-the-counter market. To list its securities on an exchange, a firm must meet qualifications relating to size, number of shares outstanding, their market value, and the like. Listed companies must register with the SEC. Advantages of listing include a certain amount of free publicity, increased prestige, a beneficial effect on the sale of the firm's products, and a favorable impact on the cost of equity capital.

Over-the-Counter Markets

Unlike the organized exchanges, the over-the-counter (OTC) market possesses no central location. The OTC markets consist of a limited number of **dealers** with their own inventories of OTC securities and thousands of **brokers** who act as agents. Prices are determined by negotiation between dealers or between dealers and investors. The dealers usually act as wholesalers for broker-agents or as principals for their own account. The brokers generally act as retailers for investors.

Dealers and brokers do not need to buy seats on the OTC market, but they must register with the SEC. To sell securities in the OTC market, companies do not have to meet any listing requirements. Any individual or firm with a small amount of capital, a telephone, a computer, and a registration with the SEC can become a participant.

What types of securities are traded in the OTC market? A greater number of stocks are traded in the OTC market, but the dollar sales volume of stocks traded is greater on the exchanges. This is because the stocks of most large companies are listed on the organized exchanges. The great majority of bond transactions occurs in the OTC markets, because OTC dealers sell large blocks of bonds to a limited number of institutional investors. In addition, U.S. government securities, federal agency securities, state bonds, and municipal bonds are important segments of the OTC market.

How to Read the Stock Quotations

Stock dealers, brokers, and investors obtain a considerable amount of information on various securities by reading the newspaper financial pages. Although big city newspapers carry the daily activities on most security markets, the Wall Street Journal is the key source of price information on these securities.

Stock quotations titled "NYSE-Composite Transactions" in the Wall Street Journal summarize all transactions in common and preferred stocks listed on the New York Stock Exchange. In fact, the stock-listing format shown below is the same for the New York Stock Exchange, American Stock Exchange and NASDAQ National Market Issue Quotations. We will use one recent American Telephone and Telegraph common stock as an illustration. Its quotation for Wednesday reads as follows.

YTD %CHG	52 WEEKS HI	LO	STOCK (SYM)	DIV	YLD %	P-E	VOL 100s	LAST	NET CHG
+11.52	56.13	45	ATT	5	9.9	6	4530	50.75	+0.75

The first column, YTD percentage of change, reflects the stock price percentage change for the calendar year to date. We see from the next two columns that ATT stock traded as high as $56.13 per share and as low as $45 during the previous 52 weeks. It should be noted that market fractions are always stated in 100ths of $1. The difference between the highest and lowest prices of ATT common stock during these 52 weeks was $11-1/8; this difference is sometimes called the range. The range represents the volatility of the stock, or the dispersion of individual prices for the stock around its average price. The wider the dispersion, the higher the risk. If the highest price and the lowest price are not widely separated from their neighboring prices, the range may be a relatively good measure of risk. If these two prices are erratic, the range should not be used as a measure of risk, because it is unreliable and misleading. Even the stocks of large, well-known corporations fluctuate widely in price from time to time. It is important to recognize the possibility that this wide fluctuation can be caused by a few extreme deviations.

In the fourth column from the left of the quotation, we find ATT, which is an abbreviated form of American Telephone and Telegraph. The 5 to the right of ATT indicates the

PART 5: LONG-TERM FINANCING

current annual rate in dollars of dividends paid or declared on a share of ATT stocks. The next entry is the yield rate. The yield rate of 9.9 percent on ATT stock equals its dividend ($5) divided by its last price ($50.75). The Wall Street Journal and big city newspapers print the P-E (price-earnings) ratios of listed companies instead of their earnings. To obtain the P-E ratio of 6 for ATT, the last price of ATT stock ($50.75) is divided by its earnings per share for the most recent 52 weeks ($8.46). "Sales 100s" states the number of shares traded in hundreds. The total number of ATT shares bought and sold is obtained by adding two zeros to the 4530. Thus, a total of 453,000 ATT shares changed hands on Wednesday.

The remaining two columns of the quotation represent the price activity of ATT stock during the day. Its last price was $50.75. The +0.75 in the net change column means that the closing price of ATT stock on Wednesday was $0.75 higher than the last price on the previous trading day.

Quotations of preferred stock and common stock are reported on the same financial pages. When there are a number of quotations for the same firm, only the first refers to the common stock and the others represent preferred stocks. Preferred stocks are identified by a pf following the abbreviated name of the firm. The format of preferred stock quotations is identical with that of common stock quotations, but the former does not contain the P-E ratio.

REGULATIONS OF SECURITY MARKETS

A variety of laws and self-regulation of stock exchanges exist to protect investors in the United States from fraud and other dishonest activities. Congressional investigations of the collapse of the stock market in 1929 and the subsequent depression found that investors suffered heavy losses for two major reasons. First, many companies had failed to disclose relevant information. Second, many misrepresentations of financial information had been made to investors.

Federal Securities Acts

The previously mentioned factors motivated Congress to enact the **Securities Act of 1933** and the **Securities Exchange Act of 1934**. The Securities Act of 1933 imposes mandatory disclosure requirements on companies that sell their new securities through the securities markets. The basic philosophy of the act is to let the issuer disclose and to let the investor beware. The Securities Exchange Act of 1934 extends the disclosure concepts to securities already outstanding.

The major provisions of the Securities Exchange Act of 1934 are as follows:

1. The Act created the Securities and Exchange Commission as a watchdog for the securities business.
2. It required listed companies to file registration statements and periodic financial reports with both the SEC and the exchanges.
3. It gave the SEC the power to prohibit market manipulation, misrepresentation, and other unfair practices.
4. It required all national securities exchanges to register with the SEC and to be under its effective supervision and regulation.
5. It gave the Board of Governors of the Federal Reserve System the authority to control margin requirements.

6. It granted the SEC the power to control short selling, trading techniques, and the procedures of the exchanges.
7. It required officers, directors, and major stockholders to file monthly reports of any changes in their stock holdings.

Margin requirements and short selling are two practices that play an important role in orderly and efficient stock market operations. **Margin requirements** are credit standards for the purchase of securities. If margin requirements are 60 percent, investors pay 60 percent of the purchase price in cash at the time of transaction and borrow 40 percent from a brokerage firm or a bank. **Short selling** means the sale of a security that belongs to another person. The short seller borrows the security from a brokerage firm, sells it, and at some later date repays the brokerage firm by buying the security on the open market.

In 1975, Congress amended the Securities Act of 1933. The major focus of the amendment was the requirement that the SEC move toward establishing a single nationwide securities market. The law did not specify the structure of a national securities market, but it assumed that any national market would make extensive use of computers and electronic communication devices. In addition, the law outlawed fixed commissions on public transactions and also prohibited banks and other financial institutions from buying stock exchange memberships to save commission costs for their own institutional transactions.

Regulation of OTC Markets

The National Association of Securities Dealers (NASD) regulates the over-the-counter markets as the SEC regulates the organized exchanges. There are many requirements that NASD members must meet. These include registration, a code of procedures and practices, limited markups on securities, the restriction of preferential treatment to members, and so forth.

State Regulation

Like the SEC, the security commissions of individual states regulate the issuance of new securities in their states and seek to prevent the fraudulent sale of securities. State regulations are particularly important for a security issue that is sold entirely to people within the state. State regulations are frequently called "blue-sky" laws, because they attempt to prevent the sale of securities representing nothing more than "blue sky."

Effect of Regulation

More than six decades have passed since the SEC was established to regulate the security industry. Has the regulation worked? To answer this question, we need to understand the two objectives of these regulations: (1) to protect investors from misrepresentation, deception, and other fraudulent practices, and (2) to ensure orderly security transactions. Although there are differences of opinion on this matter, it appears that some progress has been made on these two accounts.

The stock market regulations have at least two important implications for the financial manager. They affect the cost of new capital and they influence the riskiness of securities. You should know by now that these two factors affect the market value of the firm.

Summary

When companies need long-term external funds, they can sell their long-term securities publicly or privately. A public offering usually requires the services of an investment banker. The investment banker's major functions are advice, underwriting, and selling. For these functions, the investment banker is compensated by the spread between the purchase price of the securities and their resale price.

Two alternatives to underwriting are private placements and privileged subscriptions. Private placements are generally arranged with such institutional investors as insurance companies. Many companies offer their securities to their employees, customers, and stockholders. Normally, employees are small-scale buyers and customers are not particularly responsive investors. When the firm makes stock available to its stockholders, they receive one right for each share of stock they hold. Such a right is called a preemptive right and represents an option to buy the security at the subscription price.

Most outstanding securities are traded on either the organized exchanges or in the over-the-counter markets. Qualifying stocks of large companies are listed on the organized exchanges, whereas the stocks of small companies and the vast majority of bonds are traded in the over-the-counter markets. The organized exchanges are regulated by the SEC and by their own rules. The OTC markets are regulated by the National Association of Securities Dealers.

List of Key Terms

primary market
private placement
underwriting
best-efforts basis
privileged-subscription basis
date of record
secondary market
over-the-counter markets
unlisted securities
brokers
Securities Exchange Act of 1934
short selling

public offering
investment banker
spread
going public
preemptive right
ex-rights
organized security exchanges
listed securities
dealers
Securities Act of 1933
margin requirements

Problems

14-1 The Kemple Corporation has decided to sell 10,000 new common shares at $9 per share through a subscribed issue. Its 50,000 shares of common stock outstanding are selling for $21 per share.

  (a) Compute the theoretical value of the common stock after the sale of 10,000 new shares.
  (b) Compute the theoretical value of one right when the stock sells rights-on.
  (c) Compute the theoretical value of one right when it goes ex-rights.

14-2 The Village Company with 10,000 shares of stock outstanding wishes to raise $50,000 through a rights offering. The market price of its stock is $30 per share;

the subscription price of its new stock is $25 a share; and the number of rights required to buy an additional share of stock is 5.

(a) What is the theoretical value of one right when the stock sells with rights?
(b) What is the theoretical value of one share of stock when it sells ex-rights?
(c) What is the theoretical value of one right when the stock sells ex-rights at $30?
(d) Nancy Henning has $1,800. She believes that the price of the stock will rise to $40 by the time that the rights expire. What is Nancy's return on her $1,800 if she buys the stock at $30?

14-3 Instead of through a rights offering, the Village Company (see Problem 14-2) could raise $50,000 through a public offering at $29 per share with a flotation cost of $2 a share. The company earns $36,000 a year, 50 percent of which is paid in dividends. Assume that its price-earnings ratio is 10.

(a) Determine the earnings per share, dividends per share, and market price of the stock for the rights offering alternative.
(b) Determine the net proceeds, the number of new shares necessary to raise $50,000, earnings per share, dividends per share, and market price of the stock for the public offering alternative.

14-4 Assume that a company earned $4.50 a share during the previous 52 weeks and its stock closed at $53-1/2 with a net change of $1-1/2 for the day.

(a) Compute the company's price-earnings (P-E) ratio.
(b) What do low P-E or high P-E ratios tell you?
(c) Should investors purchase low P-E stocks or high P-E stocks?
(d) Determine the closing price of the stock on the previous trading day.
(e) Why is the current yield on some bonds less than their coupon rate?

14-5 You are given the following NYSE Composite Transactions Report, taken from the Wall Street Journal on one day in January 1996.

YTD %CHG	52 WEEKS HI	52 WEEKS LO	STOCK (SYM)	DIV	YLD %	P-E	VOL 100s	LAST	NET CHG
+10.12	45.50	37	COGER	2.50	6.25	10	250	40	+0.38

(a) How many shares of Coger stock were traded on that day?
(b) What was the price of Coger stock at the close of trading one day earlier?
(c) What was the earnings per share of Coger for the last 52 weeks?
(d) Calculate Coger's dividend payout ratio.

14-6 A company has decided to sell 100,000 shares of common stock through a public offering. The selling price is $20 per share with the company receiving $17 per share after spread. Registration fees are $25,000.

(a) Determine the dollar spread as well as the percentage spread.
(b) Determine the total expenses of the issue.
(c) If the company wants to generate $2,120,000, how many shares will have to be sold?

14-7 A company has decided to sell 20,000 shares of new common stock. The selling price is $40 per share with 8 percent spread on the offer price. Registration fees are $15,000. The company's current earnings are $200,000. The company has 75,000 shares outstanding.

(a) What is the potential dilution from this new stock issue?
(b) What is the amount of the net proceeds to the firm?

15

FIXED INCOME SECURITIES: BONDS AND PREFERRED STOCK

This chapter discusses long-term financing. A corporation's sources of long-term external funds are primarily bonds, preferred stocks, and common stock. Bonds with an original maturity of more than ten years and preferred stocks constitute the main subject of this chapter. Common stock is separately discussed in Chapter 16. Bonds and preferred stocks are usually called fixed-income securities, because they pay a fixed return.

DIFFERENCES BETWEEN BONDS, PREFERRED STOCKS, AND COMMON STOCKS

A **bond** or a bond certificate is a written promise to make payments of interest and principal on a specified future date to the holder of the bond. Bondholders are creditors to a corporation, who have prior claims on earnings and assets in liquidation. Common stockholders are owners of the corporation who have residual claims on earnings and assets in liquidation. Preferred stockholders hold a middle ground between bondholders and common stockholders. Subordinated to the various creditors of the corporation, the preferred stockholders have prior claims over common stockholders on earnings and assets in the event of bankruptcy.

Table 15-1
Differences between Bonds, Preferred Stock, and Common Stock

	Bonds	Preferred Stock	Common Stock
Status of holder	Creditor with legal claim to interest and principal	Stockholder with prior claim to declared dividends	Stockholder with residual claim to declared dividends
Order of distribution of earnings and assets if liquidation	First	Second	Last
Risk and required rate of return	Lowest	Middle	Highest

Holder receives	Fixed interest	Fixed dividend prior to common stock if declared	Residual dividend if declared
Tax treatment	Interest is tax-deductible	Dividends not tax-deductible	Dividends not tax-deductible
Maturity	Yes	No	No
Voting rights and control	No	Generally no	Yes

CHARACTERISTICS OF BONDS

When a firm issues bonds to the public, it designates a trustee. The **bond indenture** constitutes a contract between the borrower and the trustee, who represents the interests of the bondholders. It contains all the terms and conditions to which the bondholders must adhere. Some of these conditions are protective covenants similar to the various provisions contained in a term loan agreement. Chapter 18 discusses these provisions in some detail.

Face Value

Most corporate bonds carry a face value of $1,000. The **face value** is also called the principal amount, the maturity value, the denomination, and the par value. The borrower agrees to pay this full value to the bondholders at maturity. Most new bonds sell at a price very close to their par value. Old bonds, however, sometimes sell at considerably higher or lower prices than their face value. A premium occurs when the market price of a bond exceeds its maturity value. A discount arises when the bond trades at a price lower than its face value.

Maturity Date

Companies must pay the maturity value of their bonds after a specified period of time. Most bonds have maturities of 20 to 30 years. The longer the maturity, the greater the risk. Thus, interest costs rise as the maturity period increases. Although there are times when interest rates do not vary in a systematic way according to the maturity of debt instruments, the long-term interest rate is typically higher than the short-term interest rate. Hence, the financial manager must balance the unfavorable factors of short-term loans against the higher costs of bonds.

Coupon Rate

Bond issuers pay the fixed rate on the face value of their bonds. This rate is called the **coupon rate**, the stated rate of interest, or the nominal rate of interest. For example, a 10 percent bond indicates that the borrower will pay the bondholder $100 a year for every $1,000-face-value bond. The **bond's yield to maturity** is the rate of return that equates the present value of principal and interest payments with the current market price of the bond. This rate is sometimes called the internal rate of return, the annual percentage rate, the required rate of return, the effective rate of return, or the true rate of return. The yield rate depends on a number of factors such as the face value, the coupon rate, and the current market price. Thus, the coupon rate is just one of the several factors that affect the yield to maturity.

Call Provision

In an attempt to compensate for this uncertainty on future interest rates, most corporate bond issues contain a call privilege or **call provision**. This provision allows the firm to hedge against interest rate risk. For example, if interest rates fall, the corporation can invoke the call privilege and essentially refinance the debt at the more favorable, lower interest rate. On the other hand, if interests rise, the firm simply does not execute its call option. Specifically, the provision gives the issuer the right to call or buy back the bonds at a stated price before their maturity date. If the coupon rate on $200 million of 30-year bonds drops from 10 percent to 5 percent in ten years, the refund of the bonds can save the company $10 million a year in interest payments, or a total of $200 million over the life of the original bond. Because the call privilege enables the firm to manage interest rate risk, it adds value to the firm, but there is a price. Callable bonds generally will sell at lower prices and offer higher yields than other bonds that are identical in every way except that no call option is attached. The firm may even have to promise investors a higher price if the bonds are called to compensate for the interest rate risk that the bondholder now bears.

Although the call provision is beneficial to the issuer, it is detrimental to the investor. If the bonds are called during a period of falling interest rates, the investors may have no choice except to reinvest at a lower interest rate and sacrifice the higher yield to maturity on the called bond. Consequently, if a firm inserts a call provision in its bonds, it must offer something of value to offset this expected loss of yield. For example, the firm may have to offer a higher coupon rate on the bonds or promise to call them at a price much higher than their face value.

Sinking Fund

The borrowing firm can retire its outstanding bonds in a number of ways. For example, it can retire them at maturity by paying the contract value in cash, call them before their maturity, convert them into common stock, or retire them through periodic repayment. The retirement of bonds by periodic repayment is possible if the bonds are either sinking funds or serial bonds.

The **sinking-fund provision** requires the firm to pay an agreed amount of money into a special fund administered by a trustee. The trustee may invest these funds until the maturity date and then discharge the entire issue at one time. Or the trustee may use these sinking funds to buy and retire a portion of the bond issue each year. The retirement of bonds by the second approach can be done in one of two ways. First, the trustee can call a certain percentage of the bonds at a predetermined price each year. Typically bonds are numbered serially and are called on a lottery basis by their serial numbers. Second, the trustee can use the sinking-fund payment to purchase the bonds in the open market. The firm will choose the retirement method that results in the greatest reduction of outstanding bonds for a given amount of money. When the call price exceeds the market price, the trustee will elect to buy the bonds in the open market. When the call price is less than the market price, it will call the bonds.

The call provision of a sinking fund frequently works to the detriment of bondholders. Nevertheless, bondholders generally benefit from the sinking fund, because it tends to assure the orderly retirement of an issue, to support the market price of the bonds, and to reduce bondholders' exposure to risk.

Although some specific bonds in an issue may be retired before the maturity date, all sinking-fund bonds mature on the same date. In contrast, serial bonds in the issue have different maturities and are retired in serial installments. Some serial bonds have maturities as short as two or three years, and others have maturities as long as 20 or 30 years. A serial bond issue enables investors to select the maturity that best suits their needs.

Types of Bonds

There are many types of bonds. For our purposes we divide corporate bonds into three categories: secured bonds, unsecured bonds, and income bonds.

Secured Bonds

Secured bonds are those that pledge a specific type of security such as real estate or equipment. If the issuer defaults on any provisions of the secured bond indenture, the bondholders have the first claim on this property. The security may consist of land and buildings (real estate mortgage bonds), machinery (chattel mortgage bonds), stocks and bonds (collateral trust bonds), or other corporate property.

The firm can use the same property to secure several loans. When this occurs, bonds are classified into first-mortgage bonds, second-mortgage bonds, and so on. The numbers indicate the order to be followed in satisfying the bondholders' claims if the borrower defaults. The first-mortgage bondholders must recover all the money owed to them before there can be any distribution to the second-mortgage bondholders. To make up for their lack of appeal to investors, second-mortgage bonds carry a higher interest rate than first mortgage bonds.

Unsecured Bonds

Unsecured bonds are sometimes called **debenture bonds**. Because debenture bonds are not secured by specific property, debenture holders become general creditors in the event of default: they look to the nature of the firm's assets, its earning power, and its general credit strength. Although debenture bondholders are not protected by a specific pledge of property, they are protected by such safeguards as a sinking-fund provision, a conversion privilege, certain restrictions, and an extra-high interest rate.

Like second-mortgage bonds, subordinated debenture bonds rank behind senior bonds with respect to the claims on both assets and earnings. However, these subordinated debt holders still rank ahead of both common stockholders and preferred stockholders.

Income Bonds

Income bonds usually result from corporate reorganizations, and they pay interest only to the extent of current earnings. Income bonds are essentially a creditor obligation, because the interest payment on them is deductible for tax purposes. But they have some characteristics of preferred stock, because the interest payment does not have to be made unless income is actually earned by the firm. Some income bonds contain a cumulative feature with respect to unpaid interest charges, but such a clause is typically restricted to a couple of years. Therefore, income bonds are not popular with investors, and this is why they are typically used in corporate reorganizations.

New Types of Bonds

The wide swings in interest rates and rising interest rates in the late 1970s and early 1980s have made both borrowers and lenders wary of long-term, fixed-interest-rate bonds. While many innovative forms of bonds have been developed in recent years, we shall examine the two new types of bonds: floating-rate bonds and zero-coupon rate bonds.

Floating-Rate Bonds

Floating-rate bonds carry variable interest rates. In other words, the interest paid on the bond changes as market interest rates change. In 1974, floating-rate notes were first issued in the United States by Citicorp. The coupon rate on these notes was set at a minimum of 9.7 percent for ten months, then adjusted semiannually to 1 percent above the three-month Treasury bill rate.

Many other firms followed Citicorp's lead. These early issues carried rates based on Treasury bill yields, but interest rates on some other bonds are tied to other indicators. For example, the changes in the interest rate paid on the Petro-Lewis bond are based on changes in crude oil prices. Some floating-rate bonds have upper and lower limits to the rates that can be paid. Some others have only lower limits or no limits.

Zero-Coupon Bonds

Zero-coupon bonds provide all of the cash payment (interest and principal) when they mature. The bond does not pay periodic interest but is sold at a deep discount from its face value. The return to the investor is the excess of the face value over the market price. For example, in early 1982, BankAmerica Corporation sold $1,000 zero-coupon bonds with maturities of five, eight, and ten years. The market prices were $500 for the five-year bonds, $333.33 for the eight-year bonds, and $250 for the ten-year bonds. All three provided an original yield of approximately 14.75 percent.

Zero-coupon bonds have several advantages over conventional bonds. First, there is immediate cash inflow to the issuing company but no periodic interest to pay. Second, a big tax advantage exists for the issuing company because any discount from the maturity value may be amortized for tax purposes by the company over the life of the bond. For investors, zero-coupon bonds offer the luxury of a locked-in yield-to-maturity with no interest rate risk and preferential tax treatment since all income on the security would be capital gains and taxed at lower rates.

BOND RATINGS

There are several ways to analyze or compare the quality of bonds. Two financial service firms—Standard & Poor's Corporation and Moody's Investor Service—assign letter ratings to indicate the quality of bonds. Table 15-1 shows bond ratings by these two firms. Their AAA ratings indicate the highest quality of bonds. Bonds with such ratings are frequently referred to as **gilt edge** because the interest and principal are protected by substantial financial strength, thus carrying the smallest degree of investment risk. In other words, these ratings depict the estimated probability of default. Bond ratings are important because they affect the interest rate and the availability of additional long-term debt. Bonds rated Ba or lower by Moody's and BB or lower by Standard & Poor's are sometimes called junk bonds.

While there is no magic formula for rating bonds, the major rating agencies normally investigate five aspects of the company and the particular issue in question: management, level and stability of earnings, financial resources, asset protection, and indenture provisions. First, the agencies place a major emphasis on management's prudence and capability in determining bond ratings. They examine management's objectives and its policies to achieve these objectives. Second, the agencies assess the ability of companies to earn good returns consistently and to maintain adequate interest coverages (times interest earned). Stability of earnings is usually more important than the earnings level. Third, a number of specific ratios such as current ratio, inventory turnover, and accounts receivable turnover are calculated to determine a company's current liquidity. Other ratios such as debt ratio and times interest earned are used to determine a company's ability to obtain additional funds from external sources. Fourth, the degree of protection afforded by the company's assets are determined by some specific indices such as total long-term debt/net plant and net tangible assets/total long-term debt. Fifth, existing and proposed indenture provisions are reviewed to determine the repayment schedule in the event of liquidation. In addition, the bond rating agencies examine whether there are suitable safeguards against default; management is restricted in the amount of additional debt it can raise; and the terms of issue require a sinking fund.

Table 15-2
Bond Ratings by Standard & Poor's and Moody's

	Standard & Poor's		Moody's
AAA	Highest grade	Aaa	Best quality
AA	High grade	Aa	High quality
A	Upper medium grade	A	Upper medium grade
BBB	Medium grade	Baa	Lower medium grade
BB	Lower medium grade	Ba	Possess speculative elements
B	Speculative	B	Generally lack characteristics of a desirable investment
CCC,CC	Outright speculation income bonds; no interest is being paid.	Caa	Poor; may be in default
C		Ca	Speculative to a high degree; often in default
DDD, DD,D	In default	C	Lowest grade

REASONS FOR USING BONDS

There are a number of reasons why companies choose the debt alternative over the common stock alternative or the preferred stock alternative. When bonds are issued, the control of existing stockholders may be indirectly eroded by restrictive provisions and corporate earnings. But bondholders do not participate in management decisions and corporate earnings. Hence, bond financing prevents the direct dilution of both control and earnings.

Chapter 15: Fixed Income Securities: Bonds and Preferred Stock

Financial institutions such as banks and mutual savings banks are restricted by law or regulation in their holdings of common stock, but they do not have such restrictions on their holdings of bonds. The bond alternative makes it possible for the firm to tap these sources of creditor funds.

Another advantage of the debt alternative is favorable leverage. The interest payment on bonds is definitely limited. If the borrowed funds earn more than their cost, the additional earnings accrue to the stockholders. But it is important to recognize that there is always the possibility of unfavorable leverage. The advantage of the debt alternative becomes even greater when we consider the fact that interest payments are a tax-deductible expense, whereas stock dividends are not.

Unfortunately, rising prices have become a way of life in recent years. The constant value of debt decreases in a period of inflation; consequently, the debtor benefits from such a decline. For firms with considerable debt on their books, the amount of such declines may exceed the shrinkage in the purchasing power of such items as depreciation charges.

Because an increased use of debt involves a higher financial risk and a loss of policy flexibility, the financial manager must pay close attention to the mix of debt and equity in the firm's solvency itself in periods of low earnings. The right combination of debt and equity determines the ability of the firm to earn an adequate return for its stockholders and to fulfill its obligations when its earnings fluctuate widely.

HYBRID NATURE OF PREFERRED STOCK

The intermediate nature of preferred stock becomes evident when we attempt to classify it in relation to bonds and common stock. Preferred stock can be treated as debt for three reasons:

1. Like bondholders, preferred stockholders receive a fixed income and thus do not share fully in the profits of the company.
2. Like bondholders, preferred stockholders receive priority over common stockholders in the payment of dividends and assets in the event of liquidation or reorganization.
3. Because of the priority feature and the fixed dividend, preferred stockholders usually do not have a voice in management, unless the company fails to abide by its agreement with them.

Preferred stock is similar to common stock in three ways.

1. Like common stockholders, preferred stockholders are entitled to dividends only when they are declared by the board of directors. Thus failure to pay preferred dividends does not necessarily cause default of an obligation.
2. Like common dividends, preferred dividends are not deductible for income-tax purposes.
3. Call features and sinking-fund provisions are frequently established to assure the orderly retirement of preferred stock. Unlike bonds, however, preferred stock issues have no definite maturity date.

The nature of the problem under consideration will determine whether preferred stock should be treated as debt or as equity. From the purely legal viewpoint, preferred stock is a type of ownership. Accounting practice places preferred stock in the net worth section of the balance sheet. Tax law treats preferred dividends as a distribution of profits rather than as an expense of the business. For these reasons and those described in the previous paragraph, many financial analysts treat preferred stock as equity in the computation of capitalization ratios. Preferred stock and common stock quotations are also reported on the same financial pages of the *Wall Street Journal* and other newspapers.

Characteristics of Preferred Stock

Most companies have small quantities of preferred stock: the ratio of preferred stock to the firm's total capital is ordinarily quite small. Preferred stock has a variety of features.

Par Value

Most preferred stocks have a **par value**, the face value that appears on the stock certificate. It may be any amount set forth in the corporate charter, and it is used as the basis for recording the stock on the balance sheet. This par value is a meaningful quantity for preferred stockholders for two reasons. First, call prices and preferred dividends are frequently calculated as percentages of the par value. Second, par value establishes the amount that preferred stockholders can claim against their firm in the event of liquidation.

Maturity

Preferred stock does not have a maturity date, but a sinking-fund provision or a call privilege effectively creates a maturity date. Practically all preferred stock issues are callable, or redeemable. That is, the firm reserves the right to call in the preferred stock for redemption. If the firm exercises its call provision, it must pay the par value of the preferred stock, a call premium, and all accumulated unpaid dividends. A sinking-fund provision obligates the issuer to buy and retire some of the shares annually, thus assuring the orderly retirement of the stock and supporting the price of the stock on the market.

Cumulative Aspect

Preferred dividends are usually cumulative; unpaid dividends are accumulated and must be paid together with the current dividend before any dividend payment can be made on common stock. Hence, if the firm has omitted its annual preferred dividends of $7 a share for two consecutive years, it is said to be $14 per share in arrears on its preferred stock. Before it can pay a dividend to its common stockholders during the third year, it must pay $21 per share to its preferred stockholders. Unpaid dividends on noncumulative preferred stock, however, are lost forever.

It should be emphasized that preferred stockholders do not have power to force their company into bankruptcy for nonpayment of dividends. They should not be too much concerned with their lack of power to obtain unpaid dividends, however, because failure to pay preferred dividends also means failure to pay common dividends. If the amount of unpaid dividends is extremely large, it may pose a serious problem. If the firm pays current dividends and these arrears in a short period, it drains working capital severely. But a slow payment program irritates both preferred stockholders and common stockholders. Under these circumstances, the firm may decide to offer common stock to its preferred stockholders rather than to clean up its unpaid dividends.

Participating Feature

Preferred stock may be either participating or nonparticipating. If the stock is participating, which is rare, it receives its stated dividend and also shares in any additional dividends declared. The amount of additional dividends depends on the terms of the contract. For example, once the common stockholders and the preferred stockholders have received an equal amount of dividends such as $5 a share, both classes of stockholders may share equally in any additional distributions of earnings. Or the additional participation of the preferred stock may be limited in the stock contract to a specified amount of dividends per share.

Voice in Management

Because preferred stockholders have prior claims on assets and earnings, their voice in management is usually limited to certain restrictions on the payment of dividends and any subsequent issues of securities. If the company fails to pay preferred dividends during a specified period of time, however, preferred stockholders as a class may be entitled to elect a specified number of directors in order to protect their interest.

Protective Features

To protect their interest in the company, preferred stockholders normally seek certain covenants very similar to those applied to term loans and bonds. These covenants restrict common dividends and the repurchase of common stock. They generally prohibit such outlays unless the corporate current ratio exceeds a certain level or unless the accumulated retained earnings exceed a stated amount or both. The purpose of such restrictions is to increase the quality of the preferred stock.

REASONS FOR USING PREFERRED STOCK

Despite the fact that preferred dividends are not deductible for tax purposes, preferred stock is still able to provide favorable financial leverage. Preferred dividends are fixed; thus, favorable leverage occurs when the firm earns more on its preferred stock than the associated cost.

The use of preferred stocks also provides the firm with a greater degree of flexibility. From the issuer's point of view, it expands the equity base. This expanded equity base can be used as a means of supporting more long-term debt. However, if earnings are low for one or two years, the company can omit the dividend on preferred stock. Unpaid dividends can be accumulated, but they do not cause the company to go into bankruptcy. The use of preferred stock avoids the provision of equal participation in earnings and control that the use of additional common stock would require.

Preferred stock has a number of disadvantages. The fact that preferred dividends are not tax deductible severely limits its use. To attract investors, corporations usually must offer a higher yield on preferred stock than on bonds. These two characteristics make the cost of preferred stock much greater than that of bonds.

REFUNDING ANALYSIS

Most issues of corporate bonds and preferred stocks have a call provision. If interest rates or preferred dividends decline significantly, the company can call these issues and refinance them at a lower cost. Such a refinancing arrangement is called a **refund-**

280 PART 5: LONG-TERM FINANCING

ing operation. The refunding operation of bonds is identical to that of preferred stock, except that interest payments are a tax-deductible expense.

The decision to refund a bond or a preferred stock is analyzed in much the same way as an investment project. To analyze a project, we should know its initial cash outflow and its future cash benefits. By the same token, the refunding decision involves an initial cash outflow in the form of the call premium and future cash benefits in the form of interest savings. Because the interest savings occur over the life of the original security, we must determine the present value of these future interest savings and compare it with the initial cash outflow of the refunding operation. The interest savings of the new bonds are usually known with relative certainty; consequently, we have to use the after-tax cost of the new debt as a discount rate.

Example 15-1. Ten years ago the Colby Plastic Company issued $100 million worth of 30-year bonds with a coupon rate of 8 percent. Within the ten years, interest rates dropped to 7 percent. Rather than continue to pay higher rates of interest, the company plans to call in its bonds and sell a new $100 million issue of 20-year bonds with a coupon rate of 7 percent. It sold its old bonds at par and can also sell its new bonds at par; the new bonds are to be sold one month before the old bonds are called. The old bonds have an unamortized flotation cost of $1.5 million and a call premium of 5 percent. The new bonds have an underwriting spread of 2.75 percent. With a tax rate of 50 percent, is the company right to refund its $100 million worth of bonds?

The refunding-decision process requires the following computation steps:

Step 1. Determine the initial net cash outflow of the refunding decision; its gross cash outlay minus its tax saving.

(a) Gross cash outlay:

Call premium	$100,000,000 × 5.00% =	$5,000,000
Underwriting cost of new bonds	100,000,000 × 2.75 =	2,750,000
Overlapping interest on old bonds	100,000,000 × =	666,667
Gross cash outlay		$8,416,667

(b) Tax saving:

Overlapping interest on old bonds		$ 666,667
Call premium	8.00	5,000,000
Unamortized flotation cost of old bonds	12	1,500,000
Total tax deductible expense		$7,166,667
× Tax rate (50%)		× 50%
Tax saving		$3,583,333

Chapter 15: Fixed Income Securities: Bonds and Preferred Stock 281

(c) Net cash outlay = gross cash outlay − tax saving

$$= \$8,416,667 - \$3,583,333$$

$$= \$4,833,334$$

Step 2. Determine the annual interest saving of the refunding decision: the annual net cash outflow on the old bonds minus the annual net cash outflow on the new bonds.

(a) Annual net cash outflow on old bonds:

Interest expense (1)	$100,000,000 × 8.00%	= $8,000,000
Less: tax saving:		
Interest expense		8,000,000
Amortization of flotation cost	1,500,000/20	= 75,000
Total tax deductible expense		$8,075,000
x Tax rate (50%)		x 50%
Tax saving (2)		$4,037,500
Annual net cash outflow = (1) − (2)		$3,962,500

(b) Annual net cash outflow on new bonds:

Interest expense (1)	$100,000,000 × 7.00%	= $7,000,000
Less: tax saving:		
Interest expense		7,000,000
Amortization of underwriting cost	2,750,000/20	137,500
Total tax deductible expense		$7,137,500
x Tax rate (50%)		x 50%
Tax saving (2)		$3,568,750
Annual net cash outflow = (1) − (2)		$3,431,250

(c) Annual interest saving = (a) − (b)

$$= \$3,962,500 - \$3,431,250$$

$$= \$531,250$$

Step 3. Determine the present value of the interest saving for the next 20 years. Because the after-tax cost of the new debt is 3.5 percent, the present value of $7,550,125 = $531,250 × $ADF_{20,3.5\%}$ (14.212).

Step 4. Determine the net present value of the refunding decision; the present value of annual interest savings for 20 years minus the initial net cash outflow of the refunding decision. Thus, we obtain

Net present value = Step 3 - Step 1

$$= \$7,550,125 - \$4,833,334$$

$$= \$2,716,791$$

Because the net present value of the refunding decision is positive, the issue should be refunded. We can also solve this example by the internal-rate-of-return method. Because the internal rate of return is approximately 9 percent, it exceeds the required return of 3.5 percent; the issue should be refunded.

SUMMARY

This chapter described the characteristics and advantages of two fixed-income securities; bonds and preferred stocks. The principal characteristics of bonds include fixed return, definite maturity, a priority claim on earnings and assets, the call provision, and the method of retirement. This chapter also examined a number of reasons why companies use bonds in their capital structure.

Preferred stocks are a hybrid form of security that has features of both debt and equity. Preferred stocks are similar to bonds because they have a fixed return. But preferred dividends do not have to be paid unless they are declared by the board of directors. Furthermore, failure to pay preferred dividends does not bankrupt the company.

Preferred stocks are more risky than bonds because (a) companies are more likely to omit preferred dividends than to omit interest payments, and (b) bonds have priority on earnings and assets. But preferred stocks are less risky than common stocks because (a) preferred dividends are paid before common dividends can be paid, and (b) preferred stocks have a priority claim on such assets in the event of bankruptcy.

LIST OF KEY TERMS

bond
coupon rate
call provision
secured bonds
debenture bonds
floating-rate bonds
gilt edge
refunding operation

face value
bond's yield to maturity
sinking fund provision
unsecured bonds
income bonds
zero-coupon bonds
par value

PROBLEMS

15-1   A company holds a $1,000 zero coupon bond with a maturity of 15 years for $108. What is the yield of the zero coupon bond?

15-2   A company has issued a 10-year, $1,000 zero coupon bond to yield 10 percent.
   (a) What is the initial price of the bond?
   (b) If interest rates dropped to 8 percent immediately upon issue, what would be the price of the zero coupon bond?
   (c) If interest rates rose to 12 percent immediately upon issue, what would be the price of the bond?

15-3   The Park Company issued $1.5 million of 30-year, $1,000 bonds with a coupon rate of 9 percent five years ago. The bonds with a call price of $1,050 were sold at a discount of $30 per bond or with a total discount of $45,000. The initial flotation cost was $18,000. The company wishes to sell a $1.5 million new issue of 7 percent, 25-year bonds in order to retire its existing bonds. The company intends to sell its new bonds at their face value of $1,000 per bond. The flotation costs of the new issue are estimated to be $22,000. The company's marginal tax rate is 50 percent and the new bonds are sold four months before the old bonds are called.

(a) Determine the net cash outflow of the refunding operation.
(b) Determine the annual interest savings of the refunding operation.
(c) Determine the present value of the interest savings over a 25-year period at a 5 percent discount rate.
(d) Should the company refund its old bonds?
(e) Use the internal-rate-of-return approach to determine whether the company should refund its old bonds or not.

15-4 The bond indenture of a company specifies the following: (1) Bonds should not exceed 70 percent of the sum of net worth plus subordinated debt. (2) Subordinated debt cannot exceed 60 percent of net worth. (3) Preferred stock should not exceed 50 percent of common stock. What is the maximum amount of money that the company can raise if it sells $100,000 of common stock?

15-5 The four callable bonds have the following call prices and issue sizes:

Bond	Size of Bond	Call Price
A	50,000 bonds	$1,050
B	10,000 bonds	1,030
C	25,000 bonds	1,100
D	15,000 bonds	1,040

Additional assumptions are: (1) Each bond has a face value of $1,000. (2) The firm's marginal tax rate is 40 percent. Compute the after-tax cost of calling the issue for each of these callable bonds.

15-6 Reynolds, Inc., has $10 million in mortgage bonds, $14 million owed to general creditors, $1 million in subordinated debentures, and $9 million par value of common stock. The company has sold its mortgage assets for $5 million and other assets for $9 million. How would the distribution in bankruptcy be made?

15-7 Aloba Corporation has a cumulative preferred stock with a stated annual dividend of $10 per share. The company has been losing money and has not paid the preferred dividends for the last three years. There are 200,000 shares of preferred stock outstanding and 300,000 shares of common stock outstanding.

(a) How much is the company behind in preferred dividends?
(b) Assume that Aloha earns $5,000,000 in the coming year after taxes and before dividends and that all these earning are paid out to the preferred stockholders. How much will the company be in arrears?
(c) How much would be available for common stock dividend in the coming year if $5,000,000 is earned as explained in part (b)?

16

COMMON STOCK

Common stock represents the ownership of the company. In this chapter, we consider legal and accounting aspects of common stock. Convertible securities and warrants are forms of options. They are discussed along with common stock because an option is the right to buy or sell the common stock of a company within a specified period of time.

In the previous chapter, we saw that in the event of bankruptcy, claims of creditors and preferred stockholders must be settled in full before the common stockholders can have any claim on the company's assets. By the same token, interest and preferred-dividend payments should be made before dividends can be paid on common stock.

ACCOUNTING TERMS AS APPLIED BY COMMON STOCK

There are many special terms used in connection with the stockholders' equity account **(net worth)**. Investors and financial analysts must understand these terms to avoid misinterpretations and possibly costly mistakes. To facilitate our discussion of these terms, we will use the common stockholders' equity section of the balance sheet for the Clark Company.

Par Value and No Par Value

A share of common stock can be issued with a par value or with no par value. The **par value** is the face value of each share as stated in the corporate charter. When the company issues a new stock, it should not sell the stock at a price less than par value. This is because stockholders may be held liable to the creditors in the event of bankruptcy for the difference between the price they paid and the par value. It is also important to note that most state laws prohibit the company from paying dividends that would reduce the stockholders' equity below the par value. Aside from these two legal factors, the par value has little economic significance.

When the company issues stock with no par value, the board of directors frequently assigns a stated value; this stated value becomes the basis for recording the stock on the company's balance sheet. If the board of directors does not assign a stated value on the stock, its market price becomes the basis for recording it on the company books.

Authorized Stock and Issued Stock

The **authorized stock** of a company represents the maximum number of shares it can issue under the terms of the corporate charter. If the company desires to increase its

286   PART 5: LONG-TERM FINANCING

authorized stock or to change the par value, such changes require an amendment to the charter. Because an amendment requires the approval of existing stockholders and a considerable amount of time, most companies like to have a certain number of shares that are authorized but not issued. When the company sells its authorized shares of common stock, they become **issued stock**.

We see from Table 16-1 that the charter of the Clark Company authorized 1,000 shares of common stock with a par value of $50 a share and issued 700 shares. Thus, the company's common-stock account consists of $35,000. There are 300 shares that are authorized but unissued.

Paid-in Surplus and Retained Earnings

Paid-in surplus is the actual issue price of the stock minus its par value. The par values of most common stocks are set well below their market values; thus, paid-in surplus usually becomes positive. Table 16-1 shows that the company has a paid-in surplus of $14,000; it received an average of $70 per share for the sale of its 700 shares or ($49,000/700). Profits retained by the company over the years represent **retained earnings** of $69,000. The total stockholders' equity of the Clark Company is $118,000, which includes common stock, paid-in surplus, and retained earnings.

Treasury Stock and Outstanding Stock

Treasury stock is the number of shares that have been issued and subsequently reacquired by the company. **Outstanding stock** is issued stock minus treasury stock. Table 16-1 shows that the company has issued 700 shares of common stock but has purchased 200 shares at a price of $90 per share and holds them as treasury stock. Hence, the company has only 500 shares of common stock outstanding. The difference between the total stockholders' equity and the treasury stock represents the net stockholders' equity of the company.

Table 16-1
Equity Account for the Clark Company
December 31, 2000

Common stock ($50 par value; 1,000 shares authorized; 700 shares issued)	$ 35,000
Paid-in surplus or capital surplus	14,000
Retained earnings or earned surplus	69,000
Total stockholders' equity	$118,000
Less: treasury stock (purchased 200 shares at $90 per share)	18,000
Net stockholders' equity	$100,000

Book Value, Liquidation Value, and Market Value

The **book value per share** of common stock is the net stockholders' equity divided by the number of shares outstanding. The Clark Company has a net stockholders' equity of $100,000 and 500 shares outstanding; the book value of the stock is $200 per share.

Theoretically, the book value of a company should correspond to the company's actual liquidation value, but it seldom does. When companies are dissolved under bankruptcy proceedings or for reorganization purposes, many of the assets can be liquidated at depressed prices. Thus, for most companies, liquidation value is far below book value.

The current price of a stock traded in the marketplace represents the market value of the stock; it implies the existence of buyers and sellers. For those companies with listed stocks or active over-the-counter stocks, market-price quotations are readily available to investors. The market value per share of common stock is significantly different from its book value or its liquidation value. It depends on the expected earnings of the company and the risk of the stock as perceived by investors. In a strict sense, market value merely reflects the opinions of current buyers and sellers about future earnings and risk.

Legal Capital

Legal (stated) capital is the minimum amount of capital that the company cannot legally distribute to its stockholders either in the form of dividends or by the reacquisition of common stock. There are a number of variations from state to state in how the amount of stated capital is determined. Some states define legal capital as the total proceeds from the sale of stock; this amount includes common stock and paid-in surplus. However, most states define it as the par value of all par-value shares issued but not subsequently canceled plus the stated value of all no-par-value shares; this amount usually consists of only common stock. When companies issue no-par-value stocks, most states either designate a certain amount as the stated capital or allow the board of directors to designate the amount.

In general, common stockholders are not held liable for the debts of their company beyond the amount of their investment; consequently, creditors must look only to the assets of the company in liquidation. This provision has made corporate stock as readily transferrable as it is today. To obtain this provision, the state legislatures recognized a need to place a restriction on the return of capital to stockholders. The purpose of this restriction is to protect creditors from unscrupulous promoters, stockholders, or directors.

Current financial statements generally contain separate classifications for common stock and paid-in surplus, but they do not disclose the amount of stated capital. The users of financial statements may benefit from the disclosure of stated capital in the main body of financial statements or in footnotes. However, the disclosure of stated capital may be unnecessary for large and profitable companies, because their stated capital is relatively small; the entire stockholders' equity serves as a cushion for the protection of creditors.

RIGHTS OF COMMON STOCKHOLDERS

The state laws, the corporate charter, and the firm's bylaws specify the rights of common stockholders.

Rights to Income and Assets

The board of directors of a company always decides how much of the profits should be distributed to its stockholders in the form of cash dividends. Thus, like preferred stockholders, common stockholders have no rights to income until the board of directors declares dividends.

Creditors and preferred stockholders always have priorities in liquidation over common stockholders. The book value of the company represents the residual claim of common stockholders on assets, but it may be relatively unimportant in a forced liquidation. Although assets are not sold for scrap value even in the event of forced liquidation, they can be liquidated only at distressed prices; thus, liquidation values are seldom reliable standards of value. In the case of a voluntary liquidation, stockholders have a better chance to receive something, but this amount is usually far below the book value of the company.

Voting Power

To protect their claim on assets, common stockholders have the ultimate authority to determine the management of their company through the election of board members. Ordinarily, each common stockholder is entitled to one vote for each share of stock in the election of directors or in other special elections. If stockholders cannot attend the annual meeting to vote their shares, they may vote by proxy. A proxy is a form by which the stockholders assign their right to vote to another person.

The Securities and Exchange Commission closely controls the use of the proxy and frequently issues rules and regulations to improve its administration. If stockholders are satisfied with management, they usually give their written authorization to management to vote their shares. Because management is able to solicit the stockholders' proxies at the company's expense, it generally receives most of the proxies. However, if the rate of return, profit margins, and dividend-payout ratio are relatively low, outsiders have some chance to seize control of the company through a proxy contest.

Majority Voting and Cumulative Voting

There are two voting systems in common use: majority voting and cumulative voting. Under the **majority voting system**, each stockholder has one vote for each share of stock held. If a stockholder holds ten shares, he may cast ten votes for each board position. Those who receive a majority of the total votes are elected as directors. If a group of stockholders controls 51 percent of the shares outstanding, the group can select the entire board. Therefore, the majority voting system can prevent minority stockholders from electing directors who will represent their interests.

Some corporate charters require the use of a **cumulative voting system** to elect corporate directors. Under this voting system, each shareholder is able to accumulate his or her votes and cast all of them for a single director. The total number of votes for each stockholder is the number of shares he or she holds times the number of directors to be elected. For example, if a stockholder has 100 shares of common stock and five directors are to be elected, the stockholder is entitled to cast a total of 500 votes. He or she can cast 100 votes for each of the five board positions or cast 500 votes for one director.

The cumulative voting system enables minority stockholders to elect a certain number of directors. We can determine the minimum number of shares necessary to elect a specified number of directors as follows:

$$N = \frac{D \times S}{T + 1} + 1 \qquad (16\text{-}1)$$

where N = number of shares necessary to elect a certain number of directors, D = number of directors that a group of stockholders desires to elect, S = total number of shares of common stock outstanding, and T = total number of directors to be elected.

Example 16-1. John Walter and a number of other stockholders want to elect two directors. The company will elect a total of five directors and has 60,000 shares outstanding.

To elect two directors, Walter and his fellow stockholders will need at least the following number of shares:

$$N = \frac{2 \times 60{,}000}{5 + 1} + 1 = 20{,}001$$

We can alter Equation (16-1) to determine the number of directors that a group of stockholders with a certain number of shares can elect:

$$D = \frac{(N-1)(T+1)}{S} \qquad (16\text{-}2)$$

If we solve this example on the assumption that D is unknown while all other variables remain constant as before, we obtain

$$D = \frac{(20{,}000 - 1)(5 + 1)}{60{,}000} = 2 \text{ directors}$$

Classified Common Stock

Not all holders of common stock have an equal voting power. A company may have more than one class of common stock. Its common stock can be classified according to voting power. If there are Class A and Class B stocks, the **Class B stock** may have full voting rights, whereas the **Class A stock** may have limited or no voting rights. This classified common stock is used in most cases to assure the control of the company by its founders and management. Normally, the Class B stock is held by the promoters of a company and its management, whereas the Class A stock is sold to the public.

The Ford Motor Company is perhaps the most famous example of a company with classified common stock. The relatively small issue of Class B stock held by the Ford family constitutes 40 percent of the voting power. The much larger issue of common stock held by the public has 60 percent of the voting power.

REASONS FOR USING COMMON STOCK

Common stock has a number of advantages over bonds and preferred stocks. First, interest payments and preferred dividends are fixed obligations, whereas common dividends are not. Second, common stock acts as a buffer against losses for the protection of creditors; thus, the sale of common stock improves the company's ability to support more debt. Third, common stock does not have a maturity date or a sinking-fund provision. These two factors relieve the company of any eventual concern with the retirement of the issue. Fourth, common stock may be easier to sell than fixed-income securities, because it usually carries a higher expected return and provides the investor with a hedge against inflation.

290 PART 5: LONG-TERM FINANCING

Common stock has a number of disadvantages as a source of funds. Its sale results in the dilution of both control and earnings. This is because common stock gives more stockholders the right to share in both control and profits. Underwriting fees are generally greater for common stock than preferred stock or bonds. Because it is more risky than preferred stock or debt, its component cost is also higher.

CONVERTIBLE SECURITIES

Convertible securities are bonds or preferred stocks that can be exchanged at the option of the holder before the conversion privilege expires. The convertible provision is used to make certain fixed-income securities more attractive to investors and consequently to increase their marketability. Convertible securities provide investors with a steady income and an opportunity to participate in rising stock prices. Thus, the contractual (stated) rate for convertible securities is considerably below the market rate for nonconvertible securities.

The conversion privilege gives the investor a call option to hedge against risk, that is the right to convert either preferred stock or bonds into common stock at a predetermined strike price. If the firm's stock price rises in the future above the strike price, the investor can cash in on this success by converting to common stock. If the firm experiences hard times in the future, the investor avoids conversion and holds onto the more secure fixed-income security. As compensation to the firm for the call option, generally these convertible securities sell at higher prices and/or provide lower yields than their nonconvertible equivalents.

Conversion Value

The ratio of exchange between a convertible security and common stock can be stated in two ways: a conversion price and a conversion ratio.

Example 16-2. The Temple Company's convertible bonds carry a face value of $1,000 per bond and sell at par. The issue has a conversion price of $50 per share. The market price of the common stock is currently $40 per share.

Because the **conversion ratio** is the face value of the bond divided by its conversion price, we obtain

$$\text{Conversion Ratio} = \frac{\text{Face Value}}{\text{Conversion Price}} = \frac{\$1,000}{\$50} = 20$$

Thus, its conversion ratio equals 20 to 1 or 20 shares of common stock for one bond. The conversion price is established and it is usually 10 to 20 percent greater than the prevailing market price of the common stock. Generally, the initial conversion price remains constant over the life of the bond unless a reduction is essential to protect bondholders from dilution by stock dividends and stock splits.

The **conversion value** of a convertible security is its conversion ratio times the market price per share of common stock at the time of issue. The Temple Company's bond has a conversion ratio of 20, and its common stock price is $40 per share. Hence, the conversion value of the bond is $800 or (20 x $40). The difference between the actual market price of the bond and its conversion value represents the **conversion premium**. The market price of the bond is $1,000; thus, its conversion premium is $200 or ($1,000 − $800). This premium is frequently expressed as a percentage of the conversion value; the percentage premium is 25 percent or ($200/$800).

Effect of Conversion on Earnings and Control

Convertible securities are bonds or preferred stocks at the time of issuance, but they usually become common stock later. Thus, common stockholders must recognize the potential dilution in their position before conversion takes place.

Example 16-3. The Temple Company issues $20,000 of 5 percent convertible preferred stock, and the conversion price is $40 per share. The company has 2,500 shares of common stock outstanding and expects to earn $11,000 a year after taxes for many years to come. Determine the effect of conversion on both earnings and control.

The number of additional shares on conversion is 500 or ($20,000/$40); consequently, the total number of common shares after conversion is 3,000 or (2,500 + 500). Earnings per share before and after the conversion are computed as shown in Table 16-2.

Table 16-2
Temple Company's Earnings per Share

	Before Conversion	After Conversion
Earnings after taxes	$11,000	$11,000
Less: preferred dividends	1,000	0
Earnings available for common stock	$10,000	$11,000
÷ Number of common shares	÷ 2,500	÷ 3,000
Earnings per share	$4.00	$3.67

Before preferred shares are converted into common shares, the preferred stockholders receive a 5 percent dividend a year ($1,000) and have no voice in management. On the other hand, the common stockholders have earnings per share of $4 and full control of the company. After all of the preferred shares are converted into common shares, however, the common stockholders have earnings per share of $3.67. Thus, earnings per share decline by $0.33 or 8.25 percent calculated by ($0.33/$4).

Once preferred shares are converted into common shares, the original common stockholders control only 83.3 percent or (2,500/3,000) of the company. This means that they lose 16.7 percent of the voting control.

We see how conversion produces a dilution of earnings and control for the original common stockholders. It is equally important that the existing common stockholders realize that this dilution could lower the market value of the common stock. But it should be noted that the company no longer has to pay fixed dividends on the preferred stocks; this factor has a favorable impact on earnings per share when earnings are low. There are many factors that make it extremely difficult to estimate the precise impact of the conversion on the market price of the common stock. The market price of most common stocks depends on such factors as the relative size of the conversion, the importance of control, the level and stability of earnings, and expansion plans.

Companies usually expect that their convertible securities will be converted into common stock within a certain length of time. But investors do not need to exercise the conversion privilege if earnings and stock prices are unfavorable. They may prefer to retain the fixed return and greater security of their convertibles.

When securities are both callable and convertible, it is possible under certain circumstances for the issuer to force conversion. These circumstances prevail when the conversion value is significantly higher than the call price. If convertible bonds are called when the conversion value is much higher than the call price, most investors are likely to exercise the conversion option rather than accept the low call price. The company will then not have to redeem many of the bonds for cash.

Example 16-4. The conversion price of a convertible debenture is $40, and the conversion ratio is 25. The market price of the common stock has increased to $55, and the call price is $1,050. Will the call of the issue force the bondholders to exchange their bonds for common stock?

A 20 percent premium of conversion value over call price is usually sufficient to force investors to convert their securities. If the company calls the bonds, bondholders can either exchange their bonds for common stock with a conversion value of $1,375 or (25 x $55) or allow the company to redeem the bond for $1,050 in cash. The excess of the conversion value over the call price is $325 or ($1,375 – $1,050) or 31 percent. Because the premium exceeds 20 percent, conversion takes place.

WARRANTS

A **warrant** is an option to purchase a stated number of common shares at a stated price during a prescribed period. Warrants pay no dividends, have no voting rights, and become worthless at expiration unless the price of the common stock exceeds the exercise price. The exercise price is the price at which a warrant allows the investor to purchase common stock. Like convertible provisions, warrants are attached to new stock or bond issues as sweeteners to increase their price and to reduce their yield. Because bonds with warrants allow investors to share in the company growth, they are willing to accept lower interest rates and less restrictive provisions.

Convertible securities do not bring in additional funds. When convertible securities are converted, common stock increases and the convertible securities are retired. When warrants are exercised, common stock and cash increase simultaneously. Companies can force conversion, but they cannot force warrant holders to exercise their option. Hence, they are unable to control when warrants will be exercised and when there will be an infusion of additional funds into the company.

Features

The stock-purchase warrant itself contains the provisions of the option. It specifies the number of authorized but unissued common shares that the holder can buy for each warrant held. Another important provision is the date on which the option expires. Some warrants run 10-12 years; a few warrants such as those of the Tri-Continental and Allegheny Corporations never mature. But most warrants have three-to-five year lives.

The warrant also specifies the option price at which it is exercisable. The option price can be fixed or increased over time. It usually exceeds the price of the stock at the time of issuance by 15 to 20 percent. If the stock price rises above the option price, warrant holders will surrender their warrants to purchase stock at the specified price. Warrants can be detachable or nondetachable. Holders of detachable warrants can sell them separately from the bond, whereas holders of nondetachable warrants can detach them only when they exercise their option and buy stock.

Warrant Valuation

Warrants have both a theoretical value and a market value. The difference between these two values represents the **warrant premium**. The theoretical value of a warrant may be found by

$$TV = (MV - OP)N \qquad (16\text{-}3)$$

where TV = theoretical value of a warrant, MV = market value of common stock, OP = option price of the warrant, and N = the number of shares that can be purchased with one warrant.

Example 16-5. A warrant entitles the holder to buy two shares of common stock at $20 per share. The current market price of the common stock is $25.

The theoretical value of the warrant is

$$(\$25 - \$20)\, 2 = \$10$$

Warrants usually sell above their theoretical values, creating a warrant premium. If warrants are well below their theoretical values, investors buy these warrants, exercise them, and sell the stock for immediate profits. To illustrate, suppose that the current market value of the warrant in Example 16-5 is $5. You can buy it for $5, use it to buy two shares of common stock for $40, and sell them for $50; you will earn $5. This arbitrage process continues until the market value exceeds the theoretical value. For this reason, the theoretical value of a warrant represents the lowest value that the warrant will sell for in the marketplace.

Warrant Premium

Figure 16-1 shows the typical relationship between the theoretical value of a warrant (solid line) and its market value (dashed line). The figure indicates that, up to the point where the option price equals the price of the stock, the premium increases as the stock price increases, but the market value exceeds the theoretical value for all stock prices. It is also important to note that the theoretical value of a warrant becomes zero whenever the option price exceeds the market price of the common stock.

Figure 16-1
Relationship Between Theoretical and Market Values of a Warrant at Various Stock Prices

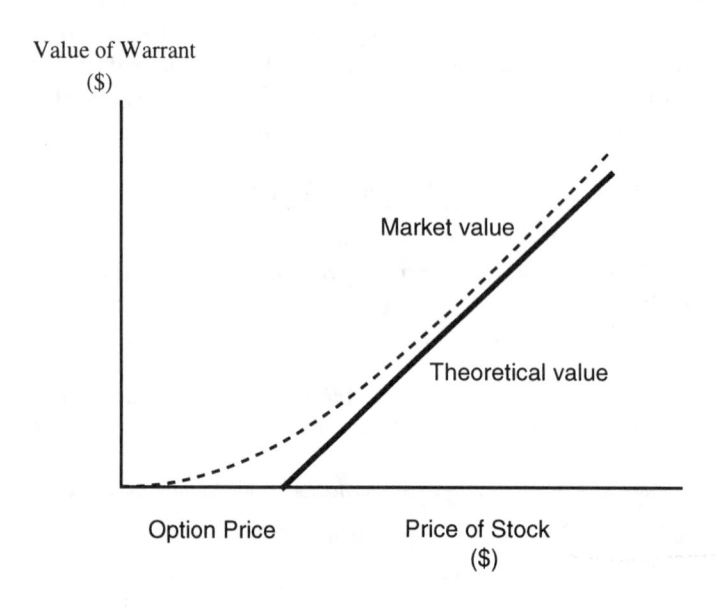

Why does the premium exist? Why should the market value of a warrant exceed its theoretical value? The answer lies in the fact that warrants are popular with speculators, because their price usually rises and falls at a faster rate than the price of the associated stock. The difference between the option price of the warrant and the stock price exceeds the change in the stock price over certain price ranges. These imbalanced changes cause the market value of a warrant to be higher than its theoretical value.

Example 16-6. A warrant entitles the holder to buy one share of common stock for $20 a share. The common stock currently sells for $25.

The theoretical value of the warrant is $5 or ($25 − $20). If the common stock rises in price by 100 percent to $50 per share, the theoretical value of the warrant increases from $5 to $30 or ($50 − $20); this increase represents a gain of 500 percent. At the same time, the amount of possible loss with the warrant is only $5, whereas the amount of possible loss with the common stock is $25. Because warrants have a greater profit potential and a smaller loss potential, they are very popular with speculators.

It is also important to recognize that the warrant premium declines as the stock price rises. This relationship occurs because the leverage of the warrant and the loss protection decrease as the stock price rises. If the common stock in Example 16-6 increases in price by another 100 percent to $100 per share, the theoretical value of the warrant increases from $30 to $80; this increase represents a gain of 167 percent. The percentage gain on the common stock remains the same, but the percentage gain on the warrant decreases from 500 percent to 167 percent. Furthermore, the loss potential on the warrant increase from $5 to $30. This $25 increase represents a 500 percent jump. A combination of the declining leverage impact and the increasing danger of losses cause the warrant premium to decline when the stock price rises.

FULLY DILUTED EARNINGS PER SHARE

Complicated economic activities and the need for a small number of comparative measurements have elevated earnings-per-share data to one of the most essential figures in financial analysis. Financial analysts and investors use earnings-per-share figures widely as a guide for making better decisions about firm valuation, expected earnings per share, and expected dividends per share. For these reasons, the Accounting Principles Board (APB) Opinions No. 9 (1966) and No. 15 (1969) recommended the disclosure of earnings-per-share data in the income statement. These two opinions played an important role in increasing the frequency of appearance of earnings-per-share figures in companies' annual reports and financial advisory services such as Moody's.

The computation of earnings-per-share ratios requires dividing earnings available for common stockholders by the associated number of common shares. If companies have such securities as convertibles and bonds with warrants, these securities may have to be counted as common stock to increase the usefulness of earnings-per-share data. Because many different types of securities exist, there could be many ways to compute earnings per share. However, the APB Opinion No. 15 suggested two separate computations: primary earnings per share and fully diluted earnings per share.

To compute the primary earnings per share, we should determine the weighted average number of common shares outstanding during the year plus the number of shares represented by common-stock equivalents. Common-stock equivalents include convertible securities, warrants, and all stock options that come within the limits of a specific formula at the time of issuance. To compute the fully diluted earnings per share, we have to know the basis of the computation employed for primary earnings per share plus the number of shares represented by those securities that have a dilutive effect but were not classified as common-stock equivalents. The major purpose of this computation is to indicate the maximum possible dilution of current earnings per share on a prospective basis. Because companies must disclose their fully diluted earnings per share in their financial statements, investors are unlikely to overlook the potential dilution that may come from convertibles and warrants.

Summary

The sale of common stock involves the dilution of both voting rights and earnings but it involves no fixed charge and no amortization. This chapter covered such important topics as accounting terms applied to common stock, rights of common stockholders, and reasons for use of common stock.

In the previous chapter and the first half of this chapter, we examined bonds, preferred stock, and common stock. In the second half of this chapter, we examined how companies can make their securities more marketable and less costly through the use of convertibles and warrants. Although the purpose of these two instruments is the same, convertibles do not bring in additional funds, whereas warrants do.

List of Key Terms

net worth
authorized stock
treasury stock
book value
majority voting system
class B stock
convertible securities
conversion value
warrant

par value
issued stock
outstanding stock
legal or stated capital
cumulative voting system
class A stock
conversion ratio
conversion premium
warrant premium

Problems

16-1 Several disgruntled stockholders intend to replace as many directors as possible. The company has nine directors and 200,000 shares outstanding.

(a) How many shares should the dissident stockholders control to elect at least one director under a majority voting system?
(b) How many shares should the dissident stockholders control to elect one director under a cumulative voting system?
(c) How many directors can the disgruntled stockholders elect if they control 80,001 shares?
(d) These dissident stockholders want to elect six board members. How many additional shares must they acquire to achieve their objective? (Assume that they own 80,001 shares at the present time.)

16-2 A company has 20,000 preferred shares outstanding and it has not paid its $4 preferred dividends for the past three years. How much in dividends can the company pay to its common stockholders under each of the following circumstances?

(a) Current earnings are $350,000 and the company intends to limit dividends to its current earnings.
(b) Current earnings are $420,000 and the company wishes to retain 20 percent of earnings available to common stockholders.

16-3 A company intends to offer $200,000 of convertible bonds with an initial conversion premium of 40 percent and with a call price of $1,050. The bonds sell at their face value of $1,000 per bond and the market price of the company's common stock is $25 per share.

(a) Compute the conversion price.
(b) Compute the conversion ratio.
(c) Determine the initial conversion value of each bond.
(d) Determine the number of new common shares to be issued if all bonds are converted.
(e) The market price of the common stock has increased to $40 per share. Do you think that the call of the issue will force the bondholders to convert their bonds into common stock?

16-4 A company intends to issue $100,000 of 6 percent convertible bonds with a conversion price of $50 per share. The company has 50,000 shares of common stock outstanding and expects to earn $500,000 before interest and taxes a year. The federal income tax rate is 50 percent.

(a) Compute the earnings per share before and after the conversion. (Assume that all bonds are converted.)
(b) Determine the effect of the conversion on the control of the firm.

16-5 A warrant entitles the holder to purchase two shares of common stock at $30 a share. The option price is adjusted downward to protect the warrants against dilution in the event of a stock dividend or when the stock price is less than the $30 exercise price. The current market price of the common stock is $35 a share. The company issues rights to purchase one new share of common stock at $20 for every two shares held.

(a) What is the theoretical value of one right before the stock goes ex-rights?
(b) What is the theoretical value of one warrant before the rights offering?
(c) What is the theoretical value of one share after the stock goes ex-rights?
(d) What is the subscription price of one warrant after the rights offering?

17

DIVIDEND POLICY AND RETAINED EARNINGS

Corporate dividend policy determines the division of earnings between dividends and retained earnings. Retained earnings are the primary internal source of long-term funds used to finance corporate growth needs. On the other hand, dividends represent the immediate cash flows that accrue to stockholders. Corporate growth and dividends, then, are desirable but conflicting goals. Thus, the important issue is how a company should divide its income between retained earnings and dividends.

This chapter has five major sections. The first section examines the key factors which affect the company's cash dividend policy. The second section considers the three major types of dividend policies commonly in use. The third section discusses the relationship between dividend policy and the price of the common stock. The fourth section discusses two noncash methods of dividend payments: stock dividends and stock splits. The last section of the chapter discusses stock repurchases as an alternative to cash dividends.

FACTORS AFFECTING DIVIDEND POLICY

The board of directors of a corporation has the discretionary power to declare dividends. When the directors declare a dividend, they specify a date of record. Holders of records on that date are entitled to receive the declared dividend. The stock is said to sell **ex-dividend** after the fourth business day prior to the date of record. That is, the buyers of the stock after the fourth business day preceding the date of record are not entitled to receive the declared dividend. When the stock goes ex-dividend, its price should decline by the amount of the dividend. But this effect is not that simple to measure, because there are many factors that influence the market price of the stock.

Legal Basis of Dividends

Although state laws and court decisions about dividend policy are complicated, they clearly state that dividends should not be paid out of capital. There are four legal restrictions that confront the company with respect to cash dividend payments: the net profit rule, the capital impairment rule, the insolvency rule, and the cash retention rule. These four rules are not important in most dividend decisions, but they affect some companies.

The **net profit rule** requires companies to pay dividends from their current and past earnings. Under this rule, no company can pay more in cash dividends than the sum of its current and past earnings. The **capital impairment rule** prohibits the payment of dividends if that would impair capital. Some states define capital as the par value of common stock, and others define it as the par value of the common stock plus the capital surplus. The **insolvency rule** forbids the payment of cash dividends if the company is insolvent, legally or technically. **Legal insolvency** occurs when liabilities exceed assets; **technical insolvency** arises when the company is unable to pay its creditors as obligations become due. The **cash retention rule** derives from the Internal Revenue Code which prohibits the undue or excess accumulation of earnings. This provision is designed to prevent the company from retaining a large portion of earnings so that its stockholders can avoid the payment of income taxes.

In addition to these legal constraints, there are many factors that influence dividend policy. Before taking up the common types of dividend policies, we will consider some of these other factors.

Liquidity

Because dividends represent a cash outflow, companies with a stronger liquidity position have a greater ability to pay cash dividends. Past earnings retained in the company are already invested in various assets rather than being held as cash. To give them flexibility and a protection against uncertainty, many companies desire to maintain some liquidity cushion. For these reasons, even some profitable companies may not be able to pay cash dividends from time to time.

Access to External Funds

The greater the ability of the company to obtain external funds, the greater its ability to pay cash dividends. Most large companies with a good record of performance have easy access to capital markets and other forms of external funds such as bank loans. In contrast, most small and new companies have a restricted ability to raise equity or debt funds from capital markets; consequently, they have to retain more earnings. Large and well-established companies are thus more likely to pay cash dividends than small or new ones.

Timing of Investment Opportunities

Investment opportunities are directly related to the company's financial requirements. Growing companies need large sums of money to finance their capital expenditures and to maintain their existing assets. Moreover, the managers of these growth companies may feel that internal expansion and continued growth are more important than the payment of cash dividends. Because retained earnings are a primary source of internal funds, the growing companies are likely to pay lower cash dividends. If investment opportunities occur sporadically, however, the retention of more earnings may not be justified to finance these investment projects.

Control

Management must also consider the effect of dividend policy on the ability of its stockholders to maintain control. Large dividend payments may make it necessary for the company to raise capital funds at a later time through the sale of stock or bonds. The sale of additional common stock may dilute the control of the dominant group in the company, because these stockholders cannot subscribe for enough additional shares. The sale of additional bonds may increase the riskiness of the company. Reliance on internal funds to maintain control reduces the amount of cash dividend payment.

Debt Repayment and Debt Contracts

There are a number of ways to retire bonds: lump-sum payment at maturity, amortization, sinking-fund accumulation, or a call provision. These debt repayment methods influence dividend policy. For example, if the company decides to call its bonds, it must retain more earnings.

Debt contracts and other forms of contract such as preferred stock agreement may restrict the ability of the company to pay cash dividends. Protective covenants in these contracts either prohibit the payment of cash dividends or limit their amount.

Tax Consideration

The tax position of the company's stockholders can have a considerable effect on its dividend policy. If a company is held by a number of wealthy stockholders in high-income brackets, it is likely to pay lower cash dividends so that its owners can take their income in the form of capital gains as opposed to dividends. Capital gains are subject to lower personal tax rates. In contrast, most low-income stockholders prefer a high payout of earnings, because their tax position is not a source of concern.

ALTERNATIVE DIVIDEND POLICIES

Although there are a considerable number of possible dividend policies, the more commonly used ones are stable dollar amounts, regular and extra dividends, and target payout ratios.

Rationale for a Stable Dividend Policy

The policy of a stable dollar amount per share is sometimes called a **stable dividend policy**. Evidence indicates that most companies tend to pursue a relatively stable dividend policy. Corporate profits have fluctuated widely with changes in the level of business activity over the years, but dividend payments have been relatively stable.

There is no conclusive empirical evidence which indicates a consistent relationship between dividend policy and stock prices. But most writers and most business executives tend to believe that stable dividend policies lead to higher stock prices.

Example 17-1. Assume that two streams of dividends are equally risky and that they have an equal present value of $6.34 (see Table 17-1). Assume further that these two companies earn the same amount of money each year and that their earnings are equally cyclical.

Table 17-1
Present Value of Companies A and B

Company	Present Value at 10%	1st Year	2nd Year	3rd Year	4th Year
A	$6.34	$2	$2.0	$2	$2.00
B	6.34	4	0.5	1	2.25

It should be clear from this presentation that Company A maintains a stable dividend over time, whereas Company B changes the absolute amount of dividend to match the underlying trend of earnings. Although the present value of dividends paid by these two companies over a four year period is identical, we may find that the market price per share of Company A is higher than that of Company B. Investors may well place a positive utility on dividend stability, and the discount rate of 10 percent does not reflect this utility. But a higher stock price reflects utility in stability.

There are a number of reasons why investors may pay a higher price for the stock of the company that maintains a relatively stable dividend over time. First, an unbroken record of dividend payments may be very important to resolve uncertainty in the minds of investors. If the company does not reduce its dividends during temporary financial reverses, investors may believe that the future of the company is better than the reduction in profits indicates. Second, many stockholders live on dividend income. To avoid inconvenience from fluctuating dividends, such stockholders may well pay a premium for the company that offers dividend stability. Third, fiduciary institutions such as pension funds and trustees are permitted to invest in only those securities that have an uninterrupted pattern of dividends; this requirement encourages pursuance of a stable dividend policy.

For these reasons, most companies follow the stable dividend policy. It is important to recognize, however, that management cannot fool the market forever. When the company has a steadily downward trend in earnings, a stable dividend cannot convey an impression of underlying stability.

Other Dividend Policies

Some companies establish a policy of a constant dollar dividend as a regular dividend. If earnings are higher than normal in a given period, the directors declare an extra dividend in addition to the regular dividend. This dividend policy is particularly suitable for companies with unstable earnings, but it fails to resolve uncertainty in the minds of investors about what their dividend income will be.

A very few companies follow a policy of target dividend-payout ratio over the long run. A dividend payout ratio refers to dividends as a percentage of profits after taxes. The company merely sets a target percentage of earnings to be paid out in the form of dividends each period. Some individuals argue that dividends are adjusted to changes in earnings with a time lag. When management is sure that the increase in earnings can be maintained, it will increase its dividend-payout ratio.

THEORIES OF DIVIDEND POLICY

The first and second sections of this chapter discussed the factors affecting dividend policy and the types of dividend policies widely used in practice. This section deals with the question of whether dividend policy affects stockholder wealth.

Dividend policy may not affect the value of the firm. This dividend policy is sometimes called the **residual theory of dividends**. Because this theory assumes that investors do not differentiate between dividends and capital gains, dividends are not paid until the company has exhausted its profitable investment opportunities. In other words, investors would prefer to have their company retain earnings as long as its investment opportunities promise a return greater than the required rate of return. If it still has earnings left over, they should then be distributed to its stockholders in the form of cash dividends.

Another school of thought suggests that a strong case can be made for the relevance of dividends, because they eliminate uncertainty in the eyes of investors. This school holds that dividends are less risky than the capital gains that will result from earnings retention, and thus, investors prefer dividends. Accordingly, investors are willing to pay a premium for the stock that pays the greater current dividend.

Optimum Dividend Policy

Because the primary objective of the firm is to maximize stockholder wealth, it must attempt to establish a dividend policy that will achieve this objective. The residual theory of a dividend policy states that, to maximize its stock price, the firm should retain as much earnings as it needs to finance all profitable investment opportunities; only the remaining amount, if any, should be distributed in the form of dividends. Another school of thought holds that investors prefer dividends and consequently place a positive utility on current dividends.

How can we reconcile these two conflicting theories on dividend policy? In theory, the optimum dividend policy should combine the company's investment opportunities and investors' preference for dividends over capital gains. There are a number of arguments to support the notion that investors have a systematic preference for current dividends over capital gains. These include the desire for current income in the form of dividends; legal restrictions that require institutional investor to buy stocks with stable dividend-payment records; and the **informational content of dividends**, which communicate information to investors about the firm's profitability.

It is important to recognize that investors invest in different firms for different purposes. Some wealthy people invest in growth firms for capital gains with an understanding that dividends will not be paid for some time. Some others invest in firms that pay large dividends in order to assure a steady source of income. Finally, there is the middle group, who invest in firms that pay not only some dividends but also promise some capital gains.

If investors have a net preference for capital gains over dividends, the company is likely to conform more to the residual theory of dividend policy determined by the profitability of its investment opportunities. In contrast, if investors have a net preference for dividends as opposed to capital gains, the company is likely to pay dividends in excess of unused earnings. Although investors have a net preference for dividends, stock price will not continue to increase with dividend payout. If we start with a zero dividend-payout ratio, share price will increase with dividend payout. This is because dividends become very important to investors when they are first declared. However, dividends become less and less important as investors receive more and more cash dividends, because cash dividends may be subject to higher tax rates than capital gains. Thus, at a critical turning point, the subsequent payment of additional dividends causes the stock price to decline. Hence, the optimum dividend policy is determined by balancing the investors' net preference for current dividends with the company's investment opportunities. The remaining portion of this chapter considers some alternatives to cash dividends.

STOCK DIVIDENDS AND STOCK SPLITS

From a management point of view, stock dividends and stock splits can be very useful tools to replace the payment of cash dividends. Although the two are similar in nature, they are quite different from an accounting point of view.

Stock Dividends

A **stock dividend** represents a distribution of additional shares of stock to the existing stockholders. It involves nothing more than a bookkeeping transfer from retained earnings to capital stock accounts (common stock plus capital surplus); a stockholder's percentage ownership remains constant.

Example 17-2. A company pays a 10 percent stock dividend, increasing the number of outstanding shares by 100. The fair market value of the stock at the time of the dividend is $50. Given the following stockholders' equity on its balance sheet, how will the balance sheet change after stock dividends?

Common stock (1,000 shares at $10 par)	$10,000
Capital surplus	15,000
Retained earnings	25,000
Net worth	$50,000

The accounting transfer from retained earnings to capital stock accounts should be based on the fair market value of the stock at the time of the stock dividend. Hence, this stock dividend requires accountants to transfer $5,000 (or $50 x 100 shares) to the two capital stock accounts. Because the par value of the stock should stay the same, the common stock account increases by $1,000 (or $10 x 100 shares); the remaining balance of $4,000 goes into the capital surplus account. The balance sheet after the stock dividend reads as follows:

Common stock (1,100 shares at $10 par)	$11,000
Capital surplus	19,000
Retained earnings	20,000
Net worth	$50,000

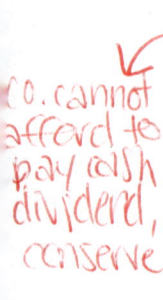

After the stock dividend, the par value per share and the net worth remain the same. But the number of common shares outstanding increases by 10 percent; consequently, both book value per share and earnings per share decrease by 10 percent. If earnings per share and dividends per share decline proportionally, the market price per share of the common stock should also decline.

Stock Splits

A **stock split** is an alternative to the stock dividend as a means of increasing the number of shares outstanding. Although the two are similar in an economic sense, there are two important differences. First, the stock split does not involve the bookkeeping transfer from retained earnings to capital stock accounts. Second, it usually involves the payment of more shares than the stock dividend. Normally, the New York Stock Financial Accounting Standards Board encourage that stock distribution in excess of 20 to 25 percent be treated as a stock split.

In a two-for-one split, each stockholder receives two shares for each one previously held. Thus, the par value of the stock, book value per share, and earnings per share are cut in half. The stock split is also likely to cut the market price of the stock in half. The common stock, capital surplus, and retained earnings accounts stay the same; the net worth, of course, remains unchanged.

There is also a **reverse split**. The reverse split reduces the number of common shares outstanding and thus involves a proportional increase in the par value of the stock, book value per share, and earnings per share.

Advantages and Disadvantages

Some argue that stock dividends and stock splits are used for different purposes. The former is generally used to conserve cash, whereas the latter is usually employed for a substantial increase in the number of common shares outstanding. In the preceding section, we also saw that the two are different from an accounting point of view. However, from a practical standpoint, there is little difference between them. Therefore, the advantages and disadvantages outlined below apply to both.

Income exists only when the increment in wealth is realized. Cash dividends represent a transfer of assets to stockholders and thus increase stockholder wealth; they represent income to the recipients. But both stock dividends and stock splits do not involve a transfer of corporate assets to stockholders; consequently, they do not represent income to the recipients. Basically, both stock dividends and stock splits have nothing to do with the accounting principles of income determination and balance sheet valuation. The two are financial maneuvers employed by some corporations to achieve a number of objectives.

Stock dividends are frequently used to conserve cash and still appease investors' desire for dividends. Some companies use stock dividends as a substitute for cash dividends and others employ them as a supplement. The availability of profitable investment opportunities and financial difficulty are the most commonly cited cases where companies use stock dividends as a substitute for cash dividends. In contrast, some companies pay cash dividends as well as stock dividends for the same period. It should be obvious that they see stock dividends as a supplement to cash dividends. Although stock dividends do not have a real value in either case, stockholders are likely to believe that the stock dividends represent something they did not have before.

Stock dividends, and stock splits in particular, are used to keep the market price of the stock within a **popular trading range**. Many companies believe in the existence of such a trading range for their stocks, and they attempt to keep their stock prices within the range. If there is such a popular trading range, a large volume of low-priced stocks should provide a broader and more stable market for the stock.

Another advantage is that stock dividends involve a transfer from retained earnings to capital stock accounts and permanently commit them to the business in a legal sense. Finally, capital gains may be realized when additional shares received as dividends are sold, and they may be subject to lower tax rates.

One of the disadvantages associated with both stock dividends and stock splits is that they are more costly to administer than cash dividends. Other disadvantages relate to a distorted report of growth rates and to an increase in dividend payments. Investment analysts adjust earnings per share for stock splits and significant stock dividends, but they do not always adjust them for small stock dividends. If earnings per share are not adjusted, the reported growth rate will be smaller than the true or adjusted growth rate. Stock dividends increase the number of shares outstanding. If the company maintains the same amount of cash dividends per share after the stock dividend, the total payment is increased proportionally.

REPURCHASE OF COMMON STOCK

The repurchase of common stock is an increasingly popular alternative to cash dividends. When companies have excess cash, they can use this money to repurchase their own shares rather than to pay more cash dividends. The Securities and Exchange Commission imposes certain disclosure requirements on companies that repurchase their own common stock. However, state laws allow corporations to buy their own common shares either in the stock market or through a direct tender offer to stockholders. (A **tender offer** is a formal offer by a company to buy a specified number of its own shares or the shares of another company within a specified time period.)

Treasury stock, as was noted in Chapter 16, is the name given to the shares of common stock that have been issued and then repurchased by the company. When the company buys its own common stock, the accounting entries involve a reduction in cash and the establishment of a treasury stock account. Because treasury stock represents a deduction from stockholders' equity, it does not play an economic role in the affairs of the company, carries no vote, and receives no dividends.

Example 17-3. A company earned $2,200 after taxes, and 50 percent of this amount turned out to be excess cash. The current market price per share of its stock is $10 and there are 1,100 shares outstanding. The company can use the $1,100 to repurchase 100 of its shares in the stock market or it can pay a cash dividend of $1 per share.

If the company decides to buy 100 of its own outstanding shares, the effect of the repurchase on the earnings per share and the market price of the remaining shares can be obtained as follows:

1. The current earnings per share is $2 = $2,200 ÷ 1,100 shares.
2. The current price-earnings ratio is 5 times = $10 ÷ $2.
3. The earnings per share after the repurchase of 100 shares is $2.2 = $2,200 ÷ 1,000 shares.

4. The expected market price after the repurchase of 100 shares is the current price-earnings ratio multiplied by the earnings per share after the repurchase, or $11 = 5 \times \$2.2$.

It should be obvious from this analysis that stockholders would receive benefits of $1 per share in any case, either a $1 cash dividend or a $1 increase in stock price. It is important to note that this result occurs only if we assume first that the company could repurchase its shares for exactly $11 per share, and second, that the current price-earnings ratio of 5 would stay the same. If the company could buy its shares for less than $11 a share, the repurchase of common stock would be better than cash dividends for the remaining stockholders. The reverse would be true if the company had to pay more than $11 a share. Moreover, the price-earnings ratio could be affected by the repurchase operation. We will take up some factors that might affect the price-earnings ratio in the following section.

Advantages and Disadvantages

If stockholders are indifferent toward capital gains versus cash dividends, the repurchase operation and the cash dividend will have the same effect on the value of the stock. But we saw in the preceding section that this indifference is debatable, because capital gains have certain tax advantages over cash dividends. Profits earned on stock repurchases are taxed at the capital gains tax rate, whereas cash dividends are taxed at the stockholders' marginal tax rate. Because the capital gains tax rate may be lower than the ordinary tax rate, there is some bias in favor of stock repurchases as opposed to cash dividends. Moreover, cash dividends are taxed immediately, but capital gains from stock repurchases are not taxed until the stock is actually sold. In other words, the repurchase operation allows stockholders to postpone the bulk of their capital gains taxes.

Repurchased stock can be used for acquisitions, the conversion of convertible securities, and stock dividends. It can also be used when warrants and stock options are exercised. Such purposes need either new shares or treasury shares. Many financial managers believe that it is more convenient and less costly to use treasury stock than newly issued stock for these purposes. Thus, although we stated in the beginning of this section that stock repurchases are used as an alternative to cash dividends, corporations can use them for many different purposes.

Most companies are reluctant to increase cash dividends unless they are confident that the new dividend can be sustained in the future. They are equally reluctant to cut cash dividends simply because earnings are not as high as expected. When surplus funds are only temporary, the company can conceal the distribution of these funds in the form of stock repurchases rather than paying more cash dividends that cannot be maintained.

There are a number of disadvantages of stock repurchases. One of them has to do with the fact that cash dividends have certain tax benefits. The Internal Revenue Code allows individuals to exclude a certain amount of their dividend income for federal income tax purposes. Also, from a legal standpoint the company must be careful not to rely on a steady program of stock repurchases in place of cash dividends. If the Internal Revenue Service concludes that the stock repurchases are an attempt to permit stockholders to avoid the payment of taxes on dividends, it may impose a penalty on the firm under the improper-accumulation-of-earnings provision.

If the company pays a high price for the repurchased stock, this is disadvantageous to the remaining stockholders. When the company makes a formal offer to stockholders to buy a given number of its shares, the bid price is usually set above the current market price in order to attract sellers. If the tender offer is used to block a takeover attempt, the price of the repurchased stock may be even higher. Suppose that company A makes a tender offer to the stockholders of Company B. Company B is likely to counter with a tender offer of its own at a higher price. Thus, to block the tender offer from the other company, Company B must pay a higher price for its repurchased shares.

The transaction costs involved in the sale of securities are another reason to favor cash dividends over stock repurchases. If cash dividends are not paid, stockholders may have to sell a part of their holdings in order to meet their cash needs. These transactions can be considerable for small stockholders, because they vary inversely with the size of the sale.

Finally, the repeated use of stock repurchases may create a climate that management is incompetent. Most stockholders know that if the company has many profitable investment opportunities, it cannot have surplus funds to buy its own shares. The location of good investment opportunities is indeed one of the most important management responsibilities. Thus, some people may feel that the announcement of stock repurchases is almost identical with announcing that management cannot identify attractive investment opportunities.

A Comment on Stock Repurchases

Regular and systematic stock repurchases should be avoided because of the associated uncertainties, such as the tax effect of such a program and the market price of the stock. Hence, they should be used only for certain specific purposes or only for a short period of time. However, stock repurchases have distinct advantages such as an increase in earnings per share, certain tax benefits, and a significant shift in capital structure within in a short period of time.

When the company intends to repurchase a specified number of its outstanding shares in the market or through a tender offer, it should offer all of its shareholders an equal opportunity to sell their shares. Similarly, the company should announce its repurchase program in advance, and it should also make all of its shareholders aware of its intentions for such a program.

SUMMARY

Dividend policy is of vital importance because it affects a company's investment opportunities, stock prices, financial structure, flow of funds, and liquidity position. Factors that affect dividend policy include legal constraints, liquidity position, access to external funds, investment opportunities, control, protective covenants in debt contracts, and tax effect. The list is not exhaustive.

There are many possible dividend policies, but the following three are most widely used in practice: stable dollar amounts, regular and extra dividends, and target payout ratios. The stable dividend policy is the one followed by most companies, mainly because it resolves uncertainty in the minds of investors.

The residual theory of dividend policy depends on the relationship between the company's investment opportunities and the investor's investment opportunities. If the company can earn a higher return on its reinvested earnings than investors can earn on their dividends received, then dividends should not be paid to maximize stockholder wealth. However, this dividend policy may not be ideal for all corporations, because there are many investors who prefer cash dividends over capital gains. Hence, the optimum dividend policy should combine the company's investment opportunities and investors' preferences for cash dividends over capital gains.

This chapter also covered such topics as stock dividends, stock splits, and stock repurchases. The first two are basically financial maneuvers that have nothing to do with the accounting principles of income determination. Normally, they are used either as a replacement for cash dividends or as a supplement to them, but they do not have any real value. Stock repurchases are an increasingly popular alternative to cash dividends. In theory, both stock repurchases and cash dividends give the same amount of distribution to stockholders. Although there are legitimate reasons for stock repurchases, they involve greater uncertainty than cash dividends.

LIST OF KEY TERMS

ex-dividend
capital impairment rule
technical insolvency
stable dividend policy
residual theory of dividends
stock dividend
reverse split
tender offer

net profit rule
legal insolvency
cash retention rule
dividend payout ratio
informational content of dividends
stock split
popular trading range

PROBLEMS

17-1 The Miller Bread Company earned $70,000 last year and retained $21,000. What is the dividend payout ratio?

17-2 The stockholders' equity portion of the Cherryhill Tire Company is as follows:

Common stock (1,200 shares at $10 par)	$12,000
Capital surplus	7,000
Retained earnings	23,000
Net worth	$42,000

The company pays a 15 percent stock dividend, increasing the number of outstanding shares to 1,380 shares. The firm market value of the stock at the time of the dividend is $18. Show the company's balance sheet after the stock dividend.

17-3 The ABC Company has 40,000 common shares outstanding. Its optimum capital structure and the after-tax cost of each capital are as follows:

	Weight	After-Tax Cost
Bonds	40%	2.5%
Preferred stock	50	6.0
Common stock	10	10.0

Current earnings are $80,000, all of which are available for reinvestment or dividends. All of the four projects under consideration are expected to earn at least 7 percent on their respective investment. The funds required to undertake these four projects are estimated to be $200,000.

(a) Compute the weighted average cost of capital.
(b) Compute the amount of dividends to be paid out if funds will not be reinvested at a rate of return less than the cost of capital.

17-4 A company has the following balance sheet:

Cash	$52,000	Common stock	
		(1,000 shares at $10 par)	$10,000
Capital surplus	20,000	Retained earnings	22,000

The company pays a 10 percent stock dividend and the fair market value of the stock is $20 per share. How would the balance sheet change after the stock dividend?

17-5 Joan Walker is a major stockholder of the Troy Company whose current earnings are $200,000, 50 percent of which is paid in dividends. The company has 25,000 common shares outstanding and Walker owns 5,000 shares. The current market price of the stock is $10 per share. Because Joan Walker has not been satisfied with managerial policy, she is willing to sell her holdings back to the company at a price of $10 a share. The valuation of the stock is based on a constant price-earnings ratio of 1.25.

(a) Determine the dividend per share before the repurchase of Walker's shares.
(b) Determine the market price of the stock while dividends are on.
(c) Determine the dividend per share after the repurchase of the shares. (Assume that dividends will not be paid on Walker's shares if repurchased.)
(d) Should the company repurchase Walker's shares?

17-6 A company has the following balance sheet:

Cash	$ 15,000	Accounts payable	$ 25,000
Accounts receivable	25,000	Common stock	35,000
Inventory	40,000	Paid-in surplus	25,000
Fixed assets	20,000	Retained earnings	15,000
Total assets	$100,000	Total claims	$100,000

The company operates in a state that defines legal capital as common stock.

(a) What is the maximum amount of dividends that the company can legally pay?
(b) What is the possible maximum dividend that the company can pay if it can reduce cash and accounts receivable by $5,000 each but it must maintain other asset balances at present levels?
(c) If the company pays out the maximum amount of dividends specified in (b), determine the balance sheet after the dividend payment.

17-7 Companies A and B are competitors. They are in the same markets and have similar characteristics in terms of size, operating leverage, and the like. Although both companies have had identical earnings per share for the past six years, the price of company A's stock has been consistently lower than the price of company B's stock. The earnings per share, dividends per share, and market price per share for these two companies during the last six years are as follows:

	Company A			Company B		
Year	EPS	Dividend	Market Price	EPS	Dividend	Market Price
1975	$5	$2.50	$20	$5	$1.75	$20
1986	3	1.50	15	3	1.75	18
1987	2	1.00	10	2	1.75	17
1988	-1	0.00	7	-1	1.75	15
1989	8	4.00	17	8	1.75	20
1990	3	1.50	14	3	1.75	19

What factors have caused the price of company A's stock to be consistently lower than the price of company B's stock?

18

TERM LOANS AND LEASES

Intermediate-term (term) loans are usually defined as debts with maturities of between one and ten years. They are sought primarily to finance fixed assets and permanent current assets. Repayment must usually come from profits rather than liquidation of the assets financed. This chapter covers three major sources of intermediate-term funds: bank term loans, other term loans, and leases.

BANK TERM LOANS

Bank **term loans** are those whose maturity exceeds one year. Although the one-year boundary is rather widely accepted, there is no definite line at the other end. The maturities of term loans depend on the type of arrangements, but they usually range from one to ten years.

Because short-term loans are highly liquid and relatively free of risk, banks had favored them in the past. But this attitude has undergone significant changes over the years. The factors that contributed to these changes include (1) increased lending capacity and higher operating expenses, (2) increased deposit insurance, and (3) the Depository Institutions Deregulation and Monetary Control Act of 1980.

Characteristics

Bank term loans are normally in the form of long-term notes and are discharged under the amortization method. The **amortization method** requires installment payments on a monthly, quarterly, semiannual, or annual basis. The repayment provisions sometimes call for an extra-large payment in the last year, known as a **balloon payment**.

The interest rate on term loans depends on many factors, such as the general level of interest rates and the financial situation of the borrower. But the interest rate on a term loan is generally higher than the interest rate on short-term loans. This is because the term loan is less liquid and more risky.

Because term loans involve more risk, banks normally require security on a greater proportion of term loans than short-term loans. Many companies may be able to obtain unsecured short-term loans but have to secure their term loans.

Although there are several different sources of funds to repay term loans, the borrower's net cash flows (earnings after taxes plus noncash charges) are the common source.

Thus, lenders are much more concerned with the borrower's earning power than any other factors. Other important credit factors include the borrower's net worth and character and the value of the collateral pledged.

Advantages and Disadvantages

Generally, notes are issued to a single lender or a relatively small number of lenders, whereas bonds are issued to a large number of public security holders. Because the borrower deals directly with a single lender or a small number of lenders, term loans provide a great deal of flexibility. Such terms as the repayment schedule and the maturity date can be revised as conditions change. Direct negotiation can enable the borrowing firm to arrange such a loan to meet its exact financing needs. Term loans are available to small firms that have no access to the capital markets. In addition, large firms may find it faster, simpler, and cheaper to obtain a bank term loan than to float a security issue publicly.

The limitations on the maturity and the amount are serious disadvantages for term loans. Some term loans have a maximum maturity of ten years, but most have maturities much shorter than this maximum. Although higher percentages are sometimes allowed for secured loans, the maximum amount a national bank can lend to a single borrower on an unsecured basis is 10 percent of its capital and surplus. Other disadvantages include kickers and an acceleration clause. **Kickers** allow the lender to share profits and to buy the stock of the borrower. The acceleration clause makes the entire loan immediately due and payable if the borrower fails to make the required payments or to live up to other loan terms.

Revolving Credits

A **revolving credit** refers to a legal commitment on the part of the bank to extend credit up to a certain amount over a specified period of time, usually two or three years. Most revolving credits require the borrower to pay a small amount of commitment fees on the unused portion of the credit. These loans are sometimes combined by banks with ordinary term loans to provide both flexibility and installment repayments. For example, the firm may arrange a two-year revolving credit convertible into a ten-year term loan at the end of two years.

Provisions of the Loan Agreement

The term loan usually involves a large amount of money for an extended period of time. The lender incorporates certain provisions into the loan agreement to safeguard itself. These provisions can be divided into three broad categories: prohibitive provisions, restrictive provisions, and affirmative provisions. The number of the provisions and their form depend somewhat on the financial strength of the borrower and the competence of its management.

Prohibitive provisions are those that prohibit certain acts of the borrowing firm unless it obtains prior consent from its lender. The objectives of such provisions are (a) to prevent the sale of assets that might weaken the financial strength of the firm, and (b) to protect the assumption of obligations that might reduce the firm's ability to repay the loan. These provisions forbid the sale of assets (including accounts receivable), the lease of assets, the pledge of assets, additional long-term debt from other lenders, and loans to other borrowers.

Restrictive provisions are those that allow the borrowing firm to do certain things but restrict their magnitude. The objectives of such provisions are (a) to increase the liquidity position of the firm, and (b) to preserve its ability to repay the loan. These provisions limit cash dividends, the amount of such payments as salaries and bonuses to employees, and capital expenditures.

Affirmative provisions are a group of obligations imposed on the borrower. The objectives of such provisions are (a) to assure the continuation of the firm's current management, and (b) to observe its financial performance on a continuous basis. These provisions require the firm to maintain a specified minimum amount of working capital, to carry life insurance on its key officers, and to submit its periodic financial statements for review.

These provisions may appear complex and strict. But such terms and restrictions are an expression of sound banking principles. They are designed to protect the bank, but they should also safeguard the financial condition of the borrower and its ability to repay the loan. It is important to note that some of the provisions should change as conditions change because they become obsolete and too restrictive.

Criteria for Evaluating Bank Term Loans

The effective use of bank credit requires the financial manager to understand a number of criteria that banks use to evaluate their loan applicants. Much has been written and said about the fundamental obligations of banks to their customers and communities. But it is important to recognize that commercial banks are not charitable institutions. They are private businesses that must make profits for their stockholders.

Most banks find their highest risks in their loan portfolio, but bank term loans are also typically the most profitable bank asset. Credit risk and liquidity pressure are two major types of risk that are usually greater for bank term loans than for most other banking assets. Credit risk is the possibility that promised payments of principal and interest will not be made. This risk depends on many factors such as credit weaknesses, wars, major economic downturns, and changes in consumer demand. Liquidity pressure is the possibility that customer demands for funds may compel banks to sell or collect credit-worthy assets at a loss. In times of high economic activity, heavy demands for loans from their customers and depositors' demands for their money may require the sale of forced collection of credit-worthy assets at a loss or without an adequate return.

Short-term bank loans are relatively free of these risks because they are inherently self-liquidating. Most short-term bank loans are designed to support seasonal buildups of inventories and receivables; thus, they generate the funds for their repayment in the normal course of business.

As noted, term loans involve greater risks than short-term loans. Thus, the criteria that banks use to set their lending policy apply more to term loans. Most important of these criteria are the suitability of repayment arrangements, the validity of the purpose of the loan, and assurances that it will be collected.

Repayment Arrangements

A sound bank lending policy requires that all loan applications include realistic repayment plans. Banks place heavy emphasis on estimates of the borrower's net cash flows in setting repayment schedules. The net cash flows are gross cash inflows less anticipated cash outlays for new fixed assets, additional working capital needs, projected dividends, and other debt service. It is also important to note that most banks are reluctant to set repayment schedules with a large balloon payment at maturity. The applicant's request for deferral of large amounts to the maturity date may be interpreted as a confession of weakness in the loan. Some writers on the subject suggest that banks match the maturity structure of loans with deposits. Under this approach, demand deposits and short-term savings deposits are used to make short-term loans. Long-term savings deposits are used to make long-term loans.

Validity of Purpose

The validity of the loan's purpose is a less obvious criterion for evaluating loans than the prospects of its repayment. It is nevertheless an essential element of soundness in the broader sense. Term loan repayments are highly dependent on profitable operations of the project to be financed by the loan. Thus, the purpose of most bank loans is either explicitly stated in the loan agreement or derived from a careful analysis of the borrower's financial statements. If credit is scarce, the purpose becomes even more important, because banks are forced to ration credit. When credit is scarce, it is more likely that banks will elect to use their limited resources to finance productive rather than speculative activity.

Collection

If loans are made for sound purposes and repayment schedules are realistic, it can be contended that little more is required to make them good loans. However, banks have certain responsibilities to their depositors and their stockholders. Moreover, most bank term loans involve sizable amounts of money and considerable periods of time. Thus, banks must take every possible precaution so that loans will be collected. The major protective measures against unexpected contingencies are the credit-worthiness of the borrower and the value of the collateral pledged to secure loans. Credit-worthiness is based largely on the five C's of credit discussed in Chapter 7: character, capacity, capital, collateral, and conditions.

Many banks obtain a lien on some asset of the borrower to support a loan. The bank's margin of safety is the market value of the security pledged minus the amount of the loan. This margin of safety is important, because the bank must sell the security to satisfy the claim if the borrower does not meet its obligations. If the collateral pledged is sold for less than the amount of the loan, the bank becomes an unsecured creditor for the amount of the difference. Thus, banks generally want security with a market value considerably higher than the amount of the loan.

OTHER TERM LOANS

In addition to banks, life insurance companies, finance companies, and the Small Business Administration lend money on a term basis.

Life Insurance Companies

Like banks, life insurance companies provide considerable amounts of intermediate-term business funds in the form of term loans. However, they prefer to lend much larger amounts of money for substantially longer periods of time than banks. Because typical maturities of insurance company term loans are 10 to 20 years, we can actually treat these term loans as long-term funds.

Bank term loans and insurance company term loans are complementary rather than competitive, because they involve substantially different maturities and amounts of funds. A bank and an insurance company sometimes share in the same loan. They may draw up a loan agreement in such a way that the bank takes the early maturity and the insurance company takes the remaining maturity.

Finance Companies

Because finance companies deal with the term loans that banks do not want or cannot legally handle, the interest charges of finance companies are usually larger than those of banks. Most finance companies provide both ordinary term loans and installment credit. Many of them also buy and lease assets to their customers.

Finance companies are very active in equipment financing. Marketable equipment represents another asset of the firm that can be used to secure its loan. There are two basic methods for financing equipment through a finance company: purchasing the equipment on installment or leasing it. In both cases there is an option to deal directly with the finance company or indirectly with it through the distributor or producer of the equipment.

Small Business Administration

The Small Business Act of 1953 established the **Small Business Administration** (SBA) as an agency of the federal government that makes loans to small businesses when they are unable to obtain money elsewhere. The underlying objectives of the SBA are (1) making last-resort loans to small businesses, (2) providing technical services on managerial problems, and (3) helping obtain government contracts.

There are two types of loans for which small businesses can apply: direct loans and participation loans. In general, direct loans from the SBA are available only when loans from other sources are not available on reasonable terms. With the participation loan, the SBA participates in a loan with a private lender or guarantees the loan up to 90 percent. Although SBA loans are term loans with an average maturity of five years, they are limited in amounts and interest rates by law.

Venture Capital

Venture capital represents funds invested in a new business by people who usually have no interest in managing the company. Most venture capitalists receive common stock in return for money invested. Venture capitalists hope that the company will thrive over time, so that they can sell their stock for many times what they paid for it. Unfortunately, new enterprises have many risks and their failure rate is high. Thus, there is a significant chance that venture capitalists will lose all their investment.

Venture capital comes from a surprisingly large number of sources: wealthy individuals, large banks such as Citicorp and Bank of America, and large corporations such as Exxon and IBM. Wealthy individuals normally form partnerships or corporations with $5 million to $30 million in order to invest in several new businesses. Banks establish small business investment companies to provide small business customers with venture capital. Large business concerns set up venture capital firms as their subsidiaries because of the prospects of higher returns on their venture capital investments than on conventional investments in their business.

New venture proposals in the high-technology area are usually most attractive to venture capitalists. For example, Boston and San Francisco are hotspots of venture capital activity due to a proliferation of electronic activities in these areas. In addition, there are many venture capital firms in New York, Massachusetts, California, Illinois, and Texas.

LEASES

A **lease** is a contractual arrangement by which the owner of an asset (lessor) allows another party (lessee) to use the services of the asset for a stated period of time. The lessee agrees to pay a periodic rent and live up to other conditions of the lease contract in exchange for the right to use the asset of the lessor for a specified period of time. After the initial period of the lease, the lessee may continue to utilize the asset at a reduced rent or may be given an option to buy it. This financing method has become increasingly popular in the last two decades, and today it is possible to lease any kind of fixed asset.

Lease versus Purchase

Many considerations become important in deciding whether to lease or purchase. They are described next.

Tax Considerations

Because lease payments are deductible as expenses for income-tax purposes, leases are competitive alternatives to loans that can be used to buy an asset. The tax law had permitted a faster tax write-off of leases than of purchased assets until the passage of the 1954 tax code, which introduced accelerated depreciation for assets. This provision wiped out the tax advantage associated with leases.

However, leases still have one advantage over loans. Many financial leases involve the lease of land. When the land is purchased, the firm cannot depreciate it for income-tax purposes. In contrast, when the land is leased, the firm can deduct it for income-tax purposes, thus allowing it to write off the cost of the land.

Effects on Future Financing

Leasing may conserve existing sources of credit for other uses. By surrendering the benefits of holding title to a fixed asset, the lessee may avoid the need to buy it. Because leasing frees funds from financing fixed assets, it permits the firm to have more cash available for alternative uses.

Some argue that leasing increases a firm's borrowing capacity, because it does not necessarily increase the assets or liabilities on the firm's balance sheet. If the lease obligation does not appear as debt on the firm's balance sheet, it does not adversely affect the firm's debt capacity. Although many creditors take the lease obligations fully into account, research indicates that they are more conscious of debt obligations than leasing commitments.

Most loan agreements for the purchase of fixed assets require the borrower to make a certain amount of down payment. Thus, the borrower receives less than the purchase price of the asset. On the other hand, leasing provides 100-percent financing, because a down payment is not required. But there is no guarantee that leasing provides more financing. Lease payments are usually made in advance and these advance payments may be viewed as a type of down payment.

There are some other effects of leasing on future financing. First, many loan indentures contain various protective covenants, but lease contracts avoid most of these covenants. Second, lease payments are fixed, thus avoiding the risks associated with short and/or intermediate financing and refinancing.

Risk of Obsolescence

Another advantage of leasing is that the lease arrangement shifts the risk of obsolescence from the user (lessee) to the owner (lessor). High rates of obsolescence for such capital assets as computers and calculating equipment increase the risk of ownership. The firm may avoid the risk of obsolescence if the lease term is quite short or if the lessor fails to accurately anticipate the obsolescence of assets in setting the lease payments.

Salvage Value

Salvage value is the value of the leased property at the end of the lease, and it belongs to the lessor. Hence, high salvage values reduce the cost of ownership. It may be wise to buy assets if they are expected to appreciate over the life of a lease agreement. Although the salvage values of many assets are highly uncertain, appreciation in the value is highly likely when land and/or buildings are involved.

Maintenance

The lease contract usually specifies the responsibility of maintenance, insurance, and taxes on the leased property. Although these charges are reduced by tax shields, they represent an expense of ownership. If the leasing arrangement requires the lessor to assume these expenses, the lessor usually passes them to the lessee in the form of increased lease payments. This makes leasing a more attractive alternative if the lessor can maintain and operate more cheaply due to the economies of scale.

Discount Rate

Although the after-tax borrowing rate is used most widely as the discount rate, it is perhaps one of the most controversial features in the lease-purchase decision. Both leasing and buying involve cash outflows over an extended period of time. Therefore, these cash outflows must be discounted for the time value of money and for risk. The problem arises because lease payments are normally fixed and certain, whereas salvage values, operating expenses, and interest charges are highly uncertain. Although we will not discuss this problem further, it can swing the decision one way or the other.

Types of Leases

There are three types of leases: (1) sale-and-leaseback arrangements, (2) operating leases, and (3) financial or capital leases. Nearly all lease arrangements fall into one of these three categories.

Sale and Leaseback Arrangements

Under a **sale-and-leaseback arrangement**, the owner of the property sells his property to another party and simultaneously enters an agreement to lease the property back under specific terms. Retail stores, office buildings, and multiple-purpose industrial structures are usually financed through this arrangement. The seller-lessee obtains the sales price in cash and retains the economic use of the property. The buyer-lessor obtains the title to the property and periodic rental payments. These rental payments are made to amortize the purchase price and to provide the buyer-lessor with a specified rate of return on the investment.

Operating Leases

This leasing arrangement allows a firm to acquire the use of an asset it did not own previously. **Operating leases** cover such types of equipment as computers, trucks, automobiles, and furniture. Operating leases have a number of important characteristics.

1. The lessor maintains and services the leased property. Thus, the lease payments include the costs of these services and maintenance.
2. The lessee frequently retains the right to cancel the agreement before the expiration of the basic lease period.
3. The lease contract usually covers a period of time that is less than the economic life of the leased property. Hence, the original lessee does not return the full value of the leased asset to the lessor.

Financial or Capital Leases

Financial leases generally require that (1) the lessee must maintain and service the leased property, (2) the lessee cannot cancel the leased contract before its maturity, and (3) the lessee must fully amortize the leased property.

Ordinarily, the lessee selects the equipment, negotiates its price and other terms with the manufacturer, arranges with a bank to buy it, and immediately leases it from the bank. A sale-and-leaseback arrangement is treated as a special type of financial lease.

The Lease-Purchase Decision

When companies acquire new fixed assets, they must make a lease-purchase decision. The present value method can be used to compare the costs of these two financing alternatives. Under this approach, we compute the present value of after-tax cash outflows for both alternatives and choose the alternative whose present value is smaller.

Example 18-1. The Long Beach Company has decided to acquire a machine with a cost of $10,000 and a depreciation period of five years. The machine is expected to have no salvage value on retirement. If the machine is purchased, the company can finance it with a loan at 10 percent; the principal and the interest are to be paid in five equal annual installments. The machine is to be depreciated on a straight-line basis. The company's marginal tax rate is 50 percent. If the machine is leased, the lessor requires that the lessee amortize the entire cost of the machine and that it provide a 10 percent return. As usual, annual lease payments are to be made in advance; the rent for the use of the machine during year 1 would be paid at the end of year 0. Because leases are analogous to loans, the after-tax cost of borrowing is to be used as an appropriate discount rate to determine the present value of the after-tax cash outflows.

Long Beach can borrow the required $10,000 on a 10 percent loan to be amortized over five years. The amount of the annual loan repayment can be calculated by solving the formula for the present value of an annuity:

$$PVA = CF \times IF_{PVA_{n,i}} \text{ or } CF = \frac{PVA}{IF_{PVA_{n,i}}} \quad (18\text{-}1)$$

where PVA = net cost of the asset to be acquired, CF = annual loan repayment, and $IF_{PVA_{n,i}}$ = annuity discount factor.

Therefore, the amount of annual loan repayment is

$$CF = \frac{\$10,000}{IF_{PVA_{5,10\%}}} = \$10,000 \div 3.791 = \$2,638$$

The five annual installments of $2,638 would retire the $10,000 loan and provide the lender with a 10 percent return. We can break down the annual payments into interest and principal repayments, as shown in Table 18-1.

Table 18-1
Term Loan Amortization Schedule

End of Year	Annual Payment	Interest at 10%	Principal Repayment	Remaining Balance
0	$10,000			
1	$2,638	$1,000	$1,638	$8,362
2	2,638	836	1,802	6,560
3	2,638	656	1,982	4,578
4	2,638	458	2,180	2,398
5	2,638	240	2,398	0

*Interest rate x the remaining balance at the end of the previous year. For example, $900 = $9,000 x 0.10.

Solved by financial calculator:

1. Hit 2nd QUIT, 2nd CLR TVM.
2. Hit 2nd P/Y, key in 1 (for one pmt per period), hit ENTER, 2nd QUIT.
3. Key in 5, hit N.
4. Key in 10, hit I/Y.
5. Key in 10,000, hit PV.
6. Hit CPT PMT.
7. PMT = -2637.97

8. To review the amortization schedule, hit 2nd Amort.
9. Key in 1 for P1 (indicates beginning of range of time interested in), hit ENTER.
10. Scroll down (down arrow) to P2 (indicates the end of the range of time interested in), key in 1 (for period one), hit ENTER. In essence, we have directed the calculator to provide amortization information for the specified range of time from P1 (beginning of period 1) to P2 (end of period 1).
11. Scroll down and view the amortization data for period 1:
    BAL = 8,362.02
    PRN = -1,637.92 (principal portion of first payment)
    INT = -1,000 (interest portion of first payment)
    Repeat steps 9–11 by adjusting P1 and P2 for the remaining periods 2, 3, 4, and 5 and observe the entire amortization schedule.

Table 18-2 shows the schedule of cash outflows and their present value. The tax shield is the interest expense plus the depreciation charge multiplied by the marginal tax rate. The after-tax cash outflow for each year is the annual loan payment minus the tax shield. The after-tax cash outflow in the first year is $1,138.

	Annual payment	$2,638
Less:		
	tax shield interest	$1,000
	depreciation	2,000
	total expense	$3,000
	x tax rate	x .50
	tax shield	$1,500
	After-tax cash outflow	$1,138

The present value of $5,672 for the buying alternative is obtained by discounting these after-tax cash outflows at 5 percent. There is some disagreement about the discount rate to be used in computing the present value of the after-tax cash outflows for both the buying alternative and the leasing alternative. However, the after-tax cost of borrowing is most widely used as a discount rate in present-value analysis of these two financing alternatives. The use of this rate is based on two assumptions: (1) that the company's marginal tax rate will stay the same, and (2) that its future taxable income will exceed the tax shield associated with lease payments.

Table 18-2
Present Value of Cash Outflows: Buying Alternative

End of Year	Annual Payment	Interest	Depreciation	Tax Shield	After-Tax Cash Outflow	Present Value at 5%
1	$2,638	$1,000	$2,000	$1,500	$1,138	$1,083
2	2,638	836	2,000	1,418	1,220	1,107
3	2,638	656	2,000	1,328	1,310	1,132
4	2,638	458	2,000	1,229	1,409	1,160
5	2,638	240	2,000	1,120	1,518	<u>1,190</u>
				Present Value		$5,672

Because the lease payments are made in advance, the first lease payment is made at the end of year 0. Therefore, we must solve for the annual lease payment that equates the cost of the machine with the first lease payment plus the present value of the remaining four lease payments. This is given as follows:

$$\$10,000 = CF + CF \times IF_{PVA_{4,10\%}}$$
$$= CF(1 + 3.170)$$
$$CF = \$10,000 \div 4.170$$
$$CF = \$2,398$$

Thus, five equal lease payments of $2,398 are necessary to amortize the cost of the machine and to return 10 percent to the lessor.

Lease payments are treated as tax deductible expenses for federal income tax purposes, but they are deductible only in the year in which the payments apply. Hence, each lease payment is deductible for tax purposes in the following year. Table 18-3 shows the schedule of cash outflows and the present value of these cash outflows. We see from the table that the present value of the total cash outflows for the leasing alternative is $5,710.

Table 18-3
Present Value of Cash Outflows: Leasing Alternative

End of Year	Lease Payment	Tax Shield	After-Tax Cash Outflows	Present Value at 5%
0	$2,398	$0	$2,398	$2,398
1-4	2,398	1,199	1,199	4,252
5		1,199	-1,199	<u>-940</u>
		Present Value		$5,710

The present value of the after-tax cash outflows for the buying alternative is $5,672. Thus, the firm should acquire the machine through the debt alternative. It is important to recognize that this conclusion occurs despite the fact that both alternatives have an interest rate of 10 percent and a discount rate of 5 percent. The advantage of the debt alternative comes from the one-year time lag between the loan repayment and the lease payment. Because lease payments are made in advance while loan repayments are not, the lease payments are multiplied by the lower discount factors; consequently, the present value of the lease payments becomes greater.

Summary

Intermediate-term funds are used to finance fixed assets and permanent current assets. Some major sources of such funds are bank term loans, insurance company loans, finance company loans, and leases. These loans have maturities of one to ten years.

Bank term loans represent the most important source of intermediate-term funds for those in a strong financial position. Ordinarily, the borrower must be able to offer security and to live up to relatively rigid restrictions. These restrictions are classified into three major categories: prohibitive provisions, restrictive provisions, and affirmative provisions.

The two main types of leases are operating leases and financial leases. Operating leases require the lessor to maintain and service leased assets, while financial leases require the lessee to maintain, insure, and pay taxes on the leased assets. Operating leases allow the lessee to avoid burdens of maintenance, risks of obsolescence, and rigid requirements imposed on bank term loans. A lease-purchase decision can be evaluated by the present value method. Under this approach, we compute the present value of the total cash outflows for each alternative and choose the alternative with the smaller present value.

List of Key Terms

term loans
balloon payment
prohibitive provisions
affirmative provisions
lease
sale-and-leaseback arrangement
financial leases

amortization method
revolving credit
restrictive provisions
venture capital
salvage value
operating leases

Problems

18-1   The Zero Company wants to acquire a machine with a cost of $200,000 and a depreciation period of five years. The machine is expected to have no salvage value at the end of five years. If the company decides to buy the machine, it can finance the project with a loan at an interest rate of 16 percent. The machine is to be depreciated on the basis of the straight-line method. The lender requires the company to repay its loan in five annual installments. The company's tax rate is 50 percent. By comparison, if the company decides to lease the machine, it will have the following characteristics: (1) The lease has a fixed noncancellable term of five years with a return of 14 percent per year. (2) Annual lease payments are made at the beginning of each year. (3) The lessee pays executory costs.

(a) Compute the present value of the after-tax cash outflows for the buying alternative at 10%.

(b) Compute the present value of the after-tax cash outflows for the leasing alternative at 10%.

18-2 Two pieces of equipment under consideration for leasing are expected to achieve the same task. These two alternatives have the following characteristics:

	Option A	Option B
Value of asset and basis of lease	$20,000	$60,000
Implicit interest rate on lease	10%	9%
Annual maintenance operating cost	$ 4,000	$ 3,000
Expected life of lease	3 years	8 years

Additional assumptions are: (1) Both options are operating leases in nature. (2) The firm will be able to re-lease assets of exactly the same characteristics as those currently being used. (3) Annual lease payments are made at the end of each year.

(a) Determine the annualized cost (annualized lease cost plus annualized maintenance-operating cost) for both lease options.

(b) Assume that B's maintenance-operating costs are a part of the lease contract, while A requires the lessee to pay all maintenance-operating costs. How large should A's annual maintenance-operating costs be before B is preferred to A?

(c) If the company really preferred the operating and other characteristics of B over A, how low should B's implicit interest rate be for the total costs of both leases to become equal?

18-3 A bank loan requires five annual payments of $27,000. The interest rate is 12 percent.

(a) Compute the face amount of the loan.
(b) Compute the balance of the loan after the second payment.

18-4 A company wants to purchase a $36,000 machine over a two-year period. Its bank has offered to lend the required amount of money in exchange for its promise to retire the loan in four semiannual installments. The loan requires a compensating balance equal to 10 percent of the outstanding balance and 9 percent interest on the unpaid balance. The seller of the machine has offered the company a sales contract with four equal semiannual payments. How large could the payments be before the bank loan is preferred to the sales contract?

18-5 A company has decided to lease a computer for a period of 10 years. Annual lease payments of $100,000 are made at the beginning of each year. The company pays taxes at the end of the year and is in the 40 percent tax bracket. If this lease is evaluated using the 10 percent discount rate, what is the present value of the after-tax cash outflows for the leasing alternative?

18-6   A company can lease a computer at $22,500 per year for 12 years and the first payment is made one year hence. The company can also buy the computer for $160,000 and borrow the $100,000 at a cost of 10 percent. Assume zero taxes and 5 percent discount rate. Should the company buy or lease the computer?

Part 6

Special Topics in Finance

Although Part Six deals with somewhat specialized topics, it draws upon the principles developed in earlier parts. These principles are the concepts by which the financial manager can maximize the market value of the firm's stock. Chapter 19 discusses the external growth of firms through mergers and acquisitions. Chapter 20 introduces the external growth of firms through multinational operations. Both mergers and multinational operations are examined from the standpoint of the firm's allocation of funds.

19

Corporate Growth through Mergers

In Part Three, we considered the purchase of an individual asset as a capital budgeting decision. When a company is buying another company, it is making an investment. Thus, the basic principles of capital investment decisions apply. But mergers are often more difficult to evaluate. First, the financial manager must be careful to define benefits and costs properly. Second, the financial manager needs to understand why mergers occur and who gains or loses as a result of them. Third, the acquisition of a company is more complicated than the purchase of a new machine because special tax, legal, and accounting issues must often be addressed. Finally, the integration of an entire company is much more complex than the installation of a single new machine.

There have been a number of major merger movements in the industrial history of the United States. The first merger movement took place in the late 1890s with the development of the oil, railroad, tobacco, and steel industries. The second major movement happened in the 1920s with the consolidation of firms in a number of industries, such as utilities and communication companies. The third one was in the 1960s with the rage of conglomerate mergers. The fourth one began in the early 1980s.

The major mania of the 1980s was sparked by several factors: the relatively depressed condition of the stock market in the early 1980s; the unprecedented level of inflation during the 1970s and the early 1980s; the Reagan Administration's tolerant attitude toward mergers; and the general belief that it is cheaper to acquire other companies than it is to expand through new product development. This merger movement was characterized by the unfriendly takeover, in which an acquiring company identifies a target company and attempts to acquire it without management permission. This led to wild bidding wars for companies.

The latest merger movement started in the early l990s and is still going strong. In 1993 and 1994, a rash of proposed or completed mergers, buyouts, and hostile takeovers swept Wall Street. This latest round of consolidation seems fundamentally different, however, from the 1980s binge, when tax legislation and easy debt financing helped propel the leveraged buyout boom. It is driven in part by strategic concerns and in part by a fear among corporate chiefs in some industries—communications and health care, for example—that they will be left behind as competitors undertake marriages designed to bolster their presence in burgeoning markets. The urge to merge is also aided by a change of attitude in Washington, where policy makers expose a more activist government role in the economy and have begun to look kindly on big business combinations.

In this chapter, we place primary emphasis on mergers from the standpoint of the acquiring firm. First, we discuss fundamentals of business combinations such as internal growth versus external growth, the types of business combinations, motives for business combinations, and the terms of business combinations. Second, we consider accounting aspects of business combinations. Third, we describe advantages and disadvantages of holding companies.

INTERNAL GROWTH VERSUS EXTERNAL GROWTH

Funds for growth can come from the retention of earnings, the accumulation of depreciation allowances, and the sale of new securities. The company grows when these funds are used to provide new capacity and new products and to serve new markets. **Internal growth** occurs when this all takes place within the same company, through the same organization, and under the same management. In contrast, external growth exists when the funds are used to acquire the ownership interests of various other companies.

Although internal growth is usually natural and economical, the process of growth may be very slow. In recent years, growth through merger with the existing business activities of another firm has received substantial publicity as an alternative to internal growth. For a variety of reasons such as antitrust prosecution, the **external growth** of business has become more visible to investors and financial analysts than year-to-year internal expansion.

Traditionally, company growth through mergers has been treated as a special topic outside the mainstream of financial management. It is true to the extent that management rarely faces the need to familiarize itself with the details involved in mergers. However, mergers should be treated as mainstream of financial management for a number of reasons. Much of the material in the preceding 18 chapters has direct bearing upon the financial manager's potential contribution to the company's external growth. Management may decide to acquire the facilities of another firm rather than to build its own. By the same token, it may enter the market for a product through acquisition rather than through the development of a substitute. All these decisions are long-term investment problems and thus they should be evaluated on the basis of discounted cash flows.

TYPES OF BUSINESS COMBINATION

The term merger refers to a combination of two or more formerly independent firms into one organization with a common management and ownership. Although in business practice other terms such as acquisition or consolidation are used in a similar context, the lines of distinction are frequently unclear. Thus, it may be helpful to begin with the clear definition of these terms. There are three basic forms of business combinations: consolidation, mergers, and holding companies.

Consolidations

The corporation laws of the various states contain formal statutory provisions for business combinations. A statutory **consolidation** takes place when two or more companies are combined to form a completely new corporation. The new company absorbs the assets and liabilities of the old companies and consequently the old companies cease to exist. Consolidations are ordinarily used when companies of approximately the same size combine. When companies consolidate, shares of their common stock are exchanged for shares in the new company.

Mergers

A statutory **merger** refers to a combination of two corporations by which one loses its identity. The surviving corporation acquires the assets and liabilities of the acquired corporation and it pays for its acquisition in either cash or common stock. Typically, this form of business combination is used when the two companies differ significantly in size. For instance, a larger company may use the merger to obtain the assets or the common stock of a smaller company.

Holding Companies

A **holding company** is a company that has a controlling interest in one or more other companies. The holding company is called the **parent company** and the controlled companies are called **subsidiaries**. The effective working control of a subsidiary by the parent company does not require a majority of the subsidiary's voting stock. The ownership of between 10 and 20 percent of the voting stock is frequently sufficient to control a company.

There are a number of significant differences between the holding company and the merger. The merger involves the acquisition of the entire company, while the holding company does not acquire the entire company. Hence, the holding company arrangement makes it possible for a company to enjoy greater asset control per dollar than a merger. The second difference is the fact that a holding company consists of a number of separate corporations called subsidiaries, whereas a merged company is a single organization.

Economic Motives for Combination

Although there are some important differences between the words merger and consolidation, their similarity should be clear at this point. In practice they tend to be used interchangeably in order to describe the combination of two or more companies. Thus, the remainder of this chapter ignores the difference between these two forms of combination.

The combination of two or more companies is economically justified only if it increases the total value of a firm. We observed in the section on optimum capital structure in Chapter 13 that the total value of the firm consists of the market value of its common stock and the market value of its debt. The traditional capitalization approach to the valuation of the firm consists of four basic steps:

1. Determine the earnings after taxes the company expects to produce over the years or earnings before taxes multiplied by (1 – tax rate).
2. Determine the capitalization rate (discount rate) for these earnings.
3. Determine the extent to which the company may be levered or the appropriate amount of debt.
4. Compute the total value of the firm from the following formula:

$$\text{Value of Firm} = \frac{\text{Earnings Before Taxes (1 - Tax Rate)}}{\text{Capitalization Rate}}$$

One can examine the effect of a merger on each of the factors that affect the total value of the firm.

Earnings Before Taxes

It should be clear from the valuation model that an increase in the expected earnings before taxes would increase the total value of the firm. A merger itself creates a larger physical size and opportunities for synergistic effects. The **synergistic effects** of business combinations are certain economies of scale from the firm's lower overhead. A synergistic effect is said to exist when the combined companies are worth more than the sum of their parts. This effect has been frequently defined as "2+2=5." That is, the two companies together produce a greater net operating income than if they had remained separate.

The merger allows the firm to acquire necessary management skills and to spread existing management skills over a larger operation. There are also opportunities to eliminate duplicate facilities and to consolidate the functions of production, marketing, and purchasing. These types of operating economies and better management can increase the profit margin and reduce risks as well.

Operating economies may best be described in combination with three forms of growth: a horizontal merger, a vertical merger, and a conglomerate merger. A **horizontal merger** occurs when firms in the same type of production or in marketing the same product are combined. Certain operating economies result from this form of combination for three major reasons: (a) it reduces the number of competitors; (b) it eliminates duplicate facilities; (c) it provides the firm with an opportunity to expand its operation in an existing product line. A **vertical merger** occurs when a company acquires its suppliers or its retail outlets. The economies achieved by this combination stem primarily from the firm's greater control over the purchase of raw materials or the distribution of finished goods. A **conglomerate merger** occurs when two or more companies in unrelated lines of businesses are combined—for example, the combination of a food processing company and an aircraft manufacturing company. One cannot expect real operating economies from this type of combination. Its key benefit is diversification which reduces risk, broadens the product base, and balances cyclical fluctuation.

Tax Considerations

Some have argued that a key motive for some mergers is to take advantage of a tax loss. The tax benefit comes from the fact that one of the firms has a tax loss carryforward. The tax loss carryforward expires at the end of fifteen years unless the firm makes sufficient profits to offset it completely. There are two situations where mergers could actually avoid corporate income taxes. First, when a profitable company acquires companies with a large tax loss carryforward, it can reduce its effective tax rate and consequently the merger increases its net operating income after taxes. Second, a company with a tax loss carryforward may acquire profitable companies in order to use its carryforward. Otherwise, a portion of the tax loss carryforward might have been lost forever for lack of sufficient profits to utilize it completely.

Capitalization Rates

An important advantage of mergers, especially conglomerate mergers, is the fact that the earnings of larger companies are capitalized at lower rates. Through conglomerate mergers companies become larger and they are more able to diversify. The securities of larger companies have better marketability than those of smaller companies. Larger companies are also better known among investors. A conglomerate merger can make all these factors happen, and they lead to lower required rates of return and higher price-earnings ratios. Since conglomerate diversification reduces the overall risk of the merged firm and thereby its capitalization rate, its value exceeds the values of the companies operating separately.

The argument for the reduction in the firm's overall risk through conglomerate diversification is exactly the same as that advanced in our discussion of capital budgeting. Most conglomerate mergers involve companies whose product lines and geographic markets are different. Therefore, their returns are not perfectly positively correlated with each other. If returns are not perfectly positively correlated, the merger of two or more companies can reduce the risk of the residual owners. Investors are basically risk averters and thus they view such a risk reduction favorably. However, it is important to recognize that they can achieve the same objective by diversifying their own investment portfolios. Thus, it is unlikely that they will pay positive utility to have their company do this for them.

Debt Capacity

The appropriate mix of debt and equity reduces the overall cost of capital and thus it raises the market value of the firm. The varying effects of financial leverage on the capitalization rates for debt and equity permit the company to reduce its overall cost of capital and thereby to increase its market value by the intelligent use of leverage. There are two situations where a merger can raise the debt capacity for the merged firm above the sum of debt capacities for the individual firms prior to merger.

First, there are companies that fail to make optimum use of debt. We observed in Chapter 13 that the company may enhance its market value by raising its utilization of debt up to its debt capacity. There are a number of ways in which the company can judge its debt limit.

1. The financial manager may examine the relationship between the cash flows of similar firms and their level of debt plus their debt service charges.
2. The financial manager may investigate their ratios of debt to equity.
3. The financial manager can have consultation with investment bankers in order to produce the approximate industry average.

The use of leverage enhances the market value of the firm primarily due to the tax deductibility of the interest on debt. Companies with an inadequate use of debt are undervalued in the marketplace. If a company acquires these companies by exchanging debt for its outstanding common stock, the market value of the merged company would then exceed the values of the companies as separate entities.

Second, sometimes it is possible for the merged firm to borrow more than the companies were able to borrow individually. If the debt capacity for the merged company exceeds the sum of debt capacities for the independent companies, a merger would increase its market value above the combined market values of the independent companies. The increased debt capacity of the merged company stems from two factors.

1. If several different streams of expected cash flows are combined through a merger, the technical insolvency of the merged firm falls because the merger

balances cyclical earnings fluctuations. Certainly, an important condition is that these income streams are not perfectly positively correlated.

2. Lenders are willing to provide more debt to a merged company than to the independent companies because the merged company can provide greater protection for its lenders than they can provide for themselves.

It should be noted that the highly levered company may become even more highly levered if it acquires another highly levered company. The merger may then cause the acquiring company's financial risk to rise and consequently the earnings may be discounted by investors at a higher rate. The net result is to reduce the market value of the owners' equity unless tax advantages and additional earnings exceed the financial risk associated with the acquiring company.

Terms of Combination

Once management has considered mergers from various aspects, it must then examine the terms of a merger. The key topics in this section are: (a) acquisition of assets versus acquisition of stock, (b) cash payment versus stock payment, and (c) the exchange ratio.

Acquisition of Assets versus Acquisition of Stock

Some companies desire to buy only a part of the assets of the selling company, while other companies may wish to control another going concern by acquiring its common stock.

Acquisition of Assets

There are some companies that desire to purchase only a portion of the assets (generally fixed assets) of the selling company. In other instances state laws make it difficult for a company to merge with other companies if the companies involved are chartered in different states. If the selling company obtains the consent of its stockholders for the sale of its assets, its assets are disposed of in exchange for cash, stock, or other securities. The proceeds from the sale are usually distributed to the stockholders of the selling company in the form of a **liquidation dividend** and the selling company then ceases to exist. If the combination allows the selling company to continue in existence, it should not be treated as a merger.

Acquisition of Stock

If a company wishes to control other going concerns, it must acquire their common stock. This method may be particularly attractive to a company that desires to obtain a controlling interest of another business gradually. There are two acquisition methods of stock: the purchase of stock in the marketplace and a tender offer. If one company seeks controlling interest in another without revealing its intentions, it may buy common shares of another company through a broker on the open market or a block of shares from one large holder on a negotiated basis.

In recent years, some companies have used the tender offer to take over another. With a **tender offer**, the stockholders of another company are asked to submit (tender) their shares in exchange for a specified price per share. To make its offer more attractive to the stockholders of the company it desires to acquire, the acquiring company sets its tender price significantly above the present market price. The tender offer makes it possible for the acquiring company to bypass the management of the company it intends to acquire, and thus the offer serves as some sort of threat to that management. Management may use a number of defensive tactics to resist the tender offer for both business and financial reasons. It may resort to some legal means as a delaying action, or it may attempt to persuade its stockholders that the tender price is too low.

Cash Payment versus Stock Payment

Mergers may involve straight cash purchase, an exchange of stock, or a combination of cash and securities. Some researchers argue that when a firm desires to acquire the assets of the selling companies or their stock for cash, such acquisitions should be treated as capital budgeting problems. The financial manager can evaluate cash acquisitions of going concerns or another company's assets as described in Part Three. When a company attempts to acquire another going concern, it must recognize that the estimation of cash flows and certain risk considerations from the changed financial structure make it difficult to apply these capital budgeting techniques.

The acquisition of another company through the exchange of common stock or other securities has certain advantages over the cash acquisition. While the acquiring company could sell its securities on the market to the public for cash, the direct exchange of securities eliminates the underpricing and flotation costs. When companies are combined through the direct exchange of stock, a ratio of exchange occurs. The exchange ratio implies the relative valuation of the companies.

The Exchange Ratio

The exchange ratio is the number of the acquiring firm's shares for each share of the acquired firm. When two companies are combined, the owners of these two companies can consider the ratio of exchange with respect to their book value per share, their earnings per share, and their market price per share.

Book values are generally meaningless as a basis for valuation in merger negotiations because they simply represent the historical investments made in the company. In other words, such investments do not reflect current prices or values, which are important in merger negotiations. However, book values have an impact on merger terms under two circumstances: (a) when they significantly exceed market values, and (b) when companies are acquired for their liquidity and asset values rather than for their expected earnings.

Mergers have potentially favorable or adverse effects on earnings, on market values of shares, or on both. The effects of a proposed merger on market values are less certain than its effects on earnings per share. There are many variables that affect market prices of shares: future earnings potential, expected dividends, growth, risk class, capital structure, asset values, managerial talent, and other factors that bear upon valuation. These future events are difficult to predict; consequently, stockholders place considerable emphasis on the immediate effects of a proposed merger on earnings per share in the bargaining process.

In addition to earnings, the major emphasis in merger negotiations is on the market-value indicator which portrays the judgement of investors concerning the company. The ratio of market prices per share is the ratio of the market price per share of the acquiring company times the number of shares offered to the market price per share of the acquired company.

Example 19-1. The acquiring firm has a market value per share of $100, while the acquired company has a market value per share of $20. What is the ratio of market prices per share if the acquiring company offers 0.2 shares for each share of the acquired company?

The exchange ratio is computed as follows:

$$\text{Exchange Ratio} = \frac{\$100 \times 0.2}{\$20} = 1.00$$

The exchange ratio of 1 indicates that the stocks of these two companies would be exchanged on a one-to-one market-price basis. In other words, the stockholders of the acquired company are able to buy a share with market value of $20 for each share of their own stock. If the market price per share of the surviving company stays the same, the stockholders of both companies are as well off as before in terms of market value. However, if the acquiring company desperately needs the liquidity of the acquired company, it must offer a price in excess of the current market price per share of the acquired company. Let us assume that the acquiring company offers 0.6 shares for each share of the acquired company. The market-value exchange ratio would then be 3.00 or ($100 x 0.6/$20). In other words, the stockholders of the acquired company are now able to purchase a share with a market value of $60 for each share of their own stock.

Some Accounting Aspects of Business Combinations

For accounting purposes, business combinations are handled either as purchases or pooling of interests. The distinction between a purchase and a pooling of interests depends upon the nature of the surviving entity. With a purchase, only the acquiring company survives and the others cease to exist. With a **pooling of interests**, companies combine to carry out their economic activities as a single entity, and nearly all of the former ownership interests would continue in the combined company.

The purchase method views a business combination as an investment for the acquiring company. The acquired assets or companies are usually recorded in the accounts of the acquiring company at the market value of the assets given in exchange. The historical cost in the accounts of the acquired company is no longer relevant. This treatment is theoretically valid because the market value of the assets given in exchange represents their current value to the acquiring company. If the acquiring company pays more than the net worth of the acquired company, the excess is treated as **goodwill**. Goodwill write-offs are not deductible for federal income tax purposes. This accounting treatment results in lower reported earnings for several years; thus, this form of business combination is not popular in practice.

If a combination of two companies is treated as a pooling of interests, the assets are carried forward at the book value in the accounts of the acquired company. Thus, the pooling-of-interests method does not change the underlying asset values of the corporate entities involved and the combination does not result in goodwill. The obvious advantage of this method is that there are no charges against future earnings and thus it would produce higher reported earnings.

Accounting policies in mergers have important implications for the reporting of value and earnings per share after the event of acquisition. There have been some allegations that acquiring companies inflated their performance records and misled the public through the pooling-of-interests method. However, on August 2, 1970, the Accounting Principles Board of the American Institute of Certified Public Accountants issued its Opinion No. 16 which significantly restricts the conditions under which a pooling of interests could take place. The most important condition is that the surviving company must issue common stock in exchange for at least 90 percent of the voting common stock of another company. Even before this opinion, the acquisition of a firm's assets or its stock for cash was treated as a clear-cut purchase. However, companies could use securities other than common stock and noncash assets to acquire another company and treat the transaction as a pooling of interests. There should be no doubt that the opinion will reduce the number of poolings of interests and thereby distortions in reported earnings.

HOLDING COMPANIES

In 1889, New Jersey became the first state which permitted corporations to exist for the sole purpose of owning the stocks of other corporations. A holding company may be a pure holding company which exists only to control other companies: it may be an operating company which exists to carry out some business activities of its own; or it may be an intermediate holding company which controls some subsidiaries but is, in turn, controlled by the parent company. Sometimes there are several layers of companies within the holding company system and one group of investors or one company can control many firms or a tremendous amount of assets for a relatively small amount of investment.

A holding company has a number of advantages.

1. It allows a company to own or control a large amount of assets with a relatively small investment.
2. The failure of one subsidiary does not cause the failure of the entire holding company because its subsidiaries are separate legal entities.
3. This form of combination does not require a formal approval from the stock holders of the acquired companies.
4. A holding company with a number of subsidiaries in different states may have some tax advantages because many state laws favor corporations chartered by the state over those chartered by other states.

A holding company also has some disadvantages.

1. It must pay a tax on 30 percent of the cash dividends it receives from its subsidiaries. A merger allows the acquiring company to avoid this tax.
2. The holding company system magnifies profits if operations are successful. However, it also magnifies losses if operations are not profitable.

3. It is a more expensive form of business organization to administer than a merged company because additional costs are necessary to maintain separate organizations and separate corporate relationships.

SUMMARY

There are only two avenues of corporate growth: internal growth and external growth. In recent years, external growth has received substantial publicity as an alternative to internal growth. There are three basic forms of external growth: mergers, consolidations, and holding companies. Although most of our discussion in this chapter centered on the first form of combination, the objective of the company in these three cases is the same: the maximization of stockholder wealth. The three types of expansion can be treated as capital budgeting decisions and their acceptance criteria are basically the same.

There are a number of economic motives for business combinations, all of which relate to the maximization of stockholder wealth. They include economies of scale, tax considerations, capitalization rates, increased debt limits, and diversification. Once management has considered a merger from various aspects, it must consider the merger terms. Important merger terms include acquisition of assets versus acquisition of stock, cash payment versus stock payment, and the exchange ratio. The exchange ratio is the relative valuation of two companies that are to be combined. This exchange ratio may be based on book value per share, earnings per share, and market value per share. The market value is more realistic than the others because it reflects the judgement of investors concerning the company.

Accounting policies in mergers have important implications for the reporting of value and earnings per share following the event of mergers. Some acquiring companies have inflated their performance records through the pooling-of-interests method. But the Accounting Principles Board Opinion No. 16 tightened the conditions under which a pooling of interests could occur. This opinion is designed to minimize distortions in reported earnings.

LIST OF KEY TERMS

internal growth
merger
parent company
synergistic effect
vertical merger
liquidation dividend
goodwill

consolidation
holding company
subsidiary
horizontal merger
conglomerate merger
pooling of interests

20

CORPORATE GROWTH THROUGH MULTINATIONAL OPERATIONS

Although business operations in foreign countries have existed for centuries, the world has recently entered an era of unprecedented global economic activity with worldwide production, distribution, and financing. There are many examples of the increasing importance of international operations. U.S. firms such as Exxon Mobil Corporation, Texaco, Inc., Dow Chemical, the Coca Cola Company, and the Boeing Company earn more than 60 percent of their total operating profit in international operations. Multinational corporations (MNC) such as Exxon Mobil, BP Amoco, IBM, American Express, and Northwest Airlines do business with more than 50 countries around the world. The value of world exports in U.S. dollars has increased from a little more than $129 billion in 1962 to approximately $5.5 trillion in 1998. According to the estimate of the U.S. Department of Commerce, U.S. exports amount to more than one-fifth of its industrial production. By the same token, international financial markets have also become increasingly important as they serve world trade and foreign investment. There has been rapid growth in international portfolio investments such as the purchase of foreign stocks and bonds, as well as direct investment by multinational corporations such as construction of plants overseas. International earning assets for the Bank of America, for example, represent more than half its total earning assets. Citibank maintains more than 250 overseas branches in over 100 countries. Simply stated, each nation is economically related to other nations of the world through a complex network of international trade, foreign investment, and international loans.

What are the differences between multinational companies and domestic companies from a financial manager's point of view? An efficient allocation of funds among assets (investment) and an acquisition of funds on favorable terms (financing) are conceptually the same for both types of companies. However, these two types of companies are different because they do business in different environments. International financial managers must understand these differences if they are to function effectively within this international environment. This chapter covers three major topics: motives for international transactions, political and exchange risks, and financing international transactions.

MOTIVES FOR WORLD TRADE

The classic economic theory of comparative advantage explains why countries exchange goods and services. The underlying assumption is that some countries can produce some types of goods relatively more efficiently than other countries can. Hence, all countries are better off if each specializes in the production of those goods which it can produce relatively more efficiently and buys those goods which other countries produce relatively more efficiently.

The Theory of Comparative Advantage

The **theory of comparative advantage** depends upon two points: (a) the factors of production such as land, labor, and capital are unequally distributed among nations, and (b) the efficient production of various goods and services requires combinations of different economic resources and different technologies. For instance, Canada has vast amounts of fertile land resources and relatively few people. In contrast, Japan has little land and abundant skilled labor. Thus, Canada may produce such land-intensive goods as wheat more cheaply than Japan, while Japan may produce such labor-intensive goods as cameras more cheaply than Canada.

The Theory of Factor Endowments

Countries are substantially different in their endowments of economic resources. This explains why Brazil is more efficient in the production of coffee and why the United States is more efficient in the production of computers. Brazil has the soil, weather, and abundant supplies of unskilled labor necessary to produce coffee more cheaply than the United States. The United States possesses the raw materials, facilities, and ample supplies of skilled labor necessary to produce computers more efficiently than Brazil.

Differences in national factor endowments explain differences in comparative costs between the two countries. Capital costs are lower in the United States than in Brazil because the United States has relatively more capital than Brazil. Labor costs are lower in Brazil than in the United States because Brazil has relatively more labor than the United States. Simply stated, the more abundant the supply of any factor, the lower the cost of the factor.

According to the **theory of factor endowments**, a country must specialize in the production and export of any good that uses large amounts of abundant factors. The country must import those commodities that use large amounts of scarce production factors at home. Most developing countries have a comparative cost advantage in the production of labor-intensive commodities. Most industrialized countries enjoy a comparative cost advantage in the production of capital-intensive commodities. Thus, specialization and trade could be mutually beneficial if industrialized countries specialize in the production and export of capital-intensive goods and if developing countries specialize in the production and export of labor-intensive goods.

Product Life Cycle Theory

All products have a certain length of life. During this life they go through certain stages. A product's life begins with its market introduction; its market then grows rather rapidly, its demand reaches maturity, its market declines, and finally its life ends. This theory attempts to explain both world trade and foreign investment.

In the context of international trade, the **product life cycle theory** assumes that certain products go through four stages.

1. A large company introduces a new product in response to some change in the home country market. After a time lag, this home country market establishes itself as an exporter with a monopoly position.

2. Increasing transportation and tariff costs make it less attractive to export the product. Thus, the firm begins to produce its product in some foreign countries. This international production replaces home country exports in certain foreign markets.
3. Some foreign companies begin to compete in third markets. This competition leads to a further reduction in home country exports.
4. Some foreign companies export the product back to the home country. Many factors such as low labor costs, economies of scale, and government subsidies make it possible for foreign companies to invade the home country market.

Other Motives for World Trade

Another important cause of international trade is the fact that costs may fall as outputs expand. If each country specializes in a limited number of products in which it has a comparative advantage, economies of mass production could be realized. Mass production and mass marketing improve skills and technologies. Opportunities to eliminate duplicate facilities occur. There are also opportunities to consolidate the functions of production, marketing, and purchasing. These types of operating economies and improved skills can lead to larger outputs of goods and services even if no differences in comparative costs between countries existed.

Even if differences in comparative costs between countries and economies of scale were absent, international trade might occur due to differences in tastes. Suppose that both Canada and Japan produce fish and meat in approximately the same amount. If Canadians prefer meat and Japanese prefer fish, then a mutually beneficial export of meat from Japan to Canada and fish from Canada to Japan would take place. Both nations gain from this exchange, because the sum total of satisfaction derived from the trade is greater than would be possible under isolated self-sufficiency without trade.

Free Trade versus Protectionism

It should be emphasized that the possibility of foreign embargo on sales of certain products and national defense needs may cause some countries to seek self-sufficiency in some strategic commodities. Political and military questions constantly affect international trade and other international business operations.

Tariffs and import quotas are the two primary means of protectionism. **Tariffs** on imported commodities may be imposed for purposes of revenues or protection. When tariffs are employed to protect domestic companies from foreign competition, they are typically high. When tariffs are used to increase revenues, they are usually modest. Although protective tariffs do not eliminate the importation of foreign products completely, they clearly put foreign sellers at a comparative disadvantage. Here consumers must pay more for foreign goods. Thus, consumers reduce their consumption of imported commodities. Domestic companies may benefit from such tariffs, but they kill all the advantage of specialization and trade.

To shield domestic producers from foreign competition, **import quotas** may also be used. They specify the maximum amounts of certain products to be imported during a given period of time, usually one year. Import quotas are sometimes more effective than tariffs in reducing the importation of certain products. Although tariffs are high, certain commodities are imported in relatively large quantities. In contrast, low import quotas totally prohibit imports beyond the quota.

Motives for Foreign Investment

The theory of comparative advantage and its corollary, the theory of factor endowments, have provided a foundation for the justification of world trade. However, similar theories for foreign investment are yet to be fully developed. Nevertheless, the product life cycle theory, the portfolio theory, and the oligopoly model have been suggested as a basis for explaining foreign investment.

Product Life Cycle Theory

The **theory of product life cycle** explains changes in the location of production. When new products are introduced in home country markets, their sales and profits tend to increase very sharply until they reach maturity. Competition increases rapidly as these products approach their maturity point. This competition narrows profit margins. At this stage, companies may utilize foreign manufacturing locations to lower production costs and sustain profit margins.

This theory assumes that large companies in highly advanced countries have a comparative advantage in new products. But companies in developing countries have a comparative advantage in the fabrication of mature products. Highly advanced technologies, highly educated labor resources, and abundant capital are essential to develop new products. They are readily available to larger firms in advanced countries. Larger markets and necessary alteration requirements in early production stages are additional reasons why larger companies in the developed areas of the world first introduce new products in the home country markets.

As products become mature, product defaults and technological imperfections, inherent in new products, are ironed out so that the production method becomes standardized. Competition begins to appear during the stage of market maturity. At this point, some companies begin to shift their standardized manufacturing method to developing countries for a number of good reasons. First, the standard production method requires many unskilled workers. Second, most developing nations have a relatively abundant supply of unskilled labor. Finally, labor costs are much lower in developing countries than in advanced countries.

Portfolio Theory

The **portfolio theory** relies on two variables: risk and return. **Risk** is the variability of returns associated with an investment project. Two projects may have the same long-term average rate of return, but one project may fluctuate widely in annual return while the other may have a stable return. A project whose returns fluctuate widely is said to be more risky than another whose returns are stable.

Typically, only a few financial variables are known in advance. Businessmen and investors are basically risk averters. Thus, they desire to minimize the overall degree of risk for their investment projects. Fortunately, there are many business situations where the risks of individual projects tend to offset each other. As a consequence, successful diversification makes it possible for a portfolio's risk to be less than the sum of the risks of the individual projects in the portfolio.

A company is often able to improve its risk-return performance by holding an internationally diversified portfolio of assets as opposed to a domestically diversified portfolio.

The key element in the portfolio theory is the correlation coefficient between projects in the portfolio. When projects with a low degree of correlation are combined with each other, a company is able to reduce its risk in relation to expected return. The portfolio theory assumes that foreign investment projects tend to be less correlated with each other than domestic investment projects. The economic cycles of different countries do not tend to be totally synchronized. On the other hand, most domestic projects tend to be highly correlated with each other because they depend upon the same state of economy.

Oligopoly Model

Oligopoly exists where there are only a few firms whose products are usually close substitutes for one another. Because a few firms dominate a market, each of these firms has a large share of the market, and its policies have repercussions on the other firms.

The **oligopoly model** offers a rationale to explain why multinational companies invest in foreign countries. The model assumes that business firms make foreign investments to exploit their quasi-monopoly advantages. The advantages of a multinational firm over a local firm may include technology, access to capital, differentiated products built on advertising, superior management, and organizational scale.

Horizontal investments for foreign production of the same goods in the home market are made to produce operating economies of scale. The horizontal investment may reduce the number of competitors, eliminate duplicate facilities, and expand the firm's operation in an existing product line. Vertical investments for foreign production of raw materials are made to control input sources. The control of input sources may make it possible for firms in an oligopolistic industry to raise barriers to the entry of new competitors and to protect their oligopoly position. Some companies make defensive investments to prevent others from getting an unanticipated advantage.

Other Motives for Foreign Investment

Companies may invest abroad to seek: (a) new markets, (b) raw materials, (c) production efficiency, and (d) new knowledge. Many companies, whose products are in a saturation stage in the home country markets, attempt to preserve or expand their markets for these products through foreign manufacturing locations. A subset of the market strategy falls within the context of the product life cycle theory. Oil companies, mining companies, and lumber companies find it difficult or costly to obtain raw materials at home. Hence, they invest their money abroad to obtain these raw materials. Some production-efficiency oriented companies look for low costs of production such as low labor costs. This is one of the most important reasons why multinational companies choose some countries in Africa, Asia, and South America for their foreign investment. Not many companies invest abroad to seek new knowledge, because multinational companies tend to have superior knowledge over local companies. However, some companies may desire to dig out news of technological developments in foreign countries through foreign investment.

The National Industrial Conference Board surveyed a sample of 60 nations and found that many developing countries have various incentive programs for private foreign investments. They include tax incentives, tariff exemptions, financial assistance, administrative assistance, protection against competitive investments and imports, remittance guarantees, and protection against nationalization and political risk. These and other incentive programs would undoubtedly motivate multinational companies to invest in those nations offering such incentives.

Yair Aharoni studied the foreign investment decision process. He surveyed 38 American companies which had invested or considered investment in Israel. This survey found that the motives for their investment in Israel were outside proposals such as those from foreign governments, fear of losing a market, strong competition from abroad in the home market, and the band wagon effect, meaning that successful foreign operations reported by a company induce its competitors to go abroad.

POLITICAL RISKS

Potential conflict between the goals of multinational companies and their host countries causes a variety of political risks for multinational companies. The primary goal of the company is to maximize the wealth of its stockholders. On the other hand, most host countries desire to develop their economy through greater utilization of local factors of production, to maintain more control over key industries through less reliance on foreign capital and know-how, and to strengthen their international position through less imports and more exports.

Operating in foreign countries involves risks that are not present in domestic operations. Such risks, for example, may be related to enforcement of contracts, repayment of loans, government restrictions of free flow of capital, and expropriation of assets. Therefore, it is important for multinational firms, commercial banks, and others who are engaged in international transactions to be able to assess a country's political risks. Country risk analysis requires the evaluation of the overall political and financial conditions of a country. *Euromoney* magazine ranks and reports countries' creditworthiness twice a year.

Types of Political Risks

Political risks are divided into two broad categories: actions that restrict the freedom of a foreign company to operate in a given host environment, and actions that result in the takeover of enterprise assets. The former category includes operational restrictions; employment policies and locally shared ownership; loss of transfer freedom, financial, personal, or ownership rights; breaches or unilateral revisions in contracts and agreements; discrimination such as taxes and compulsory joint ventures; and damage to property or personnel from riots, revolutions, or wars. The second category includes compulsory sales of business assets to local shareholders or host government units and confiscation of business assets with or without compensation.

Although there are many types of foreign environmental risks, much of the literature on this subject has concentrated on the extreme cases of expropriation or nationalization. Business operations in foreign countries are subject to the power of the host countries. It is customary that alien assets are seized for a public purpose, without discrimination, and with adequate compensation. Although these three rules are in accordance with a traditional principle of international law, they have been often ignored by many of the less developed countries.

Forecasting Political Interference

Once the nature of political risks and their implications have been examined, the focus should shift to the manager's task of forecasting these risks in foreign countries where

Chapter 20: Corporate Growth through Multinational Operations 345

his/her company has business interests. As multinational companies have become more experienced and more diversified, they have begun to maintain political forecasting staffs on a similar level as economic forecasting staffs.

In political risk analysis, a manager gives special attention to the "nationalism" of a host country. **Nationalism** represents loyalty to one's country and pride in it based on shared common features such as race, language, religion, or ideology. In other words, it is an emotion that can hinder or prevent rational dealings with foreigners. Some effects of nationalism on multinational firms are (1) requirements for minimum local ownership, (2) reservation of certain industries for local companies, (3) preference of local suppliers for government contracts, (4) limitations on number and type of foreign employees, (5) protectionism based on quotas and tariffs, and (6) expropriation or confiscation.

The task of political risk forecasting involves four basic steps.

1. The multinational company investigates the present administration's attitudes and policies toward foreign investment.
2. It assesses a country's political stability.
3. It integrates the political risk assessment into the company's strategic planning.
4. It develops strategies to reduce the company's exposure to political risks.

The first step in forecasting political interference is to understand the attitudes and policies of the present administration toward private foreign firms. The key here is to identify favorable or unfavorable trends affecting the climate in which the subsidiary will operate. There has always been evidence of a change in the government's attitude toward direct foreign investment prior to the overt act of confiscating alien assets. Other important factors to be considered include the dependency of the host country on the foreign investor's country for economic aid or political support; the types of pressures exerted on the chief governmental policy-makers; and the government's economic development plan in relation to foreign investment.

The second step in evaluating the vulnerability of a company to political risk is to understand the type of government currently in power, its patterns of political behavior, and its norms for stability. All these factors can be used to assess political stability of the host country. Political stability is in fact one of the principal preconditions for direct foreign investment by large multinational companies. The background information on the political environment of the host country goes far beyond an understanding of the administration's attitudes and policies toward direct foreign investment. The multinational company should understand the path along which all policies toward foreign investment have been made in the past.

Because political factors are subject to change, it is also important to institute an intelligence system to monitor and evaluate political developments. The intelligence system should be concerned with two things: (1) reliable in-house expertise about the host country and (2) the collection and distribution of necessary information to all relevant parties.

The third step in the process of political risk assessment is to integrate the assessment into the company's strategic planning. A multinational company may establish cutoff points for foreign projects under different conditions of political risk. In addition, the multinational company may design capital budgeting plans to reflect changes in the level of political risk.

Various political risks require multinational companies to modify their investment analysis. Because political risks are extremely high in some countries, multinational companies may decide to use a high risk premium in the cost of capital to compensate for those risks. This extra risk premium may eliminate new projects in these countries.

If foreign projects are divisible, different capital budget plans can be established to reflect different degrees of political risks. For example, oil companies may allocate their funds for oil exploration among countries with different levels of political risk. In addition, multinational companies can diversify their investment into projects with varying degrees of risk. Oil companies could invest a portion of their funds on safe projects such as pipe lines and the remaining portion of the funds on risky projects such as oil exploration.

The fourth step is to assess the relative strengths and security of the subsidiary itself. The multinational company must appraise the environment in which it operates as well as its bargaining power. The appraisal has a twofold objective: to learn how the affiliate can become a good citizen and to determine whether the host government will continue to need its presence. To become a good citizen of the host country, the multinational company may use the greatest possible amount of locally supplied raw materials, hire local people for managerial positions, and make the equity of the subsidiary available to the host country's investors. The subsidiary's ability to retain an essential status in the host country depends upon its competitive edge, the degree to which its product is valued by the host government, and the cost to the economy of local production of the product as opposed to importation.

Responses to Political Risks

Political risk forecasting is critical to the multinational company in reaching a decision on a particular project. The multinational company is not helpless in the case of political risk.

Defensive Measures Before Investment

Many host countries have recently increased their surveillance of foreign operations within their borders. To minimize subsequent political risks, it is desirable for the multinational company to negotiate concession agreements with host-country governments. The concession agreement spells out a contractual obligation on the part of both foreign investor and host country. Careful negotiation may result in contracts that address the foreign company's obligation to hire local people or agreements that provide for eventual termination of the foreign ownership. Such preinvestment contracts or agreements are very important to minimize subsequent expropriation or operational restrictions by the host-country government.

Planned divestment has been frequently suggested as one of the most important preinvestment strategies in order to avoid subsequent political risks. It provides for the sale of majority ownership in foreign affiliates to local nationals during a previously agreed-upon period of time. Planned divestment is often a necessary condition for entry into foreign markets or has been imposed on already existing companies. The major argument for planned divestment is that host countries benefit from direct foreign investment in the early years and successful foreign firms replace potential local firms in the later years. These benefits include new capital, entrepreneurship, new management, and technology. If successful foreign companies continue to dominate all the profitable growth areas, host countries tend to question what foreign companies have done for them.

The **concession agreement** specifies specific rights and responsibilities of both the foreign company and host country, but it is often revised to adapt to changing host-country priorities. When the foreign company sticks to the legal interpretation of its concession agreement, the host-country government uses pressures in areas not covered by the agreement. If these pressures do not work, the host-country government reinterprets the agreement as necessary to obtain desired changes from the foreign company. Thus, it is advisable for multinational companies to voluntarily adapt to changing host-country priorities whenever possible.

Defensive Measures After Investment

Once the decision to invest is made and defensive measures have been taken, several operating strategies can be used to cope with political risks. These are grouped for convenience into two types: strategies necessary to be a good citizen of the host country and strategies which make expropriatory actions difficult or unfeasible.

Many foreign affiliates often attempt to harmonize their policies with their host-country goals and priorities. They may hire an increasing number of local persons for positions initially held by representatives of the parent company management. They may share ownership with host-country private or public companies. They may develop and use local sources of supply for their raw materials and component requirements. They may try to export their products in order to bolster host country reserves of foreign exchange.

There are many operational policies and organizational approaches which make expropriatory actions extremely difficult or unfeasible. Foreign companies may maintain technological superiority over local companies and other competing foreign firms. The challenge here is to introduce technological improvements on a continuing basis into the host country. They may organize international operations in such a way that individual subsidiaries are integrated into a worldwide production and logistical system. Under such an integration, a subsidiary would not be able to operate or compete successfully, as is done in the petroleum industry. Examples of policy actions in this respect are: control of key patents and processes; joint-venture arrangements; capitalization with a thin equity base and a large local debt proportion; and control of key export markets for a subsidiary's products.

FOREIGN EXCHANGE MARKET AND RISKS

The efficient operation of the international monetary system has necessitated the creation of the foreign exchange market. This is a market where one country's currency can be exchanged for another country's currency. Unlike the term might suggest, the foreign exchange market actually is not a geographic location. It is an informal network of telephone, telex, facsimile, and computer communications between banks, foreign exchange dealers, arbitrageurs, and speculators. The foreign exchange market consists of a spot market and a forward market. In the spot market, foreign currencies are sold or bought at the current exchange rate for delivery (within two days after the day of trade). In the forward market, foreign currencies are currently sold or bought at an exchange rate established at the time the contract is made, but payment and delivery are not required until later (at maturity).

Foreign exchange rates represent prices of one currency in terms of another currency. The foreign exchange market employs both spot and forward exchange rates. The **spot rate** is the rate paid for immediate delivery of a currency and the **forward rate** is the rate paid for delivery of a currency at some future date. The forward exchange rate is established at the time of the contract, but payment and delivery are made at a future date. Forward rates are usually quoted for fixed periods of 30, 60, 90, or 180 days from the day of the contract. In some cases, actual contracts in major currencies can be arranged for delivery at any specified date to meet the customer's requirements. Practically all major newspapers in the world, such as *The Wall Street Journal* and the *London Financial Times*, print a daily list of exchange rates.

Foreign exchange rates are frequently given as direct quote or as an indirect quote. A direct quote is a home currency price per unit of a foreign currency, such as $0.50 per Franck franc (FF) for a U.S. resident. An indirect quote is a foreign currency price per unit of a home currency, such as FF2.00 per U.S. dollar for a U.S. resident. In France, the foreign exchange quote, $0.50 is an indirect quotation, while the foreign exchange quote, FF2.00 is a direct quote. Thus, direct and indirect quotes are reciprocals of each other. In the United States, both quotes are reported daily in *The Wall Street Journal* and other financial press.

The **purchasing power parity (PPP) doctrine** offers a rationale to explain how the exchange rate is determined in a free market. The absolute version of the PPP doctrine states that the equilibrium exchange rate between domestic and foreign currencies equals the rate between domestic and foreign prices. If one American dollar can buy two bushels of wheat and one Dutch guilder can buy one bushel of wheat, the exchange rate is 50 cents per guilder.

The relative version of the PPP doctrine indicates that, in the long run, exchange rates reflect the relative purchasing power of currencies. In other words, it relates equilibrium changes in the exchange rate to changes in the ratio of domestic and foreign prices.

Example 20-1. Let us assume that the exchange rate between U.S. dollars and British pounds is $2 per pound. Let us further assume that the United States will have an inflation rate of 10 percent for the coming year and England will have an inflation rate of 20 percent over the same period.

The PPP doctrine suggests that the U.S. dollar should increase in value by 10 percent relative to the British pound. The new exchange rate is determined as follows:

$$\text{New Exchange Rate} = \frac{\$2(1 + 0.10)}{£(1 + 0.20)} = \$1.83/£$$

Foreign Exchange Exposures

Foreign exchange risk is the risk of loss due to changes in the international exchange value of national currencies. Assume that a Japanese exporter sells TV sets on a three-month credit to U.S. citizens and invoices them in dollars. If the dollar declines in value relative to the Japanese yen three months later, the exporter suffers a loss in foreign exchange that may well wipe out the trade gain. If the dollar increases in value relative to the Japanese yen, it works to the advantage of the exporter.

Every company faces an exposure to foreign exchange risk as soon as it chooses to maintain a physical presence in a foreign country. **Foreign exchange exposure** refers to the possibility that a firm will gain or lose due to changes in exchange rates. By the same token, the firm faces an exposure to exchange risk when it chooses to finance its operations in foreign currencies. Both exchange risks are ordinarily analyzed in the context of investing and financing decisions. The three types of exchange exposure are translation exposure, economic exposure, and transaction exposure.

Translation Exposure

Companies may wish to translate financial statement items from a foreign currency into their home currency in order to prepare consolidated financial statements or to compare financial results. It is important to note that the term "conversion" should not be used in this case because we are not considering the actual conversion of one currency into another. Here we are simply restating values of financial statement items.

Translation exposure, sometimes called **accounting exposure**, measures the effect of an exchange rate change on a firm's published financial statements. Foreign-currency assets and liabilities that are translated at the current exchange rate are considered to be exposed. The difference between exposed assets and exposed liabilities is frequently called **net exposure** by accountants. Foreign currency depreciations will result in exchange losses and foreign appreciations will produce exchange gains if exposed assets are greater than exposed liabilities. On the other hand, foreign currency depreciations will lead to exchange gains and foreign currency appreciations will lead to exchange losses if exposed assets are smaller than exposed liabilities.

Transaction Exposure

Gains or losses may result from the settlement of transactions whose payment terms are stated in a foreign currency. **Transaction exposure** measures the effect of an exchange rate change on outstanding obligations which existed before the change but were settled after the change. Transactions subject to transaction exposure include credit purchases or sales of goods whose prices are stated in foreign currencies; borrowed or loanable funds denominated in foreign currencies; and uncovered forward contracts.

Receipts and payments denominated in foreign currencies are considered to be exposed. If exposed receipts are greater than exposed payments, foreign currency depreciations will cause exchange losses, and foreign currency appreciations will cause exchange gains. On the other hand, if exposed receipts are smaller than exposed payments, foreign currency depreciations will create exchange gains, and foreign currency appreciations will create exchange losses.

Economic Exposure

Economic exposure measures the impact of an exchange-rate change on the net present value of expected future cash flows. Future effects of exchange rate changes occur under the general category of economic risk. A multinational company may have established its subsidiary in a country with price stability, readily available funds, favorable balance of payments, and low rates of taxation. These positive features may disappear over time as the economic situation of the country deteriorates. Eventually the local currency will devalue or depreciate. The subsidiary is likely to face operational problems immediately if it has borrowed from abroad. Exchange rate change may also affect such economic factors as inflationary forces, price controls, the supply of loanable funds, and local labor availability.

Forecasting Currency Devaluation

Currencies are rarely devalued without prior indication of weakness. Most researchers in this area have attempted to forecast currency devaluation on the basis of some key economic indicators. Some of these indicators are balance of payments deficit, international reserves, inflation, money supply, and exchange spread between official versus market rates. These economic indicators are also used to forecast exchange controls. The use of such economic statistics depends upon the PPP doctrine. Under this doctrine combined with a freely flexible exchange rate system, if the United States had an inflation of 10 percent while Japan had an inflation of 20 percent, the Japanese yen should decline in value by about 10 percent relative to the dollar. Under a fixed exchange rate system, the difference between the forecasted and actual rates of exchange measures a currency's basic disequilibrium. Political factors and other economic factors such as relative interest rates are also considered in forecasting currency devaluation.

Managing Foreign Exchange Exposures

In the previous two sections, we focused on the types of foreign exchange and currency value forecasting. Before a multinational company decides when and by what techniques it should seek protection against exchange risk, it should identify the types of exchange exposure and then forecast devaluation or revaluation.

An arrangement that eliminates translation risk is said to hedge that risk. A **hedge** is designed to substitute a known cost of buying protection against foreign exchange risk for an unknown translation loss. One can use a variety of techniques to deal with translation exposure. Most hedging techniques designed to deal with translation exposure require a multinational company to adopt the following two basic strategies:

1. The company must increase hard-currency assets and decrease hard-currency liabilities.
2. The company must decrease soft-currency assets and increase soft-currency liabilities.

An action which removes transaction risk is said to cover that risk. A cover involves the use of forward contracts or a combination of spot market and money market transactions to protect a foreign exchange loss in the conversion from one currency to another. The term, "conversion," relates to transaction exposure because the transaction exposure involves the actual conversion of exposed assets and liabilities from one currency to another. Typical techniques to cope with transaction exposure include those described in the case of translation exposure as well as factoring accounts receivable, currency swaps, and transfer pricing.

Economic exposure is very broad in scope and affects a multinational company by changing its competitive capability profile across various markets and products. As a rule, economic exposure management is designed to neutralize the impact of unexpected exchange-rate changes on net cash flows. Diversified operations and diversified financing can be used to reduce economic exposure. They permit the multinational company to react actively or just passively to opportunities presented by disequilibrium conditions in the foreign exchange, capital, and product markets. Moreover, diversification strategies do not require that management predict disequilibrium conditions, but they require that it recognize them when they occur. In other words, the primary technique to minimize economic risk is strategic management in choosing products and markets, pricing policies, and promotion. On the financial side, the currency denomination of long-term debt, place of issue, maturity structure, capital structure, and leasing versus buying are additional tools that can be used to cope with economic risk.

When a devaluation seems likely, a company must determine whether it has an unwanted net exposure to exchange risk. If the company finds an unwanted net exposure to exchange risk, it can use a variety of techniques in order to reduce this net exposure. Adopting particular techniques to protect a net exposure depends primarily on two factors: (1) the potential exchange loss from exchange rate fluctuations and (2) the cost of buying protection against the potential exchange loss. The level of risk as measured by the potential exchange loss can be compared with the cost of providing protection against the foreign exchange loss. Essentially, management's basic objective with any exposure is to minimize the form of probable exchange losses and the cost of protection.

FINANCING FOREIGN TRADE

Foreign trade differs from domestic trade in terms of the instruments and documents used. Most domestic sales are made on an open-account credit, which does not require the buyer to sign a formal debt instrument. Under this credit, sales are made on the basis of the seller's credit investigation of the buyer. Buyers and sellers are typically farther apart in foreign trade than in domestic trade. Thus, the sellers are seldom able to ascertain the credit standing of their overseas customers. The buyers may also find it difficult to determine the integrity and reputation of the foreign sellers from which they wish to buy. The three important documents involved in foreign trade are: (1) a draft, which is an order to pay; (2) a bill of lading, which is a document involved in the physical movement of the merchandise by a common carrier; and (3) a letter of credit, which is a third party guarantee of the importer's credit-worthiness.

Drafts

A **draft** or a **bill of exchange** is an order written by an exporter that requires an importer to pay a specified amount of money at a specified time. Through the use of drafts, the exporter may use its bank as the collection agent on accounts that the exporter finances. The bank forwards the exporter's drafts to the importer directly or indirectly through a correspondent bank or a branch and then remits the proceeds of the collection bank to the exporter.

A draft involves three parties; the drawer or maker, the drawee, and the payee. The **drawer** is the person or business who issues the draft. This person is ordinarily the exporter who sells and ships the merchandise. The **drawee** is the person or business against whom the draft is drawn. This person is usually the importer who must pay the draft at maturity. The **payee** is the person or business to whom the drawee will eventually pay the funds. If the draft is not a negotiable instrument, it designates a person or bank to whom payment is to be made. Such a person, known as the payee, may be the drawer himself or a third party such as the drawer's bank. However, this is generally not the case because most drafts are a bearer instrument. Drafts are negotiable if they meet a number of conditions.

1. They must contain an unconditional promise or order to pay an exact amount of money.
2. They must be in writing and signed by the drawer-exporter.
3. They must be payable on sight or at a specified time.
4. They must be made out to order or to bearer. If a draft is made out to order, the fund involved should be paid to the person specified. If it is made out to bearer, the funds should be paid to the person who presents it for payment.

There are a number of reasons why drafts are used in foreign trade. First, they provide written evidence of obligations in a comprehensive form. Second, they allow both the exporter and the importer to reduce the cost of financing and to divide the remaining costs equitably. Third, they are negotiable and unconditional. That is, drafts are not subject to disputes which may occur between the parties involved.

Bills of Lading

A **bill of lading** is a shipping document issued to the exporting firm or its bank by a common carrier that transports the goods. It is simultaneously a receipt, a contract, and a document of title. As a receipt, the bill of lading indicates that specified goods have been received by the carrier. As a contract, it evidences the obligation of the carrier to deliver the goods to the importer in exchange for certain charges. As a document of title, it establishes the ownership of the goods. Thus, the bill of lading can be used to ensure payment before the goods are delivered. For example, the importer cannot take title to the goods until he obtains the bill of lading from the carrier.

Letters of Credit

A **letter of credit** is a document issued by a bank at the request of the importer. In the document, the bank agrees to honor a draft drawn on the importer if the draft accompanies specified documents such as the bill of lading. In a typical use, the importer asks that his local bank write a letter of credit. In exchange for the bank's agreement to honor the demand for payment that results from the import transaction, the importer promises to pay the bank the amount of the transaction and a specified fee.

The letter of credit is of advantage to both exporters and importers because it facilitates international trade. It gives a number of benefits to exporters. First, they sell their goods abroad against the promise of a bank rather than a commercial firm. Because banks are usually larger and better credit risks than most business firms, exporters are almost completely assured of payment if they meet specific conditions. Second, they can obtain funds as soon as they have such necessary documents as the letter of credit and the bill of lading. When shipment is made, the exporter prepares a draft on the importer in accordance with the letter of credit and presents it to his local bank. If the bank finds that all papers are in order, it advances the funds—the face value of the draft less fees and interest.

Although its major beneficiaries are exporters, the letter of credit also gives a number of benefits to importers. First, it assures them that the exporter will be paid only if he provides certain documents, all of which are carefully examined by a bank. If the exporter is unable to or unwilling to make proper shipment, recovery of the deposit is much easier from the bank than from the exporter. Second, the letter of credit enables the importer to remove the commercial risk for the exporter in exchange for other considerations. Thus, the importer can bargain for better terms such as a lower price. Moreover, it is comparatively cheaper to finance the goods under a letter of credit than by borrowing.

Financing Foreign Investment

The funds necessary to finance foreign investment can come from either internal or external sources. Internal sources of funds consist of retained earnings, depreciation charges, funds from the parent company, and funds from sister subsidiaries. In this section we cover external sources of funds—commercial banks, Eurobanks, development banks, joint ventures and international capital markets.

Commercial Banks

Commercial banks are not only a major financial intermediary in trade credit, but also they are the most important source of financing nontrade international operations.

Overdrafts

Overdrafts are one of the major short-term credits in Europe and Asia. An overdraft is a line of credit which permits the customer to write checks beyond deposits. The bank establishes the maximum amount of such credit based on its analysis of the customer's request, needs, and prospective cash flows. The borrower agrees to pay the amount overdrawn and interest on the credit. Although many banks waive service charges for their credit-worthy customers, some banks frequently require service charges and other fees.

Short-Term Bank Loans

Most **short-term bank loans** are made on an unsecured basis for multinational companies to cover seasonal increases in current assets. The percentages of such loans vary from country to country and reflect variations in individual bank policy and central government regulations. Most multinational firms prefer to borrow on an unsecured basis because the bookkeeping costs of the secured loans are high and they also have a number of restrictive provisions. However, some foreign subsidiaries cannot obtain loans on an unsecured basis because they are either financially weak or have not established a satisfactory performance record.

When foreign subsidiaries need short-term funds for only one purpose, they can obtain the funds by signing promissory notes. When they are in the process of obtaining long-term funds, these short-term loans may be made on a renewal basis. Such renewal short-term loans are frequently called bridge loans and are repaid when the permanent financing arrangement is completed.

Currency Swap

A **currency swap** is an agreement between parties to exchange one currency with another for a specified period of time and then exchange the latter currency with the former currency. **Arbi loans** are the best known example of such swaps. An arbi loan is arranged in a country where money is readily available at reasonable rates. It is converted to the desired local currency, but the borrower arranges a forward exchange contract to ensure conversion of the local currency into the foreign currency of original denomination at a specified future date. Thus, arbi loans allow multinational companies to borrow in one market for use in another market and to avoid foreign exchange risks. The cost of arbi loans include the interest on the loans and the charges associated with the forward exchange contract.

Link Financing

This financing permits multinational companies in weak-currency countries to tap external sources of funds indirectly. Commercial banks in strong-currency countries help subsidiaries in weak-currency countries obtain loans by guaranteeing repayment on the loans. These subsidiaries borrow money from local banks or firms with excess weak money. Certainly, the banks in strong-currency countries require some sort of deposits from the borrower's parent company and the borrower must pay local interest rates. To protect the cost against foreign exchange risk, the lender usually hedges his position in the forward exchange market.

The Edge Act of 1919

Edge Act and Agreement corporations are subsidiaries of American banks that are physically located in the United States but engage in international banking operations. The Edge Act of 1919 allowed American banks to act as holding companies and to own stock of foreign banks. Thus, these banks are able to provide loans and other banking services for American-owned companies in most countries around the world.

International Banking Facilities

Since December 3, 1981, banks in the United States have been allowed to establish **international banking facilities** (IBFs) at their offices in the United States. IBFs are vehicles that enable bank offices in the United States to accept time deposits in either dollars or foreign currency from foreign customers, free of reserve requirements and of other limitations. They can also extend credit to foreigners. Of course, U.S. multinational companies can borrow funds from IBFs to finance their foreign investment projects. IBFs are located in the United States, but in many respects they function like branch offices of U.S. banks. In other words, the creation of IBFs means the establishment of offshore banking facilities in the United States similar to other Eurocurrency market centers.

Eurocurrency Market

The Eurocurrency market consists of banks that accept deposits and make loans in foreign currencies outside the country of issue. These deposits are commonly known as **Eurocurrencies**. Thus, U.S. dollars deposited in London are called Eurodollars; German marks deposited in Paris are called Euromarks; British pounds deposited in Italy are called Eurosterling; and Japanese yen deposited in London are called Euroyen. The Eurocurrency market is free from national or domestic regulation.

Eurodollars are dollar-denominated deposits in banks outside the United States. These banks may be foreign banks or foreign branches of U.S. banks. Eurodollar deposits are either fixed-time deposits or negotiable certificates of deposit. Most Eurodollar deposits are in the form of time deposits. While maturities of these time deposits range from one day to a few years, most of them have a maturity of less than one year. A certificate of deposit (CD) is a negotiable (marketable) instrument issued by a bank. The important advantage of a CD over a time deposit is its liquidity because the holder of a CD can sell it in the secondary market at any time before the maturity date. Eurobanks issue negotiable CDs to attract idle funds from MNCs, oil exporting countries, and wealthy individuals. However, most Eurodollars are time deposits (non-negotiable).

Eurodollar loans range from a minimum of $500,000 to $100 million or more, typically in multiples of $1 million. Their maturities range from 30 days to a few years. But the major part of lending is for short-term financing. Eurodollar deposit and loan rates are determined by forces of supply and demand. These rates depend on the corresponding home country interest rates. Thus, Eurodollar interest rates on deposits and loans reflect U.S. domestic interest rates. The interest rate is usually stated as some spread over the London Interbank Offer Rate (LIBOR) and is adjusted at fixed intervals, like three months. These adjustable interest rates serve to minimize the interest rate risk to a bank. Large loans are generally made by syndicates of Eurobanks. The syndicate will be headed by a lead or managing bank; other banks wishing to participate in the loan will join the syndicate and help fund the loan.

Perhaps ironically, the former Soviet Union and other Communist countries started a large volume of transactions in Eurodollar deposits shortly after World War II. Eastern European countries were hesitant to deposit their dollar holdings in the United States for fear that these dollars might become blocked in the United States.

Eurodollars are an important source of funds for U.S. companies engaged in international business transactions. European banks with Eurodollars may use these funds in a number of ways. First, they may redeposit them in other European banks or European branches of a U.S. bank. These interbank deposits give the appearance of more Eurodollars than actually exist. Second, they may make loans to nonbank users such as multinational companies. These multinational firms can use the dollars to meet their dollar obligations or to buy local currencies. Third, they may transfer their dollars to Eurodollars in European branches of a U.S. bank, which in turn would lend these funds to the U.S. home office.

Development Banks

Development banks provide multinational companies with a broad range of financing resources. These banking organizations are established to support the economic development of underdeveloped areas through intermediate and long-term loans. There are three broad groups of development banks: worldwide, regional, and national.

World Development Banks

The **World Bank Group** is a group of worldwide financial institutions organized after the devastation of World War II to aid economic reconstruction. These institutions include the International Bank for Reconstruction and Development (IBRD), the International Development Association (IDA), and the International Finance Corporation (IFC). The IBRD was established in 1944 as the World Bank, and it provides capital when private sources are not available on reasonable terms. Its loans are used to finance such projects as schools, dams, roads, and basic industries. The IDA and the IFC were established to meet the specific needs of less developed countries. Their loans are designed to finance good projects that nonetheless are unable to support loan-repayment schedules with conventional terms.

Regional Development Banks

Groups of countries have established regional financial institutions to promote more effective economic development within the member countries. Leading regional development banks are the Inter-American Development Bank (IDB), the Asian Development Bank (ADB), the European Investment Bank (EIB), and the African Development Bank (AfDB).

The IDB was established in 1960 as a regional lending institution by the United States and 19 Latin American countries to further the economic development of its member countries. IDB loans are available only when private sources are not available on reasonable terms. It usually finances no more than 50 percent of total project cost.

The ADB was formed in 1966 by several Asian countries in partnership with the United States, Canada, Britain, Germany, and some other European countries. Approximately one-third of its subscribed capital and voting power belongs to nonregional industrial countries. The ADB makes long-term loans to private companies without government guarantees. Some ADB loans go to Asian national banks that relend to private enterprises through their respective development agencies. Some other ADB loans are used to supply risk capital.

The EIB was established in 1958 by members of the European Economic Community. Its resources are used to support the socioeconomic infrastructure of nations or basic industries. Most of these loans have maturities from 12 to 20 years. Ordinarily, three or four year intervals are established before loan repayments begin.

The AfDB was established in 1964 by the Organization of African Unity. Unlike other regional development banks, the AfDB had excluded nonregional partners in an effort to avoid undue outside influence until 1981. It makes long-term loans to industrial investors and underwrites equity offerings for projects.

National Development Banks

Many governments in industrial countries have their own development banks to foster international loans and investments. The three leading institutions for the United States are the Export-Import Bank (the Exim Bank), the Agency for International Development (AID), and the Overseas Private Investment Corporation (OPIC).

The Exim Bank was founded in 1934 as an independent agency of the U.S. government. Although the Exim Bank was originally created to facilitate trade with the former Soviet Union, its purpose has been expanded over the years. It makes the development loans to foreigners that enable them to buy American goods; it makes short- and intermediate-term loans to finance American exports; it can make loans to finance American imports; and it can finance exports or guarantee export credits which do not meet traditional criteria of reasonable assurance of payment.

The AID was established in 1961 to carry out non-military U.S. foreign assistance programs. The AID as an agency of the U.S. State Department places emphasis on assistance to friendly governments or support programs which will make foreign friends for the United States.

The OPIC was established in 1969 to handle the so-called Cooley Amendment Funds. The Funds are local currency funds received in payment for agricultural products sold by the United States either under the Mutual Security Act or the Agricultural Trade Development Assistance Act. The OPIC lends these funds to U.S. firms or subsidiaries in those countries that provided the funds by purchasing agricultural products from the United States. These loans are also extended to foreign private companies whose activities facilitate the expansion of overseas markets for U.S. agricultural products.

Joint Ventures

A **joint venture** is a corporate entity in which two or more parties; for example, a multinational firm and host country companies, have equity interest. In the past, use of a wholly owned subsidiary was the most common approach to overseas investment because worldwide strategy depended on complete control over all foreign operations. However, more and more host countries require that multinational companies have some local participation. In some situations, multinational companies will seek local partners even when there are no local requirements to do so.

Many factors may induce multinational firms to enter joint ventures with local partners. They include tax benefits, local marketing expertise, more capital, and less political risk. On the other hand, multinational companies want tight control of their foreign subsidiaries to efficiently allocate investments and to maintain a coordinated marketing plan on a global basis. Dividend policy, financial disclosure, transfer pricing, establishment of royalty and other fees, and allocation of production and marketing costs among plants are just some areas in which each owner has an incentive to engage in activities that could hurt its partners. This is why most multinational companies resist local participation. In fact, there are many cases in which multinational companies have chosen to pull out of foreign countries rather than to comply with government regulations that require joint ventures.

The International Capital Market

The international capital market consists of the international bond market and the international equity market. The three largest stock exchanges in terms of total market value are the New York, Tokyo, and London stock exchanges. The soaring yen and rapid increase in Japanese security prices caused Tokyo to surpass New York in the Spring of 1987 to become the world's largest capital market. However, the United States regained the lead in 1992 because of the recent recession in Japan.

The International Bond Market

International bonds are those bonds that are initially sold outside the country of the borrower. International bonds consist of foreign bonds, Eurobonds, and global bonds. **Foreign bonds** are bonds sold in a particular national market by a foreign borrower, underwritten by a syndicate of investment bankers from that country, and denominated in the currency of that country. **Eurobonds** are bonds underwritten by an international syndicate of investment bankers and sold simultaneously in many countries other than the country of the issuing entity. **Global bonds** are underwritten by an international syndicate of investment bankers and sold simultaneously in all major world capital markets including the country in whose currency they are denominated. Global bonds fall under the regulatory jurisdiction of national or domestic authorities, such as the SEC in the U.S. For example, a foreign bond called a **Yankee bond** is a bond issued by a foreign borrower, denominated in U.S. dollars, and sold in the U.S. A **Samurai bond** is a bond issued by a foreign borrower, denominated in Japanese yen, and sold in Japan. The Eurobond market is almost entirely free of national or domestic regulation.

Eurobonds are in bearer form rather than registered form as is the case for U.S. bonds. There are several different types of international bonds. **Eurostraight**, which dominates the market, is a fixed-rate, noncallable bond. Also, there are **floating-rate bonds** whose interest is adjusted at regular intervals, usually every six months, to reflect the short-term rates such as LIBOR, bonds with warrants, convertible bonds, and dual-currency bonds. A **dual currency bond** pays interest in one currency and the principal is paid in another currency.

The International Equity Market

In addition to debt markets such as Eurocurrency markets and international bond markets, the equity capital market is another important source of financing international transactions. Although the international equity market is the youngest segment of international financial markets, international equities have become an important segment of financial markets. International equity refers to two related activities and instruments. The term **international equity** is used for a simultaneous offering of a new issue of equity by a company in a number of countries. We may also use this term to describe foreign stocks that are registered and traded on a country's stock exchanges. Many multinational corporations' stocks are listed and traded on foreign stock exchanges. Foreign stocks listed and traded on New York markets (NYSE and OTC) are called American Depository Receipts (ADR).

SUMMARY

There are many indications that the scope of financial management should be expanded for multinational companies. Some of them are the increased world trade, the increased movement of both human and financial resources between countries, the growth in the number and size of multinational companies, and the improved capability for the collection and analysis of information. Moreover, most large and many medium-size companies in the United States have international business operations of one type or another. In recent years, it has become clear that even U.S. companies without foreign investment can be significantly affected by events in the international environment.

Essentially, the concepts of business management are equally applicable to multinational and domestic companies. However, these two types of companies are subject to environmental differences. These differences include taxes, the economic system, the political system, inflation and interest rates, and many others. Thus, the financial manager must know the institutions and environmental conditions in all foreign countries in which his company has subsidiaries and affiliates.

Chapter 20: Corporate Growth through Multinational Operations

List of Key Terms

theory of comparative advantage
product life cycle theory
import quotas
risk
oligopoly model
nationalism
concession agreement
foreign exchange exposure
accounting exposure
transaction exposure
hedge
bill of exchange
drawee
bill of lading
overdrafts
arbi loan
Eurodollars
World Bank Group
international bonds
Eurobonds
international equity

theory of factor endowments
tariffs
portfolio theory
oligopoly
political risks
planned divestment
foreign exchange rate
translation exposure
net exposure
economic exposure
draft
drawer
payee
letter of credit
currency swaps
Edge Act and Agreement corporations
development banks
joint venture
foreign bonds
global bonds

Part 7

Case Problems in Finance

Case Study 1

RATIO ANALYSIS

WAYNE AIRLINES

Susan Mary Nickerson is the new treasurer of Wayne Airlines. She graduated from a major university in Michigan with an M.B.A. in Finance. After five years of experience with one of the Big Eight CPA firms in Detroit, she joined the accounting staff of Midwest Airlines and served in a variety of accounting and finance positions for ten years. She assumed the position of treasurer at Wayne Airlines on May 3, 1986. One of her first responsibilities is to analyze the company's financial condition shortly after the airline's fiscal year, which ended on June 30, 1986.

Exhibit 1
Wayne Airlines Balance Sheets as of June 30, 1985–1986
(in millions of dollars)

	1985	1986
Cash	$ 42	$ 42
Accounts receivable	182	140
Maintenance and supplies inventory	196	210
Total current assets	$ 420	$ 392
Gross plant and equipment	1,680	2,072
Less: accumulated depreciation	700	784
Net plant and equipment	980	1,288
Total assets	$1,400	$1,680
Accounts payable	$ 63	$ 76
Notes payable	84	280
Accruals	28	50
Total current liabilities	$ 175	$406
Long-term debt	273	280
Common stock	280	280
Retained earnings	672	714
Total liabilities and net worth	$1,400	$1,680

Susan Nickerson has seen major changes in the airline industry since Congress enacted the Air Transportation Regulatory Reform Act (ATRRA) in 1978. The ATRRA, an amendment to the Federal Aviation Act of 1958, deregulated the airline industry significantly. This law, among other things, increased competition and facilitated the entry of new airlines into the marketplace. Before 1978, the Civil Aeronautics Board (CAB) had regulated fares and authorized routes for airlines. Under the 1978 legislation, the CAB was phased out by the end of 1985.

Wayne Airlines added several cities to its routes shortly after the deregulation of the industry because management felt such a move would facilitate growth. Wayne purchased a number of new airplanes to meet its expanded routes and replaced aging airplanes. These new airplanes were mostly financed by short-term bank loans to be paid from profits generated by the expansion. However, the airline encountered substantial fare and route competition from other trunk carriers. The industry's deregulation in 1978 caught Wayne with huge fixed costs and expensive labor agreements. Newer regional carriers, free of such cumbersome overhead, were able to offer lower fares profitably, but Wayne's ability to do so was strained. Furthermore, the economic downturn depressed passenger traffic, thereby causing a glut of airline capacity.

Exhibit 2
Wayne Airlines Income Statement for Year Ended June 30, 1986
(in millions of dollars)

Operating revenues		
Passenger	$1,830	
Freight	95	
Other	35	
Total revenues		$1,960
Operating expenses		
Flying operations	662	
Maintenance	212	
Equipment and passenger services	523	
Promotion and sales	209	
General and administrative	52	
Depreciation	84	
Total operating expenses		1,742
Operating Income		$ 218
Interest expense		58
Earnings before tax		$ 160
Tax		80
Earnings after tax		$ 80

Wayne, one of the largest airlines in the United States, is headquartered in Los Angeles, California. Since its establishment in 1917, the company has successfully weathered severe cyclical fluctuations characteristic of the airline industry. But as with rest of the airline industry, its sales and profitability for the last few years severely declined. The failure of Braniff Airlines reflected the serious problems facing the entire airline industry because of business slowdowns, deregulation of the industry, the air traffic controllers' strike, higher fuel costs, and intensified competition. Expanding operations had resulted in an increasingly strained working capital position for Wayne. Profits for the airline had dropped considerably since its expansion program started early in 1979 (see Exhibits 1, 2 and 3).

Exhibit 3
Industry Average Ratios

Ratios	Industry
Current ratio	3.5 times
Quick ratio	1.50 times
Average collection period	30.0 days
Asset turnover	1.20 times
Debt ratio	45.0 percent
Times interest earned	4.10 times
Profit margin on sales	4.00 percent
Return on investment	4.80 percent
Return on net worth	8.73 percent

QUESTIONS

1. Calculate the appropriate ratios of liquidity, leverage, activity, and profitability for Wayne.
2. Discuss the relative strengths and weaknesses of the airline.
3. List and discuss cautions which must be taken in using industry average ratios.
4. Prepare Wayne's funds flow statement and then explain why the company encountered an increasingly strained working capital position.
5. Discuss how to solve the airline's most pressing problems.

Case Study 2

CASH BUDGETING

CANTON TOY COMPANY

The Canton Toy Company enjoyed a rapid growth in business. In the spring of 1990, it anticipated a further substantial increase in sales. But, despite good profits and a $300,000 line of credit with its bank, Canton Toy experienced a shortage of cash. It estimated that required borrowings from July through September would add several hundred thousand dollars to its bank loan of $300,000 at the beginning of the budget period.

Robert Jordan, president of the company, scheduled a luncheon appointment with Doug Mitchell, the commercial loan officer who handled Canton's account. The two men had recently discussed the possibility of increasing Canton Toy's line of credit from $300,000 to $500,000. They agreed that $500,000 would be sufficient to handle the company's estimated working capital needs for 1990. Mr. Jordan asked that his accountant, Jean Bell, prepare a cash budget for the six months ending December 31, 1990. The cash budget would be used to support the company's request for an increased line of credit.

The Canton Toy Company manufactures a wide variety of plastic toys such as billiard sets, automobiles, trucks, guns, rockets, and satellites. The plastic toy industry was a highly competitive business, populated by many companies. New competitors easily entered the industry because capital requirements were relatively small and the technology was relatively simple. On the other hand, fierce design and price competition resulted in short product lives and numerous failures.

Canton Toy's sales forecast indicates expected sales of $6.24 million for 1990. Demand for its plastic toys has always been highly seasonal. Approximately 70 percent of sales were expected in the last six months of the year, with thirty-five percent of annual sales concentrated in September and October. The company's production schedules were also highly seasonal because it produced toys in response to customer orders. One change in this practice was that on November 7, 1989, the company decided to adopt level monthly production for 1990.

Miss Bell collected the information for a cash budget based on cash receipts and disbursements. She estimated sales for the last six months of 1990 as given in Exhibit 1. These sales are 90 percent for credit and 10 percent for cash. Analysis of past collections indicated that 20 percent of credit sales are collected in the month of sale, and 80 percent in the month after sale. At the beginning of July, Canton Toy had accounts receivable of $320,000 or (80 percent of $400,000 credit sales in June) which were to be collected in July. The company had a cash balance of $100,000 on June 30, 1990. This amount is the minimum cash balance which should be maintained throughout the budget period. Monthly purchases of raw materials are $288,000. The company buys its raw materials on 30-day terms and pays its bills on time. With level production and no projected increase during the period in wages and salaries, the payroll is expected to be $120,000 per month. Payments of overhead expenses such as heat, light and power, insurance, telephone bills, and rental payments are forecasted to be $52,000 per month. Cash outlays to cover selling expenses are estimated to be $60,000 per month. Monthly payments of general and administrative expenses are forecasted to be $30,000.

Exhibit 1
Canton Toy Company Sales Estimates for Last Six Months of 1990
(in thousands)

July	$ 500
August	600
September	1,000
October	1,200
December	400

The company's capital budget calls for the purchase of a new machine for $80,000; its payments will be made in September. Income tax payments of $38,000 each are due in September and December. A $60,000 installment payment on the principal of a $600,000 term loan is due on December 31; interest of $54,000 or (9 percent of the $600,000 term loan) is also due on December 31. A semiannual dividend payment of $50,000 is planned on December 15.

QUESTIONS

1. Prepare the cash budget of the Canton Toy Company for the second half of 1990. In preparing the cash budget, disregard both the interest on any bank loan the company may need and any income on surplus funds.
2. Estimate cumulative loan balances or surplus funds for each month during the budget period. Will a proposed $50,000 line of credit be sufficient to cover the forecasted deficits?
3. What are the values of the cash budget to the company?
4. What are advantages and disadvantages of the level production plan?

Case Study 3

Profitability Analysis

Midwest Business Instruments

In late September 1990, Eric Miller, vice president of finance for Midwest Business Instruments, was preparing for the October meeting of the finance committee. He examined various sources of funds available to finance the company's capital expansion and reviewed the company's financial statements (see Exhibit 1) with an eye toward establishing a new working capital policy.

Midwest Business Instruments was founded in 1942 by Nancy Miller to produce manual typewriters. Through the 1940s and 1950s, the company grew at a rapid pace, expanding its product line to include manual calculators and other business instruments. But the company's growth then stagnated until the late 1960s, when electric typewriters and calculators replaced their manual counterparts as the company's major products. Midwest Business has expanded rapidly since 1968, when its first plant was established in Wichita, Kansas, to produce a new generation of business instruments. The company placed two other plants on line in 1978, one in Chicago and another in Detroit.

Midwest Business' major problem has been increasing production fast enough to meet the demand for its products. The company's capacity has been expanded steadily since 1978, but it has often lost sales because of insufficient production. Recognizing this problem, Linda Schmidt, president and chief executive officer, called a meeting of the finance committee to consider ways to increase production and to review financing alternatives proposed by Mr. Miller. The meeting was attended by Linda Schmidt, president; Eric Miller, vice president of finance; Deborah Palmer, vice president of marketing; and Michael Kamanski, director and banker.

Deborah Palmer reported that the company needs a new plant to produce enough typewriters and calculators to meet market demand. She also said that the company will have to diversify into the mini and desk computer field in the near future because its major competitors have expanded their product line to include this product since 1986. Michael Kamanski agreed that it is important for Midwest Business to expand its production capacity, but he indicated that it would be very difficult to obtain long-term debt financing at the present time. Because the company's debt ratio is the same as the industry average, he felt that long-term lenders would demand a healthy risk premium on the new debt. He proposed that the capital expansion be financed by a new issue of common stock.

Linda Schmidt interrupted at this point and stated that a common stock offering was perhaps out of the question for two reasons. First, the sale of new common stock is not desirable because it was currently selling in the over-the-counter market at $12 per share, which is at least a 3-year low. Second, most current stockholders are not in a position to purchase additional common stock, and the sale of new common stock to outsiders would produce a significant dilution of earnings and control.

Exhibit 1
Midwest Business Instruments Financial Data
for Year-Ending August 30, 1990

	Midwest Business	Percent of Total	Industry Averages
A. Balance Sheet			
Current assets	$ 4,320,000	40%	30%
Net fixed assets	6,480,000	60%	70%
Total assets	$10,800,000	100%	100%
Current liabilities (8%)	$ 1,404,000	13%	13%
Long-term debt (10%)	4,320,000	40%	40%
Common equity	5,076,000	47%	47%
Total liabilities & common equity	$10,800,000	100%	100%
B. Income Statement			
Sales	$14,400,000		
Operating expenses	12,240,000		
Earnings before interest & taxes	$ 2,160,000		
Interest	544,320		
Taxable income	$ 1,615,680		
Taxes (50%)	807,840		
Earnings after taxes	$ 807,840		
C. Key Ratios			
Current ratio	3.08x		2.31x
Return on common equity	15.92%		13.85%
Operating expenses to sales	85.0%		85.0%
Debt to total assets	53.0%		53.0%

Eric Miller, who has responsibility for accounting and finance, entered the discussion at this point and stated that other financing alternatives such as leasing and the reduction of dividend payments were probably also out of the question. Restrictions in the company's long-term debt agreements made lease financing practically impossible. The company cannot reduce its dividend payments drastically without risking further declines in its stock price. Thus, Mr. Miller said that the best way to obtain funds for the company's capital expansion would be in the working capital area. Current liabilities might be increased and/or current assets might be decreased to produce the necessary funds.

Mr. Miller proposed 3 working capital policies for consideration: (1) a conservative policy that would maintain the current working capital structure; (2) an intermediate policy that calls for reducing current assets to the industry average percentage with no change in current liabilities; and (3) a liberal policy that calls for reducing current assets by 20 percent and increasing current liabilities by 20 percent. Long-term debt and common equity would be maintained at present levels under all of these policies. The intermediate policy is expected to increase sales by 5 percent, and the liberal policy is expected to increase sales by 10 percent. All finance committee members except Eric Miller indicated apprehension about any change in working capital policy, but agreed to postpone the final decision on this matter until Mr. Miller could prepare a more detailed analysis of the possibilities.

QUESTIONS

1. Prepare an exhibit that will show (a) the balance sheet, (b) the income statement, and (c) the key ratios for each policy.
2. Discuss the risk-return tradeoff among the alternative policies.
3. Which of the three alternatives should Mr. Miller recommend at the next meeting?

Case Study 4

INVENTORY MANAGEMENT

MILLER TOY COMPANY

The Miller Toy Company is a distributor of children's electronic toys in the Chicago metropolitan area. Despite the current declining birth rate and lower child population in the United States, toy sales are climbing. With an increasing trend in the number of two-income households in the economy, many couples are able to afford more spending on items such as toys and clothing. The company has been very successful in recent years due primarily to its focus on electronic toys only. Although such toys are designed for children only, people of all ages have shown interest in them. The company sells only standard electronic toys at discounted prices to other retailers in the area. Sales have more than doubled in the last two years to $12.6 million in 1990.

Lately, Glen Miller, the owner and the chief executive officer, has been somewhat concerned about his firm's ability to continue to raise the required amount of capital to finance future growth in sales. The firm is currently borrowing $1.1 million from a local bank. While Mr. Miller has always been treated as a preferred customer of the bank, Mr. Ray Scott, vice president and loan officer at the bank, showed some signs of displeasure at their recent meeting. Mr. Scott has been handling the firm's account for the last few years and is familiar with the firm's financial situation. He indicated that the money has been getting tight and the interest rates are climbing up. The bank will have to become more selective in reviewing short-term loans to smaller companies and may even have to turn down some applicants if the firm's financial ratios get too much out-of-line with the industry norms. While Mr. Scott assured Mr. Miller that his firm was not in any immediate danger of curtailment in the existing line of credit, however, such action may be forthcoming if the firm continues to operate with the existing trend in its key financial rations.

Upon returning from the bank, Mr. Miller asked his secretary Mary to call Pamela Davis, the firm's accountant, to see him immediately. Miss Davis was in the middle of discussion with a computer salesperson when she got the call from Mary. The salesperson was trying to show her the usefulness of a desk-top computer for her office. Miss Davis excused herself and rushed straight towards Mr. Miller's office. Mr. Miller told her about his conversation with Ray Scott and expressed his serious concern about some of the deteriorating financial ratios. He charged Miss Davis with the responsibility of evaluating the financial situation and to come up with her recommendations within the next three days.

Miss Davis went to work immediately and examined the most recent available income statement and balance sheet of the firm as shown in Exhibits 1 and 2. She also obtained a list of key financial ratios of other firms in the industry (Exhibit 3). While comparing the ratios for the company with those industry norms, Miss Davis noticed that the inventory turnover ratio was very low indicating excessive investment in inventory. Her observation about excessive inventory further confirmed when she compared her company's current ratio and quick ratio to industry averages. As a matter of fact, inventory turnover ratio has steadily deteriorated over the past few years. Further investigation with the purchasing department revealed that there was no inventory control system in operation and the purchasing department ordered inventory purely on the basis of guess work and quantity discounts

Exhibit 1
Miller Toy Company Income Statement for the Year Ending December 31, 1990.

Net sales	$12,600,000
Cost of goods sold	7,200,000
Gross profit	$ 5,400,000
Selling, general, & administrative expense	4,640,000
Net Operating income	$ 760,000
Interest expense	160,000
Earnings before taxes	$ 600,000
Federal income taxes at 40%	240,000
Net income after taxes	$ 360,000

Exhibit 2
Miller Toy Company Balance Sheet as of December 31, 1990

Cash and securities	$ 628,000	Accounts payable	$1,570,000
Accounts receivable	648,000	Notes payable	1,100,000
Inventory	3,140,000	Total current debt	$2,670,000
Total current assets	$4,416,000	Equity	4,946,000
Fixed assets	3,200,000	Total debts and	
Total assets	$7,616,000	net worth	$7,616,000

Exhibit 3
Miller Toy Company Industry Average Ratios

Current ratio	1.6 times
Quick ratio	0.8 times
Inventory turnover	9.0 times
Debt ratio	40.0 percent
Net profit margin	8.0 percent

Exhibit 4
Miller Toy Company
Carrying Cost as a Percentage of Inventory Value

Storage and handling	5.0%
Insurance	2.0
Financing cost	12.0
Deterioration and Obsolescence	5.0
Property taxes	<u>1.0</u>
Total carrying cost	25.0%

Exhibit 5
Miller Toy Company Stockout Costs

Safety Stock (Units)	Stockout Costs
100	$5,300
200	4,640
300	4,060
400	3,555
500	2,950
600	2,420
700	1,940
800	1,510
900	1,130
1,000	810
1,100	520
1,200	330
1,300	200
1,400	100
1,500	0

The annual sales of the company during the past year comprised of 450,000 units of toys at an average price of $28 a piece. Miss Davis interviewed the purchasing manager regarding the reordering process. Each purchase order form is typed in quadruplicate. The original is sent to the supplier, one copy is sent to the accounting department, one is sent to the warehouse staff and the last one is kept on file. When shipment arrives, the warehouse personnel verify the order and shortages are noted and the damaged items are returned back. Miss Davis estimated that the whole process costs $160 per order. Further investigation of the data helped Miss Davis to calculate the inventory carrying costs as a percentage of inventory value. For example, the company paid $157,000 in storage charges and handling fee for $3,140,000 inventory. It amounted to 5 percent or ($157,000/$3,140,000) carrying cost on account of storage and handling. It was further noted that seasonal trends in inventory were minimal. Exhibit 4 gives a summary of the various carrying costs which amounted to 25 percent of its inventory value on a cost basis. The average cost of electronic toys was $16 each for the proceeding year.

Miss Davis was aware of the fact that any inventory control model cannot work unless some estimate of safety stock is made. The purpose of the inventory safety stock is to minimize any stockout costs which may result due to more in terms of added carrying costs. Her job was to maintain a delicate balance between the carrying costs and the stockout costs. The company earned $0.80 after tax per toy sold. Miss Davis figured if the firm frequently runs out of inventory of toys when customers want to buy it, the company would lose profit as well as goodwill. Some of the customers may be lost forever to competitors. Miss Davis prepared Exhibits 5 which shows the firm's stockout costs, including loss of goodwill, at varying levels of safety stock.

Questions

1. Is Mr. Ray Scott's assertion correct that some of the ratios for the Miller Toy Company are out of line?
2. What is the firm's economic order quantity?
3. How many orders should the firm place in one year?
4. Calculate the number of toys the company should have as its safety stock.
5. What is the firm's average inventory, including the safety stock, if the EOQ (economic order quantity) system becomes operative?
6. At what inventory level should the firm reorder, including the safety stock, if it takes four days for the shipment to arrive (assume 360 days in one year)?
7. Will the introduction of the EOQ system result in the reduction of inventory? If so, by how much?

Case Study 5

SECURED SHORT~TERM FINANCING

LEWIS CLOTHING COMPANY

After a rapid growth in its business during recent years, the Lewis Clothing Company in January 1991 anticipated a further substantial increase in sales. Despite good profits, the company has experienced a shortage of cash and has found it necessary to increase its long-term dept from the City National Bank to $523,000 in January 1991. Lately, Glen Scott, the founder and chief executive officer of the company, has been somewhat concerned about his firm's ability to raise the required amount of capital to finance future growth in sales. While Mr. Scott has been treated as a preferred customer of the City National Bank, Susan Park, vice president and loan officer at the bank, showed some signs of considerable displeasure at their recent meeting.

The Lewis Clothing Company, located in Chicago, is a manufacturer of sportswear and swimsuits for men, women, and juniors. The company was incorporated in 1977, but until 1987 Mr. Scott purposely restricted his sales to the Chicago area. During the last few years, however, he did notice a decided increase in his sales volume. From 1987 on, the company's sales grew rapidly and Mr. Scott found it hard to expand the company fast enough to keep up with demand. The company has now about 720 customers (department stores and specialty shops) throughout the midwestern United States.

Keith Miller, the newly appointed vice president of finance, has been pondering the short-term financial problems of the company. Before Mr. Miller took the job, he knew that his predecessor had been fired for inept working capital management. In order to better understand this alleged ineptness, he decided to analyze the financial data listed in Exhibits 1 and 2.

Mr. Miller has noted that the company's net sales and earnings after taxes have increased rapidly since 1987. This growth has been accompanied by comparable increases in assets and liabilities. He found that, while earnings rates have continued to improve, they were below industry standards for returns on investment and net sales. Furthermore, he observed that the company's return on owners' equity has been higher than the industry norm in 1989 and 1990 simply because its debt ratio has increased steadily and has been consistently higher than the industry average.

Mr. Miller was stunned by a number of additional findings. First, the current ratio has dropped considerably to well below the industry average. Second, bad debt losses have expanded to four or five times the industry average. Third, the average collection period has been more than twice the industry standard. Fourth, while the dividend as a percent of earnings after taxes has declined somewhat during recent years, it has been approximately two times as much as the industry norm. Fifth, the company received a notice from the City National Bank which stated that the loan would be declared due and immediately payable unless the current ratio of 1.76 was not improved to meet the industry average of 2.00 within two months. The bank's notice indicated that Miller's predecessor had received a less severe notice one year earlier. Finally, the City National Bank had raised the interest rate on the loan in 1989 and 1990 mainly due to the company's request for increases in the loan and its declining liquidity.

Exhibit 1
Lewis Clothing Company Balance Sheets as of December 31, 1987 to 1990 (in thousands of dollars)

	1987	1988	1989	1990
Cash	$ 203	$ 137	$ 140	$ 161
Accounts receivable	972	1,085	1,166	1,486
Inventory	1,147	1,213	1,418	1,759
Current assets	$2,322	$2,435	$2,724	$3,406
Plant and equipment (net)	549	605	701	828
Total assets	$2,871	$3,040	$3,425	$4,234
Accounts payable	$ 600	$ 730	$ 894	$1,268
Accruals	331	368	504	668
Current liabilities	$ 931	$1,098	$1,398	$1,936
Long-term bank loan	281	262	315	520
Common stock	1,000	1,000	1,000	1,000
Retained earnings	659	680	712	778
Total liabilities and owners' equity	$2,871	$3,040	$3,425	$4,234

[1] The inventory consists of 10 percent raw materials, 80 percent work in process, and 10 percent finished goods.

[2] The long-term bank loan at an interest cost equal to the prime rate, plus 1 percent (1987-1988); 1.5 percent (1989); and 3 percent (1990).

[3] Insiders control about 40 percent of common stock.

Mr. Miller has been informed by Mr. Scott that the company will continue its plan for future sales growth and that it will not reduce its dividend payout ratio below 70 percent. Of course, he knows exactly what Mr. Scott has asked him to do: (1) quickly meet the bank's mandate of increasing the current ratio, (2) simultaneously lower the average collection period and the debt ratio, and (3) drastically reduce the amount of bad debt losses.

As Mr. Miller suspects that stockholders would not approve new preferred or common stock issues at this time, he has proposed three alternatives for the consideration of Lewis Clothing's directors. The first alternative calls for a reduction in current liabilities through increases in the outstanding long-term bank loan, the latter possibly secured by inventory. The second alternative calls for the pledging of accounts receivable with a major finance company at an interest cost equal to the prime rate, plus a 3 percent premium. In this regard, he notes that the prime rate is currently 12 percent. In addition, the company would be responsible for any bad debt losses. The third alternative calls for the factoring of accounts receivable at a commission rate of 2 percent of net sales and an interest cost equal to the prime rate, plus a 2.5 percent premium on advances before the receivables' average due date.

Exhibit 2
**Lewis Clothing Company Other Financial Data
as of December 31, 1987 to 1990**

	1987	1988	1989	1990	Industry Average
Net sales ($000)	$4,579	$5,071	$5,797	$6,896	NA
Earnings after taxes ($000)	$ 144	$ 166	$ 207	$ 259	NA
Dividend as % of earnings after taxes	90.5%	87.3%	84.5%	74.5%	40.0%
Current ratio	2.49	2.22	1.95	1.76	2.00
Average collection period	77 days	78 days	73 days	79 days	35 days
Debt ratio	42%	45%	50%	58%	40%
Bad debt losses at % of gross sales	1.5%	2.5%	4.0%	5.0%	1.0%
Return on investment (%)	5.0%	5.5%	6.0%	6.1%	7.0%
Return on owners' equity	8.7%	9.9%	12.1%	14.6%	12.5%
Return on net sales (%)	3.2%	3.3%	3.6%	3.8%	4.5%

[1]All sales on credit whose terms are equal to the industry average.

[2]The operating costs of the company's credit department are 2 percent of net sales.

QUESTIONS

1. What is the effective interest cost of the second alternative (pledging of accounts receivable) to the company?
2. What is the effective interest cost of the third alternative (factoring of accounts receivable) to the company?
3. If all accounts receivable were factored and these funds were used to pay off current liabilities, what would have been the effect on the current ratio, the debt ratio, and bad debt losses for 1990?
4. Do you think the City National Bank would increase its loan to the company, even if it were secured by inventory?
5. Which of the three alternatives should the company select?

Case Study 6

CASH FLOW ANALYSIS FOR CAPITAL BUDGETING

YORK FIBER CORPORATION

Kevin Redlin, president of the York Fiber Corporation, called to order a meeting of the Finance Committee on September 7, 1989, at 2:30 p.m. The purpose of the meeting was to review a $20 million capital budget proposal for the production of polyester fiber. The company was currently a leading manufacturer of rayon and nylon fibers for tire cord in the United States. This market was shrinking, however, because of competitive inroads made by polyester fiber manufacturers. Top management of York Fiber felt that an entry into polyester fiber could allow the company to preserve its leading market position in tire cord and also move it into the production of polyester fiber for other end uses.

On December 31, 1988, the York Fiber Corporation of Long Island, New York completed its 27th year of uninterrupted growth in sales and earnings per share. During the period 1960-1980, almost all of York Fiber's sales consisted of rayon and nylon fibers. About 70 percent of these sales consisted of rayon and nylon tire cord for use in the production of automobile tires. Polyester, the "third generation" man-made fiber after rayon and nylon, had shown very rapid growth since the mid 1960's.

The meeting was attended by Kevin Redlin, president of York Fiber; Lisa George, a member of the board of directors; Julie Wines, vice president in charge of new products; and Thomas Hampton, controller. Redlin called the meeting to order, gave a brief statement of its purpose, and then turned the floor over to Julie Wines.

Wines opened the meeting with a presentation of the cost and cash flow analysis for the polyester project. To make the discussion simple, she passed out copies of the projected cash flows to those present (see Exhibits 1 and 2). The project called for an initial investment of $19 million. About $14 million would be used to buy machinery and equipment for the production of polyester fiber, $4 million would be needed to modify nylon fiber production facilities which would be utilized to produce polyester fiber, and $1 million would be used to cover the cost for market testing which was completed in November 1988. The project had an expected useful life of 10 years with no salvage value on retirement.

Wines cautioned that the annual net cash flows in Exhibit 1 should not be taken at face value because they included those net cash flows that could be diverted from both rayon and nylon fibers. Thus, she also produced the annual net cash flows that excluded those net cash flows from sales erosion of existing products (Exhibit 2). Furthermore, she stated that these net cash flows would be more appropriate because they were incremental future cash inflows and project cash flows must be estimated on an incremental basis.

Exhibit 1
York Fiber Corporation Annual Net Cash Flows from the Acceptance of Polyester Project (including those cash flows from sales erosion of existing products)

Year	Annual Net Cash Flows
1	$2,900,000
2	3,000,000
3	3,100,000
4	3,200,000
5	3,300,000
6	3,400,000
7	3,500,000
8	3,600,000
9	3,800,000
10	3,900,000

Exhibit 2
York Fiber Corporation Annual Net Cash Flows from the Acceptance of Polyester Project (excluding those cash flows from sales erosion of existing products)

Year	Annual Net Cash Flows
1	$2,600,000
2	2,700,000
3	2,800,000
4	2,900,000
5	3,000,000
6	3,100,000
7	3,200,000
8	3,300,000
9	3,400,000
10	3,500,000

380   CASE STUDIES

Redlin noted that the nylon fiber's production facilities were to be used at only 60 percent of capacity and these facilities were to be used to produce polyester fiber. He said that the pro-rata allocation of plant facilities, based on the share of capacity used, should have been included in the proposed cash outlay for the project. His reasoning was that if an outside firm tried to rent it from York Fiber, it would be charged somewhere in the neighborhood of $7 million. Wines replied that they were sunk costs and such sunk costs were irrelevant to capital project evaluations.

Lisa George contended that if the opportunity cost of idle capacity was a sunk cost, the cost of $1 million already spent for market testing should have also been treated as a sunk cost as well. Wines responded that it was not a sunk cost because the company spent $1 million specifically to test the feasibility of polyester fiber and the cost was directly associated with the polyester project.

Thomas Hampton asked if there had been any consideration of additional working capital necessary to support the increased sales. Wines said that this project would require $2 million in additional working capital but it was not considered as an outflow because it would never leave the company.

QUESTIONS

1. Would you argue that the cost of $1 million already spent for market testing be treated as a cash outflow?
2. Do you think that the polyester project should be charged for the use of excess production facilities and building?
3. How would you deal with the question of working capital?
4. Would you suggest that the net cash flows diverted from sales erosion of rayon and nylon fibers be included in project cash inflows? If the polyester project is rejected, a competitor is expected to introduce a similar product which would divert the same amount of sales from York Fiber. How would this affect the decision by York Fiber?
5. If the company decides to finance part of this project with debt, should the interest payments of the new debt be considered as a cash outflow?
6. The company's cost of capital is 10 percent. If we include those cash flows from lost sales of existing products, what would be the net present value and the profitability index for the project? If we exclude these cash flows, what would be the net present value and the profitability index?

Case Study 7

WEIGHTED AVERAGE COST OF CAPITAL

ADVANCED TECHNOLOGY COMPANY

Until now, the Advanced Technology Company has used the payback method as a primary evaluation technique for its major investment projects. Jay Carpenter, vice president for finance of Advanced Technology, was considering two discounted cash-flow approaches (net present value and internal rate of return) for measuring proposed capital expenditures. Mr. Carpenter concluded that, once he had estimated project cash flows, his biggest problem would be to choose the appropriate discount rate to use with the net present value method or to select the proper hurdle rate to use with the internal rate of return method. He felt that it would be wise to consider a discount rate or a hurdle rate for Advanced Technology only after first discussing the company's cost of capital. Mr. Carpenter, as chairman of the finance committee, had planned to present an estimate of the company's cost of capital at the next committee meeting on January 28, 1990.

Advanced Technology manufactures office automation systems and equipment. In addition to introducing a newly designed mainframe computer during the last few years, the company has aggressively increased its research in mini-computers and word processors. These products are in high growth markets and the firm's expenditures for these projects have more than proven their worth. Advanced Technology is recognized by those in the industry as one of the leading and most successful companies in the market. Many experts in the high-tech industry have projected a potential bonanza for mini computers and word processors over the next 10 years. Thus, the company plans to invest heavily in research and development for the next 5 years.

Mr. Carpenter began his assignment by establishing the sequence of his work schedule: (1) Determine the capital structure (proportions of long-term financing); (2) Compute the costs of the individual components of the capital structure; and (3) Combine these individual component costs to obtain the weighted average cost of capital.

Mr. Carpenter identified 2 alternatives to specify the proportions of the capital structure: book weights and the current proportions of the market values of the firm's outstanding securities. Book weights can be obtained from the balance sheet in Exhibit 1. Exhibit 3 shows that in 1989 the common stock had traded within a rather narrow range and centered on the closing price of $14.50. The price of the preferred stock had remained constant for some time at $20 per share. Standard & Poor's recently upgraded the company's bond rating from Baa to A, which caused the price of the bond to increase sharply from the $80-85 range to a recent quote of $90.

Mr. Carpenter estimated that the current yield to maturity for the company's bond is 12.4 percent before taxes. The company pays $2.25 dividend (0.09 × $25) per share of the preferred stock. Interest and dividends are directly measurable component costs of debt and preferred stock. However, there is no such measurable element for the cost of common stock, because dividend declarations on common stock are made at the discretion of a firm's board of directors. Thus, the cost of common stock is more difficult to measure. Carpenter felt that there was no best way to make this estimate. After he had examined a number of methods to compute the cost of equity, he decided to use the discounted cash-flow approach (dividend growth model):

$$k_e = \frac{D_1}{P_0} + g$$

where k_e = the cost of equity capital, D = dividend per share of common stock expected at the end of one year, P = current price per share of common stock, and g = expected growth rate in dividends. Carpenter assembled the data in Exhibit 3 to help him estimate the cost of equity capital using the discounted cash-flow approach.

Exhibit 1
Advanced Technology Company Balance Sheet (December 31, 1989)

Cash	$ 1,500,000
Accounts receivable	3,500,000
Inventory	5,000,000
Total current assets	$10,000,000
Gross plant and equipment	$47,300,000
Less: accumulated depreciation	7,300,000
Net plant and equipment	$40,000,000
Total assets	$50,000,000
Accounts payable	$ 3,500,000
Accruals	1,500,000
Total current liabilities	$ 5,000,000
8% Debentures	$20,000,000
9% Preferred stock ($25 par; 400,000 shares issued and outstanding)	10,000,000
Common stock ($2.50 par; 2,000,000 shares issued and outstanding)	5,000,000
Retained earnings	10,000,000
Total liabilities and net worth	$50,000,000

Exhibit 2
Advanced Technology Company Income Statement (December 31, 1989)

Sales	$76,000,000
Cost of goods sold	55,000,000
Gross profit	$21,000,000
Operating expenses	11,600,000
Interest	1,600,000
Taxable income	$ 7,800,000
Tax (50%)	3,900,000
Earnings after taxes	$ 3,900,000
Dividend on preferred stock	900,000
Earnings available to common stockholders	$ 3,000,000
Dividend paid to common stockholders	$ 1,800,000

Exhibit 3
Advanced Technology Company Recent Financial Data

Year	Price Range	Closing Price	Dividend per Share	Earnings per Share
1984	$ 9.75-12.25	$11.00	$0.64	$1.07
1985	$11.25-14.75	13.50	0.77	1.28
1986	$10.00-14.50	11.75	0.74	1.24
1987	$12.00-16.25	13.75	0.80	1.34
1988	$12.50-17.00	14.00	0.85	1.42
1989	$13.75-15.50	14.50	0.90	1.50

QUESTIONS

1. Determine the company's book value weights and market value weights of outstanding securities.
2. Calculate the company's cost of equity capital using the discounted cash flow approach.
3. Compute the company's weighted average cost of capital using the book value weights and market value weights. Assume a marginal tax rate of 50 percent.
4. Discuss the rationale behind the use of a weighted average cost of capital as the firm's cost of capital (discount rate).
5. Discuss the pros and cons of using market value versus book value weights.

Case Study 8

VALUATION

WAYNE GIFTS INCORPORATED

Mr. Bernard Smith, 25 years old, recently graduated from a Mid-western University with a Master of Business Administration degree. Following his graduation, he got married to Mary Thomas, daughter of a real estate tycoon Mr. Mike Thomas who operated his business in the suburbs of Detroit. Mr. Smith enjoyed his MBA program and was especially moved by the learning experience he got from his case course in finance. During the course of time, Mr. Smith developed an ambition to prepare himself for the opportunity of becoming the manager and sole owner of a business with prospects for real growth.

Mr. Smith had worked at various retailing outlets during the summer months to earn his way towards his undergraduate and graduate education. During this time, he gained considerable experience in retailing and merchandising of gift stores. After consulting with his wife and father-in-law about his business plans, Mr. Smith got the feeling that he could borrow up to $200,000 from Mr. Thomas on certain terms which are to be negotiated later on. Having received such an assurance, Mr. Smith started his search for a medium-sized gift store which may be available for sale. In the course of the year, he searched into about 10 possibilities that came to his attention. Some of the stores were located in isolated areas where not much traffic was anticipated and others were in relatively low-income residential areas. Some of these possibilities were quickly rejected. Mr. Smith's persistent search led him to Wayne Gifts, Inc., a gift and decorative items store located in the suburban Dearborn Shopping Mall.

Mr. Smith quickly arranged a meeting with the current owner, Mrs. Jordan Sterling, of the store. Wayne Gifts, Inc. was established by Mr. Jordan Sterling in 1981. He operated the store until his death in early 1986, where upon his widow took it over. Mrs. Sterling continued to operate the store until the present time, 1990, but she encountered a number of problems. Profits were sliding, investments in inventories and accounts receivable were increasing, and some of high ticket gift items were not just selling. Besides, Mrs. Sterling's health was failing and she was anxious to sell the store if someone made her a good offer.

Mr. Smith quickly concluded from his discussion with Mrs. Sterling that the store had a good deal of promise and that he could do a much better of running the store than what Mrs. Sterling was doing. He observed that some of the gift items were much too expensive and were not suitable for the type of clientele one would expect to see in that particular shopping mall. Some other items were either missing altogether or did not carry a selection of patterns in at least three brand names of china, glass or flatwares. The store was heavily stocked with tablewares which are high profit items but slow to move. The store had the franchise rights to some sought-after brand name tablewares. Mr. Smith felt that he could institute an active bridal registry and do appropriate advertising to attract scores of brides, well-wishers and other gift buyers. Other customer services which Mr. Smith hoped to offer include free gift wrapping, free local delivery service, and store layaway plans.

Exhibit 1
Wayne Gifts, Inc. Balance Sheet as of December 31, 1990

Cash & securities	$ 11,000	Notes payable	$ 68,750
Accounts receivable	52,250	Accounts payable	55,000
Inventories	148,500	Other current debt	31,625
Total current assets	$211,750	Total current debts	$155,375
Fixed assets	63,250	Common stock	119,625
Total Assets	$275,000	Total L. & C.	$275,000

Exhibit 2
Wayne Gifts, Inc. Selected Data

Year	Net Sales	Profits Before Tax
1981	$166,400	$16,640
1982	174,890	18,138
1983	181,450	18,683
1984	189,630	19,803
1985	200,100	21,010
1986	185,690	12,990
1987	175,420	14,159
1988	193,890	13,900
1989	200,000	13,770
1990	198,770	14,055

Exhibit 3
Wayne Gifts, Inc.
Standard Balance Sheet for a Hypothetical Medium-Sized Gift Store

Cash	7.0%	Notes payable	15.0%
Accounts receivable	7.0	Accounts payable	16.0
Inventories	57.0	Other current debt	11.0
Total current assets	71.0%	Total current debts	42.0%
Fixed assets	29.0	Long-term debt	20.0
		Net worth	38.0
Total assets	100.0%	Total claims	100.0%

Mr. Smith examined the financial statements of Wayne Gifts, Inc. as of December 31, 1990, shown in Exhibits 1 and 2. He first sought to establish the validity of various items listed in the balance sheet. The amount of the accounts receivable shown included some questionable accounts and some accounts were past due. He estimated that the net value of accounts receivable could amount to 90 percent of its book value. The inventory consisted primarily of various gift items. Mr. Smith satisfied himself that Mrs. Sterling maintained accurate inventory records and the inventories were valued at the lower of cost or market. On the basis of a physical examination of fixed assets, Mr. Smith concluded that their value was fairly represented on the balance sheet.

In view of the location of the store, Mr. Smith felt that by altering the merchandising mix, the store's image will better suit the clientele of the shopping mall. With the oil crisis no longer a threat, Mr. Smith believed that the middle-income families will resume their shift to the suburbs and will increasingly patronize suburban malls to meet their shopping needs. It was very unlikely that any new gift store would open in the immediate proximity due to the ratio of number of gift stores to the number of inhabitants living in the area.

After gathering further information from the industry sources about a typical medium-sized gift store (shown in Exhibit 3), Mr. Smith inquired about a possible sales price for Wayne Gifts, Inc. Mrs. Sterling offered to sell her store for an asking price of $175,000. At this price, all the assets and liabilities of the firm are to be turned over to Mr. Smith, excluding the cash balance of $11,000.

QUESTIONS

1. Calculate the total investment of Mr. Smith if he was to purchase the Wayne gifts Inc. Assume a purchase price of $175,000.
2. How do you assess Mr. Smith's ability to run the store?
3. Make various estimates—high, low, and most likely—of the annual profits after Mr. Smith purchases the store.
4. Determine appropriate discount rates to capitalize the earnings estimated in Question 3.
5. On the basis of your analysis of the above questions, work out a range of possible valuations for the store.
6. Should Mr. Smith buy the store for its asking price?

Case Study 9

DEBT FINANCING

CENTRAL POWER COMPANY

The Finance Committee of the Central Power Company was scheduled to review its major financial policies in September 1990. At 2:00 p.m. on August 25, 1990, Kenneth Byrne, treasurer of the company and finance committee member, leaned back in his chair and stared off into space. His major concern was the company's debt position which had increased in the last few years to a level that placed its triple-A bond rating in jeopardy. Central Power had carefully maintained the highest bond rating for years and Mr. Byrne did not want to adopt a financing plan that might endanger its triple-A rating. However, Judy Shad, controller of the company and chairperson of the finance committee, had argued for years that it was too costly to maintain the highest bond rating. Furthermore, she argued that a depressed stock price made equity financing undesirable.

Exhibit 1
Bond Rating Guidelines for Electric Utility Industry

	AAA	AA	A	baa	ba
Debt ratio	41%	50%	55%	60%	70%
Times interest earned	5.0x	4.0x	3.5x	3.0x	2.0x

Central Power provides electric service to a large region of the northwestern United States. In the early 1970's, the company embarked on the most ambitious nuclear-power plant construction program in the nation's history. It was spurred by the Bonneville Power Administration, a federal agency that was concerned about future supply of electricity. In 1989, the company spent $250 million on new construction and $85 million to modernize existing plants. The construction program was expected to grow somewhat above the 1981 to 1989 average of 8.2 percent for the next four years.

Because demand for electric power had grown in recent years at a rate almost twice that of the overall economy, Central Power, like the rest of the electric utility industry, faced a dramatic acceleration in the need for capital to finance its growth. Mr. Byrne outlined the reasons for a sudden surge in capital expenditures facing the industry. First, the rate of growth in construction of "all electric" homes was accelerating because of an unexpectedly sharp increase in gas prices for the last few years. Second, the electric utility industry was becoming more capital intensive because of the skyrocketing construction cost of nuclear power plants. Third, the failure of the nuclear power plant at Three Mile Island had created pressure for additional spending to increase system reliability at redundant facilities.

Because Central Power had always recognized the importance of dividends to its shareholders, it had never missed a dividend payment since it was founded in 1937. Moreover, fiscal 1989 was the eleventh consecutive year in which cash dividends had been increased. This policy resulted in a payout ratio in the range of 45 to 50 percent (see Exhibit 2).

Exhibit 2
Central Power Company
Impact of Various Debt Ratios

	1990	1991	1992	1993	1994
Debt = 40% Assets by 1994					
Debt ratio	49%	47%	45%	43%	40%
Times interest earned	4.00x	4.30x	4.60x	4.80x	5.10x
Earnings per share	$5.30	$5.52	$5.76	$5.94	$6.08
Payout ratio	50%	50%	50%	50%	50%
Dividend per share	$2.65	$2.76	$2.88	$2.97	$3.04
Return on equity	10.55%	10.21%	10.02%	9.86%	9.68%
Debt = 49% Assets by 1994					
Debt ratio	49%	49%	49%	49%	49%
Times interest earned	4.00x	4.02x	3.98x	3.96x	3.95x
Earnings per share	$5.30	$5.62	$5.90	$6.24	$6.56
Payout ratio	50%	50%	50%	50%	50%
Dividend per share	$2.65	$2.81	$2.95	$3.12	$3.28
Return on equity	10.55%	10.82%	11.03%	11.36%	11.79%
Debt = 55% Assets by 1994					
Debt ratio	49%	51%	52%	53%	55%
Times interest earned	4.00x	3.92x	3.71x	3.50x	3.32x
Earnings per share	$5.30	$5.76	$6.02	$6.44	$6.90
Payout ratio	50%	50%	50%	50%	50%
Dividend per share	$2.65	$2.86	$3.01	$3.22	$3.45
Return on equity	10.55%	10.91%	11.23%	11.75%	12.03%

Note: These forecasts are based on estimates and assumptions about future capital expenditures, interest rate levels, and the allowed return on capital.

The company's debt policy was designed to maintain the highest credit rating and to maximize access to all major sources of new capital. Until the mid-1970's, its debt ratio objective had been between 30 and 40 percent. Thus, the company had obtained 60 to 70 percent of the capital needed to support growth in customer electric power requirements through a combination of internally generated funds and common stock sales. Such equity financing was possible because the company's stock price had been fairly favorable and its earnings per share had increased each year since 1937.

Central Power's debt ratio moved steadily upward from 34 percent in 1981 to 49 percent in 1989 (see Exhibit 3). During this eight-year period, the company had almost exclusively used debt to raise outside capital except for a small amount of preferred stock. The rapid increase in the debt ratio also resulted in a substantial decline in the company's stock price. The times interest earned by the company declined from 5.32 times in 1981 to 4.00 times in 1989. Standard & Poor's had recently threatened to downgrade the company's new bonds to a double-A rating, unless its debt ratio and times interest earned improved significantly in the near future.

At the end of 1989, the company was very close to the borderline for a double-A bond rating. Mr. Byrne felt that it was essential to maintain the triple-A rating because the credit rating of a bond significantly influenced both the cost and availability of long-term debt. Lower-rated bonds pay more in interest charges because they have greater long-term financial risk. In addition, lower-rated companies would find it difficult—perhaps impossible—to obtain money at times of sharply intensifying financial strain.

QUESTIONS

1. What are the letter ratings assigned by Moody's and Standard & Poor's to indicate the quality of bonds?
2. List and discuss the major determinants of bond ratings.
3. Do you think that Central Power is on the brink of losing its triple-A bond rating?
4. Why should Mr. Byrne be concerned about retaining a triple-A rating?
5. What debt policy would you recommend for Central Power?

Case Study 10

ETHICS IN FINANCE

ADVANCED TECHNOLOGY'S ETHICAL DILEMMA

The Executive Committee of Advanced Technology (AT)—Robert Smith, President; Linda Humphrey, Vice President of Finance; Sam Miller, Vice President of Marketing; and Susan Crum, Vice President of Production—scheduled a luncheon meeting on September 1, 1996 to discuss two major problems for the welfare of the company: (1) how to finance the rapid expansion of its production facilities and (2) how to cope with a growing competition in its major overseas markets. In addition, the Department of Justice requested AT to answer several questions about bribes, gifts, slush funds, and grease payments in relation to its foreign sales. This inquiry started in response to a 100-page complaint by its overseas competitor which alleged that AT violated the Foreign Corrupt Practices Act of 1977.

AT has recently enjoyed a rapid growth in business. The company anticipated substantial increases in sales for the next few years. However, it must solve two major problems—capacity and strong competition in foreign operations—if it is to maintain fast sales growth for years to come.

AT produces office automation systems and equipment. In addition to introducing a newly designed mainframe computer, the company aggressively increased research in mini-computers and word processors. These products are in high growth markets, and the firm's expenditures for these projects have more than proved their worth. In fact, the company's major problem has been to increase production fast enough to meet demand of its Asian customers. The company's capacity has expanded steadily since 1980, but it has often lost sales because of insufficient production.

The industry recognizes AT as one of the fastest growing companies in the market. Experts in the high-tech industry have projected for the next ten years a potential bonanza for mini computers and word processors. Thus, the company plans to invest heavily in research and development for the next five years. It also plans to increase production quickly by acquiring existing computer manufacturing firms and by establishing new production facilities.

AT is a multinational company with headquarters in Los Angeles, California. The company has five manufacturing locations in the United States and three abroad, with offices in 13 countries. Approximately 40 percent of its sales came from foreign operations in 1995—primarily South America and Asia where the company had recently faced stiff competition from its larger rivals, such as IBM, Digital Equipment, and Olivetti. The company depended on distributors for most of its overseas sales.

Conflict of Interest in Financial Affairs. Thomas Nickerson is a Special Assistant to the Vice President of Finance, Linda Humphrey. He graduated from a major university in St. Louis, Missouri with an MBA in Finance. After two years of experience with Ernst & Young, a major CPA firm in St. Louis, he joined the accounting staff and served in a variety of accounting and finance positions for five years. Two years ago he was appointed Special Assistant to Ms. Humphrey at an unusually high salary mainly because of his outstanding financial and communication talents. Thomas Nickerson has a large family and a home with a $450,000 mortgage. His deep debt and huge financial needs hardly matter to him because he has a promising future at the company.

Ms. Humphrey approached Thomas with a special task on August 1, 1996. She informed him that she met with other vice presidents and decided to purchase Computer Engineering to alleviate the capacity problem. She further stated that the acquisition will be highly advantageous for AT, but she needed to convince two members of the Board of Directors. Then she instructed him to prepare a report justifying the acquisition of the company. Under the terms, AT will offer Computer Engineering two million shares of its stock. The market price of the stock was $20 per share.

Normally Thomas would have welcomed the assignment, but this one made him uneasy. Computer Engineering's financial statements indicated poor performance as compared with comparable companies in the field. He knew that Ms. Humphrey and other vice presidents helped current top executives of Computer Engineering set up their company. He suspected that vice presidents of AT owned sizable blocks of Computer Engineering stock which was not publicly traded. To establish a fair market price for Computer Engineering, he has compiled the statistics presented in Exhibit 1. High Tech is more similar to Computer Engineering than any other company whose stock is traded in the public market.

Exhibit 1
Key Statistics for Computer Engineering and High Tech

Variables	Computer Engineering	High Tech
Earnings per share	$1.00	$ 2.00
Dividend per share in year 1	$0.75	$ 1.00
Annual dividend growth rate	0.04	0.09
Price per share	?	$20.00
Book value per share	$8.00	$10.00
Cost of equity	?	0.14
Number of shares outstanding	1 million	1.2 million

Ethics versus Profits in Global Business. The Foreign Corrupt Practices Act of 1977 (FCPA) has encouraged U.S. companies to introduce policies against corrupt foreign payments and to improve internal controls. The FCPA bans illegal payments to foreign officials, monitors accounting procedures, and levies heavy penalties for violations. The FCPA forced AT to think about its way of doing business overseas. The company had expanded its foreign operations very quickly. In the 1960s, less than 2 percent of its sales came from foreign operations, but by the late 1970s its foreign operations accounted for 30 percent of total sales.

Just like many other companies, AT had undertaken positive steps to prevent illegal payments to foreign officials and to improve internal control. In 1980, the company published its first corporate code, along with two separate area codes: one for the U.S. and another one for the foreign area. The code of business conduct for overseas employees reflected most provisions of the FCPA so that the company would not have any trouble with the law.

Marketing Vice President Miller has been under heavy pressure from President Smith to increase the company's foreign sales by 30 percent per year for the next five years. Mr. Miller thought that when in Rome, some do as the Romans do. In other words, he did not hesitate to call the FCPA "bad business" and "unnecessary." Miller felt that the FCPA should be repealed for several reasons. First, it forced U.S. companies to increase audit costs substantially. Second, the Department of Justice and the SEC failed to establish clear guidelines. Third, it put U.S. companies at a competitive disadvantage. Fourth, in many countries, foreign payments are not outlawed, but encouraged. Fifth, the FCPA was unnecessary because U.S. law enforcement agencies already had many statutes to prevent illegal foreign payments by U.S. companies.

Mr. Miller reflected on the report he would present to the Executive Committee. The purpose of this report was to make certain that AT was complying with its corporate code of conduct. There was, however, one situation that required a tough decision. This particular situation was considered an acceptable practice in the countries where they occurred, but he did not know how he would handle specific questions if they should come up.

Kevin Hart is the exclusive distributor for Advanced Technology products in South American countries. He had a reputation for reliability and efficiency. But the most recent audit suggested that he had corruptly influenced customs officials to obtain lower duty rates for AT's products. In doing so, he violated both the FCPA and the company's code of conduct.

AT had asked Kevin to agree in writing to abide by the code, but he refused to do so. He argued that these "grease payments" were customary in these countries. He insisted that he could not compete effectively without them. Kevin had represented AT for many years and generated approximately $10 million worth of business per year for the company. His exclusive dealership contract would be up for renewal in a few months. AT had suggested that it might refuse to renew its contract unless he agreed to abide by the code. Mr. Miller knew that it would be difficult to resolve this problem while he was under heavy pressure to increase the company's overseas sales by 30 percent per year.

QUESTIONS

1. Use the data in Exhibit 1 to estimate the market value of Computer Engineering in the following three ways: (1) price-earnings ratio, (2) market value/book value, and (3) dividend growth model.
2. List and discuss options available to Thomas Nickerson.
3. Discuss the two major sections of the FCPA—antibribery and accounting.
4. List and discuss pros and cons concerning corporate codes of conduct.
5. If you were Sam Miller, what would you do about the situation in these South American countries?

Case Study 11

INTERNATIONAL FINANCE

GM OPERATIONS IN MEXICO AND THE PESO CRISIS

Although Mexico had allowed its peso to fluctuate within a narrow band, the government had virtually pegged the peso to the U.S. dollar since 1990. However, on December 20, 1994, Mexico unexpectedly announced its decision to float the peso and a 40 percent devaluation followed in the next two days. The peso devaluation and the peso float, at first glance, seemed to have caused serious problems for General Motors, whose manufacturing facilities in Mexico depend heavily on materials and components from the United States. An emergency meeting of the GM Executive Committee was called on December 24 in Detroit to deal with the consequences of the devaluation and the float. Gary Henson, President and Managing Director of GM de Mexico since December 1992, knew that all of the company's top executives would be attending the meeting and felt certain that he would be asked why the devaluation and the float had caught him off guard. He decided to analyze economic statistics for both Mexico and the United States (see Exhibits 1 and 2) along with the news clippings in his file on the Mexican peso.

Concern over the possibility of a devaluation had existed for years from 1990 to December 20, 1994, because real exchange rates for the peso had skyrocketed. However, many observers felt that President Salinas's economic reforms improved Mexico's economy to such an extent that devaluation would not be necessary.

Henson was, therefore, not the only person caught off guard by the size of the devaluation and by the timing of the float. When Mexican Central Bank opened on December 22, it began quoting pesos at 5.5 per the U.S. dollar, then as low as 6.33; the peso dropped to 5.8 by the end of the day. By December 23, foreign exchange experts had become sharply divided on how far the peso might fall. Some said that the foreign exchange market had already overreacted, but others saw no end in sight to the peso's depreciation. Analysts also disagreed on whether the valuation and the float would be sufficient to correct the country's balance of payments difficulties and other economic problems. All these conflicting and perplexing points of view made it more difficult for Henson to assess the effects of the float and the devaluation on GM's operations in Mexico.

Although there are some historical exceptions, exchange-rate stabilization programs commonly result in a specific dynamic of consumption and investment patterns, current account deficits, and exchange rate pressures. The typical pattern of exchange-rate stabilization programs includes the following: First, despite reductions in inflation, the real exchange rate rises because some inflation remains and is not offset by nominal exchange rate movements. Second, the trade and current account balances deteriorate. Third, in the early stages of the program, capital inflows finance the excess of consumption and investment over domestic production, allowing a boom to ensue, but the inflows ultimately reverse. Fourth, with this reversal, the growing current account deficit can no longer be financed, the consumption boom ends, and the exchange-rate stabilization program collapses.

Exhibit 1
Selected Economic Indicators for the U.S. and Mexico

	1990	1991	1992	1993	3rd Q 1993	4th Q 1994
Exchange rate (pesos per $)	2.9454	3.0710	3.1154	3.1059	3.4040	5.3250
Mexico CPI	100.0	122.7	141.7	155.5	167.4	170.5
U.S. CPI	100.0	103.1	105.0	106.9	109.2	110.1
U.S. money supply	100.0	108.6	124.0	136.7	135.9	139.1
Mexico money supply	100.0	223.9	257.6	303.3	276.2	306.6

Source: International Monetary Fund, *International Financial Statistics*, June 1995.

Exhibit 2
Mexico's Balance of Payments (Millions of U.S. dollars)

Accounts	1990	1991	1992	1993	3rd Q 1994	4th Q 1994
Goods and services	-3,110	-9,369	-18,619	-16,010	-15,466	-21,054
Current account	-7,451	-14,888	-24,442	-23,400	-21,525	-28,784
International receivers	9,863	17,726	18,942	25,110	16,374	6,278

Source: International Monetary Fund, *International Financial Statistics*, June 1995.

QUESTIONS

1. Do you think that the peso had fallen far enough as of December 22 or that it will continue to lose value? (Hint: answer this question using the purchasing power parity theory.) Is the predicted exchange rate usually accurate?

11: International Finance 395

2. Could the peso float have been forecasted? (Hint: answer this question using such economic indicators as the balance of payments, international reserves, inflation, and money supply.)

3. What alternatives are available to the Mexican government for dealing with its balance-of-payments problems?

4. Assume that Mexico imposed prolonged foreign exchange controls and thus GM de Mexico, the Mexican subsidiary of General Motors, could not import crucial materials and components from the United States. Briefly outline courses of action that GM de Mexico should take to cope with the foreign exchange controls.

5. Is there any evidence that the typical pattern of exchange rate stabilization programs took place in Mexico?

Appendix A

INTEREST TABLES

Table A
Compound or Future Value of $1

Period	1%	2%	3%	4%	5%	6%	7%	8%	9%	10%
1	1.010	1.020	1.030	1.040	1.050	1.060	1.070	1.080	1.090	1.100
2	1.020	1.040	1.061	1.082	1.102	1.124	1.145	1.166	1.188	1.210
3	1.030	1.061	1.093	1.125	1.158	1.191	1.225	1.260	1.295	1.331
4	1.041	1.082	1.126	1.170	1.216	1.262	1.311	1.360	1.412	1.464
5	1.051	1.104	1.159	1.217	1.276	1.338	1.403	1.469	1.539	1.611
6	1.062	1.126	1.194	1.265	1.340	1.419	1.501	1.587	1.677	1.772
7	1.072	1.149	1.230	1.316	1.407	1.504	1.606	1.714	1.828	1.949
8	1.083	1.172	1.267	1.369	1.477	1.594	1.718	1.851	1.993	2.144
9	1.094	1.195	1.305	1.423	1.551	1.689	1.838	1.999	2.172	2.358
10	1.105	1.219	1.344	1.480	1.629	1.791	1.967	2.159	2.367	2.594
11	1.116	1.243	1.384	1.539	1.710	1.898	2.105	2.332	2.580	2.853
12	1.127	1.268	1.426	1.601	1.796	2.012	2.252	2.518	2.813	3.138
13	1.138	1.294	1.469	1.665	1.886	2.133	2.410	2.720	3.066	3.452
14	1.149	1.319	1.513	1.732	1.980	2.261	2.579	2.937	3.342	3.797
15	1.161	1.346	1.558	1.801	2.079	2.397	2.759	3.172	3.642	4.177
16	1.173	1.373	1.605	1.873	2.183	2.540	2.952	3.426	3.970	4.595
17	1.184	1.400	1.653	1.948	2.292	2.693	3.159	3.700	4.328	5.054
18	1.196	1.428	1.702	2.026	2.407	2.854	3.380	3.996	4.717	5.560
19	1.208	1.457	1.753	2.107	2.527	3.026	3.616	4.316	5.142	6.116
20	1.220	1.486	1.806	2.191	2.653	3.207	3.870	4.661	5.604	6.727
21	1.232	1.516	1.860	2.279	2.786	3.399	4.140	5.034	6.109	7.400
22	1.245	1.546	1.916	2.370	2.925	3.603	4.430	5.436	6.658	8.140
23	1.257	1.577	1.974	2.465	3.071	3.820	4.740	5.871	7.258	8.954
24	1.270	1.608	2.033	2.563	3.225	4.049	5.072	6.341	7.911	9.850
25	1.282	1.541	2.094	2.666	3.386	4.292	5.427	6.848	8.623	10.834
30	1.348	1.811	2.427	3.243	4.322	5.743	7.612	10.062	13.267	17.449
40	1.489	2.208	3.262	4.801	7.040	10.285	14.974	21.724	31.408	45.258

TABLE A
COMPOUND OR FUTURE VALUE OF $1 (CONTINUED)

Period	11%	12%	13%	14%	15%	16%	17%	18%	19%	20%
1	1.110	1.120	1.130	1.140	1.150	1.160	1.170	1.180	1.190	1.200
2	1.232	1.254	1.277	1.300	1.322	1.346	1.369	1.392	1.416	1.440
3	1.368	1.405	1.443	1.482	1.521	1.561	1.602	1.643	1.685	1.728
4	1.518	1.574	1.630	1.689	1.749	1.811	1.874	1.939	2.005	2.074
5	1.685	1.762	1.842	1.925	2.011	2.100	2.192	2.288	2.386	2.488
6	1.870	1.974	2.082	2.195	2.313	2.436	2.565	2.700	2.840	2.986
7	2.076	2.211	2.353	2.502	2.660	2.826	3.001	3.185	3.379	3.583
8	2.305	2.476	2.658	2.853	3.059	3.278	3.511	3.759	4.021	4.300
9	2.558	2.773	3.004	3.252	3.518	3.803	4.108	4.435	4.785	5.160
10	2.839	3.106	3.395	3.707	4.046	4.411	4.807	5.234	5.695	6.192
11	3.152	3.479	3.836	4.226	4.652	5.117	5.624	6.176	6.777	7.430
12	3.498	3.896	4.334	4.818	5.350	5.936	6.580	7.288	8.064	8.916
13	3.883	4.363	4.898	5.492	6.153	6.886	7.699	8.599	9.596	10.699
14	4.310	4.887	5.535	6.261	7.076	7.987	9.007	10.147	11.420	12.839
15	4.785	5.474	6.254	7.138	8.137	9.265	10.539	11.974	13.589	15.407
16	5.311	6.130	7.067	8.137	9.358	10.748	12.330	14.129	16.171	18.488
17	5.895	6.866	7.986	9.276	10.761	12.468	14.426	16.672	19.244	22.186
18	6.543	7.690	9.024	10.575	12.375	14.462	16.879	19.673	22.900	26.623
19	7.263	8.613	10.197	12.055	14.232	16.776	19.748	23.214	27.251	31.948
20	8.062	9.646	11.523	13.743	16.366	19.461	23.105	27.393	32.429	38.337
21	8.949	10.804	13.021	15.667	18.821	22.574	27.033	32.323	38.591	46.005
22	9.933	12.100	14.713	17.861	21.644	26.186	31.629	38.141	45.923	55.205
23	11.026	13.552	16.626	20.361	24.891	30.376	37.005	45.007	54.648	66.247
24	12.239	15.178	18.788	23.212	28.625	35.236	43.296	53.108	65.031	79.496
25	13.585	17.000	21.230	26.461	32.918	40.874	50.656	62.667	77.387	95.395
30	22.892	29.960	39.115	50.949	66.210	85.849	111.061	143.367	184.672	237.373
40	64.999	93.049	132.776	188.876	267.856	378.715	533.846	750.353	1051.642	1469.740

TABLE A
COMPOUND OR FUTURE VALUE OF $1 (CONTINUED)

Period	21%	22%	23%	24%	25%	26%	27%	28%	29%	30%
1	1.210	1.220	1.230	1.240	1.250	1.260	1.270	1.280	1.290	1.300
2	1.464	1.488	1.513	1.538	1.562	1.588	1.613	1.638	1.664	1.690
3	1.772	1.816	1.861	1.907	1.953	2.000	2.048	2.097	2.147	2.197
4	2.144	2.215	2.289	2.364	2.441	2.520	2.601	2.684	2.769	2.856
5	2.594	2.703	2.815	2.932	3.052	3.176	3.304	3.436	3.572	3.713
6	3.138	3.297	3.463	3.635	3.815	4.001	4.196	4.398	4.608	4.827
7	3.797	4.023	4.259	4.508	4.768	5.042	5.329	5.629	5.945	6.275
8	4.595	4.908	5.239	5.589	5.960	6.353	6.767	7.206	7.669	8.157
9	5.560	5.987	6.444	6.931	7.451	8.004	8.595	9.223	9.893	10.604
10	6.727	7.305	7.926	8.594	9.313	10.086	10.915	11.806	12.761	13.786
11	8.140	8.912	9.749	10.657	11.642	12.708	13.862	15.112	16.462	17.921
12	9.850	10.872	11.991	13.215	14.552	16.012	17.605	19.343	21.236	23.298
13	11.918	13.264	14.749	16.386	18.190	20.175	22.359	24.759	27.395	30.287
14	14.421	16.182	18.141	20.319	22.737	25.420	28.395	31.691	35.339	39.373
15	17.449	19.742	22.314	25.195	28.422	32.030	36.062	40.565	45.587	51.185
16	21.113	24.085	27.446	31.242	35.527	40.357	45.799	51.923	58.808	66.541
17	25.547	29.384	33.758	38.740	44.409	50.850	58.165	66.461	75.862	86.503
18	30.912	35.848	41.523	48.038	55.511	64.071	73.869	85.070	97.862	112.454
19	37.404	43.735	51.073	59.567	69.389	80.730	93.813	108.890	126.242	146.190
20	45.258	53.357	62.820	73.863	86.736	101.720	119.143	139.379	162.852	190.047
21	54.762	65.095	77.268	91.591	108.420	128.167	151.312	178.405	210.079	247.061
22	66.262	79.416	95.040	113.572	135.525	161.490	192.165	228.358	271.002	321.178
23	80.178	96.887	116.899	140.829	169.407	203.477	244.050	292.298	349.592	417.531
24	97.015	118.203	143.786	174.628	211.758	256.381	309.943	374.141	450.974	542.791
25	117.388	144.207	176.857	216.539	264.698	323.040	393.628	478.901	581.756	705.627
30	304.471	389.748	497.904	634.810	807.793	1025.904	1300.477	1645.488	2078.208	2619.936
40	2048.309	2846.941	3946.340	5455.797	7523.156	10346.879	14195.051	19426.418	26520.723	36117.754

Table A
Compound or Future Value of $1 (Continued)

Period	31%	32%	33%	34%	35%	36%	37%	38%	39%	40%
1	1.310	1.320	1.330	1.340	1.350	1.360	1.370	1.380	1.390	1.400
2	1.716	1.742	1.769	1.796	1.822	1.850	1.877	1.904	1.932	1.960
3	2.248	2.300	2.353	2.406	2.460	2.515	2.571	2.628	2.686	2.744
4	2.945	3.036	3.129	3.224	3.321	3.421	3.523	3.627	3.733	3.842
5	3.858	4.007	4.162	4.320	4.484	4.653	4.826	5.005	5.189	5.378
6	5.054	5.290	5.535	5.789	6.053	6.328	6.612	6.907	7.213	7.530
7	6.621	6.983	7.361	7.758	8.172	8.605	9.058	9.531	10.025	10.541
8	8.673	9.217	9.791	10.395	11.032	11.703	12.410	13.153	13.935	14.758
9	11.362	12.166	13.022	13.930	14.894	15.917	17.001	18.151	19.370	20.661
10	14.884	16.060	17.319	18.666	20.106	21.646	23.292	25.049	26.924	28.925
11	19.498	21.199	23.034	25.012	27.144	29.439	31.910	34.567	37.425	40.495
12	25.542	27.902	30.635	33.516	36.644	40.037	43.716	47.703	52.020	56.694
13	33.460	36.937	40.745	44.912	49.469	54.451	59.892	65.830	72.308	79.371
14	43.832	48.756	54.190	60.181	66.784	74.053	82.051	90.845	100.509	111.119
15	57.420	64.358	72.073	80.643	90.158	100.712	112.410	125.366	139.707	155.567
16	75.220	84.953	95.857	108.061	121.713	136.968	154.002	173.005	194.192	217.793
17	98.539	112.138	127.490	144.802	164.312	186.277	210.983	238.747	269.927	304.911
18	129.086	148.022	169.561	194.035	221.822	253.337	289.046	329.471	375.198	426.875
19	169.102	195.389	225.517	260.006	299.459	344.537	395.993	454.669	521.525	597.625
20	221.523	257.913	299.937	348.408	404.270	468.571	542.511	627.443	724.919	836.674
21	290.196	340.446	398.916	466.867	545.764	637.256	743.240	865.871	1007.637	1171.343
22	380.156	449.388	530.558	625.601	736.781	866.668	1018.238	1194.900	1400.615	1639.878
23	498.004	593.192	705.642	838.305	994.653	1178.668	1394.986	1648.961	1946.854	2295.829
24	652.385	783.013	938.504	1123.328	1342.781	1602.988	1911.129	2275.564	2706.125	3214.158
25	854.623	1033.577	1248.210	1505.258	1812.754	2180.063	2618.245	3140.275	3761.511	4499.816
30	3297.081	4142.008	5194.516	6503.285	8128.426	10142.914	12636.086	15716.703	19517.969	24201.043

TABLE B
COMPOUND OR FUTURE VALUE OF AN ANNUITY OF $1

Period	1%	2%	3%	4%	5%	6%	7%	8%	9%	10%
1	1.000	1.000	1.000	1.000	1.000	1.000	1.000	1.000	1.000	1.000
2	2.010	2.020	2.030	2.040	2.050	2.060	2.070	2.080	2.090	2.100
3	3.030	3.060	3.091	3.122	3.152	3.184	3.215	3.246	3.278	3.310
4	4.060	4.122	4.184	4.246	4.310	4.375	4.440	4.506	4.573	4.641
5	5.101	5.204	5.309	5.416	5.526	5.637	5.751	5.867	5.985	6.105
6	6.152	6.308	6.468	6.633	6.802	6.975	7.153	7.336	7.523	7.716
7	7.214	7.434	7.662	7.898	8.142	8.394	8.654	8.923	9.200	9.487
8	8.286	8.583	8.892	9.214	9.549	9.897	10.260	10.637	11.028	11.436
9	9.368	9.755	10.159	10.583	11.027	11.491	11.978	12.488	13.021	13.579
10	10.462	10.950	11.464	12.006	12.578	13.181	13.816	14.487	15.193	15.937
11	11.567	12.169	12.808	13.486	14.207	14.972	15.784	16.645	17.560	18.531
12	12.682	13.412	14.192	15.026	15.917	16.870	17.888	18.977	20.141	21.384
13	13.809	14.680	15.618	16.627	17.713	18.882	20.141	21.495	22.953	24.523
14	14.947	15.974	17.086	18.292	19.598	21.015	22.550	24.215	26.019	27.975
15	16.097	17.293	18.599	20.023	21.578	23.276	25.129	27.129	29.361	31.772
16	17.258	18.639	20.157	21.824	23.657	25.672	27.888	30.324	33.003	35.949
17	18.430	20.012	21.761	23.697	25.840	28.213	30.840	33.750	36.973	40.544
18	19.614	21.412	23.414	25.645	28.132	30.905	33.999	37.450	41.301	45.599
19	20.811	22.840	25.117	27.671	30.539	33.760	37.379	41.446	46.018	51.158
20	22.019	24.297	26.870	29.778	33.066	36.785	40.995	45.762	51.159	57.274
21	23.239	25.783	28.676	31.969	35.719	39.992	44.865	50.422	56.764	64.002
22	24.471	27.299	30.536	34.248	38.505	43.392	49.005	55.456	62.872	71.402
23	25.716	28.845	32.452	36.618	41.430	46.995	53.435	60.893	69.531	79.542
24	26.973	30.421	34.426	39.082	44.501	50.815	58.176	66.764	76.789	88.496
25	28.243	32.030	36.459	41.645	47.726	54.864	63.248	73.105	84.699	98.346
30	34.784	40.567	47.575	56.084	66.438	79.057	94.459	113.282	136.305	164.491
40	48.885	60.401	75.400	95.024	120.797	154.758	199.630	259.052	337.872	442.580

Appendix A: Interest Tables

Table B
Compound or Future Value of an Annuity of $1 (Continued)

Period	11%	12%	13%	14%	15%	16%	17%	18%	19%	20%
1	1.000	1.000	1.000	1.000	1.000	1.000	1.000	1.000	1.000	1.000
2	2.110	2.120	2.130	2.140	2.150	2.160	2.170	2.180	2.190	2.200
3	3.342	3.374	3.407	3.440	3.472	3.506	3.539	3.572	3.606	3.640
4	4.710	4.779	4.850	4.921	4.993	5.066	5.141	5.215	5.291	5.368
5	6.228	6.353	6.480	6.610	6.742	6.877	7.014	7.154	7.297	7.442
6	7.913	8.115	8.323	8.535	8.754	8.977	9.207	9.442	9.683	9.930
7	9.783	10.089	10.405	10.730	11.067	11.414	11.772	12.141	12.523	12.916
8	11.859	12.300	12.757	13.233	13.727	14.240	14.773	15.327	15.902	16.499
9	14.164	14.776	15.416	16.085	16.786	17.518	18.285	19.086	19.923	20.799
10	16.722	17.549	18.420	19.337	20.304	21.321	22.393	23.521	24.709	25.959
11	19.561	20.655	21.814	23.044	24.349	25.733	27.200	28.755	30.403	32.150
12	22.713	24.133	25.650	27.271	29.001	30.850	32.824	34.931	37.180	39.580
13	26.211	28.029	29.984	32.088	34.352	36.786	39.404	42.218	45.244	48.496
14	30.095	32.392	34.882	37.581	40.504	43.672	47.102	50.818	54.841	59.196
15	34.405	37.280	40.417	43.842	47.580	51.659	56.109	60.965	66.260	72.035
16	39.190	42.753	46.671	50.980	55.717	60.925	66.648	72.938	79.850	87.442
17	44.500	48.883	53.738	59.117	65.075	71.673	78.978	87.067	96.021	105.930
18	50.396	55.749	61.724	68.393	75.836	84.140	93.404	103.739	115.265	128.116
19	56.939	63.439	70.748	78.968	88.211	98.603	110.283	123.412	138.165	154.739
20	64.202	72.052	80.946	91.024	102.443	115.379	130.031	146.626	165.417	186.687
21	72.264	81.698	92.468	104.767	118.809	134.840	153.136	174.019	197.846	225.024
22	81.213	92.502	105.489	120.434	137.630	157.414	180.169	206.342	236.436	271.028
23	91.147	104.602	120.203	138.295	159.274	183.600	211.798	244.483	282.359	326.234
24	102.173	118.154	136.829	158.656	184.166	213.976	248.803	289.490	337.007	392.480
25	114.412	133.333	155.616	181.867	212.790	249.212	292.099	342.598	402.038	471.976
30	199.018	241.330	293.192	356.778	434.738	530.306	647.423	790.932	966.698	1181.865
40	581.812	767.080	1013.667	1341.979	1779.048	2360.724	3134.412	4163.094	5529.711	7343.715

Table B
Compound or Future Value of an Annuity of $1 (continued)

Period	21%	22%	23%	24%	25%	26%	27%	28%	29%	30%
1	1.000	1.000	1.000	1.000	1.000	1.000	1.000	1.000	1.000	1.000
2	2.210	2.220	2.230	2.240	2.250	2.260	2.270	2.280	2.290	2.300
3	3.674	3.708	3.743	3.778	3.813	3.848	3.883	3.918	3.954	3.990
4	5.446	5.524	5.604	5.684	5.766	5.848	5.931	6.016	6.101	6.187
5	7.589	7.740	7.893	8.048	8.207	8.368	8.533	8.700	8.870	9.043
6	10.183	10.442	10.708	10.980	11.259	11.544	11.837	12.136	12.442	12.756
7	13.321	13.740	14.171	14.615	15.073	15.546	16.032	16.534	17.051	17.583
8	17.119	17.762	18.430	19.123	19.842	20.588	21.361	22.163	22.995	23.858
9	21.714	22.670	23.669	24.712	25.802	26.940	28.129	29.369	30.664	32.015
10	27.274	28.657	30.113	31.643	33.253	34.945	36.723	38.592	40.556	42.619
11	34.001	35.962	38.039	40.238	42.566	45.030	47.639	50.398	53.318	56.405
12	42.141	44.873	47.787	50.895	54.208	57.738	61.501	65.510	69.780	74.326
13	51.991	55.745	59.778	64.109	68.760	73.750	79.106	84.853	91.016	97.624
14	63.909	69.009	74.528	80.496	86.949	93.925	101.465	109.611	118.411	127.912
15	78.330	85.191	92.669	100.815	109.687	119.346	129.860	141.302	153.750	167.285
16	95.779	104.933	114.983	126.010	138.109	151.375	165.922	181.867	199.337	218.470
17	116.892	129.019	142.428	157.252	173.636	191.733	211.721	233.790	258.145	285.011
18	142.439	158.403	176.187	195.993	218.045	242.583	269.885	300.250	334.006	371.514
19	173.351	194.251	217.710	244.031	273.556	306.654	343.754	385.321	431.868	483.968
20	210.755	237.986	268.783	303.598	342.945	387.384	437.568	494.210	558.110	630.157
21	256.013	291.343	331.603	377.461	429.681	489.104	556.710	633.589	720.962	820.204
22	310.775	356.438	408.871	469.052	538.101	617.270	708.022	811.993	931.040	1067.265
23	377.038	435.854	503.911	582.624	673.626	778.760	900.187	1040.351	1202.042	1388.443
24	457.215	532.741	620.810	723.453	843.032	982.237	1144.237	1332.649	1551.634	1805.975
25	554.230	650.944	764.596	898.082	1054.791	1238.617	1454.180	1706.790	2002.608	2348.765
30	1445.111	1767.044	2160.459	2640.881	3227.172	3941.953	4812.891	5873.172	7162.785	8729.805
40	9749.141	12936.141	17153.691	22728.367	30088.621	39791.957	52570.707	69376.562	91447.375	120389.375

Appendix A: Interest Tables 405

TABLE B
COMPOUND OR FUTURE VALUE OF AN ANNUITY OF $1 (CONTINUED)

Period	31%	32%	33%	34%	35%	36%	37%	38%	39%	40%
1	1.000	1.000	1.000	1.000	1.000	1.000	1.000	1.000	1.000	1.000
2	2.310	2.320	2.330	2.340	2.350	2.360	2.370	2.380	2.390	2.400
3	4.026	4.062	4.099	4.136	4.172	4.210	4.247	4.284	4.322	4.360
4	6.274	6.362	6.452	6.542	6.633	6.725	6.818	6.912	7.008	7.104
5	9.219	9.398	9.581	9.766	9.954	10.146	10.341	10.539	10.741	10.946
6	13.077	13.406	13.742	14.086	14.438	14.799	15.167	15.544	15.930	16.324
7	18.131	18.696	19.277	19.876	20.492	21.126	21.799	22.451	23.142	23.853
8	24.752	25.678	26.638	27.633	28.664	29.732	30.837	31.982	33.167	34.395
9	33.425	34.895	36.429	38.028	39.696	41.435	43.247	45.135	47.103	49.152
10	44.786	47.062	49.451	51.958	54.590	57.351	60.248	63.287	66.473	69.813
11	59.670	63.121	66.769	70.624	74.696	78.998	83.540	88.335	93.397	98.739
12	79.167	84.320	89.803	95.636	101.840	108.437	115.450	122.903	130.822	139.234
13	104.709	112.302	120.438	129.152	138.484	148.474	159.166	170.606	182.842	195.928
14	138.169	149.239	161.183	174.063	187.953	202.925	219.058	236.435	255.151	275.299
15	182.001	197.996	215.373	234.245	254.737	276.978	301.109	327.281	355.659	386.418
16	239.421	262.354	287.446	314.888	344.895	377.690	413.520	452.647	495.366	541.985
17	314.642	347.307	383.303	422.949	466.608	514.658	567.521	625.652	689.558	759.778
18	413.180	459.445	510.792	567.751	630.920	700.935	778.504	864.399	959.485	1064.689
19	542.266	607.467	680.354	761.786	852.741	954.271	1067.551	1193.870	1334.683	1491.563
20	711.368	802.856	905.870	1021.792	1152.200	1298.809	1463.544	1648.539	1856.208	2089.188
21	932.891	1060.769	1205.807	1370.201	1556.470	1767.380	2006.055	2275.982	2581.128	2925.862
22	1223.087	1401.215	1604.724	1837.068	2102.234	2404.636	2749.294	3141.852	3588.765	4097.203
23	1603.243	1850.603	2135.282	2462.669	2839.014	3271.304	3767.532	4336.750	4989.379	5737.078
24	2101.247	2443.795	2840.924	3300.974	3833.667	4449.969	5162.516	5985.711	6936.230	8032.906
25	2753.631	3226.808	3779.428	4424.301	5176.445	6052.957	7073.645	8261.273	9642.352	11247.062
30	10632.543	12940.672	15737.945	19124.434	23221.258	28172.016	34148.906	41357.227	50043.625	60500.207

Table C
Present Value of $1

Period	1%	2%	3%	4%	5%	6%	7%	8%	9%	10%
1	0.990	0.980	0.971	0.962	0.952	0.943	0.935	0.926	0.917	0.909
2	0.980	0.961	0.943	0.925	0.907	0.890	0.873	0.857	0.842	0.826
3	0.971	0.942	0.915	0.889	0.864	0.840	0.816	0.794	0.772	0.751
4	0.961	0.924	0.888	0.855	0.823	0.792	0.763	0.735	0.708	0.683
5	0.951	0.906	0.863	0.822	0.784	0.747	0.713	0.681	0.650	0.621
6	0.942	0.888	0.837	0.790	0.746	0.705	0.666	0.630	0.596	0.564
7	0.933	0.871	0.813	0.760	0.711	0.665	0.623	0.583	0.547	0.513
8	0.923	0.853	0.789	0.731	0.677	0.627	0.582	0.540	0.502	0.467
9	0.914	0.837	0.766	0.703	0.645	0.592	0.544	0.500	0.460	0.424
10	0.905	0.820	0.744	0.676	0.614	0.558	0.508	0.463	0.422	0.386
11	0.896	0.804	0.722	0.650	0.585	0.527	0.475	0.429	0.388	0.350
12	0.887	0.788	0.701	0.625	0.557	0.497	0.444	0.397	0.356	0.319
13	0.879	0.773	0.681	0.601	0.530	0.469	0.415	0.368	0.326	0.290
14	0.870	0.758	0.661	0.577	0.505	0.442	0.388	0.340	0.299	0.263
15	0.861	0.743	0.642	0.555	0.481	0.417	0.362	0.315	0.275	0.239
16	0.853	0.728	0.623	0.534	0.458	0.394	0.339	0.292	0.252	0.218
17	0.844	0.714	0.605	0.513	0.436	0.371	0.317	0.270	0.231	0.198
18	0.836	0.700	0.587	0.494	0.416	0.350	0.296	0.250	0.212	0.180
19	0.828	0.686	0.570	0.475	0.396	0.331	0.277	0.232	0.194	0.164
20	0.820	0.673	0.554	0.456	0.377	0.312	0.258	0.215	0.178	0.149
21	0.811	0.660	0.538	0.439	0.359	0.294	0.242	0.199	0.164	0.135
22	0.803	0.647	0.522	0.422	0.342	0.278	0.226	0.184	0.150	0.123
23	0.795	0.634	0.507	0.406	0.326	0.262	0.211	0.170	0.138	0.112
24	0.788	0.622	0.492	0.390	0.310	0.247	0.197	0.158	0.126	0.102
25	0.780	0.610	0.478	0.375	0.295	0.233	0.184	0.146	0.116	0.092
26	0.772	0.598	0.464	0.361	0.281	0.220	0.172	0.135	0.106	0.084
27	0.764	0.586	0.450	0.347	0.268	0.207	0.161	0.125	0.098	0.076
28	0.757	0.574	0.437	0.333	0.255	0.196	0.150	0.116	0.090	0.069
29	0.749	0.563	0.424	0.321	0.243	0.185	0.141	0.107	0.082	0.063
30	0.742	0.552	0.412	0.308	0.231	0.174	0.131	0.099	0.075	0.057
40	0.672	0.453	0.307	0.208	0.142	0.097	0.067	0.046	0.032	0.022
50	0.608	0.372	0.228	0.141	0.087	0.054	0.034	0.021	0.013	0.009

TABLE C
PRESENT VALUE OF $1 (CONTINUED)

Period	11%	12%	13%	14%	15%	16%	17%	18%	19%	20%
1	0.901	0.893	0.885	0.877	0.870	0.862	0.855	0.847	0.840	0.833
2	0.812	0.797	0.783	0.769	0.756	0.743	0.731	0.718	0.706	0.694
3	0.731	0.712	0.693	0.675	0.658	0.641	0.624	0.609	0.593	0.579
4	0.659	0.636	0.613	0.592	0.572	0.552	0.534	0.516	0.499	0.482
5	0.593	0.567	0.543	0.519	0.497	0.476	0.456	0.437	0.419	0.402
6	0.535	0.507	0.480	0.456	0.432	0.410	0.390	0.370	0.352	0.335
7	0.482	0.452	0.425	0.400	0.376	0.354	0.333	0.314	0.296	0.279
8	0.434	0.404	0.376	0.351	0.327	0.305	0.285	0.266	0.249	0.233
9	0.391	0.361	0.333	0.308	0.284	0.263	0.243	0.225	0.209	0.194
10	0.352	0.322	0.295	0.270	0.247	0.227	0.208	0.191	0.176	0.162
11	0.317	0.287	0.261	0.237	0.215	0.195	0.178	0.162	0.148	0.135
12	0.286	0.257	0.231	0.208	0.187	0.168	0.152	0.137	0.124	0.112
13	0.258	0.229	0.204	0.182	0.163	0.145	0.130	0.116	0.104	0.093
14	0.232	0.205	0.181	0.160	0.141	0.125	0.111	0.099	0.088	0.078
15	0.209	0.183	0.160	0.140	0.123	0.108	0.095	0.084	0.074	0.065
16	0.188	0.163	0.141	0.123	0.107	0.093	0.081	0.071	0.062	0.054
17	0.170	0.146	0.125	0.108	0.093	0.080	0.069	0.060	0.052	0.045
18	0.153	0.130	0.111	0.095	0.081	0.069	0.059	0.051	0.044	0.038
19	0.138	0.116	0.098	0.083	0.070	0.060	0.051	0.043	0.037	0.031
20	0.124	0.104	0.087	0.073	0.061	0.051	0.043	0.037	0.031	0.026
21	0.112	0.093	0.077	0.064	0.053	0.044	0.037	0.031	0.026	0.022
22	0.101	0.083	0.068	0.056	0.046	0.038	0.032	0.026	0.022	0.018
23	0.091	0.074	0.060	0.049	0.040	0.033	0.027	0.022	0.018	0.015
24	0.082	0.066	0.053	0.043	0.035	0.028	0.023	0.019	0.015	0.013
25	0.074	0.059	0.047	0.038	0.030	0.024	0.020	0.016	0.013	0.010
26	0.066	0.053	0.042	0.033	0.026	0.021	0.017	0.014	0.011	0.009
27	0.060	0.047	0.037	0.029	0.023	0.018	0.014	0.011	0.009	0.007
28	0.054	0.042	0.033	0.026	0.020	0.016	0.012	0.010	0.008	0.006
29	0.048	0.037	0.029	0.022	0.017	0.014	0.011	0.008	0.006	0.005
30	0.044	0.033	0.026	0.020	0.015	0.012	0.009	0.007	0.005	0.004
40	0.015	0.011	0.008	0.005	0.004	0.003	0.002	0.001	0.001	0.001
50	0.005	0.003	0.002	0.001	0.001	0.001	0.000	0.000	0.000	0.000

Table C
Present Value of $1 (continued)

Period	21%	22%	23%	24%	25%	26%	27%	28%	29%	30%
1	0.826	0.820	0.813	0.806	0.800	0.794	0.787	0.781	0.775	0.769
2	0.683	0.672	0.661	0.650	0.640	0.630	0.620	0.610	0.601	0.592
3	0.564	0.551	0.537	0.524	0.512	0.500	0.488	0.472	0.466	0.455
4	0.467	0.451	0.437	0.423	0.410	0.397	0.384	0.373	0.361	0.350
5	0.386	0.370	0.355	0.341	0.328	0.315	0.303	0.291	0.280	0.269
6	0.319	0.303	0.289	0.275	0.262	0.250	0.238	0.227	0.217	0.207
7	0.263	0.249	0.235	0.222	0.210	0.198	0.188	0.178	0.168	0.159
8	0.218	0.204	0.191	0.179	0.168	0.157	0.148	0.139	0.130	0.123
9	0.180	0.167	0.155	0.144	0.134	0.125	0.116	0.108	0.101	0.094
10	0.149	0.137	0.126	0.116	0.107	0.099	0.092	0.085	0.078	0.073
11	0.123	0.112	0.103	0.094	0.086	0.079	0.072	0.066	0.061	0.056
12	0.102	0.092	0.083	0.076	0.069	0.062	0.057	0.052	0.047	0.043
13	0.084	0.075	0.068	0.061	0.055	0.050	0.045	0.040	0.037	0.033
14	0.069	0.062	0.055	0.049	0.044	0.039	0.035	0.032	0.028	0.025
15	0.057	0.051	0.045	0.040	0.035	0.031	0.028	0.025	0.022	0.020
16	0.047	0.042	0.036	0.032	0.028	0.025	0.022	0.019	0.017	0.015
17	0.039	0.034	0.030	0.026	0.023	0.020	0.017	0.015	0.013	0.012
18	0.032	0.028	0.024	0.021	0.018	0.016	0.014	0.012	0.010	0.009
19	0.027	0.023	0.020	0.017	0.014	0.012	0.011	0.009	0.008	0.007
20	0.022	0.019	0.016	0.014	0.012	0.010	0.008	0.007	0.006	0.005
21	0.018	0.015	0.013	0.011	0.009	0.008	0.007	0.006	0.005	0.004
22	0.015	0.013	0.011	0.009	0.007	0.006	0.005	0.004	0.004	0.003
23	0.012	0.010	0.009	0.007	0.006	0.005	0.004	0.003	0.003	0.002
24	0.010	0.008	0.007	0.006	0.005	0.004	0.003	0.003	0.002	0.002
25	0.009	0.007	0.006	0.005	0.004	0.003	0.003	0.002	0.002	0.001
26	0.007	0.006	0.005	0.004	0.003	0.002	0.002	0.002	0.001	0.001
27	0.006	0.005	0.004	0.003	0.002	0.002	0.002	0.001	0.001	0.001
28	0.005	0.004	0.003	0.002	0.002	0.002	0.001	0.001	0.001	0.001
29	0.004	0.003	0.002	0.002	0.002	0.001	0.001	0.001	0.001	0.000
30	0.003	0.003	0.002	0.002	0.001	0.001	0.001	0.001	0.000	0.000
40	0.000	0.000	0.000	0.000	0.000	0.000	0.000	0.000	0.000	0.000
50	0.000	0.000	0.000	0.000	0.000	0.000	0.000	0.000	0.000	0.000

TABLE C
PRESENT VALUE OF $1 (CONTINUED)

Period	31%	32%	33%	34%	35%	36%	37%	38%	39%	40%
1	0.763	0.758	0.752	0.746	0.741	0.735	0.730	0.725	0.719	0.714
2	0.583	0.574	0.565	0.557	0.549	0.541	0.533	0.525	0.518	0.510
3	0.445	0.435	0.425	0.416	0.406	0.398	0.389	0.381	0.372	0.364
4	0.340	0.329	0.320	0.310	0.301	0.292	0.284	0.276	0.268	0.260
5	0.259	0.250	0.240	0.231	0.223	0.215	0.207	0.200	0.193	0.186
6	0.198	0.189	0.181	0.173	0.165	0.158	0.151	0.145	0.139	0.133
7	0.151	0.143	0.136	0.129	0.122	0.116	0.110	0.105	0.100	0.095
8	0.115	0.108	0.102	0.096	0.091	0.085	0.081	0.076	0.072	0.068
9	0.088	0.082	0.077	0.072	0.067	0.063	0.059	0.055	0.052	0.048
10	0.067	0.062	0.058	0.054	0.050	0.046	0.043	0.040	0.037	0.035
11	0.051	0.047	0.043	0.040	0.037	0.034	0.031	0.029	0.027	0.025
12	0.039	0.036	0.033	0.030	0.027	0.025	0.023	0.021	0.019	0.018
13	0.030	0.027	0.025	0.022	0.020	0.018	0.017	0.015	0.014	0.013
14	0.023	0.021	0.018	0.017	0.015	0.014	0.012	0.011	0.010	0.009
15	0.017	0.016	0.014	0.012	0.011	0.010	0.009	0.008	0.007	0.006
16	0.013	0.012	0.010	0.009	0.008	0.007	0.006	0.006	0.005	0.005
17	0.010	0.009	0.008	0.007	0.006	0.005	0.005	0.004	0.004	0.003
18	0.008	0.007	0.006	0.005	0.005	0.004	0.003	0.003	0.003	0.002
19	0.006	0.005	0.004	0.004	0.003	0.003	0.003	0.002	0.002	0.002
20	0.005	0.004	0.003	0.003	0.002	0.002	0.002	0.002	0.001	0.001
21	0.003	0.003	0.003	0.002	0.002	0.002	0.001	0.001	0.001	0.001
22	0.003	0.002	0.002	0.002	0.001	0.001	0.001	0.001	0.001	0.001
23	0.002	0.002	0.001	0.001	0.001	0.001	0.001	0.001	0.000	0.000
24	0.002	0.001	0.001	0.001	0.001	0.001	0.000	0.000	0.000	0.000
25	0.001	0.001	0.001	0.001	0.001	0.000	0.000	0.000	0.000	0.000
26	0.001	0.001	0.001	0.000	0.000	0.000	0.000	0.000	0.000	0.000
27	0.001	0.001	0.000	0.000	0.000	0.000	0.000	0.000	0.000	0.000
28	0.001	0.000	0.000	0.000	0.000	0.000	0.000	0.000	0.000	0.000
29	0.000	0.000	0.000	0.000	0.000	0.000	0.000	0.000	0.000	0.000
30	0.000	0.000	0.000	0.000	0.000	0.000	0.000	0.000	0.000	0.000
40	0.000	0.000	0.000	0.000	0.000	0.000	0.000	0.000	0.000	0.000
50	0.000	0.000	0.000	0.000	0.000	0.000	0.000	0.000	0.000	0.000

Table C
Present Value of $1 (continued)

Period	41%	42%	43%	44%	45%	46%	47%	48%	49%	50%
1	0.709	0.704	0.699	0.694	0.690	0.685	0.680	0.676	0.671	0.667
2	0.503	0.496	0.489	0.482	0.476	0.469	0.463	0.457	0.450	0.444
3	0.357	0.349	0.342	0.335	0.328	0.321	0.315	0.308	0.302	0.296
4	0.253	0.246	0.239	0.233	0.226	0.220	0.214	0.208	0.203	0.198
5	0.179	0.173	0.167	0.162	0.156	0.151	0.146	0.141	0.136	0.132
6	0.127	0.122	0.117	0.112	0.108	0.103	0.099	0.095	0.091	0.088
7	0.090	0.086	0.082	0.078	0.074	0.071	0.067	0.064	0.061	0.059
8	0.064	0.060	0.057	0.054	0.051	0.048	0.046	0.043	0.041	0.039
9	0.045	0.043	0.040	0.038	0.035	0.033	0.031	0.029	0.028	0.026
10	0.032	0.030	0.028	0.026	0.024	0.023	0.021	0.020	0.019	0.017
11	0.023	0.021	0.020	0.018	0.017	0.016	0.014	0.013	0.012	0.012
12	0.016	0.015	0.014	0.013	0.012	0.011	0.010	0.009	0.008	0.008
13	0.011	0.010	0.010	0.009	0.008	0.007	0.007	0.006	0.006	0.005
14	0.008	0.007	0.007	0.006	0.006	0.005	0.005	0.004	0.004	0.003
15	0.006	0.005	0.005	0.004	0.004	0.003	0.003	0.003	0.003	0.002
16	0.004	0.004	0.003	0.003	0.003	0.002	0.002	0.002	0.002	0.002
17	0.003	0.003	0.002	0.002	0.002	0.002	0.001	0.001	0.001	0.001
18	0.002	0.002	0.002	0.001	0.001	0.001	0.001	0.001	0.001	0.001
19	0.001	0.001	0.001	0.001	0.001	0.001	0.001	0.001	0.001	0.000
20	0.001	0.001	0.001	0.001	0.001	0.001	0.000	0.000	0.000	0.000
21	0.001	0.001	0.001	0.000	0.000	0.000	0.000	0.000	0.000	0.000
22	0.001	0.000	0.000	0.000	0.000	0.000	0.000	0.000	0.000	0.000
23	0.000	0.000	0.000	0.000	0.000	0.000	0.000	0.000	0.000	0.000
24	0.000	0.000	0.000	0.000	0.000	0.000	0.000	0.000	0.000	0.000
25	0.000	0.000	0.000	0.000	0.000	0.000	0.000	0.000	0.000	0.000
26	0.000	0.000	0.000	0.000	0.000	0.000	0.000	0.000	0.000	0.000
27	0.000	0.000	0.000	0.000	0.000	0.000	0.000	0.000	0.000	0.000
28	0.000	0.000	0.000	0.000	0.000	0.000	0.000	0.000	0.000	0.000
29	0.000	0.000	0.000	0.000	0.000	0.000	0.000	0.000	0.000	0.000
30	0.000	0.000	0.000	0.000	0.000	0.000	0.000	0.000	0.000	0.000
40	0.000	0.000	0.000	0.000	0.000	0.000	0.000	0.000	0.000	0.000
50	0.000	0.000	0.000	0.000	0.000	0.000	0.000	0.000	0.000	0.000

Table D
Present Value of an Annuity of $1

Period	1%	2%	3%	4%	5%	6%	7%	8%	9%	10%
1	0.990	0.980	0.971	0.962	0.952	0.943	0.935	0.926	0.917	0.909
2	1.970	1.942	1.913	1.886	1.859	1.833	1.808	1.783	1.759	1.736
3	2.941	2.884	2.829	2.775	2.723	2.673	2.624	2.577	2.531	2.487
4	3.902	3.808	3.717	3.630	3.546	3.465	3.387	3.312	3.240	3.170
5	4.853	4.713	4.580	4.452	4.329	4.212	4.100	3.993	3.890	3.791
6	5.795	5.601	5.417	5.242	5.076	4.917	4.767	4.623	4.486	4.355
7	6.728	6.472	6.230	6.002	5.786	5.582	5.389	5.206	5.033	4.868
8	7.652	7.325	7.020	6.733	6.463	6.210	5.971	5.747	5.535	5.335
9	8.566	8.162	7.786	7.435	7.108	6.802	6.515	6.247	5.995	5.759
10	9.471	8.983	8.530	8.111	7.722	7.360	7.024	6.710	6.418	6.145
11	10.368	9.787	9.253	8.760	8.306	7.887	7.499	7.139	6.805	6.495
12	11.255	10.575	9.954	9.385	8.863	8.384	7.943	7.536	7.161	6.814
13	12.134	11.348	10.635	9.986	9.394	8.853	8.358	7.904	7.487	7.103
14	13.004	12.106	11.296	10.563	9.899	9.295	8.745	8.244	7.786	7.367
15	13.865	12.849	11.938	11.118	10.380	9.712	9.108	8.559	8.061	7.606
16	14.718	13.578	12.561	11.652	10.838	10.106	9.447	8.851	8.313	7.824
17	15.562	14.292	13.166	12.166	11.274	10.477	9.763	9.122	8.544	8.022
18	16.398	14.992	13.754	12.659	11.690	10.828	10.059	9.372	8.756	8.201
19	17.226	15.678	14.324	13.134	12.085	11.158	10.336	9.604	8.950	8.365
20	18.046	16.351	14.877	13.590	12.462	11.470	10.594	9.818	9.129	8.514
21	18.857	17.011	15.415	14.029	12.821	11.764	10.836	10.017	9.292	8.649
22	19.660	17.658	15.837	14.451	13.163	12.042	11.061	10.201	9.442	8.772
23	20.456	18.292	16.444	14.857	13.489	12.303	11.272	10.371	9.580	8.883
24	21.243	18.914	16.936	15.247	13.799	12.550	11.469	10.529	9.707	8.985
25	22.023	19.523	17.413	15.622	14.094	12.783	11.654	10.675	9.823	9.077
26	22.795	20.121	17.877	15.983	14.375	13.003	11.826	10.810	9.929	9.161
27	23.560	20.707	18.327	16.330	14.643	13.211	11.987	10.935	10.027	9.237
28	24.316	21.281	18.764	16.663	14.898	13.406	12.137	11.051	10.116	9.307
29	25.066	21.844	19.188	16.984	15.141	13.591	12.278	11.158	10.198	9.370
30	25.808	22.396	19.600	17.292	15.372	13.765	12.409	11.258	10.274	9.427
40	32.835	27.355	23.115	19.793	17.159	15.046	13.332	11.925	10.757	9.779
50	39.196	31.424	25.730	21.482	18.256	15.762	13.801	12.233	10.962	9.915

Table D
Present Value of an Annuity of $1 (Continued)

Period	11%	12%	13%	14%	15%	16%	17%	18%	19%	20%
1	0.901	0.893	0.885	0.877	0.870	0.862	0.855	0.847	0.840	0.833
2	1.713	1.690	1.668	1.647	1.626	1.605	1.585	1.566	1.547	1.528
3	2.444	2.402	2.361	2.322	2.283	2.246	2.210	2.174	2.140	2.106
4	3.102	3.037	2.974	2.914	2.855	2.798	2.743	2.690	2.639	2.589
5	3.696	3.605	3.517	3.433	3.352	3.274	3.199	3.127	3.058	2.991
6	4.231	4.111	3.998	3.889	3.784	3.685	3.589	3.498	3.410	3.326
7	4.712	4.564	4.423	4.288	4.160	4.039	3.922	3.812	3.706	3.605
8	5.146	4.968	4.799	4.639	4.487	4.344	4.207	4.078	3.954	3.837
9	5.537	5.328	5.132	4.946	4.772	4.607	4.451	4.303	4.163	4.031
10	5.889	5.650	5.426	5.216	5.019	4.833	4.659	4.494	4.339	4.129
11	6.207	5.938	5.687	5.453	5.234	5.029	4.836	4.656	4.486	4.327
12	6.492	6.194	5.918	5.660	5.421	5.197	4.988	4.793	4.611	4.439
13	6.750	6.424	6.122	5.842	5.583	5.342	5.118	4.910	4.715	4.533
14	6.982	6.628	6.302	6.002	5.724	5.468	5.229	5.008	4.802	4.611
15	7.191	6.811	6.462	6.142	5.847	5.575	5.324	5.092	4.876	4.675
16	7.379	6.974	6.604	6.265	5.954	5.668	5.405	5.162	4.938	4.730
17	7.549	7.120	6.729	6.373	6.047	5.749	5.475	5.222	4.990	4.775
18	7.702	7.250	6.840	6.467	6.128	5.818	5.534	5.273	5.033	4.812
19	7.839	7.366	6.938	6.550	6.198	5.877	5.584	5.316	5.070	4.843
20	7.963	7.469	7.025	6.623	6.259	5.929	5.628	5.353	5.101	4.870
21	8.075	7.562	7.102	6.687	6.312	5.973	5.665	5.384	5.127	4.891
22	8.176	7.645	7.170	6.743	6.359	6.011	5.696	5.410	5.149	4.909
23	8.266	7.718	7.230	6.792	6.399	6.044	5.723	5.432	5.167	4.925
24	8.348	7.784	7.283	6.835	6.434	6.073	5.746	5.451	5.182	4.937
25	8.422	7.843	7.330	6.873	6.464	6.097	5.766	5.467	5.195	4.948
26	8.488	7.896	7.372	6.906	6.491	6.118	5.783	5.480	5.206	4.956
27	8.548	7.943	7.409	6.935	6.514	6.136	5.798	5.492	5.215	4.964
28	8.602	7.984	7.441	6.961	6.534	6.152	5.810	5.502	5.223	4.970
29	8.650	8.022	7.470	6.983	6.551	6.166	5.820	5.510	5.229	4.975
30	8.694	8.055	7.496	7.003	6.566	6.177	5.829	5.517	5.235	4.979
40	8.951	8.244	7.634	7.105	6.642	6.233	5.871	5.548	5.258	4.997
50	9.042	8.304	7.675	7.133	6.661	6.246	5.880	5.554	5.262	4.999

Table D
Present Value of an Annuity of $1

Period	21%	22%	23%	24%	25%	26%	27%	28%	29%	30%
1	0.826	0.820	0.813	0.806	0.800	0.794	0.787	0.781	0.775	0.769
2	1.509	1.492	1.474	1.457	1.440	1.424	1.407	1.392	1.376	1.361
3	2.074	2.042	2.011	1.981	1.952	1.923	1.896	1.868	1.842	1.816
4	2.540	2.494	2.448	2.404	2.362	2.320	2.280	2.241	2.203	2.166
5	2.926	2.864	2.803	2.745	2.689	2.635	2.583	2.532	2.483	2.436
6	3.245	3.167	3.092	3.020	2.951	2.885	2.821	2.759	2.700	2.643
7	3.508	3.416	3.327	3.242	3.161	3.083	3.009	2.937	2.868	2.802
8	3.726	3.619	3.518	3.421	3.329	3.241	3.156	3.076	2.999	2.925
9	3.905	3.786	3.673	3.566	3.463	3.366	3.273	3.184	3.100	3.019
10	4.054	3.923	3.799	3.682	3.571	3.465	3.364	3.269	3.178	3.092
11	4.177	4.035	3.902	3.776	3.656	3.543	3.437	3.335	3.239	3.147
12	4.278	4.127	3.985	3.851	3.725	3.606	3.493	3.387	3.286	3.190
13	4.362	4.203	4.053	3.912	3.780	3.656	3.538	3.427	3.322	3.223
14	4.432	4.265	4.108	3.962	3.824	3.695	3.573	3.459	3.351	3.249
15	4.489	4.315	4.153	4.001	3.859	3.726	3.601	3.483	3.373	3.268
16	4.536	4.357	4.189	4.033	3.887	3.751	3.623	3.503	3.390	3.283
17	4.576	4.391	4.219	4.059	3.910	3.771	3.640	3.518	3.403	3.295
18	4.608	4.419	4.243	4.080	3.928	3.786	3.654	3.529	3.413	3.304
19	4.635	4.442	4.263	4.097	3.942	3.799	3.664	3.539	3.421	3.311
20	4.657	4.460	4.279	4.110	3.954	3.808	3.673	3.546	3.427	3.316
21	4.675	4.476	4.292	4.121	3.963	3.816	3.679	3.551	3.432	3.320
22	4.690	4.488	4.302	4.130	3.970	3.822	3.684	3.556	3.436	3.323
23	4.703	4.499	4.311	4.137	3.976	3.827	3.689	3.559	3.438	3.325
24	4.713	4.507	4.318	4.143	3.981	3.831	3.692	3.562	3.441	3.327
25	4.721	4.514	4.323	4.147	3.985	3.834	3.694	3.564	3.442	3.329
26	4.728	4.520	4.328	4.151	3.988	3.837	3.696	3.566	3.444	3.330
27	4.734	4.524	4.332	4.154	3.990	3.839	3.698	3.567	3.445	3.330
28	4.739	4.528	4.335	4.157	3.992	3.840	3.699	3.568	3.446	3.331
29	4.743	4.531	4.337	4.158	3.994	3.841	3.700	3.569	3.446	3.332
30	4.746	4.534	4.339	4.160	3.995	3.842	3.701	3.570	3.447	3.332
40	4.760	4.544	4.347	4.166	3.910	3.846	3.703	3.571	3.448	3.333
50	4.762	4.545	4.348	4.167	3.910	3.846	3.703	3.571	3.448	3.333

TABLE D
PRESENT VALUE OF AN ANNUITY OF $1 (CONTINUED)

Period	31%	32%	33%	34%	35%	36%	37%	38%	39%	40%
1	0.763	0.758	0.752	0.746	0.741	0.735	0.730	0.725	0.719	0.714
2	1.346	1.331	1.317	1.303	1.289	1.276	1.263	1.250	1.237	1.224
3	1.791	1.766	1.742	1.719	1.696	1.673	1.652	1.630	1.609	1.589
4	2.130	2.096	2.062	2.029	1.997	1.966	1.935	1.906	1.877	1.849
5	2.390	2.345	2.302	2.260	2.220	2.181	2.143	2.106	2.070	2.035
6	2.588	2.534	2.483	2.433	2.385	2.339	2.294	2.251	2.209	2.168
7	2.739	2.677	2.619	2.562	2.508	2.455	2.404	2.355	2.308	2.263
8	2.854	2.786	2.721	2.658	2.598	2.540	2.485	2.432	2.380	2.331
9	2.942	2.868	2.798	2.730	2.665	2.603	2.544	2.487	2.432	2.379
10	3.009	2.930	2.855	2.784	2.715	2.649	2.587	2.527	2.469	2.414
11	3.060	2.978	2.899	2.824	2.752	2.683	2.618	2.555	2.496	2.438
12	3.100	3.013	2.931	2.853	2.779	2.708	2.641	2.576	2.515	2.456
13	3.129	3.040	2.956	2.876	2.799	2.727	2.658	2.592	2.529	2.469
14	3.152	3.061	2.974	2.892	2.814	2.740	2.670	2.603	2.539	2.478
15	3.170	3.076	2.988	2.905	2.825	2.750	2.679	2.611	2.546	2.484
16	3.183	3.088	2.999	2.914	2.834	2.757	2.685	2.616	2.551	2.489
17	3.193	3.097	3.007	2.921	2.840	2.763	2.690	2.621	2.555	2.492
18	3.201	3.104	3.012	2.926	2.844	2.767	2.693	2.624	2.557	2.494
19	3.207	3.109	3.017	2.930	2.848	2.770	2.696	2.626	2.559	2.496
20	3.211	3.113	3.020	2.933	2.850	2.772	2.698	2.627	2.561	2.497
21	3.215	3.116	3.023	2.935	2.852	2.773	2.699	2.629	2.562	2.498
22	3.217	3.118	3.025	2.936	2.853	2.775	2.700	2.629	2.562	2.498
23	3.219	3.120	3.026	2.938	2.854	2.775	2.701	2.630	2.563	2.499
24	3.221	3.121	3.027	2.939	2.855	2.776	2.701	2.630	2.563	2.499
25	3.222	3.122	3.028	2.939	2.856	2.777	2.702	2.631	2.563	2.499
26	3.223	3.123	3.028	2.940	2.856	2.777	2.702	2.631	2.564	2.500
27	3.224	3.123	3.029	2.940	2.856	2.777	2.702	2.631	2.564	2.500
28	3.224	3.124	3.029	2.940	2.857	2.777	2.702	2.631	2.564	2.500
29	3.225	3.124	3.030	2.941	2.857	2.777	2.702	2.631	2.564	2.500
30	3.225	3.124	3.030	2.941	2.857	2.778	2.702	2.631	2.564	2.500
40	3.226	3.125	3.030	2.941	2.857	2.778	2.703	2.632	2.564	2.500
50	3.226	3.125	3.030	2.941	2.857	2.778	2.703	2.632	2.564	2.500

Table D
Present Value of an Annuity of $1 (continued)

Period	41%	42%	43%	44%	45%	46%	47%	48%	49%	50%
1	0.709	0.704	0.699	0.694	0.690	0.685	0.680	0.676	0.671	0.667
2	1.212	1.200	1.188	1.177	1.165	1.154	1.143	1.132	1.122	1.111
3	1.569	1.549	1.530	1.512	1.493	1.475	1.458	1.441	1.424	1.407
4	1.822	1.795	1.769	1.744	1.720	1.695	1.672	1.649	1.627	1.605
5	2.001	1.969	1.937	1.906	1.876	1.846	1.818	1.790	1.763	1.737
6	2.129	2.091	2.054	2.018	1.983	1.949	1.917	1.885	1.854	1.824
7	2.219	2.176	2.135	2.096	2.057	2.020	1.984	1.949	1.916	1.883
8	2.283	2.237	2.193	2.150	2.109	2.069	2.030	1.993	1.957	1.922
9	2.328	2.280	2.233	2.187	2.144	2.102	2.061	2.022	1.984	1.948
10	2.360	2.310	2.261	2.213	2.168	2.125	2.083	2.042	2.003	1.965
11	2.383	2.331	2.280	2.232	2.185	2.140	2.097	2.055	2.015	1.977
12	2.400	2.346	2.294	2.244	2.196	2.151	2.107	2.064	2.024	1.985
13	2.411	2.356	2.303	2.253	2.204	2.158	2.113	2.071	2.029	1.990
14	2.419	2.363	2.310	2.259	2.210	2.163	2.118	2.075	2.033	1.993
15	2.425	2.369	2.315	2.263	2.214	2.166	2.121	2.078	2.036	1.995
16	2.429	2.372	2.318	2.266	2.216	2.169	2.123	2.079	2.037	1.997
17	2.432	2.375	2.320	2.268	2.218	2.170	2.125	2.081	2.038	1.998
18	2.434	2.377	2.322	2.270	2.219	2.172	2.126	2.082	2.039	1.999
19	2.435	2.378	2.323	2.271	2.220	2.172	2.126	2.082	2.040	1.999
20	2.436	2.379	2.324	2.271	2.221	2.173	2.127	2.083	2.040	1.999
21	2.437	2.379	2.324	2.272	2.221	2.173	2.127	2.083	2.040	2.000
22	2.438	2.380	2.325	2.272	2.222	2.173	2.127	2.083	2.041	2.000
23	2.438	2.380	2.325	2.272	2.222	2.174	2.127	2.083	2.041	2.000
24	2.438	2.380	2.325	2.272	2.222	2.174	2.127	2.083	2.041	2.000
25	2.439	2.381	2.325	2.272	2.222	2.174	2.128	2.083	2.041	2.000
26	2.439	2.381	2.325	2.273	2.222	2.174	2.128	2.083	2.041	2.000
27	2.439	2.381	2.325	2.273	2.222	2.174	2.128	2.083	2.041	2.000
28	2.439	2.381	2.325	2.273	2.222	2.174	2.128	2.083	2.041	2.000
29	2.439	2.381	2.326	2.273	2.222	2.174	2.128	2.083	2.041	2.000
30	2.439	2.381	2.326	2.273	2.222	2.174	2.128	2.083	2.041	2.000
40	2.439	2.381	2.326	2.273	2.222	2.174	2.128	2.083	2.041	2.000
50	2.439	2.381	2.326	2.273	2.222	2.174	2.128	2.083	2.041	2.000

Glossary
of Financial Terms

Accelerated Depreciation: Methods of depreciation that write off the cost of a tangible asset at a faster rate than the writeoff under the straight-line depreciation method. The two most common methods of accelerated depreciation are the double declining-balance and sum-of-years digits.

Acceleration Clause: A provision that makes the entire loan immediately due and payable if the borrower fails to make the required payments or to live up to other loan terms.

Accounts Receivable Turnover: The ratio of annual credit sales to accounts receivable.

Acid Test Ratio: The ratio of current assets less inventories to current liabilities.

Activity Ratios: A group of turnover relationships between net sales and various asset items. Activity ratios are used to determine how effectively the firm utilizes its resources.

Accrual Basis: The basis which an accountant uses to properly measure the net income of a business for a given period of time. Under the accrual basis of accounting, revenues are recognized when sales are made and expenses are recognized when they are incurred. This process matches the revenue of a period with the expense of that period, regardless of when, whether or how much cash has been obtained or disbursed.

Accruals: Obligations of the firm incurred during one accounting period but payable in a future accounting period. Accrued wages, accrued interest, and accrued taxes are typical accruals.

Administrative Budget: An estimate of the general office and executive requirements.

Administrative Man: A person who has a limited amount of knowledge about his decision problem and attempts to achieve a minimum level of satisfaction.

Agency Securities: Securities issued by some U.S. government agencies such as the Government National Mortgage Association.

Aging Schedule: A schedule that breaks down accounts receivable by a certain interval such as 20-day time periods. This schedule shows the age-group percentages, e.g., 60 percent of the total accounts receivable are not yet overdue, 20 percent are overdue from 1 to 20 days, etc.

Amortization: A method that retires a debt and its interest by making a set of equal periodic payments.

Annual Cleanup: A provision contained in a line of credit agreement. Under this provision, the borrower is required to clean up his loan for a specified number of days during the year.

418 Glossary of Financial Terms

Annualized Cost: The annual equivalent of a project's initial cost plus its annual operating cost.

Annuity: A series of fixed annual deposits or payments for a specified number of years.

Arrear: Unpaid dividends on preferred stocks or past due payment.

Asset Turnover: The ratio of sales to total assets.

Authorized Stock: The maximum number of common shares that the company can issue under the terms of the corporate charter.

Average Collection Period: The average number of days that the firm has waited to collect its accounts receivable.

Average Rate of Return: The percentage of average annual profits after taxes to the average net investment. The average net investment is half the original cost of the project.

Bad Debt Loss: Loss that may occur through failure to collect any of the accounts receivable. Bad debt losses are frequently estimated as a percentage of credit sales, and an allowance for doubtful accounts is established to cover them.

Balloon Payment: An extra large payment in the last year on a loan.

Bank Term Loan: A bank loan whose maturity exceeds one year.

Banker's Acceptance: A draft accepted by a bank. Banker's acceptances are usually used to finance international trade.

Bankruptcy: A legal procedure to liquidate a business. Bankruptcy usually occurs when a firm's liabilities exceed the fair value of its assets.

Bargain Purchase Option: An option that allows the lessee to buy the leased property for a price substantially lower than the expected value of the property at the time the option is exercised.

Best-efforts Sale: The sale of securities under an agreement by which investment bankers will do their best to sell the securities but they will return unsold securities to the issuing company.

Big Board: Another name of the New York Stock Exchange.

Bill of Lading: A shipping document issued to the exporting company or its bank by a common carrier that transfers the goods.

Bond: A long-term debt instrument in the form of a written promise to pay the holder a sum of money at a specified date.

Bonds Discount or Premium: A discount occurs when bonds are sold for a price lower than their face value. A premium occurs when bonds are sold for a price higher than their face value.

Bond Indenture: The contract between the corporation and the bondholder. Bond indenture specifies the rights of the bondholder and the duties of the issuing company.

Bond Value: The discounted value of all future payments. That is, the present value of the periodic interest payments plus the present value of the maturity value.

Book Value: The accounting value of an asset. The book value per share of common stock is the net worth (common stock, capital surplus, and retained earnings) divided by the number of common shares outstanding.

Break-even Analysis: An analytical technique to study the relationships among sales, fixed costs, variable costs, and profits. A break-even chart is a graphic analysis of this relationship. A break-even point or quantity is the number of units of a product that should be produced to cover its total costs.

Business Risk: The variability of operating profits or the possibility that the firm will not be able to cover its fixed costs.

Call Feature or Provision: A provision that gives the issuer the right to call or buy back the securities at a stated price.

Call Premium: The excess of a security's call price over its face value.

Call Price: The price that the company must pay when it calls its security.

Capacity: The borrower's ability to repay his obligation or his legal capacity to enter into a loan contract.

Capital Asset: An asset with a life of more than one year that is not held primarily for resale and that is not bought in the ordinary course of business.

Capital Asset Pricing Model: An approach to analyze portfolio risk.

Capital Budget: The amount of projected expenditures on assets whose benefits are expected to extend beyond one year.

Capital Budgeting: The entire process of ranking and selecting capital expenditures.

Capital Expenditure: An outlay whose benefits are expected to extend beyond one year.

Capital Gain: A profit from the sale of a capital asset or its long-term capital gains are profits on the sale of capital assets held more than one year; they are subject to the preferential tax treatment.

Capital Loss: A loss from the sale of a capital asset.

Capital Market: The market for long-term funds such as bonds, preferred stock, and common stock. The capital market consists of investment bankers, insurance companies, savings banks, and some other financial institutions.

Capital Market Line: A graphic presentation of the relationship between risk and return for a security.

Capital Rationing: The allocation of funds to a group of competing projects. The allocation problem occurs when the amount of capital expenditures required by profitable projects exceeds the amount of funds the company intends to invest in them.

Capital Structure: The sum of long-term debt, preferred stock, common stock, capital surplus, and retained earnings.

Capitalization Rate: A discount rate utilized to determine the present value of a series of future cash flows.

Carryback or Carryforward: For income tax purposes, both net operating losses and capital losses can be carried back and forward for a certain number of years.

Cash Budget: A schedule of various cash receipts and disbursements expected by the company over a specified period, usually on a monthly basis.

Cash Conversion Cycle: The length of time between when the company buys raw materials and when it collects its accounts receivable.

Cash Discount: A reduction in price allowed for early payment of a debt.

Character: The willingness of the loan applicant to honor his obligation.

Coefficient of Variation: The standard deviation divided by the expected value. The coefficient of variation measures the variability of the outcomes associated with an event.

Collateral: Assets used as a pledge for security of the credit.

Collection Policy: The procedures that the company follows to collect its overdue accounts.

Commercial Paper: Short-term promissory notes sold by finance companies and certain industrial concerns directly or through dealers.

Commitment Fee: The fee paid by a borrower to a lender on the average unused balance under a revolving credit arrangement.

Common Equity: Common stock, capital surplus, and retained earnings.

Common-size Statements: Financial statements whose accounts are expressed as a percentage of a key figure such as total assets or sales.

Common Stock: Stock held by the residual owners of the company.

Comparative Advantage: An assumption that some countries can produce certain products relatively more efficiently than other countries can.

Compensating Balance: A minimum checking accounting balance that the borrower is required to maintain with a commercial bank.

Compound Interest: Interest paid on an account which includes the initial principal and the accumulated interest of prior periods.

Computer Simulation: Computer trial runs of a process to learn its possible alternative consequences before taking a particular course of action. This method is used to determine the expected value of a project and its risk by empirical procedures rather than by a theoretical analysis.

Concentration Banking: The use of geographically dispersed banks to speed the collection of accounts receivable.

Conglomerate Merger: A combination of two or more companies in unrelated lines of business.

Conventional Investment: An investment project that has positive net cash flows over its entire life span.

Conversion Premium: The excess of the actual market price of a convertible security over its conversion value at the time of issue.

Conversion Price: The price paid for common stock when it is obtained through conversion.

Conversion Ratio: The face value of a convertible bond dividend by its conversion price. That is, the number of common shares exchanged for each bond.

Conversion Value: The conversion ratio times the market price per share of common stock at the time of issue.

Convertible Securities: Bonds or preferred stocks that may be exchanged for common stock at the option of the holder before the conversion privilege expires.

Corporation: A separate legal entity that is empowered to own assets, to incur liabilities, and to engage in certain activities. Its main advantages are limited liability, transferability of ownership, and ease of raising funds.

Cost of Capital: The required rate of return that the company must earn on its projects for the market value of its common stock to remain unchanged.

Cost of Goods Sold: The cost of goods available for sale during a period minus the cost of the unsold goods on hand at the end of the period.

Coupon Rate: The stated rate of interest on a bond, usually payable in semiannual installments.

Coverage Ratios: A group of ratios designed to measure the ability of the company to meet its fixed obligations.

Credit Period: The length of time that a customer has to pay the account in full.

Credit Standard: The minimum criterion that a customer must meet to purchase merchandise on credit.

Credit Swap: A simultaneous spot and forward loan transaction between a private company and a bank of a foreign country.

Credit Terms: The length of the period for which the company will grant credit and the size of any cash discount that it will allow for early payment.

Cumulative Preferred Stock: Preferred stock whose unpaid dividends are accumulated. These accumulated dividends must be paid before any dividend can be paid on common stock.

Cumulative Voting: A voting system that allows each stockholder to accumulate his votes and to cast all of them for a single director or any number of directors he desires to elect.

Current Ratio: The ratio of current assets to current liabilities. The traditional rule of thumb states that the current ratio should be at least 2 to 1 for the satisfactory financial position of the company.

Cutoff Point: The minimum rate of return that a project must meet to be accepted for implementation.

Date of Record: The date on which holders of record in the company's stock ledger become the recipients of either dividends or rights to buy common shares. The firm closes its stock transfer books and prepares a list of the stockholders on that date. Because it takes time for the firm to be notified of the transfer in time, stock generally goes ex-dividend or ex-rights after the fourth business day prior to the date of record.

Debenture Bonds: Unsecured bonds that are issued against the general credit of the issuing company.

Debt Capacity: The maximum amount of debt that the company should carry in order to maximize its total market value. The debt capacity or limit is expressed as a percent of the company's total assets or the owners' equity.

Debt Ratio: The ratio of total debt to total assets.

Decision Tree: A form of analyzing problems that involves a sequence of decisions.

Default: The failure of the company to fulfill its contract. Normally, the term "default" is used to mean the possibility that interest or principal on debt obligations will not be paid.

Degree of Financial Leverage: The percentage change in earnings per share divided by the percentage change in earnings before interest and taxes.

Degree of Operating Leverage: The percentage change in earnings before interest and taxes divided by the percentage change in sales.

Degree of Total Leverage: The percentage change in earnings per share divided by the percentage change in sales. The degree of total leverage is sometimes called the combined effect of operating and financial leverage.

Depreciation: The allocation in a systematic and rational manner of the cost of a tangible asset less salvage value over its useful life.

Dilution: A proportional decrease in ownership and earnings due to new issues of common stock.

Diminishing Marginal Utility: The fact that marginal utility will decrease as one obtains additional units of a specific good or service. Marginal utility is the extra satisfaction one obtains from one additional unit of a specific product.

Discount Rate: The interest rate used to compute the present value of future cash flows.

Discounted Cash Flow Approaches: Capital budgeting techniques that emphasize the time value of money. Included are the net present value method, the profitability index, and the internal rate of return method.

Dividend: The earnings that the company pays to its stockholders. Some companies frequently pay stock dividends rather than cash dividends.

Dividend Payout: The percentage of earnings distributed to stockholders in the form of cash dividends.

Dividend Yield Rate: The current annual rate in dollars of dividends divided by the closing price per share of common stock.

Double Declining-Balance Method of Depreciation: A method of allocating the cost of a capital asset over its life. Under this method, the company may deduct twice the straight-line rate.

DuPont Chart System: A system of analysis that shows the relationship among return on investment, profit margin, and asset turnover.

Earnings Per Share: The earnings available to common stockholders divided by the number of common shares outstanding.

Economic Life: The length of time that the asset is expected to produce cash flows.

Economic Man: A person who has complete knowledge about his decision problem and attempts to maximize his utility.

Economic Order Quantity: The size of the order that minimizes the total inventory costs. The total costs of inventory consist of the carrying cost and the ordering cost.

Economies of Scale: A reduction in average cost per unit as sales volume or output increases.

Effective Rate of Interest: The ratio of the total dollar interest actually earned for a one-year period to the principal.

Energy Property: Certain property designed to use fuel other than oil and gas or to reduce energy waste in existing facilities.

Equity Funds: Long-term funds provided by the owners of the company. Equity funds consist of common stock, capital surplus, retained earnings, and preferred stock.

Eurodollars: Dollar-denominated deposits in banks outside the United States. These banks may be foreign banks or foreign branches of a U.S. bank.

Exchange Ratio: The number of the acquiring company's shares for each share of the acquired company.

Expected Value: The rate of return or the net present value the company expects to realize from an investment project. The expected net present value is a weighted average of possible net present values where the weights are the probabilities.

Ex Right or Ex Dividend: The sale of stock without stock rights or a recently declared dividend. The ex right or ex dividend date is four working days prior to the date of record.

External Funds: Funds acquired through loans or through the sale of new securities.

External Growth: The expansion of a company through merger with the existing business activities of another company.

Face Value: The value stated on the bond. When a bond is redeemed at the maturity date, the bond is paid according to the face value.

Factoring Accounts Receivable: The sale of accounts receivable to a financial institution. The financial institution is called a factor.

Federal Reserve System: A system of 12 central banks created under the Federal Reserve Act of 1913 and controlled by the Board of Governors that consists of seven members.

Field Warehousing: A method of financing inventories in which a warehouse is established to control the pledged goods on the premises of the borrower.

Financial Intermediaries: Financial institutions such as commercial banks, or finance companies. Financial intermediaries act as an intermediary between savers and borrowers.

Financial Lease: A long-term lease with the following characteristics: (1) the lessee maintains the leased property; (2) the lessee cannot cancel the lease contract before its maturity; and (3) the lessee fully amortizes the leased property.

Financial Leverage: The extent to which funds with a fixed cost (debt and preferred stock) are used in a firm's operation.

Financial Risk: The variability of earnings available to common stockholders or the possibility that the firm will not be able to cover its fixed charges such as interest and loan payments.

Financial Structure: The entire right-hand side of the balance sheet which includes short-term debt, long-term debt, and equity.

Fixed Costs: Costs that remain constant as sales volume changes. They include depreciation, utilities, rent, and supervisory salaries.

Fixed Exchange Rates: Exchange rates that are fixed by a central bank or a government.

Flexible Exchange Rates (Floating Exchange Rates): Exchange rates that fluctuate with market forces.

Float: Checks in the process of collection. There are two types of float: (1) the amount of funds tied up in checks that have been deposited but are yet to be collected and (2) the amount of funds tied up in checks that have been written but are yet to be cleared.

Floating Lien: A method of financing inventories in which the company pledges its entire inventories as security for a loan.

Flotation Costs: Costs incurred in the sale of securities. These costs include underwriting spread, legal fees, and any other associated fees.

Foreign Currency Swap: An agreement between two parties to exchange local currency for hard currency at a specified future date.

Forward Market: A market that requires payment and delivery at some future date. The exchange rate is determined at the time the contract is made.

Fully Diluted Earnings Per Share: Earnings per share based on the computation used for primary earnings per share plus the number of common shares presented by all options and conversion privileges that are not classified as common stock equivalents.

Goodwill: The amount of intangible assets for the acquiring firm established by the excess of the price paid for the acquired company over its book value.

Gross Profit: The excess of sales over the cost of goods sold.

Hard Currency: Currency that may be used in international trade. Dollars and gold are most widely used in international transactions.

Hedging Approach: An approach designed to reduce or offset a possible loss. For example, the multinational company may sell forward exchange or use other means such as credit swap to offset or reduce possible losses from exchange rate fluctuations that affect values of assets and liabilities.

Holders of Record: Stockholders of the company on the date of record. They receive the declared dividend or stock rights.

Holding Company: A corporation that owns or controls one or more other companies for the purpose of united action.

Horizontal Merger: The combination of two or more companies in the same line of business.

Hurdle Rate: The minimum rate of return that an investment project must meet to be accepted.

Import Quota: The maximum amount of certain products that may be imported during a given period of time, usually one year.

Income Bonds: Bonds that pay interest only if it is earned. Typically, other fixed charges are paid first and then interest is paid on the income bonds.

Incremental Cash Flows: Net cash flows associated directly with a project.

Incremental Cost of Capital: The weighted average cost of the increment of capital raised during the year.

Insolvency: The firm's inability to meet its debt obligations.

Internal Funds: The funds provided by depreciation and retained earnings.

Internal Rate of Return: The discount rate that equates the present value of the net cash flows to the present value of the net cash investment.

Inventory Turnover: The ratio of sales to the ending inventory. There are two problems: (1) Sales are at market prices while inventories are carried at costs. (2) Sales occur over the entire year while inventories are a figure at one point in time. Thus, there are many ways of computing the inventory turnover.

Investment Banker: A specialist that acts as a middleman between the issuing company and investors. Its three major functions are advice, underwriting, and selling.

Investment Tax Credit: A credit against the income tax equal to a specified percentage of the cost of equipment in certain asset categories.

Joint Probability: The likelihood that two or more events will occur simultaneously or successively.

Lease: A contractual arrangement by which the owner of an asset (lessor) allows another party (lessee) to use the services of the asset for a stated period of time in exchange for rental payments.

Legal Insolvency: A situation where liabilities exceed assets.

Legal List: A group of securities in which certain financial institutions such as savings banks and pension funds are allowed to invest.

Letter of Credit: A document issued by a bank at the request of the importer. In the document, the bank agrees to honor a draft on the importer if the draft accompanies certain specified documents such as the bill of lading.

Leverage: The use of fixed charge obligations such as bonds and preferred stock in order to magnify profits.

Lien: A legal claim on the assets of another that are pledged for the payment of a debt.

Limited Liability: A type of liability that restricts the investor's obligation to the amount invested. Limited partners and common stockholders have such limited liability.

Line of Credit: An informal commitment on the part of a bank with respect to the maximum amount of unsecured credit that its customers will be permitted to owe during a specified period of time.

Liquidation Value: The amount that could be realized if the entire assets of a company are sold at their liquidation value.

Liquidity: The ability of the firm to meet its obligations or the relative convertibility of current assets to cash. For example, accounts receivable are more liquid than inventories.

Liquidity Ratios: A group of ratios that enable one to measure the firm's ability to meet its short-term obligations as they come due.

Listed Securities: Securities that are traded in the organized security exchanges such as the New York Stock Exchange.

Lock Box System: The operation of a system of post-office lock boxes in many cities with instruction that customers mail their payments to the lock box in their city.

Majority Voting: A voting system which allows each stockholder to cast one vote for each board position for each share of stock he holds.

Margin Requirement: The credit standard for the purchase of securities. If the margin requirement is 70 percent, investors pay 70 percent of the purchase price in cash at the time of transaction and borrow 30 percent from a brokerage firm or bank.

Marginal Cost of Capital: The cost of an additional dollar of new funds.

Marginal Rate of Return: The percentage rate of return that will result from an additional dollar of investment.

Marginal Tax Rate: The rate at which additional income is taxed. The marginal tax rate for the company with a taxable income of more than $100,000 is 34 percent.

Market Value: The amount that could be realized if goods are sold in a free and open market.

Marketable Securities: Short-term securities that can be readily sold on short notice and with a minimum loss.

Merger: A combination of two or more companies by which only one retains its corporate existence and the others lose their identity.

Money Market: Financial markets where short-term securities such as commercial paper and Treasury bills are sold and purchased.

Mortgage: A pledge of designated property as security for the payment of a debt.

Mutually Exclusive Projects: A group of projects that compete with each other in a way that the selection of one precludes all the others in the group.

Negotiable Certificate of Deposit: A formal negotiable receipt for funds left with the bank for a specified period of time.

Net Cash Flows: Earnings after taxes plus certain noncash charges.

Net Cash Investment: The next cash outlay that occurs at time zero.

Net Operating Income: Earnings before interest and taxes but after depreciation.

Net Operating Loss: The excess of tax deductible expenses over gross income.

Net Present Value: The present value of future cash inflows minus the present value of all cash outflows.

Net Working Capital: The excess of current assets over current liabilities.

Net Worth: Common stock, capital surplus, and retained earnings.

Nominal Rate of Interest: The contracted rate of interest. The nominal interest rate is sometimes called the coupon rate or the stated rate of interest.

Noncash Charges: Items that are treated as expenses for income tax purposes, but that do not require actual cash outlays. They include depreciation, depletion, and amortization charges.

Note: A paper that evidences a single-payment short-term loan.

Operating Lease: A written lease contract with the following characteristics: (1) the lessor maintains the leased property; (2) the lessee frequently retains the right to cancel the contract before its maturity; and (3) the lease contract usually covers a period of time less than the economic life of the leased property.

Operating Leverage: The extent to which fixed assets are used in a firm's operation.

Opportunity Cost: The rate of return that funds could earn if they were invested in the best available alternative project.

Optimum Capital Budget: The level of investment that maximizes the present value of the company.

Optimum Capital Structure: The combination of debt and equity that yields the lowest overall cost of capital or that maximizes the market value of the firm.

Option: The right to buy shares of a company.

Ordinary Income: Income from the normal operations of a corporation.

Organized Security Exchange: The physical location where the large volumes of selected securities are traded.

Overdraft: An arrangement that a bank allows its customers to write checks up to some limit in excess of the amount previously deposited.

Over-the-Counter Market: All facilities where unlisted securities are traded on a bid-and-ask basis.

Partnership: A business enterprise owned by two or more individuals.

Par Value: The value stated on the face of a security.

Participating Preferred Stock: Preferred stock that receives its stated dividends and shares in any additional dividends declared.

Glossary of Financial Terms

Payback Period: The number of years required for the net cash flows of a project to return its cost.

Permanent Current Assets: A minimum amount of current assets that the firm must always maintain.

Perpetuity: A series of equal periodic payments expected to continue indefinitely.

Pledging Accounts Receivable: The use of accounts receivable as security for a loan.

Pooling of Interests: A combination of two or more companies to carry out certain business functions as a single economic entity. Under this method of business combination, the assets of the merged companies are added together to form the balance sheet of the new company.

Portfolio: A collection of investments which may consist of financial assets (securities), or capital assets (machinery and equipment), or a combination of both.

Portfolio Effect: The extent to which the variations or risks of individual assets tend to offset each other.

Preemptive Right: A provision that gives the existing stockholders an ability to maintain their percentage ownership in the company. When the company sells its additional common stock, it has no choice but to offer its new issue first to its existing stockholders so that they can buy new shares on a pro rata basis.

Preferred Stock: A type of equity whose holders have a prior claim to earnings and assets in the event of liquidation over those of common stock.

Present Value: The current value of a future payment or the sum of future payments discounted at the appropriate discount rate.

Price-Earnings Ratio: The market price per share of a security divided by the earnings per share.

Primary Earnings Per Share: Earnings available to common stockholders divided by the weighted average number of common shares outstanding during the year plus the number of shares that represent common stock equivalents.

Primary Market: A market where the sale of new securities occurs.

Prime Rate: The rate of interest charged on the loan made to the most credit-worthy customers.

Private Placement: The sale of an entire issue to a single investor or a limited number of institutional investors.

Product Life Cycle Theory: A theory that all products have a certain length of life during which they go through certain stages such as introduction and maturity.

Production Budget: A projected statement that reflects the use of materials, labor, and facilities during some future period of time.

Profit Margin: Earnings after taxes divided by sales.

Profitability Index: The present value of the net cash flows divided by the net investment.

Profitability Ratios: A group of ratios that relate earnings to sales, assets, or equity. These ratios are used to measure the efficiency of management.

Pro Forma Statements: Projected financial statements. They include the pro forma balance sheet, the pro forma income statement, the cash budget, and the pro forma sources and uses of funds statement.

Proprietorship: A business organization owned by a single individual.

Proxy: A form by which the stockholder transfers his voting right to another.

Purchase Method: An accounting method used for combining the financial statements of two or more companies when they merge. If the acquiring company pays more than the net worth of the acquired company, the excess is treated as goodwill.

Purchasing Power Parity: A theory that exchange rates depend upon the relative purchasing power of currencies.

Ratio Analysis: The use of various ratios to analyze the company's immediate position. Because different ratios are used for different purposes, they are broken down into four categories: liquidity ratios, leverage ratios, activity ratios, and profitability ratios.

Refunding Operation: The sale of new bonds to replace the existing bonds. Its major purpose is to reduce financial costs.

Reorder Point: The amount of inventory at which the company places an order.

Reinvestment Rate: The rate of return at which the earlier net cash flows from a project can be reinvested. The net present value method assumes that funds can be reinvested at the cost of capital. The internal rate of return method assumes that funds can be reinvested at the internal rate of return.

Repurchase Agreement: The sale of short-term securities with an agreement to buy them back on a specified future date at an agreed price.

Required Rate of Return: The minimum rate of return required by investors.

Retained Earnings: After-tax earnings not paid as dividends.

Return on Investment: Earnings after taxes divided by total assets.

Reverse Split: The issuance of one share in exchange for more than one share of stock now outstanding.

Revolving Credit: A legal commitment on the part of the bank to extend credit up to a certain amount over a specified period of time, usually two or three years.

Rights Offering: A sale of new common stock to the company's stockholders in accordance with their preemptive rights.

Risk: The variability of returns associated with a project.

Risk-adjusted Discount Rate: A rate that consists of the riskless rate of return plus a risk premium.

Risk Premium: The excess of the rate of return on a particular risky project over the rate of return on a riskless project.

Riskless Rate of Return: The return earned on an investment project whose future benefits are known with certainty. Sometimes the rate of return on Treasury bills is treated as the riskless rate of return.

Risk-Return Tradeoff: A relationship between risk and the rate of return. That is, a schedule of the required rate of return associated with each level of project risk.

Safety Stock: Inventory that is maintained to absorb random fluctuations in purchases (delivery), production, and sales.

Sales and Leaseback Arrangement: An arrangement by which the owner of an asset sells it to another party and simultaneously enters an agreement to lease the asset back under specific terms.

Sales Budget: An estimated sales volume over a specified period of time, usually one year.

Sales Expense Budgets: Estimates of advertising, selling, and other sales expenses over the budget period.

Salvage Value: The expected value of a depreciable asset at the time of a specified period.

Secondary Market: A market for securities that have already been issued and sold.

Secured Bonds: Bonds that pledge a specific type of security such as real estate or equipment.

Self-liquidating Loans: Loans that are paid by cash from the normal operating cycle of the company.

Selling Group: A group of stock dealers and brokers formed to sell a new issue of securities.

Sensitivity Analysis: A management tool designed to measure the sensitivity of project return to individual variables such as sales price, sales volume, or variable cost.

Serial Bonds: An issue that consists of several bonds issued at the same time but with different maturities.

Short Selling: The sale of a security that belongs to another person. The short seller borrows the security from a brokerage firm, then sells it, and at some later date repays the brokerage firm by buying the security on the open market.

Short-term Securities: Securities whose maturities are less than one year. These securities are sometimes called money market instruments.

Sinking Fund: A fund into which the debtor makes equal periodic deposits to return the principal.

Sources and Uses of Funds Statement: A statement of the various sources and uses of funds during any given period.

Spot Market: A market which requires immediate payment and delivery.

Spread: The excess of the sales price for a security by an investment banker over the price paid for the security.

Standard Deviation: A statistical term that measures the dispersion of alternative net cash flows or net present values around the expected value.

Stated Capital: The minimum amount of capital that the company cannot legally distribute to its stockholders either in the form of dividends or by the reacquisition of common stock. The stated capital is frequently called legal capital.

Stock Dividend: A distribution of additional shares of common stock to the existing stockholders. It involves a bookkeeping transfer from retained earnings to capital stock accounts.

Stock Option: An option to buy a certain number of shares at a specified price over a given period of times.

Stock Split: A method of increasing the number of shares outstanding. Stock splits are similar to stock dividends but they do not involve a transfer from retained earnings to capital stock accounts.

Straight-Line Method of Depreciation: A method of depreciation that allocates the cost of an asset less its salvage value in an equal annual amount over its estimated useful life.

Stretching Accounts Payable: A strategy of paying accounts payable as late as possible without the deterioration of the company's credit rating.

Subordinated Bonds: Bonds that have a claim on assets only after senior bonds have been paid off in the case of liquidation.

Subscription Price: The price at which a share of common stock can be purchased in a rights offering.

Sum-of-years-digits Methods of Depreciation: An accelerated method of depreciation that applies a different fraction in each year to the cost of an asset less its salvage value. The denominator of the fraction is the total of the digits which represents the asset's useful life. The numerator is the number of the specific period in reverse order.

Sunk Cost: A cost that stems from a past decision. For example, the difference between the undepreciated initial cost of an old machine and its actual salvage value is such a cost.

Syndicate: A group of investment bankers formed to sell a new issue of securities. Its purpose is to spread the overall risk of the issue.

Synergistic Effect: A situation where the combined company is worth more than the sum of its parts.

Tariffs: Taxes imposed on imported goods.

Tax Anticipation Bills: Short-term interest bearing obligations issued by the U.S. Treasury that may be used as payment for taxes.

Tax Shield: Some expenditures that are deductible for federal income tax purposes.

Technical Insolvency: The inability of a company to meet its bills as they come due.

Temporary Current Assets: Current assets that vary with sales. These assets are usually reduced or converted into cash within the normal operating cycle of the firm.

Tender Offer: A formal offer by a company to buy a specified number of its own shares or the shares of another company.

Term Loan: A loan whose maturity is longer than one year. Most term loans have maturities of between one and ten years.

Times Interest Earned: The ratio of interest charges to net operating income.

Trade Credit: Credit obtained through credit sales. This credit is recorded as an account payable by the buyer and as an account receivable by the seller.

Treasury Bill: An obligation of the U.S. Treasury with a maturity date shorter than one year.

Treasury Bond: An obligation of the U.S. Treasury with an original maturity over ten years.

Treasury Note: An obligation of the U.S. Treasury with an original maturity of one to ten years.

Treasury Stock: The number of shares that have been issued and are subsequently reacquired by the company through purchase or gift.

Trustee: The third party who represents the interest of bondholders. Ordinarily, a trust department of a commercial bank acts as the representative of bondholders (trustee) and it facilitates communication between the issuer and bondholders.

Trust Receipt: An instrument used to acknowledge that the borrower holds goods in trust for the lender.

Uncertainty: A situation where the decision maker knows all the alternatives available to him but does not have enough information to assign probabilities to the set of possible consequences for each alternative. However, risk and uncertainty are interchangeably used in practice.

Underwriting: The investment banker's function of taking the risk about the new issue in exchange for certain underwriting fees. When an investment banker underwrites an issue, he actually purchases the issue by giving the issuing firm a check for the issue.

Unlisted Securities: Securities that are traded in the Over-the-Counter market.

Utility Curve: A curve that indicates risk-return preferences of a decision maker.

Variable Costs: Costs that vary with sales volume. They include direct labor, raw materials, and sales commission.

Vertical Merger: The acquisition of a company's suppliers or retail outlets.

Warehouse Receipt: An instrument which specifies inventory in a warehouse.

Warrant: An option to buy a stated number of shares at a stated price during a prescribed period.

Weighted Average Cost of Capital: A weighted average of the component costs: the cost of debt, the cost of preferred stock, the cost of common stock, and the cost of retained earnings. Typically, the weighted average cost of capital is used as the firm's cost of capital.

Working Capital Management: The management of current assets and current liabilities.

Yield: The actual rate of return on an investment. It depends on the price paid for the security and the stated rate of interest or dividend. Its basic concept is identical with the internal rate of return.

Answers to Selected End-of-Chapter Problems

Chapter 3

3-1 Current ratio = 1.0
Quick ratio = 0.6
Debt ratio = 0.6
Times interest earned = 3.0
Inventory turnover = 7.5
Accounts receivable turnover = 50.0
Average collection period = 7.3 days
Asset turnover = 2.0
Profit margin on sales = 0.05
Return on net worth = 0.25
Return on investment = 0.10

3-2 Current ratio = 2.00
(a) Current ratio = 2.25
(b) Current ratio = 1.67
(c) Current ratio = 2.40
(d) No effect
(e) No effect

3-3 Cash = $30,000
Receivables = $10,000
Inventories = $20,000
Net plant = $40,000
Notes payable = $40,000
Long-term debt = $20,000
Total assets = $100,000
Total claims = $100,000

3-4 (a)

Company	Asset Turnover	Profit Margin	Return on Investment
A	3.00	10.0%	30.0
B	1.53	12.1	18.5
C	2.53	7.9	18.3
D	1.70	7.9	13.4
E	2.14	13.3	28.6

(b) The five company averages are: asset turnover = 2 times; profit margin = 10%; and return on investment = 20%.

3-5 Sales	$100,000
Cost of goods sold	80,000
Gross profit	20,000
Operating expenses .	10,000
Operating profit (EBIT)	10,000
Interest expenses	2,000
Net income before taxes	8,000
Taxes at 40%	3,200
Net income after taxes	4,800

3-7 (a) Current ratio = 1.7
Quick ratio = 1.0
Debt ratio = 46.3%
Times interest earned = 15.0
Inventory turnover = 2.7
Average collection period = 63 days
Asset turnover = 0.77
Profit margin = 13.7%
Return on total assets = 10.5%

Chapter 4

4-1   Q = 600 units

4-2   DOL = 4

4-3   (a) EPS for all common stock = $4.00
         EPS for all debt = $4.50
      (b) EBIT = $1,800
      (c) EPS = $3

4-4   (a) DOL = 4
      (b) DFL = 2
      (c) DCL = 8

4-5   (a) Q = 1,000 units or $20,000
      (b) EBIT = $5,000
      (c) Q = 500 units or $15,000
      (d) DOL at 2,000 units = 2
          DOL at 4,000 units = 1.33

4-7   (a) SOL = 2.5
      (b) DFL = 1.33
      (c) DCL = 3.33

4-8   (a) Q = 16,000 units
      (b) Q = 15,385 units

Chapter 6

6-1 (a) EAT = $30,000
(b) Return on total assets = 15%
(c) Return on total assets = 11.4%

6-2

Current Assets/Sales	30%	50%	70%
rate of return on assets	18.2%	13.3%	10.5%

6-3

	Conservative	Moderate	Aggressive
(a) Return on equity	15.00%	15.75%	16.50%
(b) Current ratio	infinite	2 to 1	1 to 1

6-4

	Alternative A	Alternative B
Rate of return on equity	5.25%	11.07%
Current ratio	10 to 1	0.8 to 1

6-6 (a) Return on assets = 0.40
(b) Return on assets = 0.67
(c) Return on assets = 0.29

6-7 External financing required = $0.000

6-8 The expected level of sales = $72,000

Chapter 7

7-1 (a) Cash cycle = 90 days
(b) Cash turnover = 4 times
(c) Minimum cash = $500,000
(d) Savings = $20,000

7-2 (a) The amount of reduction = $3,000,000
(b) Opportunity cost = $150,000

7-5 (a) EOQ = 2,000 units
(b) Optimum number of orders = 20 orders
(c) Total inventory cost = $4,000
(d) Reorder point = 900 units
(e) Increased inventory cost = $333
    Savings = $800

7-6 (a) $1,000
(b) $833
(c) $800
(d) $820
(e) $866

7-7 (a) 7.91%
(b) 8.19%
(c) Bond yield = 8.33%

7-8 (a) $12,000
(b) 6%

7-9 (a) $4,110
(b) 632 units
(c) $1,248.68

7-10 Profit = $15,000

Chapter 8

8-1 (a) (1) 36.73%
(2) 37.50%
(3) 111.34%
(4) 12.24%

(b) (1) March 20: $490
(2) March 30: $3,360
(3) April 10: $1,455
(4) March 2Q: $4,312

8-2 (a) 24.5%
(b) 8.8%
(c) 8.9%

8-3 (a) $7,623
(b) 16.06%

8-4 (a) 11.1%
(b) 14.3%
(c) 13.3%

8-5 (a) 19.7%
(b) 28.5%
(c) 3.7%
(d) 4.4%
(e) 32.0%

8-6 10.3%

8-7 (a) $3,650
(b) 10.42%
(c) 11.5%

8-8 Wayne National Bank: 17.78%
Detroit State Bank: 14.81%

Answers to Selected End-of-Chapter Problems 439

8-9 (a) 12.5%
(b) 11.1%
(c) 18.46%

3-10 First National Bank: 12.5%
Second National Bank: 13%

Chapter 9

9-1 (a) $4,318
(b) $4,416
(c) $6,524

9-2 (a) $43,461
(b) $44,667
(c) $ 4,889

9-3 (a) $ 558
(b) $ 1,488
(c) $ 1,228

9-4 (a) $24,924
(b) $12,290
(c) $29,862

9-5 About 19 years

9-6 $1,223

9-7 7 percent

9-8 50 months

9-9 $1,171.54

9-10 $730

9-11 $29,373

9-12 $57,590

9-13 Indifferent

9-14 Take the $700,000

9-15 $2,680

9-16 $1,134

9-17 Between 3% and 4%

9-18 (a) 5%
(b) 5.25%
(c) 10.25%

9-19 $1,250

9-20 (a) $ 5,728.77
(b) $91,219.25

(c) $7,340.00

Chapter 10

10-1   (a) $16,500
     (b) $ 4,500

10-2   (a) year 1 = $11,000; year 2 = $10,500; and year 3 =9,900
     (b) year 1 = $11,700; year 2 = $10,100; and year 3 = $9,700

10-3   (a) $5,600
     (b) year 1 = $3,400; year 2 = $2,800; year 3 = $2,200; year 4 = $1,600; year 5 = $1,000; and year 6 = $1,200

10-4   (a) 5.29 years
     (b) 9.26%
     (c) $3,303
     (d) 1.09
     (e) 7.6%

10-5   Project A = 2.5 years
     Project B = 2.2 years

10-6   Project C = 25%
     Project D = 40%

10-7   (a) Project E = $2,680
         Project F = $ 177
     (b) Project E =1.268
         Project F = 1.0177

10-8   Project G = 10%
     Project H = 11.17%

10-9   (a) I= 2 years
         J = 4.2 years
     (b) I = 34%
         J = 33%
     (c) I = $450
         J = $496
     (d) I = 18%
         J = 14.55%

Chapter 11

11-1   (a) $10,000
     (b) $2,400

11-2   (a) $1,120
     (b) $1,620
     (c) $12,880

11-3   Project G = $3,259
     Project H = $2,662

Answers to Selected End-of-Chapter Problems 441

11-4   Machine A = $136,183
       Machine B = $149,796

11-5 $297,179

11-6   (a) $82
       (b) At the end of three years

11-7   (a) $1,360
       (b) $312

11-8   (a) $2,680
       (b) $2,046

Chapter 12

12-1   Expected value: Project A = $670
                                 Project B = $670

       Standard Deviation: Project A = $236
                                 Project B = $60

       Coefficient of variation: Project A = 0.35
                                 Project B = 0.09

12-2   (a) $2,900
       (b) $4,412
       (c) $1,136

12-4   (a) $13,433
       (b) $9,002

12-5 $138

12-6   (a) Net present value: Project F = $636
                                 Project G = -$364

       (b) Standard deviation: Project F = $4,000
                                 Project G = $4,000

       (c) Portfolio NPV = $272

Chapter 13

13-1   7.4%

13-2   10.5%

Answers to Selected End-of-Chapter Problems

13-3   16.4%

13-4   10.425%

13-5   12.52%

13-6   (a) $300,000
    (b) Cost of debt = 4.74%
        Cost of preferred stock = 9%
        Cost of retained earnings = 9.2%
        Cost of common stock = 10.25%

    (c) 8.137%

13-7   (a) 6%
    (b) 14.4%
    (c) 16.5%

13-8   (a) $10,500
    (b) 7.14%

13-9   (a) Undervalued
    (b) Undervalued
    (c) Overvalued
    (d) Undervalued
    (e) Overvalued

Chapter 14

14-1   (a) $19
    (b) $2
    (c) $2

14-2   (a) $0.83
    (b) $29.17
    (c) $1
    (d) $600 or 33%

14-3   (a)   Earnings per share = $3
           Dividend per share = $1.50
           Price = $30

       (b)   Net proceeds per share = $27
           Number of new shares = 1,852
           Earnings per share = $3.04
           Dividend per share = $1.52
           Price = $30.4

Answers to Selected End-of-Chapter Problems

14-4 (a) 11.89 times
 (d) $52

14-5 (a) 25,000 shares
 (b) $39-3/8
 (c) $4
 (d) 62.5%

14-6 (a) Dollar spread = $3
  Percentage spread = 15%
 (b) $325,000
 (c) 125,000 shares

14-7 (a) $0.56
 (b) $721,000

Chapter 15

15-1 16%

15-2 (a) $386
 (b) $463
 (c) $322

15-3 (a) $55,750
 (b) $14,390
 (c) $202,813
 (d) $147,063
 (e) 25.74%

15-4 $408,000

15-5 A: $1,500,000
 B: $180,000
 C: $1,500,000
 D: $360,000

15-7 (a) $6,000,000
 (b) $3,000,000

Chapter 16

16-1 (a) 100,000 shares
 (b) 20,001 shares
 (c) 4 directors
 (d) 120,001 shares

16-2 (a) $30,000

(b) $80,000

16-3 (a) $35
(b) 28.57
(c) $714.25
(d) 5,714 new shares

16-4 (a) EPS before conversion = $4.94
EPS after conversion = $4.81

16-5 (a) $5
(b) $10
(c) $30
(d) $25

Chapter 17

17-1 0.70

17-2
Common stock	$13,800
Capital surplus	$8,440
Retained earnings	$19,760
Net worth	$42,000

17-3 (a) 5%

17-5 (a) $4
(b) $14
(c) $2.5

17-6 (a) $40,000
(b) $10,000

Chapter 18

18-1 (a) $113,670
(b) $116,225

18-2 (a) Option A = $12,042
Option B = $13,840
(b) $5,798
(c) 4.4%

18-3	(a)	$97,335
	(b)	$64,857
18-4	$10,152	
18-5	$430,100	

INDEX

Accelerated cost recovery system, 30, 195
Acceleration of cash collection, 110
Accounting exposure, 349
Accounts receivable financing, 141
Accounts receivable management, 118
Acquisition of funds, 10
Activity or asset utilization analysis, 44
Activity ratios, 44
African Development Bank, 356
Agency for International Development, 356
Aggressive stocks, 244
Allocation of funds, 9
Amortization schedule, 179, 313
Annualized net present value, 215
Annuity due, 161
Arbi loans, 353
Asian Development Bank, 356
Asset turnover, 46
Authorized stock, 285
Average collection period, 44, 94
Average payment period, 45, 94
Average rate of return, 199

Balance sheet, 36
Balance sheet (simplified), 8
Balloon payment, 313
Bank selection, 139
Bankers' acceptance, 22, 116
Beta coefficient, 244
Bill of exchange, 351
Bills of lading, 352
Bond indenture, 23, 272
Bond maturity date, 272
Bond ratings, 275
Bond valuation, 183, 235
Bond yield and price relationship, 184
Bonds, 23, 272
Book value, 286
Book value weights, 246
Break-even analysis, 61
Budgets, 77
Business risk, 72

Call provision, 273
Capacity, 124
Capital, 124
Capital asset pricing model, 241
Capital budgeting process, 189
Capital impairment rule, 300
Capital leases, 320
Capital markets, 22
Capital projects with different life spans, 215
Capital rationing constraint, 206
Capital-market instruments, 15
Captive finance companies, 20
Cash budget, 80
Cash conversion cycle, 94
Cash discount, 119
Cash management, 109
Cash retention rule, 300
CBD (cash before delivery), 134
Certainty equivalent approach, 229
Character, 124
Circular flow of income, 15
Class A common stock, 289
Class B common stock, 289
COD (cash on delivery), 134
Coefficient of variation, 227
Collateral, 124
Collection policy, 122
Commercial banks, 17, 353
Commercial paper, 21, 116, 139
Commercial paper cost and evaluation, 140
Common stock, 285
Common stock ratios, 48
Common stock valuation, 237
Common stockholder rights, 287
Common-size financial statements, 52
Comparative ratio analysis, 52
Compensating balance, 113
Compound value of a current lump sum, 155
Compound value of an annuity, 160
Concentration banking, 111
Concession agreement, 347

448   INDEX

Conditions, 124
Conglomerate merger, 332
Consolidations, 330
Continuous compounding, 158
Conversion value, 290
Convertible securities, 290
Corporate income tax treatment, 28
Corporation, 26
Correlation coefficient, 231
Cost of capital, 238
Cost of common equity, 241
Cost of debt, 239
Cost of preferred stock, 240
Coupon rate, 272
Credit analysis, 124
Credit decision, 124
Credit information sources, 124
Credit period, 119
Credit risk, 315
Credit standards, 118
Credit terms, 119
Credit Unions, 18
Cumulative voting system, 288
Currency swaps, 353
Current assets, 36
Current liabilities, 37
Current ratio, 42

Date of record, 263
Datings, 135
Debenture bonds, 274
Debt analysis, 43
Debt ratio, 43
Default risk, 104, 114
Defensive stocks, 244
Degree of combined leverage, 70
Degree of financial leverage, 69
Degree of operating leverage, 65
Delay of cash disbursement, 112
Depository financial institutions, 17
Depreciation, 28
Deregulation of financial institutions, 20
Development Banks, 355
Discount rate, 151
Dividend net profit rule, 299
Dividend policy, 299
Double declining-balance method of depreciation, 29
Drafts, 112, 351

Du Pont System, 49

Earnings per share, 48, 67
Economic exposure, 349
Economic life, 191
Economic motives for merger, 331
Economic order quantity, 125
Edge Act of 1919, 354
Efficient capital markets, 242
Eurobonds, 357
Eurocurrency market, 354
Eurodollars, 354
Eurostraight, 358
Evolution of finance, 4
Exchange ratio in merger, 335
Expansion for new products decision, 194
Expectation theory, 103
Export-Import Bank, 356
Ex-rights, 263
External growth, 330

Face value, 272
Factoring accounts receivable, 142
Federal funds, 22
FIFO method of inventory valuation, 39
Finance company, 20, 317
Finance principles, 11
Financial calculators, 153
Financial decision-making model, 10
Financial institutions, 16
Financial intermediation, 15
Financial leverage, 51, 66
Financial leverage and earnings per share, 66
Financial management process, 3
Financial markets, 21
Financial planning and control, 9
Financial ratio industry cmparison, 54
Financial ratio limitations, 55
Financial ratios, 39
Financial risk, 72
Financial risk and business failure, 73
Financial statements, 36
Financing foreign trade, 351
Financing plan (aggressive), 102
Financing plan (conservative), 101
Financing plans, 99
Fisher effect, 25

Index   449

Five C's of credit, 124
Fixed costs, 61
Float, 110
Floating inventory liens, 144
Floating rate bonds, 275, 358
Forecasting currency deregulation, 350
Foreign bonds, 357
Foreign exchange exposure, 348
Foreign exchange exposure management, 350
Foreign exchange rate, 348
Foreign exchange market and risks, 347, 348
Forms of business organization, 26
Forward rate, 348
Free trade versus protectionism, 341
Fully diluted earnings per share, 295
Functions of financial management, 8
Future value versus present value, 151

Gilt edge, 275
Global bonds, 357
Going public, 261
Goodwill, 336
Gross profit margin on sales, 46

Hedge, 350
Historical standards of ratio analysis, 55
Holding companies, 311, 337
Horizontal mergers, 332

Import quotas, 341
Income bonds, 274
Income statement, 37
Indifference chart for sources of financing, 69
Industry standards of ratio analysis, 54, 55
Inflation, 24, 38, 220
Information content of dividends, 303
Insolvency rule, 300
Insurance companies, 18
Inter-American Development Bank, 356
Interest rate risk, 104
Interest versus dividend payments, 31
Internal growth, 330
Internal rate of return, 202
Internal rate of return versus net present value, 205
International Bank for Reconstruction and Development, 355

International Banking Facilities, 354
International bond market, 357
International bonds, 357
International capital market, 357
International equity market, 358
International Finance Corporation, 355
Inventory carrying costs, 125
Inventory conversion period, 44, 94
Inventory financing, 143
Inventory management, 125
Inventory ordering costs, 125
Inventory turnover, 44
Investment banker, 259
Investment banking operation, 260
Issued stock, 285

Joint ventures, 357

Kickers, 314

Lease versus purchase, 318
Lease-Purchase decision, 320
Leases, 318
Legal insolvency, 300
Legal or stated capital, 287
Letter of credit, 352
Leverage, 11
Leverage ratios, 43
Life insurance companies, 18, 316
LIFO method of inventory valuation, 39
Line of credit, 136
Link financing, 354
Liquidation dividend, 334
Liquidation value, 286
Liquidity analysis, 41
Liquidity preference theory, 104
Liquidity ratios, 41
Liquidity versus profitability, 12
Listed securities, 264
Lock-box system, 111

Management information system, 77
Management versus stockholders, 6
Majority voting system, 288
Margin requirements, 267
Marginal cost of capital, 247
Market segmentation theory, 104
Market value weights, 246
Marketable securities, 114

INDEX

Matching principle, 12, 99
Merger combination terms, 334
Mergers, 331
Money market funds, 116
Money market instruments, 15
Money markets, 21
Motives for foreign investment, 342
Motives for holding cash, 109
Mutual funds, 19
Mutual savings banks, 17
Mutually exclusive choice, 206

National Association of Securities Dealers, 267
National development banks, 356
Nationalism, 345
Negotiable certificates of deposits, 22, 116
Net cash flow, 191
Net present value, 200
Net working capital, 41, 214
New York Stock Exchange, 22, 264
No par common stock, 285
Nominal versus real interest rate, 25
Notes, 136

Objective of the firm, 5
Oligopoly model, 343
Open account, 133
Operating cycle, 94
Operating leases, 320
Operating leverage, 64
Operating risk, 72
Opportunity cost of cash management, 112
Optimum capital budget, 252
Optimum capital structure, 74, 249, 251
Optimum cash balance, 113
Optimum dividend policy, 303
Optimum investment in inventory, 125
Optimum working capital, 99
Ordinary annuity, 160
Organized exchanges, 264
OTC dealers, 264
OTC regulation, 267
Outstanding stock, 286
Over-the-counter markets, 264
Overdrafts, 353
Overseas Private Investment Corporation, 356

Paid-in surplus, 286
Par value, 285
Parent company, 331
Partnership, 26
Payback period, 198
Payout ratio, 48
Pension funds, 19
Percent-of-sales method, 85
Permanent current assets, 99
Perpetuities, 185
Phantom profits, 38
Planned divestment, 346
Pledging accounts receivable, 141
Political risks, 344
Pooling of interests, 336
Popular trading range, 305
Portfolio, 231
Portfolio effect, 12, 231
Portfolio management, 117
Portfolio risk and return, 231
Portfolio theory, 342
Pre-authorized checks, 111
Precautionary motive, 110
Preemptive right, 262
Preferred stock, 277
Preferred stock characteristics, 278
Preferred stock valuation, 237
Present value of a future lump sum, 165
Present value of an annuity, 172
Present value of unequal cash flow stream, 183
Price to earnings ratio, 48
Primary market, 22, 259
Private placement, 259, 262
Privileged subscription, 262
Pro forma balance sheet, 83
Pro forma financial statements, 79
Pro forma income statement, 82
Pro forma sources and uses of funds statement, 84
Probability theory, 225
Product life cycle theory, 340, 342
Production budget, 78
Profit margin on sales, 47
Profitability analysis, 46
Profitability index, 201
Profitability ratios, 46
Promissory note, 133

Index

Property and casualty insurance company, 19
Purchasing power parity theory, 348

Quick or acid test ratio, 42

Refunding analysis, 279
Regional development banks, 356
Regulations of security markets, 266
Replacement decision, 193
Repurchase agreements, 22, 116
Repurchase of common stock, 306
Residual theory of dividends, 303
Retained earnings, 286
Retirement decision, 217
Return on assets, 47
Return on net worth, 47
Revolving credit, 136, 314
Revolving credit agreements, 136
Risk, 6, 225, 342
Risk adjusted discount rate, 228
Risk analysis, 61
Risk-return tradeoff, 11, 96

Safety stocks, 128
Sale and lease back arrangements, 320
Sales budget, 78
Sales expense budget, 78
Salvage value, 214, 319
Samuria bonds, 357
Savings and loan associations, 18
Secondary market, 22
Secured bonds, 274
Securities Act of 1933, 266
Securities and Exchange Commission, 266
Securities Exchange Act of 1934, 266
Security market line, 243
Security markets, 264
Short selling, 267
Short-term bank loans, 135, 353
Short-term investment pools, 117
Short-term versus long-term debt, 102
Sinking fund, 181, 273
Small Business Administration, 317
Sole proprietorship, 26
Sources of operating, financial, and combined leverage, 64
Speculative motive, 110
Spot rate, 348

Spread, 259
Stable dividend policy, 301
Standard deviation, 226
Stock dividends, 304
Stock price maximization, 6
Stock quotations, 265
Stock splits, 304, 305
Stocks, 24
Straight line depreciation method, 28
Stretching accounts payable, 135
Subsidiary, 331
Sum-of-years digits method of depreciation, 29
Sunk cost, 213
Synergistic effects, 332
Systematic risk, 242

Target dividend payout ratio, 302
Target weight, 249
Tariffs, 341
Technical insolvency, 300
Temporary current assets, 99
Tender offer, 306, 334
Term loan agreement provisions, 314
Term loan amortization method, 313
Term loan repayment arrangements, 315
Term loans, 313
Term structure of interest rates, 102
Texas Instruments BA II Plus calculator, 154
Theory of comparative advantage, 340
Theory of factor endowments, 340
Time value of money, 11, 151
Times interest earned ratio, 44
Total risk, 72
Trade acceptances, 133
Trade credit, 133
Trade credit terms, 134
Transaction exposure, 349
Transaction motive, 110
Translation exposure, 349
Treasury bills, 21, 115
Treasury bonds, 115
Treasury notes, 115
Treasury securities, 115
Treasury stock, 286
Trust receipts, 144

Underwriting, 259
Unlisted securities, 264

Unsecured bank loans, 136
Unsecured bonds, 274
Unsystematic risk, 242
Uses of financial ratios, 38

Valuation, 12, 235
Valuation and cost of capital models, 254
Variable costs, 61
Venture capital, 317
Vertical mergers, 332

Warehouse receipts, 144
Warrant premium, 293
Warrant valuation, 293

Warrants, 292
Wealth maximization versus profit maximization, 5
Weighted average cost of capital, 245
Window dressing, 56
Working capital management, 93
World Bank Groups, 355
World development banks, 355
World trade motives, 339

Yankee bonds, 357
Yield curves, 103

Zero-coupon bonds, 275